D1564663

Methods of Research in

Psychotherapy

THE CENTURY PSYCHOLOGY SERIES

Richard M. Elliott, Gardner Lindzey & Kenneth MacCorquodale
Editors

LOUIS A. GOTTSCHALK, M.D.
UNIVERSITY OF CINCINNATI COLLEGE OF MEDICINE

ARTHUR H. AUERBACH, M.D.
UNIVERSITY OF PENNSYLVANIA SCHOOL OF MEDICINE

Methods of Research in Psychotherapy

NEW YORK

APPLETON–CENTURY–CROFTS
Division of Meredith Publishing Company

Contributors

ARTHUR H. AUERBACH, M.D., Associate in Psychiatry, University of Pennsylvania School of Medicine, Philadelphia, Pennsylvania; formerly Staff Member, Institute for the Study of Psychotherapy, Temple University Medical Center, Philadelphia, Pennsylvania.

FRANK AULD, JR., Ph.D., Professor of Psychology, Wayne State University, Detroit, Michigan.

SAMUEL J. BECK, Ph.D., Professorial Lecturer, Departments of Psychology and Psychiatry, University of Chicago, Chicago, Illinois; Staff Associate, Michael Reese Hospital, Chicago, Illinois.

LEOPOLD BELLAK, M. D., Director of Psychiatry, City Hospital Center at Elmhurst, New York, Department of Hospitals of the City of New York; Clinical Professor of Psychiatry, New York School of Psychiatry, New York, New York.

PAUL BERGMAN, Ph.D.,* Clinical Research Psychologist, Laboratory of Psychology, National Institute of Mental Health, Bethesda, Maryland.

EDWARD S. BORDIN, Ph.D., Professor of Psychology, University of Michigan, Ann Arbor, Michigan.

JAMES L. BREEDLOVE, D.S.W., Assistant Research Director, Family Service, Cincinnati, Ohio; now Associate Professor of Social Work, Portland State College, Portland, Oregon.

HENRY W. BROSIN, M.D., Director and Chairman, Department of Psychiatry, University of Pittsburgh School of Medicine and Western Psychiatric Institute and Clinic, Pittsburgh, Pennsylvania.

HUGH T. CARMICHAEL, M.D., Professor of Psychiatry, University of Illinois College of Medicine, Chicago, Illinois.

ROSALIND DYMOND CARTWRIGHT, Ph.D., Associate Professor and Director, Division of Psychology, Department of Psychiatry, University of Illinois College of Medicine, Chicago, Illinois.

ERIKA CHANCE, Ph.D., Research Associate, Department of Psychiatry, Mt. Zion Hospital, San Francisco, California; Consultant in Psychotherapy and Research, Sausalito, California.

JACOB B. CHASSAN, Ph.D., Head Statistician, Research Division, Hoffmann-LaRoche, Inc., Nutley, New Jersey; Assistant Clinical Professor of Psychiatry (Biostatistics), George Washington University, Washington, D.C.

FELIX DEUTSCH, M.D.,* Practicing Psychoanalyst; Consulting Psychiatrist, Men-

* deceased

v

tal Hygiene Service, Boston Veterans Administration Outpatient Clinic, Boston, Massachusetts.

ALLEN T. DITTMANN, Ph.D., Laboratory of Psychology, National Institute of Mental Health, Bethesda, Maryland.

JOHN DOLLARD, Ph.D., Professor of Psychology, Yale University, New Haven, Connecticut.

O. SPURGEON ENGLISH, M.D., Professor Emeritus, Department of Psychiatry, Temple University School of Medicine, Philadelphia, Pennsylvania.

MILTON H. ERIKSON, M.D., Editor-in-Chief of *American Journal of Clinical Hypnosis;* formerly Associate Professor of Psychiatry, Wayne State University School of Medicine, Detroit, Michigan.

JOHN A. EWING, M.D., Professor and Chairman, Department of Psychiatry, University of North Carolina and School of Medicine, Chapel Hill, North Carolina.

CHARLES B. FERSTER, Ph.D., Associate Director, Institute for Behavioral Research, Forest Glen Laboratory, Silver Spring, Maryland.

JOHN E. GEDO, M.D., Clinical Assistant Professor of Psychiatry, University of Illinois College of Medicine, Chicago, Illinois; Research Associate, Institute for Psychoanalysis, Chicago, Illinois.

GOLDINE C. GLESER, Ph.D., Professor of Psychology, Department of Psychiatry, University of Cincinnati College of Medicine, Cincinnati, Ohio.

LOUIS A. GOTTSCHALK, M. D., Research Professor and Research Coordinator, Department of Psychiatry, University of Cincinnati College of Medicine, Cincinnati, Ohio; Training and Supervising Analyst, Institute for Psychoanalysis, Chicago, Illinois.

ERNEST A. HAGGARD, Ph.D., Professor of Psychology, Department of Psychiatry, University of Illinois College of Medicine, Chicago, Illinois; Research Consultant, Institute for Psychoanalysis, Chicago, Illinois.

KENNETH S. ISAACS, Ph.D., Research Associate, Department of Psychiatry, University of Illinois College of Medicine, Chicago, Illinois.

DON D. JACKSON, M .D., Director, Mental Research Institute, Palo Alto, California.

PETER H. KNAPP, M.D., Research Professor of Psychiatry, Boston University School of Medicine, Boston, Massachusetts.

LEONARD KRASNER, Ph.D., Professor of Psychology, State University of New York at Stony Brook, New York; formerly Assistant Director and Coordinator of Training, Psychology Service, Veterans Administration Hospital, Palo Alto, California.

MERTON S. KRAUSE, Ph.D., Senior Research Associate, Institute for Juvenile Research, Chicago, Illinois.

MAURICE LORR, Ph.D., Chief, Outpatient Psychiatric Research Laboratory, Veterans Administration, Veterans Benefits Office, Washington, D.C.

RUTH G. MATARAZZO, Ph.D., Associate Professor of Medical Psychology, University of Oregon Medical School, Portland, Oregon.

Douglas M. McNair, Ph.D., Head, Clinical Unit, Psychopharmacology Laboratory, Boston University School of Medicine, Boston, Massachusetts; formerly Assistant Chief, Outpatient Psychiatric Research Laboratory, Veterans Administration, Veterans Benefits Office, Washington, D.C.

Cecil Mushatt, M.D., Assistant Research Professor of Psychiatry, Boston University School of Medicine, Boston, Massachusetts.

S. Joseph Nemetz, M.D., Assistant Research Professor of Psychiatry, Boston University School of Medicine, Boston, Massachusetts.

George H. Pollock, M.D., Ph.D., Clinical Professor of Psychiatry, University of Illinois College of Medicine, Chicago, Illinois; Director of Research, Assistant Dean of Education, and Training and Supervising Analyst, Institute for Psychoanalysis, Chicago, Illinois.

Melvin Sabshin, M.D., Professor and Chairman, Department of Psychiatry, University of Illinois College of Medicine, Chicago, Illinois; Research Associate, Institute for Psychoanalysis, Chicago, Illinois.

Leo Sadow, M.D., Associate Attending Psychiatrist, Michael Reese Hospital, Chicago, Illinois; Research Associate, Institute for Psychoanalysis, Chicago, Illinois.

George Saslow, M.D., Professor and Chairman, Department of Psychiatry, University of Oregon Medical School, Portland, Oregon.

Albert E. Scheflen, M.D., Professor and Director of Research in Psychiatry, Temple University Medical Center, Philadelphia, Pennsylvania; Senior Scientist, Eastern Pennsylvania Psychiatric Institute, Philadelphia, Pennsylvania.

Nathan Schlessinger, M.D., Associate Attending Psychiatrist, Michael Reese Hospital, Chicago, Illinois; Research Associate, Institute for Psychoanalysis, Chicago, Illinois.

William Schofield, Ph.D., Professor of Psychology, Departments of Psychiatry and Psychology, University of Minnesota, Minneapolis, Minnesota.

Philip F. D. Seitz, M.D., Staff Member, Institute for Psychoanalysis, Chicago, Illinois.

David Shakow, Ph.D., Chief, Laboratory of Psychology, National Institute of Mental Health, Bethesda, Maryland.

John M. Shlien, Ph.D., Associate Professor of Psychology and Human Development, University of Chicago, Chicago, Illinois.

Kayla J. Springer, Ph.D., Adjunct Associate Professor of Psychology, Department of Psychiatry, University of Cincinnati College of Medicine, Cincinnati, Ohio.

Hans H. Strupp, Ph.D., Professor of Psychology, Departments of Psychiatry and Psychology, University of North Carolina, Chapel Hill, North Carolina.

Seymour H. Stein, M.D., Deputy Bio-Science Officer, Headquarters Pacific Missile Range, Point Mugu, California.

George L. Trager, Ph.D., Professor of Anthropology and Linguistics, University of Buffalo, Buffalo, New York.

JACQUES VAN VLACK, M.A., Research Technologist and Cinematographer, Eastern Pennsylvania Psychiatric Institute, Philadelphia, Pennsylvania.

ROBERT S. WALLERSTEIN, M.D., Associate Director, Department of Research, and Chairman, Psychotherapy Research Project, Menninger Foundation, Topeka, Kansas.

ARTHUR N. WIENS, Ph.D., Assistant Professor of Medical Psychology, University of Oregon Medical School, Portland, Oregon.

CAROLYN WINGET, A.B., Research Associate, Department of Psychiatry, University of Cincinnati College of Medicine, Cincinnati, Ohio.

LYMAN C. WYNNE, M.D., Ph.D., Chief, Adult Psychiatry Branch, National Institute of Mental Health, Bethesda, Maryland.

FRED M. ZIMRING, J.D., Ph.D., Research Associate and Assistant Professor, Department of Psychology, Dean of Students (Social Services), University of Chicago, Chicago, Illinois.

Foreword

The prospective reader may well ask about the particular merits of this volume, especially in view of several dozen similar offerings, each with its own excellences, and of the easy availability of symposia, conferences, conventional reviews, abstract journals, and serial research reports. In spite of such other attractions, it seems to me that these 34 essays are among the most informative and stimulating which are now available *in the areas covered*. The editors have been successful in attracting new articles from many of the most prominent investigators now actively working at research in psychotherapy, who can therefore speak for themselves about what they are doing. Several of the articles have been in the preparatory stage for numerous years. Not only do they represent the vanguard of research, but because of the introduction of relatively new concepts in communication theory in the clinical setting which can be implemented by the new technology (specifically the use of sound-films and tape), they probably presage the shape of much that is to come.

It is commonplace that the history of a science is closely allied to the history of the tools available. Here we see the concepts, attitudes, and working methods on this frontier being set forth frankly and concretely in ways which avoid many of the deficiencies and evasions of previous clinical research. These investigators more than fulfill the basic requirement that problems be met intelligently: they add imagination, ingenuity, candor, humility, and, above all, methods which are publicly verifiable. The reader is afforded access to much of the best new work in this very difficult field and will be stimulated to carry on his own projects, or to read of others with renewed belief in the efficacy of the scientific method in one of the moot divisions of the behavioral sciences. Even though we have few, if any, definitive answers, there are many more realistic prospects than in 1900 or 1940. It is even encouraging to hope that for active investigators in several areas this volume will have a half-life of only five to ten years, because it will challenge them to do much better during the next decade. For historical purposes, however, this book will probably have a much longer usefulness in presenting several representative means for making small but definite progress in ways to generate and interpret data. These essays are not always consistent or congruent and some are highly controversial. Such open debate also invites new thinking and experimentation; this, indeed, is probably the major purpose of the book.

Experienced readers will miss many of their favorite authors and subject areas, but it would probably require at least ten similar books to do full justice to other methods of studying psychotherapeutic processes. Hopefully this volume will encourage the publication of similar collections at a high level of critical and experimental excellence, certainly one additional method of keeping abreast of the published work which currently appears in more than 214 psychiatric journals.

This book, however, is more than a collection of essays written by contemporary workers. Authors and editors have painstakingly attempted to provide a reasonably but selective complete bibliography which is relevant to the topic in question, and which thus provides the student with an invaluable bibliography for "gateway" reading. More importantly, a number of the essays have critical reviews of the work under discussion, so that the reader is helped to take those important steps toward an examination of both the concepts and attitudes which underlie the working hypotheses and the actual research design and methods with their strengths and weaknesses. The good critical review is generally acknowledged to be one of the best ways in which scientific information can be assimilated and synthesized. It will remain a cornerstone of such synthesis even after the new electronic devices can furnish us with any desired number of references almost instantaneously over the appropriate telephone or "talking typewriter." The sheer bulk of publications obscures the significant ones, thus making critical reviews an absolute necessity to maintain both coverage and perpective.

A word may be in order about the broad spectrum of topics covered and about the multidisciplinary character of the authors. This book is an excellent representative of the current intellectual climate in many centers which are effacing professional and ideological lines by means of interdisciplinary teams. The topics range from clinical and natural history methods through various models to those requiring intensive design. The experiments cited are more ingenious, painstaking, and far-reaching than their predecessors. We are less naive about the cost in time and energy required to verify even a single hypothesis in the areas of the measurement of changes in behavior, the problems of human controls or the "calibration" of the observer, or other aspects of process research. The new techniques are assisting in this process by compelling existing systems to re-examine their basic evidence. Searching questions from new data and conceptual frameworks have and will provoke more good research in all disciplines. It is neither possible nor desirable that single essays be characterized in this preface, but in this connection I want to point out the important contributions made by the investigators in Part II dealing with "The Process of Data Collection," particularly "Reactions of the Patient and Therapist to the Recording Procedure." These men earn our high regard for their courage and persistence in overcoming inertia, cultural lag, and prejudice against introducing new methods into a delicate situation. Paul Bergman particularly deserves high praise for his skill in discussing with exquisite sensitivity the vexing problems surrounding the introduction of a third element, such as the camera or tape-recorder, into the confidential relationship between the patient and his doctor.

It seems to me that this collection of essays may be useful as a reference source in graduate seminars and a valuable supplement in courses dealing with the study of methods in psychotherapy. For some bench workers it may have virtues as a technical guide. Established leaders who have well developed information retrieval methods of their own, and who in effect belong to DeSolla Price's "invisible college," will probably have much less use for it than younger, less experienced investigators, particularly if the latter are without the resources of a genuinely good library service in a large interdisciplinary center. If the discriminating reader utilizes these essays appropriately, he will be amply rewarded by new insights into the early foundations of the embryonic but growing *scientific* discipline of psychotherapy.

Pittsburgh, Pennsylvania   *Henry W. Brosin, M.D.*

Acknowledgments

A major acknowledgment of the editors goes to Albert E. Scheflen who had the idea of putting together such a book and took first steps in this direction. Because of the pressure of other commitments, Dr. Scheflen invited the senior editor to carry through and complete the project. Furthermore, he brought the two editors together in what turned out to be a mutually happy collaborative experience. Though the conception, organization, and contents of this book changed radically with this change in editorship, the purpose of the book—to stimulate and to further research in psychotherapy—scarcely varied from the original course set by Albert Scheflen.

The senior editor is indebted to the Research Career Award Program, U.S. Public Health Service, for the opportunity and time necessary to guide this book from the idea to an accomplished fact. He is also indebted to the encouragement and scholarly example of his chief, Dr. Maurice Levine.

The junior editor is grateful for the support provided by the Institute of Direct Analysis of Temple University Medical Center and also by the Research Career Award Program of the National Institute of Mental Health, U.S. Public Health Service.

Sincere appreciation goes also to consultants who read and provided critical views and suggestions on some of the manuscripts: John Cleghorn, M.D., Robert Downing, Ph.D., Goldine Gleser, Ph.D., Eric Hanson, M.D., Charles Hofling, M.D., Lester Luborsky, Ph.D., John MacLeod, M.D., Joseph Margolis, Ph.D., Mansell Pattison, M.D., and Henry Ricks, Jr., M.D.

In the typing and assembling of the manuscript a debt of gratitude is owed for many hours of patient and tedious work to Ann Dunston, Brenda Campbell, and Marilyn Johnson.

Permission to reprint material from their publications was graciously extended by the American Psychological Association and the Iowa Medical Society.

Contents

CONTRIBUTORS   v

FOREWORD   ix

ACKNOWLEDGMENTS   xiii

PART I   INTRODUCTION   1

1. Goals and Problems in Psychotherapy Research. Louis A. Gottschalk and Arthur H. Auerbach   3

PART II   THE PROCESS OF DATA COLLECTION   11

    A. Data Recording   13

2. Filming Psychotherapy from the Viewpoint of a Research Cinematographer. Jacques Van Vlack   15

3. Sound Motion Picture Facilities for Research in Communication. Allen T. Dittmann, Seymour N. Stein, and David Shakow   25

    B. Reactions of the Patient and Therapist to the Recording Procedure   34

4. An Experiment in Filmed Psychotherapy. Paul Bergman   35

5. Sound-Film Recording of Psychoanalytic Therapy: A Therapist's Experiences and Reactions. Hugh T. Carmichael   50

6. Subjective Reactions to Being Filmed. O. Spurgeon English   60

7. The Experience of Interviewing in the Presence of Observers. Milton H. Erickson   61

8. Filming of Psychotherapeutic Sessions as a Personal
   Experience. Don D. Jackson   64

       PART III   DATA ANALYSIS   67

           A. Process Research Focusing on Selected Variables   69

               1. Communication Variables in General   69

9. Language and Psychotherapy. George L. Trager   70

                   a. Language Variables   82

10. Measurement of Motivational Variables in Psychotherapy.
    Frank Auld Jr. and John Dollard   85

11. The Measurement of Emotional Changes During a
    Psychiatric Interview: A Working Model Toward
    Quantifying the Psychoanalytic Concept of Affect.
    Louis A. Gottschalk, Carolyn M. Winget, Goldine C.
    Gleser, and Kayla J. Springer   93

12. Content Analysis of Verbalizations about Interpersonal
    Experience. Erika Chance   127

                   b. Paralanguage and Linguistic Variables   145

13. Linguistic Techniques and the Analysis of Emotionality
    in Interviews. Allen T. Dittmann and Lyman C. Wynne   146

                   c. Kinesic Variables   152

14. Micromomentary Facial Expressions as Indicators of Ego
    Mechanisms in Psychotherapy. Ernest A. Haggard and
    Kenneth S. Isaacs   154

15. Some Principles of Correlating Verbal and Non-verbal
    Communication. Felix Deutsch   166
    A Fragment of a Sound Filmed Psychiatric Interview
    (Number 1) Illustrating Kinesic Variables
    (Demonstrating Dr. Felix Deutsch's Concepts)   170

                   2. Complex Processes   185
16. Free association: An Experimental Analogue of the
    Psychoanalytic Situation. Edward S. Bordin   189

Contents xvii

17. The Consensus Problem in Psychoanalytic Research.
    Philip F. D. Seitz   209

18. Some Methods Used in the Study of Affect in
    Psychotherapy. Kenneth S. Isaacs and Ernest A. Haggard   226

19. A Sound-Filmed Psychiatric Interview: Number 2, the
    "Temple University" Interview, Used for the
    Demonstration of Data Analysis in this Book.   240

        B. Process Research Emphasizing Investigation of
             Personality Functioning and Theory   262

             1. The Natural History Model   262

20. Natural History Method in Psychotherapy:
    Communicational Research. Albert E. Scheflen   263

        2. The Classical and Operant Conditioning Models   289

21. Behavior Modification Research and the Role of the
    Therapist. Leonard Krasner   292

22. The Repertoire of the Autistic Child in Relation to
    Principles of Reinforcement. C. B. Ferster   312

             3. The Psychoanalytic Model   330

23. Psychoanalytic Contributions to Psychotherapy
    Research. Nathan Schlessinger, George H. Pollock,
    Melvin Sabshin, Leo Sadow, and John E. Gedo   334

24. Toward the Longitudinal Study of the Psycho-
    therapeutic Process. Hans H. Strupp, J. B. Chassan,
    and John A. Ewing   361

25. Collection and Utilization of Data in a Psychoanalytic
    Psychosomatic Study. Peter H. Knapp, Cecil Mushatt,
    and S. Joseph Nemetz   401

             4. The Client-centered Model   422

26. Research Directives and Methods in Client-Centered
    Therapy. John M. Shlien and Fred M. Zimring   424

PART IV   EVALUATION OF THE EFFECTS OR
              OUTCOME OF PSYCHOTHERAPY   449

           A. Problems Regarding the Determination of the
              Pertinent Changes and How to Assess Them   451

27. Evaluative Research Design: A Social Casework
    Illustration. James L. Breedlove and Merton S. Krause   456

28. An Introduction to Intensive Design in the Evaluation of
    Drug Efficacy During Psychotherapy. Jacob B. Chassan
    and Leopold Bellak   478

29. The Psychotherapy Research Project of the Menninger
    Foundation: An Overview at the Midway Point. Robert
    S. Wallerstein   500

30. A Comparison of the Response to Psychoanalytic and
    Client-Centered Psychotherapy. Rosalind Dymond
    Cartwright   517

           B. Measurement Tools to Assess Change with
              Psychotherapy   530

31. The Structured Personality Inventory in Measurement
    of Effects of Psychotherapy. William Schofield   536

32. The Rorschach Test, Communication, and Psychotherapy.
    Samuel J. Beck   551

33. Methods Relating to Evaluation of Therapeutic
    Outcome. Maurice Lorr and Douglas M. McNair   573

PART V   RESEARCH IN THE TEACHING OF
              PSYCHOTHERAPY   595

34. Experimentation in the Teaching and Learning of
    Psychotherapy Skills. Ruth G. Matarazzo, Arthur N.
    Wiens, and George Saslow   597

AUTHOR INDEX   637

SUBJECT INDEX
                                                                  645

I

Introduction

1. Goals and problems in psychotherapy research

Louis A. Gottschalk and Arthur H. Auerbach

No new or compelling evidence is needed to establish the concept that one person can influence another's inner psychological experience or external behavior by silently listening to him, by directing toward him certain combinations of sounds and words; by various facial expressions, gestures, and gross body movements; or by various kinds of physical contacts, such as touching, holding, striking, or caressing. These are facts of common sense and experience, recognized by everyone long before he has a language to give names to such a process and is able to wonder how it works. What we call psychotherapy is one institutionalized form of this process whereby one individual attempts to influence another. Other contexts supply other names for this process of human interactions: ritual dancing, confessing, brainwashing, inciting, reassuring. This psychotherapy, this treatment involving talking and listening, has come to occupy a prominent place on the cultural scene. Many words have been devoted to describing the process, revealing its essence, demonstrating the lofty humanism in it, showing its compatibility with religion, instructing future therapists, and reassuring patients. Everyone knows what psychotherapy is. But it is easier to write a plausible and convincing book explaining the subject and the method than to prove a single assertion about it with any degree of scientific rigor.

Problems begin when one aspires to adduce principles and formulate laws concerning the ways in which psychotherapy works and to predict, evaluate, and measure changes that can be ascribed, with reasonable certainty, to psychotherapy. These problems have produced many voices of discouragement about research in psychotherapy. For example, there exists a pessimistic preoccupation about the unreliability of observations, the lack of precision in assessing change, the difficulty in controlling potentially relevant variables, and the low general predictive capacity of the theoretical framework, whatever it may be. All of these factors, and many others, serve to make research in psychotherapy a risky undertaking for a scientist who is hoping for either quick new discoveries or immediate status in the community of scientists.

There is a steady current of feeling, however, among both opponents and proponents of psychotherapy as a procedure for shaping human behavior and attitudes that research in psychotherapy needs to be pursued more vigorously and thoroughly, if only to establish more well-founded rationales for achieving various prescribed goals. Furthermore, there has been a faithful group of investigators, interested primarily in scientific progress rather than in functioning as therapists, who believe that psychotherapy is a procedure that provides rich data from which will evolve new theories relating to determinants of human behavior. These investigators have been especially interested in socially deviant behavior and in learning about factors capable of maintaining or modifying such behavior and the associated psychological experiences.

This book is addressed to that large group of persons who are seriously interested in learning more about the problems of investigating and evaluating psychotherapy and, by extension, any systematic procedure involving human relationships intended to affect human behavior, thought, and emotion. It is organized so as to provide a mosaic depicting the key perspectives and problems under the headings: data collection, data analysis (including types of variables and theoretical approaches), psychotherapy research prominently tied to personality theory, assessment and outcome research, and research on the teaching of psychotherapy. Complete bibliographical references have been provided covering the major contributions in the scientific literature under each topic. The book is also addressed to the researcher planning or already doing work in this field. Explicit statements of theoretical positions by experts selected from each major school or discipline have been provided. New research methods and approaches have been included as well as critical discussions of controversial issues.

The editors do not intend to make a critical discussion of the research design, lines of evidence, theoretical formulations, and so forth of any of the contributions in this book. In our role as editors, we have principally functioned in prevailing upon contributors to make their descriptions and their point of view as lucid as possible so that readers can grasp the ideas as readily as possible. Inclusion of a paper in this book does not necessarily represent our personal preference or endorsement for a method of studying psychotherapy or for a theoretical model. Rather, we have intended to include what we think are legitimate and potentially productive perspectives and methods. Beyond this point, each contributor is responsible to defend his own working method and thesis.

THE INTERVIEW PROCESS AS A METHOD OF GETTING INFORMATION AND AS A METHOD OF EFFECTING PERSONALITY CHANGE

The common denominator in the psychotherapies is the human transaction known as the *interview*. The interview in psychotherapy is an in-

I

terpersonal relationship lasting a variable amount of time, involving two or more persons, and having at least two principal aims: the exchange of information and the effecting of a change in personality of the interviewee by the interviewer or therapist. As we shall see later, the specific characteristics of the interview vary with the theoretical model. For example, the operant conditioning model (see chapters by Ferster and Krasner) prescribes that the interviewer employ techniques to change, to "mold and shape" the interviewee's deviant behavior. The psychoanalytic model prescribes conditions such that the patient poignantly relives with the therapist important emotional experiences with parental and other key figures. There are other foci or special interests typifying the non-directive method (see Shlien and Zimring), such as, the interviewer's aiming to elicit the interviewee's attitudes concerning some topic about which he is indecisive and mirroring these attitudes back to the interviewee so that he can reintegrate information about himself.

The reader will now begin to note that, though psychotherapies based on different theories of personality have the interview as a common denominator, the use to which the interview is put may vary considerably. It will not always make sense to compare casually or indiscriminately the amount or kind of information exchanged or the personality changes occurring with such psychotherapies. The underlying theoretical models relating both to personality and its alterations need to be identified and, if possible, categorized. Evaluative procedures should be employed that are appropriate to the personality variables that each psychotherapeutic procedure is attempting to influence. Research in psychotherapy which attempts to compare the results obtained from different types of therapies is very difficult to carry out in a meaningful way.

The chapters by Breedlove and Krause and by Cartwright provide examples of thoughtfully planned investigations which enumerate and try in their research designs to cope with some of the problems requiring consideration in comparing results from two or more types of psychotherapy.

GENERAL TYPES AND GOALS OF PSYCHOTHERAPY RESEARCH

Research in psychotherapy can be classified into at least three general categories.

1. *Research in the process of psychotherapy.* Research in the process of psychotherapy concerns itself principally with the course of psychotherapy and not with the ultimate changes in patients consequent to psychotherapy. Process research ranges from the analysis of moment by moment interchange between patient and therapist in one session to summarizing generalizations about long sequences of psychotherapy. Process research

may also involve studies of the behavior of the therapist to determine what aspects have "therapeutic" effects.

2. *Research in the effects of psychotherapy.* Research in the outcome or effects of psychotherapy deals with the assessment of all personality changes resulting from the therapy. Most investigators, of course, select for evaluation those changes which they believe have some relevance to adaptive behavior or mental health.

3. *Research in personality theory.* Psychotherapy provides a situation particularly appropriate to the investigation of the natural history of human interactions. Since the treatment setting encourages the patient to confide personal experiences and feelings not usually shared with other persons, data may be obtained which may be useful to test or amend theories of personality, learning, growth and development, memory, and psychopathology. Hence, some research in psychotherapy focuses more on discovering new information relevant to personality theory than on the process or effects of psychotherapy.

GENERAL PROBLEMS ENCOUNTERED IN RESEARCH IN PSYCHOTHERAPY

Research in psychotherapy presents a challenge to the scientific method because of the multitude of variables which can affect the process and the outcome including a sizeable number that cannot be readily controlled. Furthermore, psychotherapy research is short on reliable and valid methodologic approaches and evaluative instruments. These shortcomings can be attributed to many factors, the principal ones being that psychotherapy research obliges the investigator to exercise a degree of selection from very complex fields of knowledge about human behavior. Relevant to psychotherapy research are contributions from human anatomy, physiology and biochemistry, learning theory, communication theory, psychopathology, value theory, theory of human growth and development, theory of small groups, sociology, cultural anthropology, measurement theory, and so forth.

Let us elaborate some of the kinds of questions which the researcher in psychotherapy may have to ask himself with respect to these different areas of knowledge.

Human Anatomy

What part, if any, does the patient's anatomy, physique, sex, genetic inheritance play in his personality problems?

Human Physiology and Biochemistry

How have physiological and biochemical factors affected the patient's life history and current status? What traumatic, nutritional, metabolic, and infectious processes are relevant to his personality problems?

Learning Theory

1. How did the patient learn his symptoms or deviant behavior?
2. How can the patient unlearn, forget, give up, or live with his symptoms and deviant behavior?
3. How does the therapist play a part in the unlearning of the patient's symptoms and the acquisition of new cognitive and emotive patterns?

Communication Theory

1. How effectively does the patient communicate with himself and with others?
2. To what extent does the patient show discrepancies in what he communicates in the linguistic, lexical, paralanguage, and kinesic modalities of speech?
3. To what extent does the therapist communicate through the lexical modality of speech and to what extent does he make use of other modalities?

Theory of Psychopathology

1. What theory of neurosis and psychosis does the therapist use?
2. What are criteria of mental health and sickness?
3. Is the concept of "unconscious" emotions and thoughts useful?

Theory of Small Groups

1. In what respects are the patient's interpersonal relationships in the dyadic relationship with a therapist typical of his pathological ones with his family of origin? With his current family? With non-family members?
2. To what extent is the newly learned behavior of the patient with the therapist generalizable to interpersonal relationships outside the patient-therapist relationship?

Sociology and Cultural Anthropology

1. What are the cultural and social group characteristics that the patient has internalized?
2. How does the cultural and social background of the patient affect his personality disorder?

Value Theory

1. Does the patient have conflicts of values and are these relevant to his personality problems?
2. Is it appropriate for the therapist to impose his values on the patient or to challenge the social, political, religious, and other transcendent values possessed by the patient?

Measurement Theory

1. To what extent are quantitative measurements appropriate to the theory of personality disorder which the therapist is using? What kinds of scaling is involved in such measurements: nominal, ordinal, interval, ratio?

2. How precise are these measures? Are they absolute or relative? What degree of consensus is possible between two or more observers evaluating the same data?

3. Are directly observable phenomena distinguished from inferred entities? Are constructs, such as *intelligence, ego strength, anxiety,* used?

4. Is high-level precision (with low utility or trivial predictive significance) preserved by remaining close to observable phenomena or operationally definable phenomena (e.g., conditioned response), or is there predominant use of complex inferred entities (e.g., such structural constructs as *super ego, ego, id, ego ideal,* or topographical constructs as the *Unconscious, Preconscious,* the *Conscious*)?

These lists of questions may give some notion of the kinds of positions an investigator may find himself taking with respect to various theories pertinent to psychotherapy. Even when an investigator claims no specific theoretical point of view when launching a study in psychotherapy, it is likely that the variables which he intends to study are preselected, often unbeknown to him, on the basis of preconceptions about the fundamental theoretical backgrounds. (See also Neal E. Miller, 1959.[1])

SCOPE AND REPRESENTATIVENESS OF THIS COLLECTION OF ESSAYS ON RESEARCH METHODS IN PSYCHOTHERAPY

The editors have not entertained the idea that it is feasible to present an exhaustive coverage of the full range of research problems, theories, and strategies in psychotherapy. There has been, however, an idealistic hope that a representative view of these topics could be selected by the editors and dealt with authoritatively by experienced and reputable scholars especially qualified to be spokesmen on one or another facet of psychotherapy research. We are confident that our hope has been approximated by many splendid contributions to this book.

There cannot fail to be areas not covered in a single book on such a topic. We considered admitting additional contributions from well-quali-

---

[1] Miller states: "Pure empiricism is a delusion: A theory-like process is inevitably involved in drawing boundaries around certain parts of the flux of experience to define observable events and in the selection of the events that are observed. . . . Scientists are forced to make a drastic selection, either unconsciously on the basis of perceptual habits and the folklore and linguistic categories of the culture, or consciously on the basis of explicitly formulated theory." (p. 200)

fied investigators, but including any more of them in the present volume would have made the book cumbersome, if not encyclopaedic, in size.

There are five recent excellent books, for example, which have dealt with psychotherapy research. Greenhill, et al. (1955) have reviewed the problems and approaches in all aspects of mental health. Herzog (1959) has written an excellent monograph dealing with the problems in evaluation of psychotherapy. Reznikoff and Toomey (1959) have also discussed problems of evaluative research in psychotherapy. The American Psychological Association has sponsored the separate publication of two symposia on current research in psychotherapy, one volume appearing in 1959 and the other in 1962. Where the bibliographies of the various chapters in the book omit important pertinent references, the editors have called them to the attention of the reader. We have also commented briefly on the contributions of many of the authors and have attempted to place each contribution where it fits in a total perspective.

REFERENCES

GREENHILL, M. H., *et al.* (Eds.). *Evaluation in mental health. A review of the problem of evaluating mental health activities.* Public Health Serv. Publ. No. 413. Washington, D.C.: U.S. Dept. of Health, Education and Welfare, 1955.

HERZOG, E. *Some guidelines in evaluative research.* Washington, D.C.: Children's Bureau, U.S. Dept. of Health, Education, and Welfare, 1959.

MILLER, N. E. Liberalization of basic S-R concepts: Extensions to conflict behavior, motivation, and social learning. In S. Koch (Ed.), *Psychology: A study of a science,* Vol. II. New York: McGraw-Hill, 1959.

REZNIKOFF, M. A., and TOOMEY, L. A. *Evaluation of changes associated with psychiatric treatment.* Springfield, Ill.: Charles C Thomas, 1959.

RUBINSTEIN, E. A., and PARLOFF, M. B. (Eds.). *Research in psychotherapy,* Vol. I. Washington, D.C.: American Psychological Association, 1959.

STRUPP, H. H., and LUBORSKY, L. (Eds.). *Research in psychotherapy,* Vol. II. Washington, D.C.: American Psychological Association, 1962.

II

The Process of
Data Collection

A.

Data Recording

In the laboratory and in the field, the scientist is interested in careful and precise recording of the phenomena he is observing. In psychotherapy research, one of the first steps that was taken to fulfill a basic criterion of the scientific method was to try to obtain faithful and complete recordings of the process so the events could be examined and studied by many with ample time for scrutiny. With the development of sound recording systems, and then later with electronic sound motion picture filming techniques, the objection that psychotherapy was a process not genuinely made available to impartial examination was no longer valid.

Brilliant discoveries were indeed made without such impartial and precise recording devices, discoveries relying on the handwritten notes of a therapist sometimes written long after the psychotherapy took place. In this connection one has only to think of Freud's work. But repeated observations were also made indicating that emotional factors and the limitations of memory could interfere with the reliability of the recording of the events being investigated. Such terms as *counter-transference* and *the personal equation,* though coined from different disciplines, emphasize distortions in observations made by the investigator due to either emotional or perceptual factors. The unreliability of an observer's memory as it is manifested in the interview has not been carefully assessed until recently, probably because problems considered more crucial have attracted more research attention. The unreliability of the details of personal and developmental histories given by presumably reliable informants (MacFarlane, 1938; Haggard, et al., 1960; Wenar, 1963) raises serious questions about how accurately and how long the details of a patient's life history or the interactions of psychotherapy can be correctly recalled when recording is delayed.

As if these facts were not enough to plague the enthusiastic investigator of psychotherapy, there has occurred and grown the disturbing realization that the recording procedures are capable of provoking reactions in the patient or the therapist, psychological reactions possibly as noteworthy as the psychological changes which the therapist is aiming to observe and modify in the patient. In the laboratory, the flora, the bacteria, the mouse, the cat, dog, and the monkey have made no convincing or entirely intelligible communications indicating that the process of data observation and collection might confound or distort the raw data of natural or experimental phenomena. Even when this possibility has been suggested and pointed out, it has not been generally considered to be a situation that might vitiate or weaken the significance of observations and theories derived from scientific studies. There have been, it is true, special situations, such as that described in the Heisenberg principle of indeterminancy (which deals with the distorting effect of macroscopic observing and recording techniques on ultramicroscopic atomic particles) or the finding that animals develop conditioned reflexes to the laboratory situation itself (Pavlov, Liddell). In spite of these observations, it has been considered possible in natural history and experimental research to arrive at scientific laws, particularly in view of the fact that such laws are probabilistic approximations of natural events, rather than absolutely true or false. (See, for example, Duhem, 1954).

It has not been a widely accepted view, however, that recording procedures can be introduced into the usually confidential atmosphere of the psychotherapeutic interview without the possibility of their having major effects on what is observed.

For these reasons we have provided, first of all, two chapters on data recording, one by a trio of behavioral scientists (A. T. Dittman, S. N. Stein, and D. Shakow) and the other by a technical expert in sound motion picture photography (J. Van Vlack). These two chapters tackle the problems of data recording from two different perspectives and offer critical comments and useful suggestions.

REFERENCES

DUHEM, PIERRE. Physical law. In A. Danto and S. Morgenbesser (Eds.), *Philosophy of science*. New York: World Publishing, 1960.

HAGGARD, E. A., BREKSTAD, A., and SKARD, A. G. On the reliability of the amnestic interview. *J. abnorm. soc. psychol.*, 61: 311, 1960.

LIDDELL, H. S. Conditioned reflex method and experimental neurosis. In J. McV. Hunt (Ed.), *Personality and the behavior disorders*, Vol. I. New York: Ronald, 1944.

MACFARLANE, J. W. Studies in child guidance: I. Methodology of data collection and organization. *Monogrs. on Res. in Child Develop.*, Vol. III, no. 6, 1938.

PAVLOV, I. P. *Conditioned reflexes and psychiatry* (Trans. by W. H. Gantt). New York: International Publishers, 1941.

WENAR, CHARLES. The reliability of developmental histories. Summary and evaluation of evidence. *Psychosom. med.*, 25: 505-509, 1963.

2. Filming psychotherapy from the viewpoint of a research cinematographer

Jacques Van Vlack

The study of psychotherapeutic processes has developed a new approach to an understanding of human behavior. Studies based on the repeated evaluation of recorded behavior have led to an examination of the role of the motion picture camera as a scientific instrument. New needs challenge the professional film maker to reexamine established media of the educational, documentary, and entertainment films. For a quarter of a century interpretive films have abstracted and communicated aspects of psychotherapy, but recent developments indicate that there is a new role emerging for the motion picture which may come to be of even greater significance both for psychotherapy and for the film maker. This new role sees cinematography as a basic tool in the study of psychotherapy, with the motion picture acting as an unprecedentedly clear and complete, technically controlled abstraction of an ephemeral event. Such a tool provides a record which with limitless replication permits the observer unparalleled objectivity in the examination of nuances of psychotherapeutic interaction.

This new role for motion pictures can take full advantage of the precise tools of duplication developed by the motion picture technologist. Writing, planning, lighting, photography, sound recording, set designing, editing, printing, and distribution are all highly refined and controllable activities when performed by trained competent professionals. These have made possible the adaptation of the motion picture as a medium for scientific investigation at Eastern Pennsylvania Psychiatric Institute.

In the short history of the motion picture four roughly distinguishable types of film productions have found wide acceptance as communication forms. The motion picture as authored by recognized educators and made for classroom uses is known as a *teaching* film. The film designed to present a shaped but factual interpretation of some defined aspect of reality is a *documentary;* the *experimental* film is a creative exploration of the film medium itself; and the *entertainment* film is a speculative, highly organized production primarily produced for theatrical or television distribution. The fifth and new type of motion picture is produced under controlled, explicit conditions to produce a permanent record which may be repeatedly searched for the re-observation and re-analysis of the original ephemeral event. This film, often referred to as a *scientific film clip* or an *instrumentation film* is a *Research Document Film* (R.D.) (Van Vlack, 1965).

This chapter is devoted to a discussion of the techniques of production of the original document film in the study of psychotherapy.

Scripting is usually thought of as the first step on the way to a useful film, but in the study of psychotherapy the plans for filming must be made on the basis of the research design. In naturalistic filming for a research document film, the research design suggests the appropriate cine-matographic tool which must be made ready for the designated "cast" and location. The research design can be used with the greatest precision and objectivity under studio conditions. This paper will be limited to this phase. Non-studio or location conditions may be considered as a modifi-cation of the studio as dictated by local conditions.

In commercial production the studio must be very flexible and complex to accommodate a wide range of scripts. In the study of psychotherapy the research design calls for two or more fairly immobile persons and thus does not require a complex studio. The challenge for the set designer and the director of photography comes in preparing for the special needs of the subjects. Such subjects are not professional actors prepared to adapt to the requirements of the script or for the manipulations usually required for filming quality. Document film subjects need a low stress environment where they can behave authentically with minimal conscious or uncon-scious compensation for the technical requirements of the filming. This can be done without sacrifice of photographic quality if the usual studio procedures are simplified to suit the relatively uncomplicated needs of the research design.

Effective illumination for the study of psychotherapy requires lighting of studio quality. Basically, this type of set lighting provides a beam of light 45° from the side causing 3-dimensional molding of the face and clothing. The shadows in the folds of the clothing accentuate the minute movements that occur and differentiate one limb from another. At the same time the overall illumination must reveal some detail in the shadow area. This is the traditional *key* and *fill* lighting used in cinematography. Since the subjects are not moving about, this lighting can often be effec-tively done by one 1000-watt light bounced off the ceiling and one high 300-watt spot bulb 45° from the camera's horizontal axis focused on the set area. If the bounce fill is diffuse and the key light high enough, the lights are comfortable for the subject.

A third light for visual quality is the *accent* or *kicker* light. Illumination falls from above and behind the subject providing the highlights on the hair, face, shoulders, and knees necessary for separation from the back-ground and to improve visual quality. This illumination has little effect

on overall exposure and can be provided by small spots or a mirror behind the subjects. (See Figure 1.)

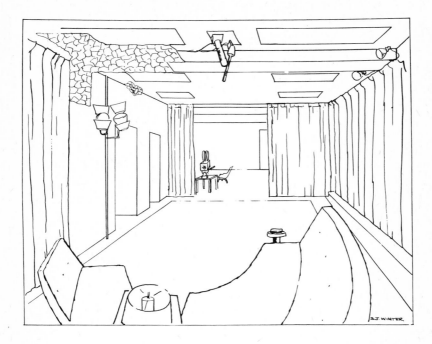

Figure 1

This lighting scheme duplicates the very advantageous effects of the
cinema studio while keeping the attractive, comfortable feeling of a normal room, about 30 feet by 10 feet by 9 feet high. Flat and otherwise inadequate lighting is not quickly recognized since the fatigue due to poor
lighting is often accepted in everyday life. For extended serious viewing a
well lit picture is invaluable.

If poor lighting is often accepted, poor sound is never tolerated. Today
the expectation of clear high fidelity sound has led the theatrical sound
engineer to make some remarkable technical innovations leading to the
wireless lavalier microphone and the highly directional "spot" microphone. The wireless can be worn around the neck and can cause as little
continuing interference as the lighting. The "spot" microphone if placed
on the ceiling as far as 12 feet from the subject can still get good reception. Isolation of the room from external and internal noise is technically
useful but extreme isolation is unnatural and adds neither to the comfort
of the room nor the reality of the subject's experience. It should be men-

tioned that even with the excellent background noise rejection of the spot microphone and the extreme proximity of the wireless microphone to the subject, theatrical quality audio cannot be expected. The sound in the entertainment films is usually recorded after the filming in a *dubbing* studio. This is out of the question in document films so the pure cinema sound is not a fair comparison for naturalistic films. Nor is pure sound uncontaminated by body and environment a goal. Such artificiality can only interfere with the subjects and distort the image received by the analyst.

Figure 2

There are three different levels of sound quality possible in the production of research document films. The least costly but lowest fidelity sound is an optical recording directly on the film at the same moment the picture is recorded. This *single system* sound is only suitable for the first "work" print to evaluate the film for further study.

A 16 mm magnetic sprocketed film recorder provides *double system* recording which is excellent for making a quality sound track but requires the synchronization of the magnetic film with the picture after development. The upper limits of this 16 mm magnetic sound recorder is set by the manufacturers with the limitations of the usual optical film projectors in mind. Most optical 16 mm projectors reproduce sound very poorly so a third original recording is made on a high quality one-fourth inch tape recorder with a synchronizing signal. High quality copies of this recording are used for making transcripts and for linguistic analysis.

A third major consideration in motion picture production is camera operation. The modalities of communication include the visual and this mode may have any part of the body and environment as its instrument. Thus, it is necessary to have the camera cover *the whole of the body* and its relevant immediate environment. *Communication constantly involves the persons present in the environmental situation.* The camera, in order to get a fairly complete coverage of the communicational environment, must include all subjects. With a normal 25 mm lens this places the camera filming a dyad about 25 feet away. Since psychotherapy does not usually involve gross movements of the subjects around a room, the camera set-up does not need to be either mobile or flexible. The camera can be placed inconspicuously but visible on a table top, with the lens at about four feet from the floor. If the camera has a 1200 ft. capacity it may be left unattended for the half hour. This has the advantage of allowing the cameraman to leave the room and the subject's environment. This is invaluable since soon after the camera is activated it is no longer necessary for the investigator to account for the cameraman's behavior.

Close-ups, cut-a-ways, and camera movements are interpretations by the film producers, which if done, must be done by a synchronized secondary camera to allow the prime camera to cover the full interaction. This filmic interpretation of the original event must be made explicit in all versions of the film.

The cinematographer in research designing must choose a laboratory and standardize his films and techniques. This is done by sending out film tests and then having the laboratory comment on the results. The standardization factors that can be checked and controlled by this procedure are: exposure, latitude, optimum grain size, frame line position, camera scratches and steadiness, lens sharpness and focus, sound quality, and printing procedures. These tests also serve to maintain laboratory quality.

Once the designing phase is over, the control of the situation passes from the cinematographer to the subjects, not as actors but as individuals behaving in any way that they find natural and appropriate for themselves.

If the experimental design and techniques are worked out cooperatively and explicitly the investigator knows the limitations of the set-up and the research cinematographer knows where his responsibilities end. With the premises firmly established the subject can proceed with minimum adaptation to the cinematography.

Unlike other filming situations the research photographer must avoid personal involvement with the problems of the actors other than that of registering the behavior so that he can better plan changes in the technique for later filming.

The investigator must learn to respect the competency of the cinematographer and to entrust him with the details of the research needs prior to each filming. The cinematographer can earn this respect by carefully stating the broad technical requirements without flooding the investigator with minor technical necessities. The cinematographer must learn enough about research to respect the competencies of the investigators. At all cost, the cinematographer must accept the requirements of the study of psychotherapy as "The Script" and keep his doubts and psychological interpretations off the set. If he is fortunate, there may be time set aside in the planning conferences for such discussion, if not, it is his obligation to discuss this only in private with the investigators. It is a frequent and disastrous occurrence for the psychiatrist to become an amateur photographer on the set and the cinematographer to become an amateur psychiatrist in the therapy session. *The mutual respect of a multi-disciplinary team can become mutual contempt when skilled professionals naively attempt to exchange roles.*

The filming itself proceeds like any professional production. If there is backstage confusion, it should never show. Normally one subject waits on the lighted set. As the remaining subjects are about to enter camera range, the film is rolled. During the approach, camera and recorder synchronization marks are established. As the subjects familiarize themselves with the situation, the cameraman goes about his job as methodically and inconspicuously as possible. He avoids noisy signals about quietness of the filming. Ducking under the camera lens, "pussyfooting," "shushing" people, overreacting to noises are all "noisy" ways of failing to be inconspicuous. If there is no technical need for the cameraman's presence he leaves the room. The audio man may occasionally check his VU meter to correct for gross level changes but there is no need for him to follow the dialogue. When the film runs out or after the subjects have left the set the equipment is turned off.

These procedures simplify technique without sacrificing photographic quality; but I would be remiss if I did not acknowledge that this simplification does sacrifice some of the film maker's traditional self-image as the focal point of all studio activities. The professional cinematographer is aware that there are also changes under way in the industry with quiet, portable, sound cameras, and light techniques which seem to reduce the importance of the camera crew. In point of fact, the adaptations of the Eastern Pennsylvania Psychiatric Institute are drawn from an earlier period of the industry where clarity of recording was a prime requisite. The precise craftsman may find filming for the study of psychotherapy less threatening than the current subjective trend in film production, in spite of certain sacrifices of his self-image at the point of actual photography.

The professional cinematographer has never had a more important and significant challenge than that of making a high quality, naturalistic recording for the purpose of intensive study.

Once the record is made the production is prepared for release, or in the case of the study of psychotherapy, the data carefully recorded in the film is made available for study. Notes are made on all available information surrounding the filming situation. The time of day, type of film, footage, exposure and volume settings, names of subjects, location of case histories, names of the crew, kind of equipment, identification of all rolls of film and tapes, products of the subjects such as drawings, etc., and finally the laboratory work order, are all part of the dossier of the research document film. These are considered as important as the film itself and great care is taken that they be preserved for immediate study and for archive storage.

All of the various materials must be identified with an information storing code on the container and on each page or portion of the material. In addition to written information, the sound tracks and magnetic tapes have an audible identification. This is carried over in every duplicate. Each *original* tape (and *only* the original tape) has the verbal identification, "This is an original recording—Start transfer now," followed by the usual code and other identification. If the listener hears the statement "This is an original recording," he knows that he must have a duplicate made for his use. An original tape recording like any other original must not be used for any purpose other than duplication.

Much the same procedure is used on films by an adaptation of the Association of Cinema Laboratories standard leader. On the films, after designation for study, titles identify the film and supply some of the filming situation information. The frame count *B roll* numbers each frame consecutively from the beginning. Titles and leaders also contain reminders that the records are only for carefully restricted showings to protect the confidentiality of the subjects. In our procedure a manual[2] is used to assign code letters to the materials so that only authorized persons have access to the materials.

After return from the laboratory of the single system frame counted print, all materials are preserved under safe conditions (see vault storage reference, Eastman Kodak Company) until the recorded event is selected for study by the investigators. This selection may have been made as a condition of the filming. But it is wise to remember that a film may not be utilized for years. Following the decision, a fine grain master duplicate is ordered. This minimizes the always present danger of damage to the original, either through normal uses or laboratory disaster.

This danger is the source of multiple cross-checking precautionary

2 "Identification of Recorded Materials in Temple Research Division," an internally distributed manual of acquisition procedures, available as a reprint.

measures. The event must still be studied even if the original documents are damaged. Any damage is serious, and the cinematographer and all involved will have to face using an inferior original document film in all its viewings and filmic generations, which could have been avoided.

The next step in making the data in the materials available, after the production documentation, is annotation. (See also Sorenson and Gajdusek, 1963.) The record, be it film, tape, or field notes, is examined and recorded. Observations are made as to the location of the possibly significant points. The frame count is used to refer these notes to a particular frame in the film. The material is labeled *research document film annotated* (R.D.[a]). Of course, on each occasion that the film is reviewed the annotation process continues.

Annotation is the point at which the content of the film often starts to be disseminated throughout the research team. The professional, whether he be physician or photographer, must always remember that document films are dealing with human lives and that through the study of the human dynamics in these films more knowledge may be gained than has previously been known about an individual. A research document film contains such a magnitude of personal information in depth as to stagger the imagination.

These data are there for the investigators of today and tomorrow to analyze and interpret. Investigation does not end with facile, early judgments and preliminary public comments about the exploratory discussions concerning the subjects in the films. Please note that I say subjects because even terms like therapist and patient may suggest a premature evaluation and over-simplification of the dynamics in the relationship.

The medical profession has a long history of respect for the confidentiality of the physician-patient relationship. The right of the patient to his privacy has been borne out in the courts; yet physicians still are being financially and professionally ruined by ethical indiscretions. The maker of document films is part of this ethic and incidentally is subject to the risks. The study of psychotherapy fantastically expands the cinematographer's knowledge of human behavior and he must be disciplined about his new knowledge. In the multi-disciplinary approach the interpretation of research documents is often not appropriately a matter of concern for the cinematographer. Unless he has good reason to trust his discretion he is well advised to choose to be blind and deaf. The interpretations that must be brought to his attention are seldom fit matters for discussion outside of the walls of the research situation. If the cinematographer finds himself privy to the patient-physician relationship he must do nothing to violate that confidence even with his most intimate colleagues and trusted acquaintances.

After the film has been exposed, the dossier prepared, and the location of some of the data in the film made accessible by annotation, the film may be analyzed. Analysis is a detailed study of an aspect of the data contained in the original document film. This can be linguistic analysis of the dialogue, a psychiatric analysis of manifest or latent content, or a kinesic analysis of the visible action. Since this analysis is also dovetailed to the frame count it may be considered an extremely detailed annotation done by a trained analyst. The term for this film, that has this degree of access to the data, is a *research document film analyzed* (R.D.A.).

It is in the analysis phase that the cinematographic quality of the production becomes most important. Many prints will be extended in frame-by-frame examinations and each improvement in the quality of the original filming will be reflected in the reduced fatigue of the investigators. As the sound is analyzed with the help of the sound spectographs, sound stretchers, and instruments yet to come, the fidelity of the recording will be utilized to its relevant limit. It is the primary obligation of the cinematographer to record the data at the absolute maximum that present techniques and skills will allow.

The findings of the study of psychotherapy must be communicated. The investigators are expected to disseminate findings through the usual media of papers, lectures, and publications. The cinematographer is equally obligated to communicate his technical and relevant personal experiences to his own colleagues while being always mindful of the confidentiality of the physician-patient relationship and the ground rules of scientific communications. Catalogue information concerning films must be made available to the Library of Congress,[3] the National Science Film Association[4] and the U.S. Department of Health, Education, and Welfare.[5]

Many of the research document films will eventually be excerpted into conventional teaching films. The pre-print material will of course be a frame counted duplication from the original. The frame-numbers will serve as references for the more serious student who will want to return to the original documents.

There is another kind of tutorial film which has introductory explanatory footage followed by the *entire uncut original* frame-numbered document film, perhaps amplified by additional commentary footage appended as the tail. The *research document film with commentary* (R.D.) is particularly useful since the student can then refer directly to the original document without additional expense. The film, at minimal cost, is double purposed.

The *research document* film makes a unique contribution to the study of psychotherapy because there is a minimum of interjection of an un-

---

[3] See "Rules for Descriptive Cataloguing in the Library of Congress," Library of Congress, 1962.

[4] National Science Film Association, 704 Seventeenth Street N.W., Washington 6, D.C.

[5] U.S. Public Health Service, Communicable Disease Center, Atlanta 22, Georgia.

known third person's personality into the record of the filmed interaction. The great success of the conventional motion picture comes from the interpretation or synthesis of a series of events into a coherent whole which inevitably must be a projection of the creator's personality. If a motion picture is produced in a manner that minimizes the manifestation of individual personalities other than the subjects before the camera, then we have a lasting record that can be seriously examined by any and all students of psychotherapy with the expectation of finding explicit common grounds for understanding human nature. This is being done by transferring the production skills of the interpretive film maker to the skillful recording of the significant data for the study of psychotherapy. In this new role the cinematographer finds himself becoming a responsible and disciplined member of the scientific community. He is badly needed. With discipline, he can meet these new responsibilities.

REFERENCES

Eastman Kodak Company. Storage and Preservation of Motion Picture Film. Rochester, New York: Motion Picture Film Dept.

SORENSON, E. R., and GAJDUSEK, D. C. Investigation of Non-recurring Phenomena: The Research Cinema Film. *Nature,* **200** No. 4902: 112-114, 1963.

VAN VLACK, J. The Research Document Film. *American Science Film Association Notes,* April, 1965.

3. Sound motion picture facilities for research in communication

Allen T. Dittmann, Seymour N. Stein, and David Shakow

In recent years there has been a growing interest in recording behavioral material by sound motion picture techniques, both for research and for educational purposes. The technical problems of constructing and equipping facilities for this sort of work, and of operating them when they are finished, are considerable. Because of our experience in building such facilities in two quite different settings, we have often been called upon to give advice in planning for this type of recording. It has seemed to us, therefore, that an outline of the requirements and some of the problems of developing such facilities might find use in the behavioral science fields. We shall take up issues of technical consultation, of the design and construction of rooms for the purpose of photographic and audio recording techniques, and finally, playback considerations.

First, there are some general problems which present themselves to subjects of such research, and to the investigators who will be using the material for their studies. Subjects, who are usually patients and interviewers, understandably feel uneasy about being photographed, as Sternberg, Chapman, and Shakow (1958) have shown, but in time they adapt somewhat to the situation. The time required for adaptation in any given case is a function of many factors, such as the personality make-up of the individual subject, the seriousness and considerateness of the investigators. Not far down the list is the nature of the physical set-up in which the recording takes place. In the case of tape recording, offices are used which differ from the usual setting only by virtue of the presence of the recording machine.[1] When motion pictures are made, however, the difference is marked by the extra lighting needed for photography, the extra equipment, the specially built room, and often by the bustle of extra personnel. All of these focus attention on the recording situation, and if there are to be many interviews of the same subjects, the physical necessities serve as a constant reminder of the fact of recording. There is no way, of course, to eliminate lights and camera if one is to have motion pictures, but it is possible to design for unobtrusiveness of the recording techniques. If the design is successful, subjects will be aided in their adaptation to the recording. Thus unobtrusiveness of the recording situation is a basic design

---

[1] For design of a suite for audio recording and observation, see Mahl, Dollard and Redlich (1954).

consideration which must be understood by many people who are unfamiliar with its necessity—lighting engineers, camera technicians, audio
specialists, and the like. We will refer back to this point in the next section of the paper.

If unobtrusiveness of recording technique is a requirement from the
subject's standpoint, high signal-to-noise ratio is even more so from the
investigator's. In this context, *signal-to-noise* is used in a more extended
sense including both visual and auditory modalities. The reason for this
requirement lies in the nature of most work with the final recordings.
Interviews or segments of interviews must be looked at and listened to
repeatedly by the investigator and by judges, and over long periods of
time. The easier it is to watch and listen, the less the observers will be
subject to fatigue and its attendant errors in this exacting and often tedious work. Sharp pictures of low grain and of good shading for easy
identification of facial contours and expression is one example of the goal.
Clear voice signal which stands out as figure against a very faint background of extraneous noise is another. In some cases, special techniques
may be used to enhance the signal-to-noise ratio, such as stereophonic
recording in playroom situations where the background level of banging
toys cannot be reduced.

It is for increase in signal-to-noise ratios that professional equipment
must be used, and that professional techniques of recording must be
adhered to. While many workers in our fields have had extensive experience
as amateurs in photography and electronics, there is a body of knowledge,
most of it unwritten, which professionals call upon in doing their jobs.
That is not to say that the ideas of amateurs have no validity. In many
cases the naivete of a non-professional can work to great advantage by
opening new approaches. After all, recording behavioral material imposes
conditions with which the professional will not have had experience. Thus
the investigator and the professional have to work together to achieve the
highest quality of recording.

TECHNICAL CONSULTANTS

When the decision has been made to construct facilities for sound motion picture recording, the first step is to consult with technical people
whose training and experience have made them competent in the various
relevant fields. The situation of recording behavioral data is very different
from the usual applications of sound motion picture techniques, and consultants will need a great deal of explanation of the aims of the work
so that they can understand fully the limitations placed upon their design.
The idea of making the recording situation unobtrusive, for example, is
quite foreign to the motion picture and television field. The artist's goal
is to perform for an audience, to make an impact upon his viewers, and he

will cooperate with technical people to further that end. In an interview situation in which the investigator is interested in interviewing techniques, on the other hand, cooperation with the technical recording people would destroy the point of the recording. Consultants must thus use their experience with the artist to develop ways of meeting the investigator's purpose. In order to serve that function best, they must have a very clear understanding of what the investigator's purpose is. It is well worth the investigator's while to explain fully, and usually to re-explain, in order to develop in the consultant a real, personal interest in the scientific or educational reasons for making the recording. For some consultants these will be the only conditions under which they will begin to design unusual facilities, any shortcomings in which they feel might reflect adversely on their reputations in their own professional community. In the past, of course, many of these fears were realistic because standard practices had not been applied in this way. By this time, however, there has been enough experience to show that useful recordings can be made under circumstances which many able people would not have considered feasible a few years ago.

Consultants from a number of fields will be needed to collaborate in the design—from architecture, heating and air-conditioning, lighting, acoustics, electronics, and photography. Since no one person has enough training and experience in all these fields to do the complete job, the final design will be the result of the work of varied specialists. The investigator will be called upon many times to make decisions he does not have the training to make, and will hope that his explanations of the purpose of the recording will be translatable into technical terms. He will also learn enough about the various fields to integrate expert advice into a final plan.

THE CONSTRUCTION OF THE ROOM

The design of the recording room will be a compromise of the interrelationships among heat, light, and sound level. Photography requires lights; lights produce heat; removing heat is noisy; but sound recording requires low background noise levels. The design from any one of these standpoints is easy: A great deal of light can be provided unobtrusively, for example, if the scene to be filmed is so short that heat build-up is not a consideration. But combining the requirements of light, heat, and sound leads to inevitable compromises. Many engineers are challenged and intrigued by such design problems.

Sound

From the standpoint of sound level, the design of the room will depend entirely upon the amount of noise in the area where the room is to be built. The investigator is fortunate if he can choose a location within the building away from built-in noise sources such as elevators, pumps, generators, and main water lines. Machinery creates low frequency noise which is far more costly to reduce than high frequency noise. While these noises may not be audible or measurable before the room is built, they may stand out after local noise is reduced.

Soundproofing is a complicated process. One thing is clear: One can never eliminate noise; one can only reduce it. How much is reduced is expressed in decibels, a ratio of one acoustic energy level to another. Even the *noise level* figure is a ratio of an existing level to a standard one (roughly the threshold of hearing.) A widely misunderstood fact about sound treatment is the difference between reduction of noise from outside the room and reduction of noise inside a room. The first concerns transmission through walls, pipes, wires, etc., while the second concerns reverberation. To reduce transmitted noise, mass of walls and insulation packed into air space between walls are used. To reduce reverberation, soft surfaces, such as acoustic tile, carpets, and upholstered furniture are used. The confusion between transmission and reverberation is very widespread. Many believe, for example, that acoustic tile can significantly reduce transmitted noise, a function for which it was not designed.

Optimum sound and reverberation levels for a room are difficult to specify in advance, since they depend on how the room is to be used. For individual interviews it will be possible to place microphones somewhat closer to the speakers than for group sessions, so the background level requirements are not so stringent. In general, noise levels below 30 db (ASA "A"-scale) are desirable but costly to obtain. Reverberation times should be as short as possible if clean speech signals are to be recorded. But there is a compromise here, too, since rooms with too short reverberation times feel artificially "dead" to subjects in them. *Optimum* reverberation times vary with room size, and the tables published in standard engineering handbooks are good guides.

Construction of acoustically designed rooms must be carried out by persons who understand the unusual nature of the specifications. Many designs, for example, call for two walls, the inner one of which floats on a separate floor which is isolated from the building. The two walls must obviously be kept separate if the isolation is to be maintained, but the plans look as if the draftsman had forgotten to include some bracing members. If he is not familiar with these peculiar techniques, even a skilled carpenter can destroy the sound reduction properties of the room with a few nails. Ideally the architect or acoustical engineer should supervise every phase of the construction; but such a practice is obviously not feasible. Proper orientation of the carpenters both by the architect and by the investigator must be relied upon. Plumbing and electrical connections from outside to inside the room must also be supervised for the same reasons.

Lighting

Providing light levels high enough for motion picture requirements presents perhaps the greatest problem for attaining the goal of unobtrusiveness in recording. Individuals involved in an interview situation could probably never adapt to the spotlights, fillers, and reflectors which characterize the traditional motion picture set. Apart from the concentrated heat from the lights themselves, such a set-up would stir movie star or third-degree fantasies even in unreflective subjects. Nevertheless, the best photographic images come from well-lighted scenes.

We have found that diffused lighting can be tolerated at extremely high levels, and while adaptation to the recording situation is not as easy as it is under "normal" room lighting, it is still possible. Fluorescent tubes now convert up to a quarter of the input electrical energy into light (the rest into heat), and a number of these tubes behind a plastic diffusing screen produce ample light for recording on relatively low-speed films. The height of the ceiling will dictate the distance between tubes—for an 8-foot ceiling, tubes mounted on 9-inch centers yield 60 foot-candles of light reflected from the face of a seated person (about 300 foot-candles incident.) Subjects say that the room is indeed bright, but has a rather cheerful brightness, as if it were illuminated by a skylight. A normally lighted corridor is very dark in comparison to the light level of a room treated in this way, and supplementary illumination for a length of hallway, say 50 feet, markedly reduces the shock of opening the door to the room.

Diffused fluorescent lighting was new to the field at the time when the interview room was built at the Illinois Neuropsychiatric Institute in the early 1950's, but it has gained wide acceptance since then. It is currently used in stores and display rooms, and will be a familiar design to most lighting specialists.

PHOTOGRAPHIC CONSIDERATIONS

The ultimate usefulness of films depends on many factors, the chief of which is resolution. *Resolution* is a relative term. If an investigator wishes to study facial expressions of several members of a group, the requirements are very stringent. He must have the very best lens and use the finest grain film available, but the image size of each face will be so small that only the grossest expressions can be studied. If he can take a close-up of an individual face, on the other hand, a great deal of grain can be tolerated, and light levels can be reduced.

Two general functional relationships are contained in this example:

(1) The relationship between film speed, light level, and grain. While tremendous gains have been made in the last few years, there is still a

relationship between film speed and grain. High speed films are characterized by large silver granules in the emulsion, while fine-grain films have
slower speeds.

(2) The field to be covered determines image size of each subject being photographed, and image size determines the grain size per subject.
If the investigator knows in advance that all of his shots will be close-ups,
he can use higher speed film, and need not design for so much light in the
room. The problems of heat and sound level will be reduced as well. But
rooms of the sort we are discussing are too expensive for special purposes
and compromises must be made.

With such expensive space, savings on the initial purchase of recording
equipment are unwise and may jeopardize the purpose of the recordings.
Professional photographic equipment is far more costly than amateur, but
the difference in image quality and most of all dependability cannot be
measured in dollars. The reason for the high cost of professional equipment can be seen at once: it is designed and built for years of constant
use. Parts are made of the highest quality materials and the workmanship
is superb. In the entertainment field, *down-time* costs money; in scientific
fields it costs irreplaceable data in addition to money.

Motion picture cameras are designed to run short lengths of film, such
as 200 feet (16 mm). Where the "takes" last 10 to 30 seconds, these lengths
are adequate and mean that the camera and attendant equipment can be
small and light. But 200 feet of film lasts about five and a half minutes at
standard sound speed (24 frames per second), and does not go far in
recording an interview. Magazines are available for many cameras for
footages up to 1200 feet, representing about 33 minutes. Greater lengths
of film would require either two cameras or a magazine built to special
order. Several firms are equipped for such construction.

Film costs for recording full interviews are high. Where many films of
an hour in length are being run, in fact, the operating costs of the project
will dwarf the costs of equipment. At this writing, negative, processing,
and printing cost in the neighborhood of $130 an hour for 16 mm black-
and-white runs. Reversal film runs about two-thirds of this cost, but leaves
the investigator with one print only, with no negative to make other prints
for replacement or for parallel uses.

To get the best out of the equipment and film, professional photogra-
phers should do the actual camera work. This includes not only taking the
pictures, but maintaining the equipment so that it will live its full life
without trouble. Regular schedules of the on-the-spot maintenance, as
well as periodic cleaning by a camera shop, must be part of the routine.
The professional photographer will also know how to make test films in
collaboration with the film processing firm so that the best balance of den-
sity, contrast, graininess, and sound exposure may be had. These tests,
too, must be routine, since film emulsions, even of the same manufacturer's

stock number, vary from one batch to the next and exposure and development time must be varied to compensate. Even the very experienced amateur photographer is not equipped to carry out all of these procedures. For the professional they are second nature, and increase enormously the probability of a high-quality final product.

AUDIO CONSIDERATIONS

Sound-on-film techniques have been undergoing improvements ever since their introduction some 30 years ago, and yet the quality of single system 16 mm optical sound as it is recorded in cameras today is low compared to the sound obtainable from tape recorders. Indeed, a significant advance has been made in motion picture sound by the application of magnetic sound to film. The chief gain in magnetic sound on film is in signal-to-noise ratio, using the term now in its technical sense. With optical sound, quiet talking is barely audible above the noise, while an emphasized phrase overloads the system and cannot be understood clearly. Magnetic sound adds to the total cost of the film, since a magnetic stripe must be deposited on the film, but the increase in quality is more than worth the increase in cost. The sound may be recorded either in the camera, on a synchronized tape recorder, or better yet, on a magnetic film recorder, and later transferred to the film.

Microphone placement is the key to clean audio signals. In general recording practice, the speaker talks into the microphone, keeping within a 6- to 12-inch range of the instrument. The recording level is adjusted so that the main signal is the voice, the background noise being barely audible. For the most part, in addition, the performer is talking in a loud voice, similar to that used to project across the footlights to an audience. Thus, the recording level may be turned down even farther, and background noise is almost inaudible on playback. The signal-to-noise ratio is then effectively the figure given for the recording system itself, over 50 db from system noise to point of three percent distortion in broadcast quality tape recorders.

In interviews the situation is radically different. The subjects are not talking to an audience, and are likely to speak softly. Further, if they are attending to the task of the interview rather than to the recording, they do not speak directly to the microphone. Thus the actual background noise level in the room must be reckoned with. Even so, however, the placement of microphones may make as much difference to signal-to-noise ratio as the acoustical construction. An informal experiment in a small office demonstrates this effect: A microphone placed one foot from a sound source produced a signal 22 db higher than the same microphone at three feet. Many hundreds of dollars in construction would have to be spent to reduce background noise that much. Thus, careful placement of microphones will increase signal quality in the best of rooms. Lavalier units developed for television use, suspended from a short cord around the speaker's neck, will make recordings possible in the most adverse circumstances. These would seem to nullify the goal of unobtrusiveness, but some are light enough so that they can hardly be felt, and are out of the normal range of vision. Subjects adapt to these units very readily.

PLAYBACK CONSIDERATIONS

On playback the audio problems are relatively simple, but the projector problems are not. Projectors are designed for continuous running of films, and it is difficult to find one which will not tear film when it is started and stopped frequently. Film must pass over so many rollers and surfaces, too, that scratches are frequent unless constant maintenance is observed carefully over all parts of the projector. In the past, remote control projectors were available only as specially modified commercial projectors, but now there are a few on the market which have the additional advantage of operating at varying speeds below the standard sound speed with little flicker, including single frame projection.[2] They are not designed for sound film, but may be modified to read optical or magnetic tracks.

The room in which films are played back presents acoustical problems if its reverberation time is too long. The sound track itself has been recorded in a room with some reverberation, and this is added to the reverberation in the playback room. In extreme cases listeners have difficulty understanding what is said, and turn the playback volume control so high that distortion results. A room with far less reverberation than the recording room is very desirable, and may be had by treating the ceiling and large areas of the walls (at the listener's position, not the loudspeaker's) with acoustic tile.

SUMMARY

In this paper we have outlined many of the problems of designing facilities for sound motion picture recordings of interviews. We have pointed to areas which need consideration (acoustics, lighting, photography, and sound recording) and included some guidelines which we have found useful. It should be clear from the number of variables we have discussed, that there are a number of possible solutions to the problem of getting good results. Consultation with designers in the various relevant fields will be easiest where the requirements can be specified the most exactly.

[2] The National Institutes of Health has had a special projector built with all of the above functions and, in addition, the possibility of running film in fast forward or fast reverse without unthreading and rethreading the film, so that portions can be rerun and other portions farther ahead can be searched for with a minimum of wasted time.

REFERENCES

MAHL, G. F., DOLLARD, J., and REDLICH, F. C. Facilities for the sound recording and observation of interviews. *Sci.*, **120**: 235-239, 1954.

STERNBERG, R. S., CHAPMAN, J., and SHAKOW, D. Psychotherapy research and the problem of intrusions on privacy. *Psychiat.*, **21**: 195-203, 1958.

B.

Reactions of the Patient and Therapist to the Recording Procedure

We have decided to give a kaleidoscopic view of the reactions of patients and therapists to the experience of being recorded in the process of the interview. To this end, we have included the reports of five psychotherapists, discussing at various length their reactions, and sometimes their patient's reactions, to being recorded during psychotherapy. It is our impression, probably well-shared, that patient and therapist vary in their life histories, personalities, and in the style depth and candor of expression of their reactions to such an event. We believe the five contributions in this section substantiate this impression.

The duration of the psychotherapy and its recording must also have a bearing on the nature and intensity of the emotional reactions of the participants in the psychotherapy. The chapter by Paul Bergman tells of how one therapist and patient reacted during hundreds of sessions of a sound filmed psychotherapy. The chapters by the other authors (Carmichael, English, Erickson, and Jackson) report reactions to much shorter episodes of filming.

4. An experiment in filmed psychotherapy

Paul Bergman

I. THE PROBLEM OF "BACKGROUND" IN PSYCHOTHERAPY

A relationship between two people can develop in any imaginable setting. A person can learn to love or hate, to trust or distrust, to understand or misunderstand another person in a crowded prison or concentration camp or in a lonely lifeboat. The external conditions become background and receive less attention as the relationship unfolds and increasingly involves the attention of the protagonists. If this holds true in other human relationships, it should also hold true in psychotherapy.

In the customary office setup of psychotherapy three conditions are taken for granted as part of the background: That the patient meets the therapist in privacy; that the meeting lasts a predetermined amount of time, no more and no less; and that the patient pays the therapist for his services. There is nothing "natural" about any of these conditions. A hundred years ago only the most "depraved" woman would have confided a personal secret to a strange man in the absence of her husband. Nor is there anything "natural" about two people talking about matters of vital importance for a set number of minutes, and interrupting the talk when that number has been reached; or about one person paying money to another in a relationship which may become one of deep personal involvement. At present, however, people of highly different sensitivities generally accept these conditions which they consider indispensable. The office setting of psychotherapy has become part of the cultural mores.

A stable background does not mean, of course, a background toward which one has no reactions. Occasionally neither the patient nor the therapist can help having reactions to some aspect of the office setting. Even the privacy of the setting can sometimes become an obstacle. Thus, one of my patients, a young man who had suffered a homosexual trauma in his early adolescence, did not want to face me for therapy in the one-to-one situation. He thought he could never talk freely if alone in a room with a man. To another patient, the fee-paying aspects became an obstacle. He considered himself unable to set aside money for the therapy, in the same unyielding way that he always had been unable to accept onerous obligations. At present I am seeing a young woman patient who struggles against all time schedules which come from me, the therapist, while she attempts to have the therapy take place at a time of her own choosing. I also remember a patient, a woman of masochistic bent, who used to feel punished, humiliated, and sexually excited when I terminated the interview at the set time.

Patients' reactions to the usual office setting have been observed and described for so long that such descriptions have become part of the psychotherapists' picture of "human nature," as if this nature would reveal itself most sharply against this particular background. Actually, human nature reveals itself against any background, yet reveals different aspects under different conditions.

The therapist also reacts to the standard office setting. His reactions, however, generally remain unrevealed, since he, who traditionally reports on the situation, tends to see himself as part of the stable background. One of the advantages of the recording or observation of therapy has been to show that the therapist is not part of the stable background, but is an individual interacting with another individual and at times very definitely reacting to the background. One observes, for instance, that some therapists show a concern with the flow of time during the therapy sessions or find it particularly difficult, if not painful, to terminate an interview. Other aspects of the standard background also may evoke reactions. When I was working with a paranoid schizophrenic young man of violent temper, I felt afraid in the privacy of my office. I did not mind seeing him on the hospital grounds where other people could observe us and I could obtain help if he were to attack me. I owe to a therapist in private practice, not a mercenary person at all, an interesting observation which he thought was pertinent to subtle differences in his attitude toward non-paying patients. He kept a dog in his office during his working hours who used to greet all his patients, except two, with a friendly wagging of the tail. The two at whom the dog invariably barked were patients who were receiving free treatment.

Although patient and therapist react to features of the standard setting of therapy, such reactions are rarely responsible for unsuccessful therapy. Patient and therapist are generally able to recognize and transcend disturbing attitudes.

If patient and therapist work under unusual conditions, such as those dictated by demands of training or research, they may react to these conditions; but again, these reactions should not, and generally do not, interfere substantially with the therapy.

Some years ago, the advisability of sound-recorded therapy was seriously questioned by many. At present, only a few retain a negative view. I doubt whether these are workers who have tried recording their own interviews. The possibility of therapy in the presence of observers has met with similar skepticism. Yet in the last few years, at various research and training institutions, observers, with the patients' and therapists' consent, have been actually sitting in the therapy room, or behind a one-way screen. Both methods have been found practicable and for the most part have had no effect upon the rate of patients' improvement, at least none apparent to the participants in these studies.

It originally came as a surprise to me that practically all patients freely accepted any proposed "unusual" features, whether these consisted of a microphone, a tape recorder, an apparatus for the recording of physiological changes, or the presence of observers. This attitude on the part of the patients did not seem related to their degree of disturbance; nor did it make any difference whether they paid or did not pay for the treatment. In the course of about fifteen years I have asked over thirty patients for permission to let themselves be recorded or observed. The only one who refused was a paranoid woman who caught me in an unwitting lie during the exploratory interview.

She asked me whether notes on her case would be available to the nurses, some of whom she knew personally. I told her what I believed, namely, that no nurse would ever see any such material. Thereupon the patient left me in intense anger. When I inquired, I learned that before the interview she had seen a note by the intake worker in the hands of the nurse at the admission desk.

Many therapists now work under conditions which would have seemed unusual and dubious a few years ago; yet no insurmountable difficulties arise. The patients do not seem to mind these conditions. They rarely request discontinuation of observation and/or recording, though in most cases they are told that they may do so if they feel unduly uncomfortable or inhibited. I have never encountered a patient who made any such request. Conceivably patients do not feel free to oppose what they (sometimes wrongly) consider to be the therapist's wish. At any rate, even follow-up interviews with the therapist or other research workers do not produce complaints about the setup of the therapy. On two occasions I had to deal with complaints of paranoid patients that hostile "powers" were listening to their recorded therapy. Both patients specifically exempted from their suspicions the microphone which was openly in their view. They accepted the setup as part of the research which I had explained to them. However, they believe that the "persecutors" had wired the room in some hidden way. For one of these patients I stopped the recording and removed the microphone. This measure did not diminish the patient's conviction that the unseen threats persisted.

Of course, patients do at times very definitely react to the peculiarities of the given background. For instance, the idea of "helping research" for some serves as a face-saving device which allows them to ask for help. The presence of observers may also be considered protection, at times even as stimulation to self-abandoned expression in order to impress the audience. Others in the same setting may delay the expression of thought and feeling, only gradually overcoming a feeling of inhibition. In any case, I doubt that the difference in background, in the long run, makes a difference for the therapy. As long as the background continues unchanged and undisturbed, most patients apparently are not overly concerned about its peculiarities. In order to secure for herself the feeling of a stable background, one of my patients declared she did not want to know whether or not observers were to attend particular therapy sessions. If she could assume that observers were always present, she could best "forget" about them.

Research patients rarely complain of being used as "guinea-pigs" and even more rarely does this issue become an obstacle to therapy. It probably obstructs research therapy as rarely as the feeling that the therapist cares only for money obstructs therapy in private practice.

To summarize, on the patient's side the obstacles to therapy in a research setup are slight and, where they do occur, can for the most part be overcome fairly easily. The paraphernalia of the technical setup—the microphone, the one-way screen, or whatever else it may be—represent to the patient a boundary beyond which no human relationship exists and from which no real threats arise.

To the therapist, however, these same paraphernalia frequently do represent human relationships and sometimes an actual threat. He knows that he may gain or lose in the estimation of colleagues who might listen to recordings or watch the actual interviews. He realizes that his own weaknesses may be pitilessly exposed in any prolonged and difficult psychotherapy. He also realizes that, at present, convictions in the field of psychotherapy are religiously held, and criticism of different strategies is frequently expressed with intense personal involvement. Several therapists of my acquaintance, persons of high integrity, have occasionally requested to be relieved of observers when they felt that they did not do well with a particular patient, or when, even though they did well, their relations with colleagues had become temporarily clouded by criticism they had received or by some other source of tension. Under similar circumstances I myself have managed to forget to turn on a recording switch, possibly because my convictions about research did not allow me a less furtive way of protecting myself from criticism.

The problem would be more manageable if it were more clearly faced. Yet I know from my own experience that this is very difficult for a therapist to do. Most of the discussion of research therapists indeed skirts the issue of their sensitivity to the criticism of colleagues, and instead stresses patients' sensitivities to some element of the setup. As I see it, the complication comes from the fact that the therapist's anxieties are displaced in several directions, and the source of the difficulty is often obscured.

To empathize with the therapist's predicament in this kind of situation, imagine yourself sitting in a dentist's chair. The headrest presses against your occiput at an uncomfortable angle, and at the same time the dentist's hand presses hard against your jaw and his drill irritates a live nerve in a tooth. Under these conditions, the more anxious you become the less you will be able to recognize and differentiate the various sources of your misery.

A research setup similarly puts the therapist in the center of a triangular field, with each point of the triangle representing a potential source of disturbance, namely, the relation with the patient, the relation with professional colleagues, and the machinery of the setup. Surely, as long as the therapist can clearly evaluate the threats emanating from each of these sources his response is amenable to rational control and repair. Under the impact of anxiety, however, he becomes less able to balance stresses, he perceives less clearly, and he tends to use pathological mechanisms of defense.

Such difficulties are not, of course, confined to the research setup. Even in a private office, where the concern about professional relations is likely to play a rather small role, a therapist may mistakenly blame some extrinsic factor for the difficulties of the therapy. A research setup, however, easily leads the therapist to displace his concern from the more sensitive sources of anxiety to the less sensitive ones. Thus, concern with colleagues' reactions can be partly or wholly transferred to concern about the patient or about the technical setup; or concern about the patient can be transferred to either or both of the other points. Later, when discussing my filming experiences, I shall bring in some relevant illustrations.

The technical setup is generally the recipient rather than the source of the therapist's concerns. By itself, the setup threatens the therapist no more than it threatens the patient. Surely therapists, like their patients, experience uneasiness about any newly introduced feature and prefer a stable background whenever possible in order to concentrate on the business at hand. For example some therapists who have not objected to being observed, nevertheless have made the same request as some patients, namely to ke kept ignorant of whether a particular session was being observed. On my part, on the rare occasions when I realized at the beginning of the session that technical difficulties were preventing the routine procedures, I felt uneasy, annoyed, letdown. Nor did I like it when regular observers failed to come. Pride and self-importance certainly entered into these feelings, but the wish for a stable background also played its role, for the presence of a new or rarely attending observer made me similarly uneasy. However, the temporary uneasiness caused by an altered background is generally soon overcome, or means are found to obviate it.

Evidently an anxious therapist will not function as well as he otherwise might. He will fare even worse when he misperceives the source of his anxiety and futilely displaces his attention and efforts. What one may do about the therapist's anxiety in a research setup will depend, of course, on the purposes of the research. If it is important that the patient get the best possible therapy then one should not expect the research therapist alone to counteract all the potential sources of tension. He should be part of a group of freely communicating, friendly colleagues. Such participation would mitigate or even eliminate one of his major anxieties, that about his professional relationships.

II. A PERSONAL EXPERIENCE WITH FILMED PSYCHOTHERAPY

A group of researchers at the University of Illinois, and later at the National Institute of Mental Health, decided some years ago that an experiment with filmed psychotherapy was worth trying (Shakow, 1960).

I became the therapist on the project at the National Institute, but I participated neither in the research planning nor in the actual research work, because the entire group agreed that the therapy should not be influenced by the hypothesis of the researchers. This paper, therefore, will not report on the research aspects of the project which have been reported elsewhere (Carmichael, 1956; Cohen, 1961; Dittmann, 1961, 1962; Sternberg, 1958). Rather I will discuss the therapy aspects as seen from the perspective of the therapist.

In the remainder of the paper I shall: (1) describe the setup in which my experience with filmed psychotherapy took place; (2) briefly present the patient's history and personality problems; (3) show how some of these personality problems were carried over into the filmed therapy situation and found expression in response to that situation; (4) examine some of my own reactions to the setup; and finally, (5) offer some evidence that therapeutic change did take place under the conditions of the experiment.

The Setup

The setup in which I was doing the filmed therapy consists of two adjoining rooms. The *scenium* is a medium large, plain, windowless room, brightly lit from a transparent ceiling. A couch, a few chairs, two small tables, one of which supports the microphone, a few books, two pictures, and a few growing plants have the task of making the room look like an ordinary office. The camera room is a smaller room which was kept dark during the filming sessions. There an operator started and stopped the film and sat by during the sessions in order to be available in case of technical emergency. From the scenium one could see the face of the camera in a window of the opaque glass wall separating the two rooms. When something occasionally went wrong, as is bound to happen where human beings and sensitive machinery are involved, the sleeve or the hand of the operator would appear there also. The operator could hear words spoken in the scenium, but generally preferred other pursuits.

The Patient

Anna, the patient I saw in this setting was a woman in her early forties, of Italian, Roman-Catholic background. Her father had been a construction worker, fiery in temperament but sick in body; her mother was a cool and competent, hard-working, "no-nonsense" person. When Anna was six years old, her father died leaving behind, besides the mother and Anna, an older girl aged twelve and a newborn baby girl. From then on, the mother worked as a clerk in a department store. A year later two more severe blows struck the family: the older sister developed diabetes, the younger one tuberculosis. A large part of the responsibility of running the home thus fell to the only healthy child, Anna. Six years after her father's death, her older sister succumbed to the diabetes. Anna suffered another six years in anxious tension, expecting a blow of fate to strike her mother, her younger sister, or herself. When it did not come, she broke down in anxiety attacks which gradually grew into a crippling phobia. In spite of this encumbrance, a few years later Anna married the owner of a small roadside motel. From then on, Anna's husband and eventually their five children became the objects of Anna's fearful concern. When Anna entered therapy she was in a state of phobic near-immobility. But it was not so much despair over her own handicap as fear that her anxieties were affecting her children which made her seek help.

The Patient's Reactions to the Setup

For many years Anna had tried to ward off the feeling that fate had singled her out for some incomprehensible, long-delayed blow. She had been accustomed to scanning her environment carefully for indications of what might be in store for herself and for her family. This set of feelings now attached itself to the new situation.

Anna unhesitatingly consented to have her entire therapy filmed for research purposes. But soon after starting she began to worry about why she of all people might have been chosen for this unusual project. There must be a "deeper" reason why she was chosen. Was it because the doctors at our institution thought her doomed to hopeless insanity or early death? Did they want a filmed record of such a person's demise? Or, on the contrary, had she been chosen because she was of completely sound mind in spite of her phobic troubles, as she had told herself for years when beset by fears for her sanity? And what did the therapist and the research staff behind him really plan to do to her? It seemed essential to her to outguess them in order not to be felled by a surprise blow. Some days the light in the scenium seemed brighter or less bright than on other days. Some days she could observe unmistakable indications in the camera room that movies were being taken. On other days it was so quiet and motionless there that she could not believe anybody was present. What could it mean? Were any of these conditions a sign that the staff and the therapist expected some dire event to happen?

Early in life, when Anna had had to take care of her sisters, there had been no other way to control her playful, dependent, passive, or aggressive needs but to keep them out of consciousness. To insure this repression, she had forced her will into a mold of responsibility-taking. Eventually this feeling of heavy and hated responsibility permeated virtually all her experiences and attitudes. Now it was transferred in full force to the therapy situation. The eyes and ears not only of the therapist but also of the research staff were upon her. What a burden to perform under the threat of some nameless catastrophe which would come about if she failed; or maybe in the eyes of the staff she had already failed. She dreaded meeting any member of the research staff; he would recognize her with a shattering look of disdain. Thus, for a very long time she hated to come to the therapy sessions, because they conveyed to her an atmosphere of inescapable disapproval and impossible responsibility.

At the time of her father's final illness Anna had passionately negotiated with God to save the threatened life. Afterwards, when it seemed to her that God had been unable to keep his part of the bargain, she lost her faith in Him. To her mind, both God and her father had proved themselves weak, unworthy of the trust that she had invested in them. From then on, all persons in authority, particularly men, seemed to her weak and pretenders to powers which they did not really hold. The real powers, she felt, were lodged in the hands of invisible, superior, fate-like forces which had no clear relation to God and which used men as puppets.

The setup allowed for a simple transfer of such attitudes. Soon after coming into therapy, Anna began to concern herself with the question of my assumed relations with my superiors at the research institute. She felt that I was weak, did not know what I was doing, and had no power to prevent any of the many looming catastrophes. My superiors breathed hot down my neck and would eventually discharge me. Whatever I did seemed to her to betray my puppet-like acting on behalf of the "real powers" who held all final decisions in their hands. I, the therapist, a deceptive pseudo-authority, could be treated with contempt, but the "real powers" were not to be trifled with.

The more distant the powers, the more dangerous they seemed to her. Anna often whispered when talking about the research staff. Even more dangerous were the politicians supposedly in control of the Institute. It took her a long time to entrust the most harmless thoughts on the contemporary political scene to the microphones. It might be safe to say such things now, but what if a change of administration should occur and the tapes should fall into the hands of yet unknown sinister powers?

In those childhood years when Anna thought of herself as responsible for the morale of the family, she had formed the conviction that she must never show her anxieties to anybody—not to her mother who had no sympathy with the expression of any emotions, not to the sisters who were ill, and certainly not to strangers in front of whom one should never lose face by admitting a weakness or a need. Anna considered being seen in an upset state, such as crying, the most intolerable humiliation. It would mean a shameful appeal for help, an admission of failure and of mental illness. She thought it quite reasonable to prefer the life-long torture of anxiety to the degradation of being seen crying. Quite often, therefore, when a tear welled up in her eye in the course of therapy, she would quickly glance at the camera and then suppress her feelings.

In spite of so much evidence that Anna reacted to the filming, I believe that the setup did not really make a difference in the amount of emotional freedom she evidenced. I unintentionally managed to quasi-test this proposition in the following way:

I had told her a number of times during the early phases of the therapy that filming would be continuous, but that probably only selected parts of the whole sequence would be studied by the researchers. Very soon, however, Anna developed the conviction that the filming had been stopped; the "powers" had lost interest in her, and I, unable to do anything about the calamity, was carrying on my routine in doomed futility. At the time I did not see the connection of this fantasy with her childhood trauma and reasoned instead that Anna expressed the need to have the filming stopped. After a few attempts to insist that we were being filmed, I began to keep silent about it and thereby confirmed her delusion. From time to time, however, Anna perceived something which she interpreted as indicating that pictures were being taken: the operator's head above the camera, the camera being moved, or noises from the camera room. So "they" had come back for more pictures, but, Anna always thought, only for a short time.

I shall comment later on Anna's and my behavior in this situation. At this point I wish to stress only that I could not at the time, nor can I now retrospectively,. detect any difference in content or emotional level between those occasions when Anna believed herself filmed and those when she did not. When I eventually corrected my attitude and insisted that Anna must realize that we were being filmed all the time she did not appear any more inhibited.

I realize that one could argue that the absence of an observable reaction to the filming was due to the fact that Anna at all times felt inhibited by the recording, even when she thought that no movies were being taken. Indeed, it is true that she never expressed the opinion that the recording had been stopped. In my judgment, however, the recording affected her only rarely, and then not very significantly, with the exception of those instances in which she was afraid of provoking the "higher powers." Whenever I asked her about her reactions, she denied that either the filming or the recording inhibited her. As to spontaneous comments, Anna rarely made any about the subject of recording; she discussed the filming more frequently. Incidentally this asymmetry of reaction was no different from that of interested colleagues, whose inquiries were preponderantly directed to the filming rather than to the recording.

The Therapist's Reaction in the Filmed Therapy

My own reactions fairly well exemplify the earlier general discussion of therapist difficulties in such a setting. I experienced several varieties of anxiety: the initial anxiety about the unusual setup and some of the more harmful varieties of displacement anxiety, namely, displacements from disturbances in my relationship with the patient transferred to concerns about the setup, and from discomfort over professional relations to irritation with the patient.

Of initial anxiety I had full measure. I perhaps suffered my worst anxiety even before the treatment started when I judged it would be a terrific strain to work under the eyes of a camera. I envisioned showing myself a fool to contemporary and future critics, or becoming accomplice to experimenting on a human being, increasing her anxiety through our observation procedures, and hurting her in the process. I thought of the expense of the project and the intense study it would receive, and I felt it would be a great burden to carry the responsibility for the fate of this therapy and research alone. Therefore, in spite of having been a supervisor myself for quite a few years, I asked for the opportunity of consultation during the course of the treatment.[1]

While my initial anxiety was high, it abated rapidly. After a while I realized that this would be in essence just like any other therapy. For quite some time, however, I remained sensitive to the presence of the movie operator in the camera room. I would feel silent irritation with him each time something went wrong with the camera and his presence became visible and/or audible to the patient and me. Only gradually did I accept him as part of the given background and discover that he did not annoy me, even on those rare occasions when he had to make an appearance.

Earlier in this paper, when I discussed Anna's delusion that the picture taking had stopped, I mentioned my faulty reaction to the situation. After scrutinizing the event more closely, I now must add that I evidently displaced my concerns from my relation with Anna onto the filming procedure. Surely, Anna was then in full negative transference, working hard and not without success at making me into the powerless pseudo-authority she felt I had to be. I realize now that my tolerating Anna's delusion that

[1] Anna and I owe much to my consultant, Dr. Edith Weigert.

she was not being filmed represented a futile attempt to improve my difficult situation.

I have no evidence that Anna ever clearly perceived this bit of "strategic withdrawal" on my part, but I do have the evidence of my own feelings during the period when I avoided taking a firm stand, and possibly
Anna perceived my feelings. I felt defensive, somewhat dishonest, and uncertain as to how to repair the situation. It seemed to me that I had lost
ground in the face of Anna's threats. It was not until I realized that the
difficulty was caused not by the filming, but by my own attitude, that I
was able to restore a better relationship. The period of my relative intimi-
dation was one of frustrating stagnancy, while the period subsequent to
my change of attitude became one of relatively quick improvement for
Anna. Looking back, I consider that I was no more justified in tolerating
Anna's delusion about not being filmed than a therapist in a private office
would have been in supporting a patient's belief that no other patients
were being seen by the therapist.

For a long while another kind of displaced concern also proved very
troublesome. In the early stages of the treatment I had fostered the interest of colleagues who inquired as to what I was doing by giving them optimistic predictions and evaluations of achieved progress. Later, when
Anna moved more slowly, slid backwards, and even became more disturbed than she had ever been, I found myself resentful of her and frequently nagged her impatiently and destructively. By this method I naturally obstructed her progress even further. My "acting-out" finally ended
when in the therapy of another, somewhat similar patient, I became aware
that I was dealing very calmly with the same kind of defensive maneuvers
that irritated me in Anna. Evidently I had reacted out of concern about
my potential loss of face.

I believe that my concern with the comment and criticism of professional colleagues created more difficulties for me than anything else in the
setup. For the most part this concern was unrealistic, since my colleagues
cared far less than I about what I did or failed to do. Yet it did make me
feel uneasy, for instance, when, several times during the course of the
treatment, I changed my ideas on how to conduct Anna's therapy. I
had planned and begun the treatment as a classical psychoanalysis. This
plan was based on an early diagnostic picture of Anna, as both the selection staff and I, myself, had seen it. When it became evident that the psychoanalytic method in the strict sense, implying use of the couch, neutrality of the therapist, and reliance on interpretation alone, would not do for
Anna, I began to grope for a more appropriate approach. However, I
made a number of false starts, partly, I think because I was anxious to
follow a method based on a definite and clear theoretical model. I reasoned at that time that researchers have a legitimate interest in seeing one

theory consistently used, because only in this way can they study the phenomena produced by the method. Eventually, however, I convinced myself that I must let the interests of the human relationship between Anna and me determine what I did, even if it reduced the researchers' chances to corroborate or refute their hypotheses. In fact, would I not make a travesty of the exigencies of research, if my behavior conformed to a theoretical model, while my disbelief in its validity, consciously or unconsciously, affected my patient?

Such uncertainties, hesitations, and conflicts are only made of the rational concerns which occupy one's attention. Much of their force and pressure derives from the ever-present basic necessity of choosing within oneself: Shall one retreat to the haven of safe but shallow acceptance by others? Or shall one attempt to satisfy higher demands and in this way try to reach out for a more meaningful relation to others? Shall one dare to be wrong, if only by that path one can hope to be right? Shall one dare to express an emotional need or to follow an irrational hunch, if one expects to reach a higher rationality only by such a detour? Shall one dare to show a reaction which others will regard as neurotic, psychopathic, paranoid, or just plain stupid? Or shall one play it safe and remain within the limits of approved practice when one believes that following approved practice will lead to stagnancy? Filmed therapy often seems to distill for a therapist the essence of this kind of issue. It is both testing ground and educational experience.

III. THE OUTCOME OF THE THERAPY

Looking back upon the course of therapy with Anna, I can discern most naturally three different phases of about equal length. In the first of these phases, as Anna experienced the crumbling of her idealized, unrealistic self-concept, she made the therapy responsible for assumedly making her mean, irritable, selfish and a host of other unpleasant qualities which she denied ever having possessed. In the second phase she still suffered from the same negatively evaluated qualities, but now she assumed the responsibility for being, and realized that she always had been, that kind of person. In the third phase of the therapy, feelings of deep weakness and helplessness gradually took the center of the stage and replaced the previously preponderant aggressive trends.

At no time of the therapy had Anna made a secret of the fact that she was solely interested in getting relief for her anxieties, and that she was not interested in achieving any particular state of insight or any other ambitious goal. She was also intensely apprehensive throughout of becoming too dependent upon therapy and therapist, and frequently declared that she wanted to leave the therapy before such a state was reached. Her childhood history makes it understandable that dependence and fear of the death of the person upon whom she would depend, and fear of her own death, would be closely associated.

At any rate, it was in the context of such attitudes that she received and welcomed an objective change which occurred in her life situation. Her husband had to sell his motel to one of the big nationwide motel chains which, as part of the deal, offered to make him manager of one of their modern motel plants in a distant part of the country, by chance close to where Anna's mother lived. Anna spoke up fervently for this plan, and it was adopted. Thus, Anna's therapy ended after four years, three months, and 632 filmed interviews.

In my opinion, the changes which the therapy brought about in Anna can be summarized in this way: The phobias (for which she originally sought treatment) have diminished markedly in number and severity, but some phobic avoidances still persist. Since these avoidances are of a kind which interfere minimally in Anna's daily life, she now has little motivation to do anything more about them. Hypochondriac somatisations in which Anna had greatly indulged before therapy have also diminished in frequency and severity. (This is an aspect of her story which I had no reason to discuss in this paper, since it did not enter into any special relationship to the filming.) Anna's "unreasonableness," a character trait based upon her excessive use of the mechanism of denial, has practically disappeared. It is possible, however, that I judge Anna so favorably in this respect because, having been inured to her earlier large doses of unreasonableness, later small doses of the same trait appear negligible to me. In a single respect one may possibly consider her in a worse state: she used to think of herself as good and normal—though beset by some mysterious trouble. Now she feels forced to view herself as neither particularly good nor as a paragon of normality, a change of self-concept which she does not much appreciate.

I consider Anna unchanged in most other aspects of her personality. She still dislikes introspection and prefers diversion when she feels tense or anxious. Her expectations in regard to people and life in general have remained low.

Readers of the report may wish to know whether the research setting of Anna's therapy provided for evaluations of the outcome of the therapy by instruments and people presumably less liable to err than the therapist, biased as he is by his subjective involvement. There were such evaluations. A team of clinical psychiatric investigators examined the initial evidence and at the end of the therapy interviewed Anna, her therapist, and other persons presumably able to contribute relevant observations. At the time of this writing, which is fifteen months after the end of the therapy, the team has not yet released its findings. It intends to have a series of follow-up investigations two years after the end of therapy, and then report in a different context.

In addition, before and after therapy Anna was given a number of psychological tests which are to be repeated two years after the end of therapy. Two psychologists examined the data of the pre-therapy and post-therapy tests, and independently wrote evaluations of them which are available to me.

The first psychologist considered that the pre-therapy data pointed to a "basic hysterical character structure, phobic symptomatology, and intrusive ego-alien, anxiety-arousing aggressive fantasies." He counseled caution in view of "the strength of certain pregenital, infantile (particularly oral aggressive) instinctual strivings, and the pervasiveness and rigidity with which the ego defends itself against the derivatives of such impulses."

The same psychologist saw in the post-therapy tests "evidence of heightened vulnerability to disorganizing anxiety" and in general a "functioning on a more regressed level than was seen at the time of initial testing." He believed that an insidious process has been set into motion "which the patient may well require further help in arresting between now and follow-up time."

The second psychologist, on the basis of the pre-therapy tests, called Anna's disturbance a "mixed neurosis with phobic, hysterical, and obsessive features." He also stressed her rigid defenses against depression and her narcissistic traits.

The same psychologist saw considerable improvement in her post-therapy tests: more directness and openness in emotional expression, more creativity and imagination, a better use of intelligence, less evasiveness, and less vanity. He thought that aggression and gloom, which were previously denied, were now conscious and openly expressed. He predicted that these changes would have beneficial consequences for Anna's interpersonal relationships.

The thorough follow-up which is planned for two years after the termination of therapy may allow some judgment as to which of these rather contradictory views is more correct. At the present time, my own perception of the course of therapy and of some informal follow-up contacts with Anna and her husband tend to make me agree more with the view of the second psychologist. In the husband's judgment Anna is considerably improved. Anna herself expresses contentment about what the therapy has done for her; she feels better than she expected to feel; and once, after mentioning evidence she found of NIH support for various worthy projects in her new location, she concludes a letter with these words: "I had no idea that so much was being done countrywide through NIH." I hope I do not unduly over-interpret this statement when I consider it revealing both a positive attitude about her experience as a research patient and an unresolved transference. It is as if Anna, who most of her life was afraid that she would lose the persons around her upon whom she depended, now feels a new kind of security in relation to the person of the therapist from whom she has separated herself but who survives and to whom she can return if she should need to do so. On the other hand, there has occurred a slight increase in phobic symptoms about a year after the end of therapy. Thus, the more pessimistic prediction of the first psychologist may still be borne out by events.

Surely, even with the best possible outcome of next year's investigation, the therapeutic change in Anna will be "nothing to crow about." But it is not the purpose of this report to "crow" about anything. Rather, its purpose is to submit evidence for the thesis that filmed psychotherapy is possible, and that in all essentials, for better and for worse, such therapy does not differ much from psychotherapy in other settings.

REFERENCES

CARMICHAEL, H. T. Sound-film recording of psychoanalytic therapy: A therapist's experiences and reactions. *J. Iowa State Med. Soc.*, **46**: 590-595, 1956.

COHEN, R. A., and COHEN, M. B. Research in psychotherapy: A preliminary report. *Psychiat.*, **24**: 46-61, 1961.

DITTMANN, A. T. The relationship between body movements and moods in interviews, *J. consult. Psychol.*, **26**: 480, 1962.

DITTMANN, A. T. Studies in expressive movements. In P. Knapp (Ed.), *Expression of emotion in man.* (In press).

SHAKOW, D. The recorded psychoanalytic interview as an objective approach to research in psychoanalysis. *The Psychoanal. quart.*, **29**: 82-97, 1960.

STERNBERG, B. S., CHAPMAN, J., and SHAKOW, D. Psychotherapy research and the problem of intrusions on privacy. *Psychiat.*, **21**: 195-203, 1958.

5. Sound-film recording of psychoanalytic therapy: a therapist's experiences and reactions

Hugh T. Carmichael

For many years, it has seemed to me that sound-film recording equipment offers unique opportunities for teaching, self-evaluation and research, and particularly for an objective evaluation of the process in psychoanalytic therapy. These potential uses were first called to my attention in 1933, when Mr. Earl F. Zinn, with whom I then began a personal psychoanalysis, was making dictaphone recordings of psychoanalytic sessions with a schizophrenic patient at Worcester (Massachusetts) State Hospital. The data so gathered was transcribed, and at the termination of the patient's analysis, the transcript had become of formidable size. When I had an opportunity to read parts of it, a few years later, it interested me, especially because I had known the patient. But the potentialities of the original sound recordings in the teaching of interviewing and psychotherapy impressed me most forcibly, and subsequently, in fact, Mr. Zinn demonstrated those possibilities.

From that time until comparatively recently, though I retained my interest in recording initial interviews and psychotherapeutic sessions and in making observations through a one-way window, the requisite equipment was unavailable to me. With a view to studying them at some future time, I kept voluminous notes of therapeutic sessions with patients in both psychoanalysis and what may be called psychoanalytically-oriented psychotherapy. I now realize, however, that as material from which to learn something of the therapeutic process, those notes were poor substitutes for sound recordings, especially since the technics for preserving conversations, complete with nuances of intonation, were being rapidly and steadily improved. Sound-film, of course, offered still greater opportunities.

Just before this country's entry in World War II, there was a brief period when it seemed possible that sound-film equipment might become available to me for my purpose, but it was not until after the close of hostilities that I obtained even the use of a room with a one-way window and sound microphone. Several years later, when David Shakow, Ph.D., came

From the *Journal of the Iowa State Medical Society* (November, 1956), pp. 590-595. Reprinted by permission.

to the University of Illinois College of Medicine as professor of psychology and director of the Psychological Division of the Department of Psychiatry, my interest in the possibilities of using sound-film for teaching interviewing and psychotherapy to medical students, interns, and residents was revived. Like me, he had been introduced to the idea by Mr. Zinn, and he was particularly attracted by the likelihood of its usefulness in the objective evaluation of the process in psychoanalytic therapy.

EQUIPMENT

With funds furnished by the institutions sponsoring the project,[1] a treatment room 19 ft. square was constructed and equipped with the special apparatus that was essential. There is a plexiglass ceiling covering 50 eight-foot and 20 four-foot fluorescent tubes capable of giving 300-335 foot candles of light on the horizontal and 130 foot candles on the vertical. This is somewhat more than 5,000 watts of light. An air-conditioning unit helps to cool the room from the heat of these overhead lights. The noise level, which was approximately 65 decibels, has been reduced to an average level of between 20 and 25 decibels. The room is equipped like a living room, rather than like an office, the furniture making it appropriate for individual interviews, group therapy, or group conferences. One wall of the room has a floor-to-ceiling decorative panel that has parts which can be removed to provide a camera aperture, and there are two one-way-vision screens between the treatment room and the adjoining camera room for use in direct viewing. Three microphones were installed to feed the optic sound track of the camera and the binaural tape recorder. Our 16 mm. camera has been modified to accommodate a single 50-minute film run of 2,000 feet.

THE PROJECT

Since 1953 our group has been using the above-described facilities in making pilot studies in preparation for an intensive study of the process of psychoanalytic therapy. Eventually, we plan to make sound-motion pictures of the whole analysis of a single patient, with his knowledge and consent and that of his therapist.

In the major project, when it gets under way, it is our intention to have successive sections of the sound film analyzed by five or six experts, some

[1] Dr. Carmichael . . . reports upon studies in which Morris Sklansky, M.D., Leon Bernstein, M.D., Joel S. Handler, M.D., David Shakow, Ph.D., Rae Shifrin Sternberg, Ph.D., Reuben H. Segel, Ph.D., and Jean P. Chapman, M.A. collaborated with him. The project, entitled "Analysis of the Factors Involved in the Psychoanalytic Therapy Process: Preliminary Studies," has been supported by research grants M-637 from the National Institute of Mental Health of the U.S.P.H.S., the Department of Public Welfare of the State of Illinois, and the University of Illinois College of Medicine.

of them psychoanalysts and others of them representatives of other theo-retical points of view in psychotherapy and experimental psychology. First, they are to be asked to do the analysis, each by himself. Later, after a certain period, they are to be asked to do it together.

The work is to have two major focuses: (1) the analysis of the psycho-analytic therapy process, and (2) the analysis of the process by which either a single conceptual formulation or several clearly differentiated conceptual formulations are arrived at by a number of people having, at the outset, varying degrees of difference in their theoretical frames of ref-erence. (Shakow, 1948) This plan was described in considerable detail by Shakow in the 1948 Round Table on the "Objective Evaluation of Psycho-therapy" published in the *American Journal of Orthopsychiatry* in 1949.

It is our assumption that the sound-film method will make available a naturalistic representation of psychotherapy and psychoanalytic therapy. We feel that the advantages of film records are clear. They are permanent, they can be reviewed at any time, and they are not dependent upon the original investigator for reliability of interpretation. They are a faithful and unbiased representation of the original events. Moreover, they afford access to the gestures, facial expressions, and bodily movements of patient and therapist. Such non-verbal, expressive data have not heretofore been available for study.

But despite these advantages, there are a number of questions that may be raised. First, is the technic valuable enough to warrant the expense that it necessitates? Before embarking upon the filming of a complete series of interviews, it is essential for us to demonstrate that the film will be worth the current minimal cost of $140 per interview for film and proc-essing only. Second, are sound-film movies of the psychotherapeutic proc-ess representative of the real thing? In other words, does the invasion of privacy (by recording and observation) distort the behavior of patient and therapist? Third, what evidence is there that the visual medium helps one understand the evidence that can be preserved by sound recordings alone? Are the non-verbal clues reliable? Do they provide information be-yond that which is to be derived from language and tonal inflection? Fourth, can one avoid the psychological effect of being overwhelmed by the sheer quantity of the data that this method affords? Some studies have seemed to support the view that increasing amounts of information served more to confound than to enlighten the individual clinician. We think such conclusions arise from faulty conceptions of how a clinician learns, and we think experiments can be designed to demonstrate that under proper conditions he can utilize all of the increments of information. Fifth, can one retain the richness of the original data while he pursues a systematic inquiry? We think that it is possible if one knows what he is looking for and can utilize appropriate methods for analyzing these kinds of data.

DISTORTIONS INTRODUCED BY THE INVASION OF PRIVACY

I do not intend to give a detailed account of our attempts to find answers to all of these questions, but I do wish to enlarge upon certain aspects of the studies we have made in trying to answer the second of them.

It has been asserted that the introduction of a third person into the psychotherapeutic setting markedly changes the quality of the experience both for the patient and for the therapist. Psychoanalysts, quoting Freud as authority, have been particularly insistent upon this point. Despite these objections, however, in recent years psychotherapists of various theoretical persuasions have been using magnetic tape recordings of psychotherapeutic interviews to provide themselves with materials for their research activities. But there are significant differences between sound recording and filming. Whereas tape recording is a push-button technic requiring the presence of no third party, a cameraman must be present when pictures are taken. There is little doubt that the camera operator's presence and the awareness, by both doctor and patient, that lasting visible images are being created do have some effect upon the therapeutic process. We have tried in three ways to determine the nature and magnitude of that effect: first, through direct inquiry of prospective patients and therapists after the filming; second, by asking patients and therapists what they think their reactions would be if they were subjected to such filming; and third, by noting the reactions of a wide segment of the general adult population to a projective cartoon series designed to tap feelings about being overheard and seen in vulnerable situations. The results obtained through these approaches will be reported in detail at another time. (Sternberg, Chapman, and Shakow, 1958.)

We have obtained information on the reactions of the three therapists (L.B., R.S.S., and H.T.C.) who have been filmed during the pilot studies, by asking them to associate freely (i.e., to voice their thoughts as unreservedly as possible) to a tape recorder immediately after each filming session. All admitted to having felt an initial anxiety about being filmed. All commented subsequently upon their adaptation to the surroundings at later filmings. They seemed to feel more vulnerable to the consequences of being recorded than did the patients.

Most revealing is the experience of a therapist who had been recorded with patients on sound film in a total of 26 interviews, and had been recorded on sound tape in an additional 30 sessions. There had been three series of interviews with three different patients: (1) a two-interview series with a patient in psychoanalytic therapy—one of them the 130th "hour," on January 30, 1954 (perhaps the first sound-film recording of a psychoanalytic interview), and the second in January, 1956, four months after the interruption of the psychoanalysis; (2) a five-interview series in the winter of 1955, beginning with the initial interview with a paranoid patient; and (3) a 19-interview series with a patient having a character neurosis, also beginning with the initial interview, in the spring and summer of 1955. (The 30 interviews recorded on tape were between the therapist and this third patient, the tape series starting where the film series ended. Thus 49 consecutive interviews had been recorded.)

The therapist reported having had some initial anxiety when he was filmed for the first time, but he said that his awareness of the situation lessened thereafter, until the series of 19 filmed interviews was well started. Then, after his relative freedom from anxiety and self-consciousness, he reported that anxiety recurred and became more intense than it had been initially. As he described it, he felt able to maintain himself in equanimity without undue strain or anxiety for a single interview or throughout a series of five interviews, or even six or more. It was when he thought of the effort he would have to exert to maintain this attitude throughout an indefinite series of recordings that he felt some dread of the never-ending exposure of himself and his technics. He later reported that these tensions subsided when he had become aware of them and had analyzed their probable origin.

We have studied the recordings of associations that the therapist made immediately after each of the 19 sound-film interviews. Some were made on sound tape in another room. Others were sound-film records made in the treatment room immediately following interviews, or were tape records made in the treatment room. Transcripts were made of all these recordings.

Six months later, the therapist was given an opportunity for the first time to look at and listen to the sound-films of the alternate sessions from 1-19 (i.e., those of the first, third, fifth, seventh, ninth, eleventh, thirteenth, fifteenth, seventeenth, and nineteenth session, ten in all). Immediately after the film showings, he made recordings on sound tape of his impressions and associations regarding what he had just seen and heard of the patient and himself in the psychotherapeutic situation. Transcripts of these recordings were made available. Comparisons were made by the therapist and one of his co-workers, R.S.S., between the recordings (we call them *introspections*) made immediately after the interviews and the recordings made six months later.

Ten categories were set up to assist in the comparison and rating: (1) the therapist's expressed degree of satisfaction with the interview; (2 and 3) his estimate of the patient's and his own awareness of recording; (4) his evaluation of his own technic; (5) his evaluation of the patient's and his own interaction; (6) his estimate of his own activity in the therapeutic interviews; (7) his estimate of the patient's and his own reactions to the physical setting; (8) his reaction to his own physical appearance; (9) his expressed attitudes toward the project; and (10) his estimate of the effect of such influences as his prevailing mood, attitude or physical state, and the weather just before each interview. The ratings under these categories were done separately by the therapist and by his co-worker, first on the introspections done immediately following the filming and thereafter on the introspections done six months later. The two of them then compared notes to ascertain the degree of their agreement before they made their final ratings.

The therapist's reactions to the physical setting in which the interviews were filmed were limited to his experiencing some discomfort from heat and humidity toward the ends of the interviews. (The air conditioning had to be turned off just before the start of filming because the noise of the unit would otherwise have been recorded on the sound track.)

The prevailing mood of the therapist just before each of the interviews was not rated as an important influence. Acceptance of responsibility as a therapist (physician) overshadowed personal feelings. His positive stimuli were anticipation of proceeding with the project, a mood level of elation, and stimulation resulting from discussion with his colleagues and visitors. Negative stimuli were fatigue, hunger, hurry, hot weather, and awareness of being a subject rather than an investigator in this phase of the research.

The therapist was sensitive to his physical appearance only at the beginning and at the end of the original series of introspections. When he saw himself six months later, he was much more concerned. Sixty percent of the later comments were adverse, 35 percent positive, and 5 percent neutral.

The therapist showed more concern about his role in the project at the time of the second series of introspections than at the first. His different position at the time of the second series probably accounts for that fact. Then he was no longer the therapist. He had distanced the original therapeutic situation and was observing it as an evaluator, critic, and investigator trying to live up to the ideal of scientific objectivity. On the other hand, he expressed less concern about his colleagues' reactions to the project during the second series of introspections. In general, his concern took the form of questioning certain aspects of his activity. When he expressed direct feelings about the project, they tended to be more positive than negative.

As recorded in the original introspections, the patient seemed to the therapist to have been largely unaware of the recording process. Six months later, the therapist saw more evidence of the patient's awareness of the filming, and so indicated in his introspections. He recalled, however, that he had thought at the time of the interviews that the patient was showing a good deal of awareness of the recording process. The accuracy of this latter evaluation was supported by the discussion we had conducted with the patient following the termination of the filming.

The therapist perceived the patient to be involved in the therapeutic process for the most part. On reviewing the films six months later, he expressed himself as seeing more evidence of resistance on the patient's part than he had seen at the time of the original filming.

The therapist's critical attitude and his dissatisfaction with himself upon reviewing the film after an interval of six months was also shown in his evaluation of the technics he had utilized in the interviews. This dissatisfaction was carried over into his characterization of his level of activity in those interviews. Upon reviewing the films, he tended to consider himself as having been overly active, whereas in the first introspections, he had tended to look upon his level of activity as relatively passive.

The therapist's awareness of the recording procedure, he said, was more or less constant. As judged in the ratings of both introspections, the awareness-unawareness ratio was approximately two to one. The ratings of the intensity of awareness fluctuated from mild to strong, the former occurring somewhat more frequently. The therapist's awareness of the observers (i.e., the co-workers who managed the camera and the binaural tape recorder) was, he thought, less than his awareness of the implications of recording for a particular interview, or in regard to the aims of the project. There seemed to be a slight tendency toward a negative correlation between the intensity of the therapist's awareness of the recording and the degree of his satisfaction with the interview.

Some further comments on the typescripts of introspections might not be amiss. Those in the second series of introspections were on the whole somewhat longer than those recording the remarks of the therapist immediately after the filmings. The lengths of the typescripts varied from three typewritten pages to a little less than one typewritten page. The shortest was one containing the therapist's introspections on an occasion when he felt under pressure to travel from the filming to a panel discussion in which he was expected to participate. We have been interested in noting the relative lack of comment in the introspections on the content of psychotherapeutic interviews, or on the psychodynamics involved, or in directly relating an interview to the immediately preceding one.

Mention should probably be made of the therapist's awareness of and comments at the time of the filmings on his own probable exhibitionistic and voyeuristic trends, as well as on their background and meaning.

DIFFICULTIES IN GETTING THERAPISTS TO PARTICIPATE

I feel inclined at this point to make some remarks about the difficulties we encountered in getting therapists to submit themselves to being filmed and recorded. The majority of those approached expressed interest in the project, but preferred to remain at a distance from it, expressing doubts about the validity with which the therapeutic process could be represented under such conditions. They hesitated or evaded, and failed to answer when asked if they would act as therapists with their patients in actual filming. They expressed a strong preference for being observers and evaluators, rather than exposing their own work to the criticism of others.

When we finally got to the point of needing a therapist and a patient for the purpose of testing the setting and equipment, we first approached members of the staff of the Department of Psychiatry. All were friendly and interested, but some begged off on the plea that they were too busy just then. Others said they would be willing to be filmed as soon as they could find suitable patients, but none of them ever seemed, simultaneously, to find the requisite time and a suitable patient. Finally, the psychoanalyst among the initial group of investigators was used for the first actual filming.

When the second series of filmings was to be undertaken, similar difficulties were encountered. Eventually, the one who volunteered and who was actually filmed, when a suitable patient had been found, was a former analyst and one of the investigators. It is assumed that this was why he consented to serve as a subject.

Still later, when no other therapist would serve for a filmed series of interviews, the investigator who had been filmed in the first actual series was used again. To date, he has been the only therapist used since the three-interview film series, although three younger psychoanalysts have now joined the project and are doing observational studies.

As has been reported in the literature, patients usually do not show resistance to being sound-recorded on tape or sound-film, whereas therapists almost all show great resistance and reluctance to having their methods and technics of psychotherapy made available for others to hear and observe. The danger of damage to their self-esteem seems to give them considerable anxiety. Yet as several of those reporting on sound recording have said (notably Gill, Newman, and Redlich in their book *The Initial Interview in Psychiatric Practice*, 1954) the playback of sound records and sound-films affords us a valuable method of improving our technic.

It may be narcissistic to let oneself be recorded and sound-filmed while doing psychotherapy or psychoanalytic therapy. Or, perhaps, should one raise a question about its being masochistic? I believe, as Shakow (1949) has pointed out, that it is necessary for a therapist to possess courage, in addition to being an expert in his particular kind of psychotherapy and a good representative of that kind of therapy.

PREVIOUS AND CONCURRENT EXPERIMENTATION

I shall not enter upon a thorough review of the literature about the reactions of therapists and patients to recordings. These deal with experiences with sound-recording only. Most of them are listed in the bibliography at the end of this article.

I know of no report on experiences in demonstrations of psychotherapy except that by Otto Fleischmann (1955) and none of sound-films for study of process other than those of Carl Rogers. Fleischmann conducted treatment of a patient before groups of psychiatric residents observing through a one-way mirror. I refer you to his article for a discussion of the details of his own, his patient's, and his observers' reactions. In a conversation, Dr. Nathaniel Apter informed me that he had been recorded on sound-film in a series of 20 interviews with a patient. He commented that he felt somewhat uneasy at the time, for the patient did not seem to realize that he was being directly observed through a one-way mirror.

At about the time we were finishing our rating of the first and second series of introspections reported above, we learned that a project roughly parallel to ours at the National Institute of Mental Health was prepared and about ready to begin filming psychotherapeutic interviews.

Finally, a word or two on the current use of sound-films. They are already being studied by experts other than the therapist who appeared in them, and a variety of methods are being employed in order to ascertain the nature of the process of psychoanalytic therapy. It is hoped that adequate methods will be devised for handling the enormous mass of data which film recording provides. There are some indications, even at this preliminary phase of our investigations, that these hopes will be realized. Reports of this aspect of the project will be released elsewhere, at a later time, by project members.

REFERENCES

APTER, N. Personal communication, 1956.

BIERER, J., and STROM-OLSEN, R. Recording of psychotherapeutic sessions; its value in teaching, research, and treatment, Lancet, 1: 957-958, Jan. 19, 1948.

BRODY, E. B., NEWMAN, R., and REDLICH, F. C. Sound recording and problem of evidence in psychiatry. Sci., 113: 379-380, Apr. 6, 1951.

COVNER, B. J. Studies in phonographic recordings of verbal material. J. consult. Psychol., 6: 105-1B, 1942.

FLEISCHMANN, O. Method of teaching psychotherapy; one-way-vision room technique. Bull. Menninger Clin., 19: 160-171, Sept., 1955.

GILL, M. M., and BRENMAN, M. Research in psychotherapy (Round Table, 1947). Am. J. Orthopsychiat., 18: 100-110, Jan., 1948.

GILL, M. M., NEWMAN, R., and REDLICH, F. C. The initial interview in psychiatric practice, with phonograph records. New York: International Universities, 1954.

KOGAN, L. S. Electrical recording of social casework interviews. Soc. Casewk., 31: 371-378, Nov., 1950.

LAMB, R., and MAHL, G. F. Manifest reactions of patients and interviewers to use of sound recording in psychiatric interviews. *Am. J. Psychiat.*, **112**: 731-737, Mar., 1956.

MAHL, G. F., DOLLARD, J., and REDLICH, F. C. Facilities for sound recording and observation of interviews. *Sci.*, **120**: 235-239, Aug. 13, 1954.

REDLICH, F. C., DOLLARD, J., and NEWMAN, R. High fidelity recording of psychotherapeutic interviews. *Am. J. Psychiat.*, **107**: 42-48, July, 1950.

ROGERS, CARL. Psychotherapy in process: The case of Miss Mun. State College, Penna.: Pennsylvania State College Psychological Cinema Register.

SHAKOW, D. Evaluation of procedure. In A. F. Bronner, Evaluation of psychotherapy (Round Table, 1948). *Am. J. Orthopsychiat.*, **19**: 463-491, July, 1949.

STERNBERG, R. S., CHAPMAN, J., and SHAKOW, D. Psychotherapy research and the problem of intrusions on privacy. *Psychiat.* **21**: 195-203, 1958.

6. Subjective reactions to being filmed

O. Spurgeon English

To the best of my knowledge I was filmed twice while treating a patient. I had had thirty years' experience appearing before audiences and also had interviewed or treated patients before groups of varying size. While being filmed by Drs. Scheflen and Birdwhistell, and possibly other observers, I was conscious of the fact that "all of me" was being scrutinized in a manner more scientific and more thorough than ever before.

My reaction to this was to think (as I have done on other occasions): "I am what I am. I do the best I can. Whatever I can learn from a study of me and the patient will help me, as well as whatever future patients I treat." I was not aware of feeling in competition with any other therapists in the Philadelphia area or elsewhere. I was not conscious of any physiological manifestations of tension (not even of dry mouth which is my most sensitive indication of anxiety). It was just one of the jobs to do that day. As I recall, my attention was focused on the patient as on other occasions. Yet, I can recall that at various periods it would flash across my mind that I was being filmed; and then I would forget it for an interval.

This is all I can remember about the experience now—six months later.

7. The experience of interviewing in the presence of observers

Milton H. Erickson

The experience of interviewing two psychiatric patients in the presence of observers and of attempting to induce hypnotic trances in them with the knowledge at the time that my efforts were being filmed for subsequent critical analysis by highly qualified persons constituted an interesting project for me. The primary consideration for me was the execution of the proposed task as adequately as possible. My own personal emotions were considered neither important nor relevant.

The emotional reactions of my patients, however, in relation to me, to the interview, to the hypnosis, to the surroundings, to the attendant circumstances, or deriving from their own psychiatric condition, were all considered to be a proper part of the proposed study. Therefore, it would be a part of my responsibilities to be as aware as possible of the patients' various emotional states, to direct and to utilize them in such fashion that the patients' attention and interest would be directed to me rather than elsewhere.

The proposed experimental procedure definitely interested me. It offered an opportunity to deal with a patient in an entirely new kind of situation that could be recorded most effectively for future and for independent study. It was also a situation that the patient presumably could comprehend to a considerable extent and to which he could quite conceivably react in a variety of interesting ways. Also, the proposed procedure gave rise in my mind to recurrent, curious questions of what manner of affective, sympathetic, and empathic responses the observers, immediate and subsequent, would make which were comparable or related to those I would experience in the actual work situation with the patient. As it later developed, now and then when I experienced one or another reaction to my patient, there would recur, momentarily only and not as a distraction, the curious question of what, if anything, the observer could possibly sense of a comparable character.

My mental set in approaching the task was that of discovering what I could understand of the patient's behavior and what I could do about it or with it. The fact that I was under observation was of no concern to me, however primary that fact might be to the observers. My task was that of observing the patient and working with him, not speculating about the possible activities of others.

To begin, my first procedure was to make a visual and auditory survey of the interview situation. I wanted to know what my patient could see and hear and how a shift of his gaze or a change of his position would change the object content of his visual field. I was also interested in the various sounds, probable, possible, and inclusive of street noises, that could intrude upon the situation. I inquired about the age, height, weight, and sex of my patient and I tested various possible seating arrangements to check relative physical comfort, the possibilities of adequate recording, and the predominant content of the patient's general field of vision. I also inquired about any special accommodations to be made to meet the requirements of the recording apparatus. As a measure of more adequately understanding my patient's possible reactions to the observers, I made special inquiries about their positioning. Since one observer (Dr. G.) was there by special request, I felt he should be placed so that he would have the least possible effect upon the others present.

Upon the arrival of my patient I immediately became intensely absorbed in the task confronting me. Occasionally I would feel momentarily oppressed by a sense of having only a limited time, followed by a strong need not to let my patient sense that hurried feeling. Now and then I became aware that I had been so attentive to my patient that I had forgotten where I was, but I would comfortably and instantly reorient myself. On at least three occasions, I became momentarily puzzled by a pair of glasses on the side of the room toward which I was facing. Each time I was astonished to discover them on a face and then to recognize the face as that of Dr. G.

Now and then I felt an urgent need to give some brief recognition to the immediate environment in some casual way so that my patient would not be given the impression of an intentional avoidance. One other intense emotional reaction on my part concerned the use of my cane at a moment when I moved it rather ostentatiously. My purpose was to force the patient to give his attention to the cane and thereby to effect a displacement of his hostility from me to the cane. As this was being done, the thought flashed into my mind that perhaps the observers would not understand the purposefulness of the maneuver. There was an immediate feeling of strong dismay that this irrelevant thinking might have altered adversely the manner in which the cane was being moved. This emotional concern vanished upon noting that the patient was responding adequately.

At the close of the first interview, I felt no particular fatigue and I was as interested in seeing the next patient as I had been in seeing the first. At the close of the second interview I had an immediate sensation of great fatigue, physical and mental, but this passed promptly. It was followed by a distressing feeling that I might have worked my patients too hard, but this was replaced by a feeling that I had completed a much longer and much more difficult task than I had realized at the outset. I then felt highly pleased that an experimental approach with adequate recording was being made to the difficult subjective, intuitive, interpersonal relationship that exists in the clinical interview. As I completed this thought a sudden wave of recollections surged through my mind. Throughout both interviews, as I noted each item of behavior, each fleeting change of expressions on my patients' faces, I had comforted myself by thinking, "But I can have a second look at that." This was later mentioned to Dr. G. in discussing the experimental project.

I consider this sound-film recording of a physician-patient interview to be a most valuable research procedure for investigating what constitutes an interpersonal relationship. It offers an opportunity to secure a fixed and reliable record of the actual occurrences, both pertinent and incidental, that record being in no way itself subject to alterations by mood, memory, bias, or any other behavioral force. Furthermore, this record is impartial in its treatment of both the interviewer and the interviewed and there can be no weighting or shading of the evidence in the record itself. It also permits a sharp and informative contrast with data obtained from the same situation by trained observers and it should reveal much concerning the nature and character of human error.

Of exceeding value is the sound-film in recording those qualitative variables of interpersonal communication such as facial expressions, gestures, intonations, inflections, mispronunciations, changes of tempo, and all the other minimal but effective modifications of speech that carry significant meanings. A sound-film is of particular value since it permits at any time a review, again and again, of any minimal manifestation, which is what I meant when, during the interviews, I comforted myself by the thought, "But I can have a second look." In the actual clinical situation, responses are often made in minimal fashion and similarly sensed; often the entire process of communication is unconscious and a sudden irruption into the conscious mind may complete a long process of unrecognized communication. Also of great significance is the fact that the sound-film permits the participant to discover many things which he did unwittingly, unconsciously, and even perhaps with no realization that he could manifest that manner or kind of behavior. I know that in the situation of dealing with patients I often wish I knew exactly what I was doing and why, instead of feeling, as I know I did with both patients, that I was acting blindly and intuitively to elicit an as yet undetermined response with which, whatever it was, I would deal.

In brief, this method of recording the interactions between selected people in a chosen setting offers a rich potential for understandings of extensive value for both therapist and patient.

8. Filming of psychotherapeutic sessions as a personal experience

Don D. Jackson

When I was asked to write of my experiences in being filmed for psychotherapeutic study, I first thought back on the total amount of experience I had. This, it would seem, is approximately six half-hour films of initial interviews with patients (largely psychotic), approximately two hours of therapy sessions with psychotic patients, twenty-five minutes of an hour long film on psychiatry during which a "stranger" was interviewed, and three half-hour RV films as a member of a three-man panel. The outstanding feature of the therapy filming experiences was my own reaction to the finished production. I did not feel well acquainted with the individual upon the screen who was masquerading as I. The voice I had become somewhat used to because of listening to hours upon hours of tape-recordings; however, the appearance was another matter. Even after six years, I am still not entirely comfortable with the recognition of myself as a psychotherapist when my image is splashed upon the screen for the instruction and criticism of psychiatric residents.

I have some feeling why this reaction is so and why it remains, although I offer this without great respect for its scientific validity. It seems to me that during the interviews, I become so involved in what the patient is saying and communicating via his body, and so involved in what I will do in response to these messages, that I have very little feeling for myself at that moment. This experience is heightened, of course, by being filmed, for one knows that one has only thirty minutes to produce an effect which will be ineradicably jotted down on celluloid for all to witness. Thus, the need to be at one's best is a decided handicap in being filmed; however it is one that lessens as the experience continues.

Despite the fact that I take a strongly transactional view toward psychotherapy, as a therapist I cannot see myself from the objective point of view which is possible through the camera lens. There is something so critical and dispassionate about the camera eye which hovers over the interview that I could never hope to take the same point of view toward myself. For example, in one interview an acute schizophrenic young man was resisting a point of view that I was offering him about one of his delusions. He sat back in his chair, with his feet together and his arms folded across his chest. And what did I do as the wise, gentle, helpful therapist? I witnessed myself on the film sitting back in my chair and folding my arms across my chest. That is, if he wanted to duel, I appeared ready to meet him. This particular body motion was quite out of keeping with the pleasant tone of voice and reassuring words that were being vocalized while the gesture was being acted out.

Thus, I would say that the experience of being filmed is a lesson in humility. I can never hope to have the uncritical attitude toward myself that the camera eye does. It would be invaluable, in my opinion, for all young therapists to have the experience of being filmed, if only to feel this kind of humility. There are additional features that make it worthwhile, including obvious points such as the availability of the material again and again for study and the ideal nature of this material as a supervisory agent.

The context in which the filming occurs probably caricatures many points that are present in the ordinary psychotherapeutic session. The pressure of time, of being wise and inscrutable while at the same time exhibiting some of the human values, can be sizeable. As an example of this, I might mention one film session, arranged without my awareness by Gregory Bateson, that is particularly memorable to me. A psychology graduate student was introduced as a patient in the Veterans' Administration Hospital; he was told that I was a patient who had the delusion that I was a psychiatrist. Unfortunately for posterity, the psychologist recognized me so that part of the experiment lost its impact. However, after interviewing him for a few minutes I was impressed by the fact that either he was not psychotic or else he was extremely cagey and resistant. I could not bring myself, because of the pressure of the situation and the feeling about the expense of the filming, to break the situation by asking him a simple question, "Are you or are you not a patient here?" Instead, unwittingly I found myself dueling with him until, after fifteen minutes of the interview, there was a decided shift in which he began to take the role of a patient. It is obvious from the film that I then became more relaxed, friendly, and efficient and at the same time protected him from telling me too much since I must have wondered whether he was a "real patient." This anomalous situation has been an intriguing one to view over and over again. Both of us were caught in a bind that was partly contextual and partly built up of our own past roles. It is interesting to me that this individual did undertake psychotherapy not too many months after our little joke.

The experience of being filmed is still a relatively rare one for psychotherapists. I do not doubt that within a few years it will be relatively commonplace and much of the "pressure" that I have described will decrease as it becomes more an accepted part of training. Our experience with an audio-visual taperecorder at the Mental Research Institute furthers this conviction.

III

Data Analysis

A.

Process Research Focusing on Selected Variables

We have tried to categorize the kinds of purposes motivating the analysis of data deriving from the psychotherapeutic interview into two broad classifications: (1) Process research focusing on selected variables; and (2) Process research emphasizing investigation of personality functioning and theory.

We have selected and placed under appropriate headings (Communication Variables in General, Language Variables, Paralanguage and Linguistic Variables, Kinesic Variables) the papers of some of the major research workers who are analyzing communication variables. It would be impossible, because of space limitations, to include examples of the works of all serious and excellent investigators working in these areas. We have based our selections of contributors, here and elsewhere, on the principle that a broad variety of styles and methods of research should be illustrated. If psychodynamic or psychoanalytically oriented approaches appear to be predominantly represented in this section, this occurs, we believe, because investigators with such orientations are probably more likely to preoccupy themselves with various aspects of the communication process than investigators starting from other theoretical positions.

1. COMMUNICATION VARIABLES IN GENERAL

In a splendid introduction and survey of the place of communication processes in cultural anthropology, George Trager clarifies and sets in order the components of the communication variables involved in the interview. Dr. Trager also reviews briefly the interdisciplinary research efforts that have taken place involving psychotherapists and linguists and offers his recommendation for fruitful collaborative endeavor.

9. Language and psychotherapy

George L. Trager

1. LANGUAGE, THE BASIC MODALITY IN COMMUNICATION

Human beings live in societies. All societies, human or nonhuman, depend on communication between their members. Communication can be of several kinds: the sender of the communication can make motions of various parts of the body, can touch the receiver in various ways, or can emit noises of various kinds; the receiver can see the motions, or can feel the touches, or can hear the noises. We may characterize these kinds of communication, for the sender, as the motile, tactile, and vocal instrumentalities; for the receiver, as the visual, sensory, and auditory instrumentalities. There is also the emission of odors and their perception—the odoriferous and olfactory instrumentalities.

Among human beings, the motile and visual instrumentalities produce the *kinesic* communication modality; the tactile and sensory instrumentalities produce the communication modality of touch, for which a name is needed; and the vocal and auditory instrumentalities produce the modalities of *language* and its accompanying *paralanguage*. Emission of odors is, for human beings, conscious and voluntary only in small degree, but olfactory reception is communicational. Language will be examined in section 2, below, and the other modalities in section 3.

In any communication system, there is the essential activity that takes place—the modality; this involves the presence of a sender and a receiver (of the reciprocal instrumentalities). And there is the function of the activity—conveying a message.

The basic, all-pervading and ever-present, and primary human communication modality is language. It is always accompanied by paralanguage and kinesics, and often enough by tactile and olfactory activities. But the primacy of language becomes evident from an examination of the intricacy, extensiveness, and independence of its structure. Paralanguage, as its name implies, occurs only with language; it has a structure simpler and less extensive, and is dependent. Kinesics can take place without lan-

This article was written during tenure of a Fellowship at the Center for Advanced Study in the Behavioral Sciences, Stanford, California, 1962-1963, and a simultaneous Research Grant from the National Science Foundation, while on sabbatical leave from the University of Buffalo. It stems in part from ideas developed in the research activities undertaken during this period. The assistance rendered by the institutions named, making possible the research and writing, is hereby gratefully acknowledged.

guage, but its availability for communication is limited to lighted places, and its structure is analogous to that of paralanguage. Tactile communication is limited by distance, as is olfactory communication. The latter is very little developed and apparently is very simply structured.

It may be added at this point that the invention of writing brought about another kind of communication, in which motile activity produces artifacts (the written signs) which can be seen. Written material, however, is always and everywhere based on and secondary to language. There is also communication by other kinds of artifacts, as will be shown in section 4.

In all human interaction it is what people say that is of first importance. It is heard, reacted to, interpreted, responded to. All other communication usually serves as background and commentary on what is said, or, in the case of the special kinds of communication by artifacts, is restricted to special situations. Language is often necessary also to make explicit and meaningful whatever other communication takes place.

2. THE NATURE OF LANGUAGE

The communication system that is language, along with the other communication modalities referred to, is not inherited. It has to be learned. Every normal human being has the biological and specifically neurological equipment to learn to talk. But a child is born without language, and must learn the language of the group within which it is raised.

At some time in the past, then, there were biological ancestors of modern man who did not know how to talk. In some way that can hardly even be speculated about, at some unknown time, some of these creatures (perhaps some australopithecines) somehow got the idea of making noises systematically and using them in ordered sequences to represent, or "stand for," or *symbolize* the world about them. With this invention—the first invention, some would call it—came the purposeful manufacture and use of tools; the control of fire; the instigation of the family, protected by rules of incest; the setting up of social hierarchies, with rules of descent and inheritance; the development of sanctions and of belief in the supernatural; and all the rest of human behavior.

All this human behavior, called *culture* by anthropologists, may be defined as the learned systems of activity by means of which human beings interact and communicate in a society (in terms of their culture).

The terms of these definitions can bear some comment. All culture is learned. Human beings have no instincts; everything they do has to be taught by precept and example, and learned by attention and observation. All cultural activities are systematic: there is no haphazard behavior. Human beings always live in societies, and have to interact. Interaction is mediated and carried on principally by language. Language consists of vocal noises that are symbols, and are arbitrary because they are symbols (that is, there is no necessary connection between a symbol and what it represents). Every language is used to communicate about the affairs of the human beings in a society. Every society has a culture (a system of cultural systems) that is its own.

As mankind grew in numbers and spread over the earth, communication between groups was often broken off because of distance and the physical difficulties of travel. The languages of isolated groups became more and more differentiated, giving rise to the multiplicity of languages now existing (some two to three thousand). The cultures of the groups also became differentiated, and this contributed further to the differences of languages. In the modern world, communication between members of different cultures and language-speaking groups can be successful only if there is understanding of the different cultural and linguistic structures. Different social and economic levels of society are also culturally and linguistically different, though sometimes only to a small degree; and the sick and the healthy constitute groups with analogous cultural variations.

The term *symbol* has been used several times. It is desirable to mention two other terms, *sign* and *signal,* and to distinguish among the three. The attempt at definition made here is based upon the general use of the terms as ordinary words of the English language, and the need to differentiate various categories of settings, events in those settings, and the functions of the events. With these definitions or descriptions, it is possible to see the nature of language behavior in the total communication situation.

A sign is an aspect of a situational setting for communication events. A sign indicates a condition of the situation, or the presence of the situation itself. It is broadly meaningful and communicative, but it is not specifically indicative, nor is it a specific, overt activity. In human beings, a perspiring brow, a nervous glance, a shaking hand, rapid breathing, sudden cessation of movement—all these are signs. Animals and human beings produce signs constantly.

With one or more signs as a setting, there can take place specific, overt acts. Such acts are signals. A cry, a sigh, a shout, a sudden gesture, a clearing of the throat, a specific noise—these are signals. Animals often produce highly diversified signals. The noises human beings make, and their gestures and movements, are, as events, signals, except when they are involuntary or accidental, in which case they may be only signs. Many human signals function as symbols.

A symbol is a representation of something. It *stands for* something. It can represent a condition, a situation, an event, a set of circumstances, an artifact, an individual or something nonexistent. A symbol may be removed in time and space from what it represents. It is independent of the physical nature of what it symbolizes. Only human beings can make symbols.

Language is a communication system that is situated in or takes place in a setting that may be interpreted as containing or consisting of signs. What takes place, what happens, is an ordered sequence of signals, relating to or stemming from the signs in the situation. These signals have a function, and that function is to symbolize, to be, or act as, or be understood as symbols.

The setting of language (the signs) is the speaker-hearer situation. The content of language consists of the signals—the noises that are made, the speaking. The function of language is conveying a message, which is accomplished by converting the signals emitted into symbols by means of systematic structuring.

The material of language can itself be looked at, or examined, or structured in a threefold way. It can be examined as sounds, or as the shapes (forms) constituted by sequences of sounds, or as the meaningful arrangements, the sense, from which the symbolizing functions arise. It appears that all languages have this basic kind of structuring, but the details of the sounds, the shapes, the senses are widely divergent.

The structural analogies make possible the science of linguistics. The sounds are studied in phonology, the shapes in morphology, the sense in semology. The subdivisions of these fields, the manner in which work on them is performed, and the details of specific languages cannot be examined here. References may be made to Trager (1964) for a summary of phonetics (a subdivision of phonology), to Joos (1958) for a discussion of semology, to Trager (1963b) for a general theoretical survey, and to Trager and Smith (1951) for a partial description of English; the articles "Language" and "Linguistics" (Trager, 1955, 1956) may also be mentioned. An introductory textbook of linguistic analysis is Gleason's (1961).

3. OTHER COMMUNICATION MODALITIES

The principal communication modalities other than language are paralanguage and kinesics.

Paralanguage (see Trager, 1958) involves a setting of voice set; this consists of an assemblage of signs which identify individuals as members of a society, and as persons of a certain sex, age, state of health, and so on, leading to identification or characterization as to age-grade, status, and other conditions. In this setting there take place certain vocalizations which do not have the threefold structure of language, and these are modified by voice qualities. The vocalizations with their accompanying voice qualities are signals, though the latter taken by themselves are of the character of signs. Paralanguage is never symbolizing in the specific way that language is. The paralanguage vocalization, *sh*, which may have voice qualities of pitch, range, tempo, resonance, and others, is a signal for silence. The language item, *hush*, is a specific word in a specific language (English), with a grammatical structure and a semology (imperative of a verb), and a symbolizing function that is its specific meaning: it is a symbol for the signal *sh*. The fact that *hush* happens to resemble *sh* somewhat does not matter; one could say *Be quiet* and be just as effectively symbolizing.

Messages conveyed by paralanguage are not specific symbols in the way that language messages are. They act as signs of the setting of language, and as supplementary and subordinate signals to the language signals. Those aspects of paralanguage that bear analogies to the sound and shape aspects of language cannot be separated from one another as can sound and form in language. And the sense aspects of paralanguage can by symbolic only in terms of the language material which they always accompany.

Kinesics (see Birdwhistell, 1952) involves a setting of body set, in which take place certain body and facial motions, which are modified by motion qualities. The total behavior, as a communication system, seems to be analogous to paralanguage. Kinesics, like paralanguage, consists of signs and signals, and produces symbolizing messages only through accompanying language items. There are, however, certain kinesic activities, which may be called gestures, that are occasionally used in such a way that they seem to resemble specific symbols.

From paralanguage there has developed the art form called music. The structure of music has not been analyzed in the terms used here (sign, signal, symbol), but it does not appear to have the kind of symbolizing force that language has. Only when accompanied by language, as in songs with lyrics, does specific symbolizing take place.

An art form stemming from kinesics and usually accompanied by music is the dance. Like the former, it does not seem to contain specific symbolizing power.

From kinesics there have been developed in modern times the communication systems of the deaf, which are calques, as it were, of writing, and therefore are secondary symbol systems.

Tactile-sensory communication has been studied very little. It probably involves signals as well as signs, but produces symbolizing only when accompanied by explanatory language. The reading-and-writing system of Braille, for the blind, is a secondary symbol system based entirely on writing.

An aspect of paralanguage, kinesics, and tactile-sensory communication is their ability to be iconic. In paralanguage this means producing signals that are close imitations of other noises in the world (and even of language). In kinesics it means motions and gestures that imitate other motions. The art forms of music and dance employ iconic material to a large extent. Tactile-sensory communication is iconic when imitating various kinds of pressures and frictions.

Olfactory communication, by perfumes and natural body odors, has not been explored to any extent as a cultural phenomenon. But there are many language items alluding to pleasant or unpleasant odors.

4. CULTURE AS COMMUNICATION

Culture has been briefly defined above in terms that are like those used in defining language, but are more general. It has also been stated that language was the first cultural system, and made possible the rest of culture. In this sense language is primary as the antecedent condition for, the vehicle of, and also an integral part of culture.

It will be useful at this point to see what cultural systems there are in addition to language, and to estimate or guess at their communication effectiveness.

It is a basic premise of this discussion that all human activity, no matter how basically biological, and no matter how seemingly dependent upon ecology, is mediated through culture. A human being does not simply see —he sees what his culture teaches him to see. He doesn't simply eat—he eats culturally approved foods. Even in early infancy he does not simply eliminate; the first diaper-change (or its analogue in non-Western societies) begins the cultural control of these activities. Culture thus has to deal with all the things that go on in the universe and to which human beings react. Every society has to deal with some aspect of all these things, and every culture develops systems for such dealings. It can be assumed that, just as extremely diverse languages have a basic commonality of structure, so extremely diverse time-systems, or kinship-systems, or philosophies may have some basic structures in common.

Anthropological theory has not developed analytical schemes for other cultural systems that are as refined and thoroughgoing as those developed for the analysis of language. But some attempts of this kind have been made. Here we can only briefly list some areas of cultural activity that seem to constitute systems that may have some analogy, in complexity, or unity of subject matter, or in expressive modality, to language. (The discussion is based on some unpublished material summarized in Trager, 1963a. See also Trager, 1962, and Hall and Trager, 1953.)

As is true for language, all culture is believed to be analyzable into processes of setting, content, and functioning. Within these processes, there are cultural foci—cultural activities dealing with and focused on certain aspects of the universe. Nine such foci may be recognized: three in the setting—space-time, the sexes, learning; three in the content—communicating, making things, setting values; three in the functioning—utilization of energy, structuring of society, and protection of individuals and groups. Each of the nine foci may be considered as having a setting, a content, and a functioning; it is accordingly divided into three cultural fields, and there are 27 fields in all in the scheme being discussed. Each field, in turn, is considered to have setting, content, and functioning, and is divided into three cultural systems, so that there are 81 cultural systems altogether. The table reproduced here from Trager (1963a) shows the 81 systems grouped under their fields and these under their foci. (The hyphens, colons, and asterisks are symbols, respectively, for setting, content, functioning; they and the figures 1 to 9, the letters A to Z and omega (Ω), and the numbers 01 to 81 are devices for coding used in the original, and are not a necessary part of the scheme.) Some further discussion of the rubrics in the table may be helpful.

Table 1
Table of Cultural Systems

- -1 Spatiotemporality
  - -A Time
    - -01 'Becoming later'
    - :02 Chronology
    - *03 History
  - :B Space
    - -04 Orientation
    - :05 Topology
    - *06 Geography
  - *C Being
    - -07 Existence
    - :08 Awareness
    - *09 Essence
- - :2 Bisexuality
  - -D Sex
    - -10 Dimorphism
    - :11 The sexes
    - *12 Reproduction
  - :E Sexuality
    - -13 Maleness, femaleness
    - :14 Sexual acts
    - *15 Sexual gratification
  - *F Gender
    - -16 Sexual conditioning
    - :17 Sex roles
    - *18 Affinity
- - *3 Doctorality
  - -G Integration type
    - -19 Neural dimorphism
    - :20 Point, line integration

- *21 Intellect
  - -H Learning
    - -22 Receptivity
    - :23 What can be learned
    - *24 Knowledge
  - *I Teaching
    - -25 Rearing
    - :26 Instruction
    - *27 Education
- : -4 Symbolics
  - -J Cerebration
    - -28 Hunch
    - :29 Coding
    - *30 Emotion
  - :K Communication
    - -31 Paralanguage, kinesics, etc.
    - :32 Language
    - *33 Stylistics
  - *L Poetics
    - -34 Modalities
    - :35 Literature
    - *36 Commentary
- : :5 Pragmatics
  - -M Motor Activity
    - -37 Stimulus-response
    - :38 Motion
    - *39 Creativity
  - :N Artifaction
    - -40 Resources

:41 Technology
°42 Exploitation
°O Technics
  -43 Design
  :44 Artistry
  °45 Art
°6 Axiomation
  -P Estimation
    -46 Teleology
    :47 Awareness of 'goods'
    °48 Differentiation of good
       and bad
  :Q Evaluation
    -49 Criteriology
    :50 Setting of standards
    °51 Ethics
  °R Values
    -52 Hierarchy of goals
    :53 Habits of action: virtue
       and vice
    °54 Incarnate values
° -7 Synergy
  -S Energy use
    -55 Availability of energy
    :56 Utilization of energy
    °57 Productivity
  :T Work and play
    -58 Division of labor
    :59 Occupation, recreation
    °60 Economics

°U Production
  -61 Want and need
  :62 Output
  °63 Distribution
° :8 Society
  -V Kinship
    -64 Relationships
    :65 Kin structure
    °66 Family
  :W Social structure
    -67 Ordering
    :68 Government
    °69 Law
  °X Hierarchy
    -70 Rank
    :71 Status
    °72 Role
° °9 Strategy
  -Y Protection
    -73 Power
    :74 Group Structure
    °75 Community Structure
  :Z Defense
    -76 Health
    :77 Welfare
    °78 'Care'
  °Ω Religion
    -79 Magic
    :80 Ritual
    °81 'Rule'

Under the space-time focus, there are systems of chronology, history, geography. Under the focus of the sexes (or, better, *bisexuality*)there are the cultural systems for dealing with reproduction, sexual acts, sex roles, and others (see Trager, 1962). Under learning are systems of knowledge, and instruction. Under communicating ("symbolics") there are systems for dealing with emotion, language, stylistics, literature. The focus of making things ("pragmatics") includes systems of creativity, technology, design, art. For setting values there are systems of ethics, and habits of virtue and vice. Under the utilization of energy are systems of productivity, division of labor, economics, want and need, distribution. Under the structuring of society we have kin structure, the family, government, law, rank, status, role. And for protection of individuals and groups ("strategy") there are systems of power, community structure, welfare, and what may be called the "rule" or "way of life" (an aspect of the field of religion).

It is believed that each cultural system is actually in some way a system of communication. There is an interaction situation, there is the behavior (the interaction events), there is the message conveyed by the interaction. No studies have yet been made in terms of this scheme which would provide analytical procedures for any of the systems other than those of communication already discussed in this paper. But some of the procedures or basic elements may be hinted at.

In a system of chronology there would be the recognition of specific periods of time and of specific times, and an awareness of them brought about not only by a terminology, but also by cyclic recurrence and accompanying affect: in our society most places look and "feel" different on a Sunday than they do during the week; one knows it is lunch time not necessarily because of physiological hunger but because one has engaged in a sufficient number of morning activities to bring on the "feeling" that it's time for lunch. That is, "Sunday" and "lunch-time" are communicated by events and appearances that we have learned as parts of a chronological system.

In technology there are the specific items of process of manufacture, materials used, methods of using them, and so on. The person who has learned a technological process receives communication from the procedures and their products about efficiency, quality, adequacy of functioning, and the like. The products of the various systems of artifaction are in themselves communicative: a chair "represents" comfort, or efficiency at work, or a period of design; a building "tells us" whether it is medieval, renaissance, or modern; a gadget is obviously for such-and-such a purpose, or just as obviously is completely mystifying.

In kin structure, the arrangement can communicate rigid patrilineal authority, or bilateral descent, or an informal feeling for all "cousins," etc.

It is suspected that the cultural systems which deal with "things"—artifacts of all kinds—and which have structures whose parts are well known and are named, are most likely to communicate directly by symbolizing as well as through the language items dealing with them. A cathedral, a sharecropper's shack; a painting, an obscene sketch on a wall; an executive's neatly cleared desk, a scholar's cluttered study; an Indian's blanket, a cowboy's high-heeled boots; a bikini on an obese woman, an all-covering "mother hubbard" on a pretty young girl; a father's admonitory gesture, a mother's caress; all these communicate. Some of them are signs, some are signals, others are symbols. Each of us receives the communication to the extent that we are participants in the particular culture; and each of us misses the point or is puzzled or upset by it, to the extent that the behavior is in a culture unknown or unfamiliar to us.

5. APPLICATIONS TO PSYCHOTHERAPY

The skilled and experienced psychotherapist, having acquired his skills as a result of his extensive experiences with all kinds of people, at many levels of the society, is able to understand intuitively the vast array of cultural differences that he encounters. He comes to *know* (though he may be completely unaware of how he knows) the significance of a gesture, of a sigh, of a pause, of a substandard expression slipping into the patient's "cultured" recital, of an ostentatious article of clothing in an otherwise tasteful array. But even the most experienced therapist, if his experiences have not included persons outside of Western society, may be completely upset by some bit of behavior that is perfectly normal in the patient's culture, and may direct his therapy at something that needs no correction, while missing completely the troublesome disturbance. The therapist may also be unaware of things in his own behavior that interfere with the patient's composure. His learned phraseology may point up a social insecurity in the patient, or his "folksiness" may irritate a patient who has generations of well-to-do city people behind him; or his foreign accent may impress one patient with his obvious competence, while utterly disgusting another patient who "doesn't like" foreigners.

It would appear to be useful, in the training of personnel for psychotherapy, to provide instruction that specifically calls attention to the existence of cultural differences and the manner in which they are manifested in the several communication systems. In the course of such instruction, sufficient information about the structure of cultural systems should be given so that the learner develops an understanding of what to look for and listen for.

Except, however, for the occasional therapist who is himself particularly interested in some one or more aspects of culture, and who wishes to develop real skill in analysis of the communication material, it would seem to be unnecessary to attempt to actually teach the details of phonetics, let us say, or of kinship analysis, or of agricultural economics. The therapist can be taught that these things exist, and how they relate to each other as parts of a total culture; and how the analogous parts of diverse cultures may differ from each other; and that there exist specialists in these fields, many of them quite willing, even eager, to apply their particular skills to psychotherapeutic materials. If the therapist learns this much, and learns how to make use of the specialists' skills and knowledge, and especially *when* he can best use the specialist, his own perceptions are likely to be sharpened, and his results to be improved, or at least to be more comprehensible.

The linguist (and the cultural anthropologist) does not, usually does not want to, and should not be allowed or expected to do any therapy.

The psychotherapist can rarely do enough analysis of communication material in a cultural setting to be more than superficially obvious; nor should he be expected to be able to or to do such analysis. But the therapist who is aware of the uses of the special skills we have discussed can set up his work so as to cooperate with the linguist who is anthropologically trained and who is aware of psychotherapeutic problems. Between them they may achieve progress.

For over a decade there has been work done involving collaboration of psychotherapists and various kinds of social scientists along some of the lines suggested. A survey of some of what has been done may be useful at this point.

Psychotherapy has been carried on for a long time by clinical psychologists as well as by medically trained psychiatrists. In many cases there has been contrast and disagreement between these two kinds of therapists. But even where there has been collaboration, there has been little in the way of infiltration of one discipline by the ideas and methods of the other; rather it has been a case of doing the same things in the same way, starting from very much the same premises. Where social workers and sociologists have been brought in, they have been utilized principally as a kind of auxiliary, a technician, rather than as real participants in the therapeutic process. Some anthropologists have long been addicted to psychologizing and even psychiatrizing, but it is they who have exploited the therapists—not too intelligently in most cases—and not psychotherapy that has utilized their knowledge.

As long ago as 1932, Edward Sapir wrote on the relation between cultural anthropology and psychiatry (Sapir, 1932). This article is programmatic and general, but still remains very well worth reading, because so little has been done to implement it since.

More specifically, collaboration of psychotherapists with anthropologically oriented linguists has been done to some extent. A prime example is found in *The First Five Minutes.* (Pittenger, Hockett, and Danehy, 1960). The psychiatrists, Pittenger and Danehy, associated the linguist, Hockett, to the work of analyzing minutely the opening minutes of a therapeutic interview recorded on tape. Hockett transcribed linguistically and paralinguistically. Pittenger and Danehy carefully followed the details of transcription and then came to therapeutic conclusions by evaluating what they heard in their own medium of analysis, and in relation to the data the linguist supplied. As in any pioneer work, there are errors in the linguistic part, and no doubt also in the psychiatric part of the work. The two psychiatrists are actually themselves competent in linguistic coding (the present author worked with them on material similar to that in the book for several years up to 1960 and can testify to this), and could have done much the same work as Hockett did, though there might well have been more transcription errors. But by bringing in a linguist they kept the levels of analysis apart and avoided mixing their roles. In this way they were able to do the therapeutic aspects of their work unencumbered by much detail that was only secondarily pertinent. Acquaintance with and understanding of the linguistic material by the therapists was essential; but the detail of linguistic coding points up the irrelevance (or rather non-relevance) of many of the linguistic items except as background material. One lack in this work is any record of the accompanying kinesics of the interview. It is clear that not many more such works will be published, if indeed any. But the skills and activities displayed must be part of the background for therapy. Collaborative effort can bring about their efficient and effective use.

A clinical psychologist and a psychiatrist worked with the present author for several years on the communication aspects of psychotherapeutic interviews. In a brief report (Dittmann, and Wynne, 1961) they state that the details of linguistic analysis are reliably describable, but "probably have little psychological relevance" (p. 203), while paralinguistic phenomena "have higher psychological relevance, but cannot be coded reliably." It is probably true that linguistic details as such have little psychological relevance, though they are basic to the sociocultural placement of the speaker in therapy; and the paralinguistic phenomena are of much higher psychological relevance in psychotherapeutic situations, though it must be understood that as behavior events they occur in a matrix of language. But I must question the conclusion that paralinguistic details cannot be coded reliably. At the time that the work was done with Dittman and Wynne, the analysis of paralanguage was still in a very preliminary stage, though good agreement was reached by the three of us in evaluating the material. Since their study, a notation system for paralanguage has been worked out, and work has been done in recording minutely the paralinguistic phenomena in English as well as in some other languages. More research and field analysis are urgently needed to test and expand the system. Moreover, this points up still more strongly the desirability of collaborative work rather than attempts by either therapists or linguists to assume each others' roles.

It is unfortunately not possible to report any work along the lines discussed in which detailed analysis of some cultural system other than language or paralanguage was carried out as an aid to psychotherapeutic work. In the case of some ethnic groups, for instance, detailed study of the actual working of kin-relations might have great bearing on therapy. Generalizations have been made about authority structures and about kin groups, as well as about other aspects of culture, but systematic collaboration, with the kind of detailed point-by-point evaluation evidenced in *The First Five Minutes*, let us say, has been completely absent. Such work would, of course, be highly desirable.

REFERENCES

BIRDWHISTELL, R. L. *Introduction to kinesics.* Washington, D.C.: U.S. Dept. of State, Foreign Service Institute, 1952. (Reprinted by the University of Louisville, 1954. Out of print.)

DITTMANN, A. T., and WYNNE, L. C. Linguistic techniques and the analysis of emotionality in interviews. *J. of abnorm. soc. Psychol.,* **63**: 201-204, 1961.

GLEASON, H. A., JR. *An introduction to descriptive linguistics.* New York: Holt, Rinehart and Winston, 1955 (2nd ed., 1961)

HALL, E. T., JR., and TRAGER, G. L. *The analysis of culture.* Washington, D.C.: American Council of Learned Societies, 1953. "Prepublication edition." (Out of print.)

JOOS, M. Semology: A linguistic theory of meaning. *Studies in linguistics,* **13**: 53-70, 1958.

PITTENGER, R. E., HOCKETT, C. F., and DANEHY, J. J. *The first five minutes: A sample microscopic interview analysis.* Ithaca, N.Y.: Paul Martineau, 1960.

SAPIR, E. Cultural anthropology and psychiatry. *J. of abnorm. soc. Psychol.,* **27**: 229-242, 1932. Reprinted in D. G. Mandelbaum (Ed.). *Culture language and personality, selected essays.* Berkeley and Los Angeles: Univ. of California Press, 1956. Pp. 140-163.

TRAGER, G. L. Language. In *Encyclopaedia Britannica,* Vol. 13, 696 703, 1955.

TRAGER, G. L., Linguistics. In *Encyclopaedia Britannica,* Vol. 14, 162 A-H, 163, 1956.

TRAGER, G. L. Paralanguage: A first approximation. *Studies in linguistics,* **13**: 1-12, 1958.

TRAGER, G. L. *Phonetics: glossary and tables.* (*Studies in linguistics: occasional papers,* 5), 2nd ed., 27, Buffalo, N.Y., 1964.

TRAGER, G. L. A scheme for the cultural analysis of sex. *SW J. of Anthrop.,* **18**: 114-118, 1962.

TRAGER, G. L. *A schematic outline for the processual analysis of culture.* Stanford, Calif.,: Center for Advanced Study in the Behavioral Sciences, May, 1963. (a) (Multilithed; unpublished.)

TRAGER, G. L. *Linguistics in linguistics.* (*Studies in linguistics: occasional papers,* 10), Buffalo, N.Y., 1963. (b)

TRAGER, G. L., and SMITH, H. L., JR. *An outline of English structure.* (*Studies in linguistics: occasional papers,* 3), Norman, Okla., 1951 (6th printing, New York: American Council of Learned Societies, 1965.)

a. *Language variables*

Several examples of types of content analysis in psychotherapy have been provided, such as those by Auld and Dollard; Gottschalk, Winget, Gleser, and Springer; and Chance. A review and collection of content analysis methods and findings is available elsewhere by Pool (1959) and also by Marsden (1965).

Content analysis is a relatively established method of studying psycho-therapy. It was inevitable that researchers would try to reduce the com-plexity of psychotherapy to a number of variables which could be studied individually and in their relationship to each other. In this connection, Scheflen will, in a later section of this book, present his arguments against the isolation and quantification of variables occurring in psychotherapy. Ultimately, the value of content analysis methods depends on the meas-urability, pertinence, and predictive capacity of the variables chosen. These methods differ in the level of inference required to identify the variables and the extent to which quantification is featured.

The contribution by Auld and Dollard is an updated joint effort by these two authors of their book *Scoring Human Motives* (1959), and the present report places relatively more emphasis on unconscious motivation and psychoanalytic theory and less on learning theory and general science theory. In this connection, these authors provide, in succinct form, a set of operational criteria for inferring unconscious motivation which is one of the clearest statements in the literature of these criteria. (See also Mac-Intyre, 1958.) Their method of analysis of content requires the use of psy-chotherapists experienced in psychodynamic theory, and with such re-searchers quite satisfactory inter-rater reliability coefficients are found. Also reported in this contribution are some validity findings with the use of their method.

Gottschalk, *et al.* have attempted in their contribution to define affects operationally from typescripts of the psychotherapeutic interview. The authors have derived, from psychoanalytic theory, a procedure for quanti-tatively assessing the magnitude of a number of immediate affective reac-tions. The method has been developed to the point where technicians un-trained in the skills or theories of psychotherapy can carry out the content analysis procedures required with adequate inter-judge reliability. The applicability of these scales to research in psychotherapy and to psycho-somatic interrelationships appears to be promising. The use of the verbal behavior analysis method is illustrated in detail on the *Temple* sound-filmed interview which begins on page 241.

Chance describes a content analysis system designed to measure a pa-tient's interpersonal strivings. These strivings are classified according to the Leary circle, with the polarities of love-hate and dominance-submis-sion. The data under study are, of course, the patient's words, and the unit of analysis is any phrase which expresses an interpersonal experience. The unit approximates the grammatical clause, which is the communication unit used by Auld and Dollard and by Gottschalk *et al.* Chance's chapter also contains an application of her method to the "Temple" interview. Using it, she is able to construct a profile of the patient's personality based on one minute of interaction.

REFERENCES

MACINTYRE, A. C. *The unconscious. A conceptual analysis.* London: Routledge,
    1958.
POOL, I. (Ed.) *Trends in content analysis.* Urbana, Ill.: Univ. of Illinois Press,
    1959.
MARSDEN, G. Content-analysis studies of therapeutic interviews: 1954 to 1964.
    Psychol. Bull. 68: 298-321, 1965.

10. Measurement of motivational variables in psychotherapy [1]

Frank Auld Jr. and John Dollard

Among many psychoanalysts *quantification* has acquired a bad reputation. They think of *quantification* or *measurement* as a destruction of the meaningfulness of the therapeutic interaction, as an insensitivity to vital processes of therapy, as a rather stupid and arrogant use of numbers. One can understand why they feel this way; there have been many misguided attempts at measuring psychoanalytic concepts. But in these misguided attempts, the troubles arose not from quantification, but from the erroneous applications of analytic theory. For example, the easy assumption that repression can be equated with forgetting is just plain wrong; and whether an investigator making this erroneous assumption uses quantification or not is quite beside the point.

Disregarding the negative connotation that *quantification* has acquired, we find it necessary to move toward the quantification of psychoanalytic variables; for science demands objective observation and reliable measurement. The work of the authors in developing a system for coding the sentence of a therapeutic interview (reported in our book, *Scoring Human Motives*) is intended as a first step toward the measurement of psychoanalytic variables. We wished to measure such events and processes as *resistance, transference, unconscious motive, anxiety, inhibition, dependence, hostility,* and *interpretation*.

As we became involved in the task of measuring variables in the therapeutic interview, it became clear to us that the central problem in doing this is: How does one make inferences about unconscious processes? To answer this question, we looked at what we ourselves did when we arrived at the formulation, "Something unconscious is determining the patient's behavior." We observed, also, the grounds on which psychoanalysts arrived at such a formulation during discussions at case seminars. From such observations a set of criteria for designating unconscious motives emerged.

The basis of these criteria is the assumption that mental life is lawful

---

[1] The first draft of this chapter was written by Frank Auld, Jr., who is therefore listed as senior author. The material of this chapter is based on John Dollard and Frank Auld, Jr., *Scoring Human Motives* (Yale University Press, 1959), but various new data relating to the validity of the content-analysis system have been added.

and intelligible. Thus, if there are seeming discontinuities in mental life—inexplicable features that do not fit with the rest—we assume that with added information, or with appropriate hypotheses, we can make a coherent and complete explanation of the individual's mental life. The gaps that we observe arise in this way: what the patient tells us about himself is insufficient to account for his behavior. With the best of will to cooperate with the therapist, what he says about his behavior is inadequate to account for it; his private verbalization even falls short of describing accurately and fully the wishes and fears that have determined his behavior. It is not that the patient for the moment neglects to mention some aspect of his motivational structure; rather, he is unable to do so at all. There is some motive, some response he is making, some cue to which he is responding, or some reward he is experiencing that he cannot name at all. The unconscious is the unnameable or unlabelable. There may be a rationalization replacing the ideally accurate description; or there may be in the patient only a sense of puzzlement: "I can't understand what made me do that."

We say, therefore, that where there is a mystery—an aspect of the patient's behavior for which he cannot account adequately—we are justified in speaking of an unconscious motive.

GUIDELINES FOR INFERRING UNCONSCIOUS MOTIVATION

We have identified four situations that permit the inference of an unconscious motive: (1) The situation in which the patient is participating is expected to evoke a particular motive, but the patient communicates little, if any, evidence of experiencing the motive. (2) The patient responds with bodily mobilization appropriate to a particular motive, but the patient is not aware that the motive is influencing his behavior. (3) An avoidant response is reported, without report of adequate provocation in the environment. (4) The patient talks about the activities or feelings appropriate to a motive, while denying that he experienced the related affect.

1. *Evocative situation.* Strife evokes angry emotions; situations of danger evoke fear. There are limits to this principle, but one will be right most of the time if he imputes to a participant that motive which the situation is expected to evoke.

2. *Bodily mobilization.* A virtuous housewife may experience the quickened pulse which accompanies the weekly chat with the cheerful trashman but have no knowledge that she is experiencing, and responding to, a sexual temptation. We, however, may be willing to make the inference that she has an unconscious sexual reaction, the naming of which is inhibited.

3. *Avoidant response.* An attractive young married woman fell into con-

versation with the bachelor who occupied the ground-floor apartment in her apartment house. She mentioned that she was in psychotherapy; he inquired whether she had a sexual problem; she began to tell him the details of her sexual problem. Then, frightened, she fled back to her apartment; thereafter, she avoided the bachelor. We infer that this young woman would not have avoided the man unless she had been unconsciously attracted to him, unconsciously disposed to become seduced by him.

4. *Naming with denial.* If the patient speaks of actions and feelings related to a motive, while denying that the motive determines his behavior, we are paradoxically led to say he cannot name the motive. What we mean, of course, is that he cannot name the motive as active within himself. We will often have the most compelling reasons for believing that the patient would not talk about the motive unless it held importance in his life; therefore, we infer an unconscious motive. This principle is not entirely satisfactory, but we believe it will lead to correct inferences more often than not.

CATEGORIES FOR PATIENT'S SENTENCES

As we then attempted to measure significant variables in the therapeutic interview, we decided to code each sentence of the interview according to a system of classification that represents such variables. We decided to assign each sentence to one, and only one, category—that category which expresses the most significant aspect of the sentence.

How did we decide on the categories to use? We were influenced by our knowledge of psychoanalytic theory, of behavioristic learning theory, and of cultural anthropology; but we did not start by putting down a complete list of concepts drawn from these disciplines, subsequently trying to find examples of these concepts. Instead, we started by looking at the material of the therapeutic hour; we adopted tentatively a few obvious concepts; we applied these categories to the therapeutic material; then we revised the categories and added new ones. Though we did not consciously examine psychoanalytic theory to see how to construct our content-analysis system, after the fact it can be seen that from analytic theory we took its motivational schema, which assigns importance to libidinal development (through the psychosexual levels), to the contrast between libido and aggression, to an understanding of the vicissitudes of libidinal and aggressive impulses, and to a theory of defense mechanisms and of resistance. From psychoanalysis, too, we acquired a theory of the therapeutic action of psychotherapy. According to this theory, better functioning of the ego is a primary goal of psychotherapy. Psychoanalysis also emphasizes the importance of the distinction between conscious and unconscious mental functioning.

The categories for the patient's sentences are as follows:

A: anxiety
Conf: confirmation of an interpretation
Dep: dependence
Dream: the report of a dream (the manifest dream)
H: hostility
H/self: self-criticism
L: aim-inhibited love
Lf: laughter (which may be further classified as *anxious* or *relaxed* laughter)
Mob: strivings for social mobility
N: a simple negation, unless it is considered resistant
Obs: obsessional thoughts and acts
PSS: report of a psychosomatic symptom
r: rewarding experience (usually added to another sign; e.g., *A:r* means that one feels relief from anxiety)
Reas: reasoning, insight
Res: resistance
S: Sex
Sigh: a sigh
W: weeping
Y: a simple agreement which cannot be scored otherwise
Unsc: unscorable, does not fit any of the other categories

When the patient is in mental conflict, we can represent this fact with a combination of signs: for example, *H-A* to mean that the patient is hostile but is restrained by anxiety from acting on his hostile feelings.

We use codes beginning with capital letters to designate conscious motives (*A, Dep, H, H/self, L, Mob, S*) and codes beginning with small letters to designate unconscious motives (*a, dep, h, h/self, l, mob, s*).

CATEGORIES FOR THERAPIST'S SENTENCES

The therapist categories derive largely from the psychoanalytic theory of the action of analytic psychotherapy, which tells us that the aim of therapy is to make the unconscious conscious, creating ego where id was; that the therapist must overcome resistance; that he does this by means of interpretations; that he utilizes the positive transference to bind the patient to the therapeutic task; that he at times directs the patient's attention to fruitful areas for exploration; and that he can err by allowing countertransference to distort his actions, by failing to make use of appropriate technical maneuvers, by making premature or wrong interpretations, by failing to interpret when he should, or by giving a wrong structure to the therapeutic situation. Our categories for the therapist allow us to code some of his actions which are relevant to these variables.

The categories are:

Interp: interpretation (of anything unconscious, including resistance)

D: any motivating statement of the therapist (including criticism of patient, asking patient to do something or to think about something, asking patient a question)

R: any rewarding statement (including reassurance, kind comments, expressions of interest in patient)

M: signal of continued attention (Mmm-hmm)

Pretni: a therapeutic error (of any of the types mentioned above in the statement of theory)

Unsc: unscorable

THE UNITIZING TASK

Any study of the therapeutic process requires some sort of division of the material into units. Quantitative study requires a *precise* division of the material. Many different kinds of units are possible. Because for our research we desired a unit that is very small, we chose the sentence. Linguists call this "a single free utterance," *free* in the sense that it is not included in any larger structure by means of any grammatical device (see Fries, 1952, and Bloomfield, 1933).

The rules that we developed for dividing interviews into sentences are presented in our book, *Scoring Human Motives* (1959).

RELIABILITY OF THE CODING

We say that a method of measurement is *reliable* if it gives consistent results, i.e., if any scientist using the method on a particular body of data gets the same result as any other scientist. Developing reliable measures of the events in psychotherapy is no pious and empty exercise, nor is it a compulsive absorption in minutiae. It is, instead, a necessary step in the development of a science of psychotherapy.

Because the scoring on which our book was based was done by the authors, the data on reliability of scoring reported therein came from a limited experience. We reported excellent agreement on assignment of the therapist's sentences to the various categories: tetrachoric *r*'s averaged about .91. We reported somewhat lower correlations for the patient categories, with an average of .89 for one case and .78 for another case, in the main categories. Such a level of agreement on coding would be sufficient for many research aims.

Others who have subsequently used the category system or parts of it have obtained levels of agreement about the same as those reported in *Scoring Human Motives*. Goldenberg (1964), Snyder (1963), Hampton (1963), and Klein (1965) have all achieved scoring reliability that was good enough to make the system useful for their purposes.

Extensive definitions and examples are offered in our book, so that a researcher who wants to extend or to sharpen the measurement can use our work as a starting point.

VALIDITY OF THE CODING SYSTEM

Auld and White (1959) made use of the coding system to investigate four hypotheses:

1. The patient's speech hangs together; he is likely to continue in the next sentence with the same category as the present one.

2. Resistant sentences are likely to precede silence, and silence is likely to precede resistant sentences. Such a correlation would be taken to mean that when the patient is resistant during a particular period of time, it will be manifested at one moment by silence and at another moment by resistant utterances.

3. Whether the patient is speaking resistantly influences whether the therapist will intervene, in particular whether he will intervene by making an interpretation.

4. Interpretive interventions of the therapist are no more likely to evoke immediate resistance by the patient than are noninterpretive interventions.

Four therapy cases, carried by four different therapists, provided the material for this study. All of the hypotheses were confirmed.

Goldenberg (1964) repeated the portion of the Auld and White study that dealt with the correlation between silence and resistant sentences, in order to rule out the possibility that the scorer's knowledge of where silences occurred could bias his scoring. With this more careful research design, Goldenberg confirmed the original findings.

Snyder (1963) has made use of the coding system for the patient's sentences, finding it useful for the description of the ongoing therapeutic process in a case that he studied in great detail. Hampton (1963) ingeniously adapted the coding system for scoring sentence-completion responses, and believes that his approach yields useful information.

The definitions of the coding system provided Klein (1965) with a method for identifying resistant segments in psychotherapy interviews. Klein compared five-minute segments of the interview that were highly resistant with segments that showed unstable resistance and segments characterized by minimal resistance. It was Klein's hypothesis that patients are relatively comfortable when resistance is strong and stable, that they are quite anxious and aroused in periods of unstable resistance, and that they are somewhat labile but not extremely anxious during periods of low resistance. His findings, in which continuous measurement of electrical skin conductance has furnished data about physiological arousal, have been consistent with this hypothesis.

Finally, we note the work of Tourney and a group of his co-workers at

Lafayette Clinic (1963). These researchers have taken the categories of *Scoring Human Motives,* have added other categories, and have developed rating scales for all of them. The ratings can be made for each five-minute segment of an interview, or, of course, for a shorter or longer period.

Much of the work at Lafayette Clinic has been focused on the study of therapist errors. Errors have been classified as errors of omission (failure to ask appropriate motivating questions, failure to interpret, lack of empathic response) or of commission (unnecessary advice, wrong or ill-timed interpretations, over-identification with the patient). Among the findings of the first eleven cases to be studied are these:

After the therapist makes an error of commission, the patient is more-than-usually hostile to the therapist, and more depressed. After an error of omission, the patient is more anxious and more hostile to the therapist. There is, of course, some variation among patients in how they respond to actions of the therapist; thus we find some patients who become more resistant after a therapeutic error, though this correlation cannot be stated yet as a general finding.

Errors of commission by the therapist are preceded by hostility, resistance, and negative arousal in the patient, while errors of omission are not preceded by significant changes in the patient's emotional expression. We can speculate that the hostile, resistant, or anxious behavior of a patient provokes the therapist to intervene somehow, and that if he is a beginner in doing therapy (as these therapists were) he may intervene by making some kind of error.

Lest we leave the impression that the Lafayette Clinic researchers were concerned solely with the therapist's mistakes, we want to describe one case they studied in which a timely and appropriate interpretation was followed by lessened resistance and lessened expression by the patient of hostile feelings toward the therapist. In an interview with a patient who was diagnosed in the category *conversion reaction,* the psychiatric resident responded to the patient's strong resistance and moderate expression of hostility toward therapist, at the very beginning of the hour, by making an interpretation. He continued with interpretive comments until halfway through the session, when the resistance diminished considerably and the hostility abated almost completely.

EVALUATION OF THE CODING SYSTEM

The coding system of *Scoring Human Motives* provides a method for the measurement of a considerable number of the variables believed by psychoanalysts to be important in the therapeutic interaction. When each sentence is scored, this method gives a detailed description of the therapeutic interaction. Those researchers who do not need so detailed a picture of the therapy can adapt the method, by choosing larger units to be scored, or by selecting a few from the whole set of variables. The work of Tourney and his co-workers demonstrates the value of our system in stimulating research on the dynamically important variables in psychotherapy.

We believe, also, that our approach to the task of quantifying the events in therapy has illuminated the problem of defining unconscious motives, that we have made a beginning toward the solution of this difficult problem.

Finally, we would make the point that we have demonstrated the feasibility of getting reliable measures not from simple, objective features of the therapy situation, but through a procedure that makes use of the empathic understanding of an observer. There is a way, we believe, to harness the power of that empathy which Greenson (1960) and others have written about.

REFERENCES

AULD, F., JR., and WHITE, ALICE M. Sequential dependencies in psychotherapy. *J. abnorm. soc. Psychol.*, **58**: 273, 1959.

BLOOMFIELD, L. *Language*. New York: Holt, Rinehart and Winston, 1933.

DOLLARD, J., and AULD, F., JR. *Scoring human motives: A manual*. New Haven: Yale University Press, 1959.

FRIES, C. C. *The structure of English*. New York: Harcourt, Brace & World, 1952.

GOLDENBERG, G. M. and AULD, F., JR. Equivalence of silence to resistance. *J. consult. Psychol.* **28**: 476, 1964.

GREENSON, R. R. Empathy and its vicissitudes. *Int. J. Psychoanal.* **41**: 418, 1960.

HAMPTON, P. A study of hidden motives and conflicts in university counseling. In *VII Congreso Interamericano de Psicologia*. Mexico, D.F.: Sociedad Interamericana de Psicologia, 1963. Pp. 437-441.

KLEIN, L. S. *Correlation of resistance with GSR of patients in psychotherapy.* Doctoral dissertation, Wayne State University, 1965.

SNYDER, W. U. *Dependency in psychotherapy*. New York: Macmillan, 1963.

TOURNEY, G., LOWINGER, P., SCHORER, C., BLOOM, V., and AULD, F., JR. The measurement of psychotherapy. Paper presented at American Psychiatric Association divisional meeting, New York, November 8, 1963.

11. The measurement of emotional changes during a psychiatric interview: a working model toward quantifying the psychoanalytic concept of affect

Louis A. Gottschalk, Carolyn M. Winget, Goldine C. Gleser, and Kayla J. Springer

INTRODUCTION

The advantages to psychoanalysis as a science of some means of quantifying a few of the key psychoanalytic concepts have been referred to by many authors, including Fenichel (1945), Kubie (1952), Jacobson (1953), Rapaport (1953, 1960), Knapp (1957), and others. Rapaport (1960), for example, has reminded us that all sciences, in striving to make their assertions precise, move toward a mathematization of the relationships they establish by their procedures, and that "quantification may prove to be the mathematization appropriate to psychoanalysis" (p. 91). Eloquent pleas have been made for exploratory quantification, on even an *a priori* basis, of the concept of cathexis and other psychoanalytic constructs, but there have not been offered any practical methodologic solutions to attain these ends.

A team of research workers at the Department of Psychiatry, University of Cincinnati, has been involved for several years in exploring one method of quantifying some psychoanalytic concepts, utilizing certain characteristics of verbal behavior as indicative of the intrapsychic state. Some headway has been made toward developing a reliable and valid method of quantifying the concept, as we structure it, of affect or emotion. In this paper we plan to review and illustrate our approach (Gleser, *et al.,* 1961; Gottschalk, *et al.,* 1963).

We have recognized, and others (for example, Reid, 1950; Rapaport, 1950; and Jacobson, 1953) have pointed out, that there are terminological confusions, theoretical divergencies, and a lack of precision in the definition of emotions and affects. We intend to sidestep rather than to resolve

These studies have been supported in part by a research grant (MH-K3-14,665) from the Public Health Service, Department of Health, Education, and Welfare and research grants (T 57-74 and B 59-21) from the Foundations Fund for Research in Psychiatry.

these issues. Furthermore, we have not adhered strictly to some of the proposed terminological distinctions between emotions, affects, and feelings. We have the impression that many of the theoretical and definitional arguments in this area cannot be resolved by discussion alone but that some of these concepts may be clarified by further empirical research. Accordingly, we have formulated working concepts of the emotions or affects we have intended to study and are quite prepared to modify our concepts and relevant assumptions about them, after obtaining further convincing empirical data or after gaining new and persuasive theoretical viewpoints.

Two affects that we have studied in detail are hostility and anxiety. With respect to hostility, it has been the hostility-anger portion of the complex hostility concept which has invited our attention. (See Gottschalk, *et al.*, 1963, for a full discussion of this point.) We have focused our interest, furthermore, on the direction of hostility, distinguishing between hostility directed away from the self, hostility directed toward the self, and *ambivalently* directed hostility. The hostility outward measure provides a scaling of the intensity of adversely critical, angry, assaultive, asocial impulses and drives toward objects outside oneself. The hostility directed inward measure scales degrees of self-hate and self-criticism and, to some extent, feelings of anxious depression and masochism. The ambivalently directed hostility measure, though derived from verbal communications denoting destructive and critical thoughts or actions of others to the self, assesses not only some aspects of hostility directed inward but at the same time some features of hostility directed outward. From validation studies, this measure appears to be capable of varying independently from either the hostility outward or hostility inward measure and, hence, it seems to deserve separate classification.

Our measure of anxiety includes an assessment of what is customarily thought of as both anxiety and fear, for the procedure used in making these measurements does not provide a differentiation between these affects. There has been an attempt to include in this measurement different qualities of anxiety depending on the affective context in which the anxiety is being generated, for example, death, mutilation, guilt, shame, and separation.

Before going into more detail about our procedure for assessing the relative magnitude of affects, particularly transient affects, it is appropriate to describe and discuss first our working definitions and assumptions.

QUANTIFICATION OF AFFECTS

General Problems

One of the general problems involved in the quantification of affect is the formulation of a satisfactory working definition of affect. Theoreticians and experimentalists have approached this problem in different ways, and these differences, as we have mentioned, have sometimes led to varying conclusions.

We have chosen to define affect from an intrapsychic frame of reference, and we have based our assessment of immediate affect on two types of verbal communications. One type is the direct verbal report of the subjective experience of a feeling state. The other type of verbal communication provides indirect evidence of the occurrence of affect. Only by inference, using clinical psychoanalytic theory, can the latter type of verbal statement be taken to signalize the presence of affect. These are affects which the individual is either aware of but does not care to acknowledge or which he does not recognize as a specifiable emotional feeling but experiences as a feeling tone that, nevertheless, influences the quality and intensity of the individual's general feeling state, ideation, and behavior.

There are many other kinds of behavioral and psychologic manifestations besides verbal communications that have been used by investigators to determine the presence of affects. The signs used have been external behavior, including facial expression, criteria frequently used by investigators experimenting with subhuman animals (Massermann, 1943; Seitz, 1954, 1959; Mirsky, 1958); physiological measures (Darrow, 1929; Cannon, 1936; Lacey, 1959); biochemical indicators (Funkenstein, 1956, 1957; Persky, 1958, 1961; Mason, 1961); the report of subjective experience alone, as in the Taylor Anxiety Scale (1953) and Cattell Scale (1956), and in various adjective check-lists (Nowlis, 1956; Zuckerman, 1960); speech disturbances (Mahl, 1961); and so forth.

It is our opinion that the essential, psychologic feature of affects is that they are qualitative feelings of varying intensity about which the individual has various degrees of verbal articulateness or discriminatory capacity, these depending on the relative amounts of awareness he has about these feelings and drive states.

We presume that, at a neurophysiologic level, the qualitative and quantitative differences typifying emotional states are associated with the activation of different configurational patterns of the cerebral cortex and the visceral brain. (See, for example, Gellhorn and Loofbourrow, 1957; or MacLean, 1955.) Though the nature of the neurophysiologic concomitants of affects are of serious interest to our working concept of affect and affect quality and intensity, an integration of neurophysiologic and psychologic theories and facts related to affects is not our aim at this time. Neurophysiologic bases of affects require even more research than the psychodynamic features of affects, and it is premature and pretentious to attempt to invent a workable, unified psychophysiologic theory of emotion. In our opinion, it is a wiser procedure at this time to sketch out only roughly the principles afforded by our overlapping knowledge of emotions at the psychologic and neurophysiologic levels and to maintain a tentative position about the principles governing their psychophysiologic interrelationships.

The usual objection to using an intrapsychic frame of reference as a vantage point from which to determine the amount or intensity of an affect is that subjective and intrapsychic data have not generally been considered suitable for scientific investigation. There is sound evidence to support the viewpoint, however, that such data can be used as reliably and validly as any other phenomena subjected to scientific scrutiny provided adequate research designs and controls are used. (Auld and Murray, 1955; Gottschalk, et al., 1956; Beecher, 1959; Sargent, 1961; and others.)

Our working definition of *affect*, in summary, is as follows: Affects are feeling states that have the dimensions of quality and quantity. Affects and emotions have subjective, purely psychologic components as well as physiological, biochemical, and behavioral concomitants. Continual mixtures of affects of relatively long duration occur and these constitute what is ordinarily designated as mood. Upon this background of mood, feeling states of relatively high intensity and variability may play, and these are generally referred to as emotions. Relatively smaller fluctuations of feeling states which occur irregularly are sometimes referred to, in a narrower sense, as affects. We do not intend here to differentiate between affects, emotions and feeling states—as previously indicated. But since we are attempting to develop an instrument to measure immediate affect rather than the more prolonged feeling states usually referred to as mood, we do want to point out that we are not here equating affect with mood.

To go from verbal behavior to an estimate of the relative intensity of certain affects experienced by an individual during brief units of time has required a series of assumptions that should be made explicit at this point. Some of these assumptions have been partially substantiated. Some have not and, perhaps cannot be, for they may be more in the nature of representational models than testable hypotheses. It would require more space than is appropriate to take at this time to give here in detail the evidence that tends to favor one assumption or another; instead, references will be made, here and there, to investigations providing supportive data for some of our working assumptions.

1. The relative magnitude of an affect can be validly estimated from the typescript of the speech of an individual, using solely content variables and not including any paralanguage variables. In other words, the major part of the variance in the immediate affective state of an individual can be accounted for by variations in the content of the verbal communications (Gottschalk, et al., 1958a, 1958b, 1961a, 1961b, 1962; Gleser, et al., 1961).

Features other than the content of verbal behavior, especially pitch, volume, tone of voice, accent, rhythm, cadence, stress, and so forth, constitute paralanguage concomitants of the affect being measured. These aspects of speech also provide signals by means of which this affect can be detected and measured. We are assuming that the increments in affect experienced and communicated by these particular paralanguage variables are roughly proportional to the affect experienced and communicated via verbal content variables alone. We have some evidence in the present report to support this assumption in that we found our anxiety scores to be similar on an ordinal scale when the scorer used only a typescript of speech, as compared to when both the typescript was read and a tape recorded transcription was played. Paralanguage variables probably serve to clarify and emphasize quantitative differences in the emotional feelings occurring, rather than to differentiate them. One of the most important reasons that paralanguage variables are not useful in systematically assaying the magnitude of affective reactions in spoken language is that no one has yet been able to devise a reliable method to measure affects using these variables. (See, for example, the report of the excellent and careful investigations of Dittmann and Wynne.)

2. On the basis of verbal content alone, the magnitude of any one affect at any one period of time is directly proportional to three primary principles: (a) The frequency of occurrence (per unit of time) of categories of verbal themata listed in our affect scales as compared to the occurrence of all types of thematic statements in a language sample. (b) The degree to which the verbal expression represents directly or is pertinent to the psychologic activation of the specific affect. (For example, to say that one is killing or injuring another person or wants to do so is regarded as a more direct representation of hostile aggression than to say that one simply disapproves of another person.) (c) The degree of personal involvement attributed by the speaker to the emotionally relevant idea, feeling, action, or event.[1]

3. The degree of direct representation (also called *centrality* by H. Sargent) of the specific affect in the verbal expression (2b above) and the degree of personal involvement attributed by the speaker (2c above) can be represented mathematically by a weighting factor. Higher weights have tended to be assigned to scorable verbal statements which communicate affect that, by inference, is more likely to be strongly experienced by the speaker. Completely unconscious or repressed hostility of any kind is not, by our method of weighting, considered to signify affect of high magnitude, but rather to amount to zero affect. This numerical weight, which is assigned to each thematic category, designates roughly the relative probability that the thematic category is associated with our construct

---

[1] By inspection one can see that the affect scales we are using and illustrating in this report (See Schedules I, II, III, and IV) have used principles (b) and (c) in somewhat varying proportions. For example, the hostility scales do not employ principle (c) to the extent that the anxiety scale does.

of the affect. Initially, weights were assigned deductively on the basis of clinical psychoanalytic judgment. Subsequently, the weights have been modified and revised whenever empirical evidence has been sufficient to warrant such a change (Gottschalk, *et al.*, 1961a, 1963 and 1964).

4. The occurrence of suppressed and repressed affects may be inferred from the content of verbal behavior by the appearance of a variety of defensive and adaptive mechanisms. Like the psychology of the dream and dream work, we assume that the verbal content of spontaneous speech contains the workings of primary and secondary process thinking, though speech employs presumably different proportions of these kinds of thinking than the dream. Thus, the immediate magnitude of an affect is considered to be approximately the same, whether the affectively toned verbal thematic reference is expressed in the past tense, present tense, or future tense, as a conditional probability or as a wish. Some of the defensive and adaptive mechanisms signalizing the presence of suppressed and repressed affect in language are: (a) affect or its associated location or behavior attributed to other human beings; (b) affect or its associated ideation or behavior occurring in subhuman animals or in inanimate objects; (c) affect and its equivalents repudiated or denied; (d) affect and its equivalents acknowledged but reported to be present in attenuated form.

5. The product of the frequency of use of relevant categories of verbal statements and the numerical weights assigned to each thematic category provides an ordinal measure of the magnitude of the affect.

In other words, the greater the specific kind of affect of a speaker over a given unit of time, the more verbal references will be made, as compared to thematic statements of all types, to experiences or events of the types that we have classified in relevant categories of varying weights. Thus, multiplying the weight for the category by the number of references in the verbal sample classified in that category, and then summing up all the content categories pertinent to the specified affect provides an ordinal index of the intensity of the feeling state. (See Schedules I, II, III, and IV for examples of thematic categories and weights.)

6. Individuals differ considerably in rate of speech, and the same individual may vary in rate of speech from one unit of time to another. Since our numerical indices of magnitude of emotion can vary with the number of words spoken per unit time, the numerical score derived from one verbal sample may be compared to the score derived from another verbal sample composed of a different number of words by using a correction factor which expresses the affect scores of speakers in terms of a common denominator, namely, the score per 100 words. We have learned that affect scores are essentially the same proportionately, whether we express the scores per number of clauses (thematic references of all types) or number of words.

In previous studies we have made this correction by dividing the total raw score by the number of words spoken, and multiplying by one hundred. Recently we have investigated correcting all raw scores for correlation with number of words spoken by using as the corrected score the differences between the observed score and the score linearly predictable from the number of words. These differences, suitably scaled, give a more continuous distribution than does a simple ratio score, when the raw scores include many zeros (signifying no relevant content items were spoken). But unless the correlation is determined separately for each sample studied, correlations still persist between the corrected affect score and number of words in some samples. We have finally decided that the most satisfactory and simplest way to take into consideration rate of speech is by adding 0.5 to the raw score, multiplying by 100 and dividing by the number of words spoken. This method avoids the discontinuity occurring whenever the scorable items have occurred in some verbal samples. It also provides a uniform transformation over all samples and, with rare exceptions, reduces the correlation between the affect score and number of words essentially to zero.

A further transformation is made to obtain the final score, using the square root of the corrected score. This transformation is intended to reduce the skewness of the score distributions, thus making the measure more amenable to parametric statistical treatment. This square root transformation tends to make the ordinal scale approximate the characteristics of an interval scale.

The mathematical formula we are using to derive the magnitude of an emotion is: Magnitude of an emotion per 100 words =

$$\left[\frac{100 \, (f_1 w_1 + f_2 w_2 + f_3 w_3 \ldots f_n w_n) + 0.5}{N} \right]^{\frac{1}{2}}$$

where f_n is the frequency per unit of time of any relevant type of thematic verbal reference, w_n is the weight applied to such verbal statements, and N is the number of words per unit time. The weights are based on the degree of direct representativeness or centrality and the degree of personal involvement to the specific affect indicated in the verbal content.

A RÉSUMÉ OF SOME OF THE RELIABILITY AND VALIDITY STUDIES OF THE VERBAL BEHAVIOR METHOD OF MEASURING ANXIETY AND HOSTILITY

Our verbal samples are usually obtained by asking the subject to speak for five minutes, with as little interruption as possible, about any interesting or dramatic personal life experiences (Gleser, et al., 1961; Gottschalk, et al., 1955, 1961a, 1963). In some of our studies the subjects have simply been asked to talk for five minutes about anything that comes to their mind (Gottschalk, *et al.*, 1962) or to write for ten minutes about how they are feeling (Gottschalk, *et al.*, 1963). For spoken verbal samples, the subjects speak into a tape recorder and the material is later transcribed verbatim by a secretary. The typescript is then scored by one or two trained technicians, who note and score each grammatical clause in which the content is covered by one of the categories in the scale. The scoring enables us to determine the number of references to each content category and the type of reference. As previously indicated, the score for any particular category is obtained by summing the weights of all the verbal references made within that category during some time period; the total raw score for any affect is the sum of scores over all categories.

In the study presently being reported, we are extrapolating our findings derived from such investigations to the somewhat different situation of the psychotherapeutic interview. We have made such extrapolations before, in earlier studies (Gottschalk, *et al.*, 1958b, 1961b, 1963), realizing that the aims of the psychotherapeutic interview are in some respects different from those of our basic investigations, and realizing also that the continuous sequences of five-minute units of speech prevailing in the interview may obey principles different from single five-minute verbal samples in regard to revealing affect magnitude. Naturally, we would not make such extrapolations if we did not think there were important features in common. We are sure, however, that the psychotherapist's verbal behavior, structured by training and therapeutic design as it is, is more likely to reflect a major proportion of the patient's emotional reactions than that of the therapist. In this important respect, and possibly others, the verbal behavior in the interview differs from simple five-minute verbal samples produced by patients, because the therapist's contribution to the interview usually tells us more upon which area of the patient's emotions the therapist is focusing than which emotions the therapist is personally experiencing.

For the reader who prefers experimental studies and evidence before he feels comfortable looking at illustrative material, we are providing a résumé of some of our reliability and validity studies resulting from the use of our verbal behavior method of measuring emotional states. For readers who become fatigued with statistics before demonstrations, we suggest skipping over the following section on reliability and validity and returning to it later if the demonstration appears interesting.

RELIABILITY OF SCORING VERBAL SAMPLES
FOR ANXIETY AND HOSTILITY

In the development of thematic content scales for scoring anxiety and hostility from verbal material we have paid considerable attention to the consistency of scores obtained by different technicians using our scales.

Such concern reflects our aim to develop content categories which are as clearly defined as possible so that scoring might be objective rather than intuitive and idiosyncratic, and based more on literal rather than on figurative assessment of content. Moreover, since our investigations have been continuing over several years, it has been necessary to insure comparability of scores obtained at different periods and using different scoring technicians. Thus, not only have we utilized a training period to insure comprehension of the content categories, but we have also set up criteria of minimal intercorrelations and mean differences of overall scores which we have considered at a satisfactory level of precision. We have also revised categories and established rules to clarify scoring as a result of encountering ambiguous or controversial verbalizations. In addition, we have adopted the routine of using the average of two independent scores for all our data. Our goal with these measures of affect has been to achieve a scoring reliability of at least .85 for the average total scale score. We have reported elsewhere evidence showing that the scoring reliability of the anxiety scale (Gleser, *et al.*, 1961) and of the three hostility scales (Gottschalk, *et al.*, 1963) meets this standard.

SUMMARY OF VALIDATION STUDIES OF THE ANXIETY SCALE

Anxiety scores derived from verbal samples differentiated a normative sample (90 gainfully employed people from the Kroger Co.) and 24 psychiatric patients (a mixed group of schizophrenic and neurotic patients all seen shortly after hospitalization) (Gleser, *et al.*, 1961). The difference in mean scores (.98) was significant beyond the .001 level.

The above 24 psychiatric patients were independently rated on a clinical scale of anxiety by two psychiatrists just prior to the time each patient gave a five-minute verbal sample. The clinical anxiety scale provided a rating of the magnitude of immediate anxiety evidenced in current motor and autonomic activity as well as by the patient's verbalizations of anxiety symptoms. The average of the clinical ratings by the two psychiatrists correlated .66 with the anxiety scores derived from the verbal samples, which is significant beyond the .001 level. The clinical ratings of autonomic signs and motor signs of anxiety correlated as highly with the verbal behavior measure of anxiety as did the clinical rating based on verbal reports of the subjective experience of the patients.

A comparison was made between *verbal behavior* anxiety scores and scores on paper and pencil tests, namely the MMPI psychasthenia scores, on 14 patients with dermatoses. Although some disparity would be expected on comparing two such measures, the correlation (.51) was found to be significant at the .03 level by a one-tailed t test. On this same group of patients, the scores from the anxiety dimension (A) proposed by Welsh and derived from the MMPI were compared to the verbal behavior anxiety scores derived from these 14 patients and the correlation was found to be .68, which is significant at the .01 level.

The total anxiety scores on 43 verbal samples obtained from 28 medical patients correlated .37 (Sholiton, *et al.*, 1962) with their total scores on the IPAT Anxiety Scale (Cattell, 1957).

The verbal behavior anxiety scores of a group of ten hypertensive patients were found to differ significantly from that of a group of nonhypertensives (P = .02) (Kaplan, *et al.*, 1961).

In a study (Gleser, Gottschalk, and Springer, 1961) of 90 gainfully employed white men and women between the ages of 20 and 50, including 45 men and 45 women stratified for I.Q., anxiety scores derived from verbal productions were compared. While there were no significant sex differences for overall anxiety level, some interesting differences did occur in the type of anxiety expressed as indicated by separate category scores. It was found that females, as compared to males, had significantly higher scores for *shame* anxiety and lower scores for *death* and *mutilation* anxiety. A significant negative trend was also noted with I.Q. (P = .05), the lowest I.Q. groups having the highest anxiety score.

Recently, anxiety scores derived from verbal samples were found to correlate significantly (r = .49) with average plasma-free fatty acid levels in a group of 24 men. This finding was completely substantiated in a second group of 20 men (r = .44). In both groups of men no significant correlations were found between plasma-free fatty acids and the hostility indices derived from the same verbal samples (Gottschalk, *et al.*, 1965). The importance of such findings is that plasma-free fatty acid levels, in the fasting individuals, can serve as indirect indicators of catecholamine activity or autonomic arousal, and hence the verbal behavior anxiety measure does assess a psychologic variable associated with biologic activity, namely catecholamine secretion. Furthermore, this study (and others we cannot take the time to describe here) points out that different affects at low levels of arousal, e.g., anxiety and hostility, are associated with different biochemical and physiological processes. To corroborate this further, certain hostility scores have been found to correlate significantly with plasma 17-hydroxycorticosteroids, whereas anxiety scores derived from speech samples had no significant correlations with this biochemical substance (Sholiton, *et al.*, 1963).

SUMMARY OF VALIDATION STUDIES OF THE THREE HOSTILITY SCALES

Six different samples of subjects have been used in validation studies of these three measures and the samples have been drawn from normative, neurotic, and psychotic populations (Gottschalk, *et al.*, 1963). Criterion measures have included self-report and personal inventories as well as assessment procedures made by someone other than the subject. Results of comparisons made between scores from criterion measures and hostility scores derived from verbal behavior have varied, to some extent, with the sample of subjects examined. Certain typical and recurring findings have appeared, however, and these point to the conclusion that it is statistically, as well as heuristically, valid to separate the affect of hostility into three types based on the direction of the drive or impulse.

The psychological state assessed by our measure of hostility directed outward is similar to the assaultive and angry impulses and feelings of which a person is aware and can describe in various self-report test procedures. And it is also similar to the harmful, asocial, and destructive behaviors and attitudes toward objects outside oneself that an external observer can perceive or infer. The emotional phenomena measured are dissimilar to the psychological constructs measured by the depressive scales of various adjective check-lists, the Beck depression inventory (1961), and the depression and paranoid subscales of the Wittenborn system of ratings (1955).

Our verbal behavior procedure of assessing hostility outward and the two other types of hostility tends to preclude a subject's covering up and not revealing his hostility. This is evidenced by the lack of correlation between the verbal hostility scales and the MMPI lie scale which is essentially a measure of the tendency to give socially acceptable responses.

The measure of hostility directed inward is a similar construct to the psychological constructs of *depression* and *fatigue* as assessed on adjective check-lists, the *depression* and *acute anxiety* scores derived from the Wittenborn rating scales (1955) and the scores obtained from the Beck depression inventory (1961), and a clinical depression scale designed by Gottschalk (1963). It measures a psychological construct dissimilar to that measured by the Oken hostility scale (1960) and other assessment procedures designed to measure anger or outwardly directed hostility.

Our construct of ambivalent hostility overlaps both the constructs of hostility directed inward and the hostility directed outward, the overt much more than the covert portion of the latter measure. This has been demonstrated elsewhere (Gottschalk, *et al.*, 1963) by the intercorrelations between our different hostility measures, but also by the positive correlations between ambivalent hostility scores and the various criterion measures labeled: *hostility, depression, indirect hostility, suspicion, negativism,* and so forth. These correlations might be expected and understandable from a clinician's point of view if one pauses to recall that the patient who feels adversely self-critical and expresses this self-criticism (such a patient would obtain a high hostility inward score) often tends to assert that he is criticizable by others (verbal behavior which is associated with a high ambivalent hostility score). Furthermore, it is clinically commonplace for psychiatric patients with strong consciences, who overtly express their hostility, to feel they should be criticized adversely. And it is not uncommon for a patient to express his anger by complaining that others are hurting or criticizing him, thus trying to provoke a possibly sympathetic listener to feel angry at those who have wronged him.

THE PROCEDURES USED IN ORGANIZING THE DATA OF THE PSYCHIATRIC INTERVIEW FOR VERBAL BEHAVIOR ANALYSIS

In this report we are limiting the scope of our presentation to an illustration of the methods we have developed for the measurement of the emotional dimensions of anxiety, hostility outward, hostility inward, and ambivalent hostility. Here, we have applied our tools to the tape recorded give-and-take of a psychiatric interview to illustrate some features of our approach. In so doing, we have tried to mathematize the sequential changes in these affects as they appear in the verbal content of the psychiatric interview.

Affect Measurements Derived from Only the Typescripts of the Interview[2]

The procedure followed has been described elsewhere in more detail (Gottschalk, et al., 1961a). In brief, the typescript of the interview was divided into successive five-minute sequences. Since both patient and therapist may speak within a five-minute sequence, the number of words spoken by the patient was tallied separately from the number of words spoken by the therapist. The total number of words for the five-minute sequence, regardless of speaker, was also tabulated. These word counts were used as correction factors (namely,

$$\left[\frac{\text{raw score} \times 100 + 0.5}{\text{number of words spoken in five minutes}}\right]^{1/2} = \text{corrected score}) \text{ to trans-}$$

form the score to a common denominator so that an affect score derived from one five-minute segment could be compared with the score derived from another segment having a different number of words. (See assumption number 6.)

There are several different ways to examine the sequences of emotional changes verbally expressed by patient and therapist during a psychiatric interview; and we intend to illustrate here several possible perspectives. For theoretical or possibly practical reasons, some investigators may prefer one way over another of looking at these emotional changes.

1. For instance, an investigator may prefer to regard the emotional reactions expressed in the language used during the interview as representing the summation of the transactional or interpersonal experiences of the

[2] This psychiatric interview was a consultative interview between a patient and a psychoanalyst, but it was not, in any sense, a classical psychoanalytic session.

patient and therapist; such a viewpoint might hold that any ordinal estimate of affect magnitude must be attributed not to either patient or therapist taken singly but to the dyad. (See, for example, Jaffe, 1961.) Investigators attracted to this theoretical persuasion will be interested to see that we computed affect measures per five-minute sequences of the interview in terms of the dyad. We have also derived the level of the separate contribution of each single participant to the total (dyadic) emotional index.[3]

2. Investigators who would prefer to examine the sequence of emotional changes occurring within patient and therapist separately per five-minute sequence will find that we have made suitable computations for this purpose.[4]

The ordinal magnitudes of a sequence of emotional assessments in an individual during an interview calculated by these two methods of computation are similar, but not exactly equal, for participants in an interview do not regularly speak proportionately the same percentage of words during equal time sequences. The former method of computation assumes that the proportion of time a participant speaks from interval to interval during an interview is unimportant insofar as the intensity of the emotion he is expressing verbally, since the intensity of emotion is thought to be an attribute of the dyad. The latter method of computation assumes that how much a person speaks in a given unit of time is associated with how strongly he is feeling and that the intrapsychic process can be validly measured without counting how many verbal units (words) another person spoke during these same units of time of an interview.

Details of Scoring Verbal Samples

The typescript of the interview was divided into clauses, the smallest unit of verbal communication, except for expletives or elliptical expressions. The literal content of each clause was then examined, in its surrounding context, by one member of our research team (C.M.W.) to determine whether its content fell into the scorable categories of our Anxiety Scale. If the content could be classified into one of the thematic categories, the clause was tallied with the appropriate weight according to our scale. Otherwise, the clause received no score for anxiety. (See the Anxiety Scale, Schedule I.)

---

[3] The index of the emotional feeling of the dyad and the index of the contribution of each participant in the interview to this dyadic measure have been computed by using the total number of words per five minutes spoken by both patient and therapist as a correction factor.

[4] The index of the discrete (intrapsychic) emotional feelings of the participants has been computed by using the separate word count per five minutes of the patient and therapist to derive different correction factors for the scores of the patient and therapist respectively.

Schedule I
Anxiety Scale

1. *Death anxiety:* references to death, dying, threat of death, or anxiety about death experienced by or occurring to:
   a. self (3)°
   b. animate others (2)
   c. inanimate objects destroyed (1)
   d. denial of death anxiety (1)
2. *Mutilation (castration) anxiety:* references to injury, tissue or physical damage, or anxiety about injury, or threat of such experienced by or occurring to:
   a. self (1)
   b. animate others (2)
   c. inanimate objects (1)
   d. denial (1)
3. *Separation anxiety:* references to desertion, abandonment, ostracism, loss of support, falling, loss of love or love object, or threat of such experienced by or occurring to:
   a. self (3)
   b. animate others (2)
   c. inanimate objects (1)
   d. denial (1)
4. *Guilt anxiety:* references to adverse criticism, abuse, condemnation, moral disapproval, guilt, or threat of such experienced by:
   a. self (3)
   b. animate others (2)
   d. denial (1)
5. *Shame anxiety:* references to ridicule, inadequacy, shame, embarrassment, humiliation, over-exposure of deficiencies or private details, or threat of such experienced by:
   a. self (3)
   b. animate others (2)
   d. denial (1)
6. *Diffuse or nonspecific anxiety:* references by word or in phrases to anxiety and/or fear without distinguishing type or source of anxiety:
   a. self (3)
   b. animate others (2)
   d. denial (1)

° Numbers in parentheses are the scores or weights.

After the interview material was scored for anxiety, each clause was then rescored for hostility directed outward. (See the Hostility Outward Scale, Schedule II.) And then the whole interview was rescored by the same technician for hostility directed inward and ambivalently directed hostility (See the Hostility Directed Inward Scale and the Ambivalent Hostility Scale, Schedules III and IV.)

Schedule II
Hostility Directed Outward Scale

(Destructive, injurious, critical thoughts and actions
directed to or occurring to others)

Thematic Categories	Thematic Categories
Weights (I) Overt Hostility	Weights (II) Covert Hostility
3 (a) Self killing, fighting, injuring other individuals, or threatening to do so.	3 (a) Others (human) killing, fighting, injuring other individuals, or threatening to do so.
3 (b) Self robbing or abandoning other individuals, causing suffering or anguish to others, or threatening to do so.	3 (b) Others (human) robbing, abandoning, causing suffering or anguish to other individuals, or threatening to do so.
3 (c) Self adversely criticizing, depreciating, blaming, expressing anger, dislike of other human beings.	3 (c) Others adversely criticizing, depreciating, blaming, expressing anger, dislike of other human beings.
2 (a) Self killing, injuring or destroying domestic animals, pets, or threatening to do so.	2 (a) Others (human) killing, injuring, or destroying domestic animals, pets, or threatening to do so.
2 (b) Self abandoning, robbing domestic animals, pets, or threatening to do so.	2 (b) Others (human) abandoning, robbing domestic animals, pets, or threatening to do so.
2 (c) Self criticizing or depreciating others in a vague or mild manner.	2 (c) Others (human) criticizing or depreciating other individuals in a vague or mild manner.
2 (d) Self depriving or disappointing other human beings.	2 (d) Others (human) depriving or disappointing other human beings.
	2 (e) Others (human or domestic animals) dying or killed violently in death-dealing situation, or threatened with such.
	2 (f) Bodies (human or domestic animals) mutilated, depreciated, defiled.
1 (a) Self killing, injuring, destroying, robbing wild life, flora, inanimate objects, or threatening to do so.	1 (a) Wild life, flora, inanimate objects, injured, broken, robbed, destroyed, or threatened with such (with or without mention of agent).
1 (b) Self adversely criticizing, de-	1 (b) Others (human) adversely crit-

Schedule II *(Continued)*

Weights	Thematic Categories (I) Overt Hostility	Weights	Thematic Categories (II) Covert Hostility
	preciating, blaming, expressing anger or dislike of subhuman, inanimate objects, places, situations.		icizing, depreciating, expressing anger or dislike of subhuman, inanimate objects, places, situations.
1 (c)	Self using hostile words, cursing, mention of anger or rage without referent.	1 (c)	Others angry, cursing without reference to cause or direction of anger. *Also* instruments of destruction not used threateningly.
		1 (d)	Others (human, domestic animals) injured, robbed, dead, abandoned or threatened with such from any source including subhuman and inanimate objects, situations (storms, floods, etc.).
		1 (e)	Subhumans killing, fighting, injuring, robbing, destroying each other, or threatening to do so.
		1 (f)	Denial of anger, dislike, hatred, cruelty, and intent to harm.

Schedule III
Hostility Directed Inward Scale

(Self-destructive, self-critical thoughts and actions)

Weights	I. Thematic Categories
4 (a)	References to self (speaker) attempting or threatening to kill self, with or without conscious intent.
4 (b)	References to self wanting to die, needing, or deserving to die.
3 (a)	References to self injuring, mutilating, disfiguring self or threats to do so, with or without conscious intent.
3 (b)	Self blaming, expressing anger or hatred to self, considering self worthless or of no value, causing oneself grief or trouble, or threatening to do so.
3 (c)	References to feelings of discouragement, giving up hope, despairing, feeling grieved or depressed, having no purpose in life.

2 (a) References to self needing or deserving punishment, paying for one's sins, needing to atone or do penance.

2 (b) Self adversely criticizing, depreciating self; references to regretting, being sorry or ashamed for what one says or does; references to self mistaken or in error.

2 (c) References to feelings of deprivation, disappointment, lonesomeness.

1 (a) References to feeling disappointed in self; unable to meet expectations of self or others.

1 (b) Denial of anger, dislike, hatred, blame, destructive impulses from self to self.

1 (c) References to feeling painfully driven or obliged to meet one's own expectations and standards.

Schedule IV
Ambivalent Hostility Scale

(Destructive, injurious, critical thoughts and actions of others to self)

Weights	II. Thematic Categories

3 (a) Others (human) killing or threatening to kill self.

3 (b) Others (human) physically injuring, mutilating, disfiguring self, or threatening to do so.

3 (c) Others (human) adversely criticizing, blaming, expressing anger or dislike toward self, or threatening to do so.

3 (d) Others (human) abandoning, robbing self, causing suffering, anguish, or threatening to do so.

2 (a) Others (human) depriving, disappointing, misunderstanding self, or threatening to do so.

2 (b) Self threatened with death from subhuman or inanimate object, or death-dealing situation.

1 (a) Others (subhuman, inanimate, *or situation*) injuring, abandoning, robbing self, causing suffering, anguish.

1 (b) Denial of blame.

These coded clauses scored for each one of the three affects were re-examined by another member of our research team (K.J.S.) and wherever it was considered advisable changes were made in the original coding, differences in scoring being resolved by discussion to reach a consensus between the two scorers.

The clauses (or elliptical clauses) actually classified as scorable for free anxiety on our Anxiety Scale, and the coding each clause obtained, are given in Table I. Tables II, III and IV have similar information for hostility outward, hostility inward, and ambivalent hostility respectively.

Table I

Verbal Items in the Interview that
Received Scores for Anxiety-fear

(After each clause is a symbol in parentheses, which designates the category, by letter and number, of the Affect Scale into which the clause was classified; and this is followed by the weight assigned to the content item. The coded statements are reproduced below in chronological order.)

First Five Minutes

D: How anxious do you feel . . . ? (6b2)
   I found I froze a little with Rosen (6a3)
P: . . . this sounds very awkward (5a4)
   It sounds so silly . . . I feel (5a4)
D: You'd rather talk about the way you feel . . . (5b2)
P: I feel very much out of context (5a3)
   . . . you don't know exactly who's going to see it (5a3)
   . . . and what they're gonna think (5a3)
   (speaking of actor reading reviews) he doesn't know whether it's a good
       production (5b2)
   . . . he's gotta find whether it is (by reading newspapers) (5b2)
   I feel the same thing (3a3)
   We hadn't done too well (5a3)
   I was really quite concerned (6a4)
   I'm not gonna be with a dead organization (1c1)
   She says, you shouldn't park your car there (4b2)
   She says, well what are ya doing (woman criticizing man) (4b2)

Second Five Minutes

P: I get real tense (6a4)
   . . . really tense (6a4)
   I don't even know who I'm going to introduce (5a3)
D: Are you disappointed that Al didn't stick around (3b2)
P: Sure (3a3)
D: I felt that way myself (3a3)
   . . . he walked out on us (3a3)
P: I feel too uncertain of myself (5a3)
   . . . I feel sort of at sea (3a3)

Third Five Minutes

P: I usta feel so guilty (4a4)
   I would just mess up in something else (4a3)
   . . . pretty strong feeling . . . of wanting to be included (3a3)

Fourth Five Minutes

D: . . . you had guilt (4b2)
   . . . you're not sure it's right (4b2)

P: well, he's not either (sure it's right) (4b2)
  . . . he's got guilt (4b2)
D: . . . sure he's got guilt (4b2)
  . . . you have your rational guilt (4b2)
  . . . he has both irrational guilt and real guilt (4b2)
P: . . . trying to translate his irrational guilt (4b2)
  . . . make them (guilt feelings) more explicit (4b2)
  . . . get punished for them (4b2)
  . . . hope they (guilt feelings) go away (4b2)
D: . . . this boy who hasn't got a father to learn from . . . (3b2)
  . . . therefore he steals (4b2)
P: . . . only I do it (stealing) in a more socially acceptable way (5a3)
  . . . I think with no more light (5a3)
  . . . the same flooky way I used to perform (5a3)
  . . . I don't know from nothing (5a3)
  . . . I'm still the same dopey guy (5a3)
  . . . who snarls up in everything (5a3)
I'm still his dopey kid (5a3)
  . . . idiotic judgments on my part (5a3)
  . . . stupid, stupid, stupid stuff (referring to self) (5a3)
  . . . I've been doing stupid things ever since (5a3)
D: . . . you really haven't stolen anything from him (4d1)
  . . . you would feel guilty as hell (4b3)

Fifth Five Minutes

P: . . . he isn't gonna like me at all (3a3)
That's right (I'm a scene stealer) (4a3)
I hate myself for it (4a3)
  . . . but I do this (scene stealing) (4a3)
I really hog it (4a3)
D: You'd get sore as hell at 'em (4b2)
P: Sure, and . . . the other guys got sore at me (4a3)
  . . . I thought at the time you shouldn't (get annoyed) (4a3)
  . . . might be even heresy (4a3)
D: the question is why it bothers you (being competitive) (6b2)
P: I feel sorta bad about being competitive (4a3)
  . . . if you win the men all crumble up (1b2)
  . . . they just all faded away and died (1b2)
  . . . didn't really die (1d1)
  . . . got little and shriveled up (2b2)
  . . . and that bothered me (6a3)
D: . . . this is . . . you don't feel comfortable about (6b2)
P: . . . Al characterized him as having the most vicious subconscious (4b2)

Sixth Five Minutes

P: . . . he'd been trying to undercut Al (thru criticism) (4b2)
  . . . all the mistakes he made (4b2)
  . . . he makes some cutting comment (re Al) (4b2)

Table I *(Continued)*

D: . . . you can really puncture him (4b2)
P: . . . then he doesn't talk to me (4a3)
   . . . he's been having . . . fight with this other woman (4b2)
   . . . this undercurrent is about ready to kill her (6b3)
   . . . she's afraid to slap him (2b2)
   . . . this guy's gonna cut me out (3a3)
   (He says) tell me when I'm doing things wrong (4b2)
   . . . he loses his job (3b2)
   . . . not too many more jobs open to him (3b2)
   . . . he's scared stiff (6b3)
D: . . . the father topples (3b2)

Last Three Minutes
D: You're saying . . . he has to come off his high horse (4b2)
   . . . why you're anxious (6b2)
P: . . . if he's not as good as his father (5b2)

Table II
Verbal Items in the Interview that Received Scores for Hostility Outward

(See Schedule II for explanation of symbols in parentheses.)

First Five Minutes
P: I get so annoyed (Ic1)
   That's enough of that nonsense (Ib1)
   I'm not going to be with a dead organization (Ib1)
   She says to him, "You shouldn't park your car there" (IIc2)
   . . . she says, "Well, what are ya doing" (IIc2)

Second Five Minutes
D: You really told them where to head in at. (IIc1)

Third Five Minutes
D: . . . recent acquisition . . . that you can push people around (IIc3)
P: . . . or at least if I ever did it (push people) (Ic3)
   . . . I get very mad (Ic1)
   . . . I get annoyed (Ic1)

Fourth Five Minutes
P: (He) makes them explicit and gets punished for them (IIc3)
D: . . . therefore he steals (IIb3)
P: I do too (steal) (Ib3)
   (I) tell him I'm not listening to what you say (Ic2)
D: Why do you say I don't understand a word of what you say? (IIc2)

P: Everything went wrong yesterday (Ib1)
D: . . . Compete . . . some way offensive to him (IIb1)

Fifth Five Minutes

D: . . . you're a . . . scene stealer (Ic2)
P: . . . if I saw it in somebody else I would say that (he was hog) (Ic3)
D: You'd get sore as hell at 'em (IIc3)
P: Sure I would (get sore) (Ic3)
P: There's always some excuse (criticizing men with whom patient made picture) (Ic2)
　I usta get annoyed at this (Ib1)
　I thought . . . you shouldn't get annoyed (IIf1)
　The men all crumble up (IId1)
　They . . . all faded away and died (IId1)
　. . . they just got little and shriveled up (IId1)
　I got pretty hostile thoughts (Ic1)
　. . . a guy who's got fierce hostility (IIc1)
　. . . really fierce internal hostility (IIc1)
　Al characterized him as having the most vicious subconscious (IIc3)
　. . . he's a real charlatan (Ic3)
　. . . he palms himself off (Ic3)

Sixth Five Minutes

P: I know . . . we were gonna tangle (Ic3)
　. . . (he said) after all he's gone through two wives (IIc2)
　. . . (he said all the mistakes he made (IIc3)
　(He's not a big guy) I mean physically as well as otherwise (Ic2)
　. . . I just sorta slaughter him (Ic3)
D: You can really puncture him (IIc3)
P: He makes some cutting comment (about Al) (IIc3)
　I say . . . a little guy like you (Ic3)
　. . . hasta say things like that (IIc3)
D: You really fix 'im (IIc3)
P: . . . he starts to boast on . . . (Ic2)
D: The next time . . . he starts out again (criticizing Al) (IIc3)
P: He's been having a terrible fight with . . . (IIc3)
　He's completely unsuited for the job he's in (Ic3)
　He has no business being in this (Ic3)
　She . . . has all of her hostility too (IIc1)
　She doesn't have an awful lot (hostility) but what she has (IIc1)
　She wants to keep good feelings toward people (IIf1)
　She's about ready to explode (IIc3)
　This undercurrent . . . about ready to kill her (Id1)
　She's afraid to slap him (IIa3)
　She doesn't know quite how to do it (slap him) (IIa3)
　He . . . came to a break with the head . . . (IIc3)
　This guy hasn't functioned well (Ic2)
　. . . he's not suited for this job (Ic2)

Table II *(Continued)*

I have no feeling . . . he should be in this job (Ic2)
He's been spouting about . . . (Ic3)
I knew this guy didn't have an analysis (Ic3)
I said . . . knowing what your problems are and doing something are quite another thing (Ic3)
I don't think that this is too profitable (Ic2)
. . . then he was kowtowing (Ic3)
I says . . . this was a lot of bull (Ib1)
. . . he loses his job (IId1)
(Keeps him) from making life difficult for this woman (IIc2)

Last Three Minutes

P: . . . if I'm in the situation I'm gonna tell ya (Ic2)
D: You're saying he's gotta come off his high horse too (IIc2)
   Bobby's problem . . . better than his passive beaten-down father (Ic2)
P: . . . then he's gonna be stuck with his mother (IIb1)
D: . . . whereby he doesn't get stuck with his mother too (IIb1)
   . . . just the fact that he's obnoxious (Ic3)
   . . . your motivation . . . for pushing him around (IIc3)

Table III

Verbal Items in the Interview that Received Scores for Hostility Inward

(See Schedule III for explanation of symbols in parentheses.)

First Five Minutes

P: It sounds so silly (referring to his voice) (Ib2)
   . . . we hadn't done too well. (Ia1)
   I felt so depressed. (Ic3)
   It wasn't (crowd didn't show up for meeting) (Ic2)

Second Five Minutes

P: Sure (I'm disappointed Al didn't stick around) (Ic2)
D: I felt that way myself (Al didn't stick around) (Ic2)
P: I feel too uncertain of myself. (Ib2)
   (When I'm in a situation where I don't know what the coloration is) I feel sort of at sea. (Ic2)
   This is the ultimate in conformity (speaking of self) (Ib2)

Third Five Minutes

P: I usta feel so guilty (Ib3)
   I would just mess up in something else (Ib3)
   . . . big block has been this conformity (of mine) (Ib2)
   . . . I don't know what to do. (Ia1)

Fourth Five Minutes

P: I think with no more light or anything else. (Ib2)
    (I) went about in the same flooky way. (Ib3)
    I deny all of it (my success) (Ib3)
    I don't know from nothin' (Ib3)
    I'm still the same dopey guy (Ib3)
    . . . who just snarls up in everything (Ib3)
    I'm still his dopey kid (Ib3)
    . . . who's never gonna get to be independent (Ia1)
    . . . idiotic judgments on my part (Ib3)
    stupid, stupid, stupid stuff (on my part) (Ib2)
    I've been doing stupid things ever since (Ib2)
    Sure (I would feel guilty as hell) (Ib3)

Fifth Five Minutes

P: . . . That's right (I'm a scene stealer) (Ib2)
    Sometimes I hate myself (Ib3)
    . . . I do this (scene stealer) (Ib2)
    I really hog it. (Ib2)
    I thought at the time you shouldn't (get annoyed) (Ib2)
    I feel sorta bad about being competitive (Ib3)

Sixth Five Minutes
    None

Last Three Minutes
    None

Table IV

Verbal Items in the Interview that received Scores for Ambivalent Hostility

(See Schedule IV for explanation of symbols in parentheses.)

First Five Minutes

P: . . . you don't know who's gonna see it and what they're gonna think (IIc3)

Second Five Minutes
D: He walked out on us (IIa2)

Third Five Minutes
    None

Fourth Five Minutes
    None

Table IV *(Continued)*

Fifth Five Minutes

P: . . . he isn't gonna like me at all (IIc3)
   . . . let the other guy get sore at me too (IIc3)
   . . . his always got at the top (Patient's name went on film last) (IIa2)
   . . . his name always happened to end up first (IIa2)

Sixth Five Minutes

P: I knew sooner or later we were gonna tangle (IIc3)
   . . . he doesn't talk to me for another three months (IIc3)
   . . . he disappears and never comes back (IIc3)
   . . . this guy's gonna cut me out sooner or later (IId2)
   . . . how to get him off my back (IIc3)

Last Three Minutes

  None

It will be noted that some statements have received a score for two affects, and in rare instances, for all affects measured. This should not be surprising if one pauses to realize that this signifies simply that a person has communicated more than one affect via his verbal behavior. By introspection and observation of others, it becomes obvious that having more than one affect at the same time is more the rule than the exception; one affect, however, is usually predominant, i.e., has greater magnitude than the others present.

Scoring Procedures for Including the Sound and Inflection of the Participants' Voices in Assessing the Magnitude of Various Affects

One scoring technician (C.M.W.) listened carefully to the electronic tape recording of the interview to reassess the scoring, one month after all the scoring was completed on the basis of using only the typescript by itself. The tape was heard twice in estimating the changes in each affect. On the first listening the order of scoring affects was: (1) hostility outward; (2) anxiety-fear; (3) hostility inward and ambivalent hostility. The second listening occurred three to four days later and the order of scoring affects was reversed.

Criteria for scoring verbal items included the same content categories delineated in each affect scale plus any cues as to emotional nuances provided by changes in pitch, tone, rhythm, cadence, accent, intensity and so forth. No scored verbal items were discounted on the basis of listening to the speaker's voice, although it was the technician's impression that there were some verbalizations that had been coded for anxiety where the sound of the voice gave no evidence of anxiety. In a few instances, there were some verbalizations scored as hostility inward, on the basis of the typescript alone, which were given an additional score of hostility outward on the basis of the tone or inflection of the voice.

No attempt was made to obtain consensus between two scorers when the sound of the speaker's voice was used as an additional cue, besides content, for quality and quantity of the affect. Therefore, the reader must realize that the affect scores based on sound of voice, as well as on verbal content, represent the impressions of only one technician. This portion of the demonstration of our approach to measuring affect from speech represents a research direction in which we have not hitherto gone. This is so for many reasons, the principal one being the technical problems involved in obtaining findings which can be replicated. We consider this brief exploration of the part played by vocal sound in affect expression to be a quite preliminary test of our assumption (number 1) that sound of voice is most often a redundant factor or a factor of secondary importance in determining affect magnitude. We do not regard this brief exploratory study as conclusive or crucial or definitive in any respect.

RESULTS

Sequential Changes in Anxiety-fear

The changes in the patient's anxiety scores per five minutes, as well as the changes in the anxiety level of the dyad, are diagrammed in Figure 1. This figure shows the differences obtained in calculating the separate anxiety scores per five minutes for the patient in terms of the word count of the dyad versus the word count of the individual patient. The rank order correlations among these three sets of scores are extremely high, ranging from .89 to .96. In this particular interview, which was a relatively brief one, there is not a great deal of ordinal difference resulting from calculating the anxiety-fear scores in these different ways.

Looking at the successive five-minute anxiety scores of the patient, one can see that they are primarily derived from references to himself ("overt" anxiety-fear) ·rather than from references to others ("covert" anxiety-fear), except in the last two five-minute periods.

When the technician scored anxiety-fear by listening to the tape recording of the interview as well as reading the typescript, she found some additional evidences of anxiety from the sound of the patient's voice occurring with about equal frequency for content references to the self and to others. The rank ordering of scores remained essentially unchanged when the tape recorder was used. These findings are illustrated in Figure 2 where the scores have been adjusted to the same mean and standard deviation.[5]

[5] Without this adjustment, scores obtained using the sound of the patient's voice are all greater than or equal to the scores on the typescript alone, since no codings were rejected or eliminated on the basis of sound cues.

The amount of anxiety by types experienced by the patient was calculated for each five-minute sequence of the interview. Figure 3 illustrates these features. In the first five-minute period the relatively high score for shame anxiety is accounted for by the patient's discussion concerning how he feels about having his psychotherapeutic session filmed and tape recorded. In the fourth five minutes the large shame-anxiety score is related

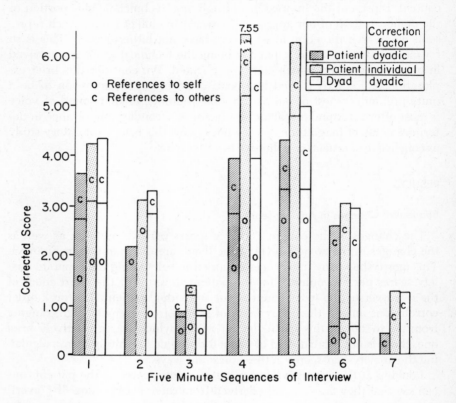

Figure 1

Comparisons of Anxiety-Fear Scores of the Dyad (therapist and patient) and of the Patient

to the patient's many references depreciating himself and expressing his inadequacy. The separation anxiety during the second five-minute period stems from the discussion of the participants at being "walked out on" by "Al." The relatively increased guilt anxiety during the fifth and sixth sequences can be accounted for by the content of the clauses labeled *4a3* and *4b2* in Table I during the fifth and sixth five-minute sequences respectively.

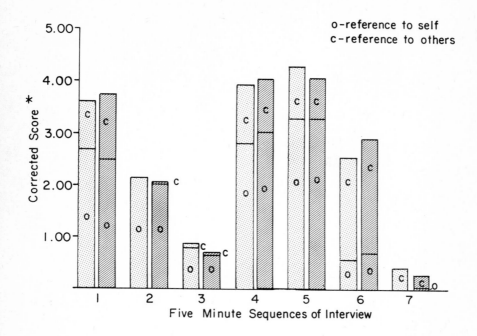

Figure 2

Comparative Anxiety-Fear Scores of Patient Based on:
1. Reading typescript of interview alone
2. Listening to tape recording while reading typescript

° Computed on basis of correction factor of the dyad. Scores adjusted to the same mean and standard deviation.

Sequential Changes in Hostility Outward

Figure 4 illustrates how the patient's hotility-outward score builds up during the interview to reach a high peak total score 6.72 using the typescript only) during the sixth five-minute segment. If a score at this level were to occur under our usual testing procedure, in which separate five-minute verbal samples are obtained in response to standard instructions (Gottschalk and Hambidge, 1956; Gottschalk, *et al.*, 1958a, 1959, 1960, 1961a, 1961b), it would be at or above the scores obtained by 97 percent of a *normative* sample of individuals. Figure 4 shows, also, the proportions of the total amount of hostility outward that is overtly and covertly expressed.

The patient's scores on this affect are considerably higher than the therapist's, and the therapist's scores fall primarily into the covert classifica-

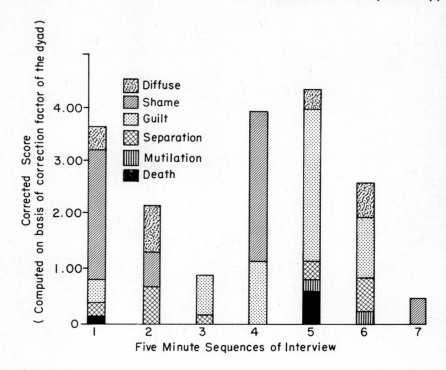

Figure 3

Sequential Changes Per Unit Time in Types of Anxiety-Fear
Expressed by Patient

tion. Here the therapist is tending to reflect what the patient has said. The hostility-outward scores obtained for the therapist do not represent his changing hostility levels, we presume, but rather the degree to which the therapist is selecting out and mirroring the patient's outwardly directed hostility. We suspect this, not just from some special characteristics of the affect scores themselves, but from an understanding of the process of dynamic and expressive psychotherapy where the typical function of the psychotherapist is to work toward eliciting, clarifying, pinpointing, and making verbally articulate the affective reactions of the patient. Even during the last five-minute period, where the therapist's level of overt hostility seems high, the therapist is simply repeating criticisms of another person made by the patient. (See also Table 2.) In other words, our procedure does not really measure the therapist's affect in the context of the psychotherapeutic interview, but it does indicate how the psychotherapist

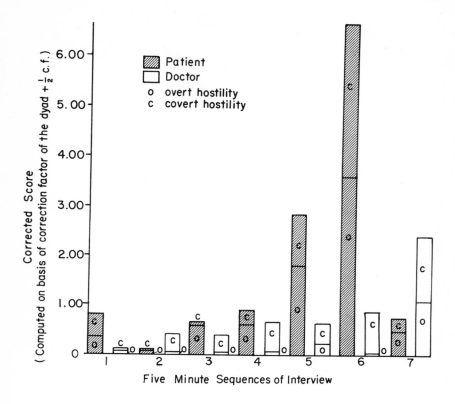

Figure 4

Changes in Hostility Outward Scores of Patient and Doctor

is going about his work and to what extent he is participating in his usual function of evoking the patient's emotional expression.

Sequential Changes in Hostility Inward and Ambivalent Hostility

An examination of Figure 5 reveals that the patient exhibits more hostility inward than ambivalent hostility. We think this means that the patient has a fair degree of awareness of his own adversely self-critical and disapproving perspectives, that he can report these, and that he is not inclined to project these adversely critical attitudes to others or to require much hostility from others. The latter would be scored as ambivalent hostility. The intensity of his hostility inward reaches a relatively high level during the fourth and fifth five-minute periods of the interview.

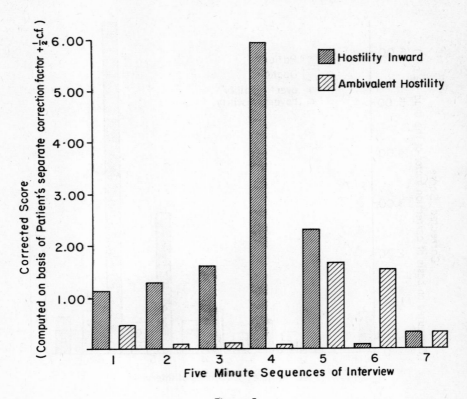

Figure 5

Changes in Patient's Hostility Inward and Ambivalent Hostility Scores

DISCUSSION AND SUMMARY

We have attempted to illustrate some features of a method of measuring changes in certain emotional states during the psychotherapeutic interview. This interview material affords us a favorable opportunity to elucidate the theoretical basis of our approach, to review some of the reliability and validity studies we have carried out, and to demonstrate some of the kinds of mathematical analyses of interview data that can be made. On several other occasions we have used our verbal behavior approach to analyze interview material. In one such study, we used the first 500 words of the patient in a series of patient-therapist interviews in order to assess the relative magnitude of masochistic conflict in an experimental psychophysiologic investigation. (Gottschalk and Kaplan, 1958b.) In another such study, we measured the sequential changes in a variety of emotional and attitudinal variables in order to demonstrate some of the advantages and possible usefulness of our method (Gottschalk, *et al.*, 1961b, 1963).

An idea of the versatility of our method of verbal behavior analysis can be gained when one realizes that our general approach to the problem of quantification has been found sensitive and valid enough to differentiate: the severity of schizophrenic social alienation and personal disorganization (Gottschalk, *et al.*, 1958a, 1961a, 1964), genuine suicide notes from false ones (Gottschalk and Gleser, 1960b), the changes in anxiety and hostility associated with phases of the menstrual cycle (Gottschalk, *et al.*, 1962), the effects of perphenazine as compared to a placebo on the hostility outward level of a group of dermatologic patients (Gottschalk, *et al.*, 1960a), anxious from non-anxious individuals (Gleser, *et al.*, 1961), and many other studies (Gottschalk, *et al.*, 1955, 1956, 1957, 1958, 1963, 1965; Gleser, *et al.*, 1961; Kaplan, *et al.*, 1961).

Besides the fact that there are no other systematic methods that can provide running estimates of the intensity of various affects during an interview, our method has other advantages. The tape recording and scoring of the interview material can be done by technicians who are not psychiatrically or psychologically trained. The necessary interpretive inferences and other assumptions involved in the process of assessing affect intensity from verbal behavior are built into the affect scales, so that the technician need only classify the interview content into categories of the scales on a literal rather than on a figurative basis.

A shortcoming of our approach to affect quantification is that the procedure does not provide a simultaneous evaluation of the psychodynamic origins of the affect. Furthermore, the affect scores for each time unit represent a summation of some specific type of emotional experiences, triggered potentially by several different psychodynamic routes, and these routes cannot be differentiated via the score alone. Our procedure does provide, however, some psychologic context relevant to the affect, such as the type of anxiety, for example, death, mutilation, separation, guilt, and shame. Another shortcoming is that the measurements are, of necessity, on an ordinal and not on an interval scale. The mathematical transformation of the affect scores, by obtaining their square roots, tends to make our scale approach some of the features of interval scales. We know of no way, at this time, to devise a true interval scale type of measurement of such psychologic variables. Finally, at this stage of our investigations the numerical units of our different affect scales are not directly comparable to each other, so that one cannot say which affect is predominant at a given time. We are satisfied, however, that we have made several major advances along the uncharted route toward measuring the magnitude of emotions as adjudged from verbal communication. We hope we can provide a working model that may prove useful in quantifying other psychologic and psychoanalytic concepts.

REFERENCES

AULD, F. JR., and MURRAY, E. J. Content analysis studies of psychotherapy. *Psychol. Bull.*, **52**: 377-395, 1955.

BECK, A. T., WARD, C. H. MENDELSON, M., and ERBAUGH, J. An inventory for measuring depression. *A.M.A. Arch. gen. Psychiat.*, **4**: 561-571, 1961.

BEECHER, H. *Measurement of subjective responses.* New York: Oxford, 1959.

CANNON, W. B. *Bodily changes in pain, hunger, fear, and rage.* (2nd ed.) New York: Appleton-Century-Crofts, 1936.

CATTELL, R. B. *Handbook for the IPAT Anxiety Scale.* Champaign, Ill.: Institute for Personality and Ability Testing, 1957.

DARROW, C. W. Differences in the physiological reactions to sensory and ideational stimuli. *Psychol. Bull.*, **26**: 185-201, 1929.

DARROW, C. W. Electrical and circulatory responses to brief sensory and ideational stimuli. *J. exp. Psychol.*, **12**: 267-300, 1929.

DELAY, J. DENIKER, P., and HARL, J. M. Traitement des états d'excitation et d'agitation par une méthode medicamenteuse derivée de l'hibernotherapie. *Ann. Med-Psychol.*, **110**: 267-271, 1952.

FENICHEL, O. *The psychoanalytic theory of neurosis.* New York: Norton, 1945.

FUNKENSTEIN, D. H. Norepinephrine-like and epinephrine-like substances in relation to human behavior. *J. nerv. ment. Dis.*, **124**: 58-67, 1956.

GELLHORN, E., and LOOFBOURROW, G. N. *Emotions and emotional disorders. A neurophysiological disorder.* New York: Hoeber-Harper, 1963.

GLESER, G. C., GOTTSCHALK, L. A., and SPRINGER, K. J. An anxiety measure applicable to verbal samples, *A.A.A. Arch. gen. Psychiat.*, **5**: 593-605, 1961.

GOTTSCHALK, L. A., CLEGHORN, J. M., GLESER, G. C., and IACONO, J. M. Studies of relationships of emotions to plasma lipids. *Psychosom. Med.* **27**: 102-111, 1965.

GOTTSCHALK, L. A., and GLESER, G. C. Distinguishing characteristics of the verbal communications of schizophrenic patients. *Proceed. Ass. Res. nerv. ment. Dis. Disorders of Communication.* Baltimore: Williams & Wilkins, 1964

GOTTSCHALK, L. A. and GLESER, G. C. An analysis of the verbal content of suicide notes. *British J. med. psychol.* **33**: 195-204, 1960b.

GOTTSCHALK, L. A., GLESER, G. C., DANIELS, R., and BLOCK, S. The speech patterns of schizophrenic patients: A method of assessing relative degree of personal disorganization and social alienation. *J. nerv. ment. Dis.*, **127**: 153-166, 1958. (a)

GOTTSCHALK, L. A., GLESER, G. C., and HAMBIDGE, G. JR. Verbal behavior analysis: Some content and form variables in speech relevant to personality adjustment. *Arch. Neurol. Psychiat.*, **77**: 300-311, 1957.

GOTTSCHALK, L. A., GLESER, G. C., MAGLIOCCO, E. B., and D'ZMURA, T. Further studies on the speech patterns of schizophrenic patients: Measuring interindividual differences in relative degree of personal disorganization and social alienation. *J. nerv. ment. Dis.*, **132**: 101-113, 1961. (a)

GOTTSCHALK, L. A., GLESER, G. C., SPRINGER, K. J. Three hostility scales applicable to verbal samples. *A.M.A. Arch. gen. Psychiat.*, **9**: 254-279, 1963.

GOTTSCHALK, L. A., GLESER, G. C., SPRINGER, K. J., KAPLAN, S., SHANON, J., and Ross, W. D. Effects of perphenazine on verbal behavior: A contribution to the problem of measuring the psychologic effect of psychoactive drugs, A.M.A. Arch. gen. Psychiat., 2: 632-639, 1960a.

GOTTSCHALK, L. A., and HAMBIDGE, G., JR. Verbal behavior analysis: A systematic approach to the problem of quantifying psychologic processes. J. proj. Tech., 19: 387-409, 1955.

GOTTSCHALK, L. A., and KAPLAN, S. M. A quantitative method of estimating variations in intensity of a psychologic conflict or state. Arch. Neurol. Psychiat., 79: 688-696, 1958. (b)

GOTTSCHALK, L. A., KAPLAN, S. M., GLESER, G. C., and WINGET, C. M. Variations in the magnitude of anxiety and hostility with phases of the menstrual cycle. Psychosom. Med., 24: 300-311, 1962.

GOTTSCHALK, L. A., KAPP, F. T., Ross, W. D., KAPLAN, S. M., SILVER, H., MacLEOD, J. A., KAHN, J. B. JR., VAN MAANEN, E. F., and ACHESON, G. H. Explorations in testing drugs affecting physical and mental activity. J. Amer. Med. Ass., 161: 1054-1058, 1956.

GOTTSCHALK, L. A., SPRINGER, K. J., and GLESER, G. C. Experiments with a method of assessing the variations in intensity of certain psychologic states occurring during the psychotherapeutic interview. In L. A. Gottschalk (Ed.), Comparative psycholinguistic analysis of two psychotherapeutic interviews. New York: International Universities, 1961. (b) Pp. 115-138.

JACOBSON, E. The affects and their pleasure-unpleasure qualities in relation to the psychic discharge processes. In, R. M. Lowenstein (Ed.), Drives, affects, behavior. New York: International Universities, 1953.

JAFFE, J. Dyadic analysis of two psychotherapeutic interviews. In L. A. Gottschalk (Ed.), Comparative psycholinguistic analysis of two psychotherapeutic interviews. New York: International Universities, 1961. Pp. 73-90.

KAPLAN, S. M., GOTTSCHALK, L. A., MAGLIOCCO, E. B., ROHOVIT, D. D., and Ross, W. D. Hostility in verbal productions and hypnotic dreams of hypertensive patients: Studies of groups and individuals. Psychosom. Med. 23: 311-322, 1961.

KNAPP, P. Conscious and unconscious affects: A preliminary approach to concepts and methods of study. In Research in affects, Psychiat. Res. Rep. 8. Washington, D.C.: American Psychiatric Association, 1957.

KUBIE, L. A. Problems and techniques of psychoanalytic validation and progress. In E. Pumpian-Mindlin (Ed.) Psychoanalysis as science. Stanford, Calif.: Stanford University Press, 1952.

LACEY, J. T. Psychophysiological approaches to the evaluation of psychotherapeutic process and outcome. In E. A. Rubinstein and M. B. Parloff (Eds.), Research in psychotherapy. Washington, D.C.: National Publishing Co., 1959.

MacLEAN, P. D. The limbic system (visceral brain) in relation to central gray and reticulum of the brain stem. Evidence of interdependence in emotional processes. Psychosom. Med., 17: 355-366, 1955.

MAHL, G. F. Measures of two expressive aspects of a patient's speech in two psychotherapeutic interviews. In, L. A. Gottschalk (Ed.), Comparative *psycholinguistic analysis of two psychotherapeutic interviews.* New York: International Universities, 1961. Pp. 91-114.

MASON, J. W., MANGON, G., JR., BRADY, J. V., CONRAD, D., and RIOCH, D. Concurrent plasma epinephrine, neorepinephrine, and 17-hydroxycorticosteroid levels during conditioned emotional disturbance in monkeys. *Psychosom. Med.*, 23: 344-353, 1961.

MASSERMAN, J. H. *Behavior and neurosis.* Chicago: Univ. of Chicago Press, 1943.

MIRSKY, I. A., MILLER, R. E., and MURPHY, J. V. The communication of affect in rhesus monkeys: I. An experimental method. *J. Amer. Psychoanal. Ass.*, 6: 433-441, 1958.

NOWLIS, V., and NOWLIS, H. H. The description and analysis of mood. *Ann. of the N.Y. Acad. of Sci.*, 65: 345-355, 1956.

OKEN, D. An experimental study of suppressed anger and blood pressure. *A.M.A. Arch. gen. Psychiat.*, 2: 441-456, 1960.

PERSKY, H. Adrenocortical function during anxiety. In R. Roessles and S. Greenfield (Eds.), *Physiological correlates of psychological disorders.* Madison, Wis.: Univ. of Wisconsin Press, 1961.

PERSKY, H., HAMBURG, D. A., BASOWITZ, H., GRINKER, R. R., SABSHIN, M., KORCHIN, S. J., HERZ, M., BOARD, F. A., and HEATH, H. A. Relation of emotional responses and changes in plasma hydrocortisone level after stressful interview. *A.M.A. Arch. Neurol & Psychiat.*, 79: 434-447, 1958.

RAPAPORT, D. *Emotions and memory.* New York: International Universities, 1950.

RAPAPORT, D. On the psychoanalytic theory of affects. *Int. J. Psychoanal.*, 34: 177-198, 1953.

RAPAPORT, D. The structure of psychoanalytic theory. In *Psychological Issues*, Vol. II, no. 2, New York: International Universities, 1960.

REID, J. "Introduction" to S. Cobb, *Emotions and clinical medicine.* New York: Norton, 1950.

SARGENT, H. D. Intrapsychic change: Methodological problems in psychotherapy research. *Psychiat.*, 24: 93-108, 1961.

SEITZ, P. F. D. The effects of infantile experiences upon adult behavior in animal subjects: I. Effects of litter size during infancy upon adult behavior in the rat. *Amer. J. Psychiat.*, 110: 916-927, 1954.

SEITZ, P. F. D. Infantile experience and adult behavior in animal subjects. II. Age of separation from the mother and adult behavior in the cat. *Psychosom. Med.*, 21: 353-378, 1959.

SHOLITON, L. J., WOHL, T. H., and WERK, E. E., JR. The correlation of two psychological variables, anxiety and hostility, with adrenocortical function in patients with lung cancer. *Cancer*, 16: 223-230, 1963.

TAYLOR, J. A personality scale of manifest anxiety. *J. abnorm. soc. Psychol.*, 48: 285, 1953.

WITTENBORN, J. R. *Wittenborn psychiatric rating scales.* New York: The Psychological Corporation, 1955.

ZUCKERMAN, M. The development of an affect adjective check list for the measurement of anxiety. *J. consult. Psychol.*, 24: 457, 1960.

12. Content analysis of verbalizations about interpersonal experience

Erika Chance

SOME CONSIDERATIONS IN THE CHOICE OF A CONCEPTUAL MODEL FOR STUDYING PSYCHOTHERAPY

It is a truism to say that the complete and accurate observation of a human being is impossible. Perception of other persons, just as the perception of the world around us, must utilize some ways of reducing and ordering the impact of a myriad of sensory messages upon the observer. These processes are vitally important biological defenses even to the researcher who strives so constantly for complete and accurate appraisal of the data under study. As Robert Oppenheimer (1958) has said so aptly:

> There is much more that one might know than any of us are ever going to know. . . . This has nothing to do with the trivial fact that we don't work hard enough; nor . . . that things are difficult to learn. It is, rather, that any form of knowledge really precludes other forms; that any serious study of one thing cuts out some other part of your life. Narrowness is not an accident . . . but a condition of knowledge—by the very techniques, powers, and facts of its acquisition and by the way it organizes the chaos that is the world around us. (p. 7)

If, then, we must be content with partial and selected observations dependent upon the observer's approach to the data, it is necessary to formulate the assumptions and principles which have guided the selection.

My selection of problems in psychotherapy and the development of methods to explore them comes from a conviction that the most useful questions about pathology and treatment can be derived from listening to patients and therapists. Ideally such "listening" should use non-verbal clues as well as content. But the problems of devising a systematic approach to the data which is both meaningful and practical led me to the decision to restrict my observations to the content of the patients' and therapists' formulations. This can be studied and easily replicated wherever recorded and transcribed treatment sessions are available. Even when the field of observation is so restricted, the problems of a systematic approach to it are legion. What kinds of formulations by patients and therapists are most crucial to the study of the treatment process? How can these be translated into operational terms so that they become amenable to objective study?

In our studies (Chance, 1959) it was possible to demonstrate that among the many possible variables for the content analysis of the patients' and the clinicians' formulations, the description of interpersonal experience held a strategic place. Psychotherapy can be defined as the planned use of a professional relationship to help the patient toward better, more socially adaptive functioning, that is, to the experience of less conflict-laden, more rewarding interpersonal relationships. This means that interpersonal experience is crucial to the understanding of illness, treatment, and recovery. What methods might be devised for the systematic investigation of the patient's interpersonal experiences?

Systematic observation of data requires a point of reference, a classification or system, and a clearly defined process of classification.

The choice of a point of reference did not present a problem in view of the clinician's extensive training in empathizing with patients. The researcher must follow in the clinician's footsteps and infer what the patient feels, experiences, and intends.

Various workers have devised similar methods to classify interpersonal experiences, all of which involve an empathic rating of the smallest possible units of observed behavior. This method limits and defines the basis upon which inference is made. Because it considers these small units in context, it involves clinical judgment in miniature. Like all actuarial methods (Meehl, 1954) this process has the disadvantage of leaning heavily on frequency as a criterion of importance. This defect can be remedied only partially by weighting each item for intensity of affect inferred and by describing the individual in terms of the relative proportion of items falling in a given class of behavior. At present this seems to be the best compromise between exactness of rating and the sweep of clinical judgment yet devised.

The selection of a system to classify interpersonal experiences presents far greater difficulties because of the great variety of possible experiences to be included and because various personality theories have emphasized different kinds of experience. This situation challenges the researcher to construct a system based on small units that are immediately related to manifest phenomena, simple to observe, which can serve as the common denominator of various clinical theories permitting alternate ways of grouping them. For such a system it would be necessary to categorize data into a fairly large number of discrete classes, each relating to different kinds of interpersonal experience. Such a classification becomes a system only when the discrete categories are arranged to represent the focal dimensions of a particular clinical theory. It should be possible to represent another theory by rearranging the same units into a different pattern. If such a system can be devised, it would be possible to compare the interpretations of various schools about the same data, thus providing a means of communication between various workers which would further a better understanding of the many "angles" from which an individual can be viewed. This process of trying a number of ways of "construing" the environment has been aptly described by Kelly (1955):

> Man looks at his world through transparent patterns or templets which he creates and then attempts to fit over the realities of which the world is composed. The fit is not always very good. Yet without such patterns the world appears to be such an undifferentiated homogeneity that man is unable to make any sense out of it. Even a poor fit is more helpful to him than nothing at all. . . .
>
> In general man seeks to improve his constructs by increasing his repertory, by altering them to provide better fits, and by subsuming them with superordinate constructs or systems. In seeking improvement he is repeatedly halted by the damage to the system that apparently will result from the alteration of a subordinate construct. Frequently his personal investment in the larger system, or his personal dependence upon it, is so great that he will forego the adoption of a more precise construct in the substructure. (pp. 8-9)

In testing clinical hypotheses, the investigator is engaged in just such a search for improved and "better fitting" constructs. What, then, should determine the researcher's choice of units for the intensive study of interpersonal experience?

The various personality theories can be considered alternative systems for organizing clinical data. Even though they may emphasize different facets of human experience, they have in common certain ways of arranging clinical evidence and certain conceptual constructs to describe and explain patients' behavior. The investigation of these common constructs seems of primary importance because it is from them that the most fundamental relationships between various aspects of the clinical picture can be learned. Theories of psychiatry developed since the 1940's have focused more and more on exploring the interpersonal relationships which characterize the patient's functioning. Thompson (1950) has summed up this trend:

> Whatever theory in the long run proves to be most adequate . . . by establishing the idea that the habitual attitudes provide the resistance to cure, a new era in treatment has begun. . . . The way the person defends himself in his daily relations with people has become the main object of study. . . . (p. 77)

There has always been a good deal of interest in the individual's habitual, characteristic ways of relating to others, as illustrated by the *character types* of various theoretical schools. These types reveal similarities between the various theories in the way in which they group certain kinds of interpersonal behavior and in the patterns upon which their constructs are based.

Among Freudian theorists, Karl Abraham (1927) and Wilhelm Reich (1945) have emphasized that the patient's habitual ways of reacting are useful in understanding him. The character traits emerge as defensive measures against instinctual strivings predominant at a certain developmental level. Thus, the anal character is described as motivated chiefly by the desire to control and dominate things and people and is characterized by orderliness, frugality, and obstinacy. The oral character type also relates back to the individual's early development: "Usually pronounced oral satisfaction results in remarkable self-assurance and optimism. . . . Exceptional oral deprivation, on the other hand, determines a pessimistic (depressive) or sadistic (redress demanding) attitude" (Fenichel, 1945, p. 489). Freud (1950), in his discussion of the vicissitudes of instinct, has shown how this theory posits that each defensive process involves a switch in the motivation of the individual's interpersonal experience along the three polarities of self-other, activity-passivity, and friendliness-hostility.

Jung defines a type as "a characteristic model of a general attitude . . ." (Jung, 1932, p. 612). Four basic psychological functions (thinking, feeling, intuition, and sensation) are characterized by their motivational direction into extraversion or introversion. Introversion is an attitude which is characteristically self-centered, but not in the evaluative sense. Extraversion is "other-directed," though not in Riesman's (1950) sense.

For Adler, the basic conflict of neurosis lies in the individual's achievement of superiority. This can be traced to the fact that "throughout the whole period of development, the child possesses a feeling of inferiority in its relation both to parents and the world at large" (Adler, 1950, p. 13). In order to cope with these feelings, each individual develops a "life style" which is comprised of his habitual interpersonal attitudes. Adler holds that the child's ordinal position in the family is an important factor in determining the life style.

The individual's basic neurotic conflict, according to Horney (1937), is in the fundamentally contradictory attitudes toward other persons he has acquired while trying to cope with feelings of isolation and helplessness, even from early childhood. These conflicting, habitual attitudes are characterized by contrasting motivations, the desire to move toward, against, and away from people.

Fromm distinguishes four neurotic character types in *Man for Himself* (1947). The *receptive* and *exploitative* orientations are outcomes of the symbiotic resolution of the feeling of loneliness, the *hoarding* and *marketing* character types, the result of withdrawal. Fromm is one of the few theorists to spell out the adjustive as well as the pathological manifestations of these basic character traits. His method of definition for the exploitative orientation is: *Positive* aspect, active, able to take initiative, able to make claims, proud, impulsive, self-confident, and captivating. *Nega-*

tive aspect, exploitative, aggressive, egocentric, conceited, rash, arrogant, and seducing. (Fromm, 1947, pp. 114-116)

The discrepancy between the real self and the one which the individual may present under social pressure plays an important role in a number of personality theories. Jung (1932) has defined the concept of *persona* as a form of *dissociation* or *character splitting*.

> . . . a definite milieu demands a definite attitude. Corresponding with the duration or frequency with which such a milieu-attitude is demanded, the more or less habitual it becomes. Great numbers of men of the educated classes are obligated to move in two, for the most part totally different, milieux —viz.: in the family and domestic circle and in the world of affairs. These two totally different environments demand two totally different attitudes, which, in proportion to the degree of identification of the ego with the momentary attitude, produce a duplication of character. In accordance with social conditions and necessities, the social character is oriented, on the one hand by the expectations or obligations of the social milieu, and on the other by the social aims and efforts of the subject. . . . Through his more or less complete identification with the attitude of the moment, he (the individual) at least deceives others, and also often himself, as to his real character. (pp. 589-591)

Horney (1937) has discussed similar phenomena under the heading of the idealized self-image in which the conflicting parts are so transfigured that they no longer appear in conflict, but as various aspects of a rich personality. Fromm speaks of the pseudo-self as "essentially a reflex of other people's expectations of him . . ." (1941, p. 206).

Despite the marked differences among schools, there are certain common features. Experience of intrapsychic conflict is accompanied by feelings of tension, discomfort, and dissatisfaction with the self. It is, in most schools, traced to the individual's relationships with parents and siblings in early childhood. The person attempts to escape these feelings of tension and self-rejection by a variety of security operations or defense mechanisms. His habitual way of relating to others is in large part the outcome of such efforts. The habitual attitudes or characteristic orientations toward people singled out for emphasis by the various schools require a classification which will describe interpersonal experience in terms of contrasting variables. For Freud's theory, we need to place interpersonal relations on the dimensions of activity-passivity and friendliness-hostility. To portray Horney's neurotic solutions, interpersonal experience must be divided into movement toward, away from, and against people. For Fromm's classification, indifference and destruction must be contrasted with symbiotic, mutually dependent relationships.

RESEARCH METHODS DESCRIBING INTERPERSONAL EXPERIENCE

The way personality theories describe conflict and the individual's ways of coping with it suggests that a system for classifying interpersonal experience must contain at least two kinds of polar dimensions; it should describe interpersonal experiences in terms of the opposites the schools have singled out and it should differentiate between experiences which are acceptable and those which the individual rejects in himself and others. In this area of research the methods developed by Mowrer (1953), Rogers (1949, 1950), Bales (1950), and Freedman and his collaborators (1951) are outstanding. In examining the classifications devised by these workers, it was believed that each method contributed to the exact evaluation of data in the treatment situation, either by focusing primarily on the content of interpersonal experience (Bales, Freedman) or by focusing on the acceptable quality of that experience (Rogers, Mowrer). Because it was believed that both represented crucial factors in the understanding of the patient, a method was devised which attempted to emphasize both the content and the quality of the individual's interpersonal experience.

Those aspects of clinical theory which portray conflict are represented in terms of the acceptability or unacceptability of each unit of interpersonal experience. The manner in which the individual relates himself to others is classified in terms of the circle shown in Figure 1. This circle represents an extension of the system originally devised by Freedman, Leary, Ossorio, and Coffery (1951) and indicates how the 20 categories used might be grouped to represent the polarities favored by Freud. Adlerian polarities can be represented by omitting the vertical axis of the wheel and using only the horizontal division into active versus passive participation in interpersonal experience. The Horney school would require division of the circle into unequal parts; the category of retreat and withdrawal representing one division, the other negative categories representing movement against others, and the positive section representing movement toward others. The Jungian extraversion-introversion typology depends upon the self- or other-directed nature of the individual's motivation. The active and passive versions of this can be represented by omitting the vertical axis. Fromm's "positive aspects" of the "receptive orientation" can be found in the positive passive quadrant, while the negative aspects are for the most part represented in the negative passive quadrant. All of the negative aspects of the "exploitative orientation," except the item "seducing," are included in the negative active quadrant. The positive aspects of this orientation are chiefly represented in the positive active quadrant. This system was constructed in the hope that workers with a variety of theoretical preferences might pool their clinical material and submit it to systematic analysis in which the same units are used, but are arranged differently to suit each theory.

In many ways the classification developed leaves much to be desired. The most obvious omission is that it ignores the contextual clues of gesture, facial expression, and tone, indeed, all behavior except verbal productions. Also important is its inability to deal directly with the division of mental functioning into conscious and unconscious experience. This is a conundrum for which no direct solution has yet been found, since, by definition, the unconscious is not manifest and the researcher is committed to using manifest phenomena for inferences.

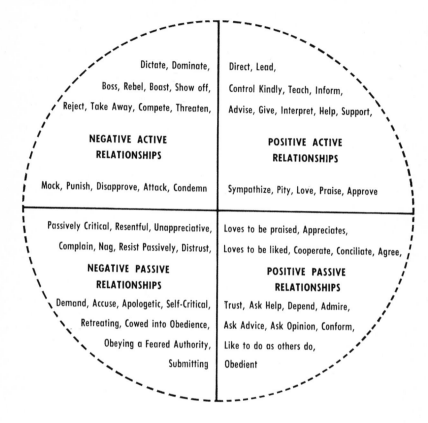

Figure 1
A System for Classifying Interpersonal Experiences

The third most important omission in the system is the absence of categories for much used clinical concepts such as anxiety, depression, ambivalence, tension, etc. This lack is less significant than the others because these clinical concepts describe intrapsychic states which can be considered the outcome of interpersonal processes. Clinical thinking has made a test of this hypothesis relatively easy. Ambivalence is a state in which two intrapsychic processes operate simultaneously but antithetically in relation to the same object. The system denotes ambivalence toward the self as simultaneous acceptance and rejection of the self. Ambivalence toward others is also measured in these terms. Depression is designated clinically as hostility turned inward upon the self. Depressed patients should, therefore, show a tendency to retreat, withdraw, and condemn the self, and their verbalizations about interpersonal experience should be characterized by high self-rejection. Tension and anxiety states are harder to codify in this system. These states are characterized by the individual's pervasive discomfort in a wide variety of experiences. They seem to entail considerable fluctuations and disruptions of that enduring system of behavioral tendencies called personality. Perhaps the best description of such states could be achieved by observing the extent to which the individual fails to maintain a consistent self-evaluation in a wide variety of experiences (e.g., simultaneous self-acceptance and self-rejection pervading all categories), and by noting just how labile and variable his pattern of relating might be.

In the selection of these categories it is clear that personal bias cannot be entirely eliminated. That other workers have thought these phenomena important is reassuring. My own bias is demonstrated by the inclusion of the category of "competitive behavior" among negative interpersonal experiences in Figure 1. Such an evaluation of competitive behavior is, perhaps, more natural to an investigator of European extraction than to one born in America. The way the flexibility of the system provides the opportunity to express bias through multiple arrangement of the categories is viewed as a methodological advantage since it permits definition and testing of a series of such biases. Recent studies (Chance and Arnold, 1960) have shown that the classification of interpersonal experience into polar dimensions of activity-passivity and hostility-friendliness is highly meaningful to psychoanalytically-trained psychiatrists assessing the verbalizations of the same patient. Whether this system of classification is equally appropriate for Freudian clinicians from other disciplines remains to be seen. Some evidence in our current work suggests that psychiatrists who cite Sullivan, Horney, or Fromm as the most important influence upon their thinking may group these categories differently from analytically-trained psychiatrists.

APPLICATION OF THE MODEL TO DATA ANALYSIS

In the light of the foregoing, application of this method of data analysis requires classification of the patient's verbalizations about interpersonal experience in three frames of reference. The smallest unit descriptive of an interpersonal experience is first classified into one of the 20 categories. Next, it is rated for intensity of the experience, from 1 (minimal or understatement) to 3 (maximal or extreme intensity), and last, it is judged as entailing self-acceptance or self-rejection by the patient. Table 1 is an example of this coding technique applied to the illustrative case.

Methodological problems in coding transcribed material have for the most part been satisfactorily resolved. Defining the smallest unit in the transcript of an interpersonal experience is the researcher's decision. That reliability on this decision can be achieved has been shown by Freedman, et al. (1951), but no attempt seems to have been made to date to test whether different research teams working independently utilize similar sections of the material or to test whether differences in approach might account for differences in findings. Similarly, it became apparent in training raters that the amount of context taken into consideration appears to vary from one rater to the next. Despite this, however, satisfactory reliability was established on all the dimensions outlined, as shown in Table 2 (Chance, 1953).

Table 1
Coding Sample for the Illustrative Material

A. *Transcript*:

Dr. B: Are you getting set?

Pt: Now, I'm (not completely certain about)[1] Al, in what he—I mean, he talked about this a lot, for what he wants to use it for.

Dr. B: And we don't know how genuine an hour you can have with your picture.

Pt: (The movie begins) Well, I think this is a very unusual situation to be in.

Dr. B: Yea. How anxious do you feel about being in front of a camera?

Pt: Well, (I like it,)[2] as a matter of fact.

Dr. B: Well, that's what I think; it might be fine.

Pt: I used to (repress my feelings about this. In fact, it used to be a thing.)[3] (I don't think I ever had a picture taken.)[4] (I did get in one)[5] (film I produced.)[6] I was just (talking about that)[7] a little while back. But, (I think it's great.)[8] You know, (I was surprised)[9] at the transformation that comes over Al, too.

Dr. B: Yeah.

Pt: He looks very different when this is going on. This is very exciting and (I can sort of feel with him.)[10]

Dr. B: Well, I've been kidding everybody that this ought to be a lot of fun being in the movies.

Pt: Oh.

Dr. B: How have you been?

Pt: (Pretty good.)[11]

Dr. B: Have you had anything particular on your mind since I saw you last? We'll try to get into what we were talking about before.

Pt: Okay, but (this sounds very awkward.)[12] (It sounds so silly,)[13] you know.

Table 1 (Continued)

B. *Classification:*

Item Number	Content	Intensity	Category	Quadrant	Accepted	Rejected
1	not completely certain about	1	Distrust	Negative Passive	❋	
2	I like it	2	Appreciate	Positive Passive	❋	
3	repress my feelings . . . it used to be a thing	3	Retreat	Negative Passive		❋
4	I don't think I ever had a picture taken	1	Conform	Positive Passive		❋
5	I did get in one	1	Cooperate	Positive Passive	❋	
6	film I produced	1	Lead	Positive Active	❋	
7	talking about that	1	Inform	Positive Active	❋	
8	I think it's great	3	Admire	Positive Passive	❋	
9	I was surprised	2	Admire	Positive Passive	❋	
10	I can sort of feel with him	1	Sympathize	Positive Active	❋	
11	Pretty good	1	Appreciate	Positive Passive	❋	
12	this sounds very awkward	2	Condemn self	Negative Passive		❋
13	It sounds silly	3	Condemn self	Negative Passive		❋

Table 3 shows the simplest kind of grouping which results when this method of data analysis is confined to the patient's verbalizations about his own interpersonal experiences. It affords an opportunity for a number of generalizations about the way in which he describes himself. We can determine which areas of interpersonal experience dominate his verbalizations and which appear to receive least attention. Profiles describing his preoccupation can be constructed from either the percentage or the rank columns. Next, we can determine the extent to which this patient describes conflict-charged interpersonal experiences. This can be described on three levels: First, the number of categories in which self-rejection occurs may give a measure of the pervasiveness of conflict. Next, the intensity of conflict may be measured by the proportion of the individual's total verbalization about his interpersonal experience which he tends to reject. This measure is known as his self-rejection score. Last, it is of importance to know what kind of interpersonal experiences (identified by category and quadrant) are conflict-charged for this patient.

Table 2
Correlations Between Ratings of Two Independent
Raters for the Method of Content Analysis Used

$(N = 20$ categories$)$

Case Number†	Scores Rated "Accepted"	Scores Rated "Rejected"	Total Category Rating
A. Nonpatient Sample of 36 Fathers (5)			
Frequency Correlations Obtained			
e 10	r = .96**	r = .52*	r = .97**
e 9	r = .98**	r = .83**	r = .97**
e 17	r = .96**	r = .82**	r = .96**
Intensity Correlations Obtained			
e 10	r = .96**	r = .43	r = .95**
e 9	r = .98**	r = .84**	r = .96**
e 17	r = .97**	r = .78**	r = .97**
B. Patient Sample of 34 Families			
Frequency Correlations Obtained			
M 11	r = .90**	r = .71**	r = .91**
M 12	r = .95**	r = .51*	r = .96**
F 9	r = .93**	r = .66**	r = .93**
Intensity Correlations Obtained			
M 11	r = .91**	r = .74**	r = .93**
M 12	r = .91**	r = .58**	r = .94**
F 9	r = .93**	r = .66**	r = .92**

* Significant at .05 level.
** Significant at .01 level.
† The three most difficult transcripts from both the nonpatient and patient samples were used for reliability tests.

The following inferences about the illustrative case emerge from an examination of Table 3. The column of ranks shows that he is most concerned with retreating and self-blame and secondly with criticism of others and complaints. Concern with rejecting and competition are followed closely by liking to be liked. Preoccupation with conforming and kindly leadership receive the relatively high ranks of fourteen and fifteen. It is as if he vacillated between a concept of himself as an active, somewhat hostile, but also benevolently superior kind of person and, on the other hand, a notion that he could not perform adequately, was much put upon by circumstances, and was forced to withdraw from the world. Such ambivalence in self-perception is very likely to lead to inner conflict.

Table 3
Analysis of Illustrative Material in Terms of
Interpersonal Experiences Described by the Patient

Category	Frequency	Intensity				
		Accepted	Rejected	Total	%	Rank
Lead	9	17	2	19	6.3	14
Teach	1	2		2	.7	3
Give	1	1		1	.3	2
Support	5	8		8	2.7	8
Love	7	14		14	4.7	12
Positive active quadrant	23	42	2	44	14.7	
Appreciate	10	22		22	7.4	16
Cooperate	9	16		16	5.3	13
Trust	0			0		1
Admire	6	12		12	4.0	10
Conform	20	11	10	21	7.0	15
Positive passive quadrant	45	61	10	71	23.7	
Boss	2		4	4	1.3	4
Rebel	3	7		7	2.3	7
Compete	11	18	7	25	8.4	17
Punish	4	6		6	2.0	5.5
Hate	17	32	4	36	12.0	18.5
Negative active quadrant	37	63	15	78	26.0	
Resent	7	8	5	13	4.3	11
Complain	20	32	4	36	12.0	18.5
Distrust	4	6		6	2.0	5.5
Retreat	19	27	15	42	14.0	20
Submit	4		9	9	3.0	9
Negative passive quadrant	54	73	33	106	35.3	
TOTALS	159	239	60	299	99.7	

Self-rejection score $= 60/299 = 20.1\%$

It will be recalled that each unit of interpersonal experience is rated for implied self-acceptance or -rejection as shown in Table 1. The third column in Table 3 summarizes the frequency of self-rejection (weighted by intensity) in any one area of interpersonal experience. Turning aggression inward upon the self elicits most self-disapproval and conforming to a benign authority or submitting to a hostile one seem next most conflict-charged for this patient. In this fragment of therapy he appears to be most conflicted in experiences which put him in a passive position. Indeed, he rejects such experiences twice as much as those which involve his active participation in relationships.

If this patient makes an attempt to turn away from the passive roles in which he experiences so much contempt, he seems to seize upon interpersonal experiences which are likely to lead to further conflict. For the most part these involve hostile transactions such as criticism and rejection of others and competition with them. So far as friendly relationships with others are concerned his score pattern suggests preoccupation with status goals such as leadership without due concern with the instrumental transactions which would make this functional (e.g., helping, advising, etc.) and with affective goals such as liking to be liked without the instrumental experience of trust, which is essential for gratification of the need for love.

We do not know how representative this fragment of therapy might be of his behavior in other treatment sessions and his functioning in everyday life. It is of course not possible, therefore, to infer from this score pattern the implications of such preoccupations for the development of the patient's problem or his current functioning. It may be that the switch from a male to a female therapist, indicated in the data supplied to participants in this study, has increased those of his concerns which have their source in a problem-laden mother-child relationship. Concerns with status and striving for power, for example, may receive greater emphasis in this therapeutic context than in therapy with a male analyst. This may be related to the patient's attachment to a socially ambitious, upward mobile mother.

Assuming that we have ascertained that this kind of preoccupation is characteristic of the patient's concerns with interpersonal experience, it is also possible to ask to what extent he is like and how he may differ from other patients with similar socioeconomic backgrounds. In order to illustrate such a comparison, I have drawn upon the score profiles of sixty parents attending a child guidance clinic who were seen shortly after the beginning of treatment for the child. These patients came from a socioeconomic background very similar to that of the illustrative case. The method of data analysis used was the one described and resulted in the profiles shown in Figure 2.

Comparison of the profile for the illustrative case with the mean profile for these sixty patients shows that he seems more concerned with hostile and less with friendly relationships. He differs most sharply from the kind of people who may well represent his congregation in that he shows marked concern with competitive relationships and also with experiences involving retreat, withdrawal, and self-condemnation. This comparison should not be used in order to make inference concerning the typical or atypical character of the patient's verbalizations. It merely illustrates how one might usefully compare the productions of a single individual with those of a group to which he can be meaningfully related.

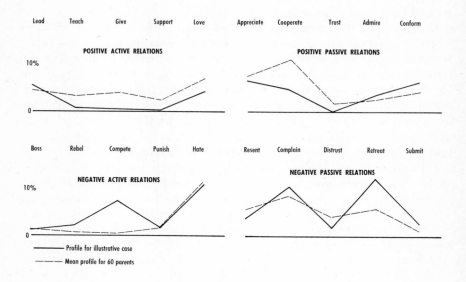

Figure 2

Comparison of Profiles (percent verbalizations about interpersonal experience) for the Illustrative Case and 60 Parents Attending a Child Guidance Clinic

SOURCE: See Table 5, Chance, 1959.

Such an approach to the data of therapy offers opportunities for many other comparisons which may throw light upon the process of treatment. If it were possible in this case to take comparable samples of the patient's productions at the beginning, middle, and end of the treatment year, one could begin to describe the fluctuations in his concerns. Continuous recording of analytic sessions would permit closer study of the patient's responses to special situations such as cancellations of hours by the therapist, treatment sessions with another therapist, etc. Throughout it should be borne in mind that the research method described here is clearly limited to minimal inference about the patient's intrapsychic life. Each reported interpersonal experience is utilized, and complex clinical concepts such as ambivalence, conflict, repression, identification, etc. have to be "reconstituted" in terms of constellations of such verbal reports. This is a laborious procedure in which theoretical formulations must be operationally defined.

EXTENSIONS OF THE METHOD ILLUSTRATED BY OPERATIONAL DEFINITIONS FOR SOME CLINICAL CONCEPTS

If interpersonal experience is a crucial variable in the process of treatment, it should be possible to define important clinical concepts in these terms. In the following a few examples will be given of the kind of translating that has to be done before a clinical concept can be defined operationally in terms of this variable. First, it is possible to describe diagnostic syndromes in terms of the kind of interpersonal experiences which characterize the patient's verbalizations about himself. The term *Passive Aggressive Character Disorder* is one instance in which clinical word-usage and the classification of interpersonal experience shown in Figure 1 are clearly identical. The categories of resentment, complaint, distrust, withdrawal, and submission to a hostile world which are grouped in the Negative Passive quadrant of the figure describe the syndrome. The diagnosis of "Sado-masochism" could be represented by extreme concern with categories in both the Negative Active and the Negative Passive quadrants of the figure. By comparing self-descriptions obtained from a group of patients in a given diagnostic category, it is possible to determine what profile of concern with interpersonal experiences might characterize their productions.

If we turn next to concepts describing the treatment relationship, it is possible to demonstrate how operational definitions may assist in the more detailed study of clinical phenomena, but also how the use of such definitions falls short of some aspects of meaning in clinical terminology. Transference has been defined by Freud (1925) as follows:

Every human being has acquired a special individuality in the exercise of his capacity for love, that is in the conditions which he sets up for loving, in the impulses he gratifies by it, and in the aims he sets out to achieve in it. This forms a cliché or stereotype in him which perpetually repeats and reproduces itself. . . . Of the feelings which determine the capacity to love only a part has undergone full psychic development. This part is directed toward reality . . . the other has been held up in development, withheld from consciousness and from reality. . . . Each new person will inevitably arouse expectant libidinal impulses in anyone whose need for love is not being satisfactorily gratified in reality. . . . The patient will weave the figure of the physician into one of the "series" already constructed in his mind, it will be attached to one of the prototypes already established. (pp. 312-313)

If this sensitive, poetic, and infinitely human description of how the patient becomes involved in therapy is translated into operational terms, it can be rephrased as "the patient's tendency to respond to the therapist with irrational feelings, attitudes, and behavior which are stereotypes or clichés of his childhood experiences with significant others." The first object of these reactions can be called the transference origin or source, while the second can be considered as the transference object. In a study attempting to assess the degree of transference in group psychotherapy (Chance, 1952) it was possible to demonstrate that patients varied in the extent to which they equated their image of the therapist with that of a person significant in early childhood. However, this study also pointed up the limitations of substituting equivalence in the description of transference source and transference object for the rich and elusive phenomenon first described by Freud. It was not possible to determine just how and where the patient's perception of the therapist in terms of the feelings and attitudes attributed to a person significant in early childhood was indeed irrational. Very possibly some of the characteristics attributed to the therapist existed in fact and were not projections. Furthermore, in any psychotherapy the clinical phenomenon of transference may have its origin in several important childhood relationships and the relationship to the therapist may be a replicate of a succession of these or represent a composite of these. Much further study in this area needs to be done before we can rely on an operational definition of this kind.

The concept of countertransference describes the same process applied to the therapist's attitude toward his patient. In our studies it was possible to demonstrate that therapists had a tendency to generalize across their caseloads. These generalizations varied in degree and content from one clinician to the next (Chance, 1959, Chap. VII). There was no doubt that some of the therapists studied showed a tendency to stereotype in their expectations about the kind of interpersonal concerns which would characterize the verbalizations of their patients. In so far as this was not indicated by the actual verbalizations of the patients the irrational component of transference was probably involved. To what extent could the content of such a stereotype be equated with the therapist's own experience, feelings, and attitudes vis-à-vis important persons in his childhood? The exploration of this question would require data which were not available to us at the time of the study.

Last, every clinician hopes that in the process of therapy the patient will not only show shifts in his preoccupations with certain kinds of interpersonal experience, but also changes in the kind of intrapsychic organizations and mechanisms which have characterized his functioning. Questions about shifts in the preoccupation of a patient with certain kinds of interpersonal experience can be explored by comparing his description of relationships to others at various points in therapy. If at the beginning of treatment he was most preoccupied with complaints, resentment, and distrust, will his concern with these relationships diminish? If at the outset of therapy his feelings of resentment, his stream of complaints, and his accusation of others appeared to him as a fully justified response to a hostile world, will these reactions to others become less acceptable and more conflict-laden for him as therapy progresses?

Questions about the role of such intrapsychic organizations as the Superego, the Idealized Self-image, or the Persona may be explored by utilizing a patient's self-description given under contrasting conditions. It can be assumed that a patient may feel more free to reveal his socially unacceptable characteristics and experiences in therapy and less free to do the same under anxiety-arousing test conditions. Differences in the patient's productions at these two levels may be understood as areas of actual or potential conflict between intrapsychic organizations. This reasoning was explored in our studies (Chance, 1959). It was possible to determine "how acceptable" each of the 20 categories of interpersonal relationships (Figure 1) might be for a group of patients coming from a homogeneous social background. The categories were arranged along a scale according to the degree of acceptability in middle class U.S.A. as estimated by five clinicians. Because of high agreement among the clinicians it was possible to combine their judgments into the previously mentioned Acceptability Scale. It was discovered that while the patient's concern in the confiding situation of treatment showed no relationship to this scale, when put in a test situation he presented a social façade highly correlated with the Acceptability Scale. While patients showed no change in their response under test conditions in the course of therapy, their concern with the 20 categories of interpersonal experience in treatment changed in the direction of greater similarity to this scale.

Questions about the patient's use of intrapsychic mechanisms such as projection or introjection can be investigated by defining these operationally and then tracing them in the course of therapy. Operational definition of these mechanisms involves not only the individual's perception of himself, but also that of another. Projection may be defined as the individual's need to externalize and attribute to another those characteristics of his own which are unacceptable to him. Similarly, introjection may be defined as the individual's incorporation into his self-perception of characteristics attributed to him by another. For an exploration of these phenomena this method of content analysis has to be expanded to include the individual's self-description as well as his description *of* another (in the case of projection) or his description *by* another (in the case of introjection). Thus, in a study of families in treatment (Chance, 1959) exploring the phenomenon of introjection it was found at the beginning of treatment that there was a close and significant relationship between the child-patient's verbalizations of conflict and self-rejection during his hour and the mother's rejection of the child in sessions with her own therapist. In the course of treatment it was possible to demonstrate how the child's rejection of himself became increasingly independent of the mother's child-rejection.

There are many other ways in which this method of data analysis can be extended or adapted to fit the focus of interest of a particular investigator. These extensions are, of course, limited by the choice of the crucial variable of interpersonal experience and by the extent to which rich and colorful clinical concepts lend themselves to operational redefinition in terms of this variable. It is hoped that the limitations of the method as well as its rewards have become more evident by the discussion of its relationship to clinical theory, to the illustrative material, and to concepts frequently employed in clinical practice.

REFERENCES

ABRAHAM, K. *Selected papers on psychoanalysis.* Translated by D. Bryan and A. Strachey. London: Hogarth, 1927.

ADLER, A. *The practice and theory of individual psychology.* Translated by P. Radin. London: Routledge, 1950.

BALES, R. F. *Interaction process analysis.* Reading, Mass.: Addison-Wesley, 1950.

CHANCE, ERIKA. A study of transference in group psychotherapy. *Int. J. Group Psychother.,* **2**: 40-53, 1952.

CHANCE, ERIKA. The father's perception of his first child. Unpublished doctoral dissertation, Stanford University, 1953.

CHANCE, ERIKA. *Families in treatment.* New York: Basic Books, 1959.

CHANCE, ERIKA, and ARNOLD, JACK. The effect of professional training, experience, and preference for a theoretical system upon clinical case description. *Human Relations,* **13**: 195-213, 1960.

FENICHEL, O. *The psychoanalytic theory of neurosis.* New York: Norton, 1945.

FREEDMAN, M. B., LEARY, T. F., OSSORIO, A. G., and COFFERY, H. S. Interpersonal dimensions of personality. *J. Pers.,* **20**: 143-161, 1951.

FREUD, S. The dynamics of the transference (1912), *Collected papers,* II. London: Hogarth, 1925.

FREUD, S. *Collected papers.* London: Hogarth, 1950.

FROMM, E. *Escape from freedom.* New York: Holt, Rinehart and Winston, 1941.

FROMM, E. *Man for himself.* New York: Holt, Rinehart and Winston, 1947.

HORNEY, KAREN. *The neurotic personality of our time.* New York: Norton, 1937.

JUNG, C. G. *Psychological types or the psychology of individuation.* London: Routledge, 1932.

KELLY, G. A. *The psychology of personal constructs,* Vol. I: *A theory of personality.* New York: Norton, 1955.

MEEHL, P. E. *Clinical versus statistical prediction.* Minneapolis: Univ. of Minnesota Press, 1954.

MOWRER, O. H. Further studies utilizing the discomfort relief quotient. In,

O. H. Mowrer (Ed.), *Psychotherapy, theory, and research.* New York: Ronald, 1953. Pp. 257-295.

OPPENHEIMER, J. R. A talk to young scientists. *Sci. Perspectives,* 1 (2): 6-7, 17, 1958.

REICH, W. *Character analysis, principles, and techniques for psychoanalysts in practice and in training.* Translated by T. P. Wolff. New York: Orgone Institute Press, 1945.

RIESMAN, D. *The lonely crowd.* New Haven: Yale University Press, 1950.

ROGERS, C. R. *A study of the process and outcomes of client-centered therapy.* Mimeographed first and second interim reports. Chicago: Counseling Center, Univ. of Chicago, 1949, 1950.

THOMPSON, CLARA. *Psychoanalysis, evolution and development.* New York: Hermitage House, 1950.

b. Paralanguage and linguistic variables

There is available today a variety of approaches to the analysis of paralanguage, linguistic, and kinesic variables. In this connection an excellent review article dealing with the nonverbal properties of speech has been published elsewhere by Kramer.*

A chapter by Dittmann and Wynne describes a crucial investigation of paralanguage and linguistic variables. This is one of two contributions to this book reprinted from other sources, and it is included herein because of its importance as a landmark on the current status of linguistic and paralinguistic analysis in psychotherapy research. Dittmann, a psychologist, and Wynne, a psychiatrist, conclude that the details of linguistic analysis can be reliably described but apparently do not have any psychological pertinence; whereas paralanguage phenomena have some psychological relevance but cannot be reliably evaluated. Their observations have gone essentially unchallenged in the literature. Trager, a linguist and cultural anthropologist writing in this book, sounds a more hopeful note and reports that a notational system for paralanguage has recently been worked out which appears to have satisfactory reliability. He also recommends that more collaborative research involving linguists and psychotherapists will be bound to overcome some of the unsolved problems in this research area.

* E. Kramer, Judgment of personal characteristics and emotions from nonverbal properties of speech. *Psychol. Bull.,* 60: 408-420, 1963.

13. Linguistic techniques and the analysis of emotionality in interviews

Allen T. Dittmann and Lyman C. Wynne

For many years clinicians and researchers alike have been searching for some way aside from content to conceptualize and measure the emotionality that is expressed in interviews. There is general agreement that while content, or *what* is talked about, is very important, and gives many clues to the inner life of patients, the manner of speech, or *how* things are talked about, enriches the communication immeasurably. Recently the field of linguistics has been seen by many workers to offer the hope of capturing the vocal aspects of communication. Many of the references to linguistics have been impressionistic and programmatic: investigators have been enjoined to study systematically the effects of "tone of voice" in communications. To date only one published research (McQuown, 1957)[1] has used linguistic techniques in analyzing interview material. The study is a pioneering one, but does not attempt to evaluate the techniques in a systematic way.

In the light of the present status of the field, we should like to report our experiences in using microlinguistic techniques in studying interviews. Our results are limited to only one aspect of linguistics, and a very microscopic one at that; so what we have to say must be regarded as a progress report rather than a final evaluation of the entire field.

We wanted several kinds of help from linguistic techniques. First, at the lowest level of abstraction, we wanted some measure of the degree of disturbance shown in the speech. Disturbance in this sense may mean any deviation from the speaker's normal, calm, controlled state, be the deviation the result of anxiety, fear, anger, elation, or whatever. Speech disturbances as a measure of anxiety have been used by Mahl (1956) and Dibner (1958), but their methods were more closely based upon content and grammatical form than we wished them to be for our purposes. One sign used by both Mahl and Dibner, for example, is Sentence Change (Mahl) or Breaking in with New Thought (Dibner). The judgment of this sign depends on the meaning of the words and their syntactical sequence, not on how the words are spoken, and Dibner could thus use typescripts to

From the *Journal of Abnormal and Social Psychology*, 63: 201-204, 1961. Reprinted with permission.

[1] Since this study was completed, a report of another investigation has appeared using linguistic analysis (Pittenger, Hockett, & Danehy, 1960).

make judgments of speech disturbances. Our wish was for a technique that would depend less on content, through which we could delineate very slight disturbances, and thus catch changes more immediately as they occur in the interview.

The second kind of judgment we hoped linguistic techniques could give was that of type of expressed affect. Is the patient asking this question challengingly or from puzzlement? Is the therapist offering this interpretation as an hypothesis or as a foregone conclusion? Answers to questions like these would call upon linguistic techniques not only to tell whether affect is present, but also to specify the meaning of the affect.

The third kind of judgment we hoped for was the most general, that of specifying styles of communication which are important in the development and maintenance of psychopathology. Contradictions and confusions between messages simultaneously or sequentially communicated have recently been stressed as contributory to the etiology and perpetuation of schizophrenia (Bateson, Jackson, Haley, and Weekland, 1956; Ruesch, 1958; Wynne, Ryckoff, Day, and Hirsch, 1958). Statements at this level of abstraction, if they are to be based upon linguistic coding, obviously demand a great deal of the coding system in all of its aspects.

The system of linguistic analysis we have used was developed by Trager, Smith, and Hall. G. L. Trager served as a consultant to our program for 2.5 years, and the writers learned techniques of coding from him directly.[2] Descriptions of the system may be found in Trager and Smith (1951), Pittenger and Smith (1957), and Trager (1958). Only certain aspects of the total system were considered for this study, those which seemed most pertinent to what is usually called "tone of voice." These are parts of spoken language as much as other sounds, even though they are not generally included in the teaching of grammar and style. The elements we coded may be grouped under Linguistic and Paralinguistic phenomena. The Linguistic phenomena were coded in terms of phonemes, which are speech sounds grouped together so that despite local variation, each group has the same meaning to all native speakers of the language. Linguistic methodology makes use of the psychological discontinuity between the phonemic groupings; a same-or-different criterion enables linguists to analyze and code language in terms of phonemes. The Paralinguistic phenomena are superimposed upon the phonemes of speech. They include very diverse phenomena, only some of which lend themselves to discrete coding. Others are not discriminated into discrete groups, but have the character of continua.

Those linguistic phenomena that were coded in this study are juncture, stress, and pitch:

---

[2] The authors wish to extend their thanks to G. L. Trager for the painstaking work which he undertook both in teaching us the techniques and in submitting them to this analysis. The responsibility for this report, however, is entirely ours.

A. *Junctures* are dividing points in speech by which "clauses" are separated from one another. The word clauses is put in quotes, since these may be quite unrelated to clauses as defined by traditional grammar. There are three types of junctures, defined by the amount of lengthening or stretching of the material beginning with the primary stress, and by the pitch phenomena at the very end of the clause.

B. *Stress* refers to the pattern of increase and decrease in loudness within clauses which is additional to the accents on different syllables of multisyllabic words. There are four degrees of stress in English. Each clause must have one and only one primary stress, and may have one or more secondary, tertiary, or weak stresses, depending on the length of the clause and the meaning to be conveyed.

C. *Pitch* refers to the rise and fall of fundamental frequency of the speaker's voice within a clause. There are four pitch levels in English. Most clauses have three pitches although some short ones have only two, and a small minority up to four. The three usual pitches occur at the beginning, at the primary stress, and at the end. Pitch changes in the juncture definitions mentioned above are fine pitch changes superimposed upon the end pitch for a clause.

The Paralinguistic phenomena are grouped under vocalizations, voice quality, and voice set:

A. *Vocalizations* may be of three types:
   1. Vocal Characterizers: laughing, crying, voice breaking.
   2. Vocal Segregates: sounds other than "words" which have specific communicative value, such as "um-hmm," "huh?," and the like.
   3. Vocal Qualifiers: extra increase or decrease in loudness, pitch, and duration beyond what are needed to convey juncture, pitch, and stress patterns.
B. *Voice Quality* carries baseline information about an individual's speech such as tempo, rhythm, precision (or sloppiness) of articulation, breathiness, register range, intensity range, rasp and openness, nasality, and resonance. Changes in these qualities can be indicators of the effects of current situational factors on the usual speech of an individual.
C. *Voice Set* refers to physiological characteristics current in the speaker—fatigue, immaturity, and the like.

METHOD

Sample

The speech samples used for the present study were excerpts from six interviews with a single patient and excerpts from the recording of a radio program. The interviews were chosen for their variability in emotional expression, including direct anger at the psychotherapist, anger about an incident in the past, anxiety in relation to the psychotherapist, panic about an episode of "crazy" acting out, a calm discussion of vocational plans, and a discussion of a novel in an interview conducted by another person. In addition to the interviews with this one patient, we also used excerpts from one session of the NBC radio program *Conversation*, in which Clifton Fadiman and three guests talked in a completely unrehearsed situation about a topic of general interest. This conversation seemed to be an enjoyable "thinking out loud," with the normal tensions of discussion among well-informed people and of the knowledge of the broadcast situation.[3]

Procedure

Excerpts of about 3-minutes' duration from each of the interviews were typed and coded for the Linguistic and Paralinguistic phenomena listed above. Six excerpts from four of the interviews were coded again after a period of 6 months for reliability study. Coding was always done by a group of three coders. While this procedure is subject to the influence of any dominant member of the coding group, it does serve to insure constant alertness to the task, which is at best a tedious one, approximately an hour being required to code one minute of speech material in this detail.

Reliability was checked by comparing the codings of the judges at the two different times. For juncture patterns all possible places where a juncture could occur (usually between words) were tabulated as to presence or absence of junctures, and if one was present, which one was coded. For stress and pitch patterns and for the Paralinguistic phenomena a different unit was necessary for determining reliability. Tallies were made of those places where the codings were made at each session, and agreement between codings was tabulated. Results are reported in terms of percentages of agreement.

For those phenomena which turned out to have high reliability, we next pursued the question of validity, comparing the distribution of the different phenomena among the interview samples of different emotional expression. We also compared the distributions of codings of the patient's speech with those of the speakers in the excerpts of the radio program.

RESULTS

The Linguistic phenomena held up well in the reliability studies. On juncture patterns the agreement on the two of the codings done 6 months apart was very high. The decision as to whether to code a juncture or not produced 93% agreement (the χ^2 was 304.7 for 1 df). Where a juncture was coded both times there was agreement as to which juncture 87% of the time (the χ^2 was 89.5 for 4 df). Complete agreements for pitch and stress were 76% and 87%, respectively.

While the Linguistic phenomena proved to be reliably codeable, the Paralinguistic did not. Vocal Qualifiers such as overhigh and overlow pitch, overloudness and oversoftness, fared less well in the reliability check than did Linguistic phenomena, and there was great variability in agreement between interviews: for example, type of vocal qualifier (not counting differences in onset and cessation) produced agreements of 31% and 77% for the two samples recorded after a 6-months' interval.

---

[3] Kind permission has been given by the program's producer for the use of this material.

For Voice Quality agreement percentages varied even more widely, both from one code to another and from one interview to another for the same code. Often a voice quality was noted at one coding and nothing at all was recorded at the other time. In other instances the label for the voice quality differed; this was not surprising since such clinically impressionistic terms as "petulance" had been used to describe what seemed to be recurring combinations of voice qualities. In the unusual instances when the same label was used in both codings, the points of onset and cessation often differed. Comparison of the elements of voice quality which made up such overall descriptions as "petulance" resulted in different components for the two occasions of coding. Vocal Characterizers and Vocal Segregates were too infrequently occurring in the sample to be subjected to reliability study.

Each time the coding was done there was group consensus as to the description finally made. McQuown (1957) has claimed that settling differences in coding by consensus establishes "verifiability" of the techniques. "Without such a demonstration of methodological reliability, any steps in the characterization [of persons on the basis of the coding]—will run the risk of being unconvincing" (p. 80). We agree that group consensus is necessary for such complex coding, but group consensus is not a test of reliability, and the consensus itself must be subjected to reliability check.

The Linguistic phenomena, juncture, pitch, and stress, which proved reliable enough for further investigation, were next subjected to validity comparisons across the samples of the interviews, and between the samples of the patient speech and those of the conversationalists recorded from the radio program. Our most thorough efforts to find any relation between the variety of emotional expression and the kinds of profiles of Linguistic phenomena coded met with failure. There was no tendency, for example, for any pattern of intonations and junctures to appear more frequently with anger than with calmness. Similarly, judgments of "appropriateness" of these patterns were unrelated to the widely different affects expressed in the interviews. Finally, the participants of the radio program could neither be differentiated from each other nor from the patient by the Linguistic codings.

DISCUSSION

Our studies indicate that the Linguistic patterns (juncture, stress, and pitch) can be described reliably with presently available coding techniques, but that these aspects of speech probably have little psychological relevance. By contrast, the Paralinguistic phenomena (vocalizations, voice quality, and voice set) presumably have higher psychological relevance, but cannot be coded reliably. Our explanation for these findings is that the methods developed in traditional linguistic analysis may not be applicable to the analysis of emotional expression, not because of deficiencies in the field of linguistics, but because of fundamental differences in the nature of language and emotional expression.

The difference lies in the fact that language is made up of discrete elements, while emotional communication in speech consists of continuous phenomena that have more complex interrelations. The elements of any language are usually described as phonemes. Under the definition given previously, these elements are seen as either present or absent, and may be coded as such by the linguist. Phonemes are put together according to a long, but finite, series of rules into words, and words in turn into more complete structures to convey cognitive messages. While there are many words which have different "meanings" in different contexts, still all the elements of language, and to a large extent the meanings they convey, are discrete, and lend themselves to codings of Present or Absent.

Emotional aspects of speech, on the other hand, are different from the cognitive aspects. They have not yet been so completely studied that we can tell if they are describable in Present-Absent terms: it may be that emotional communication is always present in speech. Our experience does show, however, that where these emotional factors occur, they are best described as continua. Seen in this way, coding techniques taken from linguistics are inappropriate to the analysis of emotional factors in speech. Similarly the search for elements of emotional expression, analogous to phonemes in classical linguistics, may be just as inappropriate, or so time consuming as to defeat its own purpose. Global judgments of emotionality in speech where cognitive messages are filtered out electronically, as used by Starkweather (1956a, 1956b), may prove useful in the analysis of interviews long before the elements which form the basis for these judgments are understood. In developing methods for such judgments, the techniques designed for scaling data which fall on continua seem more appropriate than does the search for discrete elements. Trager (1958) has recognized the need for scaling in his most recent formulation by assigning degrees to vocal qualifiers (p. 6). We may hope that linguists, who have extensive experience in listening carefully to speech, will contribute to the application of scaling techniques to this purpose, and may, in the course of this work, find fruitful avenues for further linguistic analysis of emotionality in speech.

SUMMARY

To test the applicability of linguistic techniques to the analysis of emotional expression in speech, excerpts of six psychotherapeutic interviews of markedly different emotional tone and excerpts from an unrehearsed conversation recorded from a radio program were studied. These excerpts were coded on those aspects of the linguistic system developed by Trager and his associates which were presumed to have relevance to "tone of voice": the Linguistic phenomena of juncture, pitch, and stress, and the

Paralinguistic phenomena of vocalizations, voice quality, and voice set. Coding was done by three coders working as a group, and a sample of excerpts was selected for recoding by the same group 6 months later for reliability check. The Linguistic phenomena proved to be highly reliable, while the Paralinguistic did not, but the reliable Linguistic codings were independent of the emotional expression in the different interviews and of the individual differences among the speakers represented by the interviews and the radio program. Explanation for these results was sought in the difference between language proper and emotional expression as communicated by vocal means other than language.

REFERENCES

BATESON, G., JACKSON, D. D., HALEY, J., and WEEKLAND, J. Toward a theory of schizophrenia. *Behav. Sci.*, **1**, 1956, 251-264.

DIBNER, A. S. Ambiguity and anxiety. *J. abnorm. soc. Psychol.*, **56**, 1958, 165-174.

McQUOWN, N. A. Linguistic transcription and specification of psychiatric interview materials. *Psychiatry*, **20**, 1957, 79-86.

MAHL, G. F. Disturbances and silences in the patient's speech in psychotherapy. *J. abnorm. soc. Psychol.*, **53**, 1956, 1-15.

PITTENGER, R. E., HOCKETT, C. F., and DANEHY, J. J. *The first 5 minutes: A sample of microscopic interview analysis.* Ithaca, N.Y.: Paul Martineau, 1960.

PITTENGER, R. E. and SMITH, H. L. A basis for some contributions of linguistics to psychiatry. *Psychiatry*, **20**, 1957, 61-78.

RUESCH, J. The tangential response. In P. H. Hoch and J. Zubin (Eds.), *Psychopathology of communication.* New York: Grune & Stratton, 1958. Pp. 37-48.

STARKWEATHER, J. A. The communication value of content-free speech. *Amer. J. Psychol.*, **69**, 1956, 121-123. (a)

STARKWEATHER, J. A. Content-free speech as a source of information about the speaker. *J. abnorm. soc. Psychol.*, **52**, 1956, 394-402. (b)

TRAGER, G. L. Paralanguage: A first approximation. *Stud. Linguist.*, **13**, 1958, 1-12.

TRAGER, G. L., and SMITH, H. L. *An outline of English structure.* Norman, Okla.: Battenberg Press, 1951.

WYNNE, L. C., RYCKOFF, I. M., DAY, J., and HIRSCH, S. I. Pseudomutuality in the family relations of schizophrenics. *Psychiatry*, **21**, 1958, 205-220.

c. *Kinesic variables*

Haggard and Isaacs, research workers involved in the University of Illinois Psychotherapy Research project, have singled out micromomentary facial expressions as a kinesic variable of interest. These fleeting facial changes last only one-eighth to one-fifth of a second and, as in other types of psychotherapy research, the investigators were obliged to examine the reliability with which different observers could detect the same phenomena. The study of such changes was made possible only by sound-film recordings and running the film at the slow speed of 5 frames per second. Haggard and Isaacs took care to ascertain the degree of confidence one can have in accurately perceiving these subliminal facial movements. They observed that these micromomentary facial expressions can be adjudged, three-fourths of the time, to be incompatible with the contextual affect expression in which they have occurred. Their theoretical formulations to account for these interesting kinesic phenomena provide several hypotheses worth testing in further investigations.

The chapter by Deutsch illustrates a skilled psychoanalyst's attention to the totality of the patient's communication, that is, to the kinesic modality as well as to language. Deutsch is largely responsible for the present awakening of interest in body communication. He finds in the patient's gestures and postures evidence for underlying drives and defenses, such as conflicts between masculine and feminine tendencies. The reader will want to compare Deutsch's approach to kinesics with that of Scheflen. Deutsch finds meaning in each individual gesture. This meaning can be understood if one possesses the key, as in translating hieroglyphics, and to a large extent he perceives a one-to-one relationship between the gesture and the underlying drive. For Scheflen, however, matters are more complicated. He holds that only rarely is the meaning of a single gesture clear and then only in the simplest cases. Instead, he notes complex patterns of communication in which the body language is one element, and to be understood it must be considered in its complicated interaction with the patient's verbal behavior. Whereas Deutsch finds that a bit of behavior indicates, for example, underlying hostility, Scheflen studies that piece of behavior and fits it into a larger pattern which may extend over 15 minutes. The evidence for Deutsch's system for interpreting kinesics consists of its plausibility, internal coherence, and consistency with some aspects of psychoanalytic theory. Like other more or less personal systems, it will of course have to be tried and tested by others.

14. Micromomentary facial expressions as indicators of ego mechanisms in psychotherapy

Ernest A. Haggard and Kenneth S. Isaacs

In psychotherapy research, one is often hard pressed to make sense out of the many behaviors, processes, and other phenomena which can be observed in the therapy situation. The present report is concerned with one class of behaviors and processes which cannot be observed—namely, facial expressions which are so short-lived that they seem to be quicker-than-the-eye. These rapid expressions can be seen when motion picture films are run at about one-sixth of their normal speed. The film and projector thus become a sort of *temporal microscope*, in that they expand time sufficiently to enable the investigator to observe events not otherwise apparent to him.

We first noticed the existence of micromomentary expressions (MMEs) while scanning motion picture films of psychotherapy hours, searching for indications of non-verbal communication between the therapist and patient. Although we discovered something new each time we ran the film at normal speed, we also found it instructive to run the film silently backward or forward, faster or slower, or even frame-by-frame. In fact, such procedures often seemed to give a more vivid picture of the non-verbal aspects of the therapist-patient interchange than when the film provided a reproduction of the events at the same speed with which they transpired in the therapy. During such explorations, for instance, we noted that occasionally the expression on the patient's face would change dramatically within three to five frames of film (as from smile to grimace to smile), which is equivalent to a period of from one-eighth to one-fifth of a second. We were not able to see these expression changes at the normal rate of 24 frames per second (f.p.s.). Being intrigued by this phenomenon, we set out on a long and tedious attempt to study the occurrence and meaning of these micromomentary expression changes and to relate them to other aspects of the therapeutic process.[1]

This investigation was supported by a Public Health Service Research Grant (MH-00637) and a career program award to the senior author (MH-K6-9415), both from the National Institute of Mental Health.

[1] We are grateful to the therapists and patients who contributed the basic records and to Ellis G. Olim, Jean Kavanagh, Edward M. Brown, and Robert W. Lissitz for their assistance in translating them into the data used in this report.

METHODS AND MEASURES

Methods of "Measuring" the Phenomenon

Initially, we scanned the films in an attempt to locate all the instances of identifiable changes of facial expression which occurred in not more than five frames of film; to identify the presumed affective content (e.g., anger, disdain, pleasure) of these expressive bursts; to locate their precise occurrence during the hour; and, by running the film at regular speed, to collate them with the concurrent verbal statements. This procedure had several drawbacks. It was not only very time consuming but, in addition, we quite frequently obtained inconsistent findings in terms of both inter-judge and intra-judge agreement. In other words, often two different judges could not agree on the occurrence of a given MME and, occasionally, the same judge could not "see" it again. Presumably, the inherent subtlety and fleetingness of the phenomenon, the difficulty of pinpointing the start and end of the MME, differences in the judges' ability to perceive it, differences in their subjective definition of it, and fluctuations of attention (sometimes due to boredom) accounted for the unreliability and instability of the findings obtained by these procedures.

On the basis of our initial work, we adopted the following scoring conventions in order to increase the ease of scoring and the objectivity and reliability of our measures:

1. The judge should assume a mental set of passive alertness, which in the visual modality is similar to "listening with the third ear" or "free-hovering attention" in the auditory modality. That is, the judge should not focus directly on any specific muscle group or look for specific facial movements, but should observe the face as a whole (as in conversation) for changes of facial expression.

2. During their training period, judges should work in groups of two or more, each viewing the film together at slow speed (4 f.p.s.) and at normal speed (24 f.p.s.). As any judge observes a change of expression the projector should be stopped and the film segment rerun to help make explicit the exact location of the change and the cues used to identify it. After training, judges may work separately, using the following *scoring rules*:

3. Each *film segment* should be divided into *judgment units* which are to be viewed at both slow and normal speeds. For a two-minute film segment judged at slow speed (4 f.p.s.), each judgment unit runs six seconds (i.e., 24 frames), giving 120 judgments for each film segment. At normal speed (24 f.p.s.) each unit runs five seconds, giving 24 judgments for each film segment.[2] With the film running silently, the *total number of*

---

[2] We found 4 f.p.s. to be optimal for slow-speed viewing. At slower speeds it was difficult to maintain the perception of the constant flow of expression; at faster speeds it was difficult to observe all changes of expression. Viewing-time intervals of 5-6 sec. were used so as not to tax the attention or memory span of the judges. It should also be noted that the films of the patients were *close-ups* (i.e., head and torso); the difficulty of judging changes of facial expression increases as the image size of the subject decreases.

changes of expression per judgment unit should be observed and recorded independently for both slow and normal speeds.

4. Each expression change should involve a shift from one identifiable expression to a qualitatively different expression, involving some motion of the facial muscles as evidenced by motion of the overlying skin and features. Movements of only the eyes or movements of the mouth, tongue, or jaw involved directly in speech, for example, should not be scored as changes of facial expression.

5. If the subject's face is turned away from the camera, or his hand covers at least half of the face (e.g., when his mouth and/or eyes cannot be seen) for at least half of a judgment unit, a "no score" is to be assigned to that judgment unit.

6. The codings for expression changes at both slow and normal speeds are to be collated with the concurrent verbal transcript. (The collation of the various measures—verbal content and expression changes—is greatly facilitated if the film is edge-marked at one-foot intervals at the time of development.)

The data obtained by our initial and revised scoring procedures are not strictly comparable. In the former we sought to identify the MMEs directly; in the latter we *subtracted the number of expression changes observed at normal speed from the number observed at slow speed.* The resultant *difference score* is correlated with, but is not identical to, the occurrence of MMEs. It may be assumed, however, that a large difference score, which indicates a series of rapid expression changes, will contain some expressions which are not observable at normal speed. When it was desirable to isolate instances of MME, using the criterion that they should be visible at slow but not at normal viewing speed, the revised scoring procedure served as an intermediate step: MMEs presumably occur more frequently in the segments with large difference scores.

Reliability of the Measures

To obtain estimates of the reliability of the judgments of the changes in facial expression which can be observed from films run at slow and at normal speeds, we set up the following design: films of two therapy hours (one from each of two patients) were divided into fifths, and a *two-minute segment* was taken (as a sample) from each fifth of each hour. Two judges, after a preliminary training period, independently viewed each of the ten segments at slow (4 f.p.s.) and at normal (24 f.p.s.) speeds, and noted the number of changes of facial expression which could be observed during each judgment unit, as described above. The findings of this study, involving 1,440 pairs of judgments, are summarized in Table 1.

The reliability of the judgments can be viewed either in terms of the correlation coefficients which indicate the extent to which the two judges

Table 1

Estimates of Inter-judge Reliability for Judgments of Expression Change

Speed of Film	Film Segments		Reliability Coefficients[a]		Changes Observed[b]		"No Change" Observed[c]	
	Judgments Per Segment	Number of Segments	Range	Average	Range	Average	Range	Average
Slow								
(4 f.p.s.)	n = 120	10	.30-.70[d]	.50	38-91	55.2	37%-77%	62.6%
Normal								
(24 f.p.s.)	n = 24	10	.14-.89[d]	.55	5-27	20.7	31%-84%	46.6%

  a Coefficients of intraclass correlation were computed to estimate the inter-judge reliabilities for each of the 10 segments at both speeds. (See E. A. Haggard. *Intraclass correlation and the analysis of variance.* New York: Holt, Rinehart and Winston, 1958.)
  b Average number of expression changes (adjusted for "no scores") observed per judgment unit.
  c Percent of judgment units during which no expression change was observed.
  d For the degrees of freedom involved, correlations above .21 for segments run at slow speed, and above .46 for segments run at normal speed, are statistically significant at the .01 level.

agreed on the occurrence and number of observed expression changes or the extent of their agreement that no change occurred. From Table 1 it is clear that many of the coefficients for individual segments are not so high as one would like them to be. One is also struck by their range (e.g., .14 to .89 for the ten segments at normal speed). However, when the coefficients are averaged (via the z transformation), the values of .50 and .55 are *statistically significant* well beyond the .01 level. Table 1 also shows that in a large proportion (on the average, around half) of the judgment units, no change of expression was observed. Some evidence for inter-judge reliability is seen in the fact that the judges tended to agree regarding the proportion of judgments in which no change was observed when viewing the ten segments at the slow and normal speeds ($r= .73$; $P = .02$).

Since the judges viewed the ten film segments at both the slow and normal speeds, it is instructive to compare these two sets of data. Perhaps the clearest difference is in the number of observed changes of facial expression: about two and a half times as many changes were observed when the film was run at slow speed, with no overlap between the two distributions (e.g., 5-27 for normal and 38-91 for slow speed).[3] It is pointless to do a *significance test* on such data. These findings clearly indicate that many of the expression changes which could be observed at the slow speed eluded the judges when the film was run at normal speed—that is, the rate which reproduced what occurred during therapy.

  [3] There were also 16 percent more *no change* judgments made when the film was run at the slow than at the normal speed. But this difference may be (in part) an artifact of our method. Since there were five times as many judgment units for the slow as for the normal speed, it is to be expected that some brief expression changes were split between two different judgment units, and hence were not observed.

The information loss which occurs at normal speed is not a matter of simple decrement. If it were, we would expect the number of changes observed at the two speeds to be proportional, which would be indicated by a correlation (r) of 1.00 between these two measures. But this r is only .75. Also, even though the averaged reliability coefficients of .50 and .55 do not differ much, the range and variability of the coefficients for the ten segments viewed at normal speed are appreciably greater than the corresponding values for slow speed. When these two distributions are compared (via z) in terms of their variances, the difference is significant (F for 9/9 d.f. $= 4.70$; $P = .05$). Finally, in considering both the percentage of judgment units when *no change* was observed (e.g., 62.6%) and the *average number* of observed changes (e.g., 55.2%) at the slow speed, it is apparent that the expression changes frequently occurred in *bursts*, so that many of them were too rapid or fleeting to be observed at the normal viewing speed.

The factors which determine the wide variation in the observation of expression changes at the two film speeds are complex and largely unknown. But from the data in Table 1 it is clear that the different portions of the film are anything but uniform. The number, speed, and type of expression changes in any judgment unit no doubt influence the ease and accuracy with which they may be observed, and hence judged. It is also to be expected that individual judges will differ in their ability to observe accurately those expression changes which do occur, and that under the more difficult condition of viewing the film at normal (as opposed to the slower) speed, such individual differences will be accentuated.

SOME REPRESENTATIVE FINDINGS

Our investigation of rapid changes of facial expression and their correlates has been relatively unsystematic thus far—partly because we lacked clear theoretical or methodological guidelines when we began and partly because of the time required to analyze carefully even short segments of film. Our strategy has been to explore a series of hunches or leads, several of which are still in the process of being investigated.

Some of the findings presented in this section are based upon our initial scoring procedure; others are based on our revised procedures. It should also be noted that in some instances *reliability checks* were not conducted—that is, the data are based on the judgments of a single trained observer. But the accuracy or reliability of the judgments will vary with the phenomena to be judged. Satisfactory agreement among judges can be obtained when the task is merely to designate the occurrence of an expression change; it is more difficult to obtain satisfactory agreement when the task is to identify and designate the impulse or affect which presumably underlies any particular expression or expression change. (The task of designating affective states from facial expressions would be simplified if only single and discreet affects were involved and if all individuals expressed them similarly.) To avoid excessive detail, the findings reported in this section are limited to those in which the measures are judged to be at least reasonably stable and reliable.

The Variability of Rapid Expression Changes

As we have already seen from the reliability data, variability seems to be the most characteristic feature of rapid changes of facial expression. As one might expect, we found large individual differences from patient to patient. These differences are illustrated by the following study. We divided the transcripts of the therapy hours of two patients into content segments (based on changes of manifest content) and determined: the rate of expression change observed at normal film speed, the difference in rate observed at slow and at normal speeds, and the percent of time the patient was speaking during each segment of the therapy hour.

The data for the two patients, both in psychotherapy with training analysts, are given in Figure 1. For Patient A we see that the three measures tend to be parallel over the hour (the average r for the three measures over the 12 content segments is .87), so that they tend to rise and fall together (tending to rise after the segments during which the therapist is active). For Patient B, on the other hand, the three measures are much less concordant throughout the hour (the average r over the 24 content segments is .21) and the r between the two measures of expression change is -.44 for the first 12 segments—but is .68 for the second 12 segments.

Patient B also showed great variability from session to session. During the hour represented in Figure 1, this patient emitted 98 MMEs, but only three could be observed during another hour which was marked by a stubborn depressive mood, long silences, and little movement or expressiveness of any kind.

Some Correlates of Rapid Expression Changes

Initially, we had the impression that rapid changes of facial expression occur most often during a phase of general expressiveness, as indicated by gestures, overt bodily movement, and speech—especially during the discussion of affective states or content.[4] From our findings to date, this

[4] Speech, more than other forms of expression, seems to "pull the cork" on otherwise controlled impulses and affects. Thus, for Patient B in Figure 1, rate of speech was correlated with the difference score .43 ($P = .05$), but rate of expressions observed at normal speed was correlated only .18 with the difference score and .00 with speech.

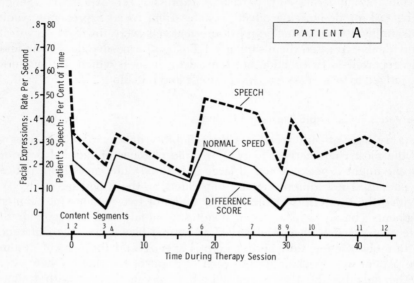

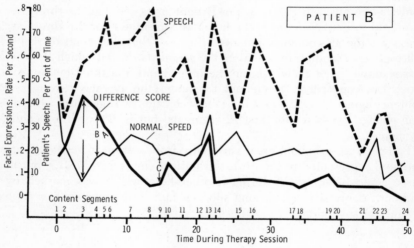

Figure 1

Relationships Among Measures of Rate of Patient's Speech, Facial Expressions
Observed at Normal Film Speed, and Difference Between Expressions Observed
at Slow and Normal Speeds During Representative Therapy Hours of
Two Patients

generalization seems to be valid when the individual's normal controls (or defenses) are functioning effectively; it is not necessarily valid when the individual is in active conflict—that is, anxious or ambivalent with respect to his (conscious or preconscious) feelings and impulses and how he wishes to express them.[5]

Several findings suggest that MMEs tend to occur in a context of conflict. For example, when the content of one therapy hour was categorized in terms of 14 major themes, we found that the MMEs tended to be associated with both denial statements by the patient (e.g., "I was *not* angry at . . .") and with instances of verbal blocking ($r = .61$). The MMEs also tended to be incongruent with the concurrent verbal content and the adjacent facial expressions. Thus, the patient may show a micromomentary burst of anger while talking about liking someone ($\chi^2\ 1_{d.f.} = 8.29$; $P = .01$) and, similarly, the MME tends to be incompatible with the facial expressions which precede and follow it—as from pleasure to anger to pleasure ($\chi^2\ 1_{d.f.} = 8.18$; $P = .01$).[6]

Rapid changes of facial expression can be evaluated from a clinical as well as from a theoretical point of view. This can be done in several ways. In one case (Patient B, Figure 1), the therapist re-viewed the therapy hour by watching the motion picture film of it. The film, which had been divided into the 24 content segments, was run at normal speed until the end of each segment, then stopped while the therapist commented on it.[7] During the first part of this hour (when the patient related a conflict-ridden dream) there was an unusually high incidence of rapid changes of facial expression. Coincidental to the data in Figure 1, the therapist

[5] In a related study from this project (MH-00637), a psychoanalyst (Dr. Leon Bernstein), in collaboration with the authors, rated single therapy hours of two patients for several types of expressive behavior. These ratings included the patient's defensive maneuvers during the hour (e.g., whether at any particular time the patient was in an "expressive," "defensive" or "wavering" phase) from the typescripts; verbal behavior (e.g., language disturbances) from the tape recordings; and overt behavior (e.g., postural shifts) from the films of these hours. In this study, language disturbances ($\chi^2\ 2_{d.f.} = 10.76$; $P = .01$) and postural shifts ($\chi^2\ 2_{d.f.} = 8.73$; $P = .05$) tended to occur during the wavering phase more frequently than during the expressive or defensive phases. Although these films have not been studied for the occurrence of MMEs, from our other findings we would expect them to occur primarily during the wavering phase when the patient is "on the fence" or in conflict regarding the acceptance or non-acceptance of his impulses and affects, which are neither openly expressed nor well controlled.

[6] The MMEs were judged to be incompatible with their context in about three-fourths and compatible (but different from) their context in about one-fourth of the observations in the two samples used to compute these chi-squares. Usually the compatible MME was an exaggeration of its context expression, as a more emphatic expression of the impulse or affective state.

[7] For each segment, the therapist's remarks covered, for example, the latent meaning of what the patient had said during the segment, the nature and strength of conflict, the relation between the content of the segment and earlier or subsequent material, the nature of any transference and counter-transference phenomena, etc. In all, the therapist spent about three hours discussing this 50-minute therapy session.

made the following independent observations: At point A (i.e., the end of segment three), the therapist remarked, "It appears to me that waves of anxiety, perhaps, are crossing (the patient's) face, and are being brought under control only with (the patient's) restless movements." At point B the therapist said, "It is very interesting that while (the patient) is telling this material, (the patient's) facial expression changes. The tension and anxiety go out of it." Again, at point C the therapist noted that "at this point I think there has been a great deal of relaxation of the hostile tension in the mother transference with which the hour opened up and the first part of the dream was told. (The patient) seems very relaxed, very comfortable toward me." Although this therapist's remarks may not "prove" anything, they strongly suggest that meaningful relationships exist between the data in Figure 1 and the content and dynamics of the therapy hour.

The proposition that micromomentary changes of facial expression appear to be related to the individual's intrapsychic dynamics is supported by a comparison of the occurrence of MMEs and the manifest content with which they are associated. In one case, for example, we classified the patient's verbal material in terms of the significant persons (or surrogates of them) discussed during the therapy session, and tallied the number of MMEs which occurred while each of them was being discussed. Part of these data are given in Table 2.[8] These data indicate that the MMEs tended to be associated with some classifications much more than with others, suggesting that the high relative occurrence of MMEs was associated with particular foci of cathexis and/or conflict in this patient. The inferences implicit in the data in Table 2 are, incidentally, congruent with the therapist's formulation of the case.

Table 2
Example of Disproportionate Occurrence of Micromomentary Expressions to Content Areas During One Hour of Therapy

Representative Areas of Verbal Content	Number of Micromomentary Expressions	Total Number of Verbal References to Content Areas	Relative Occurrence of Expressions*
Parental role	4	38	10.5
Spouse	0	12	0.
Children	6	26	23.1
Blond women	35	57	61.4
Brunette women	0	7	0.
Sensuality: women	10	15	66.7
Sensuality: men	5	20	25.0

* The relative occurrence (i.e., percentage) values are obtained as follows: $4/38 = 10.5$ percent.

[8] Because of our intent to present our findings on the level of processes rather than personalities, those classifications which might identify the patient were omitted.

CONCLUDING COMMENTS

Some Methodological Considerations

Various approaches might be taken to explore further the phenomena discussed in this report. For example:

1. It would be useful to check the occurrence of MMEs with a *phonetic control,* such as an actor (matched for age, sex, and general facial features) who can reproduce verbal passages taken from the sound films of the therapy hours which contain a high incidence of MMEs. Although we cannot be certain at this point, we doubt that the actor would show MMEs in the same number or in the same location as the patient, for two reasons. One is that the occurrence of MMEs seems to be associated with the patient's own intrapsychic processes; the other is that MMEs are non-functional (and even may interfere with) the straightforward production of speech sounds, although MMEs may be functional in other ways.

2. Films of persons in situations other than psychotherapy should be studied to determine the extent to which rapid changes of facial expression occur and some of the personal and situational factors which appear to elicit them. In a pilot study of non-therapy films, character structure and situational stress seemed to be reflected in expression changes of the sort which we have discussed but, unfortunately, clinical, personality, and related types of data were not available to collate with the occurrence of the MMEs.

3. It would be interesting to sample segments of the film over the duration of several therapies, with special reference to major themes as they wax and wane during the therapy. It may be that MMEs serve the function of "trial balloons," by means of which the patient preconsciously finds out whether he can openly express particular affects without retaliation or rejection; if so, MMEs may be precursors of affects to be expressed more openly later in the therapy.

4. Another type of approach would be to study the concurrent or sequential facial expressions of the therapist and the patient in vis à vis psychotherapy. It may be possible by this means to determine whether, or to what extent, they respond to each other in terms of either MMEs or the somewhat slower expression changes. If the therapist and patient do respond in this manner, does the sequence of such expression changes vary over different phases of the therapy (as during the early, middle, and final stages of it, or when they are working effectively together or are at loggerheads, or when transference or counter-transference phenomena are in evidence)?

5. Finally, the comments of the therapist of Patient *B* in Figure 1 who, on seeing the film of the hour, reported that "waves of anxiety, perhaps,

are crossing (the patient's) face" suggests that sensitive observers are aware of much more than the manifest expressions in the face of the person they are observing. It would be useful to determine the extent to which observers differ in their ability to perceive accurately rapid changes of facial expression and the major correlates of this ability.

Some Theoretical Considerations

We believe that many MMEs occur so rapidly that they are subliminal. From our experience to date, judges have been quite unaware of facial changes that came and went in from three to five frames (about 1/5 sec.) when the film was run at normal speed (24 f.p.s.). For expressions lasting from about six to ten frames (about 2/5 sec.), careful observers were aware that "something happened," but could not identify the content of the expressions.[9] Expressions of longer duration usually were identified, although sometimes their content was ambiguous and different observers interpreted them differently.

The phenomenon of subliminal changes of facial expression raises a variety of theoretical issues and questions. One set has to do with the observer; another set has to do with the person who is observed. For example:

1. Have we, as adult observers, learned *not* to see some aspects of what occurs "before our very eyes?" Or, more specifically, is our inability to perceive MMEs inherent or acquired? In this connection Lorenz, on the basis of his naturalistic observation of animals, speculated that man's ability to perceive very rapid and subtle expression changes has degenerated because of his reliance on language in communicating with others.[10] From his findings, however, there is no reason to believe that man's ability to perceive (or not to perceive) subtle expression changes is due to a decrement of inherent perceptual capacity.

If children are notorious for their ability to see through the mask of the stereotyped expressions and gestures that go with what we call "socialized behavior," it suggests that certain of their capacities become dampened and their expression stylized as they grow up. Creativity in art productions, or an unbridled fantasy life, may be similar instances of capacities

---

[9] It is quite possible that the therapist of Patient *B* referred to expressions in this second category, partly because many of the expressions of three to five frames duration during segment three appear to express anger more than anxiety.

[10] Lorenz states that "The mysterious apparatus for transmitting and receiving the sign stimuli which convey moods is age-old, far older than mankind itself. In our own case, it has doubtless degenerated as our word-language developed. Man has no need of minute intention-displaying movements to announce his momentary mood: he can say it in words. But jackdaws or dogs are obliged to 'read in each other's eyes' what they are about to do in the next moment. For this reason, in higher and social animals, the transmitting, as well as the receiving, apparatus of 'mood-convection' is much better developed and more highly specialized than in us humans" (pp. 77-78). See K. A. Lorenz, *King Solomon's Ring*. New York: Crowell, 1952.

that seem to diminish with the passing of childhood. Perhaps as an individual acquires the ability to master socially unacceptable impulses and to develop ordered and stable interpersonal relationships, he also sacrifices some of his potentialities, including perceptual ones. It is also possible that an ego mechanism such as "perceptual defense" may interfere with the perception of objects or events which, if one were to observe them fully, would activate impulses, conflicts, or anxieties which one had succeeded in forgetting.

2. Why does the patient (or anyone for that matter) "emit" MMEs, since it is a contradiction to say that one consciously intends to communicate something that cannot even be perceived? There are at least two possible explanations for the occurrence of MMEs. One is that the individual unconsciously intends to communicate the content of the MME as well as its context expression. If this were the case, we would assume that, more often than not, the individual intends to communicate ambivalence or conflict since, according to our findings, the MME usually was incompatible with its context expression. Another (and more likely) possibility is that MMEs are merely expressions, without intent to communicate. In this case, the occurrence of MMEs would indicate the existence of an ego mechanism which we may call *temporal censorship*. Thus, in addition to the ego controls which regulate (or even inhibit) the expression of particular impulses or affects or the awareness of particular fantasies or memories, we assume that these controls also have a temporal dimension. Consequently, the MME may serve as a safety valve to permit at least the very brief expression of unacceptable impulses and affects. From this point of view the MMEs have a double benefit to the individual: he may indulge in some impulse expression with minimal risk of retaliation or rejection by the observer, and without arousing the anxiety that would ensue if he himself were aware of, or of having expressed, the unacceptable impulse or affect.

In conclusion, our findings suggest that the study of MMEs may increase our understanding of the psychotherapeutic process. If, as one assumes, therapy results in intrapsychic as well as behavioral changes, one would expect to find during therapy some instability in the balance of forces between the previously established controls and the newly released but as yet unintegrated impulses and affects. This transitional stage of instability may lead to an increased occurrence of MMEs during therapy; if so, MMEs may be indicators of therapeutic change. One would expect that as therapy succeeds, the individual will achieve a more flexible intrapsychic balance—or, in less abstract terms, greater inner harmony which also permits more effective relationships with others.

15. Some principles of correlating verbal and non-verbal communication

Felix Deutsch

In an exploratory associative interview I try to find out how bodily non-verbal expressions are related to the personality and the emotional condition of the patient, because such a correlation may add to the understanding of our entire therapeutic approach to patients in general. The object of psychotherapy is to ease the inner conflicts of the patient and to strengthen his ego—to help him adjust to life better with fewer defenses to the reality in which he lives. I approach him not only as he presents himself as an adult with his struggles, but as he has been in the past, and as he has developed. I try to take him back into the past where his conflicts originated and developed. In recalling them he can then use them for a confrontation with himself as an adult, see himself in another light, and attempt to resolve his conflicts consciously and maturely.

This paper will deal with observations of the relationships of verbal and postural behavior of the patient and therapist during the psychotherapeutic interview. The underlying theories and deductions used during the process of psychotherapy in our research will be illustrated by the presentation of the transcript of the first half of a psychotherapeutic interview, including notations and comments about the postural patterns of both the patient and therapist. The non-verbal behavior of an individual includes not only postural behavior but also physiological responses; a consideration of the latter will not be included in the present report.

Before presenting the transcript of the interview it will be well to set forth the rationale for studying the patient's postural behavior along with his words. The heart of the argument is the fact that the patient will evoke his recollections of the past not only in words but also by his behavior. His bodily reactions will contain the residues of past emotional struggles. Conflicts which may be hidden by ego defenses will nevertheless be revealed by his motility and postural patterns. Such patterns may thus indi-

This paper is a partial report from the Veterans Administration Outpatient Clinic, Boston, Massachusetts, on the project P4-256, "Correlation of Non-verbal Communication with Verbal Communication in Clinical Interviews," and Project M-282, "Correlation of Verbal with Non-verbal Communication in Associative Anamnesis."

These projects were carried out with the assistance of the staff of the Outpatient Clinic and of Morris Adler, M.D.

cate the depth of the patient's illness and the extent of his improvement. A more detailed discussion of these concepts and theories can be obtained from other publications (Deutsch, 1949, 1950, 1951, 1952, 1953, 1955, 1959).

The patient's contact with the interviewer evokes the process of transference, which means a revival of relationships to figures of the past whom the interviewer may catalyze for the patient. The psychotherapeutic situation also revives for the patient the relationships of the patient to himself in the past, memories which determine his present symptoms, what he feels, and what he thinks of himself. These feelings and thoughts are often only incompletely expressed in words. In the process of the interview, it is essentially the patient's motor behavior which compensates for the incompleteness of his verbalizations. For this reason the motor behavior should be closely observed, in the context of what he says, to establish a meaningful and reliable correlation with verbal data, and to arrive at an understanding of the underlying psychodynamics of the patient's symptoms. Although we cannot always recognize in a face-to-face interview to what extent the verbal behavior of a patient is consciously determined, we can take it for granted that postural behavior is always unconsciously conditioned. Postural associations might even have a deeper-rooted meaning than the verbal ones. The goal of such an interview is to clarify the meaning of the symptoms, which can best be achieved by deciphering the code of postural communication. A closer scrutiny will always reveal that these communications are not randomly chosen, but that their elements are assembled in a fixed form which will occur again and again in a specific sequence.

The movements of the therapist will also be reported in our transcript. The reason we do so is that if we claim that the patient expresses with his body that which he does not verbalize, we have to postulate that the interviewer has similar, though controlled needs. The patient's motility patterns are not voluntary expressions; they are involuntary, and they accompany the verbal expressions as an unconscious stimulation of the motility sphere. A greater measure of control enters into the interviewer's movements. These are, to a certain extent, consciously designed to facilitate the flow of free associations. They are part of the total interchange between therapist and patient.

If the importance of postural patterns is granted, there is still the question of how they are to be understood. What do postures and movements mean? The interpretations we place on them are derived from three basic principles:

1. Unconscious emotional needs which cannot be discharged in words lead to motility and postural behavior. Transference attitudes are an especially important example of these needs.

2. The nature of certain postural activities is revealed when they occur in association with specific verbalized mental contents. This is particularly

true where there are repetitive patterns of simultaneous body and thought expressions.

3. Our knowledge of the patient's personality make-up helps to clarify the meaning of his gestures. Here we refer both to the relatively permanent aspects of personality and to short-lived states such as temporary identifications with internal objects. The patient's motility patterns may change as he alternately identifies with and rejects various incorporated objects. Postural behavior, once understood, throws further light on the patient's personality structure. The process of understanding thus proceeds in two directions at once.

The transcript of the interview also illustrated the method of associative anamnesis. In this method of interviewing, the patient's free associations lead to expression of his emotional and bodily feelings in words and behavior. The therapist, through his words and behavior patterns, creates an atmosphere which is optimal for the flow of the patient's associations. The therapist does not introduce any words which the patient has not already uttered; in this way the patient is not induced to use the interviewer's verbiage. The application of these principles will be illustrated in the commentary to the transcript.

SUMMARY OF PATIENT'S HISTORY

This 37-year-old patient was seen for the first time on October 11, 1956 when he presented himself for help with pains in the chest and the stomach. A recent medical examination had disclosed no physical causes to account for these symptoms. The patient felt that his nervousness was undoubtedly related to his somatic symptoms and told of a general feeling of restlessness and anxiety.

In appearance the patient was a large, well groomed, well dressed, polite, readily talkative individual who showed extreme evidence of anxiety with excessive perspiration and cold skin.

He readily slipped into the past as he talked about his difficulties, feeling that they were all due to his childhood. He gave a past history replete with many instances of neurotic behavior, memories of extreme unhappiness in his home, and marked feelings of insecurity. As far back as he could remember everyone in his family was screaming and yelling, and fighting with each other. He told of an Italian Catholic father and of a mother who belonged to the "Holy Jumpers Church." The mother was so religious that she would not permit the patient, his oldest sister, and his younger brother to attend movies, constantly reminding them that the devil might infect them at any time. The patient related an incident in which his older sister was having a convulsion on the floor and people ran into the house screaming, "She's got the devil! She's got the devil!" They all shouted and pointed at her, and it was finally decided that the sister had attended a movie and "got the devil" from the movie. Subsequently she was converted to the mother's church. His father could neither read nor write and went on welfare when the patient was 12. The mother worked. The patient did much of the cooking. The father always ridiculed the patient, comparing him to a pig, and constantly encouraged him to get married so that the father could have somebody who could adequately take care of him. The patient did marry, and stated that he, his wife, his daughter, six, and his son, two, got along quite harmoniously.

The patient worked as the manager of a women's hairdressing parlor and earned $5500 a year. He claimed he could make much more if he just had the courage to go out and get a better job. He was on 70 percent government disability due to a psychoneurotic condition. He feared financial insecurity as a result of which he might be in a helpless, dependent situation. He was constantly trying to figure out ways that he could avoid this.

A sister about ten years older than he died in the Cocoanut Grove fire. The younger brother was living. The sister had considerable influence on the patient's upbringing, but she preferred the younger brother. The mother devoted a great deal of the time to her religious activities and taking care of sick people. The patient said she seldom was home to get food for them. If they complained she would sometimes get angry and beat them. When he was a child he feared his mother and he blamed more of his difficulties on the mother than on the father.

REFERENCES

DEUTSCH, F. *Applied psychoanalysis: Selected objectives of psychotherapy.* New York: Grune & Stratton, 1949.

DEUTSCH, F. Thus speaks the body. I. An analysis of postural behavior. Trans. by *N. Y. Acad. Sci., Series 2*, **22**: 2, 1949.

DEUTSCH, F. Thus speaks the body. II. A psychosomatic study of vasomotor behavior. *Acta. Med. Orient.*, **9**: 8-9, 1950.

DEUTSCH, F. Thus speaks the body. IV. Some psychosomatic aspects of the respiratory disorder asthma. *Acta Med. Orient.*, **10**: 3-4, 1951.

DEUTSCH, F. The art of interviewing and abstract art. *Am. Imago.*, **9**: 1, 1952.

DEUTSCH, F. Thus speaks the body. III. Analytic posturology. *Psa. Quart.*, **20**: 1952.

DEUTSCH, F. Basic psychoanalytic principles in psychosomatic disorders. *Acta Psychother.*, **1**: 2, 1953.

DEUTSCH, F. On the formation of the conversion symptom. In, F. Deutsch (Ed.), *On the mysterious leap from the mind to the body.* New York: International Universities, 1959.

DEUTSCH, F., and MURPHY, W. F. *The clinical interview.* New York: International Universities, 1955.

A Fragment of a Sound Filmed Psychiatric Interview Demonstrating Dr. Felix Deutsch's Concepts.

Number 1:

Illustrating Kinesic Variables

Interview Data	Veteran-Patient's Postural Movements and Changes	Therapist's* Postural Movements and Changes	Dr. Deutsch's Comments
Dr. D. How do you do?	Enters room. Sits and clasps hands; moves head and body to right. Left thumb moves up while hands clasped.[1]	Stands up; shakes patient's hand. Sits down; left elbow on arm of chair; both hands holding eyeglasses; hands resting over lap.	1. Any patient entering an interpersonal relationship with an interviewer who is almost a complete stranger needs to assemble his defenses. His unconscious feelings have to be controlled. The initial postural configuration illustrates the adjustment which the patient's ego finds most tolerable. In the present case the patient's need for control is expressed through the clasping of his hands. The initial posture taken in an interview is very often only a try-out, the basic one not being displayed until a secure personal interrelationship is established, which finally leads to minimal defensive postural configurations.
Pt. How do you do, Doctor?			
Dr. D. Will you take a seat here?			
Pt. Yes.			
Dr. D. I am much interested in seeing you again and to hear how everything is going.		Bends forward.	
Pt. Oh, it's coming along pretty good. I'm trying very hard.			
Dr. D. What did you say?		Looks at patient, moving head to the right.	
Pt. I'm trying very hard.			
Dr. D. In what way?			
Pt. And, uh. . . Well, to understand my problem.			

CODE:
     ' = Minutes
     " = Seconds
     - - - = Word at which 15" interval occurs
     ———— = Word or words emphasized by therapist or patient
* *Observers of movements:*
     Therapist—Dr. Mary Eichhorn
     Veteran-Patient—Miss E. Katz
NOTE: Superscript numbers in "Interview Data" column refer to Dr. Deutsch's comments.

Time	Patient / Therapist	Movement		Interpretation
	Dr. D. What do you mean by your problem?[2]			2. The therapist repeats the word "problem," thus inducing the patient to develop associations. The latter responds by saying "inferiority complex." "Problem-inferiority complex" become the first key words.
Pt. 30" 45"	Well, my, uh, inferiority complex that I've developed. I'm trying to correct it, and, uh, what I always wanted to do was to recapture what I lost in my, in the childhood days, like, uh, not doing well in school, and, as you[3] know, I told	Moves body forward	Nods head	3. The patient moves his body towards the therapist when he says that he always wanted to recapture what he lost. The movement towards the therapist is an unconscious attempt to get from the therapist what he has "lost."
1'	you the last time,—I believe I did, that, uh, I only want, well, I've only gone as far as the sixth grade, and I was sixteen years old when			
1'15"	I left the sixth grade. Today I feel kind of bad about that, and I've felt I should have done better,[4] if I'd had the proper bringing up, and I was held back four year. . . -four times in	Moves head forward Right thumb moves up	Nods head	4. Moves his head toward therapist when the latter nods. The therapist's nod of course conveys acceptance. The patient's movement of his head in response is already a transference manifestation. To "I should have done better," he moves right thumb up. This display of a phallic symbol is a compensatory, masculine-aggressive gesture. There is probably identification with the interviewer as well as unconscious aggression directed toward him. "I want to be as strong as you. I want to be like you and have what you have."
			Nods head	
1'30"	school, and I was just a complete failure in[5] school, and, uh, and I was thinking that, uh, maybe there's a way of recapturing that,—to	Moves head to left		5. "I was a failure" is accompanied by head movement to the left. Since the patient is right-handed,

171

Interview Data	Veteran-Patient's Postural Movements and Changes	Therapist's Postural Movements and Changes	Dr. Deutsch's Comments
1'45" learn my basic English, basic math,[6] and, uh, and to me it does not,—I don't feel comfortable, don't feel at ease knowing that I was a failure in school. And I dream about them; they bother me; I think about them, and, uh, and that's why I come here[7]. I want to find out if there's a way of my recapturing that. If there isn't, I'll just have to forget about it, I guess. Do you follow me? If I can recapture that. I feel kind of bad about it, and I feel resentful, too, and, and I, well, I blamed it on my parents,[8] maybe I shouldn't have, for being ridiculed as a child and for being ignored,—no help,—and I remember when, when I was a child and I went to school, the first day in school I didn't even	Moves hands forward	Nods head	his left side symbolizes passivity and femininity. The gesture thus expresses the same sense as the verbal content. This may be a reaction to the previous show of strength expressed with the right thumb.
2'			6. "There is a way of recapturing"—he moves hands forward.
2'15"	Moves hands forward	Bends forward	7. "I come here to recapture" he says and moves first both hands and then 3 times the right hand upward. The movement of the right hand again symbolizes the aggressive, masculine drive.
	Moves right hand up right hand is up		
2'30"	Clasps hands		8. "I blamed it on my parents," who ignored him and he brings the hands together and clasps them. One hand is holding down the other, which expresses the humiliated, repressed status that he is describing. He tried to be on his own and moves right thumb up.
2'45" know how to speak English, and the teacher gave me a hard time. And in those days, they used to call us "Guineas," all the Italian extraction. Of course, my folks were, at that time, probably in this country only four or five years; they could not express themselves. They brought me to school, and that was it; I was on my own from then on, and I remember the teachers[9] and they would just consider us a bunch of "Guineas," and any idiosyncrasies that my	Moves hands up Clasps hands	Nods head	
	Right thumb moves up		
3'	Hands up		9. He turns to the teacher: 3 times hands up.
	Hands up 2 more times		

172

Time	Transcript	Movement	Interpretation
3'15"	folks had, you know, have passed on, like,—I remember the teacher in the first grade gave me a very difficult time because my mother believed that during the winter I should wear[10] a shirt, I mean, that's a sweater—made out of wool, and that would pret you,—protect you	Moves hands outward	10. He tried to fight off mother sissyfying him and covers the mouth and moves hands outward as if to ward her off.
3'30"	from pneumonia, you know, respiratory diseases, and the teacher insist that I don't wear it, and, uh, she kept harping[11] on me all during the winter, but my mother insist that I wear it. You know, those things like that were em-	Nods head / Right hand in air	11. "Teacher . . . kept harping." He repeats these outward gestures when saying
3'45"	barrassing situations, and, uh, of course, at that time, I didn't unders. . . . —you know, it was beyond my comprehension. I was just a child, and were very annoying: all those things were	Clasps hands	
4'	very annoying[12] to me, and, uh. And today, I'm, I'm not satisfied with my work[13] although I'm makin' a good week's salary. I feel I don't be-	Outward movements (both hands) / Clasps hands / Hands outward / Nods head	12. "It was very annoying"—"I don't belong in the job I'm doing" or "I'm not satisfied with what I earn." In his references to both past and present, the patient reacts against his humiliated, helpless (feminine) status by making active, aggressive movements.
4'15"	long in the job I'm doing. I don't like to go to work in the morning, although I do perform my work. I perform it well. I execute it very well, but I don't care for it, and I'm not satisfied with it. To me, it's just earning a living, that's all. But	Hands outstretched	13. Clasps hands as if trying to pull himself together.
4'30"	there is no gratification in it, don't enjoy it, don't enjoy it, and, uh, I was thinking that, uh, I mean, uh, I don't know how to evaluate myself; what am I fitted for? I figure every man has a purpose on this earth, and what am I fitted for?	Right hand outward / Both hands toward self	14. Saying "I don't like to listen to the nonsense of women" he moves both hands up and then the right hand. In this context, the movement of both hands up symbolizes his occupation, since this is the movement which he characteristically makes in his work. This illustrates that the same gesture may have different meanings, and
4'45"	And I don't believe that I'm fitted to do the work I'm doing, hairdressing, I, I don't like to listen to a lot of nonsense[14] from the women coming in,—'My permanent's too tight, it's too soft.' What am I accomplishing? I mean, the people come in, they're,—if you give it too tight, they aggra. . . , they aggravate you, they com-	Hands up / Right hand out / Moves head left, then right	

	Interview Data	Veteran-Patient's Postural Movements and Changes	Therapist's Postural Movements and Changes	Dr. Deutsch's Comments
5'	plain. If it's too soft, 'My permanent don't last,' and you try to explain to them about a permanent wave and they try to argue back, and, uh, and it's a lot of nonsense. I'd rather do something more substantial,[15] something I could put my finger on, like maybe mechanical drawing, or something or other. I don't know if I got the	Left hand out		may express different parts of the personality: in this case an ego activity, in others an id drive, and so on. The principle of overdetermination applies to postural behavior just as it does to verbal expressions and symptoms. Then rejecting women's nonsense, he moves left hand away from body.
5'15"		Clasps hands near chest		15. "I would rather do something more substantial"—he clasps hands near chest (breast). This body-language reference to breast contradicts his stated desire for a more masculine occupation, and reveals the unconscious conflict over masculine or feminine identity. The extent to which a patient uses postural behavior to convey what he cannot verbalize will depend on the transference and on the strength of the ego to master repressed, unconscious feelings.
	capacity. I'd even go to school nights if I could be evaluated to find out what I'm fitted for. But I never, never get ar . . , never seem to			16. Moves the right hand to the mouth when saying he wants to hit the right thing for which he is fitted. Placing his hand to his mouth expresses an unconscious desire to bite off his mother's breast.
5'30"	(5'30") make connections or, uh, hit the right thing or person to tell me what I'm fitted for or[16] what I should do, 'cuz my whole life's always been in confusion, always in a turmoil. Get	Slight movement		
5'45"	up 3:00 o'clock in the (5'45") morning. I've got up 3:00 o'clock in the morning since I was	Right hand out and back to mouth	Nods head	

6'

15, 16, 17, 18, 19, 20, 21, and I'd just ring[17] doctors' doorbells to find out what's wrong with me, with heart palpitation, sweating, and, uh, there was nobody I could talk to, and no . . . no . . . I mean, in fact, if I want to go to my brother-in-law, he would only ridicule you, make the matters worse. I would keep it in myself, you know. There was no cousin or

6'15"

uncle or somebody that was understanding;[18] they were all ignorant, uneducated. Who could I go to? I'd go to a doctor; all he would give me was phenobarbital, and one time I went to see,—I went to a police station, and I was 21 years old before I went into the service. My mother had passed away, and I got up about 3:00 in the morning with heart palpitation and skipped beat and, uh, perspiring, and I was just

6'30"

a real, uh,—just like I was being attacked by somebody, a fear, an anxiety, and uh, I went to the police station. I wanted help.[19] I mean, I had to go to somebody for help, and I went to the police station, and, uh, he, he dispatched an ambulance, poli. . . , patrol car, and I went to City Hospital. They examined me and they told me I was all right, and that was it. I was there for about a half-hour. But there was no-

6'45"

body that'd understand, you know. I mean, they looked at it medically, humph, and that was all. "You're, you're all right. Your heart's all right; your lungs are all right; your,–you're low temperature and we can't admit you" and that's all. Home I went and I stayed awake all night, lookin' in the mirror, takin' my own pulse[20] and something is wrong,–I don't know

7'

7'15"

Body movements

Right hand up and down

Moves body forward

Moves head slightly backward

Right hand back and forth to mouth

Nods head

Right hand outward movement

Both hands raised up

Hands clasped

Hands outstretched

Hands outstretched and clasp again

Notes

17. This movement he repeats several times when saying "I'd just ring doctors' bells," or "I want to go to my brother-in-law," whom he calls ignorant. The unconscious meaning here is the same except that in this instance it is an aggressive desire to bite off the doctor's or his brother-in-law's penis. One of the patient's problems is latent homosexuality.

18. He could only turn to himself since mother died. He moves the right hand back and forth to mouth. In his case the movement of the hand to the mouth is a symbolic turning to the mother. The oral cavity stands for the mother.

19. Alternately clasps hands or stretches them out when saying "I had to go to somebody for help." The stretched out hand expresses the plea for help.

20. During this long monologue, the therapist avoids interrupting the free flow of associations. His aim is to elicit a sufficient number of highly charged terms from which he can select those which can best be linked with the first key

175

Interview Data	Veteran-Patient's Postural Movements and Changes	Therapist's Postural Movements and Changes	Dr. Deutsch's Comments
7'30" what! Humph. Just was not comfortable. And that went on and on and on and on, till I went into the service, and I was preoccupied in the service, but I had the heart palpitation, anxiety			words "problem-inferiority complex."
7'45" in the service[21] but I felt pretty occupied, more maneuvers, and going into combat and all that. And that was actual combat, also,—Guadalcanal, and I weathered that pretty good. I weathered the going overseas, and back again.	Left thumb keeps moving		21. When speaking of his anxiety in the service his left thumb keeps moving. The left side symbolizes the feminine, weak part of his personality, the part which experiences anxiety.
8' But these palpitations,[22] I always kept them to myself, all the time. I felt there was nobody there to understand them, and, uh, while I was	Circular gesture with hands		22. ". . . palpitations, I always kept them to myself . . ." There was an unconscious longing for his mother and this is expressed by the circular gesture which symbolizes her breasts.
8'15" in the service, I knew there, there was a psychiatrist there,—I've forgotten his name,—and I was in the Public Relation. I was a photographer, Public Relation, and I got well acquainted[23] with the psychiatrist and, uh, spoke to him about my problems for about five min-	Moves body forward	Nods head	23. "I got acquainted with psychiatrist"—moves body forward, closer to the present psychiatrist, and thus dramatizes his moving closer to the psychiatrist in the service.
8'30" utes, and he didn't seem, uh interested and I just let it go and from then on, I just kept 'em to myself, and uh, until I came out of the service, and then I came here.[24] And uh, then I	Circular gesture with hands	Nods head	
8'45" stopped coming, Came here for a while, but now, I am more determined than ever, and I've been coming here frequently, that's in the last year and a half. I've had standard appointments, and I've been feeling pretty good. My heart	Circular gesture (one hand circling other)	Nods head	24. As if coming here he got what he lost; he makes repeated circular gestures and put the right hand to the mouth.
9' palpitations subsided down to, uh,—I've got more insight now, more foresight and, uh,—but I'm still not satisfied. I, I, I feel that I haven't	Outward gesture (hands)	Nods head	

176

Time	Patient speech	Body/hand movement	Head movement	Notes
9'15"	touched something that's not being touched; I haven't hit and, uh, given me what you'd say, well, peace of mind in a normal way, and uh, (pause), I remember when I would have disturbed dreams particularly every night, disturbed dreams, and it was always like I said, pertaining to death.25 It was always death, embalming, death, undertakers, and uh,—but now if, uh—and that's because I've had a lot of dreams about war; that's Japanese and Russia, and all that. I had one last night, but they don't get my heart going like they used to. I had one last night; was attacked by the Russians, and two or three years ago I would have got up in anxiety; I would	Right hand to mouth	Nods head / Moves head to left	25. Right hand to mouth several times in quick succession accompanies the talk about death dreams (oral activity is killing).
9'30"			Nods head	
9'45"	have got excited about it but I took it pretty good. I figured it was just a dream and that's it and uh,—I remember when I first came out of the service I had this kind of a nightmare every night, practically every night; used to get up screaming, yelling, and my father would come in the room and say, 'What are you going, crazy?'	Right hand to mouth / Right hand to mouth / Circular movement with hands	Nods head	
10'		Clasps hands	Moves head to left	
10'15"		Moves right leg close to left and up		
Dr. D.	What did he say?			
Pt.	He would say, 'What are you going, crazy?' You know, he's a, an Italian, 'Quest tu, pacci?' (Chuckles). And uh, I would just stay awake all			
10'30"	night after that, with just palpitation. Always felt that there was something I was gonna see, something was th-e-re, there, and not there that	Moves left hand up / Moves right hand back to mouth and makes outward gesture with hands		
10'45"	I was going to see that was gonna be unpleasant. I didn't want to see it. That's the provincial nightmare, always the same thing. Something then was there; you couldn't touch it, and it was calling for me, but I didn't want to see it; I			
11'	never saw it in the dream, and it was very annoying and uh, it left me with tremors, diarrhea. I'd get up and I'd have the tremors, shakes, cold	Both hands in air and clasps near waist		26. In the dream he was fearful of what would be done to him, and therefore in telling it the left (weak) side of his body is in action.

177

Interview Data	Veteran-Patient's Postural Movements and Changes	Therapist's Postural Movements and Changes	Dr. Deutsch's Comments
11'15" sweats, diarrhea, and the next day I was all shook up. I couldn't concentrate very good but I seem to have held my own[27] and uh, (pause), now I'm trying to find out, uh, how to recapture what I lost. What can be done? How to go	Moves right leg on top of left and holds left leg with left hand—right hand moves upward		27. The nightmare is over: "I . . . held my own" and . . . "how to recapture what I lost." And now he moves the right leg up on top of left and holds with right hand the left leg. In these movements the general conflict between masculine and feminine drives is apparent. He recaptures, so to speak, his manhood. As if now self-assured in the transference, he moves right hand continually in air and lets the right foot move repeatedly upward. The therapist at this point repeats the words "recapture what you have lost" as the next key phrase. It was selected because it occurred frequently during the patient's associations, and seemed most significant.
11'30" about it? I don't know. Maybe I should or I shouldn't, I don't know. That's why I come here every week.	Both hands in air	Nods head	
Dr. D. To recapture what you've lost? Pt: 11'45" Yeah. What I lost. Can it be done? I don't know. How should I go about it? Have I got the capacity? What was it? Was I a failure in school because of a mental deficiency, or was	Right hand in air		
12' it because of my environment? I don't know. I, I got a sneaky suspicion it was because of my environment. I don't know. I mean, I don't want to blame everything on my environment, but I	Right foot moves upward		
12'15" feel, I, I've, uh, when I take an I.Q. I score low. Like in the Army I scored very low but I felt it was due because I didn't[28] do well in school and I got confused, other . . . uh, I didn't know how to take an examination. See? And I feel that if I could be trained in how to take an	Right foot moves upward Left hand in air		28. As if to offset the low performance in school and in the Army, he moves the right hand upward and forward.
12'30" examination and uh, how to concentrate, I think I can score pretty high in an I.Q., in intelligent test and, and I'm willing to uh, subject myself	Right hand folded and moves in air		29. The transference has taken root. The patient is exhibiting his right hand and foot, stretching them out toward the therapist to get in contact with him. The therapist joins in and answers nonverbally by putting his glasses conspicuously on the desk, moves his right
12'45" to the psychiatrist[29] and, uh, as a, well, as a guinea pig, to find out is there a history or any-	Right hand moves in air		
13' thing you know, find out: Is it environment? Is	Left hand moves in air toward doctor	Moves leg and foot;	

leg over the left and his right hand down on the lap. Finally, he spreads his legs i.e., uncrosses them. Patient reacts with increased right hand movements, makes circular gestures and putting his own right hand to the mouth thereby expressing what he wants. The therapist's movements are sometimes planned consciously and sometimes unconsciously determined. They are designed to test the nature and strength of the transference. The patient's response reveals a good deal: he may, by imitating the therapist's movements, demonstrate his identification with him. The patient may reveal part of his body, or generally assume a more "open" posture; this would express the fact of his receptiveness to the therapist. Or his posture and gestures may indicate his opposition and resistance to the therapist. The more the patient drifts into transference, the more his postural behavior will express his core conflicts.

30. "Why does it bother me (i.e., poor report cards)?" he asks, and as if explaining, he keeps moving the left hand in the air.

31. Then he says, "I don't want it to bother me" and proving it, he adds verbally "I want to check it"

13'15" it me,—my low I.Q. intelligence, inborn intelligence? What is it that made me fail in school, being held back, poor marks? Very bad marks; they were very bad marks, I remember, I had a very poor report card, all D's and E's, general report card D's and E . . . and it's, uh,—why?

right knee over left knee; puts glasses on desk with right hand; then right hand down on lap. Left arm continues resting on left arm of chair. Right leg uncrossed; both legs straight ahead and feet on floor.

13'30" My brother went right through school. We were brought up in the same house, and, uh, his report cards were average, normal report cards, good marks. They bother me; these things bother me, to know why. I mean, it, uh,—I know some people can shake it off—they don't care, but I know, uh, several fellows brought up in my environment with, say, I don't kn. . , I won't say the same situation but they were

Both hands—circular gesture — Right hand and foot move

14' brought up and they had poor remar. . report cards. Today they've got mediocre jobs but they're happy. They don't care; it doesn't seem to bother them. But why does it bother me?[30]

Right hand moves to mouth — Right foot moves — Large circular gesture — Left hand keeps moving in air

14'15" And if it does bother me, I want to look into it. And, and it doesn't bother me that I want it to bother me: well, I won't say I want it to bother me, it just comes in to me.[31] And if it

Left hand keeps moving in air

14'30" does, then I want to check it. And, uh, in modern science of psychiatry, I feel they have the,

Right hand on foot — Right hand points toward self

179

	Interview Data	Veteran-Patient's Postural Movements and Changes	Therapist's Postural Movements and Changes	Dr. Deutsch's Comments
	the proper people to go to to help me. I've tried religion,—it didn't work. I've gone to, uh, priests, and uh, I don't like the suggestion,—what they want me to do. They felt that my problem was			and posturally he puts the right hand on the foot and points with this hand to himself.
14'45"	sin. I don't go for that.[32] To me it doesn't register,—I can't see it,—and they said it was sin because I was practicing birth control and I	Hands clasped at finger tips		32. Religious belief he unconsciously expressed by clasping the hands at finger tips, thus keeping all impulses under control. He rejects it and moves the separated hands up and down.
15'	should sleep with my wife at certain times of the month and uh, I should get twin beds or a new bedroom and uh, see, I didn't go for that. And uh, every one I've gone to was because I	Hands up and down		33. Demonstrating objections to the demand for confession, he puts right hand on right leg. He clasps hands only to repeat their separation. His unconscious impulse at this point in his recital is to be aggressive with his right hand. The right hand is therefore held down on his leg or clasped to the left hand, in order to restrain this impulse.
15'15"	should go to confession, they wanted me to confess right there and then; I wouldn't do it.[33] To confess, you made sins; you have to wash your sins from your mind, see? That's why I	Right hand on right leg and left hand on arm of chair		
	haven't been troubled,—I don't believe in it, because uh, er, if I do have a guilt complex, I don't think it's due to sin, that,—I mean, I, I don't feel I, I have committed sin.[34] I mean, any, anything that I have done in my life I think was normal. I don't think that birth con-	Hands clasped		34. Denying that he considers what he did in life as sinful, he scratches with the right hand as if showing that it is not sinful. The unconscious meaning is: "I am only scratching, not clawing or tearing off."
15'30"				
15'45"	trol is a sin. (Pause). Uh, my wife's gonna have a child now; we planned that child. I've been practicing birth control for a time—I felt that we'd bought a new house, I had to. I'm lookin'	Right hand scratches head		
16'	at the money angle. Now I'm makin' more money, a little more money. My house is five	Right hand moves		

180

years old; it was a brand new house when I bought it. It's five years old, and now I can afford another child, and we want another child;35 we have two,—a girl, 8, and a boy, 4, and I want another child. I know I can afford

16'15" it. I've got the money put away for it. I think that's logical. But I don't think I've committed a sin36 because I practiced birth control. I think, sometimes, you have to control nature and, uh, that's it. And, uh, I tried religion; it

16'30" didn't work. I mean, I couldn't see,—I couldn't get out of religion like some people claim. They claim they can feel God or touch God;37 I don't get that feeling. I looked for it; I've prayed but

16'45" I can't seem to get that; it doesn't ring a bell with me. So now I'm trying psychiatry, which has done more for me than anything else and

17' uh, and I wish and uh. . .

Dr. D. But you want to recapture what you have lost?

Pt. Because I feel that there's longevity in my

17'15" family. My father lived to 81 and my aunt—lived to 88; my uncle lived to 98.38 I am 38. What if I should live another 40 years? I can do a lot in another 40 years, if I should live to 80, 85. It only takes 5, from 5 to 6 years to learn a good,

17'30" soun. . . , you know, if I can recapture and go to school. Say it takes 6, 7 years,—it's worth doing, and get away from hairdressing. That's the way I look at it, uh, I mean, uh, there are times I fear death, I feel I'm gonna die but yet

Nonverbal behavior (center column):

Left knee over right knee. Left hand gestures outward.

Hands outstretched up and down

Both hands move back and forth

Right hand to mouth

Body moves forward

Both hands in air

Moves left hand

Right hand on mouth

Right hand out

Right hand on mouth

Body moves forward

Nods head

Interpretive notes (right column):

35. "We want another child" he says and stretches the hands out.

36. Another denial of seeing in it a sin, he moves the right hand to the mouth. This is a symbolic statement that his sexuality is only oral, therefore he need feel no guilt over genital activity.

37. Moving his body forward, he accompanies it verbally by the words, "I tried to touch God." He accentuates it by stretching the hands out in the air. When he did it the therapist asked, "You wished to recapture what you lost?" The patient answered nonverbally by putting the right hand on the mouth. In this instance the right hand represents the therapist's penis which the patient wants to bite off, and in this way regain what he has lost.

38. Mentioning the objects whom he lost, like father or uncle who died, he stretches out the right hand, moves it to his mouth, moves the body forward and repeats these movements several times saying "I can recapture." Losing these objects through death is equivalent to losing the penis. Stretches out his right arm as he says "I can re-

Interview Data	Veteran-Patient's Postural Movements and Changes	Therapist's Postural Movements and Changes	Dr. Deutsch's Comments
17'45" I know I'm healthy, I've got a good heart; I got good lungs; I've—physically, I'm strong.[39] And, uh . . . Well, that's the mental part, now, to go on with my . . . And if all that can be done, I'm, I'm willing to cooperate. If that can be evalu-ated. I mean I'm able to concentrate and study,	Right hand to center of chest Right hand on mouth Right hand moves out	Nods head	capture" as an aggressive move-ment which denies the loss; or at least denies that the loss is per-manent. He assures himself that he has lost nothing by saying "I am healthy."
18'			39. "I am strong." All that is accom-panied by right hand movements.
and I don't think it should take long to learn the basic of what I lost, like math, and I'd say arithmetic, multiply, divide, and subtract,—grammar,—I don't think it should take long if, if I can just break through the mental blocks,—if it is a mental block. But if it isn't, I'm willin' to go along and stay as a hairdresser. What else can I do? But if I feel that there is an inmade or inborn intelligence,—if there is in me, that I can learn something else within 5 or 6 years, I'm willin' to go along with it. And why shouldn't I? And, and, and I feel that hairdressing—I'm, I'm not satisfied. It's uh, there's nothing there.			40. The nonverbal responses of the therapist to that need for feeling strong is that he put his right hand to his chin and moves his head toward the patient by nodding; and finally acceptingly moving his left hand outward, continuing to hold his chin with the right hand. The chin, like other pro-tuberances, symbolizes masculin-ity, and the therapist is thus ex-pressing masculinity by holding his chin with his right hand. Mov-ing the left hand outward signifies an extrusion of the passive, femi-nine elements of the personality.
18'15"	Right hand moves out Right hand moves out	Right hand to chin[40]	
18'30"	Right hand moves out Right hand moves out	Nods head	
18'45"	Both hands out-stretched[41]	Left hand gestures outward Right hand contin-ues on chin	41. The therapist's gestures intensifies the right hand movement of the patient; that is he responds to the masculinity of the therapist with a display of his own masculinity.
Dr. D. You want to recapture something else? Pt. Yes. 19'	Hands down		
Dr. D. Mm hum. If you would know what you want to recapture.	Right hand to side		

182

Speaker / Time	Transcript	Movement	Movement	Commentary
Pt. 19'15"	I don't. Is it the basic or, I mean, wha...., what is it? Is it what I lost in school? I can't put my finger on it, and I don't, uh.... I want to recapture what I lost in my childhood. I don't mean fun, or play. I mean, uh academically. You know, an, an intelligence or a learn-ing.[42] I don't know what it is.[42] It, uh, uh	Right hand to side Body moves forward	Right hand continues on chin	42. The therapist here links together the ideas "recapture what you have lost" and "inferiority complex." The need for making contact with the therapist becomes more and more apparent. He makes 9 movements in 1 minute first with the right hand, then with the whole body toward the therapist, when he is asked what he wants to recapture and what, as he said, he can't find on the woman.
Dr. D. 19'30"	To recapture what you lost, and what, uh, might be the cause of your inferiority complex.	Right hand in air Right hand on knee	Circular gestures to self with left hand; then makes an outward circular gesture with left hand Nods	
19'45" Pt.	That's right. (Pause). I mean, I have a dif..., a very deep inferiority complex, and now and then, I, of getting late, I feel that I've lost, you know,[43] I, I've ...	Nods		43. "I feel that I've lost, you know," he exclaims, simultaneously holding his knee with the right hand while the therapist holds his chin. Moreover, the therapist sets his left hand in motion by making the same circular movements which the patient had made previously. The patient's movements fade out when he can verbalize that he has the inferiority complex because he has lost something. This is another instance in which the verbal and bodily forms of communication are in a reciprocal relationship to each other: what he can put into words he does not need to express through his body.
Dr. D.	Complex?			
20' Pt.	I haven't got it now, but then it hits you. Yes.	Hands out and clasped in air	Right hand down from chin	
Dr. D.	What do you mean?			
Pt. 20'15"	The inferiority complex. I'll go along two days feeling great, I feel like I've got the world, but then all of a sudden, past! I go right down again. I can't seem to shake it off, that inferiority complex. I feel inferior (Pause), to other people. I mean if, uh, to a doctor or lawyer or dentist, or an engineer. I feel inferior to them. I am just a hairdresser. What the	Hand back on knee		44. He begins to talk about women derisively, shows off simultaneously what he has by moving the right foot up, touching his head
20'30"	heck's a hairdresser?[44] I mean, it's not the high plane elevations,—make a bunch of pin-curls, you comb out. I'm, oh, there's a lot to it but	Right foot moves up Right hand to head	Hands fold on each other; then right el-	

183

Interview Data	Veteran-Patient's Postural Movements and Changes	Therapist's Postural Movements and Changes	Dr. Deutsch's Comments
20'45" there isn't that much to it. 'Cuz I, I was a photographer. There was more to photography than hairdressing, a lot more.	Right hand and then left hand in air	bow rests on arm of chair; right hand dangles down; left arm rests on left chair arm and left hand dangles down	and then his mouth as if to say that he has what a man has as well as what a woman has. Both sides are now in motion, then the therapist does the same. The patient stares at him as if fascinated.
Dr. D. What do you mean?			
Pt. In photography. I mean, there was a lot more and, uh, I don't know,—the people that I had			
21' contact with, that I worked with in, in, in photography are of a higher plane than hairdressers.	Right hand on mouth and foot up		
Much of a higher plane. Hairdressers are just a			45. A movement occurs only every 15", but his depreciating remarks about his female customers become uninhibited. He ridicules their complaint to have lost their permanents.
21'15" service, doing business so they can tip you. And if they feel like bawlin' you out, a customer, they will; they think nothing of it. I	Looks to doctor		
mean, there's nothing to it. It's uh, it's just a bunch of complaints, that's all.45 I mean, it's,	Right hand keeps moving		
some of the things they come in with is idiotic, —you do a, a customer's hair, you give her a			46. The character of his movements becomes repetitive. He finds himself in agreement with the therapist who joins him in his delight by repeating the word "lost."
21'30" permanent, you set her hair and then she goes out in the rain and gets the hair wet,	Hand out—right hand to head		
she blames you for it.			
Dr. D. That she lost it.46			

The film of this interview can be rented for teaching purposes without charge from the Mental Hygiene Clinic of the Boston Veterans Administration, Court Street, Boston, Mass.

184

2. COMPLEX PROCESSES

There are many complex events and activities occurring during the psychotherapeutic procedure that defy simple classification. We have included papers dealing with a few of these complex variables or procedures under the heading of *complex processes*.

Bordin has described an interesting experimental study of free-association, a process which is a fundamental part of the psychoanalytic method. He has developed measures of the adequacy of free-associative responses, and these consist of three scales, *Involvement*, *Spontaneity*, and *Freedom*, which can be rated at acceptable levels of agreement among raters. Practicing psychoanalysts may observe that some of the categories at the lower end of Bordin's scales which denote relatively inadequate free-association are typically perceived by the psychoanalyst (and eventually by the analysand) as signals of or clues to neurotic problems and unconscious conflicts. For example, sudden silences or preoccupations with the task or immediate surroundings are clues to inner conflicts, *defense transference*, and other psychodynamic phenomena of possible interest. Bordin is well aware of these facts, and in other research in which he is engaged he is concentrating on the manifestations of *resistance* to free-association and the effects of interpretive interventions on these phenomena.

Seitz, using the *focal conflict* concept derived from the interpretive method of Thomas French, has illustrated the problem of reliability in assaying complex processes occurring during the psychotherapeutic situation. He reports research on what is perhaps the most basic and important problem in psychoanalysis: consensus among analysts in the interpretation of clinical material. Six trained analysts compared the interpretations which they placed on patients' productions. They attempted to develop a systematic method of interpretation which could be used reliably and thereby increase consensus among analysts. This effort was not successful. However, a failure in the purely formal sense may be highly valuable in the light it throws on some fundamental issues.

The failure to reach satisfactory consensus calls for some comment. Before reaching the conclusion that psychoanalytic interpretations are idiosyncratic and arbitrary it would be well to remember that there are certain features of research and of the phenomena under study which make a high level of agreement unlikely. The psychoanalyst-judges were asked to examine a segment of the therapeutic interaction and then to state what they thought was the event precipitating some particular behavior of the patient, what focal conflict the patient had at that time, and what were the defenses against and efforts at solution of the focal conflict. Focal conflict refers to the preconscious conflict which is dominant at the time, and consists of a *disturbing motive* and a *reactive motive*. The interpretations of the judges for each of these categories were compared.

There are certain obvious difficulties in achieving high consensus, and Seitz considers these. The first is the concept of overdetermination, which holds that behavior is the result not of one easily discerned motive, but of many motives acting in concert. If this is so then each observer may point to a different motive in the patient, each will be correct, yet consensus among them will be zero. In dealing with this difficulty Seitz draws upon the psychoanalytic theory of mental functioning, with emphasis on French's notion of focal conflict. According to this view, the overdetermined motives are in the unconscious; they emerge by way of a final common path to a single preconscious focal conflict, and it is this which the judges were asked to identify. But the judges tended to interpret the *un*conscious motives; the distinction between an unconscious and a preconscious drive may at times be a rather fine one.

One kind of overdetermination which can cause particular difficulty for raters is the coexistence of opposite motives. Psychoanalytic work provides innumerable instances of this. For example, our explorations may reveal that a patient simultaneously desires and fears a given situation. Thus it is quite possible for raters to place exactly opposite interpretations on clinical material. An illustration of this is found in Seitz's example. Three of the judges perceived the patient as motivated during the interview by "hostile, competitive impulses toward Al," whereas a fourth saw "passive, homosexual feelings toward Al." Seitz points out that in such cases one of these attitudes is serving as a defense against the other, but he admits that it may not be easy to determine which is which. In the present instance the reader can turn to the transcript of the "Temple" interview (p. 241) and decide this question for himself.

It will be noticed that Seitz has in no way attempted to gloss over the difficulties in obtaining agreement among judges. He explains clearly the definition of what constituted "agreement"; it was a rather stringent one. He points out where agreement was not reached, gives thoughtful consideration to why not, and suggests how future efforts may be more successful. The general impression is that he and his coworkers have felt sufficiently secure in their understanding of psychoanalytic methods that they could tolerate the harsh light of scientific inquiry directed at their work.

In addition to the report on consensus, his chapter contains his own attempt to understand the material of the "Temple" interview according to the principles of French's interpretive method. Seitz gives an impressive demonstration of systematic reasoning from the patient's verbalizations to the inferences regarding his motives. Evidence is presented at each point in the reasoning process. Finally, the author gives careful consideration to those data which do *not* fit his interpretive framework, and discusses their implications. This type of systematic combing of clinical material will do a great deal to improve the scientific status of psycho-analysis.

With regard to the difficulty in reaching agreement among judges, it should be pointed out that the search for consensus among psychoanalysts has not been uniformly unsuccessful. Other researchers have achieved satisfactory reliability in their assessments of variables derived from psy-choanalytic personality theory. For example, Auld and Dollard; Gotts-chalk, *et al.*; Bordin; Isaacs and Haggard; Cartwright; Strupp, *et al.*; and Knapp, *et al.*, in this volume have reported adequate reliability co-efficients for interjudge evaluations. Elsewhere, Bellak and Smith (1956)[1] have reported modest success in reaching satisfactory agreements on clin-ical psychoanalytic inferences concerning interview material. With Seitz the editors agree to the need for a systematic method of interpretation, with critical scanning of all the clinical material, rather than intuitive hunches based on part of the material, as steps toward improving con-sensus. There are a number of other steps that could improve the relia-bility of interobserver agreement which, if fully utilized in a study similar to Seitz's, could lead to acceptable consensus. Some of these would be: (1) lucid definition of all observables and inferables to be measured or categorized so that each judge fully understands the substance and limits of each item and dimension on which he is making an evaluation; (2) a period of practice making the required assessments, so that misinterpreta-tions can be corrected; (3) an avoidance of the assessment of highly in-ferential variables, that is, second or third order abstractions, and the preferential use of first order abstractions or directly observable events; (4) the specifying of variables in advance rather than calling for free-wheeling descriptions from different judges and trying to match these; (5) the use of already established rating and statistical approaches, such as Stevenson's Q technique; (6) probably foremost, consultation with behavioral and social scientists well trained in test and measurement theory and technique.

Isaacs and Haggard describe a variety of methods they have used in studies of affect in psychotherapy. A brief summary of some of their find-ings will help to illustrate their methodological concentration on the complex and subtle affective processes and phenomena of interest to a psychodynamic theoretical orientation.

They first describe investigations involving the construct *relatability*, which is a dimension marked by six levels designating the relative capac-ity of an individual "for 'object relations' and interpersonal relations." They have assumed that the higher the level of relatability, the greater the variety of affects an individual may potentially experience. In one

---

[1] L. Bellak and M. B. Smith, An experimental exploration of the psychoanalytic process, *Psychoanal. Quart.*, **25**: 385-414, 1956.

study they found that patients at higher levels of relatability have a much greater likelihood of showing improvement with psychotherapy carried out at either client-centered or psychoanalytically-oriented settings. In another study, they found that persons with higher levels of relatability change with psychotherapy in some ways which are different from the ways in which patients at lower levels change.

In another series of studies, Isaacs and Haggard examine what they call the *meaningfulness* of statements, and by this they refer to interview content revealing factors shaping the personality and life of the patient. An inter-judge reliability study of this dimension, involving 20 therapists, gave satisfactory correlations. *Meaningful* patient statements were found more likely to have been elicited by therapist interventions containing affective words. Furthermore, therapeutic interventions containing affective verbalizations were found more likely to elicit spontaneous returns to this subject matter by the patient during the remainder of the interview.

The resourcefulness of these authors and their collaborators in finding methods to assess affects and relate them to other pertinent variables is well exemplified in this chapter and other publications given in their bibliography.

16. Free association: an experimental analogue of the psychoanalytic situation

Edward S. Bordin

This paper will describe an experimental situation analogous to the conditions of psychoanalysis and offer rating devices for use in studying some of the issues surrounding psychoanalysis in particular and psychotherapy in general. Before doing so, however, I propose to examine the history of methodological developments in research in psychotherapy and to consider the requirements for avoiding violation of the phenomena under study.

THE PROBLEM OF CONTROL AND SIMPLIFICATION

After a long period of depending upon participant observations[1] by the therapist or the patient of the nature and results of psychotherapy, psychologists and psychiatrists have initiated a gradual shift to other modes of increasing their understanding of this process through which the behavior and experience of one person is modified by his interactions with another. Only a little over twenty years ago, Rogers and his collaborators launched a series of studies of psychotherapy which broke away from a dependence on observations by either of the two participants (Rogers, 1947). Electrically recorded psychotherapeutic interviews and their verbatim transcriptions make the phenomena of psychotherapy directly accessible to a third party. Gradually, other substitutes for relying on the reports of the participants have been developed. As a means of obtaining access to the inner processes underlying overt communications between therapist and patient, the client-centered group initiated the use of Q-sorts (Rogers and Dymond, 1954). At some point or points in time, prior to, during, or after the course of therapy, but not during the therapeutic hour, the patient, therapist, or both, orders a series of descriptive state-

The research on which this article is based was supported by a grant from the National Institute of Mental Health (M-5029) which is gratefully acknowledged.

[1] Though participant observations are extremely important data, they are also one-sided, especially when the observer has a strong set such as is represented by strong adherence to a theory regarding the phenomena under observation.

ments according to their degree of applicability to himself as he is, would like to be, or whatever other object of interest to the researcher.

A big and controversial step was the introduction of experimental controls and the attempt to utilize experimental analogues. In the first Conference on *Research in Psychotherapy* (Rubinstein and Parloff, 1959), Snyder's (1959) report of studies in which therapists were asked to respond in ways incompatible with their own theoretical orientation or pragmatically adopted modes of behavior in therapy was met with reactions of doubt about the representativeness of therapeutic methods tested under such conditions[2] and uncertainty as to whether it was ethical to ask a therapist to act against his convictions. (Rubinstein and Parloff, 1959, pp. 267-275). Similar reservations have been expressed in response to the utilization of experimental analogues. Keet's (1948) study was one of the earliest examples. Via word association methods he identified words tapping conflicts in volunteer subjects and established the presence of blocks toward remembering these words during word association learning. The experiment proper consisted of a comparison of the efficacy of reflection versus interpretation in aiding the subject to overcome the memory block. This experimental technique suffered a fate other than that of being criticized; other experimenters failed to replicate the preliminary condition of establishing a memory block tied to characteristics displayed during word association. (Merrill, 1952; Grummon and Butler, 1953.) Whether the experimental conditions in verbal operant conditioning studies represent analogues or substitutes for psychotherapy depends partly on the investigator, his interests, and convictions. In verbal operant conditioning, the subject is given the task of talking, usually about some general subject (e.g., his life history) or is given some other task that includes verbalization. The experimenter reinforces a preselected class of the subject's verbal behavior by carefully controlled verbal or nonverbal cues. Krasner (Strupp and Luborsky, 1962, p. 103) has argued that these techniques should not be viewed as experimental analogues of psychotherapy but as part of the broader psychology of behavior control, of which psychotherapy is a special class. Making use of typescripts and motion pictures drawn from psychotherapy, Strupp has studied factors influencing the therapist's responses. The subject-therapists are asked to offer their own responses at selected points in the interview. This device has the virtue of comparing therapists under standard conditions. Strupp (1962) has himself offered an excellent analysis of the reasons that a reserved answer must be given to the question of how related are a therapist's responses in this situation

---

[2] It should not be overlooked that the biggest decision is that involved in *any* invasion by a third party into a therapeutic relationship, whether by recording in which a third person is implied or by collection of data after therapeutic sessions. Experience suggests that, where skillful therapists are involved, the influence of these invasions becomes only one more incident around which transference and resistance cluster and, as such, is dealt with in the usual manner (Greenblatt, 1959).

to those he would give in actual psychotherapy. Finally, there are the various efforts to study interview phenomena, the latest example of which is the series of studies conducted by Saslow, Mattarazzo, and their collaborators (1959). Here, too, their applicability to psychotherapy is questionable.

The advantages to be gained through the experimental control of aspects of the psychotherapeutic situation, either in an actual process or in an experimental analogue, are obvious. Control represents an important tool for the ruling out of alternative explanations and provides an opportunity to test the power of our formulations. This is especially true for the analogue, because freed of the restrictions imposed by the use of patients, the problems of invading a highly personal relationship, and the ethics of doing so, the investigator can carry out many experiments in the time it takes to do one in the clinic. Therefore, it is worthwhile pausing to examine the characteristics essential to a therapeutic relationship. What is it that sets psychotherapy off from other interpersonal relationships? In what ways is it similar? The answer to these questions can provide us with a guide for designing analogues and with criteria for deciding on the relevance of any given one to psychotherapy.

At the outset we must state the principle that how far an experimental situation can depart from the original and still be considered relevant depends, in part, on the level of our understanding. Highly sophisticated theory and highly refined knowledge permits physicists to move freely between events observed in the laboratory and events in every day experience. Given the crudity of our present understanding of psychotherapy, the investigator will soon strain credulity in departing from the conditions that obtain in either theoretical statement or every day practice.

We turn now to the hallmarks of this interpersonal situation. One defining characteristic is the motivations of the patient. His request for psychotherapy ultimately rests on dissatisfaction with himself which has led him to seek change. Most psychotherapists include in the preparation for psychotherapy the clarification and strengthening of the patient's awareness that it is with himself that he is dissatisfied and that in seeking psychotherapy he has acknowledged his commitment to change. Psychoanalytic theory specifies that this awareness and commitment to change is an important part of the *rational ego* to which therapeutic interpretations must appeal and which gives them the leverage they need to play a part in change. Closely related to this commitment is the patient's willingness to accept the task that the therapist gives to him. The basic rule of free association imposed in psychoanalysis, being a radical departure from our usual modes of social interaction, would be accepted only under very special motivating conditions such as are created by the experience of protracted psychic suffering that customarily precede the patient's entrance into analysis. Finally, the role definition of the healer, especially of the psychological variety, includes the characteristics of a trustworthy person who is committed to the patient's welfare. The patient is usually aware that the members of the profession subscribe to a code of ethics which reinforces this responsible attitude. Fulfilling these conditions, which refer primarily to the patient, creates certain working conditions for the psychotherapist. To the troubled person desperately seeking change in a situation defined to focus on inner events, his relationship to the helper inevitably becomes highly charged. This follows whether or not one accepts the theory of transference. It follows, then, that one of the defining conditions of the psychotherapeutic situation for the therapist is that his reactions take place in a relationship which is, at least on one side, highly charged and which can hardly avoid being provocative in some degree.[3]

SIGNIFICANCE OF THE FREE ASSOCIATIVE TASK

As is well known, the technical specifications of psychoanalysis include the basic rule that the patient must say whatever comes to mind without selection, whether to avoid embarrassment, to make sense, or to be realistic. As a centralist theory of personality, psychoanalysis sees the important determinants of behavior as being centered about native and acquired drives and motives which are organized into cognitive, affective, and action systems. The intent of the basic rule is to provide a situation maximally conducive to laying bare these internally organized systems by minimizing the influence of external (situational) determinants. Many other theories of psychotherapy, even those not considered neo-psychoanalytic, proceed from a centralist assumption and, consequently, give the patient a task which is ambiguous because it sets relatively few limits on his range of response. In an earlier paper (Bordin, 1955), I discussed this point and suggested that while all personality oriented therapies tended to make use of ambiguity in the therapeutic relationship, the orthodox form of psychoanalysis through the rule of free association most definitely and most fully relies on this mechanism.

Were it possible, as I believe is the case, to successfully reproduce in the laboratory this basic part of the process, we would have a valuable device for investigating many of the theories regarding the psychic phenomena surrounding inner experience and, even some aspects of the impact on them of interventions by another person. When we consider that Freud supplemented his experiences with patients with those obtained through casual encounters, this aspiration does not seem far fetched. In discussing the forgetting of foreign words, Freud (Brill, 1938) described an encounter with a casual acquaintance while traveling on vacation and

---

[3] If this argument is accepted, it follows that we may not accept without empirical demonstration that a therapist's response by insertion into the typescript or sound film of a therapeutic interview is representative of his behavior in psychotherapy.

the process of free association by means of which he met successfully the young man's challenge to account for his having forgotten a word in a quotation from Virgil. This kind of incident underlines the fact that important intrapsychic aspects of the process of free association can be captured in situations that do not reproduce precisely the psychoanalytic one. It suggests that it is sufficient for the person to be willing to accept the basic rule even though his motivations may not be safely assumed to be that of achieving psychological change.[4] It is, of course, unlikely without a very strong motivation such as that stimulated by neurotically based discomfort, that a person would be willing to endure the pain and strain involved in penetrating very deeply through self-erected barriers to experience and to impulse expression.

Considering its central position in psychoanalysis, it is surprising that so little research on free association has been attempted. What work there is has been centered on word association. My search of the literature at the beginning of my own interest in such research uncovered only two studies involving free association, one an unpublished doctoral dissertation, and remarkably little effort to deal directly with the process. Writers on psychoanalysis as treatment have been mainly concerned with resistance, the ways that patients circumvent the basic rule, and little concerned with free association per se. Both of these early studies made use of the therapist's ratings in investigating characteristics of the patient associated with the ability to free associate. Temerlin (1956) found that good free associators showed greater variability in the autokinetic effect than poor free associators, which has not been supported in my own studies.[5] Schneider (1953) devised a Rorschach measure of capacity to free associate centered around the various indices of balance, e.g., movement and color, form and color, which was found to be related to therapists' ratings of their patients' response in psychotherapy. Though the study was marred by failure to insure that the ratings were made without knowledge and, therefore, uninfluenced by the Rorschach, this finding was supported by my own studies.

THE EXPERIMENTAL ANALOGUE

My reading of psychoanalytic theory suggests that the prototypic psychic process in free association is one which stretches over a period of time, permitting the successive development of conventional anxieties

---

[4] While it is not safe to assume a motivation for change, it is not unlikely that the threat of his love's pregnancy may have motivated Freud's young friend to challenge the master in a dimly felt hope of change. We find that volunteers for psychological experiments, especially for those labelled as related to personality and psychotherapy, often are anxious persons, consciously hoping for some kind of relief.

[5] A paper reporting these studies is in simultaneous preparation.

about the listener (i.e., is he friendly? protective? punitive? moralistic? etc.), anxieties arising as the flow of associations inevitably moves toward drive invested and conflictual areas, and finally the investment of the analyst with characteristics associated with objects of infantile fixations. One of the initial decisions is how long to make each session. One could, of course, choose the traditional 50 minutes, but our preliminary trials of free association in a single session gave us the distinct impression that the shorter time of 30 minutes did not modify appreciably the subject's performance. Somewhat later, Colby (1960), without knowledge of my work, also chose 30 minutes for the length of sessions in his studies of the effects of the presence of an observer on free association.

One of the variations in the situation is in the preparation of the subject. Our initial studies have been directed toward the question of how personality influences response to free association. We felt that response in a single session was a natural starting point, but we wanted to keep out the influence of material prepared specifically in anticipation of the task. So we did not warn our subjects of the task we would give them. Instead, they were told during recruiting-selection interviews that they were to participate in a study of different methods of measuring personality. The methods were to include laboratory perceptual tasks, clinical personality tests, and "an interview such as is sometimes conducted in psychotherapy." On the other hand, Colby (1960) whose research design required four sessions a week for three weeks, informed his subjects of the task during the recruiting interview.

What are the motives of subjects recruited for such studies? How are they comparable and how different from those who participate in psychotherapy? When the subjects are paid, as was the case in Colby's studies and in my own, there is, of course, an economic motive. It has already been suggested that interest in therapeutic effects is likely to be stimulated, often by the process itself and by the subject's awareness of the therapeutic responsibilities and competencies of the experimenters in their other roles.[6] It seems likely that unpaid volunteers are more certain to be moved by therapeutic interests, whether or not self-acknowledged. One prominent motive, especially to be expected with subjects recruited from a university population and probably likely with most other segments of the general population, is that of contributing to science and of sharing in the discovery of knowledge.

Our recruiting interviews gave special attention to the activation of this motive and to relating it to willingness to conform to the task. Subjects were given to understand that participation in the experiment committed them to revealing themselves. They were asked to give thought to the question of their readiness to cooperate because it would interfere

---

[6] Those subjects who had experienced psychotherapy or were currently in it were automatically excluded.

with the purposes of our study were they to prove constrained. We gave the prospective subject time to struggle with his doubts, helping him to voice them. Almost without exception these doubts consisted of concern about how the data would be used and by whom. Naturally, we gave assurances of the confidentiality of our data, that we were aware of our responsibilities, that our interest was in the relationships of measures, and that individuals would not be identified. Evidence of some success in stimulating this motive to fulfill one's obligation and to contribute to science is found from time to time in our interviews when a subject, finding himself unable to communicate and complaining of his mind being a blank, will comment on the fact that this was interfering with the purposes of the experiment. For the most part these appeared to be expressions of genuine regret rather than purely hostile taunts.

In comparing the motivations of the patient in psychotherapy and those of the volunteer for experiments in free association, our purpose is served by focusing on his motivations with regard to the task. It is clear that the patient has a deeper intrinsic motivation for accepting and conscientiously complying with the task than does the volunteer, especially where the therapist has taken care to establish a clear cognition that in his expert opinion the performance of this difficult and often painful chore is a crucial part of the treatment. We may say that the patient's ego has been allied with the therapeutic effort and is available for aid in the process of overcoming resistance. If some internalized source of motivation is to be appealed to in the volunteer, it will more likely come from his superego. He is being paid, and conscientious effort to comply with the task is his part of the contract. Further, when his idealism is engaged, he would be interfering with the march of science by failing to comply. Thus, we may conclude that in experimental studies of the free associative task, as compared to psychotherapy, we have an opportunity to study the interaction of a weaker motivation to comply with the task *with* whatever counter forces toward performing the task are created for the particular subject and by interventions by an experimenter (therapist). Through selecting subjects with strong latent interests in therapeutic change, it might be possible to come very close to achieving conditions of motivation comparable in strength to those in psychotherapy, thus making accessible to experimental study those therapeutic phenomena which become accessible only under such conditions.

The physical conditions of the sessions should, ideally, be close to those of psychoanalysis in that the room be more like an office than a laboratory. While the microphone and recorder are not hidden, they are unobtrusively placed. A reasonably comfortable couch is provided and the experimenter is seated to the side and rear so that he is out of the subject's sight unless he makes a special effort to turn and look.

Our version of the basic instructions is:

"What we are going to do here is conduct a session similar to those sometimes used in psychotherapy. It will be about 30 minutes long, and what you are to do is say whatever comes to mind—say anything and everything that comes to your mind, even if it seems trivial, irrelevant, unpleasant, or not the kind of thing you would customarily say in polite society. Lie back and begin."

Since our studies were concerned with the subject's response to the task, we wished to keep the experimenter's interventions unvaryingly at a minimum. He kept silent as much as possible and responded to questions by saying, "whatever comes to mind," implying that questions would not be answered but the subject could speak them if they came to mind. If the subject continued to press for answers, this point was made explicit. Silences were handled in the following manner: during the first five minutes of the interview, the experimenter waited three minutes before speaking; with silences after the first five minutes, he waited at least five minutes before speaking. In both cases his first comment was to remind the subject to say whatever came to mind. If the subject responded that he had no thoughts, the experimenter waited a few minutes, then said, "it's very difficult to go so long without any thoughts" or "out loud" or "any thoughts?" These latter comments were said more insistently than the first intervention.

Ratings of Performance

To study the vicissitudes of free association, we must have rigorously standardized methods of differentiating performance at different times by the same person and between persons. In developing such methods, we could draw on previously developed measures of resistance in psychotherapeutic interviews by Speisman (1959) and Gillespie (1953) but had to adapt our thinking to the onesidedness of the interactions in our experimental situation. Further, we wished to orient ourselves toward what free association is, rather than what it is not, as is the case in resistance. Bellak's (1961) discussion of free association would have been helpful, had it been available earlier. He points out that the instruction to say whatever comes to mind without selection is an invitation to relax those functions (perceiving, reasoning, etc.) that we exercise in adapting to reality. This is an invitation to regress to a primary process mode of experiencing. Yet this regression, while sharing many of its characteristics, is not identical with the regression exhibited, for example, in schizophrenic thinking, in that the best working analytic patient is "able to oscillate between reduction and increased adaptive functions while exercising the synthetic functioning and thereby producing new insights, working through and reintegrating previous apperceptive distortions" (p. 14.). In short, the analysand regresses "in the service of the ego." One might expect that the psychoanalytic situation would foster a state of emotional detachment. The patient's supine position and the analyst's passivity, all with the intent of creating the maximum opportunity for the patient to experience himself, to hear the inner messages emitted in response to his relaxed posture and the echoes of immediate and remote past experience, certainly create conditions favorable to detachment. Bellak argues that the patient's awareness of his personal difficulties prevents it from developing.

Our thinking followed roughly along the above lines. After considerable discussion among our research staff[7] and many trial ratings, a series of rating scales were developed. One of them was a global scale of the adequacy of response which we defined as follows:

Table 1
General Scale of Free Association

1. *Severely blocked:* Many, many pauses. Long silences, perhaps with remarks about nothing coming to mind, or complaints or questions about the task. Often (but not necessarily) obviously upset by/about the task. Silences or intellectual argument and/or query about task predominates.
2. *Uninvolved listing:* Primarily describing, with minimal overt affective involvement (though much tension and strained inhibition may be evident), the room or physical details related to it. Or leafing through a series, be it of events, places, people, etc., which are fairly clearly dealt with as a class/ category of objects, this with minimal overt affective involvement. Emphasis here is ordinarily *less* on meaningful interpersonal or experiential "categories," and the impression is mainly one of listing, of marking time in an avoidant fashion. Cool, often somewhat stiff.
3. *Selected, little-involved, light conversation:* Emphasis here on conversational quality. Coherent, spoken in customary everyday fashion, with no notable spontaneity. Sentences, fairly standard pacing, deliberate. Note: wider range, *more* involvement and less obvious "categories" (if any) than Number 2, but still on impersonal side, could be casual talk with acquaintance.
4. *Relaxed, animated conversation:* Spontaneous, only moderately censored, dealing with emotionally significant matters with at least medium involvement. Little concern with connected, related-topic, organized narrative. But selection and editing still easily evident, and still slight relaxation of ordinary secondary processes—with no or only occasional breakthrough of sudden, tangential transitions and ruptured sentence structure.
5. *Mixed conversation-associate:* Spontaneous, unprepared, little-selected, strongly involved and meaningful, primarily conversational in nature, but permitting significant fragmentation of sentences and overtly "incoherent," unusual transitions.
6. *Loose-free association:* Irregularly paced, spontaneous, highly involved and meaningful, fragmented non-conversational form with "illogical" transitions, unprepared and not studied or deliberate.

[7] Dr. Albert Cain made distinct contributions in the formulation of the rating scales. Others who participated were Drs. Edward Lichtenstein, Robert Mendelsohn, and Robert Ryder and Mr. Martin Timin.

As we examined this scale and began to apply it, we became convinced that it was not unidimensional. Out of it we evolved three hopefully purer dimensions, all of which were fairly obviously embedded in
descriptions of the six points in the general scale. The part characteristics
of free association are Involvement, Spontaneity, and Freedom which
were defined by the following five-point scales:

Table 2
Involvement*

To be evaluated in terms of the subject's attitude toward the material spoken,
how much he cares about material spoken, as well as how much overt affective
expression there is. Affect here refers to the full scope of feeling (fondness,
anger, hurt, exasperation, joy, sorrow, etc.), but specifically *excludes* anxiety,
tension. Amount he "cares" is to be judged on the face, the surface of the material, deeper inferences *not* to be made (e.g., rater must not say "It's cool,
neutral, and half-hearted, but he spends a lot of time telling about it, so he
must really care greatly about it. . . .").

1. *Minimal:* virtually no concern or feeling visible, generally cold, flat, impersonal, half-hearted indifference (tension may or may not be visible).
2. Not totally gutless and icy, but generally neutral, cool, with only occasional evidence of significant feeling and concern.
3. *Moderate:* Affect and personal import often visible, though always well-
   modulated and balanced by cooler material.
4. Frequently strong concern and affect, clearly visible, but not passionately so.
5. *Intense:* reaching sharp peaks of affect, literal outbursts of emotion, and
   deeply felt concern almost always visible.

* Affective expression about or care about the task itself, e.g., angry rejection or
overwrought perplexity about why such a task, etc., is *not* to be evaluated on this
scale (Cf. Ego vs. Task-Orientation Scale). Where there is such strong task rejection
or such strong blocking that there is little material remaining/emerging on which to
base an "Involvement" rating, simply rate *XI.*

Table 3
Freedom—Inhibition*

To be evaluated in terms of degree of blocking, caution and circumlocution,
censorship, and stiffness/constriction. . . .

1. *Strongly inhibited:* rarely or never loose, free, unchecked; but loose
   enough so can still talk, even if haltingly. Often with a few quite long, or
   many, many short periods of silence; much constraint, reserve.
2. *Moderately inhibited:* notably restrained, relatively stiff, at least everyday

* As a given period of silence approaches 30 seconds, the presumption of inhibition
is great. With silences less than 30 seconds, inference is required as to its nature—
which may or may not be inhibitory. Many of the briefer silences, often amidst relatively freely flowing material, *may* simply represent genuine fallow moments as subject awaits next thought.

censoring. Few significant periods of silence, no marked halting quality, fairly smooth flow.

3. *Moderately informal, only somewhat less than ordinary:* everyday censoring, checking, restraint. Restraints noticeable but not predominant feature.

4. *Distinct departure from normal conversational quality:* visibly pushing beyond ordinary constraint, cautions, hesitancies or delicacies, but not severely so.

5. *Notably unguarded, rarely blocking or stiffening control for any length of time:* little checked, or qualified but *not* necessarily to any degree approaching anarchy.

Table 4
Planned—Spontaneous

To be evaluated in terms of degree to which prepared, deliberate, formally structured and ordered, polished. If severe blocking, etc. permits so little material that a meaningful rating cannot be made, rate "XO."

1. *Highly formal, well-ordered, well-connected, and even integrated, polished.* Perhaps even lecture-like. Virtually no peripheral irrelevancy admitted, almost no unrelated bits or splotches.

2. *Relatively formally ordered, connected, balanced presentation.* Occasional drifting off, disconnected material, and less delay/unembedded pieces of expression, but these still playing quite a minor role. Notably deliberate.

3. *Ordinary conversational quality.* Mixture of moderately organized and related material, with relatively relaxed, little-structured, unembroidered talk.

4. *Quite irregular, brief comments not formally presented.* Much tangential relating of material, minimal polishing: some manifest structuring efforts still visible, but much overshadowed.

5. *Almost "chaotic" from ordinary rational view.* Scrambled, seemingly unrelated, scattered quality, highly irregular in form, unforeseen and unexplained switches, bits and fragments of expression.

In addition to the above ratings, which concentrated on the formal characteristics of free association, we felt that a classification of content should be included to make the analysis of performance more complete. Five content categories were defined as follows:

Table 5
Content Categories*

A. *Inability to talk—Silence:*

Represented by dots, and in the case of relatively long silences, by parentheses within which total time of silence is set. Examples: "And that was about it. . . . . Well, wait now. . . . don't see what else . . . . . .

---

* Where categories (A), (B), and (C) involve fairly precise determinations of time, number of lines, etc., categories (D) and (E), while having suggested rough guidelines, are meant to be used with more reliance on rater judgment.

Table 5 *(Continued)*

. . . . . (33 secs.) This morning—" Each dot, beyond punctuation, represents three seconds of silence.

B. *Communications primarily about the task:*

Subject questions, suspects, derogates, battles, complains about the task. "Personal" reactions to the task, such as comments about being anxious, frightened, confident, worried about adequacy in it, are *not* generally to be included here (rather in *D*), except where the comments are made in repetitive fashion. Intellectual argument, analysis, or suspicion of the task *do* belong here. May be with very strong feeling. Examples: "Well, but, what's the purpose of it really?" "I just don't see how anyone could do th-that. Sometimes you just—I simply don't have any thought in my mind, not that I know of, not that I can sort of 'hear'. . And others, well, it's silly . . ." "You people hadn't mentioned something like this. You're not going to ask me any questions? . . . How-where are you supposed to start? If this is really is a measure of personality like you people said, I'm not sure I see . . . . I'm just supposed to start talking, and you'll take it down on something, and from it . . ."

C. *Communications primarily about discrete immediate environmental stimuli:*

Subject talks about the experimental room, its construction, wonders about its details. "I didn't know they had rooms like this in . . . is that a . . . I'll bet it's a one-way mirror. The couch is comfortable enough. . . maybe I'll go to sleep (laughs). Those wall and ceiling things, they're for the sound, the holes do it I guess, though I never exactly knew how . . ."

D. *Communications about interpersonal experience:*

1. *Relates actual interpersonal experiences.* Examples: speaks of girlfriends, outings with fraternity brothers, arguments with roommate, trouble with parents, tangle with police, landlord, teacher, sister.

2. *Speaks of emotive reactions to interpersonal experiences or fantasied or planned future ones.* Examples: speaks of feelings about roommate, kind of girl he dreams of being married to, guy he might room with, hopes for different attitudes among his peers toward him, way he is going to handle forthcoming battle at fraternity house meeting, thoughts about interpersonal aspect of jobs he's considering.

3. *Speaks of self as involved in specific object-less acts (e.g., painting, driving) or feelings (e.g., sadness) or events in which he's personally involved. Must be primarily concrete quality to discussion,* not *becoming a matter of abstract ideation.* Example: speaks of where he went, what he painted, how good it felt to be painting again vs. speaks of the essence of painting, its relationship to photography, conventional vs. artistic perception, etc. "Went to the movies, enjoyed heck out of it" vs. critique of current acting techniques and simple-minded movie "morals." Work on own play vs. abstract discussion of problems inherent in three-act play construction.

E. *Communications primarily about abstract ideas:*

1. *Ideas in and of themselves.* Even when ideas are discussed with a great

deal of feeling, even when subject identifies it as "my idea" and as an important "part" of himself, as long as what appears is essentially statement of abstract ideas, score here. Examples: subject states views on labor corruption, politics, conventionality, modern poetry, Emily Dickinson, types of jazz, etc.

2. *Self as related to classes of people solely in terms of ideas.* Examples: subject contrasts own views with those of faceless communists, bohemians, pacifists: "they" say, "a socialist would argue . . .", etc.

3. *"Pure" description of places, things, or another person's actions.* Examples: tells of waterfall he has heard of, describes other person or persons (*not* in terms of their interaction with subject) either as people or in various actions, e.g., two guys in dorm who are always fighting, adventures of friend in Asia, etc. Where person described appears to be mentioned essentially as a contrast or juxtaposition to the subject, or is someone intimately related to the subject, the material gains more of a (D) flavor.

Both the tape recording and the typescript were available to the raters. They were asked to listen to at least ten minutes of the tape, four at the beginning and end and two in the middle while following along with the typescript. They were encouraged to listen more when in doubt or to sense more fully some significant passages. The general rating was to be done first, then the three part scales, but ratings of content could be made at any point. For the raters' use, the amount of silence was timed and written in. This was especially useful in classifying content because we asked the raters to differentiate between primary and secondary content classifications of a performance. Fifteen minutes of silence automatically required a primary classification of "Silence." The rater could decide that there were no secondary or more than one secondary content themes. Table 6 shows the complete instructions given to the raters.

Table 6
Content Category Rating Instructions

Each interview is to be given a "primary" rating: what category the predominant portion of the interview fits in. Only convention here is that 15 minutes or more of silence *automatically* requires a primary "silence" (A). Where the silence constitutes less than 15 minutes, it *may or may not* deserve a primary; this is a question for the rater's judgment. An interview may have *no* "secondary" rating, or *one* or *more than one* secondary rating. Secondaries are not ranked as to importance where there are more than one: both are simply entered as secondaries.

The following constitute the criteria for gaining a secondary rating:

A. *Silence:*° when the sum total of all silences (15) seconds or more amounts to four minutes or more.

° Amount of silence will be totalled by us, and noted at the top of each typescript. Also note, in estimating one-sixth for categories D and E, ignore silences unless there was enough silence for a secondary rating.

Table 6 (Continued)

B. *Task:* roughly 18 *lines* of task communications. Single isolated lines here should be given little weight.

C. *Environs:* roughly 12 *lines* which are primarily "room-environment" reactions. Single, isolated sentences here should be given little weight.

D. *Interpersonal:* roughly one sixth of the *total time* (not just of the spoken words) of the transcript is to be in this category for it to obtain a secondary rating. This one-sixth is a rough guide, to be taken figuratively, not literally. If the material in this category is somewhat less than one-sixth but carries obviously intense feeling or is accompanied by much material right on the border of this category, give it a secondary rating.

E. *Abstract ideas:* same as D.

TRAINING AND AGREEMENT OF JUDGES

Our judges have been advanced students in clinical psychology, all of whom have had diagnostic and psychotherapeutic experience. As part of their training for use of the scale, judges were taken through six trial interviews and, when they seemed to be reaching a satisfactory level of agreement, were tested on another set of six interviews. In the latter trials we have obtained average percentage of agreements of .75.

In most of our studies we have had each interview rated by at least three judges and used either the consensus or a new rating consisting of the sum of their respective ratings. Since there were three judges rating different interviews, the usual average inter-judge correlation could not be computed. One alternative was to compute the percentage of agreement for the raters by finding the ratio of agreements, taken two at a time, to the total possible number of agreements. Knowing the number of scoring categories for each scale, one can compute the agreement expected by chance, and, using the expected distribution for number of interviews on which all three agreed, two out of three and none, a chi-square can be computed. The results of such an analysis in two of our studies are displayed in Table 7. As can be seen our raters agreed substantially better than chance.

Another indication of the agreement among our raters was obtained on a sample of interviews where the subject had five successive daily sessions. In all, 20 subjects were involved, two of them having four instead of five sessions, so that ratings of 98 interviews were available. This time Horst's (1949) expression for the case of unequal numbers of ratings was employed with the results shown in Table 8. Summarizing the two analyses, we can say that it is possible to obtain substantial agreement among raters who are relatively inexperienced clinicians.

Table 7
Obtained and Chance Percentage Agreement
for Free Association Rating Scales

Scale	Obtained Agreement		Chance Agreement	Chi-Square	
	Study 1	Study 2		Study 1	Study 2
General Scale	70	63	23.6	341.0*	292.3
Involvement	60	56	23.6**	118.5	92.0
Spontaneity	61	53	23.6**	160.9	78.1
Freedom	72	59	28.0	177.4	130.4
Content	85	82	28.0	385.8	558.5

* Chi-square of 9.2 is significant at .01 level
** It was possible to treat Involvement and Spontaneity as "Unratable" because of insufficient material. This judgment was treated as a sixth response category.

Intercorrelation of Free Association Ratings

In formulating ratings of the three part characteristics of free association we hoped to identify relatively independent attributes. An analysis of the intercorrelations among the general rating scale and the three part scales, which is given in Table 9, shows that we were not very successful. At the same time, there is sufficient gap, especially in the case of spontaneity, between the common variance and the variance reflected in reliability to leave some room for a variance specific to each part characteristic.

Table 8
Reliabilities (Horst Method) Among Six Raters in Rating
Each of Five Successive Free Association Interviews for Twenty Ss

Variables	Interview Number				
	1	2	3	4	5*
General Scale	.90	.80	.91	.68	.85
Involvement	.85	.80	.69	.68	.85
Spontaneity	.79	.78	.80	.92	.93
Freedom	.87	.81	.86	.85	.85

* N = 18

AREAS NEEDING INVESTIGATION

The vast literature of theoretical and clinical psychoanalysis represents a potentially rich source of inspiration for the research applications of the above described analogue. Three broad areas of investigation have al-

Table 9
Intercorrelations Among Free Association Rating
Scales Based on Sample I
(N = 40)

	I	S	F
Six Point Scale	.62	.69*	.88
Involvement		.42	.49
Spontaneity			.68
Freedom			

° Correlations in which Involvement or Spontaneity participate are based on 32 cases.

ready been foreshadowed in our preceding discussions: the links between personality differences and free association, dissection of the psychic components of the process, the influence of interventions.

Personality Differences and Free Association

Both Bellak and Rapaport have discussed the relevance of personality organization to response to free association. We have here the possibility of empirical verification of joint assumptions about psychopathology and the nature of psychic processes. Bellak (1961) points out that ". . . in certain types of associative disturbances, those found in obsessives, for example, the patient presents the analyst with a 'travelogue,' a faithful account of realistic events; he does not focus upon internal observation, nor does he regress topologically to preconscious levels or give up his cognitive vigilance. On the contrary, he often increases it, much like the sexually disturbed person who becomes excessively aware of every thought, every feeling and every action during intercourse—even the ticking of the clock" (p. 14). In discussing the oscillating function of the ego in free association, he suggests that some kinds of patients are better in the regressive phase while others are better in adaptive and synthesizing phases. Hysterics and schizophrenics are better able to regress, but obsessives are better able to adapt and synthesize. Of course, any imbalance makes for ineffectiveness in reaching the ideal of free association as a creative activity, one that results in new perceptions and in change.

In his concept of the autonomy of the ego of inner and outer-environments, Rapaport (1958) introduces ideas that point toward an understanding of how personality organization can influence response to the associative task. In essence he underlines the fact that psychic structures useful for memory storage, inhibition and delay, and reasoning, evolving out of native sensory-motor-cortico-neural equipment, are interposed between the individual and the pressures from drives and external stimuli. Since complete independence of either drives or external reality is inconceivable, Rapaport speaks of the relative autonomy of the ego. A necessary condition to effective functioning is the organism's capacity to maintain this relative autonomy and thus escape slavery either to drives or external stimulation. He points out that sudden intensification of drives (e.g., in puberty) or conditions of curtailed stimulation and information (e.g., sensory deprivation,) especially when coupled with humiliating, degrading, and guilt-arousing information, (e.g., in brainwashing,) all diminish ego autonomy. When it comes to an examination of how personality organization influences vulnerability to loss of autonomy, Rapaport seems to argue that personalities tend to be organized to maintain one side of the autonomy at the expense of the other. Again, we find obsessive-compulsives used as the example. He emphasizes the increased elaboration of the secondary process in this condition which makes for the substitution of intensified observation and logical analysis for affective and ideational signals. "Obsessive-compulsive defense thus maximizes the ego's autonomy from the id, but it does so at the cost of ever-increasing impairment of the ego's autonomy from the environment: the suppression of affective and ideational cues of drive origin renders the ego's judgments and decisions increasingly dependent upon external cues" (p. 23). Conversely, borderline and psychotic patients are seen as instances where reduction of the ego's autonomy of drives results in loss of touch with reality.

Thus, we can arrive at the general formulation that the balance of personality organization between autonomy of drives versus external stimulation will predict how an individual will respond to the task of free association. Other than broad statements regarding diagnostic categories such as obsessive-compulsive, psychotic, or hysteric, this formulation does not permit more precise specification of the personality attributes and the measures to be used to obtain them that will be predictive of response to free association. It seems likely that the gap can only be bridged by empirical investigations such as I have already undertaken. The surface has been only scratched. There are suggestions that certain kinds of laboratory perceptual tasks, (e.g., the number of reversals seen while fixating on a reversible figure,) and certain diagnostic clinical measures, (e.g., aspects of the Rorschach and the Minnesota Multiphasic,) will prove to be related.

In another paper (Bordin, 1963) I have argued that the logic of psychoanalysis calls for demonstration that performance in free association is related to the person's functioning in his daily life. This is necessary in order to lay down the network of evidence that will make possible meaningful investigations of the influence of psychoanalysis or other psychotherapies upon the various desiderata of "good mental health," e.g., the capacity to work effectively or to relate to others in a mutually gratifying and constructive fashion. In a sense, a comparison of the free associative responses of schizophrenic and non-psychiatric subjects would represent one form of this class of evidence. But studies will need to proceed beyond such crude means of describing daily functioning to much more intensive analysis of behavior which can penetrate the complexities behind the facade of "non-psychiatric" or "normal" status.

Dissection of the Free Associative Process

The most important feature of the free associative process is that, according to theory, it lays bare certain subtle aspects of psychic process which under more usual circumstances are not evident. With some ingenuity, it should be possible to verify some of these theories of psychic functioning. For example, one feature of primary process is a lessening of influence and control by space-time coordinates. By obtaining estimates of the passage of time under different levels of adequacy of free association (our Spontaneity measure seems the most relevant one), a test of part of the theory might be made. We would expect, of course, that those who achieved more adequate levels of response would show greater underestimation of the passage of time during the free associative period and those least adequate would show the greatest overestimation. This last error would arise from their experienced discomfort and eagerness to have the session come to an end.

Of both methodologic and theoretic interest is an investigation of the influence of different conditions of preparation and duration on free association. In exploratory studies, we found some evidence of the effects of these differences on ratings of free association. We compared ratings based on a single session in which the subject had no forewarning of his task with those based on four subsequent sessions and found differences, even though there was also considerable correlation. Moreover, there was a suggestion that the above-mentioned differences in ratings reflected different patterns of relationships with other measures, in that the relationship with reversible figures found in a single interview was reversed when ratings were based on the four subsequent interviews.

Influence of Interventions

In the long run, progress in psychotherapy depends upon the specificity of our knowledge of the influence of the therapeutic conditions and of the therapist's interventions. Colby (1960) started by investigating the basic question of the influence of the presence in the room of the experimenter and found effects on the content of free association.

Our analysis of the motivations of subjects in free association experiments suggested that a milder form of the dynamics of psychotherapy could be achieved. In our explorations with multiple sessions we have seen subjects troubled by their lack of freedom to associate. It would seem possible to design studies in which modes of intervention and experimenters (therapists) could be varied independently. Is it emotional support or interpretive activity that enables a person to overcome the inner obstacles toward free association? If it is the interpretive activity, can it be accomplished in a single disclosure? If not, is a specific order of disclosure needed to unlock the door?

SUMMARY

In the beginning our knowledge of psychotherapy depended upon the participant observations by patient and therapist. Gradually, methods of making possible direct observation by a third party have been introduced. Some of these methods have included the development of experimental analogues which raises the question of what it is that distinguishes the psychotherapeutic relationship from other relationships. Reflection on this question suggests that this relationship is marked by the special motivations of the patient for change, his conviction that it is he that should be changed, and his consequent willingness to accept the unusual task set by the basic rule. The intense reaction that this situation sets off in the patient creates an unusually provocative situation for the therapist.

With the above background, an experimental analogue of the psychoanalytic situation was described and the results of the development of measures of adequacy of free associative response was reported. A general scale of adequacy, and the specific scales, Involvement, Spontaneity, and Freedom, could be rated at acceptable levels of agreement among raters. While the specific scales fell far short of independence, it was judged that sufficient statistical specificity existed to encourage further exploration and improvement.

Several areas of study opened by this analogue were discussed. These included links between personality differences and free association, dissection of the psychic components of free association, and the influence of interventions on the free associative process.

REFERENCES

BELLAK, L. Free association: Conceptual and clinical aspects. *Int. J. Psychoanal.*, **42**: 9-20, 1961.

BORDIN, E. S. Ambiguity as a therapeutic variable. *J. consult. Psychol.*, **19**: 9-15, 1955.

BORDIN, E. S. Response to the task of free association as a reflection of personality. Paper read at Seventh International Congress for Scientific Psychology, Washington, D.C., August, 1963.

BRILL, A. A. *The basic writings of Sigmund Freud.* New York: Modern Library, 1938.

COLBY, K. M. Experiment on the effects of an observer's presence on the imago system during psychoanalytic free-association. *Behavioral Sci.*, **5**: 197-210, 1960.

GILLESPIE, J. F., JR. Verbal signs of resistance in client-centered therapy. In W. U. Snyder (Ed.), *Group report of a program of research in psychotherapy*. State College, Penna.: Pennsylvania State University, 1953. Pp. 105-119.

GREENBLATT, M. Discussion of methods of assessment of change. In E. A. Rubinstein and M. B. Parloff (Eds.), *Research in psychotherapy*. Washington, D.C., American Psychological Association, 1959. Pp. 209-220.

GRUMMON, D. L., and BUTLER, J. M. Another failure to replicate Keet's study: two verbal techniques in a miniature counseling situation. *J. abnorm. soc. Psychol.*, 48: 597, 1953.

HORST, P. A generalized expression for the reliability of measures. *Psychometrika*, 21-31, 1949.

KEET, C. D. Two verbal techniques in a miniature counseling situation. *Psychol. Monogr.*, 62: No. 14 (Whole No. 287), 1948.

MERRILL, R. M. On Keet's study, "Two verbal techniques in a miniature counseling situation." *J. abnorm. soc. Psychol.*, 47: 722, 1952.

RAPAPORT, D. The theory of ego autonomy: A generalization. *Bull. Menn. Clinic*, 22: 13-35, 1958.

ROGERS, C. R. The organization of personality. *Amer. Psychologist*, 2: 358-368, 1947.

ROGERS, C. R., and DYMOND, ROSALIND F. (Eds.) *Psychotherapy and personality change*. Chicago: Univ. of Chicago Press, 1954.

RUBINSTEIN, E. A., and PARLOFF, M. B. (Eds.) *Research in psychotherapy*. Washington, D.C.: American Psychological Association, 1959.

SCHNEIDER, S. F. Prediction of psychotherapeutic relationship from Rorschach's test. Unpublished doctoral dissertation, Univ. of Michigan, 1953.

SNYDER, W. U. Some investigations of relationship in psychotherapy. In E. A. Rubinstein, and M. B. Parloff (Eds.), *Research in psychotherapy*. Washington, D.C.: American Psychological Association, 1959. Pp. 247-259.

SPEISMAN, J. C. Depth of interpretation and verbal resistance in psychotherapy. *J. consult. Psychol.*, 23: 93-99, 1959.

STRUPP, H. H. The therapist's contribution to the treatment process: Beginnings and vagaries of a research program. In, H. H. Strupp and L. Luborsky (Eds.), *Research in psychotherapy*. Washington, D.C.: American Psychological Association, 1962. Pp. 25-40.

STRUPP, H. H., and LUBORSKY, L. *Research in psychotherapy*. Washington, D.C.: American Psychological Association, 1962.

TEMERLIN, M. K. One determinant of the capacity to free associate in psychotherapy. *J. abnorm. soc. Psychol.*, 53: 16-18, 1956.

17. The consensus problem in psychoanalytic research

Philip F. D. Seitz

The consensus problem in psychoanalytic (and psychotherapeutic) research refers to the difficulty that clinicians have in agreeing upon the interpretation of the same set of (interview) data. This problem exists in every field of science, although some sciences necessarily depend more upon interpretation than others. Archeology and paleontology are examples of sciences that must utilize considerable interpretation in attempting to synthesize and reconstruct total pictures from fragmentary observational data. Psychodynamic research, which includes research in psychotherapy, is another such example. Psychoanalysis has shown how extensively the phenomena of personality and behavior tend to occur without direct, straightforward, objectively observable manifestations. The investigator of psychological dynamics must develop methods for "reading between the lines" and "piecing things together"—i.e., for interpreting certain aspects of the total situation that are not immediately apparent, may only be alluded to indirectly, or may even be conspicuous by their absence from the manifest behavior.

The consensus problem arises when several observers of the same behavior attempt to compare their individual interpretive formulations. As often as not, they interpret differently. Even highly experienced and skilled clinicians who are trained in the same clinical discipline (e.g., a group of senior analysts) may have difficulty in agreeing upon the interpretation of the same psychodynamic material.

What does this mean? The most extreme view would be that with such glaring lack of agreement among the experts of a field, there can be no science. Possibly that is true, at least in the sense that psychodynamics is still more of an art than a science. But what else might account for this lack of agreement among the experts? It might conceivably result from the various observers focusing upon different parts of a total picture. If that were the case, the various observers would not necessarily all be completely wrong in their interpretive formulations; each might be only partly right.

Research in psychoanalysis is one of the subjects hardest hit by the consensus problem since psychoanalysis depends so extensively upon interpretive methods. Since the psychoanalytic process serves as a "laboratory" for investigating many subjects, it is most in need of consistent and systematic interpretive methods that can make consensus possible among different observers.

Although research in the dynamics of the therapeutic process has become widespread in recent years, the trend in most such research has been to approach these problems with the strategy of attempting to improve the methods of observation, collection, and recording of interview data. Relatively little attention has been paid to the problem of how these data are to be analyzed and interpreted. A group of psychoanalysts under the leadership of Leopold Bellak (1956) attempted to make independent formulations of the same case material. That research did not focus upon the consensus problem, however, nor did it attempt to develop an improved system of interpretation. The researches of Carl Rogers (1949) and his associates utilize various objective tests of the therapeutic process, rather than attempting to analyze and interpret the interview data themselves. Louis Gottschalk (1963) and others (Dollard and Mowrer, 1947; Dollard and Auld, 1959; Kaufman and Raimey, 1949) have attempted to develop systematic methods for interpreting interview data by quantitative analysis of verbal samples. The present writer knows of only two reports, both of which are unpublished, that deal directly and specifically with the consensus problem in psychoanalytic and psychotherapeutic research. One is a report by French, presented to the American Psychoanalytic Association in 1954; and the other was a report by this writer (1956) to the Rockefeller Foundation.

In the fall of 1956, with the aid of a research grant from the USPHS, six analysts at the Chicago Institute for Psychoanalysis formed a research group to study the consensus problem. The present writer was the coordinator of the project. Other members of the group (for variable periods of time) were Doctors Thomas M. French, Louis B. Shapiro, Fred P. Robbins, George Pollock, Roy M. Whitman, Joseph G. Kepecs, and William C. Lewis. The researchers continued for three years and then disbanded because of inability to make progress in developing a reliable interpretive method—i.e., a method that would yield greater consensus among a group of analysts in making independent formulations of the same case material. In a sense, therefore, this chapter reports the failure of a research, although not necessarily of the research method that was used. Although the results of this investigation are largely negative, the research method may be worth reporting.

The basic plan of the investigation was for the members of the research group to make independent interpretive formulations of the same psychologic case material, and then to study the reasons for their difficulties in obtaining agreement. Systematic study of the reasons for our lack of consensus helped us to discover defects and discrepancies in our individual ways of interpreting psychologic data. Theoretically, knowledge of these deficiencies in our interpretive techniques should have provided us with opportunities for improving our methods of interpretation.

Two types of case material were used: small units of material, such as first dreams, from different cases; and ongoing material from a single, continuous case. First dreams were used because of their frequent clarity and ease of interpretation. The reason for using a continuous case was that we wanted to have the advantages of studying one case intensively enough to enable us to examine the validity of our interpretations by attempting to make predictive tests. At the same time, we wanted to expose ourselves to a large enough variety of cases so that we could become familiar with the problems of our interpretive techniques in patients with different types of psychopathology.

The case material used by the Consensus Group was in the form of mimeographed interview notes. The notes had been written by the treating analyst during and after each interview.

The continuous case was that of a patient on whom very complete notes had been kept and typed. The cases from which only small units of material (such as first dreams) were studied came from various sources, but primarily from the teaching case seminars at the Institute.

The project coordinator arranged for the secretary to make copies of the case material to be studied each week. The copies were distributed to the members of the Consensus Group. Each member did independent work on this case material, and sent to the coordinator an interpretive formulation of it. The secretary typed up these formulations in enough copies so that each member could receive a copy of every other member's formulation. The names of the different members were not put on the typewritten copies of their formulations. The latter procedure was an (unsuccessful) attempt to avoid being influenced by each other personally.

Upon receiving the anonymous copies of everyone's interpretation, each member did further independent work preparing a revision of his original formulation. The second interpretation utilized clues obtained from the other formulations, in addition to one's own ideas. The purpose of the second formulation was to provide us with an opportunity to make independent syntheses of several interpretations, prior to coming together as a group and attempting this.

We experimented with two types of write-ups for the independent formulations. One was a mimeographed form to be filled out by the investigators. The other was an essay-type of write-up, in which emphasis was given to an explanation of the investigator's *interpretive reasoning,* i.e., it described how the investigator arrived at his interpretation and the steps he took in reaching his conclusions. The latter type of write-up proved most useful, and we adopted it. We did agree, however, to give specific answers to the following series of questions in our write-ups:

1. What is the precipitating situation or event?
2. What is the focal conflict? (This refers to the preconscious conflict with which the patient is most intensely preoccupied at that time, and is broken down into a "disturbing motive" and a "reactive motive.")
3. What are the defenses against and efforts at solution of the focal conflict?
4. What was your interpretive reasoning in arriving at this formulation?
5. What evidence supports your formulation?
6. What evidence is opposed to, or not accounted for, by your interpretation?

A word may be said at this point about the concept of *focal* conflict. In attempting to interpret the events of an entire interview, the psychoanalytic investigator is confronted with the problem that multiple motives may be operative at any given time (overdetermination of mental events). French's concept of focal conflict assumes that during any one time period such as a single interview, the Preconscious tends to be focused upon one principal (but highly condensed, overdetermined) problem at a time. As the present writer has discussed and attempted to demonstrate in another report (1962), associated, unconscious, genetic conflicts are activated during the same time period, the emotional charges of which are characteristically transferred[1] to the single, hypercathected, *focal* conflict in the Preconscious. It is the present writer's concept, therefore (not fully shared by T. M. French) that the focal conflict usually consists of the current transference to the analyst, and is best understood theoretically in terms of the dynamics of day-residues. Because these hypercathected, preconscious conflicts constitute points of convergence of dynamic forces within the mind, they provide a useful focus for unifying and integrating interpretive formulations of the complex, seemingly heterogeneous associational material of individual interviews. In the present research, the interpreters agreed to interpret what they considered to be the *focal* (i.e., most hypercathected, preconscious) conflict in each interview, as well as the factors and events giving rise to it (i.e., precipitating stimuli), and the principal defenses against and attempted solutions of the focal conflict.

Soon after we began our research, a fairly high level of interest and enthusiasm developed. We found ourselves waiting impatiently to compare our own formulations with those of the other investigators. The temptation was strong to ask each other about our respective interpretations before the scheduled meetings. At the meetings themselves, heated discussions and arguments would develop, each investigator passionately championing and defending his own formulation. If this phase of the work had no other result, it certainly did get the group off to an enthusiastic start.

[1] For discussion of Freud's original, metapsychologically more precise, endopsychic (in contrast to his later, interpersonal) definition of *transference,* see Kohut (1959), and Kohut and Seitz (1963).

As time went on, this original exuberance about the project mellowed into a more sober attitude of puzzlement and curiosity about why we were having so much difficulty in obtaining agreement. The character of our write-ups and of our consensus meetings began to change. The formulations became more tentative, the meetings more restrained. Often, investigators would state in their write-ups that they were uncertain about the interpretation, and began to include data that could not be accounted for by the tentative formulations they submitted. The group adopted a rule that in the consensus meetings only one formulation could be considered at a time. A corollary of this rule stated that the formulation under discussion could not be criticized by a suggestion that some other formulation fitted the facts better. Each interpretation came to be studied on its own merits. This was accomplished by the group's choosing one of the interpretations at a time for critical discussion. While this formulation was being evaluated, no other interpretation could be considered or brought into the discussion. Comparison of differing interpretations was postponed until each interpretation had been reviewed and discussed individually.

The group functioned as a totality, not as a conglomeration of individuals, in these critical evaluations, systematically studying one point after another in the interpretation to determine the evidence for or against it. No one individual necessarily became protagonist for or antagonist of the interpretation being evaluated. If someone saw evidence supporting a point he mentioned it, and whoever felt doubt about the adequacy of the evidence indicated so. The project coordinator kept running notes of the discussions, which were useful in reviewing what points had been covered and what points remained to be considered.

The group's definition of *agreement* was fairly stringent. In the weekly meetings, the entire group had to decide whether and how two interpretations agreed or disagreed. When two interpretations were compared, it was not enough for the two interpreters involved to conclude that they were in agreement or disagreement concerning particular points. The rest of the research team also participated, somewhat like "referees," in the discussions and debates comparing individual interpretations. Frequently the referees took sides in these discussions; the group then tended to become deadlocked in disagreement. This outcome was considered "agreement that we had disagreed." Occasionally we could "agree that we had agreed."

There was very little, if any, tendency in this group to take sides based upon personal loyalties, status positions, etc. Sides were taken which tended to agree with one's own interpretation of the moment. Narcissistic investment in one's own interpretive ideas appeared to be a considerable (some of us believe, a formidable) obstacle to progress in improving our interpretive methods in psychoanalysis.

Eventually the group developed more zeal for detailed *microscopic,* point-for-point analysis of how all of the dream and associational data could be accounted for, rather than being satisfied with an interpretation that could account for only part of the data. This led to a sustained interest in repeated meetings on a continuous case.

Predictions about future developments in the continuous case were made both independently by the different members of the group, and by the group as a whole, when consensus could be reached about such predictions. Predictions were recorded by the coordinator in his notes, and also in a separate "List of Predictions," which was kept up-to-date by the coordinator and secretary, and which was on hand for all members of the group to see each time they met.

Following each consensus meeting, the project coordinator attempted to make an analysis of the agreements and disagreements on the first and second attempts at independent formulation of that week's material. He did this in two principal ways: by a detailed tabulation of each member's interpretation, broken down according to categories; and by a more "gestalt" approach in which he attempted to summarize, in brief condensed statements, the patterns and trends of agreement and disagreement. The main purpose of these data analyses was to search for clues about the nature of our disagreements and possible reasons for them. A less important reason for doing this was to keep a sort of "scoreboard" of our consensus results.

The results of our research, if viewed only in terms of consensus obtained, would hardly deserve mention. Our results in this respect are strongly negative. On very few of our attempts at independent formulation did we reach satisfactory consensus. The positive results of our work were of three kinds. First, we demonstrated that there is a consensus problem; second, we established a working concept of the basis for this problem—the inadequacy of our interpretive methods; and third, we made some progress in discovering and correcting certain errors and deficiencies in our interpretive procedures.

How are our difficulties in obtaining interpretive consensus to be explained? Overdetermination of mental events is doubtless one of the principal reasons for this result. On the other hand, psychoanalytic theory postulates that condensed, overdetermined contents from the dynamically repressed Unconscious transfer themselves across or through the repression barrier to particular day residues in the Preconscious—which, theoretically at least, should produce a kind of *final common pathway* effect in the form of preconscious transference *carriers.* As discussed previously (p. 212), the concept of *focal conflict* implies dynamic processes of this kind, the focal conflict in a well-proceeding analysis usually consisting of the current transference to the analyst. The participants in the Consensus Research Project were not asked to interpret the unconscious overdeterminants of the focal (preconscious) conflict, however, but only to specify the currently most highly cathected derivatives of such (endo-psychic) transferences. Our consensus difficulties had to do with the inter-pretation of these focal, preconscious derivatives which, being more unitary mental contents and nearer the surface, theoretically should be easier to interpret and to agree upon. Instead, we found that participants often tended to interpret at levels *deeper* than the focal conflict in the Preconscious, frequently singling out a specific *unconscious* overdeter-minant of the focal conflict and organizing an entire interpretive formula-tion around that particular dynamic trend.[2] This finding led to our conclu-sion that difficulties in reaching consensus are due, not so much to the various interpreters being *all wrong*, but to the fact that each of us tends to be *only partly right*.

Various kinds of overdetermination probably contribute to problems of interpretation and interpretive consensus. One might be the occurrence of genuine complementarities of motives: e.g., a particular form of be-havior simultaneously serving id, ego and super-ego motives, all of which complement each other. Another type of overdetermination involves the co-existence of opposite motives. In the Temple University interview, for example (see below), "hostile-competitive impulses toward Al" and "pas-sive homosexual feelings toward Al" may be present and condensed in the same element of behavior.

On the other hand, the exact dynamic relationship between a configura-tion such as hostile-competitive and passive-homosexual feelings needs to be determined at the particular time that it occurs and in the specific context in which it is imbedded. Is the passive attitude a defense against conflict about competitive feelings; or *vice versa;* or is each serving alter-nately as a defense against the other? Theoretically, there should be ways of making such distinctions interpretively. The art and science of psy-choanalysis have not yet advanced to the point, however, at which we can do that consistently and reliably.

Another possible reason for our difficulties in obtaining consensus was the fact that we attempted to interpret material from relatively early phases of on-going analyses, during which conflict and defense patterns were still very disguised and obscure. As the present writer has discussed and illustrated elsewhere (1962) concerning retrospective, research anal-ysis of psychoanalytic interview data, in a treatment that proceeded well, the dynamics of the analytic process are much clearer and more easily interpretable toward the end of the analysis, when the intensity of de-fenses had been reduced markedly. For this reason (and others), it is important to use cases for research purposes in which the end phases of

---

[2] This finding is reminiscent of a related observation found in Bellak and Smith (1956, Table 1, p. 403); viz. at times their raters agreed more on the patient's uncon-scious motives than on his conscious ones!

treatment were reached and completed satisfactorily—preferably cases
in which considerable resolution of defenses and conflicts occurred, with
associated clarification of dynamics. In the retrospective, research analysis
and interpretive reconstruction of data from such analyses, the author has
found it useful, after reading or listening to the records of the entire treatment, to start at the end of the analysis, where the dynamic processes
and sequences are easier to interpret, and then to work back toward the
beginning of the case.

Since, as French (1954, 1958)[3] has shown (supported by my own
studies), the analytic process follows repetitive dynamic cycles which become shorter as the treatment proceeds, it is sometimes possible to reconstruct one entire dynamic cycle near the end of the treatment, and then
to use it as a *template*, pattern and guide for interpreting and reconstructing earlier cycles in the analysis.

The principal (but certainly not the only) defect that we discovered
in our respective interpretive approaches was excessive reliance upon
intuitive impressions and insufficient attention to the systematic and
critical checking of our interpretations. Some of us found that formerly
we had used highly subjective ways of attempting to gauge the correctness of an intuition; e.g., by noting the strength or subjective impact of
the *hunch*. More and more, we were forced to the conclusion that intuitive impressions must be tested in more objective ways than that. Intuition cannot be dispensed with in this type of interpretive scientific work.
It requires systematic, critical checking, however, in order to control the
factor of personal idiosyncratic bias, which exists in any subjective process.

Our interpretive technique evolved toward an essentially two-step procedure: first, giving free rein to the intuitive imagination in search of possible interpretations; and then, having hit upon an interpretation which
appeared to have possibilities, going to the actual interview data to see
whether and to what extent this hypothesis fit the facts. The more interview data that could be accounted for by the interpretation, and the more
internal consistency that could be shown to exist among the data by applying this interpretation, the more likely it was considered to be correct. We
considered it a mark of progress in our work when we were able to see
data that did not fit our interpretive hypotheses.

As far as a consistent system of interpretation was concerned, the closest
we came to that was French's interpretive method, which we attempted to
test for reliability. It was not a fair test, however, since we repeatedly
came upon inconsistencies and misunderstandings in our various ways of
applying that method. Consensus on the principles and procedures of a
method is necessary before the results of applying the method can be

[3] See especially Vol. II (1954), pp. 299-304, 308-312; and Vol. III (1958), pp.
107, 113-135, 287-302, 403-404, 451-453.

tested. Since French (1952, 1954) has described his method elsewhere, it will not be repeated here.

Summarizing, in this research we attempted to work toward an improved interpretive method in psychoanalysis, tested for reliability by the method of consensus, and for the validity of its results by the methods of internal consistency and prediction. Despite the largely negative results statistically, a number of observations, findings, and conclusions from the investigation provide some basis for encouragement that interpretive consensus among psychoanalysts may be possible some day. We know now that this problem exists. Once the problem is more out in the open, it is almost certain to be investigated more extensively. Eventually, improvements in our methods of interpretation should result.

At this point, schematic summaries of the Consensus Group's interpretations of the "Temple University" interview will be presented, followed by a more detailed interpretation of that interview by the present writer in which he attempted as far as possible to follow the principles of French's interpretive method.

All five of the interpreters agreed that the precipitating situation was the patient's feelings and fantasies about the consultation, and the effect upon these of Al's sudden and unexpected leaving. Three interpreters agreed that the disturbing motive of the focal conflict was hostile competitive impulses toward Al, while the other two interpreters each postulated different disturbing motives. Some agreements and overlaps are seen among the postulated reactive motives, but there is even more disagreement here. The same may be said about the postulated principal defenses and attempted solutions.

It might be mentioned in this connection that, taking all of our experiments in interpretation over a three-year period, we found most agreement on disturbing motives, least on principal defenses and attempted solutions, with precipitating situations and reactive motives being about equal in consensus and intermediate between the two extremes. Why we were most successful on disturbing motives and least on defenses and solutions is not entirely clear and warrants further study. The present writer has theorized in another report (1962) that the reason for this finding may be because focal conflicts, although complexly overdetermined, are more unified, unitary, condensed mental contents; whereas the patient's repertoire of defense mechanisms against and attempted solutions of a particular focal conflict may be more discrete; i.e., the various defenses cathectically less connected or condensed directly with each other. According to this concept, the seeming heterogeneity of associative material from any one interview may not result so much from serial activation of successive conflicts, but from multiple attempts to ward off and solve a single focal conflict. Considered in this way, the manifest content of an analytic interview may be interpreted in terms of *multiple*

Table 1

Schematic Summary of the Focal Conflict in the "Temple University" Interview

Interpreter	Precipitating Situation	Disturbing Motive	Reactive Motive	Principal Defenses and Attempted Solutions
A	Al's absence from interview interferes with defense of pleasing Al by performance, and gives rise to anxiety about competitive feelings toward Al.	Destructive competitiveness toward Al.	Fear of punishment.	Maintain close, dependent relationship to analyst.
B	The consultation, with sudden, unexpected absence of Al.	Hostile competitive impulses toward Al.	Fear of inadequacy.	Identification with aggressor. Pseudo-rebellion. Pseudo-compliance. Self-depreciation.
C	Interview made him feel inferior, which he hoped to relieve by appearing superior to Al in the eyes of the woman consultant. Al's leaving frustrated this hope, left him feeling inferior, which activated hostile rivalrous feelings toward Al.	Hostile phallic-Oedipal rivalry toward Al (as father-figure) for the admiration and favor of the woman consultant (as mother-figure) with the fantasy of cutting off Al's penis and using it to gain superiority over Al.	Fear of retaliative castration from Al (father).	Self-abnegating reaction-formations. Dependent regression. Rationalization. Projection.
D	Disappointed that Al left because he wanted to impress him. In the absence of Al, he turns to the interviewer for cues.	Wish to please the woman interviewer who urges him continually to be aggressive.	Wish to remain on the good side of Al, who will know the content of this interview.	Denial of his successes and dependence upon Al.
E	Disappointed that Al left because he wanted to use this opportunity to continue a warm, younger colleague-type relationship with Al.	Passive homosexual feelings toward Al.	Shame.	Pseudo-aggressive protests.

defenses against and attempted solutions of a *single* hypercathected conflict with which the patient is struggling preconsciously at that time. The *multiplicity* of defenses and solutions, in contrast to the singleness of the focal conflict, may help to account for our finding that psychoanalytic interpreters agree more on focal conflicts (at least, on the disturbing motive of the focal conflict) than they do on mechanisms of defense against and solution of conflicts.

Eight two-hour meetings were held at weekly intervals to discuss the interpretations of this interview; but rather than reaching more agreement from these discussions, if anything, more disagreements were discovered. Along these lines, our overall trends for all interpretive experiments (over the three-year period) revealed that as a group, and considering all interpretive categories combined, we modified our interpretations 30 percent of the time. Individually, the interpreters varied over a fairly wide range in how often they modified their interpretations. One interpreter changed his formulations 54 percent of the time. Another interpreter modified his formulations only 8 percent of the time. As the group continued in its work together, the individuals did not change much in how frequently they modified their interpretations. Most changes were made in the category of reactive motives, least in precipitating situations. Disturbing motives and attempted solutions were about equal and between these two extremes.

Differences in reliability were also found between our efforts to interpret entire interviews, in contrast to more discrete bits of material such as individual dreams. Usually it was more difficult to obtain consensus about a more discrete bit of material. The longer the time span studied and interpreted, the more abstract the dynamic formulations became, and the easier it was to fit various interpretations into a general scheme.

The following is this writer's detailed interpretation of the "Temple University" interview, which attempted to follow the principles of French's interpretive method (1952, 1954, 1958).

Parallel[4] *1.*

A. Patient expected Dr. Scheflen to be present at the interview, but Dr. Scheflen didn't come.
B. He speaks of a meeting at which he felt "so depressed . . . 'cause had these fantasies of walking in and the auditorium packed, but it wasn't (3'5"–3'6")* it was just a couple of people sitting here" (a slip, which he then changes to "there").
   Inference: Patient is disappointed that Al is not present. (The interviewer came to this same conclusion [6'0"–6'4"].)

_____
* Elapsed time of the "Temple University" interview in minutes and seconds. (See pp. 241 of this book.)
[4] Searching for implicit parallels and contrasts in the clinical data is a feature of French's interpretive approach.

The question arises in my mind now: Exactly what is the nature of his disappointment? To answer this, we would have to know exactly why the patient hoped Al would be present. He says that he wanted Al there so he would get clues from him about how to act (8'1"-8'5"). However, this is his conscious reason, and therefore this explanation is likely to be a defensive-solution rationalization (for an underlying reason about which he is in conflict). With this interpretive reasoning in mind, I look for other parallels and contrasts.

Parallel 2 (via contrast).

A. He pictures self as rather helpless and unable to function without Al present to provide the cues (10'4"—11'9").
B. Yet at 12'1" to 13'1" the example he gives (of being "like the kid who wants to do what his father does") is one in which Al had a problem and "wanted me to tell him what to do."
C. (The example pictures him as anything but helpless; in fact, if anyone is helpless and in need of help, it is Al. Cf. also that patient is "helping Al out" by agreeing to have this filmed-recorded interview, which will assist Al in his researches.)
   Inference: Patient's picturing self as helpless without Al to provide the cues is a coverup for feelings and fantasies of wanting to reverse the roles with Al and be in a superior position to him.

I then wonder: What is the source of this fantasy and wish? The material (13'2"-14'3") suggests a possible answer: He recalls something Al told him about his son, an incident in which the son taught the father something. His fantasy of "child being father of the man," therefore, probably has a father-son origin.

Parallel 3.

A. The man he spoke of "tangling with" (27'6"—28'2") "didn't go far enough in his analysis to get all his problems worked out."
B. Patient is being interviewed by consultant because results of his analysis with Dr. Scheflen were not entirely satisfactory.
   Inference: The man he spoke of tangling with refers to himself, and what he accuses this man of represents largely a projection of his own feelings.

What did he accuse this man of? The following: (1) ". . . a guy who's got really fierce internal hostility." (2) ". . . the most vicious self-conscious(ness) of anybody he knew." (3) ". . . palms self off as a great deal more than he is." (4) ". . . trying to undercut Al." (5) ". . . makes cutting comments." (6) ". . . a little guy, physically not very big" (who is envious of Al's big size). (7) ". . . he's going to cut me, up underneath." These associations suggest a hostile-rivalrous attitude toward Al; and the repeated references to cutting and undercutting (up underneath) suggest more specifically hostile-castrative impulses toward Al's penis.

Parallel 4.

A. Material about man wanting to undercut Al (24′6″–25′3″).
B. He has fantasy of Al cutting out part of film (32′1″).
   Inference: The reactive motive to his castrative impulses toward Al is fear of retaliative castration from Al.

At this point in my interpretive reasoning, I wonder whether the hostile phallic rivalry toward Al (and fear of retaliation) occur in connection with, or independently of, Oedipal fantasies. I look for material that might help to answer this question.

Parallel 5.

A. In the material about the man he "tangled with," he brings up a woman, speaks of her "breaking with the head of the organization" (26′5″–26′8″) and of his being asked to "iron out the problem between them." (Here again—this time in a situation involving two men and one woman—he pictures self being not the one who needs help, but the one who gives it.)
B. He had the fantasy that present interview would involve three people: woman consultant, Al, and himself.
C. He had been asked to undergo this interview for research purposes, which would assist Al and possibly also the woman consultant.
   Inference: He reacted to the present interview (unconsciously) as an opportunity to compete successfully with Al for admiration and favor in the eyes of the woman consultant.

The last parallel and inference appear to round out the interpretive picture, which I shall now try to formulate schematically as follows:

Precipitating Situation.

A. Being interviewed by woman consultant about the incompleteness of his analysis (and therefore, by implication, his lack of maturity) makes him feel inferior.
B. Hope of relieving the inferiority feelings by appearing superior to Al in the eyes of woman consultant is facilitated by reality of Al's having asked patient to help him in this research project; by reality of Al's not having "succeeded" in his analysis of patient; and by reality that patient is more experienced in this sort of situation (movie-recording-performing before audience) than Al is.
C. He is disappointed in this hope when Al is not present at interview. Since this hope was a fantasied solution for inferiority feelings, its failure to materialize left him more exposed to the inferiority feelings, and activated hostile-rivalrous feelings toward Al.

Focal Conflict.

Hostile phallic-Oedipal rivalry toward Al (as father-figure) for admiration and favor of woman consultant (as mother-figure), with reactivation of boyhood fantasy of achieving this by cutting off Al's penis and using it to produce a reversal of roles with Al—himself becoming the father and Al the child—*versus* Fear of retaliative castration from Al (father).

Defenses and Attempted Solutions

1. (8'1"-8'5") Rationalizes that disappointment about Al's not being present is due to inability to get cues from Al. This condenses both:
   A. that he wants to get something from Al, feels unable to function effectively without Al's power; and
   B. (10'4"-11'9") and (18'2"-18'4") defensive attitude that he is just a helpless little boy who needs Daddy to tell him what to do.
2. (18'7"-19'3") Rationalizes that he just wants to "identify" with Al, "be like him" (not take anything away from him).
3. (18'6") Now pictures self not only as helpless little boy, but also as bungling, clumsy, "idiotic." The emphasis is on how harmless he is—no threat to anyone.
4. (21'1") "Heee did it." Pretends he wants Al to have all the glory. "He's really running it, off the scene." The defensive emphasis is still on keeping his own light hidden under a bushel.
5. (21'6") "Al will be famous in 10 years, I in 11." Assures everyone he will stay one jump behind Al—another self-abnegating defense.
6. (24'1") The preceding series of rationalizations and self-abnegating defenses appear to fail, because associations now refer directly to "fierce, vicious hostility"—which apparently can no longer be kept repressed and disguised and can therefore only be projected or denied. He projects it—to a rival at work—and the form this takes [25'3"-28'8"] has both the Oedipal content which was referred to in the postulated focal conflict, and allusions to inferiority and rivalry about who is the most adequately analyzed.
7. (24'7" and 32'2") The phallic rivalry with Al (about their penises) is displaced to rivalry about who is the best analyzed in two places (24'7" and 32'2"); he subtly depreciates Al: "After all, Al's been through two wives and uh—he didn't get his—insight the easy way, you know. All the mistakes he made. . . ." "It was quite a while after the end of his (Al's) analysis before he caught on that (he was copying his analyst's likes and dislikes about people)."
8. (32'1") Fear of castrative retaliation from Al is displaced to fantasy of Al cutting out the part of film in which patient depreciated him as incompletely analyzed.

Material not accounted for, and observations about this interpretation.

1. There is too much associative material in the interview to make a point-by-point comparison of the fit between each manifest content

and the present formulation. The principal section of material that may not fit this interpretation is that from 27'6"-28'9": his acrimonious discussion with the man at work about how completely analyzed the man was. Since I have postulated that the material about this man represents mainly a projection of his own feelings, then it should follow that these particular associations also refer to himself; he must feel that he himself needs more analysis.

This does not fit my formulation of the rest of the interview very well. Why should he shift suddenly from his hostile-rivalrous feelings toward Al to tell himself forcefully that he needs more analysis? The only way I can integrate this with my present interpretation (and avoid an "and . . . and . . . and" interpretation) is to postulate that he introduced this as a possible solution to the focal conflict—a solution which may have come from the more rational part of his ego. Since this possible hope of solution did not reach consciousness directly, but was projected, I have to assume that it produced a supra-focal (solutional) conflict (possibly with his pride, to admit that he was incompletely analyzed), and that this momentary hope of solution therefore had to be repudiated. If this additional interpretation were unable to account satisfactorily for the material about how much analysis the man had had, then this should be considered a discrepancy and the present interpretation modified as necessary to relieve the discrepancy.

2. The material from 25'3"-27'5" which I have interpreted as having triangular Oedipal connotations, is somewhat ambiguous; and, actually, there are more than three people involved in the incident reported: the woman, the man he tangled with, the "head of the organization" and the patient himself. My interpretation of the Oedipal components in the focal conflict depends upon a postulated parallel between his being asked:

A. to iron out the problem between the woman and the head of the organization, and

B. his fantasy that the present interview would consist of three people —Al, woman consultant, and himself and that he was in position of doing both a favor.

More minute analysis of the parallel in these two incidents reveals two distinct areas of overlap:

A. In both cases, he is in the position of being asked to do a favor for a man and a woman who might easily represent father and mother figures.

B. In both cases the favor he is asked to do would have the effect of bringing harmony or cooperation between the man and woman. (He would "iron out the problem" between the woman and the head of the organization at work; and he would facilitate the research collaboration of Al and woman consultant in the interview.)

This is an interesting parallel, and one not adequately accounted for by the present interpretation. Although he might react to both of these situations with some pride in being "looked up to" and "turned to" for help, the prospect of facilitating harmony between the man and woman should be objectionable to him if he really is intent upon competing with the man for the woman's admiration and favor. This discrepancy should cause some modification of the present interpretation. I shall mention only two possible avenues of approach to modify it:

A. This discrepancy might point the way to a different focal conflict— e.g., something like: Pleased by opportunity to do analyst and woman consultant a favor (by having his interview filmed) because this gives him prideful feeling of being "looked up to" and "turned to" for help from parent figures *versus* Reluctant to do anything that would enhance harmony or facilitate collaborations between the parent-figures, whom for other reasons he would like to separate and come between.

B. Another possible way this discrepancy might modify the present interpretation is by making the present precipitating situation more specific—perhaps something like this: Being asked to help in this research interview may have reactivated a primal scene type of fantasy in which he does not want to exclude father (in present, Al) or get rid of father. In fact, he would be pleased to facilitate the relations between parents (in present, Al and woman consultant). But he would like the situation to be one in which he is included (cf. 14'3"). ". . . that's a strong feeling I have, of wanting to be included" and in which he is in a superior, looked-up-to, admired, respected position (cf. 28'3"). ". . . then he was kow-towing to me," of helping and assisting them in their (sexual) relations with each other. Al's not coming to the interview may, by frustrating this hope, have led to the emergence of more primitive, hostile feelings and fantasies of castrating Al and reversing father and son roles with him.

3. Aside from the above discrepancies, my principal reservations about the present interpretation concern the disturbing motive of the focal conflict. The postulated Oedipal connotations (regarding rivalry over a woman who represents specifically his mother) could easily be wrong. The phallic rivalry with Al may occur independently of Oedipal connections, and it is possible that if women come into the rivalry at all, it may be only incidentally—perhaps as a means to the end of measuring who is the most manly.

Is the rivalry specifically about the penis, and the reactive motive specifically fear of retaliative castration? There are so many allusions of this kind in his associations that it seems necessary to postulate a specific rivalry concerning the penis.

REFERENCES

BELLAK, L. An experimental exploration of the psychoanalytic process. (Presented at the midwinter meeting of the American Psychoanalytic Association, New York City, Dec. 2, 1955.) *Psa. Quart.*, **25**: 385, 1956.

DOLLARD, J., and AULD, F., JR. *Scoring human motives: A Manual.* New Haven: Yale University Press, 1959.

DOLLARD, J., and MOWRER, O. H. A method of measuring tension in written documents. *J. of abnorm. and soc. Psychol.*, **42**:3, 1947.

FRENCH, T. M. The problem of consensus. (Presented at the mid-winter meeting of the American Psychoanalytic Association, New York City, Dec. 2, 1954).

FRENCH, T. M. *The integration of behavior:* Volumes I, II, and III. Chicago: University of Chicago Press, 1952, 1954, 1958.

GOTTSCHALK, L. A., GLESER, G. C., and SPRINGER, K. J. Three hostility scales applicable to verbal samples. *A.M.A. Arch. gen. Psychiat.*, **9**: 254-279, 1963.

KAUFMAN, P. E., and RAIMY, V. C. Two methods of assessing therapeutic progress. *J. abnorm. and soc. Psychol.*, **44**: 379, 1949.

KOHUT, H. Introspection, empathy, and psychoanalysis—an examination of the relationship between mode of observation and theory. *J. Amer. Psychoanal. Ass.*, **7**: 459-483 (see esp. pp. 471-472), 1959.

KOHUT, H., and SEITZ, P. F. D. Concepts and theories of psychoanalysis. In J. M. Wepman and R. W. Heine (Eds.), *Concepts of personality.* Chicago: Aldine, 1963. Pp. 113-141 (see pp. 120-123).

ROGERS, C. R. A coordinated research in psychotherapy. *J. consult. Psychol.*, **13**: 149, 1949.

SEITZ, P. F. D. Research in psychotherapy—A progress report to the Rockefeller Foundation, 1956.

SEITZ, P. F. D. Notes on research utilizing the psychoanalytic process; some theoretic and methodologic considerations. Presented to the Seminar on Current Research, Doctor of Medical Science Program, Department of Psychiatry, Downstate Medical Center, State University of New York, Brooklyn, March 30, 1962. (Revised April, 1964; unpublished manuscript.)

18. Some methods used in the study of affect in psychotherapy

Kenneth S. Isaacs and Ernest A. Haggard

The early psychoanalytic formulations were primarily in terms of affectivity. *Catharsis* is a prime example of just such a formulation (Freud, 1955). Later the major concern of the psychoanalytic formulations was in regard to other aspects of psychic life. The genetic, dynamic and structural viewpoints provided a focus which overshadowed interest in the affect theory. Further exploration of the place of affect in normal and abnormal development of personality was relegated to passing references in the literature on technique. Nevertheless, affect remained a central focus in psychic function, psychopathology, and psychotherapy. Brierly, in 1951, pointed out that patients always forced this on psychoanalysts. The appearance of essays on affect in recent years suggests some revival of primary interest in affective states and processes (e.g., de Saussure, 1950, 1959; Greenson, 1953; Lewin, 1950; Novey, 1959; and Rangell, 1955). Some recent papers from our own group may be added to the list (e.g., Alexander, 1960; Alexander and Isaacs, 1963; Isaacs, Alexander and Haggard, 1963; Alexander and Isaacs, 1964; and Isaacs and Alexander, in press).

The central position of affect in psychic life would suggest a central position for affect in the technique of psychotherapy and theory of technique. Therefore, it seems worthwhile to attempt to delineate the part played by affectivity in psychic life through substantive study.

Two aspects of affectivity which we have studied are: (1) The relationship between affective capacities of individuals and the resulting differential capacities for participating and profiting from psychotherapy, and (2) The relationship between verbalization about affective experience and the psychotherapy process. A number of studies of affect in relation to psychotherapy were undertaken. Our main emphasis in this paper will be on methods and approaches which we used in studies of these problems.

This investigation was supported in whole by Public Health Service Research Grant MH-00637 and by a research career program award to the second author (K6-MH-9415), both from the National Institute of Mental Health.

RELATABILITY

One notion of the developmental aspects of affectivity was described in the construct *relatability* (Isaacs, 1956). The term *relatability* is intended to connote a hierarchy of six levels of potential capacity of an individual for *object* relations and interpersonal relations. A basic assumption is that the repertoire of affects and affective attitudes increases as the individual moves through a step-wise development in relatability. Ego development is thought of in terms of a multidimensional hierarchy including increasing complexity of object relations, shifts in ego boundaries, increased interpersonal perception, increasing feeling-understanding of self and others, changes in the bases for the *self* concept and the *other* concept, and the development of ego control systems. Each advance to a higher potential level for any individual is marked by the epigenetic appearance of new affects and affective attitudes.

The appearance of the new affect is seen as the central event in the developmental progression of each individual to his new maximum potential level. Some aspects of this developmental process are outlined elsewhere in more detail (Alexander and Isaacs, 1963; Isaacs, et al., 1963; Alexander and Isaacs, 1964; Isaacs and Alexander, in press).

It may be assumed that in order to participate in the psychotherapeutic process the patient must have certain capacities. In the developmental sense, the patient must have achieved a capacity for trusting others or he will not be free enough to reveal himself fully enough to his therapist to permit psychotherapy to take place. He must have sufficient empathic capacity to realize that it is possible for the therapist to recognize him as an individual. He must have sufficient objectivity about himself to be able concomitantly to experience and to observe himself. Without the presence of these capacities in the patient, psychotherapy seems likely to revolve around either anxiety alleviation or the development of these psychotherapy prerequisites within the patient.

The relatability construct may be described briefly in terms of clusters of characteristics as follows:

Zeta (ζ). Prior to perception of others, the person is at the level of oneness with the cosmos and has not yet made self-other distinctions. Others are seen only as extensions of the self. Ego boundaries are as yet unformed. The world is not affectively understood. There is no felt distinction between human and non-human nor animate and inanimate. Feeling experience is imprecise. This level is rarely seen except in severe illness, pain, or stress.

Epsilon (ϵ). The individual sees others as distinct from self, but without interactions among them. This stage is the beginning of sensory and intellectual awareness that others exist separately from the self, but without a sense of interaction. Feeling experience is related to satisfactions and gratifications within self, rather than to, from, or with others. Affects experienced at this level are highly personal.

Delta (δ). The individual sees others as potential need-satisfiers or satisfaction-preventers. Concerns are about establishing ego boundaries and of one person influencing another. Affects are related to controlling or being controlled (e.g., security, ownership) and hence, greed, envy, fear, shame, disgust, and grief are characteristics. Pity for others occurs through projection across ego boundaries. There is interaction with others but not understanding of or consideration for them.

Gamma (γ). The individual sees others as potentially having needs. Concern is with content of ego boundaries—what the self is. Two-way interaction is recognized and thus provides the possibility of cooperativeness and tenderness. Trust develops together with trustworthiness. Sympathy supplants pity. Feeling consideration for others develops, with understanding of others having feelings different from one's own.

Beta (β). The individual is concerned about himself as an individual. The major intrapsychic process is reworking of introjects—i.e., disidentification and integration of introjects. Capacity for self-observation develops, allowing greater objectivity about self. Empathy supplants sympathy and allows appreciation of both self and others as individuals.

Alpha (a). The individual has achieved individuation. There is a recognition of the compounded multiple interactions of several persons. There is a sense of individuality of self and of others.

The research questions in relation to relatability had to do with the issue of the maturity of patients in relation to both their participation in therapy and the outcome of psychotherapy. For purposes of the studies of psychotherapy outcome, relatability was considered as a dichotomy (Alpha, Beta versus Gamma, Delta, Epsilon, Zeta). The reason for this was the theoretical assumption that although trust develops earlier (Isaacs, Alexander and Haggard, 1963), Beta level is the minimal level at which the observing function of the ego and empathic capacity are both present and is, therefore, the minimal level at which *insight* therapies are likely to be successful (Miller, Isaacs and Haggard, 1965). Measurement of relatability was of necessity by inference, since relatability is defined as having to do with potentiality rather than with current behavior. The inferences were made from projective tests—in this instance the Thematic Apperception test (TAT).

CRITERIA FOR RESEARCH ON OUTCOME OF PSYCHOTHERAPY

Psychotherapy research dealing with outcome must meet the problems of the criteria for improvement. Under one set of criteria a patient may be "improved" and under another set of criteria the patient may be "unimproved." Some of the issues are: How much is "enough" improvement? What is the significance of symptomatic improvement? What should be the duration of treatment until improvement? What duration of improvement assures us it is *real*—i.e., durable—improvement?

In these studies of psychotherapy outcome different approaches were used with different samples. For instance, in the University of Chicago Counseling Center Block I sample (Rogers and Dymond, 1954) a variety of measures of improvement were described. For that sample, various comparisons with these criterion measures were possible. Some of these will be described below.

In other samples, in order to maximize the differences between the improved and unimproved conditions, it was decided that the screening of a sizeable number of patients would yield, at the extremes of improvement and unimprovement, a small group of markedly improved and a small group of clearly unimproved patients. The judges were instructed to consider improvement in terms of changes in the patient's character structure. Anxiety alleviation or disappearance of symptoms were to be regarded as insufficient evidence of change unless they appeared to be the result of a shift in the basic elements of character defenses. Such selection of patients at the extremes of improvement and non-improvement is illustrated with one sample of seven improved and eight unimproved. Out of 200 cases from the Mental Health Centers (Chicago) which were screened by one judge, 24 were chosen as the 12 most clearly improved and the 12 most clearly unimproved. These cases were presented in mixed order to each of two new judges who were required to categorize each case as being markedly improved, (as, for instance, in the sense of a character change), or not improved, (except, perhaps, in the sense of some alleviation of anxiety). It was required that their judgments also agree with the first screening judge and the psychotherapist. That sample reduced to seven improved and eight unimproved. Pre-therapy TAT's for the selected patients were retyped and coded story-by-story and distributed to the judges for blind rating of relatability.

In another sample of 33 patients, 11 high and 22 low relatability patients were found (See Table 1). In this sample the high relatability patients fared much better in psychotherapy than the low relatability patients.

Table 1
Relatability and Improvement—Mental Health Center Sample I

Reliability Rating	Marked Improvement	Little or No Improvement	Total
Alpha or Beta	6	5	11
Gamma, Delta, Epsilon, or Zeta	1	21	22
Totals	7	26	33

$P = .001$—level based on Chi-square

In the four samples in which this approach was taken, significant P values based on Chi-square ranged from .10 to .001.

The findings in each of the samples studied lend credence to the hypothesis that persons at the higher levels of relatability have much greater likelihood of showing improvement in psychotherapy than persons at the lower levels of relatability. For example, as in the sample illustrated in Table 1, the chance of a patient at the lower levels of relatability to improve appears to be 1 out of 22, while the chance of a patient at the higher levels of relatability to improve appears to be 6 out of 11. We might expect that not all of the high relatability patients would improve since high relatability is looked upon as a necessary but not sufficient condition for improvement. Accordingly, the prediction we can make is negative, viz., without high relatability, there is little likelihood of improvement in psychotherapy.

In a comparison of the patients in the Counseling Center Block I sample, some further corroboration of our hypothesis was found. Since pre- and post-therapy TAT's as well as a number of measures were available for this sample, many comparisons could be made. The comparisons with the measures on the John Scale 22[1] (Rogers and Dymond, 1954, Chapter 9) and the Dymond Scale of Adjustment[2] (Rogers and Dymond, 1954, Chapter 8) provided further support for the hypothesis that high relatability is related to improvement from psychotherapy. Three comparisons were possible: (1) the pre-therapy TAT relatability ratings; (2) the post-therapy TAT relatability ratings; and (3) the 77 percent of cases in which identical relatability ratings were received on pre-and post-therapy TAT's. In all three comparisons, the higher relatability patients (Alpha, Beta) tended to be higher on the Dymond Scale of Adjustment than the lower relatability patients (Gamma, Delta, Epsilon, Zeta). The pre-therapy relatability ratings selected patients at non-significantly different levels. The post-therapy and the stable relatability ratings selected patients at significantly different levels ($P = .01$ and $P = .03$). The suggestion is that there is a relationship between relatability level and the scores on the Dymond Scale of Adjustment. Those relatability ratings which did not change with treatment selected patients at significantly different levels on both the John Scale 22 and the Dymond Scale. Both of these latter scales measured changes with treatment. The Dymond and John Scales studies suggest that the patients in that sample tended to improve with therapy. The relatability measures predicted the level at which that improvement occurred. The patients at the higher levels of relatability improved over

[1] The John Scale 22 is a summary scale of adjustment based on TAT ratings of how well adjusted the individual is in terms of *overt* behavior.

[2] The Dymond Scale of Adjustment involves judgments on a seven-point scale ranging from "Severe disturbance bordering on psychotic or psychotic" to "Well-integrated, happy person, socially effective."

a more favorable range of the John and Dymond Scales of health. It seems, therefore, that persons at higher levels of relatability change in some ways which are different from the ways in which persons at the lower levels of relatability change. Again, it may be speculated that the distinction may be along the lines of the difference between stress relief through anxiety alleviation at the lower levels of relatability, as opposed to stress relief from actual shift or growth in the psychic structure for patients at the higher levels of relatability. The tendency for greater improvement with higher relatability holds for cases from either the client-centered or the psychoanalytically oriented settings.

AFFECT VERBALIZATION AND CLINICAL INTERVIEW PROCESS

In the studies in the second area of research we are reporting (affect verbalization in the interview process) we turned from the study of outcome to the study of process. We will describe here studies of the relation of affect verbalization to meaningfulness of patient verbalizations, to the relationship between categories of interviewer and patient verbalization, and to the facilitation of spontaneous return to the content of psychotherapeutic interventions.

Talking therapies rely on the verbalizations of the patients for guidance about what the patient is working on, and how well he is working. Patient verbalization also forms the most common basis for judging when and how to make therapeutic interventions. Consequently, it seems reasonable to expect that the more meaningful the verbal material is, the greater is the prospect for efficient therapist participation and, hence, for therapeutic progress. In diagnostic interviews, the importance of the meaningfulness of the verbalization by the patient is even more apparent. Since decisions in such circumstances are based on small samples of information, often derived from only a single interview, it is of considerable importance that the interview be meaningful, that is to say, packed with material significant for understanding the patient.

In our studies the following categorization of the content of therapist and patient statements was used:

(1) *Affect words:* those directly expressing subjective feeling experience, e.g., the intensity or purity of joy, sadness, love, hate, loneliness, etc.
(2) *Emotionally toned words:* those which are mixtures of affective and cognitive elements, dilute or less specific affects, e.g., being worried, upset, disturbed, thrilled, etc.
(3) *Non-affective words:* those which have no affective connotations.

In the several studies on affective verbalization, scales designating the above were utilized varying somewhat in the number of scale points some with a dichotomy (affect versus non-affect), and others with as many as seven defined scale points representing variations in purity and intensity of the affect in the material.

It was hypothesized that the affect verbalizations by interviewers would result in elicitation of more meaningful verbalizations by patients. The study required, therefore, a measure of meaningfulness of patient verbalization in addition to the categorization of *affectivity* of statements described just above.

THE "MEANINGFULNESS" OF PATIENT STATEMENTS

Some of the statements made by patients during diagnostic or therapy hours are highly meaningful in that they reveal the factors which shaped their life and personality, including personal and interpersonal problems. Other patient statements are practically meaningless in this sense. We therefore sought answers to two questions: (1) Can judges agree on the relative meaningfulness of patient statements? and, if so, (2) What are some of the major components of *meaningfulness*?

With respect to the first question, a sample of five patient statements from each of five diagnostic interviews and five early treatment interviews was drawn, with an attempt to provide a range of meaningfulness in the statements from each interview. These 50 patient statements were randomized and presented to 20 experienced therapists who rated them on a five-point scale of meaningfulness. The judges included seven clinical psychologists, seven psychoanalysts, and six social workers. The extent to which the judges agreed as to the relative meaningfulness of the 50 items is indicated by the reliability coefficients in Table 2. Although the degree of agreement in the ratings was in all cases statistically significant $(P = .001)$, the members of each group differed among themselves as to the appropriate rating for particular items. However, when the group ratings for each item were averaged, and the means for each group compared, we find that the different groups agreed quite well on their overall meaningfulness ratings. Or, in other words, the within-group variation appears to be greater than the between-group variation, as indicated by the fact that the inter-group coefficients are much higher than the intra-group coefficients. In any case, when the average meaningfulness ratings of all three groups are compared, the coefficient of .90 indicates the high degree of consensus in their judgment of the relative extent to which the 50 items are clinically meaningful.

Another indication of the fact that the members of the three professional groups did not differ appreciably in their judgment of meaningfulness was obtained by intercorrelating the ratings of all 20 judges, factor analyzing the correlation matrix, and determining the extent to which the members of the three groups were distributed over the factors. Three orthogonal factors were obtained by the varimax method, and each judge

Table 2
Inter-judge Reliabilities of Ratings of
"Meaningfulness" of Patient Statements

Groups of Judges	Intra-group Reliabilities*		Inter-group Reliabilities*	
	R	(n)	R	(n)
1. Psychologists	.53	(7)	—	—
2. Psychoanalysts	.33	(7)	—	—
3. Social Workers	.52	(6)	—	—
1-2. Psychologists and Psychoanalysts	.47	(14)	.95	(2)
1-3. Psychologists and Social Workers	.51	(13)	.66	(2)
2-3. Psychoanalysts and Social Workers	.36	(13)	.84	(2)
1-2-3. All Judges	.45	(20)	.90	(3)

* Reliabilities are estimated by coefficients of intraclass correlation (Haggard, 1958). The intra-group reliabilities are based on the scores of each judge to each item; the inter-group reliabilities are based on the item means of each group of judges. For the degrees of freedom involved, all R's in this table are statistically significant beyond the .001 level.

was categorized in terms of the factor on which he obtained the highest loading. The results of this analysis are given in Table 3, which indicates that the members of the three professional groups rated the meaningfulness of the items neither idiosyncratically, nor in a pattern determined by professional discipline.

Table 3
Distribution of Members of Professional Groups Over Factors Based on Their Ratings on a Scale of Meaningfulness (50 Items) of Patient Verbalizations

Professional Group	Varimax Rotated Factors*			
	I	II	III	Total
Psychologists	4	1	2	7
Psychoanalysts	3	2	2	7
Social Workers	2	2	2	6

* The proportion of the variance in the correlation matrix which was accounted for by the three factors was: 39, 31, and 30 percent, respectively.

Is the judgment of clinical meaningfuless of patient statements necessarily based upon an intangible, global impression, or can some of its components be identified? Since the 20 therapist-judges were asked only to rate the items for meaningfulness, we asked three clinical psychologists independently to rate each of the 50 items on nine characteristics considered to be relevant to the theory and practice of psychotherapy, viz., the degree of affect and the use of affect words, the indications of impulse, the conflict and symptoms, the patient's ability to observe his intrapsychic processes and inform the therapist of them, the interpersonal relationships, and the time orientation. A tenth characteristic, item length, was objectively determined by a word count of the items. The (averaged) ratings on these 10 characteristics and the (averaged) meaningfulness rating over the 50 items were intercorrelated and the resulting matrix factor analyzed by the varimax method. The three orthogonal factors which were extracted are given in Table 4.

The data in Table 4 indicate that a variety of relatively specific characteristics are positively correlated with the *meaningfulness* of patient statements (some more than others, of course), and that these characteristics or components of meaningfulness can be grouped in terms of at least three *factors*. Loosely defined, these factors may be described as: (1) the extent of the patient's concern with himself and his problems; (2) his concern with and his ability to relate to others; and (3) his current motivational state. In future work, it may be desirable to analyze data in terms of the components of meaningfulness as well as the more global rating of it.

RELATION OF SIGNIFICANCE OF PATIENT STATEMENT TO CATEGORY OF PRECEDING INTERVIEWER STATEMENT

After finding that it was possible, within limits, to determine the psychological meaningfulness of the verbal content, the next task was to determine whether there were differences in the meaningfulness of patient statements in response to categories of interviewer interventions. The interviewers' eliciting statements were divided into two categories, viz., (1) an affect group which contained affect words, and (2) a nonaffect group which contained no affect words. Thus, we compared the relation of the category of therapist and diagnostician statements to the meaningfulness of the patients' immediate responses to each of them. The difference between the two affect categories resulted in a significant difference (t for 48 d.f. $= 4.375$, $P = .001$). That is to say, there is a clear difference in the mean values (of meaningfulness) of patients' immediate responses to the two types of therapist statements. The affect group of interviewer interventions is clearly more productive of meaningful patient statements.

In this study the meaningful patient material was more likely to have been elicited immediately by interventions containing affective words. The presumption, not tested, was that the affect words were in each instance relevant to the patient content. There was no distinction made regarding the interviewer's specific therapeutic or diagnostic orientation which might lead him also to refer to impulse, defense, or cognitively organized structures.

Table 4
Relation of Independently Judged Components of Meaningfulness to the 50-Item Meaningfulness Scale

Variable	Inter-judge Reliability (R)*	Correl. (r) with Meaningfulness	Varimax Factors**		
			I	II	III
1. Meaningfulness	(.45)	—	.77	.46	.16
2. Symptoms	.75	.72	.88	.01	.24
3. Affect words	.56	.66	.81	.11	.26
4. Self-observing	.29	.70	.70	.17	.52
5. Conflict	.57	.60	.65	.20	.31
6. Item length	—	.76	.65	.59	-.15
7. Interpersonal relations	.62	.47	-.01	.93	.14
8. Informing	.66	.69	.43	.68	.46
9. Time orientation	.71	.36	.16	.06	.84
10. Degree of affect	.61	.65	.44	.54	.60
11. Impulse	.61	.67	.49	.43	.58

* The inter-judge reliabilities are based on the ratings of three judges, except for the variable of meaningfulness, which is based on the ratings of the 20 therapist-judges (see Table 2). All of the coefficients of intraclass correlation (R) are significant at or beyond the .01 level, as are all of the product-moment coefficients (r) indicating the correlation between the variables and meaningfulness.

** The proportion of the variance in the correlation matrix which was accounted for by the three factors was: 46, 29, and 25 percent, respectively.

Since the meaningful patient responses tended to be elicited by affect verbalizations of the interviewer, the question was raised as to the relationship between the affect categories of the patient and the interviewer. Using the same interviews as in the study just described, every statement of both patient and interviewer was categorized as to affectivity or non-affectivity.

In this set of interviews there was a broad range of affectivity in the sense that we are using the term. The interviewer affectivity ranged from one and one-half percent to 77 percent of the statements within an interview. Patients ranged in affectivity almost as broadly—seven percent to 62 percent of their statements included affective content. The relationship between the patients' affective statements and the interviewers' eliciting statements provides some information on the proportionate utility of interviewer attention to patient's affective or non-affective content in eliciting further affective content from the patient. In response to the total of 257 affective interventions in 10 interviews, 102 or 39.7 percent of the patients' immediate responses were affective. This is in sharp contrast to patient responses to the 1,054 non-affective interviewer interventions to which 135, or only 12.8 percent, were affective. (Chi-square for 1 d.f. $= 98.6, P = .001$).

Table 5
Proportionate Utility of Interviewer Attention
to Affective or Non-Affective Content

Interviewer Intervention	Patient Response		Total
	Affective	Non-Affective	
Affective	102	155	257
Non-Affective	135	919	1054
Totals	237	1074	1311

Chi-square $= 98.6, P = .001$

Within each of the individual interviews examined, the relationship between the overall level of interviewer affective statement and overall level of patient affective statement is also close. Expressed in terms of rank order coefficient of correlation, rho $= .80$. That is to say, when the interviewer deals with affective material, the patient tends to do so as well.

The number of verbal interactions between each interviewer and his patient is highly correlated (inversely) with the affect percentage of the interviewer (rho $= -.62, P = .06$) and even more so with the affect percentage of the patient (rho $= -.79, P = .01$). In other words, the tendency is for overall response patterns to be: high interviewer affect percentage with fewer and longer patient responses, and low interviewer affect percentage with more and shorter patient statements. This finding is quite consistent with our clinical knowledge that involvement in some types of subject matter impels longer discussion, and that interviewers will generally not intervene if a patient appears to want to continue imparting meaningful material.

FACILITATION OF PATIENT'S SPONTANEOUS RETURNS TO THE CONTENT OF INTERVIEWER INTERVENTIONS

The two studies just reported have to do with the measurement of immediate effects of interviewer interventions according to the degree of affectivity in those interventions. It was thought that somewhat longer term effects of interviewers' affective probes might also be measurable. The question of the duration of the effects was raised. Spontaneous returns to the subject matter of interviewers' interventions after a time lag were considered to be indicators of preconscious working-over by the patient.

For this research task a method which has the merit of relative directness and objectivity, although quite tedious to carry out, was selected. First, the content of the interviewers' verbalizations and all following patient content were compared. Then, the time lapses between each interviewer verbalization and later patient response to that verbalization were measured within the remainder of the interview. The basic data for the study of the part played by interviewer content in facilitation of spontaneous returns to interviewer content by patients after a time lag were the following: (1) content which was not returned to by the patient; (2) content to which the patient spontaneously returned; (3) record of time elapsed; and (4) type of content.

The hypothesis was that affective material facilitates patients' spontaneous return to previous interviewer content. The general findings were as follows: (1) Immediate (less than 10") relevant response to interviewers for any type of material by patients was high. The mean of 39 comparisons of various combinations of order of interview and specific interviewer type was 87.52 (range = 76 to 100). (2) Affectively-oriented interviews had a higher relative rate of delayed spontaneous return than objectively-oriented interviews. The ratios were over two-to-one. (3) Regardless of interviewer and interviewer type, specific interventions containing affective material yielded more spontaneous returns, and did so in the ratios shown in Table 6.

In these interviews, the spontaneous returns by patients to subject matter brought up by the interviewer appear to be rare events. Within the range of these rare events, the spontaneous returns by the patient were increased at least two-fold when the interviewer verbalized about the patient's affects than when he focused on the patient's non-affect verbalizations. In the interviews studied, patients returned to the subject matter more frequently when it dealt with their affects. Furthermore, when the general tone of the interview was affective, patients tended to return more frequently to previous interviewer content.

Table 6
Rates* of Immediate Responses and Delayed Spontaneous
Returns to Combined Interviewers' Specific Content

Type of Interviewer Intervention	Rate of Immediate Response	Rate of Spontaneous Returns
Affect	85.25	1.97
Emotionally Toned	87.05	1.74
Other (Non-Affect)	90.65	0.81

* Rate = returns/opportunity for returns

All of these studies result in a set of findings which indicate the importance of the affective experience in psychological functioning. From the studies of relatability, it seems clear that the development of a certain level of affective capacity is a significant prerequisite for participation by the patient in insight therapies.[3] In brief, the studies of affect verbalization support the position that when the interviewer verbally responds to the patient's affect words, he will tend to elicit patient responses which have qualities differing from those following a non-affective intervention.

Other findings suggest that the results reported here are not limited by the interviewer's concomitant orientation toward symptoms, history, interpersonal relations, cognitive structures, or other substantive concerns. Rather, they suggest that if the interviewer, regardless of orientation, includes response to the patient affect verbalization, he is likely to elicit more meaningful patient response, affective verbalization in that response, fewer and longer patient responses, and greater numbers of spontaneous returns to the content of his interventions after a time lag. Studies not described here also suggest that there will be an increase from the general baseline level of discussion of affect by the patient, and that the factual information about the patient will be at least as great as it is when the therapist steers the patient toward factual material. At least, by "following the patient's affects," the therapist or interviewer learns about the factual data which are meaningful in an affective sense, because they are elicited as part of a totality of affectively-oriented discourse.

[3] Speculatively, it seems likely that the same affective development is a prerequisite for the participation of the therapist in the psychotherapeutic process.

REFERENCES

ALEXANDER, J. M. The psychology of bitterness. *Int. J. Psychoanal.*, **41**: 514, 1960.

ALEXANDER, J. M., and ISAACS, K. S. On seriousness and preconscious affective attitudes. *Int. J. Psychoanal.*, **44**: 23, 1963.

ALEXANDER, J. M., and ISAACS, K. S. The function of affect. *Brit. J. Med. Psychol.* **37**: 231, 1964.

BRIERLY, MARJORIE. *Trends in psychoanalysis.* London: Hogarth, 1951.

FREUD, S. Studies in hysteria. In J. Strachey (Ed.), *The standard edition of the complete psychological works of Sigmund Freud*, Vol. II, 1893-1895. London: Hogarth, 1955.

GREENSON, R. R. On boredom. *J. Amer. Psychoanal. Ass.*, **1**: 7, 1953.

HAGGARD, E. A. *Intraclass correlation and the analysis of variance.* New York: Holt, Rinehart & Winston, 1958.

ISAACS, K. S. Relatability, a proposed construct and an approach to its validation. Unpublished doctoral dissertation, Univ. of Chicago, 1956.

ISAACS, K. S., and ALEXANDER, J. M. Affect in ego development. In press.

ISAACS, K. S., ALEXANDER, J. M., and HAGGARD, E. A. Faith, trust, and gullibility. *Int. J. Psychoanal.*, **44**: 4, 1963.

LEWIN, B. *The psychoanalysis of elation.* New York: Norton, 1950.

MILLER, A. A., ISAACS, K. S., and HAGGARD, E. A. On the nature of the observing function of the ego. *Brit. J. Med. Psychol.* 1965.

NOVEY, S. A clinical view of affect theory in psycho-analysis. *Int. J. Psychoanal.*, **40**: 94, 1959.

RANGELL, L. On the psychoanalytic theory of anxiety: a statement of a unitary theory. *J. Amer. Psychoanal. Ass.*, **3**: 389, 1955.

ROGERS, C. R., and DYMOND, ROSALIND F. (Eds.), *Psychotherapy and personality change.* Chicago: Univ. of Chicago Press, 1954.

DE SAUSSURE, R. Present trends in psychoanalysis. *Congres Int. de Psychiatrie.* Paris: Rapport, **5**: 95, 1950.

DE SAUSSURE, R. The metapsychology of pleasure. *Int. J. Psychoanal.*, **40**: 81, 1959.

19. A sound-filmed psychiatric interview: number 2, the "Temple University" interview

Used for the Demonstration of Data Analysis in this Book

One of the original conceptions of this book, when Albert Scheflen[1] was first working on the idea of compiling the material, was that it would be comprised of a collection of papers each illustrating a research method applied to the same sound-filmed psychiatric interview. That organization of the book was not adopted because the editors decided it might limit the types of significant contributions to research methods in psychotherapy that could appropriately fit in this book. A number of groups of research workers in psychotherapy across the nation, however, had access to transcripts or films of this sound-filmed interview, recorded under the direction of Dr. Scheflen at Temple University Medical Center. Of these researchers, several did, in fact, use this recorded interview to illustrate their methodological approach. Four chapters in this book (those by Erika Chance, Louis A. Gottschalk, *et al.*, Philip F. D. Seitz, and Albert E. Scheflen) made use of what we will call the "Temple University" interview.

A transcript of the "Temple University" interview is included in this book and follows immediately after these introductory comments. It deserves a place here for two main reasons. The reader can examine the total transcript and determine for himself the usefulness, accuracy, meaningfulness or any other pertinent aspect of the research procedure applied to the recorded interview by contributors to this book; the approaches illustrated are essentially assessments of change in psychological content at varying levels of complexity. Second, the reader can apply to this interview his own method of evaluating relevant changes and, if he likes, compare his results with others who have used the same raw material.

The patient was a 35-year old man who held degrees in several fields and had made brilliant but spotty contributions in still other fields of intellectual endeavor even when he was still an adolescent. He had, however, not developed any progressive or focused career line and hardly earned a living. Each accomplishment was followed by a period of severe depression and non-productivity. He had no friends, no social or recreational life,

[1] See the Acknowledgments for a further explanation.

and no sexual experience. These difficulties brought him to analysis with a male analyst.

In analysis he was extremely aggressive and rebellious. He denied hearing any interpretations and consciously tried to conceal any evidences of relationship or transference. Nonetheless his depression disappeared. He married, and by focusing his career activities he attained in three years a remarkable success, prestige, and income. These things, too, he attempted to conceal. He insisted upon dressing and acting like a laborer despite important professional status and considerable financial holdings. He retained various feminine elements of speech and mannerisms to conceal marked aggressiveness and his general manner belied his unusual intelligence and high education. The incongruity between his presentation of himself and his career attainments characterizes the interview reproduced below and is most likely to mislead the reader.

This picture and his driving, unrelaxed competitiveness were features of his unresolved transference. After three years of analysis he was referred to a woman training analyst for consultation and she conducted a series of weekly psychotherapy sessions with him. One of these was filmed for the research and the transcript of this session follows.

Transcript of the "Temple University" Interview

Pt: Well, I think this is a very unusual situation to be in.

Dr: Yeah. (*Drawled*) [4"]²

Pt: But I think it's interesting. (*Very softly*)

Dr: How anxious (*loudly*) do you feel about being in front of a camera? (*Rasping*) (*Hesitance before* "camera." *Holding laughter?*) [8"]

Pt: Well, I like it, uh, as a matter of fact. (*Through laughter*)

Dr: Well, that's what I think, it might be fun. [16"] (*Through laughter*)

Pt: Oh gee, I, I, ya know (*smooth flow*) I usta, I usta repress my feelings about this. (*Softly, heavy rasping*)

Dr: Um hum. [22"] (*Softly*)

Pt: Ya know, (*very softly*) in fact it usta be a thing . . . I, I don't think I even had a (*high-pitched and boyishly*), I don't think I ever had a picture taken. [27"] Uh, I did get in one film, (*over fast and competently*) I produced [32"] (*Ambiguous intonation: (a) coyly, femininely (b) earnestly pleading*) Uh, I was, was just talkin' to Al about that. [34"]

Dr: Yeah. (*Softly*)

Pt: Uh, but I think it's great, ya know. I was surprised at the transformation that comes over Al, too. [39"]

Dr: Yeah.

Pt: Ya know, (*rapidly and softly*) he looks (*boyishly and high-pitched*)

² These numbers indicate, in minutes and seconds, the elapsed time in the interview.

very different when this is going on, (*rasping*) that uh [44″], this is, ya know, very exciting 'n great and I can (*Softly*)

Dr: Yeah. (*Softly*)

Pt: (*Con't*) sorta feel with 'em [48″] (*Softly*)

Dr: Um, well I've been kidding everybody, this oughta be a lot of fun to be in the movies. (*Laugh*)

Pt: Yeah.

Dr: We'll see, I found I froze a little with Rosen half an hour ago (*softly*). Uh I was in a picture with him.

Pt: Oh, um hum.

Dr: How've ya been? [1′0″]

Pt: Pretty good. Think so. (*Softly*)

Dr: Have ya had anything particular on your mind since I saw ya last . . . we'll try to get into what we were talking about before. [1′2″]

Pt: Okay, but this just sounds very awkward. It sounds so silly. I feel. . . .

Dr: Uh huh.

Pt: (*Con't*) ya know. I . . . (*trails off*)

Dr: Ya'd rather talk about the way ya feel about . . . [1′3″]

Pt: Well, I think I would for a while. I . . .

Dr: Ok.

Pt: I can almost hear myself, ya know.

Dr: Hum hum.

Pt: This sounds to me like, like a recording. [1′4″] (*Loudly*)

Dr: Yeah.

Pt: (*Loudly*) Like ya feel, when, ya know, ya . . . a bunch of people get together 'n in a party . . . you're gonna (*rapidly*) make a record of what's going on in the party. [1′5″]

Dr: Yeah.

Pt: (*Con't*) an you record it, . . . an' this (*hesitates*) feels just about like that. [1′6″] But I suppose there's not much we can do about it. (*No fall in pitch*)

Dr: Yeah, well . . . I don't think ya can do anything about it. I don't know, (*drawling*) ah, ah, well why don't cha talk about the feeling (*high-pitched and uneven*) because partly you look(ed) forward to having your picture takin' 'n this is why you offered to do it, but partly ya begin to feel as though ya weren't being yourself. [1′9″]

Pt: Yeah. I feel very much out of context. This is a, well this is not the sorta (*spoken rapidly*) place where I normally find myself. [2′1″]

Dr: Yeah.

Pt: An' I think that (*rapidly*) there are a lot of fantasies attached to it because ya like to feel that (*soft rasping*) you're in the center. [2′2″]

Dr: Um hum.

Pt: (*Loudly*) I do. I mean I want a tremendous amount of (*increasingly heavy rasp*) narcissistic gratification.

Dr: Yeah, well of course your (*drawl*) career in a way gives you a good deal of narcissistic gratification. [2'3"]

Pt: Yeah, yeah. I think it, it affords tremendous opportunities for it. (*Increasingly heavy rasp*) [2'4"]

Dr: Why don't cha enjoy this, then? Na' what's unreal about this when . . .

Pt: Well. (*Loudly*)

Dr: (*Con't*) it isn't unreal when y're speaking in front of the public? [2'5"]

Pt: I think the big, the big part of unreality here is that you don't know exactly who's, who's gonna see it, an' what they're gonna think. [2'7"]

Dr: Um hum. (*Softly*)

Pt: Ya know it's sorta like the, the actor who uh, puts on the performance and then, then he jist can't go to sleep until he reads (*loudly*) what the uh critics say. [2'8"] (*High-pitched*)

Dr: Yeah.

Pt: 'Cause he doesn't know whether it's a good production or not (*spoken very rapidly*). He gotta find (*clipped*) whether it is and he hasta read it in the newspaper, ya know. [2'9"]

Dr: Um hum. (*Softly*)

Pt: And I feel the same thing (*loudly*) that this is, ya know, quite detached. (*Loudly*) [3'0"]

Dr: Yeah.

Pt: Uh, the point is ya see, u, uh, normally I, I (*loudly*) know what's happening. (*Rasp*)

Dr: Oh, because ya had the feel of the audience.

Pt: Yeah, (*loudly*) ya have, ya get used to it after a while an' ya have the feel of the audience you know how they're . . . going what they doing an' . . . [3'2"]

Dr: Um hum.

Pt: Ah, you react to it. (*Lip smack*) 'Cause last night I had a pretty interesting experience too.

Dr: Yeah.

Pt: I . . . I was sort of interested in thinking it through. This was a, an open meeting of this organization an' we hadn't done too well in . . . in other meetings we had an' I was really quite concerned because we had some very . . . ah important people coming. [3'5"]

Dr: Um hum.

Pt: But it's difficult to involve the neighborhood (*snapping noise*) in it.

Dr: Yeah.

Pt: An' ya know, I got there at eight o'clock and boy I felt depressed . . . (*high-pitched*) . . . ah 'cause I had these (*loudly*) fantasies of walking in, ya know, havin' (*indistinct, spoken rapidly*) (an) havin' an auditorium packed. (*Very loudly*)

Dr: Um hum. [3'6"]

Pt: Well, it wasn't (*very rapidly*) it uz just a couple people sittin' here, a couple people sitting there. I get (*high-pitched, loudly*) so annoyed ya know, an I think. . . .

Dr: Um hum.

Pt: (*Con't*) boy that's enough of that nonsense, I'm gonna resign [3'8''] (*drawled*) (*loud snap*) Ah . . .

Dr: Um hum.

Pt: I'm not gonna be with a dead organization. (*Heavy rasp*) It did (*loudly*) turn out extremely well. [3'9''] (*Loudly*)

Dr: Did more people come or . . . ?

Pt: Oh yah, a lot more people came . . .

Dr: Oh, they gradually drifted in . . . um [4'0'']

Pt: Yah, they're jist, that's the way they are, they jist don't uh . . .

Dr: Um hum.

Pt: They don't feel that if it's supposed to be eight o'clock promptly this means if you get there by nine that's doin' great. [4'1''] (*Loudly*) [Auto horn] Ya know. (*Through laughter*)

Dr: (*Soft laughter*)

Pt: Like the one woman was sayin' to me she said, I was . . . talkin' (*spoken very softly*) about something about this and so on she (*rapidly and indistinctly*) (*says it's*) like her brother-in-law . . . [4'2'']

Dr: Um hum.

Pt: She said he jist parks his car (*loudly*) anywheres you know . . .

Dr: Um hum.

Pt: An' she says to 'im that, you know, you shouldn't park your car there an' he looks up 'n says, yes, but the sign (*high-pitched*) just says uh, no parking. [4'4'']

Dr: Um hum.

Pt: An' she says, well what are ya doing, he says well (*spoken rapidly*), it doesn't say positively (*loudly*) no parking.[4'5''] [Snap or slap]

Dr: (*Laughter*)

Pt: So . . . (*Laugh*)

Dr: (*So*) that one of your problems with these groups is that, (*slowly*) uh, ah, ya can't set it up you s . . . ya sorta respond to whatever the group does. [4'8'']

Pt: Yeah, and you get used to that after a while. That I . . . (*high-pitched*), I really do that very well. Ah [4'9'']

Dr: Um hum. Y . . . you're able to improvise you mean.

Pt: Yeah, well you know I do that entirely. I don't prepare . . . [5'0''] (*spoken softly*) for any of the . . . the lectures or other times. (*Rasp*)

Dr: (*Increased softening*) Well, what did ya do last night then . . . in the way of . . . getting the group going when there were so few at the first, at the beginning. (*Softly*) [5'1'']

Pt: Well, ah, (*loudly*) (*expiration*) one of the members of the organization (have) plays the autoharp, and . . . [5′2″]

Dr: Um hum.

Pt: So we decided that . . . we jist skip the beginning of the . . . (*rapidly*) I mean not start the beginning of the program yet and uh, have
some group singing, so we decided to have some group singing.
[5′4″]

Dr: Yah.

Pt: An' it worked out fine, we had a great time, and . . . (*softly*)

Dr: Um hum.

Pt: Ah, I mean, I get real tense . . .

Dr: 'M . . .

Pt: Really tense. [5′5″]

Dr: Um hum.

Pt: And, I'm not exactly sure (*drawled*) what's, what's gonna happen,
and I don't even know who I'm gonna introduce, ya know. [5′6″]

Dr: Yeah.

Pt: But there were . . . [slap] a councilman showed up, we didn't know
he was gonna come an', and uh, the director of the Philadelphia Cotil-
lion Society showed up, [5′8″] we weren't sure he was gonna come
an' . . .

Dr: Um hum.

Pt: Uh, you know, heads of various city departments came, [5′9″] we
weren't sure they were gonna come.

Dr: Yeah.

Pt: Uh, it was pretty much sitting there all the time writing notes back
and forth between different people. [6′0″]

Dr: Yeah.

Pt: And in never knowing what the next thing was gonna be, but then
you'd get up an' . . .

Dr: Say, I have an idea. Are you disappointed that Al didn't stick around?

Pt: Sure. (*High-pitched*)

Dr: Well, ya know, I felt that way myself. He said I'm not gonna give ya
any choice.

Pt: (*Laughter*) Yeah.

Dr: And he walked out (on us). (*Through laughter*) Might've been easier
if we had a group then. (*Softly*)

Pt: Yah, well I think this is, uh . . . [6′4″] I think there's certain pro-
lems in that part of the relationship. (*Heavy rasp*)

Dr: Yeah.

Pt: That I feel . . . too . . . (*slowly with hesitation*) uncertain of myself [6′6″] (*Loudly*) . . .

Dr: Yeah.

Pt: (*Softly*) And I gauge pretty much what's going on . . . by what someone else does. [6'7"]

Dr: Yeah. (*Softly*)

Pt: See, I think there's one of the problems too (*rapidly and high-pitched*) we came out, . . . I remember I took a . . . (it) was some kind of a, just, it wasn't a very exacting psychological test . . . one of these (*rapidly*) in this, *This Week* magazine . . . [6'8"]

Dr: Oh, yah.

Pt: (*Con't*) ya know, and I tried this when I was quite (*laughter*), quite amazed, it was one of "complete the picture" [7'0"], and the work had broken lines, and you're supposed to see what it is . . .

Dr: Yeah.

Pt: (*Con't*) that this represents . . . [car horn outside] and it was, I think, there were twenty . . . (check) possibilities. [7'1"]

Dr: Um hum.

Pt: And they said something like, uh, you know, twelve was about par. [7'2"]

Dr: Um hum.

Pt: And eighteen was out of this world, well I got twenty. (*Laughter*)

Dr: Yeah. (*Laughter*)

Pt: And we were talking about it 'un, gee, I think, ha know, what it really says is (*hesitates*) do an incredible amount of conforming. I don't think I do it as much as I used to but I take on the coloration . . . of the situation and when I'm in a situation where I don't know what the coloration is I feel sort of (*high-pitched*) at sea. [7'5"]

Dr: Um hum. Oh, so you think that . . . fact that you could . . . do twenty of 'em meant that you could imagine every possible situation.

Pt: No, no, no, no, (*rapidly*) quite the contrary, I, I, I, think what it means, ah, is that, ah . . . (*slowly*) my own ideas and feelings don't enter in at all. [7'9"]

Dr: Um hum. Oh, that, that . . .

Pt: This is the ultimate in conformity, . . . other words, (*rapidly*) I saw them for exactly what they were. [8'0"]

Dr: Um hum.

Pt: I didn't, uh, ya know I wasn't inclined to read anything into it. [8'1"]

Dr: Oh, yeah. (*Softly*) Oh, so that the idea is that if Al was here the thing 'ud be set 'cause you'd know what to do.

Pt: (*Lip smack*) That's right.

Dr: Um hum. (*Softly*)

Pt: But this is a (*indistinct*) (si)tuation in which, ah, . . . I have a little difficulty in adjusting at picking up the cues. [8'3"]

Dr: Yeah . . . Oh, w-th- (*rapidly*) that well then this is what would make you a good public performer . . . in case you can pick up the (cues). (*Trails off*)

Pt: Yeah, I play by ear all the way through. [8′5″]

Dr: Yeah, well really you leave yourself out of it an awful lot, then. (*Trails off*)

Pt: Yeah, (*loudly*) sure, this is what happens.

Dr: Um hum. (*Softly*)

Pt: The, this is what really completely happens. [8′6″]

Dr: Yeah.

Pt: This is the reason why I always want to be in a situation where . . . ah, the situation is the kind . . . of . . . environment in which I'm happy. (*Very rapidly*) in other words, if I'm in a certain situation I, I'll conform to whatever situation I'm in. But its, I, the only way I have of controlling . . . [8′9″] my (*loudly*) behavior is by selecting the situation.

Dr: Yeah. (*Softly*)

Pt: (*Rapidly*) It doesn't originate in me, it originates in the situation . . . if I pick the right situation then . . . (*loudly*) it's fine. [9′1″]

Dr: Yeah, but on the other hand you told me last time I saw you that, ah, you can change the situation. For instance, in the case of the parents of this boy. [9′2″]

Pt: Sure.

Dr: Ah, you really told them where to head in at [9′3″], you didn't let them set the, ah, . . . tone for (him).

Pt: Oh, yeah, sure, I, I can do this. I mean this thing I was talking about was some time ago.

Dr: Yeah.

Pt: And I think this, . . . this . . . change has been pretty recent. [9′5″]

Dr: Oh, you mean it's a recent acquisition of yours that ya (*loudly*) can push people around instead of only conforming.

Pt: Yah, it's a very recent one.

Dr: Um hum.

Pt: Sure, or at least if I ever did it before I usta feel so guilty that I couldn't (*rasping; trails off*) uh. [9′7″]

Dr: Um hum. (*Softly*)

Pt: Then I, then I would just mess up in something else. [9′8″]

Dr: Is there anything about this situation that makes ya need to conform more, because I think this is where your problem is today [9′9″], is that you're lookin' for clues.

Pt: Ts' right.

Dr: Whereas you weren't looking for any clues (*through laughter*) when we, when I saw you (*stumbles*), oh, oh, oh, well let's say not so much so anyway. You were able ta more or less initiate what you thought oughta be going (in/on). [10′1″]

Pt: Um hum.

Dr: Is that because of Al . . . I'm jist raising the question because this

. . . that the presence of the three of us, or having seen Al and me to-gether . . . makes ya more or less look to him for cues, or wish he was here so you'd get a cue. Or is it s-, or is it (*softly*) something else? [10'4"]

Pt: (*High-pitched*) Well, I think that's a very interesting, uh (*softly*), I think that's a very interesting thing to think about. [10'5"]

Dr: Yeah. (*Softly*)

Pt: Ah, . . . (*loudly*) I'd be very pleased ah, . . . if that were so. [10'6"]

Dr: Um hum.

Pt: Ah, I don't think it the end but I think it, it would be very healthy if it were. [10'7"]

Dr: Yeah.

Pt: I think if I looked to Al for cues this is, I don't know if I'm doing (*loudly*) this, but I think it would be very nice if I were. (*Loudly*) [10'8"]

Dr: Yeah.

Pt: (*Expired laugh?*) I, I'd like to think I was doing this. (*Rasping*)

Dr: Well, w . . . why don't cha talk about that a little (*softly*) [10'9"] more.

Pt: Well, you know, it, . . . it's very interesting because, ah, . . . I think there's a tremendous amount of transference . . . [11'0"]

Dr: Um hum.

Pt: Ah, that goes on. I, . . . you know, I just, just thinking about it now that I think one of the big, . . . (*drawled*) blocks . . . that has been in (*loudly*), in my analysis with (*loudly*) Al. [11'5"]

Dr: Um hum.

Pt: Ah, has been this conformity.

Dr: Yeah.

Pt: That actually what (*loudly*) happens is that, ah, when I don't have anything much to go on (*voice trembles*) with Al, ah, I get very mad (*loudly*), ya see, I, I get (*high-pitched*) annoyed because I'd, ya know, I don't (*increasingly high-pitched*) know what to do. (*Loudly*) [11'6"]

Dr: Um hum.

Pt: Ah . . . and the times I think when (*precise articulation*) I have functioned . . . fairly well, at least I felt (*loudly*) very good about analysis and about Al, have been the times when I've . . . ah, seen him in a different relationship. [11'9"]

Dr: Yeah. (*Softly*)

Pt: Yeah, I, it's very (*softly*) interesting.

Dr: Oh, you spoke of his feeling so good about having 'is pictures taken . . . jist (*firmly*) today. [12'0"]

Pt: Well, yeah, sure but I . . .

Dr: Well, this would, see, be in a different relationship than (*increasingly softer*) the analytic relation.

Pt: That's right, yeah. (*Rasping*) [12'1"]

Dr: Well, uh, the, then in a way part of your feeling toward Al would be that like the kid who wants to do what his father does.

Pt: Yeah. (*Loudly*)

Dr: Did (*very loudly*) that sound like it? [12'3"]

Pt: (*Very loudly*) yes, I think that's what it is, I think (*soft with increasing rasping*) it's very close to that . . . I can remember one time (*rapidly*) I was very pleased because he had some, he had some problems . . . an, or was thinking about how to work out, ah, a way of . . . modifying the projector to (*loudly indistinct*) these films. [12'7"]

Dr: Yeah.

Pt: And was very interested (*rasp*) in that. And, so he (*loudly*) asked me, well what do ya do? [12'8"]

Dr: Um hum.

Pt: (*High-pitched, rapidly*) And, I was (*loudly*) very pleased about this, (*soft rasp*) you know.

Dr: Yeah.

Pt: I was very (*high-pitched*) happy about the fact that he wanted me to ta tell him what he might do.

Dr: Um hum.

Pt: (*Very high-pitched, drawled*) And, I was thinking of how . . . when he was saying . . . ah, two days ago, Wednesday he was remarking, about some of the advantages of having children. [13'1"]

Dr: Yeah.

Pt: Some of the ways in which it is gratifying, and he was talking about, I think his boy, twelve, John, I think it is.

Dr: Yeah.

Pt: Who [13'2"] ah, he said you know that you can get information from children.

Dr: Yeah.

Pt: And that how John would (*loudly*) tell 'im, ah, a lot about different kinds of insects. [13'3"]

Dr: Um hum.

Pt: And it's kinda funny, ya know, he was saying, you know, I'd see a bug go by and he'd say, ah, "well John what is it?" you know and (*rapidly*) John would tell him 'aw [13'5"] just a so-and-so (*rasped*) you know . . .

Dr: Um hum.

Pt: And how, it wasn't to the point where it could help (*loudly*) him in any of his research, you know, but, still, it sorta kept him on his toes. [13'6"]

Dr: Yeah, I remember the first time my (*loudly*) child, he was five years old, the first time he told me something, I didn't know, and I remember how startling and how, I (*can*) still remember what it was, ah, we were out walking and we heard a bird and he looked at me and said, 'oh, that's a purple grackle' well, I'd never even seen one before.

Pt: (*Laugh*)

Dr: Or (*through laughter*) heard one before and, it, it, it's (*high-pitched*) very pleasing even if the information isn't practical, you do get a lot of practical information . . .

Pt: Yeah.

Dr: from kids as they get older, though.

Pt: But you see, I think that that's not (*drawled*) unlike this . . . relation . . . that I had when he a . . . asked me, well (*softly*) you know, how would you go about doing this?

Dr: Yeah.

Pt: 'Cause I think that's a s . . . that's a pretty (*high-pitched*) strong feeling that I have . . . [14'3"] of wanting to be included.

Dr: Uh hum (*Softly*)

Pt: I think this ties in with Bobby, this whole thing that, you know, Bob the boy. [14'4"]

Dr: Yeah.

Pt: Ah, of my being able to understand what he's doing, because this is exactly what (*loudly*) I'm doing. [14'5"]

Dr: Well, he's, he's doing in a psychopathic way what you're doing in a perfectly . . . good way (*softly*) only for you . . . ya had guilt about it you're not sure . . . it's right. I mean he (is) . . . he

Pt: (*Loudly*) Yeah.

Dr: (*Loudly*) feeling (*Very loudly*)

Pt: (*Loudly*) Well, he's not either. Yeah. He's got guilt too.

Dr: Yah, [14'8"] (*annoyed*) oh sure he has guilt but the point is that you have your rational guilt and he has both irrational guilt and real guilt.

Pt: Yeah, well, he's trying (*loudly*), I th . . . I think sorta trying to . . . to, ah . . . to translate his irrational . . . guilt, guilt feelings into (*softly, rasped*) rational ones, I mean . . . [15'0"]

Dr: Yah, I . . .

Pt: make them explicit (*loudly*) get punished for them and hope they'll go away. [15'1"]

Dr: Yeah, but I think that the real problem with him is that he wants to know what you're doing and how you're doing it, he wants to (*loudly*) identify with you.

Pt: Sure.

Dr: And, oh this is a very interesting thing . . . you'll see it in little kids who take their father's keys, you know, and (*softly*) put 'em in holes and . . . so to imitate the father, even on a very small level . . . (softly) I (wondered) . . . I never forgot one of my . . . boys was under two, not much . . . between eighteen months and two years old, he was down in the basement, he'd learned to turn the lights on and off and we had a light that was on a big, uh . . . wire, ya know, and you plug it in before you can light it to walk under the furnace and things like that . . . and this kid picks up the light . . . and looks at it, and he takes hold of the (*loudly*) plug and he goes and plug it in and he lights it . . . and he had picked that up from his father. (*High-pitched*)

Pt: Um hum.

Dr: And (*high-pitched and uneven*) it was just amazing to see him do it with such accuracy. And I think this is the sort of thing . . . that, that you see in a psychopathic way with this boy who hasn't got a father to learn from . . .

Pt: Um hum.

Dr: and, uh, therefore he . . . steals, he does it in a magical way.

Pt: Sure. Oh, of course, I, I do too (*loudly*), only I do it in a . . . more socially acceptable way. [16'3"]

Dr: Yeah. Well you see the, the, the (*loudly*) real point of this is to learn in such a way that you can (*loudly*) use it. [16'4"] There's no point in/to watching somebody do something if you can't do it, do it (*loudly*) yourself. I mean, let's say, occasionally you enjoy a (*loudly*) ballet or something . . .

Pt: Yeah.

Dr: but by and large unless you get something . . . that you can use yourself. Maybe the ballet is an inspiration to do something different (*loudly precise articulation*), for instance.

Pt: Yeah . . . But you know very practically that what I do is essentially with Al is tell him I'm . . . (*rapidly*) not listening to what you say. (*Indistinctly*) I don't understand (*rapidly*) a word you're saying . . . ah, and then act on it. [16'8"]

Dr: You mean you pick it up unconsciously (*increasingly softer*) even though you don't understand it.

Pt: I'm not so sure it's . . . so unconscious any more.

Dr: Um hum.

Pt: (*Rapidly*) I mean I kinda know I'm doing this. I don't always know I'm doing it at the time, but this of course (*loudly*) must be what's happening. [17'0"]

Dr: Why do you say I don't understand a word of what you say . . .

Pt: Well, I don't always, you know, think of it. I, at sometimes I actually believe this. But, ah, I obs . . . obviously, this is not happening 'cause it always sort of, you know, amazed me because you figure that . . . as far as . . . (*slight tremble*) the way I act and the fact, I was thinking in terms of the way I was . . . the session went (*loudly*) yesterday approximately like the first (*slight rasp*) session I ever (*loudly*) had with him went. [17'4"]

Dr: Yeah.

Pt: I think with (*loudly*) no more light or anything else. You know, this was just, it was nothing . . . and the whole of (*loudly*) yesterday as a day, up until . . . the evening, went (*very loudly*) about . . . in the same . . . flooky way that . . . I usta perform five years ago. But the difference is . . . [17'7"] that . . . I, an awful lot has happened, I mean.

Dr: Um hum.

Pt: You know, I'm married, I'm . . . I have (*loudly*) four times the income I had before. I just got a two thousand dollar raise. [17'8"] and . . .

Dr: Again? (*Loudly*)

Pt: And I'm president of a couple of organizations.

Dr: Um hum.

Pt: And, you know (*high-pitched*), a lot of things have happened.

Dr: Yeah.

Pt: I mean I'm no more, you know, no, no longer a kid.

Dr: Um hum.

Pt: And yet (*loudly*) . . . I deny all of it. [18'0"]

Dr: Yeah.

Pt: It . . . didn't (*very loudly*) happen, ya know.

Dr: (*Through laughter*) Yeah.

Pt: (*Loudly, through smile*) I don't know from nothin', ya know. (*Loudly*) I'm still the same very dopey (*very loudly*) guy who just snarls up in everything. [18'2"]

Dr: Oh, well you must be thinking you're doing Al a favor if you don't . . . (*softly*) or . . . show that you can handle the thing (*trails off*)

Pt: Yeah (*softly*) . . . See I'm still his, his dopey kid, you know, who's never gonna get to be independent. [18'4"]

Dr: Yeah (*through laughter*) You're like Prometheus who said, "I never did learn how to make the fire." (*Laughter*)

Pt: Yeah (*laughter*). Well, it's true, 'cause, gee, it's, it's really remarkable . . . I mean . . .

Dr: Um hum.

Pt: . . . (*High-pitched*) everything went wrong yesterday and [18'6"] most of it was all just (*loudly*) idiotic judgments (*rasp*) on my part, just stupid (*high-pitched*).

Dr: Yeah.

Pt: Stupid, stupid stuff. And I've [18'7"] been doing stupid things ever since . . . yesterday. (*Softly*)

Dr: Yeah (*softly*). Yeah, well I think you're saying, I think this is why you want Al here now because you're saying if he would tell ya . . . whether the way you're identifying with him is O.K. and ya haven't really stolen anything from him, then this 'ud be fine. But if you should . . . identify with him or compete with him in some way that was offensive to him then you'd feel guilty as hell.

Pt: Sure, because very, very deeply underneath this is this clue. Well, suppose they see the way this film comes out and they decide . . . other people decide, "Gee, that's great, you know. This involves this, this guy in (*loudly*) other things . . . you see, (*increasingly softer*), then he's gonna really get sorry. [19'3"]

Dr. (*High-pitched*) He'll be sorry for what?

Pt: Oh he'll be real sorry because if people pay more attention (*softly and rapidly*) to the film than they pay to him then he isn't gonna like me at all. (*Loudly*) [19'4"]

Dr: Ah, you're s . . . you're a, whadaya call it, you're (*through laughter*) a scene-stealer.

Pt: (*Loudly*) That's right, I am.

Dr: (*Laughing*) [slapping noise].

Pt: Sometimes I (*loudly*) hate myself for it but in our local . . . in our local group I do this.

Dr: Yeah.

Pt: Boy, I really (*loudly*) hog it.

Dr: Um hum.

Pt: I mean, uh . . . it's just for, you know, it's . . . if I saw it in somebody else (*through laughter*) [19'7"] I would say that.

Dr: You'd get sore as hell at 'em.

Pt: Sure I would. . . . Let the other guys . . . [19'8"] you know . . . get sore at me too . . .

Dr: Um hum.

Pt: 'cause everything ends up being at our place.

Dr: Yeah.

Pt: We get the plums.

Dr: (?)

Pt: And I always get the plums. I always get the (*rasp*) top billing. [20'0"]

Dr: Um hum.

Pt: (*Loudly*) by accident.

Dr: Oh, I wouldn't say that . . . (*Laughter*)

Pt: (*Laughter*) I wouldn't either. Ever since I got in that thing with Ted [20'2"] in that film we made, and we were co-producers of the film.

Dr: Um hum. (*Softly*)

Pt: And, uh . . . he said doesn't make any difference, you know, how these titles went on but (tha . . .) his always got up at the top you know. [20'3"]

Dr: Yeah.

Pt: Just 'cause his last name came before mine. He'd always decide, "Well, lets put these things on (*loudly*) alphabetically," you know . . .

Dr: Yeah. (*Laughter*)

Pt: or something like that. [20'4"] There's always some excuse but his always happened to end up first. (*High-pitched*) I usta get annoyed at this.

Dr: Um hum.

Pt: Only I thought at the time you (*loudly*) shouldn't.

Dr: Yeah. Well now you know you can't.

Pt: (*Loudly*) Now I just cut it off, you know, and put my own in. [20'6"]

Dr: Yeah. (*Laughter*)

Pt: (*Through laughter*) Yeah.

Dr: Every place but here, ya don't wanna (*Laughter*).

Pt: (*Through laughter*) No, 'cause I mean . . . and, see, this is even worse. [20'8"] (It, it) might be even real heresy.

Dr: Um hum . . . You mean y, you'd like to fix this some way so Al gets the top billing whether he's here or not.

Pt: Yeah. [20'9"]

Dr: Uh hum. Well, that's great, we'll tell Al that. (*Laughter*).

Pt: You know I can say he (*loudly drawled*) did it [21'0"] you know. (*Inspiration through laughter*)

Dr: Yeah (*through laughter*). . . . So that you're identi— . . . (*trails off*)

Pt: He's just (*loudly*) off, you know, off the scene, really running it. [21'1"]

Dr: Yeah. (*Softly*) Yeah, I guess that's the problem.

Pt: Of course, the way he's floated around today sort of encourages this fantasy. [21'2"]

Dr: Oh, sure. He puts these glasses on you (*Softly*) in case you're interested. (*Through laughter*)

Pt: (*Through laughter*) I know he did.

Dr: Yeah, um hum. [21'4"] END OF REEL NUMBER 2.

Pt: (*Gasp, high-pitched*) . . . Well, I guess he figures that since, in ten years he's going to be a very famous man . . . that maybe in ten years from now no (*loudly*), not in (*very loudly*) ten, eleven . . . eleven years from now I might be famous too. [21'6"]

Dr: Yeah, that's what he told ya. (*Loudly*)

Pt: Oh yeah. (*Loudly*)

Dr: Um hum.

Pt: (*Very rapidly*) No, he didn't tell me about the (*loudly*) eleven years, he told me about the ten years. He said [21'7"] that ten years from now he (*loudly*) was gonna be very famous . . . and, ah.

Dr: He said t—, he said ten years from now (*loudly*) you were gonna be very famous and that you might therefore be recognized in this movie. [21'9"]

Pt: Well (*very rapidly*), I don't think he s . . . did he say ten? (*loudly*)

Dr: I don't remember. (*Annoyed*) (*Trails off*)

Pt: (*Very loudly*) No, no, see, see I figured tha' he told me I said something about, ah, you know, at the rate I'm going (*rapidly*) I'll be

. . . get past him sometime, he said (*very rapidly*), uh uh nope, he said remember (*loudly*) he said, uh, uh you know I'm learnin' as quick as you are [22'1"] or he says . . .

Dr: Al.

Pt: at least I'm learning new things every year (*loudly*) too . . . you know, so . . . when you catch up to where I am. (*Loudly*)

Dr: Ah huh.

Pt: I'll be past there. So I figures since . . .

Dr: (*Muffled*) Um hum. You're not so sure of that, huh. Are ya gonna take that?

Pt: No (*loudly*) course I'm not gonna take it, but (*laughter*) but I think (*softly muffled*) maybe if he feels better. [22'4"]

Dr: Um hum. Oh, y, we're gonna kid 'im along, huh.

Pt: No (*softly and rasped*). No, you (*don't listen*) I mean it's . . .

Dr: (*Laughter*)

Pt: pretty (*loudly*) evident how competitive I am. (*heavy rasp*)

Dr: Oh sure.

Pt: (*Softly*) Oh.

Dr: The, the only question is why it bothers you . . . let's say when you know this is the, the (*softly*) . . . problem. Um hum.

Pt: Yeah (*softly*) Yeah, well I think uh . . . well (*high-pitched*) I feel sorta bad about being competitive, 'cause I figure that . . . [22'8"] that if you win (*loudly*) the, the men all crumble up.

Dr: Um hum.

Pt: Least all the men I knew whenever you won . . . they . . . jist . . . all faded away and died. [23'0"]

Dr: Um hum.

Pt: They didn't really die but they just got little and shriveled up.

Dr: Yeah.

Pt: And that bothered me.

Dr: Yeah, well ya see, there's another way of looking at it, and that is that if ya win ya can teach somebody something. . . . That's tough but that's the way it is. [23'3"]

Pt: Yeah, that's a (*through laughter*) possibility.

Dr: Oh sure.

Pt: I can see where it's a possibility.

Dr: Yeah.

Pt: I just . . . have, have trouble believing this would ever happen. (*Rasp*)

Dr: Um hum . . . at any rate, this is the reason you don't uh . . . feel comfortable about, uh . . . free floating . . . because you're not so sure what's gonna happen to Al.

Pt: Well, yeah, and I got pretty hostile thoughts (*high-pitched and rasped*) you know. [23'8"]

Dr: Um hum hum.

Pt: I think something else that's revitalized this is there's a mutual . . . acquaintance . . . that, ah both Al and I know (*softly*) a guy who's got . . . (*very loudly*) fierce hostility really (*loudly*) fierce internal hostility and it's oh I . . . Al characterized him as having the most . . . (*precise articulation*) vicious subconscious . . . [24'1"]

Dr: Um hum.

Pt: of (*rasp*) anybody I know.

Dr: Um hum.

Pt: Well (*drawled*) this guy's (boy he's he's) a real . . . charlatan, you know. [24'2"]

Dr: Yeah.

Pt: And he (*loudly*) palms himself off as being a (*slowly and softly*) great deal more than he is. [24'3"]

Dr: Yeah.

Pt: And, uh Al (*softly and rasped*) Al knew him from . . . here I think and, uh, . . . so, . . . he's in . . . the organization I'm in now. One of the organizations. [24'5"]

Dr: Yeah.

Pt: And . . . came at lunch yesterday. I knew sooner or later we (were) gonna tangle. [24'6"] Because he'd been trying to undercut Al.

Dr: Oh, yeah.

Pt: By telling me about, you know . . . well, you know, he oughta know what he's doing . . . after all he's gone through two wives. [24'7"]

Dr: Um hum.

Pt: And uh . . . he didn't get his insights the easy way, you know . . .

Dr: Yeah.

Pt: all the mistakes he (*loudly*) made on the way, (*Through laughter*)

Dr: (*Laughter*)

Pt: and the way I been handling it so far is just . . . he's not a very big guy anyhow. [24'9"] I mean physically as well as (*rasp*) otherwise an' . . . .

Dr: Um hum.

Pt: So I just sorta slaughter 'im ya know.

Dr: You can really puncture him huh?

Pt: Yeah (*loudly*) he tells me some, he tells me some . . . he makes some . . . cutting comment and I say well, you know (a) little guy like you hasta say things like that, then he doesn't talk to me for another three months. [25'2"]

Dr: You really fix 'im. But the next time you see him.

Pt: Where he starts to . . .

Dr: He starts out again, doesn't he?

Pt: Yeah (*loudly*) or he starts to boast on how much money he makes, you know. [25'3"]

Dr: Yeah.

Pt: And I say, well frankly, you know, it's not terribly important to me as long (*softly and slowly*) as I get more than fifteen thousand a year I don't care. [25'4"] And he disappears and never comes back ya know. (*Rapidly through laughter*)

Dr: (*Laughter*)

Pt: So, uh . . .

Dr: Yeah (*laughter*).

Pt: He's he's been having terrible fight with . . . this . . . other, er, woman he works with. [25'6"] I mean they both . . . in the same . . . uh, job, same kind of . . . work, you see.

Dr: Yeah.

Pt: And he, oh he's (*loudly*) completely unsuited for the job he's in.

Dr: Um hum.

Pt: He's working with people. [25'7"]

Dr: Oh yeah.

Pt: And he had (*loudly*) no business being in this . . . position at all. And the woman . . . that he's working . . . or works for him actually, . . . [25'9"]

Dr: Um hum.

Pt: Although they both have the same title.

Dr: Yeah.

Pt: Ah . . . she's awful nice, she's sweetness and light (*sigh*).

Dr: Um hum.

Pt: Member of the Society of Friends and feels that reconciliation and friendship are very important.

Dr: Um hum.

Pt: Very compassionate sort of person, you know . . .

Dr: Yeah.

Pt: And she internalizes all of her hostility, too. (*loudly*) [26'1"]

Dr: Um hum.

Pt: She (*rapidly*) doesn't have an awful lot but what she does have she puts in. [26'2"]

Dr: Um hum.

Pt: But she still wants to keep, you know . . . feeling . . . good feelings towards people [26'3"] [thump] Well, she's up against a stone wall. (*Loudly*) I mean she's about ready to explode (*loudly*) 'cause . . .

Dr: Yeah.

Pt: all this undercurrent here is just about ready to kill her.

Dr: Um.

Pt: And she's afraid to slap him.

Dr: Um hum.

Pt: (*Softly and rapidly*) You know she doesn't know quite how to do it. So (*indistinctly*) he finally came to a break with the head of the organization (*rasped*) about this. [26'5"]

Dr: Um hum.

Pt: And so, at lunch (*loudly*) he was asking me what I thought should be done about (*rapidly*) the situation. Would I iron the problem out between the two of them. And so I thought I might as well lay my cards on the table because this guy's gonna cut me out sooner or later underneath [26'8"] so we might as well get in the open.

Dr: Um hum.

Pt: And I said, and I asked Al about whether it's all right to, you know, to quote him [thump] and he said yeah, he would talk (about him) [26'9"]

Dr: Yeah. . . .

Pt: So, uh . . . I just said well, you know, . . . this (*softly*) guy uh . . . this guy hasn't functioned well where he was before and this is the kind of problem he was involved in all along. [27'1"]

Dr: Um hum.

Pt: So . . . I'm not surprised. I know how I (*loudly*) react to him.

Dr: Yeah.

Pt: And I don't think he's suited for this job and I don't feel that I can possibly iron out the difficulties because (*inhale*) I don't . . . I don't see any point ironing the difficulties out because I . . . I have no feeling that he should be in this job in the first place. [27'4"]

Dr: Yeah.

Pt: So how can I, you know [thump] straighten the job out. . . . So I don't think I can do this. [27'5"]

Dr: [Thump] Yeah.

Pt: And uh (it) was pretty hard to come right out, you know.

Dr: It's (*loudly*) very hard to do that because then this guy's left with his problems. [27'6"]

Pt: Then I, you know, and, and, when the other . . . the head . . . fellow went away I said . . . well look . . . ah, he's been spouting about how he had an analysis and so on. (*Rasped*) (*Softly and rasped*) I knew this guy didn't have an analysis. So I said well, you know, who did you have it with and when. Well, it turns out that he (*loudly*) started with somebody. [27'9"]

Dr: Yeah.

Pt: He says, but I went far enough at what some of my problems are.

Dr: Um.

Pt: And, I said, well sure, I don't doubt that (*loudly*) . . . [28'0"]

Dr: Yeah.

Pt: but, you know, knowing what your problems are and doing something are quite another thing. (*Loudly*)

Dr: Um hum.

Pt: And if you go you know, into analysis, until you're confronted with a problem that you can't manage and drop out I don't think that this is too profitable. [28'2"]

Dr: Um hum.

Pt: So then he was kowtowing, so suddenly he flips the other way (*rasp*), you know . . . [28′3″] (*loudly*). Please tell me, you know, anytime I go overboard and tell me when I'm doing things wrong and (*softly, rapidly*) everything else and (*rasped*) I says (*this was*) a lot of bull.

Dr: Um hum.

Pt: You know as well as I do that's not gonna work. [28′5″]

Dr: Yeah. Well, so the worse that happens is you drive him back into analysis.

Pt: That's right.

Dr: Aw. (*Annoyed*)

Pt: Well that's what I'm gonna do, I mean he . . .

Dr: Yeah.

Pt: He . . . he's confronted with the fact now that he either gets analysis or he (*loudly*) he loses his job. [28′7″]

Dr: Um hum.

Pt: Ah, I don't think there are too many more jobs open to him.

Dr: Yeah.

Pt: And one thing, it certainly pulls him down off of the position of making life difficult for this woman. [28′8″]

Dr: Yeah.

Pt: I mean it gets him off her back (*loudly*) . . . And, of course, now to get him off my back. I mean, he's scared stiff, he won't even come near me. (*Loudly*) [28′9″]

Dr. Yeah . . . Yeah, well I think that the problem is, is that you feel that if you're successful I mean, this what we're talkin' about, Father topples. [29′1″]

Pt: Sure.

Dr: And, uh, the . . . this is something that you gotta face. But as I said, this is why I say the worse that happens is he goes into analysis. . . . If he doesn't go into analysis that's his problem. [29′2″]

Pt: That's right, yeah, it is. . .

Dr: Um hum. (*Softly*)

Pt: Um hum. (*Softly*) . . . I felt a little better at least by putting the cards on the table and (*rasped*) saying, you know. . . .

Dr: Um hum.

Pt: I preferred not to be forced into this situation but if I'm in the situation I'm gonna tell ya. [29′4″]

Dr: Yeah (*softly*) . . . O.K. Well, now it seems to me that you probably got something . . . like that going with Al that you haven't yet solved.

Pt: Yeah.

Dr: But it's the same business of you're saying he has magical thinking and he's gotta come off his high horse, too (*through laughter*). And

I'd say that's what you're headed for with him, you know, and that, uh, probably that's why you're anxious. Well, ah . . . see, because behind that is the whole problem of your father. And the whole problem as to whether what you're doing is being like . . . Bobbie (*loudly*) is his name? [30'1"]

Pt: Bobby, yeah.

Dr: Yeah . . . 'cause that's the way kids learn, by picking their old man's brain and then they compete with them. (*Softly*) [30'2"]

Pt: Um hum.

Dr: . . . And so, uh, I think you need to have 'im around. Is, is just so you won't go too far. Now, whatever your fantasies are of going too far I think they're important. [30'5"]

Pt: Um hum. (*Very high-pitched*)

Dr: . . . You (*softly*) wouldn't want to volunteer one . . . So what would happen if you went too far. [30'8"]

Pt: . . . I don't think I (*cough*) even let myself formulate them. [30'9"]

Dr: (*Softly*) Yeah . . . Well, I could tell ya, ah, if ya go back to Bobbie and have 'im . . . just discussing a family situation you described to me (*loudly*) . . . that, uh Bobby's problem is really being better than his passive . . . beaten down father. [31'1"]

Pt: That's right . . . And he, I don't think he can separate out . . . I think if he feels that he's gonna be better than his father then he's gonna be stuck with his mother. [31'3"]

Dr: Um hum.

Pt: And if he's not as good as his father then what's he gonna be?

Dr: Yeah.

Pt: How do you get out of this (block) and of course, he's I think looking to me to figure out a way to [31'4"] help him.

Dr: Well then you got to . . . ah . . . ah, figure out some way whereby he doesn't get stuck with his mother too. [31'5"]

Pt: That's right, yeah.

Dr: You really have to pull a double, double maneuver there.

Pt: Yeah.

Dr: And this leads me back to this other fellow. The question is whether your motivation uh . . . for ah pushing (*loudly*) him around . . . isn't uh, partly to rescue the mother instead of just the fact that he's obnoxious. [31'9"]

Pt: Yeah, I think this is an element. . . . I think there's another element, too, which Al and I discussed which is . . . ah, he said . . .

Dr: Um hum.

Pt: that . . . after his analysis . . . ah (*rasp*) [32'1"] He, h . . . now the thing that I think about here is that I wonder Al wouldn't wanna cut this part out.

Dr: Cut what part out?

Pt: 'Cause I just wonder whether this is kosher though . . .

Dr: Sure, it's kosher! This is just a gamble. They can cut the film.

Pt: Yeah, it was quite a while after the end of his analysis before he caught on that, that many times when his analyst said that he didn't like somebody Al would proceed to not like him and get rid of him (*both laugh*). And when his analyst said he liked somebody, why, Al would proceed to like him and hire him. [32′2″]

Dr: Yeah, well I think this is the problem of identification.

B.
Process Research Emphasizing Investigation of Personality Functioning and Theory

In this section we, have provided a series of chapters dealing primarily with process research methods emphasizing investigation of personality functioning and theory or relational (or communicative) structure.

1. THE NATURAL HISTORY MODEL

The chapter by Albert Scheflen is a critical essay decrying what he believes is an overemphasis in psychotherapy research on quantitative approaches and the selection and isolation of a few variables for study. Dr. Scheflen pleads vigorously for a *natural history method* which strives to examine patterning of meaningful variables in their context. Scheflen's approach to kinesic analysis has already been compared, above, to Deutsch's approach. Scheflen describes the method of "context analysis" and illustrates it with data from the Temple interview.

20. Natural history method in psychotherapy: communicational research

Albert E. Scheflen

THE SEARCH FOR APPROPRIATE METHOD

Since 1956 our research group at Temple University Medical Center has been studying the processes of psychotherapy. We originally attempted two approaches: (1) isolating and counting variables; and (2) clinical observation, group discussion, and formulation through consensual validation.

The statistical approach did not yield information about the continuity of the processes or the relationships of the events we were studying.

Discussion failed to reach any consensus. First of all, each of the investigators used a different conceptual framework. One formulated in topographic terms: ego, id, superego. Another used psychosexual frameworks. Another thought in terms of interpersonal relationships, and so on. But the problem was deeper than this. Even when two investigators *were* able to reach common conceptual ground it was generally found that they did not agree; they conceived of different intrapsychic processes to account for what they had observed and often they had been watching different behaviors.

This was a serious problem. All theories of intrapsychic processes are based upon inferences made from the visible behavior. Even if various researchers could get themselves to observe precisely the same behavior, they still had multiple conceptions about its intrapsychic roots or concomitants. The trouble was that we were *dealing in methods based upon psychodynamic inference applied to processes that could not be observed directly.* The degree of consensual validation seemed to depend upon how similarly the various observers had been trained.

There is also a serious mixing of levels in most clinical studies. Research in psychotherapy is, at one level, research in social processes, i.e., research in interaction and communication. Such social level phenomena fall in the

The work was done in daily collaboration with Dr. Ray L. Birdwhistell, who generously declined co-authorship; but so inseparable are his contributions that the pronoun "we" is used throughout the paper.

province of the social scientist. In order to use his skills in making inferences about intrapsychic processes, the clinician is apt to unwittingly reduce group processes to personality operations, thereby producing in the research a great confusion in levels. When these difficulties became apparent we split our research staff into two subteams. A clinical, psychoanalytic group was to continue the study of intrapsychic processes. The other team was to find means of systematically studying the interactional processes of psychotherapy. This development in our thinking occurred at the time that context analysis was being developed for the purpose of studying the interview by natural history methods. In 1958 we brought Dr. Birdwhistell, who had pioneered this development, to the Temple University project in research in psychotherapy. In 1959 a collaborative project for research in human communication was established at the Temple Research Division of the Eastern Pennsylvania Psychiatric Institute.

Ultimately researchers will have to integrate the intra-organismic (intrapsychic) and the social (communicational) processes for a holistic understanding of psychotherapy. This integration will depend upon the development of research methods which can deal with the complexity and organization of interaction and communication. Since modern natural history methods show promise of filling this need, this chapter will describe one variant of modern natural history research which is being applied to communication and psychotherapy.

CONTEXT ANALYSIS: A NATURAL HISTORY METHOD

The Modern Evolution of Natural History Method

For centuries it has been a fundamental step in scientific methods to select some element of an item under study, separate the element from the larger whole, and examine the abstracted element in isolation. The isolate is often measured or analyzed and its frequency is counted or correlated with other selected isolates. This quantitative approach was introduced into psychiatry from chemistry and experimental psychology. Since World War I it has so dominated formal psychiatric research that two generations of psychiatric researchers have grown up believing it is the *only* method of *scientifically* approaching human behavior.

Applied to research in psychotherapy this tradition has produced, in the name of science, a plethora of counts and correlations of isolated variables such as words per minute, noun-verb ratios, foot taps, therapists' interpretations, and so on. It is not surprising that such data and their analyses have tended to divide the psychiatric clinician and the psychiatric researcher. Such scores and statistical categories seem unfamiliar and unsatisfying to the clinician who has experienced the unity and flow of the psychotherapeutic session. This world of bits and pieces does not represent the richness of his experience. Concepts like rapport or empathy are destroyed rather than captured or sharpened by such dissection.

Yet the pressure in psychiatry to be "scientific" silences the clinician's protests. He withdraws from formal research or he reluctantly bows to quantitative procedures. All too often he abandons productive insights about methodology to obtain a grant or to achieve status as a "scientific" researcher.

It is not our purpose to deny the value of isolating variables and of treating them statistically. The value of this procedure has been amply demonstrated in the modern history of science. The point is that this approach is not appropriate to *all* kinds of research. In particular, as Brosin has said, it is not appropriate to many questions in research in psychotherapy (Brosin, 1966). In situations where the larger picture is clear and the relations within an element established, it is useful to use isolation and quantification to analyze some specific detail. But analysis into components is not useful if a research question involves relations and integration *per se*. For example, such techniques have dubious value in studying how a doctor and patient are related or how an interpretation relates to the history and/or to transference behavior. Quantitative techniques may tell us about the incidence of components but they will tell us little about meaning, function, and reference. In other words, quantification will not allow us to reconstruct ideas of systems, interaction, or processes. Such reconstruction is possible only through synthesis (Schneirla, 1949).

The clinician's objection to much current research procedure has substance. He wants to know how his actions are integrated and how they affect the patient and the relationship. It does not help him to know *how many* verbs or scowls he uses. He turns from research not solely because he fears scrutiny. In part, his research colleagues have alienated him by the rigidity and impoverishment of their techniques. His identity becomes machine not sentient organism.

But this criticism of quantification is not an endorsement of traditional clinical approaches to research. The dissatisfaction with statistics does not mean we can place our reliance on anecdotes nor upon team judgments about them. The clinical appraisal is capable of dealing with complexity and integration and it may be empirically accurate. However, a research method which relies upon free association and intuition is incomplete from another direction. Science demands that its operations of exploration and test be explicit and reproducible.

To deal with psychotherapy we must have research strategies which avoid atomism, on the one hand, and purely intuitive search operations on the other. There must be a way to deal with a complex structure systematically. Perhaps we can turn to other sciences for methodological suggestions. They have dealt with analogous problems. Not only human relationships, but all phenomena in nature exist in an integrated universe.

Life is not found in atoms, but *emerges* only with their organization into macromolecules which are in turn organized into cells. It is in the cell that we can trace those processes we term *life*. Mobility by means of musculature is not a cellular activity but exists two levels above in the behavior of total organisms which are complex organizations of organ systems.

During the past century broad outlines of human behavior have been sketched. By 1900, the place of man in society had been tentatively formulated in a way which at least gave lip service to the monistic, deterministic canons applicable in the older sciences. Psychology, anthropology, sociology, and psychoanalysis had been formulated in a general way. Data, facts, details, confirmations were demanded by both teachers and students. The focus of investigation and self-justification as "sciences" prompted the movement to the study of elements and components. Perceptual experiments, isolated stimulus response-correlations, demographic counts, and skeletal measurements were needed to fill in and test the sweeping generalizations of the previous century.

Thousands of counts of percepts, concepts, attitudes, responses, stimuli, and associations now have been made. We have learned much about the individual isolated human being out of the context of society, his natural milieu. Now there is need to re-examine ideas of intrapsychic processes in terms of interpersonal processes, social organization, and culture. Greater sophistication and the exhaustion of detail seem to be reasons for the return of science after science to concepts of organization, relations, i.e., to the larger picture. With this trend has come a necessary revival of the natural history method, vastly advanced through systems concepts, capable of testing relations and determining organization seen in equilibrium and in change.

Astronomy has moved from concepts of gravitation (in relationship to individual bodies) to a unified field theory. Cybernetics was deliberately formulated as a science for dealing with complexity (Ashby, 1956). Anthropologists deal not only with cultural elements but with patterns of culture (Benedict, 1946). General systems theory (Bertalanffy, 1950), modern molar biology (Simpson, 1962; Novikoff, 1945), structural linguistics (Gleason, 1955; Hockett, 1958), field theory (Lewin, 1951), and gestalt theory (Koffka, 1935) emphasize the integrated system and the organization of parts in the whole. Freud, for psychoanalysis, emphasized that dream elements are not interpretable apart from their relation to the current life, the past history, and the relationship of patient and analyst (Freud, 1913).

Despite this trend, the adoption of systems concepts and natural history observation of them has been very slow in the psychological sciences. The dogmatic insistence upon quantitative procedures is only one manifestation of this resistance. Authors, conversant only with the methods of isolation and/or quantification, insist that we have no way to deal scientifically with nuance or subtlety in psychotherapy; no way to deal with complexity and integration in psychotherapy research. Many psychiatric and psychological researchers and officials of granting agencies misunderstand natural history methods, and seem to believe that such methods are based on purely clinical description, intuition, and consensual validation.

Natural history methods are used today, *when appropriate,* in every science (including the physical sciences). It should not be surprising that specific types have been developed to study human interaction: psychotherapy, human communication, and interviewing.

In 1956 the Palo Alto group[1] formulated a natural history method specifically for study of communication in the interview and Birdwhistell and Scheflen have further developed this method. This approach is called "Context Analysis."[2]

The Application to Human Communication

Theoretically the basic principles of context analysis apply in the study of any natural phenomenon. We have applied them to human small group behaviors abstracting those which belong to a communicational frame of reference.

Given a field of behaviors, the investigator chooses a frame of reference and abstracts only those elements that are demonstrably part of this framework (Scheflen, 1963). For example, suppose he is studying the behaviors of a group of college students. He may observe that in a day's time they carry out a great many diverse kinds of activities. The investigator may choose some particular set of their activities as part of a particular context in which he is interested. For example, he may study only the courtship behaviors of the students. The context chosen determines which behaviors he will use. (In this sense of the term, frame of reference, it is a context).

The observer notes that the students walk and talk. The behavioral components of these activities are in the service of multiple frames of reference (they walk to get to class, to have lunch, to engage in campus activities, and to entertain coeds). The behaviors that the investigator will abstract (courtship being his frame of reference) are those that demonstrably belong to the context, courtship.

Similarly, we can conceptualize the behavior of a patient in psychoanalysis in any of several frames of reference. We may look at his actions from a standpoint of the level of psychosexual development and characterize them as oral, anal, or genital. We may look at patient behavior in terms of his apparent libidinal objects, abstracting those that indicate

---

[1] G. Bateson, R. L. Birdwhistell, H. Brosin, F. Fromm-Reichmann, C. Hockett, N. A. McQuown, at the Center for the Advanced Study in the Behavioral Sciences.

[2] *Context* analysis must be distinguished from *content* analysis, a method of studying words and ideas only.

narcissism or object love (Freud, 1933). We could, furthermore, differentiate his behaviors on the basis of whether they appeared motivated by or reflective of various affects like guilt, shame, or anxiety.

The Communicational Frame of Reference

In this chapter context analysis will be applied to behavior in the communicational frame of reference, especially as it is seen in that specific variant of the communicational system, psychotherapy.

Our communicants will be patients and therapists. The criteria for abstracting given elements will be that they are communicative. We will not, however, decide a priori that a given behavior is communicative. *The crucial criterion for calling a behavior communicative is that its presence or absence accompanies an observable relation to the presence or absence of some particular behavior of an interactant or relationship.* In this sense, context analysis is operationalism. If a given behavior regularly is related to a given pattern of activity, then it has presumably been perceived or experienced by the membership at some level. Communication has taken place.

Let me hasten to say that, while we abstract the communicative quality of a behavior, this does not mean that the behavior does not have other functions and implications. The behavior is still an expression of a motive or defense or other intra-organismic process. An action can be a message in the communicational frame of reference and also represent a motive or a defense or a technique in the psychoanalytic frame of reference (Gottschalk, 1961; Strupp, 1957). A behavior is communicative at the social level; it is subject to intrapsychic inference at the organismic level. In communication research in psychotherapy, it is the social effect we study, while the psychoanalysts in our group work with the personality implications of the behavior. It is important to realize that communicational theories are in no way competitive or alternative to personality theories. They are complementary and methodologically they are at a different level of description. As Freud suggested, the observer's feelings may offer some clue to meaning (Freud, 1940) but the criteria we have established are *observable* relations between occurrences. In this way, the final reliance upon inference is reduced and we have made a tactical gain in research method.

Communication as an Abstract System

Our view of communication differs from the one ordinarily held in the psychological sciences. Generally, the psychologically oriented researcher necessarily begins with examination of the *performers* in an interaction. He focuses upon the view that Mr. *A* sends a message to Mr. *B*, which *B* decodes and so on. Such models, based on S-R theory and statistical information theory (Shannon and Weaver, 1949; Cherry, 1961) can be called interactional or action-reaction or coder-decoder models. Menninger has described psychotherapy in this model, speaking of party of the first part, party of the second part and so on (Menninger, 1958). This is also the model of Colby's machinomorphized version of communication in psychoanalysis (Colby, 1960).

We agree with Percy, who suggested that his colleagues ask what communication is instead of trying to force it into an S-R model (Percy, 1961). We approach human communication from a different direction beginning with the communicational system itself. Using a systems view, we see communication as an organization of abstractable structural units, standard, and shared by members of a common culture. These structural units are related in a hierarchy of levels. This system gives continuity, generation to generation. Each child born into the culture must learn these units and how to arrange them in order to communicate.

In a particular situation, certain of these units are selected out of the repertoire and arranged in certain ways. Another situation will call for a different set of units and a different organization of them. For example, courtship calls for different units and order from those of a court trial. Psychotherapy is a unique but regular system whose units are borrowed from the language and kinesic patterns of a given culture and from other institutionalized forms like doctor-patient, teacher-student, and parent-child reciprocals. A given session of psychotherapy will show some type of deployment of these standard units. Each psychotherapy is unique, to be sure, but we seek to abstract the commonalities. We try to reconstruct through comparative studies the basic ground rules, the units, and the arrangement characteristic of this institutionalized and transmissible interaction.

Basic Assumptions of Context Analysis

These ideas can be formulated as a set of basic assumptions which underlie the research. These are:

1. That communication (for a given group or culture) like all natural phenomena, has a regular, ultimately predictable structure consisting of definite units arranged in particular ways.
2. That the structural units of communication have a regular set of components and organization which must be performed the same way (within a given range) by all members of an ingroup or else communication will not occur. For example, of billions of possible combinations of phonemes, only a relatively small number actually constitute English words; and these are shared with some minor variations by all English speakers.
3. That these structural units, consisting of communicational behaviors, are themselves merely components of larger units in a hierarchy of levels. For example, in language, phonemes are organized into morphemes which are organized into syntactic sentences.

4. That institutionalized activities like psychotherapy use the basic communicational system of the culture modified in certain specialized but lawful ways.
5. That all participants have learned and know (mostly without consciousness) the system of communication for the groups in which they have membership.
6. That the communicative system of any type of group can be abstracted by context analysis.

This paper will describe how the communication system is derived, illustrating the procedure with excerpts from the Temple Experimental Film. Four steps will be described: (1) recording and transcribing; (2) ascertaining the structural units; (3) synthesizing the larger picture to determine meaning or function; and (4) setting up the natural history experiment.

STEP 1. RECORDING AND TRANSCRIBING

Sound Motion Picture Recording

Since context analysis requires that we search and research the data and deal with each element of a unit, it is essential that we have a complete and consistent record. We cannot depend upon our memories or those of the therapist or patient because many components may be forgotten or distorted in these recollections. We cannot use a tape recording alone because the non-linguistic behaviors are not picked up. At present, a sound motion picture is the necessary record for a context analysis.

This record of the interaction must be complete. Often the vital interchange at some second may involve the hands or feet of the interactants. In context analysis all actions are examined in terms of all others present. Accordingly, the cameraman must not pan the room or move in for a closeup, thereby cutting off some of the scene. These principles are described by Mr. Van Vlack in another paper in this volume.

Transcribing Data from Film

Not only must we record all of the scene we wish to study, but we must include all the communicative elements in the analysis. The very behavior we think can be dispensed with may be the signal to take all of the other behaviors metaphorically and our omission of it may make it impossible to comprehend the meaning of the whole. The element we neglect may signal that one unit has been completed and another begun or it may be a parameter that changes the implications of all that will follow. *Just as we must not decide a priori what to leave out of the film we must not select arbitrarily what can be omitted from the analysis and synthesis.* We do not decide beforehand what is trivial, what is redundant, or what alters the system. This is a *result* of the research.

Not only must we record elements of language but of posture, body movement, touch, facial expression, dress, and decor. If we could record odors, vibration, and pressure we would do so. The communicational system uses all of the sensory modalities.

The recording of so many behaviors becomes feasible because we can record structural units as single entities (see below). Most of the larger structural units of communication have not yet been described but units of the size of the syntactic sentence and smaller are already well known through twenty-five years of linguistic research and ten years in kinesic research.

What we end up with in such microrecordings[3] are transcripts of syntactic sentences and familiar units of kinesics and posture for each interactant recorded on a time graph. Those elements of behaviors which we do not find familiar cannot be plotted in the beginning but will first have to be studied (see below). Such a plot shows us the order in which the communicative behaviors occurred. We can use it in several ways. If we attend to which person performed the behavior, we can reconstruct the interaction of the session through time. We can examine the time graph to spot patterns and repetitions. But such a description of sequence is not a determination of structure and system. It tells us only that events were or were not contiguous in time. It does not tell us the function of any behavior. It does not reveal how behaviors are integrated into a larger system. To do this we will have to use a synchronic approach determining the structural units and how they are put together. This approach will now be described.

STEP 2. ASCERTAINING THE STRUCTURAL UNITS

The Characteristics of a Structural Unit

The structural unit can be defined as a regular organization or complex of components occurring in specific situations or contexts. A structural unit, then, has: (1) a given set of component parts; (2) a definite organization; and (3) specific location in a larger system. For example, an immediate family consists of a mother, father, and children with prescribed relationships and a definite position in a larger family or kinship system. Morphemes (words) consist of given phonemes arranged in regular ways and having set locations in the sentence.

A structural unit is recognized by three criteria. These are: (1) its components; (2) their arrangement; and (3) the neighborhoods or contexts in which it occurs.

Sometimes a component or unit is so well known and so characteristic that we can identify it by itself, i.e., even when it is not located in a larger

---

[3] Birdwhistell (1952, 1966) has published details of more refined and exact microrecording of kinesics and the structural linguistics have developed exact recording for speech modalities (Gleason, 1955, Hockett, 1958).

unit or in a context. The anatomists would have no difficulty identifying the human brain in isolation. There are people we know so well that we would immediately recognize them no matter where we saw them; others we would be uncertain about unless we saw them in some familiar context such as in their shop or at the office.

Structural units can be seen as entities belonging to larger systems or they can be looked at in terms of their components. To look at a unit as a set of components is to analyze it. To examine a unit in relation to the larger systems to which it belongs is called syntheses (Simpson, 1962). In context analysis we both analyze and synthesize. Analysis in this usage does not merely mean to break down into components as the term often is used in chemistry or psychology. Analysis here, as in logic and in psychoanalysis, means to separate into units which are seen in relation to the whole.

Structural units, then, are parts of larger units, which are parts of still larger units, and so on. Such an arrangement is called a hierarchy of levels, (Bertalanffy, 1950, 1960; Feibleman, 1954; Simpson, 1962; Scheflen, 1963). This relation of units in a hierarchy of levels can be represented schematically as follows:

Level I

Level A.B ... N

Level 1.2 ... N
Level a.b.c. ... n
Level (1) (2) (3) ... (N)

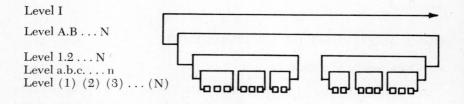

One example of a hierarchy of levels is the ascending order of complexity and inclusiveness of electron, atom, molecule, cell, organ, organism, and group. Another is phoneme, morpheme and syntactic sentence (Gleason, 1955; Hockett, 1958).

How Units are Identified and Tested

The method for ascertaining or identifying the structural unit is based upon its three characteristics, i.e., its components, their organization, and the context(s) in which they occur. We begin by inspecting the behaviors and grouping, as a tentative unit, those that occur together in time. We then test this tentative formulation by three tests, reformulating the unit over and over by trial and error until we have determined the relations of components. When we have found the combination that is a structural unit each of its components will occur together every time. They will have consistent arrangement and appear invariably in the same context. If not we must begin again. The procedure becomes simple with practice and experience in the nature of communication units.

Three aspects of the relations of communicative behaviors are tested. They are:

1. *Delineation:* which components invariably occur together.
2. *Contrasting:* which components are not interdependent in this way.
3. *Testing in Context:* which context(s) or shifts in context regularly accompany the occurrence of each tentative unit.

The relations are determined by what in mathematics is called the *Method of Agreement and Difference* (also formulated as *Mill's canons*).[4] Simply stated, if *A* appears every time *B* appears, and vice versa, and if *A* does not appear when *B* is absent, then *A* and *B* have relations of interdependence and represent an entity. These relations are examined by direct observation of multiple instances of occurrence and non-occurrence.

Identity and Substitutability

All units which have the same components and arrangement and which occur in the same situations are said to have relations to identity. They are merely different performances or occurrences of the same structural unit. Units which do not have identical components or arrangements but which occur in the same contexts, i.e., their occurrence has the same *effect*, are substitutable for each other in communication.

Illustrating the Operations with a Sample of Psychotherapy Behaviors

Operation 1
Delineation or Formulation of the Tentative Unit

Three times in the experimental session the therapist engaged in a behavior that looked like it might be a structural unit. She lit a cigarette. Each time this action was followed by a consistent change in the patient's behavior.

Cigarette-lighting occurred as follows:

1. From 00 minutes, 00 seconds—00 minutes, 20 seconds
2. From 12 minutes, 18 seconds—13 minutes, 36 seconds
3. From 20 minutes, 30 seconds—21 minutes, 31 seconds

---

[4] Ordinarily in the psychologic sciences we think of determining relations by scattergram or product moment correlation. This would be possible in context analysis. We could take more film to obtain a larger *n*, set up intervals, and determine the frequency of each component. We could then determine the correlation. But this procedure is unnecessary. We are interested in occurrence and non-occurrence, not in measuring degrees of difference. We want to know what pieces go together. In pattern and natural structure, co-occurrence is not probabilistic. We do not bother to assess the probabilities that human beings have hearts or that the word *heart* has an *a* in it.

The tentative unit can be described through time as follows:

The doctor reached to a table on her left and took up a pack of cigarettes and matches. With her right hand she removed a cigarette which she eventually placed between her lips. Holding the match cover in her left hand, she struck a match with her right hand, applied it to the cigarette, inhaled, and blew a puff of smoke. She then shook out the match with her right hand, transferred it to her left hand, and discarded it in an ash tray on the table to her left.

There are many things that we can do with this tentative unit. We can make a linguistic analysis of the associated speech (Pittenger, Hockett, and Danehy, 1960). We can measure the actions in any of several ways. Since we have motion pictures, we can superimpose standard grids and measure excursions of movement or distance between participants or measure any other dimension that interests us, for that matter. Since each motion picture frame is numbered, and there are twenty-four frames per second, we can accurately measure the duration of each act or pause or comment. There is, however, no point in making any detailed description of a tentative unit. We wait until we are sure we are dealing with a structural unit.

How do we determine whether the complex cigarette-lighting *is* a structural unit? We first analyze cigarette-lighting into its component behaviors at the level below.

The components of cigarette-lighting were:

1. Taking out a cigarette and bringing it and a pack of matches to her lap.
2. Waiting until the patient has finished a story.
3. Putting the cigarette in her mouth.
4. Waiting until the patient looks away.
5. Lighting up.
6. Discarding the match.

Each of these elements can, in turn, be analyzed. For example, *lighting up* has the following elements:

1. Holding match cover in left hand.
2. Removing a match.
3. Watching the patient until he diverts his eyes.
4. Striking the match with her right hand.
5. Applying the match to the cigarette.
6. Inhaling and exhaling smoke.

Operation 2
Contrasting or Distinguishing Between Units

Reciprocal to the procedure of finding what elements go together is the operation of finding what elements are not part of the tentative unit.

An example will clarify the concept. Suppose we are observing a colony of bees and have a chance to witness the fascinating dance by which these insects communicate the distance and direction of food supplies (Von Frisch, 1953). The dancing bee will carry out a series of movements in a given set of directions. If we test the relations of these movements we will find them interdependent; they invariably occur together. We have found a structural unit that occurs in a given context, i.e., when the unit occurs the bees will fly in a given direction. Another dancer will move in a different set of directions on the hive frames. These movements also prove interdependent and make up a unit which occurs in a context of flying in some other direction. In the same dance, the bee does not intermingle behaviors of Unit *A* and Unit *B* or his message would be ambiguous. We can distinguish Unit *A* and Unit *B* by the component movements of each, by the configurations of each whole dance, and by the context of each, i.e., the subsequent directions of flight.

There were several units on the same level as cigarette-lighting but which are contrasting and distinguishable from it. Consider at the moment only one other example.

Looking up: Frequently the therapist extended her neck and looked upward at the ceiling. She adopted a quizzical look, furrowing her brows and staring off into space as though deep in thought. In a second or two she looked back at the patient and started to speak.

Sometimes contrasting units have the same elements but they are organized differently. Other contrasting units have a similar set of components and a very similar organization, only one component being different. Yet these similar units are functionally different and occur in different contexts. For example, the one additional element may be a signal not to react to the unit. To consider structural units together just because they appear similar is to court the kind of trouble we had when we considered all psychoses to be the same or when all renal disease was called Bright's disease. Appearance is deceptive. We must test each structural unit and contrast those we delineate.

Contrasting provides us with a second test of our tentative unit. That a unit *X* is not unit *Y* is part of distinguishing its characteristics. Later we will see that units at the same level which contrast in their structure are likely to be co-components in a larger structural unit.

Operation 3
Examining in Context(s)

It is possible to use an approximate and a definitive concept of the context. Loosely, we can define the context in terms of some aspect of it; some single component of the larger system which appears whenever the structural unit appears. For example, the earth appears in the context Solar System, but the earth might be identified for some space explorer by locating it in relation to Mars or Venus. The occurrence of some aspect of context in conjunction with the unit is useful in identifying the unit. Later we will have to define and determine contexts more precisely.

We now test the tentative unit's relation to an element of the context. The technique is already familiar. If the tentative unit, $(a.b.c.d. \ . \ .n)$ occurs each time in the same context and it does not occur without this context, then the tentative unit and the contextual event are interdependent.

A shift was noticed after cigarette-lighting. Let, for a moment, a single event stand for the context. The patient stopped relating anecdotes from his current life and spoke more of his feelings and attitudes. In doing so his manner changed from expansive bravado with over-loud and editorial paralanguage to a more hesitant, slightly childlike presentation. He began to speak of more personal matters. In clinical terms, the patient stopped acting like a conversationalist and adopted a stance more typical of the psychotherapy patient.

We carefully observed the relation of this shift to each occurrence of cigarette-lighting. *The test failed. The shift did follow cigarette-lighting but was not interdependent with it.*

We will have to search the data again and reformulate.

The tentative unit, cigarette-lighting, did have interdependent components and gave every evidence of being a structural unit,[5] but it was not in reliable relation to the shift in the patient's behavior. There are two possibilities: (1) that cigarette-lighting is not a *complete* unit because we have overlooked elements of it that do relate to the shift of the patient; or (2) that cigarette-lighting is a unit, but one that belongs to another context, a context that we have not yet uncovered. This second possibility proved to be the case.

Cigarette-lighting belonged to a context in which the therapist temporarily stopped conversing and began to try to interrupt the patient's story. Also the patient began to talk more rapidly and use more single bar junctures (a linguistic activity that discourages interruption).

We can now diagram the tested structure unit as follows:

[5] There are two exceptions to the generalization that a given communicative unit invariably contains the same elements. First, a unit may be "incorrectly" performed, whereupon it does not have its customary effect in context and it will "fail" communicationally. Second, in established human relationships there tends to be abbreviation of units as members develop short-cuts and private languages. The units in such a relationship may be incomplete or lack some of their usual components. Such incomplete units are nonetheless regular for *that* relationship.

Cigarette-lighting:	Occurring in a context A:
a set of regular interdependent behaviors in a given arrangement	in which therapist shifts to refraining from conversation and tries to interrupt the patient's stories.

Recording and Visualizing Become Feasible

Context analysis is not a simple progression of steps, but a moving backward and forward through operations. The last step makes it possible to complete the first. Now we know how to go back and finish recording. We have the key which makes the transcribing of data from the motion picture film feasible. You may remember that our method called for inclusion of all the communicative behaviors. Without comprehending the structural units this task seems absurdly arduous. The microrecording of communicative elements involves 120 variables each ⅛th second for each participant; over 100,000 elements a minute.

What are we to record? Therapist blinks right eye, mutters "ah," looks down, wiggles toes. Patient sighs, looks up, flushes, says "a," then "d." How can we deal with such complexity let alone make any sense out of it?

The secret is that we do not have to record or examine each bit. The pieces are organized into standard structural units, many of which are known through other research, recognizable at a glance and recordable with a stroke. This is the nature of a communicative system. If its units were not highly regular with little deviation there would be no mutual recognition and therefore no communication.

This standardization may strike the psychiatrist as incredible. He is used to looking for individual differences, not similarities. He has always focused upon the *content* of the syntactic sentence. There are hundreds of thousands of different words that can be placed in this structural unit, but the truth is that all syntactic sentences follow one of a mere half-dozen forms. There are probably no more than thirty American gestures.

An analogy may help explain the point. Suppose you are at a baseball game and you are to record every behavioral event. If you do not know the structural units of the game you will have to record thousands and thousands of fragments, e.g., Player Number 1 opens mouth, scratches arm, lifts bat, looks at player Number 7, and so on. But if you do know the units and the system of notation you can codify the entire game on a single sheet of paper and later reconstruct the game in sufficient detail for a lengthy newspaper account. You note hits, walks, and outs and you codify just how each was made.

But you have to be willing to abstract similarities. If you dwell on the individuality of human behavior and see each communicative behavior as a piece of creative inventiveness you will have an endless list of units. Actually, it takes conformity to be a communicant. The forms of a communicative unit have only the narrowest allowable deviation. Exceed this range and you will not communicate. If I make up one new word I will get a questioning letter from the editor. If I ask for another martini in a creatively novel pitch pattern I will be likely to be served coffee. There are, to be sure, stylistic and dialectical variations but the sine qua non of communicative behavior is its reliability. As an American I can recognize lawn mowing, embarrassment, and the New York skyline at a glance. I can sense the slightest deviation in stress or pronunciation. *This regularity in the communicative system permits the researcher to recognize known structural units quickly and to record them with a single symbol.*

It is true that we do not know all the units of the communicative system, but those that are unfamiliar can be determined by context analysis.

STEP 3. SYNTHESIZING THE LARGER PICTURE: THE APPROACH TO MEANING

The Concept of Contexts

If we were interested only in defining the one structural unit, cigarette-lighting, we might stop here—short of knowing more about its context and therefore of knowing accurately about its meaning or function. Since we have only three instances we might go on to study other sessions to accumulate a larger number of cigarette-lightings for a more creditable sample. We might also make conjectures about cigarette-lighting, e.g., maybe it is part of the therapist's self-discipline in refraining from conversation with her patient.

If, however, we wish to determine the structure of other units and the organization of the larger picture, if we wish to accurately determine the meaning of these actions, we must go on. We will have to identify the other contrasting units and the more complete contexts. We are already familiar with how this is done. We again formulate tentative units and test them. All such units, once identified, that are interdependent with each other (at the same level) are the components of the larger unit at the next higher level in the hierarchy. At the same time such units constitute the immediate context for any one of them. The *immediate* context, then, of any unit is the more inclusive unit at the level above.

The *mediate* context is the unit at the next higher level. The units at still higher levels constitute the *remote* contexts of a unit. The immediate context of a therapy session, for example, might consist of other sessions in the course of a particular psychotherapy or psychoanalysis. The mediate contexts might prove to include all psychotherapy and psychoanalysis, the institutional environment, and schools of psychiatric thought. Remote contexts might turn out to include the evolution of cultural ideals, middle-class values, and the economic situation in the community.

Other Units at the Level of Cigarette-lighting

There were two other tested structural units at the level of cigarette-lighting. These were:

1. *Interpreting:* You remember that I described the therapist's tendency to look up at the ceiling with a quizzical expression. The action was interdependent with the lexical actions typical of the clinical technique of interpreting and with actions that encourage the patient to discuss the point. This unit I will call *interpreting.*

2. *Tactical Shifting:* The shift in the patient's behavior from bravado and story-telling to acting like a patient was related to three activities of the therapist.

(a) *Discarding ashes and shifting the cigarette to the left hand:* In the act of taking a drag on the cigarette and discarding the ashes in the ashtray on her left, the therapist would shift the cigarette from her right to her left hand. This shift presumably made it easier for her to reach the ashtray. It is important to note that she sometimes took a drag without discarding ashes. Therefore, discarding and dragging were not interdependent. They were separate elements that belonged to different structural units. It was discarding that occurred with shifting the cigarette that is part of the unit we are now reconstructing.

(b) *Shifting posture:* After the therapist lit her cigarette she shifted her entire body in two ways. First, she would rotate slightly to her left (away from the camera) and more directly face the patient. Second, she would slouch slightly, becoming less erect in the chair. This postural shift brought her pelvis forward and nearer the patient. It would have brought her upper body farther from him except that she also bent slightly at the waist and inclined toward him.

We have already told you that in the act of discarding her match she shifted from a position of arms or hands crossed to one of uncrossed upper extremities. Collectively, these shifts bring a person slightly closer to and more open or accessible to a vis-à-vis. The shift also gives a person the appearance of greater ease and relaxation.

This postural shift was either durable or transient. Either she made this postural shift only to quickly go back to her original position or she maintained this new position until she finished smoking. *Only the maintained shift* was associated with the shift in the patient's presentation.

(c) *Instructing the patient:* During this sequence of behaviors the therapist made a comment to the patient. Either she told him to talk about his problem, or she asked him about it, or she talked about an anecdote from her own life as if providing him with an example of what to talk about.

None of these elements was new to us. We have seen them all before in our research in psychotherapy. Instructions to act more like a patient we have called *structuring maneuvers* (Scheflen, 1960). The use of the left, rather than the right, hand in holding a pipe proved to be an important signal of rapport and openness in the Whitaker and Malone method (Scheflen et al., 1965). Postural shifts of this same type and context have been observed in each of twelve psychoanalytically-oriented psychotherapies that we have studied. In each case unfolding the arms and/or the legs and moving toward the patient was associated with an offer to help or an invitation to talk about personal problems. *Postural shifting, then, is a regular element in offering rapport.*

Often two of these elements would occur but not the others. The configuration was, therefore, not complete. *When all of the components had been complete and when the therapist was smoking, the shift in the patient's presentation invariably and immediately occurred.* These actions are the components of a tested structural unit. We will call the unit *tactical shifting.*

It was like putting together a puzzle consisting of four pieces. It does not matter which piece is put down first. The gestalt appears when all four have been placed.

The doctor often delayed in supplying one of the three pieces or performed a component and then retracted it. It was as though she was hesitant to complete the unit that would prematurely signal the patient to shift. For example, she might transfer the cigarette to her left hand, instruct the patient, shift toward him, and then shift back again. A moment later, she would again shift forward and repeat her instruction, but she would delay discarding the ashes and shifting the cigarette to her left hand. In either case, this configuration remained incomplete.

It was apparent that these delays and backtrackings were related to the patient's refusal to accept interruption and his insistence on prolonging his stories and his anecdotes. Later, the therapist reported that her principle preoccupation during the session was her difficulty in getting the patient to relate to her and talk about himself. In reading the transcript it is evident that he kept talking about his previous therapist and avoiding the subject of his relationship to her, a fact that she commented upon and interpreted. Presumably, she delayed completion of the unit until she picked up some readiness in her patient. The cue appeared to be a pause in his narrative.

The multiple false starts in this sequence of behaviors, however, were useful to the context analysis. Unlike the cigarette-lighting, where there were only three instances, there were recurrences of the discarding, postural shifting, and instructing components of tactical shifting. There is considerably more evidence of a relation between tactical shifting and the patient's modification.

Whenever the therapist finished her cigarette she tamped it out in the ash-tray and then step by step undid or reversed the steps in tactical shifting. She moved back to her erect posture (more distant from the patient) and again folded her arms across her chest. As she did so, she also stopped her passive listening and began a period of active interpreting to the patient. He promptly responded to the reversal of her sequence by again reverting somewhat to his non-patient behavior.

This sequence of behaviors could be diagrammed as follows:

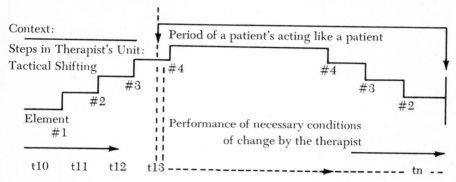

You will note an analogy in these findings to the work of the ethologists in animal interaction, where the innate releasing mechanisms are dependent upon exact configurations of behavior. You will also note that our method is quite parallel to those the ethologists have used (Klopfer, 1963; Lorenz, 1952). Apparently the human infant smiles at four to six months in response to, and only in response to, the eye-nose-mouth configuration (Spitz, 1951). This is one example of a precise configuration acting as a signal or *releaser*.

Now that the structural unit has been tested, it is possible for us to describe it in great detail. We could describe it diachronically as a series of components in sequence as they occurred through time. Or we could describe synchronically the organization of components, the duration, the contextual conditions for its occurrence, variations in its form, its regulation by the patient's behaviors, and so on. But you have suffered enough detail. Those qualities of the unit have been recorded for future comparison with similar structures in other psychotherapies.[6] We can now put the parts together.

The Larger Units (or the Contexts) to Which Cigarette-lighting Belongs

Lighting up, tactical shifting, and interviewing proved to be interdependent. They belong to a shift in context in which patient and therapist

[6] There is every indication so far that psychotherapists who smoke use their cigarettes or pipes as important props in regulating and signalling their tactics. For the most part, this relation appears to be nonconscious. It may be borrowed from general communicational practices or learned by identification in psychiatric training.

change from conversation to the typical psychotherapy relationship involving free association and interpretation. Suppose I call this unit *structuring therapist-patient reciprocals*.

The unit can be diagrammed as follows:

UNIT I							
STRUCTURING THERAPIST-PATIENT RECIPROCALS							
A. Refraining from Conversation		B. Tactical shifting			C. Interpreting		D*
1. Cigarette-lighting	2. Smoking etc.	1. Shift to left hand	2. Postural shift	3 Instructing	1. Looking up	2. Offering Interpretation	1. etc.
‖ ‖ ‖ ‖	‖ ‖ ‖ ‖	‖	‖	‖ ‖	‖ ‖	‖ ‖	‖ ‖

* Unit *I* also seemed to contain another unit or two which were not tested. It also often contained more than one repetition of unit *C* and an occurrence of tactical shifting in reverse (see above).

There is something else we can say about this unit. Like other units, it has *markers*, i.e., definite actions which indicate its beginning and end (Scheflen, 1964). It begins with lighting a cigarette and ends with extinguishing the cigarette.

In this way, we synthesize *upward*, level by level in successive contexts, as if we were building a pyramid, until the multiple events of an interaction come together as components of a single overall unit.

By gross inspection the structural unit, structuring therapist-patient reciprocals, seemed to contrast to three other tentative units which in clinical terms appeared like "working through," "telling anecdotes," and "discussing advice." These units, however, were not tested.

In this way the synthesis continues repeating the same operations until a whole session has been described or until certain units have been studied comparatively in multiple sessions.

Meaning

Only when we know the organization of the systems and the relation of components to larger entities can we systematically determine the meaning or function of any unit. In clinical work we often seek meaning by intuiting what we have observed about the organization of behavior. There is little doubt about the intuitive abilities of the experienced clinician but his operations are private.

Meaning can be defined operationally as the relation of a specific unit and its context or contexts (Bateson, 1966). The meaning of a unit x is that it is not y or z and that it regularly occurs in the contexts X or Y, but not in contexts A or B. For example, the meaning of psychotherapy, it might be postulated, is that it is not child-rearing or courtship, and it occurs in the contexts of correction of deviancy and treatment of psychophysiological disorder, but not in evangelism or political indoctrination. The operations for confirming this guess would be: determination of the structural units and contexts of each of these large social units and making the necessary contrasts.

The concept of meaning can be explained in another way. Consider meaning as a relative quality. Bateson (1966) has said that meaning increases as ambiguity decreases. Operationally then, the meaning of a unit is approached by decreasing the ambiguity of its relations to contexts. For example, if the tentative unit, psychotherapist behavior, were to be found only in the context correction of deviancy systems, then the ambiguity would be small. A specific role interdependent with a single specific context (precisely defined) would not allow for possible alternatives to the fact that psychotherapy behavior was an activity in deviancy correction.

Here is another application of the idea that meaning is inversely proportional to ambiguity. Suppose we were given the letters *b.b.* and asked about their meaning. The great ambiguity would lead us to throw up our hands. If we were supplied contextual elements (e.g., that *b.b.* occurred as part of the phrase "big boy") we could start making guesses about contexts: gangster movies, large artillery, child-rearing, and so on. If we, then, learned that the word was said by a father to his son upon viewing a job well done, the ambiguity is considerably reduced. We would then only need to know whether the paralanguage indicated sarcasm or approval and the meaning would be determined through excluding other possibilities.

If an event is stripped out of the context in which it actually occurred, its meaning is at the mercy of the imaginary contexts that we supply for it. In Langer's terms, we form a conception rather than a concept (Langer, 1953). We may try to objectify free associations about meaning by using judges and correlating their guesses, but the fact that they may agree may mean little. Fifty million Frenchmen *can* be wrong. If a particular understanding is shared by a group, it may be a doctrinal or cultural misconception rather than a private illusion; the number of people in agreement do not verify the understanding. In the past, consensual validation has been achieved about phlogiston, N-Rays, witches, a flat earth, and a geocentric universe. Today some researchers in psychotherapy seem to examine all events in psychotherapy in the light of a private conception of morality or proper practice. Meaning, thus, becomes little more than value judgment.

The answer to the problem of meaning lies in not ripping events out of context in order to study them. To avoid the ambiguity that results from the replacement of known contexts by imaginary ones we must *observe the units in the contexts in which they actually occurred.*

Function

We can also translate the language of context analysis into the more familiar terms of experimental medicine. The principles were laid down a century ago by Bernard (1927). The development of the modern concept of the adrenal will serve as an example. Based on the anatomy, the adrenal gland was once conceived of as an entity, even though the type of components (cells) and their arrangements were known to differ in the two sections of the adrenal, the medulla, and the cortex. When the cortex of the adrenal was selectively extirpated a very different physiology obtained from when the medulla was removed. These two parts of the adrenal were then known to have different functions in the physiological system. The context of the unit, cortex, we could then say, is different from that of the unit, medulla.

If, however, we are examining a stream of events or structures which we cannot manipulate, we may not have information about what happens when one event is removed. What we can see is that A occurs in given contexts. We can observe through time (as we did with the tactical shifting) and wait until A does not occur at its expected place in the pattern. We then learn what happens in its absence. Thereby, we can gain information analogous to that of the extirpation experiment. We can confirm such relations by natural history experimentation (see Step 4).

In this way the meaning or function of any unit is found by examining its relation to the larger system or contexts to which it belongs. Thus we find the transforms between three ideas: meaning, function, and place in the larger system. We are also warned against reductionism: the tendency to explain a thing in isolation or in terms of its parts or mechanisms. Reference and explanation require examination of the level above, of the larger picture.

STEP 4. SETTING UP THE NATURAL HISTORY EXPERIMENT

When we have ascertained the structural units and their relations in a hierarchy of levels, we can experiment to determine more exactly their role in a system. We can find out what will happen in the larger picture if we remove a unit or if it changes or fails to occur. In this sense, the natural history method ultimately uses a classical technique. But after a natural history description has been made, relations and organization have been determined systematically and the smallest change becomes quickly apparent when a system is thoroughly known.

SUMMARY

1. Some shortcomings (in terms of research in psychotherapy) of quantitative methods and clinical evaluation are described.

2. The growth of modern natural history methods are traced, and basic concepts of one type of natural history research are described. It is called *context analysis*.
3. The application of this method to studying communication in psychotherapy is elaborated.
4. The operations of context analysis are described and explained, using illustrations from the experimental psychotherapy film.

REFERENCES

Ashby, W. R. *An introduction to cybernetics*. New York: Wiley, 1956.

Barker, R. G., and Wright, H. F. *The midwest and its children: The psychological ecology of an American town*. New York: Harper & Row, 1954.

Benedict, R. *Patterns of culture*. Mentor MD 89, 1946.

Bateson, G. The message, "This is play." In B. Schaffner (Ed.), *Group processes*, Vol. II. Madison, N.J.: Madison Printing Co., 1955.

Bateson, G. Chapter I. Communication. In N. McQuown (Ed.), *The natural history of an interview*. New York: Grune & Stratton, 1964.

Bernard, C. *An introduction to the study of experimental medicine*. New York: Abelard-Schuman, 1927.

Bertalanffy, L. V. An outline of general systems theory. *Brit. J. for Phil. of Sci.*, 1: 134, 1950.

Bertalanffy, L. V. *Problems of life*. New York: Harper & Row, 1960.

Birdwhistell, R. L. *Introduction to kinesics*. Louisville, Ky.: Univ. of Louisville Press, 1952.

Birdwhistell, R. L. Chapter 3, In N. McQuown (Ed.), *The natural history of an interview*. New York: Grune & Stratton, 1964.

Brosin, H. In N. McQuown (Ed.), *The natural history of an interview*. New York: Grune & Stratton, 1964.

Butler, J. M., Rice, L. N., and Wagstaff, A. K. On naturalistic definition of variables. In H. H. Strupp and L. Luborsky (Eds.), Research in Psychotherapy. Washington: Psychological Association, Inc., 1962.

Cherry, C. *On human communication*. New York: Science Editions, Inc., 1961.

Colby, M. K. *An introduction to psychoanalytic research*. New York: Basic Books, 1960.

Feibleman, J. K. Theory of integrative levels, *Brit. J. Phil. Sci.*, 5: 59, 1954.

Freud, S. *The interpretation of dreams*. New York: Macmillan, 1913.

Freud, S. *New introductory lectures in psychoanalysis*. New York: Norton, 1933.

Freud, S. A note upon the mystic writing pad. *Int. J. Psychoanal.*, 21: 469, 1940.

Gleason, H. A. *An introduction to descriptive linguistics*. New York: Holt, Rinehart and Winston, 1955.

Gottschalk, L. A. *Comparative psycholinguistic analysis of two psychotherapeutic interviews*. New York: International Universities, 1961.

Hockett, C. F. *A course in modern linguistics*. New York: Macmillan, 1958.

LANGER, S. K. *Introduction to symbolic logic* (2nd ed.), New York: Dover, 1953.

LEWIN, K. Field theory in social science. In *Group Dynamics: Research and Theory*. Cartwright D. (Ed.), New York: Harper & Row, 1951.

LORENZ, K. *King Solomon's ring*. New York: Crowell-Collier, 1952.

KLOPFER, P. H. *Behavioral aspects of ecology*. Englewood Cliffs, N.J.: Prentice-Hall, 1962.

KOFFKA, K. *Principles of gestalt psychology*. New York: Harcourt, Brace & World, 1935.

MENNINGER, KARL. *Theory of psychoanalytic technique*. New York: Basic Books, 1958.

NOVIKOFF, A. B. The concept of integrative levels and biology. *Sci.*, **101**: 209, 1945.

PERCY, W. The symbolic structure of interpersonal process. *Psychiat.*, **24**: 39, 1961.

PITTENGER, R. E., HOCKETT, C. F., and DANEHY, J. J. *The first five minutes*. Ithaca, N.Y.: Paul Martineau, 1960.

SCHEFLEN, A. E. *A psychotherapy of schizophrenia: A study of direct analysis*. Springfield, Ill.: Charles C Thomas, 1960.

SCHEFLEN, A. E. Research in psychotherapy. In J. Masserman (Ed.), *Current psychiatric therapies*, New York: Grune & Stratton, 1963.

SCHEFLEN, A. E. Context analysis. In *Strategy and structure in psychotherapy*. English, O. S. (Ed.) In press.

SCHNEIRLA, T. C. Levels in the psychological capacities of animals. In E. W. Sellars, *et al.* (Eds.), *Philosophy for the future*. New York: Macmillan, 1949.

SHANNON, C. E., and WEAVER, W. *The mathematical theory of communication*. Urbana, Ill.: Univ. of Illinois Press, 1949.

SIMPSON, GEORGE GAYLORD. The status of the study of organisms. *Amer. Scientist*, **50**: 36-45, 1962.

SPITZ, R. *No and Yes*. New York: International Universities, 1951.

STRUPP, H. H. A Multi-dimensional system for analyzing psychotherapeutic techniques. *Psychiat.*, **20**: 293, 1957.

VON FRISCH, K. *The dancing bees*. New York: Harcourt, Brace & World, 1953.

ADDITIONAL REFERENCES RELATED TO CONTEXT ANALYSIS

1. On Levels of Organization and Integration

BERTALANFFY, L. V. General systems theory: A new approach to unity of science. *Human Biology*, **23**: 302-312, 1951.

GROBSTEIN, C. Levels and ontogeny. *Amer. Sci.*, **50**: 46-58, Mar. 1962.

HAWKINS, D. *Design for a mind*. Daedalus, 1962.

KOEHLER, W. Gestalten problems und Anfaenge Einer Gestal and theorie. *Jakresber ges Psychiol.*, **3**, 1925.

MILLER, G. A., GALANTER, E., and PRIBRAM, K. H. *Plans and the structure of behavior*. New York: Holt, Rinehart and Winston, 1960.

NOVIKOFF, A. B. The concept of integrative levels and biology. *Sci.*, **101**: 209-215, 1945.

REDFIELD, R. (Ed.) *Levels of integration in biological and social systems.* Symposium No. 8. Lancaster: Cottell Press, 1942.

2. On Naturalistic Observation

BARKER, R. G. *The stream of behavior.* New York: Appleton-Century-Crofts, 1963.

BATESON, G. *Naven* (2nd ed.), Stanford: Stanford University Press, 1958.

BERNARD, G. *An introduction to the study of experimental medicine.* New York: Abelard-Schuman, 1927.

BOCK, P. B. *The social structure of a Canadian Indian reservation.* Doctoral Thesis, Harvard University, 1952.

EVANS-PRITCHARD, E. E. *Social anthropology.* London: Cohen and West, 1951.

HARRIS, Z. *Methods in structural linguistics.* Chicago: Univ. of Chicago Press, 1951.

LORENZ, K. *King Solomon's ring.* New York: Crowell-Collier, 1952.

McQUOWN, N. A., BATESON, G., BIRDWHISTELL, R. E., BORONSEN, H. W., and HOCKETT, G. F. *The natural history of an interview.* (To be published).

TINBERGEN, N. *Social behavior in animals.* London: Methuen, 1953.

3. On Information Theory, Communication and Cybernetics

BAVELAS, A. Communication patterns in task-oriented groups. *J. Acoust. Soc. Amer.,* **22**: 725, 1950.

BERLO, D. K. *The process of communication.* New York: Holt, Rinehart & Winston, 1960.

DEUTSCH, K. On communication models in the social sciences. *Public Opinion quart.,* **16**: 356-380, 1952.

DEWEY, J., and BENTLY, A. F. *Knowing and the Known.* Boston: Beacon Press, 1949.

LAWSON, C. A. Language. Communication and biological organization. In L. Bertalanffy and A. E. Rapoport (Eds.), *General systems,* 8: 107-115, 1963.

LATIL, P. DE. *Thinking by machine.* Boston: Houghton-Miffiin, 1957.

MARUYAMA, M. The second eybernetic: Amplifying mutual causal processes. *Amer. Scientist,* **51**: 164-180 (June), 1963.

RUESCH, J., and BATESON, G. *Communication, the social matrix of psychiatry.* New York: Norton, 1951.

WEINER, N. *Cybernetics.* New York: Wiley, 1948.

4. On Language

BIRDWHISTELL, R. L. Paralanguage: 25 years after Sapir. In H. Brosin (Ed.), *Lectures on experimental psychiatry.* Pittsburgh: Univ. of Pittsburgh Press, 1961.

BLOOMFIELD, L. *Language.* New York: Holt, Rinehart & Winston, 1933.

DUCKERT, A. R. The acquisition of a word. *Lang. and Speech,* **7**: 107-111, 1964.

HARRIS, Z. S. *Structural linguistics.* Chicago: Univ. of Chicago Press, 1951.

HARRIS, Z. S. Discourse analysis. *Language,* **28**: 1, 1952.

Joos, M. Description of language design. *J. Acoust. Soc. Amer.*, **22**: 701-708, Nov., 1950.

Mandelbaum, D. G. (Ed.) *Selected writings of Edward Sapir.* Berkeley: Univ. of Calif. Press, 1949.

McQuown, N. A. Linguistic transcription and specification of psychiatric interview materials. *Psychiat.*, **20**: 79, 1957.

Osgood, C. E. (Ed.) *Psycholinguistics: A survey of theory and research problems.* Baltimore: Waverly Press, 1954.

Pike, K. L. *Language.* Glendale, Calif.: Summer Inst. of Linguistics, 1954.

Pittenger, R. E., and Smith, H. L., Jr. A basis for some contributions of linguistics to psychiatry. *Psychiat.*, **20**: 1, Feb., 1957.

Trager, G. L. Paralanguage: A first approximation. In W. M. Austin (Ed.), *Studies in linguistics* **13**: 1 and 2 Spring, 1958.

5. On Kinesics, Posture and Tactile Communication

Birdwhistell, R. L. Contribution of linguistic-kinesic studies to the understanding of schizophrenia. In, A. Auerback (Ed.), *Schizophrenia.* New York: Ronald, 1959.

Birdwhistell, R. L. Kinesic analysis in the investigation of the emotions. *Address:* Amer. Ass. Adv. Sci., Dec., 1960.

Birdwhistell, R. L. Kinesics and communication. In E. Carpenter and M. McIuhan (Eds.), *Exploration in communication.* Boston: Beacon Press, 1960.

Birdwhistell, R. L. Body signals: Normal and pathological. *Address:* Amer. Psychol. Ass., Sept., 1963.

Charney, E. J. Postural configurations in psychotherapy. (In press.)

Darwin, C. R. *The expression of emotion in man and animals.* New York: Philosophical Library, 1955.

Deutsch, F. Analytic posturology. *Psychoanal. quart.*, **21**: 196-214, 1952.

Frank, L. K. Tactile communication. In E. Carpenter and M. McIuhan (Eds.), *Exploration and communication.* Boston: Beacon Press, 1960.

Hewes, G. W. The anthropology of posture. *Scientific Amer.*, **196**: 123-132, Feb., 1957.

Scheflen, A. E. Communication and regulation in psychotherapy. *Psychiat.*, **26**: 126, May, 1963.

Scheflen, A. E. On the significance of posture in communication systems. *Psychiat.*, **27**: 316, 1964.

6. On Meaning or Semiotics

Bar-Hillel, Y. Logical Syntax and semantics. *Language*, **20**: 230-277, Apr.-June, 1954.

Carnap, R. *Meaning and necessity.* Chicago: Univ. of Chicago Press, 1947.

Ogden, C. K., and Richards, J. A. *The meaning of meaning.* London: Routledge, 1949.

Sebeok, T. A., Hayes, A. S., and Bateson, M. C. *Approaches to semiotics.* London: Mouton and Co., 1964.

7. On Research in Communicational Behavior in Psychotherapy

BELLAK, L. An experimental exploration of the psychoanalytic process. *Psychoanal. quart.*, 25: 385, 1956.

CHAPPLE, E. D., and LINDEMANN, E. Clinical implications of interaction rates in psychiatric interviews. *Appl. Anthro.*, 1: 1-11, 1942.

DeMASCIO, A., BOYD, R. W., GREENBLATT, M., and SOLOMON, H. C. The psychiatric interview. *Dis. nerv. sys.*, 16: 2-7, 1955.

ELDRED, S. H., and PRICE, D. B. A linguistic evaluation of feeling states in psychotherapy. *Psychiat.*, 21: 115-121, 1958.

JAFFE, J. Language of the dyad. *Psychiat.*, 21: 249-258, 1958.

GOTTSCHALK, L. A. (Ed.) *Comparative psycholinguistic analysis of two psychotherapeutic interviews.* New York: International Universities, 1961.

GOTTSCHALK, L. A., and GLESER, G. C. Distinguishing characteristics of the verbal communications of schizophrenic patients. In *Disorders of communication*, Vol. XLII. Research Publ. ARNMD, 1964.

PITTENGER, R. E., HOCKETT, C. F., and DANEHY, J. J. *The first five minutes.* Ithaca, New York: Paul Martineau, 1960.

PENNICKER, R. E. Microscopic analysis of sound tape. *Psychiat.*, 23: 347, Nov, 1960.

SHAKOW, D. The recorded psychoanalytic interview as an objective approach to research in psychoanalysis. *Psychoanal. quart.*, 29: 82, 1960.

STRUPP, H. H. A multidimensional system for analyzing psychotherapeutic techniques. *Psychiat.*, 20: 293-312, 1957.

8. On Motion Picture Recording for Research

MICHAELIS, A. R. *Research films in biology, anthropology, psychology, and medicine.* New York: Academic, 1955.

SPOTTISWOODE, R. *Film and its techniques.* Berkeley and Los Angeles: Univ. of Calif. Press, 1951.

VAN VLACK, J. D. The Research Document Film. *J. Society of Motion Picture and Television Engineers,* Spring, 1964.

2. THE CLASSICAL AND OPERANT CONDITIONING MODELS

The papers by Krasner and Ferster illustrate the application of learning theory to the problems with which the psychotherapist struggles. Such applications are of potentially great significance, both theoretically and therapeutically. Dollard (1959) has said: "In the present confusion of social science theory, learning theory is a rock." And Hathaway (1959) noted with approval the trend toward uniting learning theory and psychotherapy. In his view, the significance of this trend was that learning theory is part of the well-established body of knowledge of academic psychology. If this knowledge could be applied to psychotherapy, then "psychology might undergo a kind of renaissance as a basic science to the practice of psychological healing." We are still a long way from this highly desirable state of affairs, but the work of Krasner and of Ferster represents some firm steps in the right direction.

Krasner views the psychotherapy process within the broad context of behavior modification. This approach is an appealing one because it has generated a great deal of new research and because it is well grounded in psychological theory. According to it, psychotherapy has elements in common with learning, attitude change, hypnosis, and operant conditioning. Krasner presents the rationale for placing psychotherapy within the social psychology of behavior modification. He describes verbal operant conditioning experiments which have, for good reason, aroused much interest. The special relevance of this work for psychotherapy researchers is that it permits the investigation of variables important in psychotherapy, for example, the effect of the subject's (or patient's) mental set, the implicit conveyance by the experimenter (or therapist) of his expectations, and those personality characteristics associated with high conditionability or high ability to condition others.

The learning theorist's approach to psychotherapy differs from the psychoanalyst's. The learning theorist is more willing to work for symptomatic improvement, and he perhaps values it more than the psychodynamicist does. The analyst is more interested in helping the patient achieve self-knowledge, including the relationships of unconscious processes to symptoms and other surface behavior; to achieve these goals the analyst carefully selects patients whose personalities and motivations make such goals feasible. The learning theorist thinks in terms of response hierarchies and repertoires, and therefore believes that the substitution of one response for another is a meaningful change. The psychoanalyst evaluates the meaningfulness of symptom substitution from the context of the patient's psychologic conflicts, overt and covert, and from the context of the subculture in which the patient moves and lives.

Krasner believes that most people underestimate the extent and variety of ways in which the therapist influences the patient in psychotherapy. It is probably true that some therapists are reluctant to think of themselves as influencing the patient in any active way; rather, they conceive of their role as facilitating the patient's growth, with the implication that this growth will occur naturally when the patient's pathologic defenses are undone. This question is likely to spark much lively discussion in the years ahead.

There are some areas where psychodynamic theory may be closer to the facts of life than learning theory is. An example is the patient-therapist relationship. As Krasner points out, some behavior therapists have overlooked the importance of this relationship. If a therapist concentrates on the orderly, systematic extinction of response A and the substitution of response *B*, he runs the risk of equating his patient with a machine. Many behavior therapists are coming to realize the importance of the patient-therapist relationship. As other theoretical models for psychotherapy have evolved and matured, for example, not only the psychoanalytic model but also the client-centered model, more attention has been paid to the effect that the therapist's genuine interest and respect for the patient has had on the outcome.

Ferster uses the autistic child to demonstrate the cogency of Skinnerian principles of reinforcement (operant conditioning) in understanding human behavior disorders. The key concepts which he discusses are: (1) the child's behavior repertoire; (2) how stimuli serve as reinforcers to develop and maintain behavior; (3) the mutual influence between the child and his environment in the differential reinforcement of behavior; (4) the development of chains or sequences or responses, with conditioned reinforcement of each step, leading to the final reinforcement which maintains the whole sequence; (5) the significance of generalized reinforcers: for example, the friendly interest of an adult is a generalized reinforcer for a child because it may lead to a great variety of more specific reinforcements; (6) the importance of all reinforcers which are mediated through adults.

Few would argue with the facts that Ferster presents or the conclusions that he draws from them. But it may seem a far cry from the relatively simple situation he discusses to the intricacies of psychotherapy. This distance is partly bridged by Krasner's paper. A recent critical review of "learning-theory" approaches to psychotherapy is recommended as additional background reading for the student and the researcher (Breger and McGaugh, 1965).

REFERENCES

Breger, L. and McGaugh, J. L. Critique and reformulation of "learning-theory" approaches to psychotherapy and neurosis. *Psychol. Bull.* **63**: 338-358, 1965.

Dollard, J., and Auld, F., Jr. *Scoring human motives: A manual.* New Haven: Yale University Press, 1959.

Hathaway, S. R. Clinical methods: Psychotherapy. In *Ann. rev. psychol.*, **2**: 259-280, 1951.

21. Behavior modification research and the role of the therapist

Leonard Krasner

In recent years there has been a growing tendency to view the psychotherapy process within the broader context of behavior modification research. These research approaches have given fuller recognition to the fact that the therapist's behavior is a major influence in the therapy process. This chapter will discuss some underlying assumptions about psychotherapy from a behavior modification point of view and illustrate the relevance of this approach with two types of behavior modification research, verbal conditioning, and behavior therapy.

The term *behavior modification* is used to cover a multitude of research approaches to changing behavior. These studies derive from basic psychology and more often than not represent an extension of learning theory as applied to the influence of one individual's behavior upon another. Watson (1962) used the term to include structured interviews, verbal conditioning, the production of experimental neuroses, and patient-doctor relationships. "In a broader sense, the topic of behavior modification is related to the whole field of learning. Studies of behavior modification are studies of learning with a particular intent—the clinical goal of treatment." (p. 19)

In describing research relevant to psychotherapy, a term such as behavior modification, or behavior influence, is to be preferred to terms such as *learning* or *reinforcement* because it allows for broader conceptualization and for the inclusion of behaviorally defined and relevant concepts such as modeling, role taking, expectancy, awareness, and values in addition to the more standard learning concepts of conditioning, extinction, scheduling, discrimination, etc.

The development of a broad psychology of behavior influence can eventually be conceived. It would include those fields primarily investigating the ways in which human behavior is modified, changed, or influenced and would include research on learning, operant conditioning, psychotherapy, attitude change, hypnosis, sensory deprivation, modeling, and education. In effect, it would be a social psychology of behavior modification,

From the Behavior Research Laboratory, VA Hospital, Palo Alto, Calif. Preparation of this report was supported, in part, by Public Health Service Research Grant M-6191 from the National Institute of Mental Health, through Stanford University.

with emphasis on the variables in common to these fields. Behavioristic therapy results from the application of these techniques for deliberate modification of the behavior of specific individuals in a clinical setting.

The use of such techniques represents a view of personality as being primarily a function of events outside the body: environmental stimuli, social interactions, social roles. It is both a highly optimistic, as well as a highly threatening view of man. The optimism is represented through the belief in the modifiability of behavior. The threat lies in the danger of *imposing behavior* on others, even in socially sanctioned *behavior imposition* situations such as psychotherapy. It is the implications of *behavior control* studies for the psychotherapeutic process which have recently been creating more and more interest and concern (Krasner, 1962a, 1963a; May, 1963; Patterson, 1958).

In recent years, this *behavioristic* point of view has become increasingly prominent in a wide range of both theoretical and research papers. A series of earlier papers and books had placed psychotherapy within the framework of learning or social reinforcement theory (Dollard and Miller, 1950; Mowrer, 1953; Rotter, 1954; Shaffer and Lazarus, 1952; Shaw, 1948; Shoben, 1949). However, learning theory approaches until recently have usually limited themselves to the reinterpretation or translation of the ongoing therapy process into learning theory terminology, and as such, offered little in the way of relevant new research techniques into the process. More recent works (Bandura, 1961; Eysenck, 1960; Frank, 1961; Kanfer, 1961; Krasner, 1955; 1962b; Lundin, 1961; Marmor, 1961; Murray, 1963; Shaw, 1961; Wolpe, 1958) have moved in the direction of interpreting the therapist as one who manipulates and controls the therapy situation by his knowledge and use of learning techniques in a social reinforcement situation; and out of these works useful research techniques and clinical applications have been developing.

This approach to behavior modification research is typified in verbal operant conditioning studies (Greenspoon, 1962; Krasner, 1958a; Salzinger, 1959). These studies have features in common that distinguish them as a unique body of research. In verbal operant conditioning the subject is required to emit verbal behavior as part of a given task. The examiner reinforces a pre-selected class of the subject's verbal behavior by carefully controlled verbal and/or non-verbal behavioral cues (Krasner, 1958b). The conditioning of verbal behavior is developing as a major technique for systematically exploring variables of interpersonal situations.

Verbal conditioning is a research technique which grew out of an unlikely marriage of Skinnerian operant conditioning and clinical interest, especially in psychotherapy. The early Skinnerian reinforcement techniques concentrated on developing basic laws of behavior using animals such as rats and pigeons. The viewing of speech as *verbal behavior* (Skinner, 1957), following the same degree of lawfulness as other behaviors, represented a major advance opening the way to studies of an important human behavior.

Thus investigators in this field started with two different but overlapping orientations and interests. The first was an interest in basic laws of learning, and was laboratory oriented. The work was primarily with students, to study the variables which affect verbal behavior, or to test out learning models. The second and larger group of investigators was primarily interested in an objective approach to the treatment process. Here, at last, seemed to be a laboratory situation in which you could investigate the complexity of the human treatment process by taking one variable at a time and exploring its effects. However, the argument that verbal conditioning is an "analogue" of psychotherapy is less defensible than at first seemed to be the case.

Rather verbal conditioning research studies are "prototype" situations of the broader human influencing process. They are an excellent way to investigate, in a carefully controlled manner, how verbal behavior is influenced by situational events, what are the most effective ways of changing verbal behavior, and what other kinds of behaviors are associated with these changes. Viewed thusly, there are some similarities and some differences between these two situations, verbal conditioning and psychotherapy, but they are not the same process, nor is one an "analogue" of the other. Rather, both belong to the family of behavior-modifying techniques which include attitude change, placebos, role taking and modeling, milieu control, and brainwashing.

In comparing the two situations it is sometimes argued that verbal conditioning is an artificial laboratory situation created for research purposes, whereas psychotherapy is a "natural" process. Such a view of psychotherapy can be highly misleading and can result in false conclusions about the nature of the therapy situation. Psychotherapy, as the planned behavior of a professional person to assist or aid another person seeking help, is a highly artificial and even an experimental situation. It is a situation with historical origins that has as its basis certain specific concepts about how human behavior can be changed, and it is very much rooted in time and place and is not inherently part of a "natural" order of life.

The verbal conditioning studies place major emphasis on the role of verbal behavior in mediating change. There are several reasons for this. First is the comparative ease of specifying verbal response classes as against non-verbal response classes. Verbal behavior can be isolated, categorized, labeled, and manipulated. Verbal behavior is also the basic element in interpersonal influencing situations such as psychotherapy. There is a good reason for this. Verbal behavior is in itself a *real* behavior, and changes in verbal behavior reflect *real* changes in behavior. Physiological correlates are influenced by verbal behavior change. Changes in verbal behavior generate changes in other kinds of behaviors in other situations.

Certain types of verbalizations are considered *therapeutic* in and of themselves because of their *insight* value. Furthermore, Skinner's (1957) view of verbal behavior as being "reinforced only through the mediation of another person" points up the importance of social learning in verbal behavior. In verbal conditioning studies the reinforcement itself is usually also verbal, and ranges from a minimal verbal cue such as "mm hmm" to "psychoanalytically derived interpretations."

In order to define the basic variables of the verbal conditioning situation, we must first examine the structure of the situation as presented to the subject by the examiner. The structure of this situation is presented both implicitly by the setting and subtle examiner cues and explicitly by instructional set. Most frequently the setting is that of research. Once we have placed the situation within a research context, certain behavioral attitudes on the part of the subjects are brought into focus. The investigations of Orne (1962) on the "demand characteristics" of "research" situations, of Rosenthal (1963) on "examiner biases," and of Goldstein (1962) on "patient-therapist expectancies" are all relevant for the social psychology of "research" situations.

Orne (1962) demonstrated the remarkable control over behavior that results when a situation is labeled as "research" or as an "experiment." Once an individual is accepted in the role of experimenter, he can do a considerable amount of behavior manipulation often without even being questioned. Orne demonstrated this by having the subject doing boring, unrewarding tasks with few errors or decrement in speed on their part. Orne states "it became apparent that it was extremely difficult to design an experiment to test the degree of social control in hypnosis, in view of the already *very high degree of control in the experimental situation itself.*" Orne feels that generally subjects are very strongly motivated to be good subjects because they are ego-involved enough to want the experiment to be a success and to play the role of the "good subject." "The subject's performance in an experiment might almost be conceptualized as problem-solving behavior; that is, at some level he sees it as his task to ascertain the true purpose of the experiment and respond in a manner which will support the hypotheses being tested. Viewed in this light, the totality of cues which convey an experimental hypothesis to the subject become significant determinants of subjects' behavior. We have labeled the sum total of such cues as the *'demand characteristics of the experimental situation.'*" (p. 779)

These demand characteristics enter the verbal conditioning situation especially in the investigation of *awareness*. Some studies have demonstrated a relationship between verbalized awareness of the contingencies of the situation and conditionability (Dulany, 1961; Spielberger, Levin and Shepard, 1960). But these studies have usually used college students, and a verbal conditioning task of selecting a specific pronoun in making up sentences (Taffel, 1955) which is most conducive to effective hypothesizing as to the real nature of the study. Students who are able to solve the demands of the situation, who have the information to play the role of the "good subject," and who have no strong reason not to, such as being made hostile, will then comply and "play the game."

In the therapy situation it is the therapist who deliberately creates the demand characteristics. It may not be the demands of a particular therapist, but by now, the role of the patient has been repeatedly presented to the general public in the analytical model. There are probably few educated people who could not describe in detail what the demand characteristics of the psychotherapy situation are.

In another series of studies of importance to behavior modification research, Rosenthal (1963) points out that when an examiner undertakes an experiment, even if it is not very explicitly formulated, he has some hypotheses or expectancies about the outcome. The very fact of his having selected a particular variable for study rather than another is a clue to the nature of his expectancy. Rosenthal demonstrated the effects of examiner biases in obtaining desired results with animal as well as with human subjects.

Rosenthal utilized two studies of verbal conditioning to point up the biasing effects. One related examiner bias to report of awareness. Rosenthal trained 18 examiners to condition their subjects to give high positive ratings of the success of persons pictured on photographs. Half of the examiners were told that their subjects had personality test scores such that they would afterward be aware of having been conditioned. The other half of the examiners were told that their subjects would not be aware of having been conditioned. Each of these two groups was further divided into a group of examiners whose subjects' instructions favored their seeing through the experimental situation, and a group who received standard instructions. Subjects of the examiners biased to expect higher rates of awareness and subjects who had been given a set to see through the experiment tended to be more aware, though this latter effect was not as reliable as the effect of examiner bias. The obtained effects were most powerful when they were operating conjointly.

In another study, Rosenthal set out to investigate how the biasing was accomplished. The first hypothesis was that it was via verbal conditioning, a very subtle way of doing it. The results indicated that it was *not* via verbal conditioning that biasing occurred since the effects were already in evidence at the beginning of the study before conditioning could take place. They concluded that they probably had to look for the mediating of the bias in the brief pre-data gathering interaction during which the examiner greets, seats, *sets*, and instructs the subject. In a later study Rosenthal and his collaborators wanted to determine if verbal conditioning could drive the ratings of photos up and down according to the will of the examiner. "Results showed clearly that this was possible, and that it worked best with certain types of Ss. We may therefore conclude that, while verbal conditioning is neither a necessary nor a necessarily frequent antecedent of biasing, it nevertheless could be." (p. 275)

One seemingly clear implication from such verbal conditioning studies is that the therapist shapes the behavior of the patient to his own biases. This has repeatedly been pointed out even by analysts, e.g., Stekel (1951); one of the early analysts points out that every therapist gets the kinds of dreams that fit his own theory. Marmor (1961) goes so far as to credit, or blame, verbal conditioning as the technique of manipulating or shaping patient behavior to match therapist biases.

Next, what is the nature of the verbal conditioning *task* itself? There are, broadly, two types of tasks involved. There is, first, the restricted task which offers the subject a choice of a limited response category, such as the Taffel Sentence Completion Task (1955). The choice is usually between a noun, pronoun, or verb to be put in a sentence. This Taffel task has become the most popular in the verbal conditioning studies, primarily because of the limited response possible and the consequent ease of scoring. However, for matters of interpretation and extrapolation to more general behavior influence situations, this type of task is not too useful because of its obvious artificiality and limited response repertoire. This task has been criticized as not really representing a true operant conditioning situation, but rather a discrimination learning task. Greenspoon (1962, p. 546) says, "it appears to the writer that some questions may be raised concerning the inclusion of research using the Taffel-type situation with the operant conditioning paradigm. The writer has serious doubts about its conclusions because an essential element of operant conditioning is missing. Skinner emphasized the importance of the generic nature of the concept of response. The essence of Skinner's approach to the concept of response is that a single response is unique and it is necessary to conceive of a class of responses, the members of which have certain common characteristics. The Taffel-type situation in which a specific personal pronoun is reinforced certainly does not provide for generalization within a class of responses. The modification of the Taffel-type situation in which hostile verbs, bodily active verbs, etc. are reinforced does provide opportunity for generalization within the class of hostile or bodily active verbs. Some of the confusion in the results of research in verbal conditioning may be a product of apparatuses, materials, and procedures that do not fit within the operant conditioning paradigm."

The other type of task is that of an interview or story-telling situation in which the subject can freely emit a series of responses (Greenspoon, 1955; Salzinger and Pisoni, 1960). The task is structured as either an interview or test-like situation in which the subject can respond to the stimuli before him out of a wide response repertoire. Illustrations of this type of task include instructions such as "say all the words you can think of" (Greenspoon, 1955), "tell a story" (Krasner and Ullmann, 1958), "what do you see in these ink blots?" (Fahmy, 1953).

The free operant verbal task is usually presented in a somewhat disguised form. The instructions must give the appearance of role validity. The task must make sense as an experimental task or the subject will attempt to give it meaning. Thus, it must sound plausible, such as "I'm interested in how people tell stories, use their imagination." Furthermore, the task is usually one in which the subject is preoccupied, e.g., interview, conversation, making up a story. There is little time or energy left over to hypothesize about the nature of the task, and if this is done, the speculations are usually in relation to the given task, e.g., "you were saying 'mm hmm' to hinder me, to interfere with my story telling."

The advantages of this type of task are that it more clearly approximates real life and other behavior influence situations such as psychotherapy; the verbal units are more real-emotional words, self-reference affect statements, or a particular content area. Furthermore, the relationships are more complex, and there is less likelihood of the subject reporting awareness of the purpose of the study and thus introducing further complications.

As in any other experimental situation, the performance of the subject is determined, to a large extent, both by the specific instructions he receives and by his expectancies of the situation. These expectancies can be manipulated to influence his subsequent susceptibility (Di Vesta and Blake, 1959; Forgays and Molitor, 1962; Simkins, 1963).

Usually the instructional set is manipulated to either inhibit or facilitate awareness. Instructional sets are also used to influence the situation and to label as *awareness* the procedure of structuring the information given to the subject. Ekman, Krasner, and Ullmann (1963) found that responsiveness to verbal conditioning could be influenced by information describing the task given either in positive or negative terms. When the task was described as measuring "personal problems and difficulties," no conditioning resulted. Significant conditioning did result when the task was described as one measuring "warmth and feeling."

An important function of the instructional set is to increase or lower the amount of involvement of the subjects. This is a major variable about which very little is done in most psychological experiments with humans, most of whom are college sophomores who are "going through the motions" of getting their required research time out of the way.

The next major variable is that of the reinforcer. Here a pragmatic view would define a reinforcer as a behavior or stimulus which follows a specific behavior and increases the likelihood of that behavior occurring again. Stated very simply, it is a rewarding act or stimulus. At first, in verbal conditioning studies isolated reinforcements were used. For example, a specific bit of behavior such as "mm hmm" was used systematically following certain behaviors such as self-references, and these behaviors would appear to increase as a function of the use of the reinforcer "mm hmm." The emphasis in most studies was on the reinforcer; the "mm hmm," or the "good," or the light, or the candy. Early studies attributed a magical quality to these reinforcers. When negative results were reported investigators were puzzled because the "mm hmm" did not work for them. It is obvious that in social reinforcement research you cannot divorce the reinforcement from the reinforcer. This point is not stressed enough or is ignored even by learning therapists who place great emphasis on the role of the reinforcement. It is recognizing a fact that clinically is obvious; some people are more effective behavior modifiers than others. The reason for this can offer a very fascinating series of investigations.

Sapolsky (1960) started a line of research with further implications for the role of the reinforcer. His study pointed up the relationship between the interpersonal attractiveness of the examiner and his resultant effectiveness as an influencer. Bloomberg (as reported in Iverson, 1962) tried to demonstrate vicarious verbal conditioning in a quasi-group therapy situation, and related it to the "set for interpersonal attraction" between the two subjects. The vicarious conditioning was accomplished by reinforcing one of the two students seen in a group setting while the other students received no reinforcement. Although there were no vicarious results, there were differential effects depending on level of attractiveness.

As to the specific stimuli used as reinforcers in verbal conditioning studies, they have included a wide variety of cues and objects including head nodding, tokens, candy, cigarettes, and verbal statements of reflection and of interpretation. A very interesting type of reinforcement has been developed by Adams, Noblin, Butler, and Timmons (1962), which has direct implications for the therapy situation. The subjects received a psychoanalytically-derived interpretative statement which was designed specifically for the sentence which the subject emitted. For example, if the subject chose "I" rather than "He" to complete the sentence fragment "sought for truth," the examiner responded "your early religious training is in conflict with your true self." Their results indicated that psychoanalytically-derived interpretations may be used as verbal reinforcers to raise the frequency of a selected response class. On a more qualitative level, interpretations may be noxious stimuli, as most subjects become quite emotional and annoyed during the acquisition phase of the experiment. In a second study (Adams, Butler, and Noblin, 1962), the most striking finding was the apparent resistance to extinction of responses conditioned by interpretations. In a third study by this group (Noblin, Timmons, and Reynard, 1962) they investigated whether *any* interpretive statement by the examiner, even if the content of the interpretation were unrelated to the subject's statement that it followed, could act as a reinforcer. This was in contrast to the previous two studies in which each interpretation was specifically designed to relate to the content of the particular incomplete sentence which served as its stimulus. Colby (in a personal communication) had suggested that much of the effect of interpretations may depend upon their "truth-status." To investigate Colby's hypothesis, the interpretations were listed separately from the stimulus cards and shuffled to yield random pairing of stimulus sentences and interpretations. The learning curve for the subjects receiving "shuffled interpretations" was quite similar to that of subjects who received the logically fitting interpretations following "correct" responses. The data supported the hypothesis that the "truth-status" or relevance of interpretations is *not* the central factor in whether interpretations lawfully modify verbal behavior in a verbal conditioning situation.

Another interesting variation is to study the effect of prior examiner-subject interaction, the kind of interaction, the length and frequency of such interaction, and the effect on the consequent social influence situation. Kanfer and Karas (1959) illustrate how social deprivation, as any other kind of deprivation, results in the individual being more susceptible to those stimuli of which he had been deprived. Would psychotherapy be more effective if it were expected, as part of the procedure, that prior to entering the room with the therapist the patient was required to sit in an empty antechamber for one hour?

Of all the variables of the verbal conditioning situation having relevance for psychotherapy, investigation of awareness is of paramount relevance. The immediate connection is with *insight*, and the relationship between *insight* and behavior change. It has been axiomatic that it is necessary for therapists to have emotional insight into behavioral contingencies before behavior can change.

The complexities of the relationship between conditioning and awareness are many, just as there is between insight and changed behavior in psychotherapy. Based on a series of verbal conditioning studies and those reported in the literature, Krasner and Ullmann (1963) concluded that: the level of awareness reported by subjects is influenced by the informational cues given to the subjects; the verbal behavior of reporting awareness may itself be conditioned; the personality of the subjects and the atmosphere of the experiment are both relevant variables in the reporting of awareness; and the same variables which influence conditionability, such as subject and examiner personality, and situational set, also influence the level of reported awareness, and as such, a positive correlation between the two does not necessarily imply that awareness mediated conditionability.

The research reported by Sarason and Minard (1963) is a good illustration of the complex interactions and interrelations among subjects, experimenters, and situational variables. They used not only samples of subjects, but also samples of examiners. The examiner's characteristics studied were sex and scores on a hostility scale. The same subject variables were also employed. Degree of personal contact between subject and examiner and the examiner's prestige value were the two experimentally manipulated variables. The results indicated that reinforcement did lead to an increase in personal pronouns, but non-reinforcement failed to result in extinction effects. Analyses of both the reinforced and non-reinforced trials demonstrated significant results involving every one of the individual differences and experimental variables. It was concluded that approaching experimental situations such as verbal conditioning from the point of view of interpersonal transactions possesses considerable potential for researchers interested in personality and social psychology.

In a series of verbal conditioning studies Krasner and Ullmann found that verbal behavior of both normal subjects and psychiatric patients can be changed by the selective application of reinforcing stimuli cues. Further, the effectiveness of the examiner in the manipulation of verbal behavior can be enhanced or lowered by alterations of the conditions of the experimental situation. They focused on problems of the relationship between behavior change and: awareness (Krasner, Weiss, and Ullmann, 1961); generalization (Ullmann, Krasner, and Collins, 1961; Ullmann, Krasner, and Ekman, 1961; Ullmann, Weiss, and Krasner, 1963); atmospheres (Weiss, Krasner, and Ullmann, 1960; Weiss, Krasner, and Ullmann, 1963); instructional set (Ekman, Krasner, and Ullmann, 1963); examiner variables (Krasner and Ullmann, 1958; Krasner, Ullmann, Weiss, and Collins, 1961); changes in response class characteristics (Ullmann, Krasner and Gelfand, 1963); and relation to other influence processes (Weiss, Ullmann, and Krasner, 1960). Their results have been consistent with the growing mass of data coming from verbal conditioning studies which are reviewed elsewhere (Krasner, 1962b). These studies, taken as a whole, indicate clearly that change in verbal behavior is a function of social reward and manipulation of environmental stimuli. It would be difficult to avoid the conclusion that there are elements of verbal conditioning in all interpersonal situations including psychotherapy.

The behavior modification research with its major implications for psychotherapy is proceeding at several levels. In addition to the verbal conditioning studies with their emphasis on comparison of performance of large numbers of subjects, important research is proceeding at the individual level, particularly with a view to modifying deviant behavior. These studies involve the growth of utilization of learning principles in actual therapeutic endeavors. Here there have been at least two different approaches, one theoretically derived from Hullian theory, and based on the work of Wolpe (1958), with a growing number of reports from England, Australia, South Africa, and Canada using techniques described as reciprocal inhibition, desensitization, relaxation, aversion conditioning, negative practice, avoidance learning. This research is usually with various forms of neurotic behavior. Reports along these lines have come from Lazarus (1963), Rafi (1962), Yates (1958), Bond and Hutchinson (1960), and Lang and Lazovik (1963), among others. Reports of their work have appeared in Eysenck's *Behavior therapy and the neurosis* (1960), and in a new journal edited by Eysenck, *Behavior research and therapy*.

A second group studying the application of learning principles is very rapidly growing up in this country, and its members are influenced to a considerable degree by Skinnerian operant conditioning. Their work represents a blending of research within a therapeutic context and has had wide applicability including mental hospitals, psychiatric wards in general hospitals, outpatient clinics, hospitals for mental defectives, etc. Literature reports include the studies of Ayllon and Michael (1959), Ferster and De Myer (1961), Lindsley (1960), Goldiamond (1962), Rickard, *et al.* (1960), Saslow and Matarazzo (1962). The emphasis is thus far on the hospitalized patients because of the greater control possible of the environment in a total setting such as a mental hospital.

A few illustrations of operant conditioning research as treatment will be cited. Specific social reinforcement techniques have been used by Ayllon and Haughton (1962) and Ayllon and Michael (1959) in a hospital setting. They "programmed" nurses as "behavioral engineers" by instructing them in the effects of social reinforcement and particularly in the effect of withholding of attention toward those behaviors considered to be undesirable (e.g., psychotic talk). Ayllon points out that many of these undesirable behaviors are shaped and maintained primarily by the reaction of the aides and nurses, and can be changed within a few days to a few months by appropriate behavioral engineering techniques. Some of the desirable patient behaviors being "shaped" include knitting, playing piano, sweeping, singing, "normal" verbal responses, going to a dining room, and feeding oneself. Isaacs, Thomas, and Goldiamond (1960) describe the use of operant conditioning to "reinstate verbal behavior in psychotics" primarily by the use of reinforcement of successive approximations to the behavior that is desired. Ferster and DeMyer (1961) describe the use of reinforcements delivered through vending machines, such as food and candy, in the control of the performance of autistic children. Lindsley (1960) has been investigating the control of psychotic's behavior with a variety of programmed reinforcement. Saslow and Matarazzo (1962) describe the organization of a psychiatric service in a general hospital which is set up to elicit new behaviors from their patients and to maintain the new behaviors with social reinforcement. They place major emphasis on the utilization of a variety of intermediate social learning situations to enhance generalization of the newly learned behavior outside of the hospital situation. Slack (1960) describes the technique of using "Examiner-Subject psychotherapy" as an approach to the treatment of "unreachable" cases, such as delinquents. This consists primarily of the use of reinforcements, such as money, for specified behaviors with the role-taking situation of "being a subject." In effect this is an application of the technique of successive approximations in that reinforcements are used to differentially affect behaviors as they get closer to the "real therapy role."

Ullmann, Krasner, and Collins (1961) report a study in which patient behavior in group psychotherapy, as rated by the therapist, is used as an outside criterion situation of the effectiveness of verbal conditioning of emotional words. Those patients who had been exposed to social reinforcement (approval-indicating cues such as "mm-hmm") in a storytelling situation "improved" in their subsequent behavior in group therapy as compared with control groups of patients who had been in the storytelling situation, but who had not received the social reinforcement.

Rickard, Dignam, and Horner (1960) used verbal conditioning with an individual therapeutic case. In that study, the therapist rewarded non-delusional responses and "mildly" punished delusional responses. The results were a drop in delusional content with the therapist, though the high delusional content returned when a second and a third therapist were introduced to test generalization of this response. Dinoff, Horner, Kurpiewski, and Timmons (1960) were able to condition psychiatric patients to respond to different aspects of their environment. This was done in a group situation where a therapist reinforced personal responses, environmental responses, group responses, or responses about the therapist. The therapist's behavior was limited to the reinforcing of the appropriate response clues. A reliable and scorable index of patients' behavior was thus developed. Salzberg (1961) found that silence on the part of the therapist was highly correlated with patient verbal interaction in a group therapy situation.

It should be noted that there are sharp differences between the Hullian and the Skinnerian applications in terms of different theoretical models, classical versus operant conditioning, differences in emphasis on verbal versus motor behaviors, a physiological versus a non-physiological orientation, differences as to the role of and usefulness of the concept of *anxiety*, differences in the use of hypnosis and auto-suggestion, in the use of drugs, and in the type of problem behavior or behavior deficit for which each is more appropriate.

Another way of distinguishing within the learning group has recently been suggested by Murray (1963), who uses Boring's Biotrophic vs. Sociotrophic dichotomy and cites various differences. Murray contends that the biologically-oriented investigators such as Eysenck and Wolpe lean heavily on classical conditioning, hypnosis and other authoritarian forms of control, and the impersonal manipulation of primary drives. They see

the ultimate causal factors in psychopathology as constitutional and genetic, such as innate differences in conditionability. Murray contends that
this group, despite their protests, still cling to an implicit disease concept
of neurosis that sees symptoms as bad things which one has to get rid of
rather than motivated responses subserving some function in the life-goals
of the person which he may not wish to change. Murray contrasts this
group with other learning theorists such as himself, Shoben (1949), Mowrer (1953), and Dollard and Miller (1950) who try to account for the
phenomenon of therapy by extrapolating laboratory concepts to the verbal
and emotional material in therapy. Murray points out that they stress
reinforcement, extinction, symbolic processes, therapeutic relationship,
and cultural forces. They are seen as reinterpreters of traditional therapy
in learning terms.

Briefly, some of the attitudes and techniques which distinguish both
types of learning approaches from the psychodynamic approaches are:
the view that therapy is a learning process; the emphasis on what are
described as scientific procedures; the willingness to view the symptom as
the behavior to be changed; the emphasis on current behavior in contrast
to the dynamic past and conversely little interest in the unconscious as a
useful concept. The kind of questions asked are more like, "What are the
reinforcements that maintain current behavior?" rather than "What are
the dynamics?" Eysenck (1960), for example, describes the symptom as
an "unadaptive conditioned response." Others see the symptom as evidence of "faulty learning" rather than representing "repression." The
operant conditioning group would talk in terms of creating consequences
which affect the production of current behavior. Therapy goals are
phrased around environmental manipulation to elicit new behaviors and
to reinforce and maintain them.

Of major importance is the likelihood that in viewing behavior as
learned the behavior therapist is apt to reject the medical, disease model
of psychopathology and all the consequences that follow from such a
model. Historically the disease model, in its day, represented a major
advance for mankind. From man's point of view, considering unusual or
deviant behavior as the result of a disease process represented a step
forward, in contrast to the previous notions that the unusual behavior represented the work of witches, demons, or even criminal behavior. Now most
of the current jargon and labels which are so widespread in our society follow from a disease model of abnormal behavior. These include terms such
as *mental illness, emotional illness, psychotherapy, mental health, mental
hospital, mental patients, diagnosis, prognosis, psychotherapy, treatment.*

Therefore, the psychotherapy situation consists of one person in the
sick role, labeled *patient,* and another person in the role of *healer,* the
psychotherapist. The disease model views the specific behavior of an individual as symptomatic of an underlying disease process. This implies

that there are internal mediating forces within the individual that are responsible for the observable behavior. These forces are often represented as being unconscious, or having psychodynamic significance. All too frequently illness itself becomes an explanatory concept; an individual behaves a certain way because he is ill, sick. In psychotherapy the verbal behavior one is dealing with is not the primary data or of primary importance. It is a means of getting at something else, that which underlies it. The undesirable behavior one sees is a symptom of the underlying dynamic or disease process. It is the underlying process that must be changed, brought out, or dealt with in some way. In verbal conditioning, by contrast, the primary datum is the verbal behavior with which one is dealing. As it is changed we are interested in changes that may occur in other situations associated with this verbal behavior, not because we made any underlying changes, but because of the change in the behavior itself.

The attacks on the disease model come, in part, from learning theorists who view behavior as the results of lawful events in a person's life. This includes all behavior including so-called *abnormal,* and there is no sharp distinction between *normal* and *abnormal* except insofar as society labels behavior with these terms. The strongest attack, however, comes from a psychiatrist who is not necessarily identified with learning theory, Thomas Szasz, in a series of papers which culminate in his book (1961), *The Myth of Mental Illness.* Szasz would prefer to put emotional problems in communications terms. He is quite willing to discourage the inner world of man. He feels that the concept of mental illness is unnecessary and misleading since it implies a disease of the brain, and *neurosis* and *psychosis* are definitely not diseases of the brain. He suggests that the phenomena now called mental illness be examined afresh, that they be removed from the category of illness, and that they be regarded as the expression of man's struggle with the problems of existence.

What are the implications of the behavior therapist of seeing his role differently? His goal is to change behavior, not to help insight, self-actualization, or growth, or to lessen anxiety. All of these may be useful to him in achieving his goal, but they are means to the end, not the end in itself. With this goal, he is immediately faced with a value problem; he cannot deny it, evade it, or hide behind meaningless terms which obscure his role (Krasner, 1963a). He has taken the responsibility of changing another human being's behavior and must be able to face the implications of such responsibility. He will be less able to hide behind the reassuring view that "growth" is up to the patient.

The behavioral therapist finds himself in the role of an optimist regarding the changeability of human behavior in contrast to the basic pessimism of many dynamically-oriented therapists. It is the behavior therapist who refuses to acknowledge the limitations, so long accepted, of changing the behavior of mental defectives, physically handicapped, brain-injured, chronic schizophrenics, overweight, and other previously untouchable groups. Here can be cited recent work of a growing number of investigators including Bijou and Orlando (1961), Barrett and Lindsley (1962), Barnett, Pryer, and Ellis (1959), Ayllon and Haughton (1962), and Wolf, Mees, and Risley (1963).

Furthermore, the behavioral therapist continually has to defend himself against the charge of "robotism," which depicts him as cold, impersonal, mechanical in approach, destroying the patient's freedom, and more interested in research than in people. This conceptualization has been expressed recently in Murray's (1963) statement that "part of the antipathy to examining the relationship aspects of therapy, on the part of some learning-oriented individuals, is a conception of the therapist as E—the detached, unimpassioned, objective experimenter. But this is an unnecessary confusion of the therapist and scientist roles" (p. 255).

Shoben (1963), in his critique of behavior therapists such as Wolpe, expresses the view that the behavior therapists "are arguing that the patient is a malfunctioning machine; eliminate the malfunction and the machine is repaired. The only question is one of what procedures will accomplish the repair job. Obviously, the relationship of the mechanic to his broken down device is a ridiculous thing to discuss, and it is comparable nonsense to waste time with such matters as the manipulativeness or the authoritarian qualities of the repairman's work" (p. 265).

Shoben's "machine" description is a fine example of the projection of the "robot" image onto the behavior therapists. In actual fact, the behavior therapists are no more mechanical in their approach than any other therapists, perhaps even less so. In fact, it is true that behavior modification research results in a picture of the therapist who sees his role somewhat differently than that of the traditional therapist. However, the therapist is still a human being, not a machine (Krasner, 1963b), a human being programmed by his society and profession for a very specific task. He is aware of his own effects on others; he is familiar with current research on the social influence process. He is trained to consider the value implications and consequences of his professional role; he knows the type of individual with whom he most effectively interacts. He is able to decide the most appropriate form of treatment to modify patient behavior and is flexible enough to consider trying different techniques such as desensitization or *shaping* behaviors. He thinks of freedom in terms of making available to patients alternative responses in a role repertoire. He uses his own humanness to give of himself, contingently, in terms of attention, approval, and interest. Finally, he sees his function primarily in non-medical terms working with behavior or living problems, not disease entities.

Perhaps the result of lasting significance that will emerge from behavior modification research is that at last the therapist can become effective in his treatment procedures. If nothing else, the research described, as well as future research spawned from it, will enable the therapist to approach his task differently and thus eventually to break through the present log-jam of uncertainty and inefficiency which characterizes psychotherapy.

REFERENCES

ADAMS, H. E., BUTLER, J. R., and NOBLIN, C. D. Effects of psychoanalytically derived interpretations: a verbal conditioning paradigm. *Psychol. Rep.*, 10: 691-694, 1962.

ADAMS, H. E., NOBLIN, C. D., BUTLER, J. R., and TIMMONS, E. O. The differential effect of psychoanalytically-derived interpretations and verbal conditioning in schizophrenics. *Psychol. Rep.*, 11: 195-198, 1962.

AYLLON, T., and HAUGHTON, E. Control of the behavior of schizophrenic patients by food. *J. exp. Anal. Behav.*, 5: 343-352, 1962.

AYLLON, T., and MICHAEL, J. The psychiatric nurse as a behavioral engineer. *J. exp. Anal. Behav.*, 2: 323-334, 1959.

BANDURA, A. Psychotherapy as a learning process. *Psychol. Bull.*, 58: 143-159, 1961.

BARNETT, C. D., PRYER, M. W., and ELLIS, N. R. Experimental manipulation of verbal behavior in defectives. *Psychol. Rep.*, 5: 593-596, 1959.

BARRETT, BEATRICE H., and LINDSLEY, O. R. Deficits in acquisition of operant discrimination and differentiation shown by institutionalized retarded children. *Amer. J. ment. Defic.*, 67: 424-436, 1962.

BIJOU, S. W., and ORLANDO, R. Rapid development of multiple-schedule performances with retarded children. *J. exp. Anal. Behav.*, 4: 7-16, 1961.

BOND, I. K., and HUTCHISON, H. C. Application of reciprocal inhibition therapy to exhibitionism. *Canad. med. Ass. J.*, 83: 23-25, 1960.

DINOFF, M., HORNER, R. F., KURPIEWSKI, B. S., and TIMMONS, E. O. Conditioning verbal behavior of schizophrenics in a group therapy-like situation. *J. clin. Psychol.*, 16: 367-370, 1960.

DI VESTA, F. J., and BLAKE, KATHERYNE. The effects of instructional "sets" on learning and transfer. *Amer. J. Psychol.*, 72: 57-67, 1959.

DOLLARD, J., and MILLER, N. E. *Personality and psychotherapy*. New York: McGraw-Hill, 1950.

DULANY, D. E., JR. Hypotheses and habits in verbal "operant conditioning." *J. abnorm. soc. Psychol.*, 63: 251-263, 1961.

EKMAN, P., KRASNER, L., and ULLMANN, L. P. Interaction of set and awareness as determinants of response to verbal conditioning. *J. abnorm. soc. Psychol.*, 66: 387-389, 1963.

EYSENCK, H. J. *Behavior therapy and the neuroses*. New York: Pergamon Press, 1960.

FAHMY, SUMAYA A. Conditioning and extinction of a referential verbal response class in a situation resembling a clinical diagnostic interview. *Dissertation Abstr.*, 13: 873-874, 1953.

FERSTER, C. B., and DEMYER, MARION K. The development of performances in autistic children in an automatically controlled environment. *J. chron. Dis.*, **13**: 312-345, 1961.

FORGAYS, D. G., and MOLITOR, HAZEL. Reinforcement as a function of instructional set. *J. Psychol.*, **53**: 193-198, 1962.

FRANK, J. D. *Persuasion and healing: A comparative study of psychotherapy.* Baltimore: Johns Hopkins Press, 1961.

GOLDIAMOND, I. The maintenance of ongoing fluent verbal behavior and stuttering. *J. Mathetics*, **1**: 57-95, 1962.

GOLDSTEIN, A. P. *Therapist-patient expectancies in psychotherapy.* New York: Pergamon Press, 1962.

GREENSPOON, J. The reinforcing effect of two spoken sounds on the frequency of two responses. *Amer. J. Psychol.*, **68**: 409-416, 1955.

GREENSPOON, J. Verbal conditioning and clinical psychology. In A. J. Bachrach (Ed.), *Experimental foundations of clinical psychology.* New York: Basic Books, 1962. Pp. 510-553.

ISAACS, W., THOMAS, J., and GOLDIAMOND, I. Application of operant conditioning to reinstate verbal behavior in psychotics. *J. speech hear. Dis.*, **25**: 8-12, 1960.

IVERSON, M. A. Interpersonal comparability and verbal conditioning. In Symposium on interpersonal variables and verbal conditioning, Annual Meeting, Amer. Psychol. Ass., St. Louis, Sept., 1962.

JOURARD, S. M. I-thou relationship versus manipulation in counseling and psychotherapy. *J. Indiv. Psychol.*, **15**: 174-179, 1959.

KANFER, F. H. Comments on learning in psychotherapy. *Psychol. Rep.*, **9**: 681-699, 1961.

KANFER, F. H., and KARAS, SHIRLEY C. Prior experimenter-subject interaction and verbal conditioning. *Psychol. Rep.*, **5**: 345-353, 1959.

KRASNER, L. The use of generalized reinforcers in psychotherapy research. *Psychol. Rep.*, **1**: 19-25, 1955.

KRASNER, L. Studies of the conditioning of verbal behavior. *Psychol. Bull.*, **55**: 148-170, 1958. (a)

KRASNER, L. A technique for investigating the relationship between the behavior cues of the examiner and the verbal behavior of the patient. *J. consult. Psychol.*, **22**: 364-366, 1958. (b)

KRASNER, L. Behavior control and social responsibility. *Amer. Psychologist,* **17**: 199-204, 1962. (a)

KRASNER, L. The therapist as a social reinforcement machine. In H. H. Strupp and L. Luborsky (Eds.), *Research in Psychotherapy*, Vol. II. Washington, D.C.: Amer. Psychol. Ass., 1962. Pp. 61-94. (b)

KRASNER, L. The behavioral scientist and social responsibility: no place to hide. In symposium on "Social responsibilities of the psychologist." Annual meeting, Amer. Psychol. Ass., Philadelphia, Sept., 1963. (a)

KRASNER, L. The therapist as a social reinforcer: man or machine. In symposium on "Social influence, counseling and psychotherapy." Annual meeting, Amer. Psychol. Ass., Philadelphia, Sept., 1963. (b)

KRASNER, L., and ULLMANN, L. P. Variables in the verbal conditioning of schizophrenic subjects. (Abstract) *Amer. Psychologist,* **13**: 358, 1958.

KRASNER, L., and ULLMANN, L. P. Variables affecting report of awareness in verbal conditioning. *J. Psychol.* **56**: 193-202, 1963.

KRASNER, L., ULLMANN, L. P., WEISS, R. L., and COLLINS, BEVERLY J. Responsivity to verbal conditioning as a function of three different examiners. *J. clin. Psychol.*, **17**: 411-415, 1961.

KRASNER, L., WEISS, R. L., and ULLMANN, L. P. Responsivity to verbal conditioning as a function of awareness. *Psychol. Rep.*, **8**: 523-538, 1961.

LANG, P. J., and LAZOVIK, A. D. Experimental desensitization of a phobia. *J. abnorm. soc. Psychol.*, **66**: 519-525, 1963.

LAZARUS, A. A. The results of behaviour therapy in 126 cases of severe neuroses. *Behav. Res. Ther.*, **1**: 69-79, 1963.

LINDSLEY, O. R. Characteristics of the behavior of chronic psychotics as revealed by free-operant conditioning methods. *Dis. nerv. Syst.*, **21**: 66-78, 1960.

LUNDIN, R. W. *Personality—An experimental approach.* New York: Macmillan, 1961.

MARMOR, J. Psychoanalytic therapy as an educational process: common denominators in the therapeutic approaches of different psychoanalytic "schools." Presented to Academy of Psychoanalysis, Chicago, Ill., May, 1961.

MAY, R. R. Individual freedom and social values. In symposium on "Social responsibilities of the psychologist." Annual meeting, Amer. Psychol. Ass., Philadelphia, Sept., 1963.

MOWRER, O. H. *Psychotherapy: theory and research.* New York: Ronald, 1953.

MURRAY, J. Learning theory and psychotherapy; biotropic versus sociotropic approaches. *J. counsel. Psychol.*, **10**: 250-255, 1963.

NOBLIN, C. D., TIMMONS, E. O., and REYNARD, M. C. Psychoanalytic interpretations as verbal reinforcers: importance of interpretation content. *J. clin. Psychol.*, **19**: 479-481, 1963.

ORNE, M. T. On the social psychology of the psychological experiment. *Amer. Psychologist*, **17**: 776-783, 1962.

PATTERSON, C. H. The place of values in counseling and psychotherapy. *J. counsel. Psychol.*, **5**: 216-223, 1958.

RAFI, A. A. Learning theory and the treatment of tics. *J. psychosom. Res.*, **6**: 71-76, 1962.

RICKARD, H. C., DIGNAM, P. J., and HORNER, R. F. Verbal manipulation in a psychotherapeutic relationship. *J. clin. Psychol.*, **16**: 364-367, 1960.

ROSENTHAL, R. On the social psychology of the psychological experiment. *Amer. Scientist*, **51**: 268-283, 1963.

ROTTER, J. B. *Social learning and clinical psychology.* Englewood Cliffs, N.J.: Prentice-Hall, 1954.

SALZBERG, H. C. Manipulation of verbal behavior in a group psychotherapeutic setting. *Psychol. Rep.*, **9**: 183-186, 1961.

SALZINGER, K. Experimental manipulation of verbal behavior: a review. *J. gen. Psychol.*, **61**: 65-94, 1959.

SALZINGER, K., and PISONI, STEPHANIE. Reinforcement of verbal affect responses of normal subjects during the interview. *J. abnorm. soc. Psychol.*, **60**: 127-130, 1960.

SAPOLSKY, A. Effect of interpersonal relationships upon verbal conditioning. *J. abnorm. soc. Psychol.*, **60**: 241-246, 1960.

SARASON, I. G., and MINARD, J. Interrelationships among subjects, experimenter, and situational variables. *J. abnorm. soc. Psychol.*, **67**: 87-91, 1963.

SASLOW, G., and MATARAZZO, J. D. A psychiatric service in a general hospital: a setting for social learning. *Int. J. soc. Psychiat.*, **8**: 5-18, 1962.

SHAFFER, G. W., and LAZARUS, R. S. *Fundamental concepts in clinical psychology.* New York: McGraw-Hill, 1952.

SHAW, F. J. Some postulates concerning psychotherapy. *J. consult. Psychol.*, **12**: 426-431, 1948.

SHAW, F. J. (Ed.) Behavioristic approaches to counseling and psychotherapy. Southeastern Psychological Association Symposium, University of Alabama Studies, No. 13, 1961.

SHOBEN, E. J., JR. Psychotherapy as a problem in learning theory. *Psychol. Bull.*, **46**: 366-392, 1949.

SHOBEN, E. J., JR. The therapeutic object: men or machines. *J. counsel. Psychol.*, **10**: 264-268, 1963.

SIMKINS, L. Instructions as discriminative stimuli in verbal conditioning and awareness. *J. abnorm. soc. Psychol.*, **66**: 213-219, 1963.

SKINNER, B. F. *Verbal behavior.* New York: Appleton-Century-Crofts, 1957.

SLACK, C. W. Experimenter-subject psychotherapy: a new method of introducing intensive office treatment for unreachable cases. *Ment. Hyg., N.Y.*, **44**: 238-256, 1960.

SPIELBERGER, C. D., LEVIN, S. M., and SHEPARD, M. The effects of awareness and attitude toward the reinforcement on the operant conditioning of verbal behavior. *J. Pers.*, **73**: 239-247, 1960.

STEKEL, W. *How to understand your dreams.* New York: Eton, 1951.

SZASZ, T. *The myth of mental illness: Foundations of a theory of personal conduct.* New York: Hoeber-Harper, 1961.

TAFFEL, C. Anxiety and the conditioning of verbal behavior. *J. abnorm. soc. Psychol.*, **51**: 496-501, 1955.

ULLMANN, L. P., KRASNER, L., and COLLINS, BEVERLY J. Modification of behavior through verbal conditioning: effects in group therapy. *J. abnorm. soc. Psychol.*, **62**: 128-132, 1961.

ULLMANN, L. P., KRASNER, L., and EKMAN, P. Verbal conditioning of emotional words: effects on behavior in group therapy. Palo Alto, Calif.: Research Reports of the Veterans Administration of Palo Alto, No. 15, 1961.

ULLMANN, L. P., KRASNER, L., and GELFAND, DONNA M. Changed content within a reinforced response class. *Psychol. Rep.*, **12**: 819-829, 1963.

ULLMANN, L. P., WEISS, R., and KRASNER, L. The effect of verbal conditioning of emotional words on recognition of threatening stimuli. *J. clin. Psychol.*, **19**: 182-183, 1963.

WATSON, R. I. The experimental tradition and clinical psychology. In A. J. Bachrach (Ed.), *Experimental foundations of clinical psychology.* New York: Basic Books, 1962. Pp. 3-25.

WEISS, R. L., KRASNER, L., and ULLMANN, L. P. Responsivity to verbal conditioning as a function of emotional atmosphere and pattern of reinforcement. *Psychol. Rep.*, **6**: 415-426, 1960.

WEISS, R. L., KRASNER, L., and ULLMANN, L. P. Responsivity of psychiatric patients to verbal conditioning: "success" and "failure" conditions and pattern of reinforced trials. *Psychol. Rep.*, **12**: 423-426, 1963.

WEISS, R. L., ULLMANN, L. P., and KRASNER, L. On the relationship between hypnotizability and response to verbal operant conditioning. *Psychol. Rep.*, **6**: 59-60, 1960.

WOLF, M., MEES, H., and RISLEY, T. Application of operant conditioning procedures to the behavior problems of an autistic child. Paper presented to Western Psychol. Ass., Santa Monica, Calif., Apr., 1963.

WOLPE, J. *Psychotherapy by Reciprocal Inhibition.* Stanford, Calif.: Stanford University Press, 1958.

YATES, A. J. The application of learning theory to the treatment of tics. *J. abnorm. soc. Psychol.*, **56**: 175-182, 1958.

22. The repertoire of the autistic child in relation to principles of reinforcement

C. B. Ferster

Childhood schizophrenia is a model psychosis in that it is a profound behavioral disturbance occurring in a very young child without the long and elaborate histories of experiences of the adult. This less complex behavioral history makes the child an ideal subject for experimentation with psychotic debilitation, since the relevant data in the child's history are closer at hand, the number of individuals who can potentially influence the child fewer, and the behavioral control by the parents virtually absolute. When we understand the ways in which behavioral deficiencies occur in young children, and the techniques for ameliorating them, we will have developed tools which have, at least, general relevance for understanding and treatment of the adults, even though the procedures and responsible variables will not be exactly comparable in the two cases. The general method of procedure is to understand how behavior develops in the new child, the variables of which it is a function, and how it is maintained. When we can make a functional analysis of the behavior of the child in relation to its controlling environment, we will have identified the relevant variables which may be potentially responsible for weakening or disrupting behavior, or otherwise producing behavioral deficiencies.

Since reinforcement is the key concept (Skinner, 1953) in describing how new behavior is developed and how it is maintained by the environment, a description of the processes will clarify the deficits observed in the autistic child (Ferster, 1961). Reinforcement is, in most general terms, the major cause of behavior. By reinforcement is meant, first of all, the immediate consequences of the performance in question. The behavior of the child in reaching for a block is almost immediately reinforced by the tactile contact of the block in the child's hand. The stimulus, *block in the child's hand,* however, may in turn be reinforcing because of further relationships to the child's repertoire. The essential point is that the reinforcement of a performance is specific, immediate, and an identifiable consequence. To find the cause of behavior, we analyze the effect of that behavior on the environment. Conversely, to determine which events are reinforcing, we examine those environmental consequences which maintain the child's behavior. Although reinforcement is relevant to almost every behavioral process, it is especially concerned with a question of "Where does the rapidly developing complex repertoire come from?" The two major phenomena are the shaping of new behavior and its maintenance by already developed reinforcers, and the processes by which new stimuli become reinforcers. Many stimuli reinforce behavior without any explicit behavioral history, as for example, many of the events which maintain the behaviors of the infant. Many visual changes are potential reinforcers for the young infant as, for example, movement of the hands and fingers in the field of vision. Once we have identified an effective reinforcer or as soon as a new reinforcer is developed by the processes described below, it may be used by the process of differential reinforcement to successively approximate new forms of behavior never before occurring in the organism's repertoire.

The *shaping* of behavior by differential positive reinforcement occurs continuously in almost every stage in the development of the infant. Consider, for example, weaning the infant to a cup. Here, a new set of performances reinforced by the ingestion of milk is to be developed. At first, the repertoire which the child brings to bear upon drinking out of the cup is almost entirely appropriate to the behavior developed previously when it sucked its milk or put other objects in its mouth. If this performance is at all successful in producing some milk in the mouth the behavior will be sustained, and conditions will be present for the differential reinforcement and shaping of the behavior in the direction of the complex performance eventually required in drinking. Any variation in the infant's behavior which will produce more milk in the mouth will increase in strength, and those activities which have no effect will gradually extinguish. The likelihood of developing the new performance depends upon (1) the physiological development of the organism, so that it is ultimately capable of the behavior; (2) a current repertoire which contains at least the minimal elements to produce at least some food in the mouth and, hence, maintain the behavior necessary for the further shaping of the final drinking performance; and (3) a sufficient level of food deprivation, so that the appearance of given quantities of milk in the mouth from the cup will be sufficiently reinforcing to continue to maintain the performance. Just after having completed a meal, for example, the likelihood is smaller that a child will learn to drink from a cup.

By similar applications of the differentially reinforcing effects of the child's physical environment, there is a continuous shaping of many kinds of behavior, such as picking up objects, eating from a spoon, crawling, walking, sitting erect, focusing the eyes, and manipulating objects with the hand. The young infant acquires control over its limbs as the various movements are differentially reinforced when the child's hand passes through its field of vision or results in the tactual contact with a part of the crib. The final repertoire of playing with its hands in front of its eyes is approximated by the diffuse arm movements occasionally passing the field of vision. The first change in performance is a gross increase in the general level of arm activity, but the performance becomes differentiated progressively as closer approximations to the maximally effective performance have more direct effects in the visual field. All of these are performances which initially have only limited effects upon the environment, and later develop progressively as successive approximations to more effective forms which have more direct reinforcing effects in shaping up the movements of the sensitive parts of the fingers.

Naturally, these processes operate in the context of a physiologically maturing organism. The effect of the differential contingencies of reinforcement in developing the increasingly complex repertoire of the growing child is paced by the state of muscular, neurological, and biochemical maturation. Operant reinforcement in the newborn infant often acts in the context of reinforcing behaviors which are originally reflex, for example, crying and eating. Originally, the infant's sucking is elicited, as in a reflex. After experience, however, the operant control resulting from the differential effects of different degrees of sucking "shapes" the behavior. Originally, the infant's cry is an unconditioned effect of food deprivation, gastric distress, etc. Later, however, crying comes under the control of operant as well as respondent reinforcement because it is a response of striated muscle and amenable to control by its consequences.

REINFORCEMENT OF THE AUTISTIC CHILD'S BEHAVIOR

Direct Effects on the Physical Environment

The reinforcers maintaining the greater part of the autistic child's behavior are simple and direct effects, either on himself or on the physical environment as, for example, in rocking back and forth; producing a noise by shuffling the feet over the floor; genital manipulation; oral manipulation of the hands, body, or small objects; playing with food; rubbing a sticky spot on the floor; breaking physical objects; scribbling on paper or walls with colored crayons; tearing paper; throwing sand or toys; climbing; urinating and defecating. In all of these cases, it is probable that the very simple and direct physical effects of the performance on the environment or on the child himself are maintaining the behavior. The reinforcer maintaining the autistic child's behavior is least ambiguous in performances involving self-stimulation, but it is also probably true in behaviors such as breaking toys, tearing paper, and throwing things. In these latter cases, there is some possibility that the behavior may also be maintained, as might be the case in a normal child, by an effect on the adult community. But in the case of the autistic child, it is probably true that the actual reinforcer is little more than the change in the physical environment as the toy goes into several pieces, or the paper is torn, or the colored marks appear as a result of moving the crayon back and forth. All of these performances which are seen are normal in very young children. More complex consequences are also effective in maintaining the behavior of the autistic child, but these maintain a relatively small part of the child's total activity. Examples of more complex reinforcers are playing with water in the toilet or water playroom, swimming in the pool, or riding in a car. Food is, by and large, the major consequence maintaining the strongest and most durable behavior in most autistic children's repertoires, although this is by no means a complete rule.

Shaping the Autistic Child's Repertoire

The possibility of differentially reinforcing new forms of behavior depends upon a behavioral repertoire in the autistic child in which there are relevant reinforcers whose frequency, amount, or kind of effect will increase by new performances which produce them. Thus, the whole process of differential reinforcement of new behavior is mostly irrelevant in respect to the autistic child, except where there is strong behavior maintained by significant reinforcers. Only in the area of behaviors maintained by food and those behaviors strongly affecting the adult by aversive control, such as a tantrum, is there a strongly enough maintained effect which is potentially sensitive to change by the manner of its effect on the environment. In general, the hospital or parental community of the autistic child does not adjust its reinforcement contingencies sensitively in respect to the child's existing repertoire, as is usually the case with the normal child. One of the problems in applying the process of successively approximating a complex repertoire is that the hospital and parental community in general apply their contingencies in terms of the physical appearance of the child, as they do successively with the normal child, rather than in terms of its behavioral repertoire, which would ordinarily be appropriate for a much younger child. This gross discrepancy between the appearance of the child and the kinds of reinforcers which are, in fact, applicable, makes it difficult to deal consistently with the autistic child.

Reinforcement from the Social Environment

Some of the autistic child's behavior is maintained by its effect on other persons, adults and children, usually by the application of some aversive state of affairs such as a tantrum, kicking, biting, poking fingers into ears or eyes, or throwing and spitting. As with non-social reinforcers, the distinction must be made as to whether the reinforcer is simply the immediate effect of the performance (the ratchet effect of the stick on the picket fence) or whether the reaction of the adult or other child to aversive stimulation occurs because of more complicated relations to the autistic child's repertoire as, for example, in counter-control or teasing.

Estimating the Strength or Durability of a Reinforcer with an Autistic Child

In spite of the major importance of the frequency of occurrence of a response as one of its main dimensions, it is impossible to judge the strength or overall effectiveness of a reinforcer simply by the frequency of occurrence of the related response. The frequency of occurrence of a given item of behavior is also a function of other variables, such as its schedule of reinforcement. The most direct way of gauging the durability of a reinforcer is to maintain the behavior under intermittent reinforcement. A pigeon, for example, will peck many thousands of times per day when the behavior is reinforced by food under large orders of magnitude of food deprivation, such as 75 to 80 percent of its free-feeding body weight. When the level of deprivation is reduced to an order of magnitude of 12 or 24 hours, the reinforcing effect of the food will disappear entirely. By increasing the frequency of reinforcement (most optimally every response is reinforced), the bird will begin responding again even at nearly free-feeding conditions and normal body weight. Thus, one of the main tests of the strength or durability of a reinforcer is how much behavior continues to be maintained when the performance is reinforced intermittently. Relatively weak reinforcers may maintain a high frequency of behavior if the reinforcement is continuous, and very effective reinforcers are required to maintain a response whose reinforcement is highly intermittent. Experiments with autistic children's behavior confirm the general weakness of the child's behavior when it is intermittently reinforced (Ferster and DeMyer, 1961).

Behaviors maintained by simple effects on the physical environment (such as flipping a cup back and forth) may, in fact, not be maintained very strongly, despite their high frequency. The frequent occurrence of these responses may be related to their continuous reinforcement. Each occurrence of the behavior has a very predictable continuous and direct effect. Also relevant to how much behavior will be maintained by a weak reinforcer is the competition from other reinforcers maintaining other items in the child's repertoire. A pigeon experiment will clarify the behavior principle involved. In a standard experiment, a pigeon may produce food by pecking either of two keys for which the schedules of reinforcement are independent. On the left key every fiftieth peck, for example, produces food; on the right key, on the average, a response every ten minutes produces food. Under these conditions, the bird will respond predominantly on the left key (180 pecks per minute) because of the very high frequency of reinforcement. An occasional response on the right key will occur, but at a very low rate (five pecks per minute) because of the very unfavorable schedules of reinforcement. The same bird, however, with only the right key available, will respond at a much higher rate, perhaps 180 responses per minute, instead of five responses per minute, when there was the alternative of working on the more optimal schedule on the left key. In a similar fashion, the rate of responding on the right key can be increased by raising the work requirement on the left key. As a bird is required to peck 100, 200, or 300 times per reinforcement, the rate of responding on the right key increases continuously.

In general, the experiments with autistic children showed a decline in the amount of repetitive, simple performances as an increasing amount of their behavior came under the control of durable reinforcers in the experimental environment. Behaviors such as flipping a cup, rubbing a spot on the floor, rocking back and forth, or climbing, initially occurred frequently in the experimental room before strong behavior developed under the control of the reinforcement supplied in the experiment. As the child's behavior came under the control of the experimental environment, these performances declined and, in some cases, disappeared. The most durable items in the repertoires of most autistic children in the normal ward ecology appear to be behaviors maintained by the routines involved in feeding and by simple effects on the behavior of the attendants and parents. For example, opening the door at lunch time will support a great deal of crying, vocalization, and locomotion which is apparently maintained by its effect on ward attendants.

The Problem of Specifying the Reinforcer

We usually infer the reinforcers maintaining the autistic child's behavior from direct observation. Ultimately, the specification of the reinforcer maintaining the various elements in the child's repertoire is an empirical problem, the solution of which depends upon being able to manipulate the consequences of the behavior and observe its change in frequency. To determine whether the behavior of the child playing with a doll is maintained by the crying sound which comes out of the doll, we have only to arrange the mechanism so that the sounds no longer occur. If the frequency with which the child moves the doll falls, there is evidence that the doll's sound is a reinforcer. Many of the maintaining consequences for most of the items in the autistic repertoire, however, are inevitably tied to the behavior itself, and it is virtually impossible to manipulate the reinforcer independently of the behavior. When the child manipulates its genitalia or manipulates objects in its mouth, the feedback to the child cannot be prevented without physiological intervention, except by preventing the performance. The analysis of the reinforcing effect of stimuli also becomes very difficult in social behavior. The performance maintained, for example, because it has an aversive effect on an attendant, is very difficult to study because the reaction of the attendant is fairly rigidly determined by the effect of the aversive stimulus on him. To extinguish such behavior would require the attendant to show absolutely no reaction to being spit at or poked in the ear or eye. In actual application, this is difficult, if not impossible. Even if the attendant could feign indifference to being kicked, poked, or thrown at, there would still be the reaction of other persons in the neighborhood or generalization effects from other individuals who still react normally to being kicked, for example.

Growth and Development as the Successive Approximation by the Reinforcing Community of the Complex Repertoire of the Adult

The community in general adjusts its reinforcement contingencies so as to make contact with the repertoire of the young child. The young child, for example, who says, "Wawer" will be given water by the parent, even though the accepted form of the word is "Water." At a later age, the same response would *not* be reinforced and perhaps, even punished by the same community. This gradual shift in the reinforcement contingencies in the direction of more complex performances shapes, by successive approximation, the complex repertoires of the young adult. The community, beginning with some performance already in the repertoire of the child, maintains it by reinforcing almost any recognizable approximation to the community practices. The reinforcement is then gradually shifted in the direction of variations which approximate the required repertoire very closely. The community at large also carried out the same practice in explicitly adjusting reinforcement contingencies in education in respect to the repertoire of the child. Almost any behavior of a young child will be reinforced by most persons in most situations without regard to the importance of the child's behavior to the person who reinforces. As the child grows older, however, the community requires a closer and closer adherence to its practices before it will reinforce. The development and maintenance of the final complex repertoire of the adult depends upon the rate at which the community restricts its reinforcing contingencies. In general, the restriction occurs with age and physical development of the individual rather than in terms of the actual behavioral repertoire existing at the moment. This progressive restriction in the forms of behavior the social community will reinforce as the child grows older has special relevance for the autistic child whose repertoire is usually deficient compared with other children of the same age.

INTERMITTENT REINFORCEMENT

Whenever the reinforcements maintaining the behavior of one organism are mediated through another organism, there is a likelihood that the behavior of the first organism will be intermittently reinforced. This intermittent reinforcement occurs because the occurrence of the reinforcement depends upon a process in the behavioral repertoire of the reinforcer which is under only limited control of the reinforced individual. The physical environment also frequently reacts intermittently. The child digging a hole in the earth must operate with its shovel the required number of times before the hole appears in the required depth; or he must reach for a certain number of blocks before the structure he is erecting can be completed. The usual social environment introduces intermittency very gradually to its children. Most parents reinforce much of the behavior of the infant almost continuously at first, but as the child matures more and more intermittency occurs as the community becomes less and less disposed to reinforce forms of behavior which do not conform exactly to its reinforcing practices. The narrowing of the community's requirement occurs both in respect to the form of the behavior that will be accepted ("waw waw" for "water"), and the disposition of the audience to listen. We frequently pay attention to the very young child, whether or not the child's behavior is intrinsically interesting to us. As the child grows older, however, its verbal responses will be reinforced only in the presence of appropriate audiences, and then, only if the behavior is relevant to the repertoire of the listener. This necessity of conforming to the reinforcing practices of the community provides another source of intermittent reinforcement as the child matures. Educational systems frequently adjust the schedule of reinforcement explicitly, depending upon the extent to which the educational reinforcements are maintaining the child's behavior. When the child is "doing very well," we generally withhold reinforcement. When it becomes discouraged (disinclined to study), we reinforce more frequently, until the disposition to study increases.

When a child whines, annoys, or otherwise aversively stimulates the parent, the aversive control of the parent by the child represents an intermittent (variable-ratio schedule of reinforcement) reinforcement of the teasing behavior. The nature of this aversive stimulation is such that its effect is cumulative and depends upon its continuation. The parent will reinforce the whining behavior by providing the required reinforcement whenever the whining is continued sufficiently long to constitute an intense enough aversive stimulus from which escape is reinforcing. The extent of aversive stimulation necessary to reach the parent's *threshold* will vary widely, however, depending upon the general state of rest of the parent, the number of other sources of aversive stimulation, other positively reinforced or aversively maintained behavior which might be prepotent even temporarily, etc. As a result, there is considerable variation in the amount of teasing, nagging, or annoying which will produce the required effect upon the parent. This schedule of reinforcement is one which generates a high and sustained rate of behavior, as well as a very strong disposition to continue behavior for some period even after reinforcement is discontinued. The high frequencies of atavisms in the autistic repertoire, taken with their generally direct aversive effects on adults, make it highly probable that this form of social control will emerge in the autistic repertoire. It is, in fact, likely to be the main form of social interaction between the autistic child and its adult environment. Crying and tantrums may be so strongly maintained by an intermittent schedule of reinforcement provided by the parent, that cases have been reported of parents who stood next to an autistic child's bed all night to avoid precipitating the child's tantrum by leaving.

The specific history by which the child is introduced to the various intermittent conditions of reinforcement is of crucial importance in determining whether or not the behavior will be, in fact, maintained under the schedules, particularly those which may be unoptimal (Ferster and Skinner, 1957). A schedule of reinforcement which, under many conditions, will maintain behavior very strongly, may fail to maintain behavior, or may maintain it very weakly, if the appropriate developmental conditions are not present. In the development of the repertoires associated with sports (for example, baseball), the early history of the child is of crucial importance in determining whether or not he will be disposed to play subsequently. The activities involved in the game constitute essentially a fixed-ratio schedule in which a certain amount of activity is necessary in order for events like hitting the ball, catching a fielded ball, etc., to occur. If the first exposure of a child to a baseball occurs with children who are considerably more skilled and older, and if the appropriate skills in the child are not sufficiently developed, then the first contingencies of reinforcement may not occur frequently enough to sustain enough behavior to keep the child in a situation so that further skill can develop. Similar considerations are also relevant to the development of whining, or the complex behaviors required in the older child for adequate social adjustment, or the successive approximation of any complex performance.

In general, the effects of intermittent reinforcement constitute one of the major factors in determining an individual's disposition to behave. The stubborn child, the industrious child, the child who discourages easily are individuals who reflect, to a large extent, optimal or unoptimal schedules of reinforcement, or histories of reinforcement which establish performances under strong control of the schedules.

CONDITIONED REINFORCEMENT

While it is often convenient to speak of food as the reinforcement for a pigeon pecking at a key or for the child opening a door leading to a dining room, a more detailed analysis of these behaviors shows that we are dealing in these cases with long chains of responses maintained by conditioned reinforcers which support the intermediate performances leading ultimately to the final consequence maintaining the total behavioral episode. The processes involved are more simply explained with examples from the pigeon. The behavior of the pigeon pecking at the key is understood best by reviewing the conditions under which the performance is originally established. The first stage in the training procedure is simply to open the food dispenser and allow the bird to eat. The behavior of pecking at the grain and swallowing it is already in the bird's repertoire, so that all that needs to be reinforced (by the sight of food in a position where pecking at it will result in food in the mouth) is walking toward the food dispenser. After the bird eats readily from the food magazine, the bird's behavior is brought under the control of a special stimulus, a light which comes on only when the food dispenser is available. Approaching the closed dispenser in the absence of the light weakens that behavior, approaching the food dispenser in the presence of the light results in the sight of the grain in the open magazine, and the bird eats. After a small amount of exposure to these procedures, the bird stops approaching the magazine in the absence of the light (extinction), and rapidly approaches the food dispenser whenever the light is on. This behavior is maintained by the sight of food and, in turn, by food in the mouth, etc., leading ultimately to the digestion of the food following the chain of gastrointestinal reflexes. The light accompanying the open food dispenser can now be used as a reinforcer for producing new responses not yet in the pigeon's repertoire. The bird occasionally faces the key at which he is to peck as he moves about the cage. At this instant, the light over the feeder is turned on, and the already-established chain of responses occurs. As a result of one or two reinforcements of this kind, the frequency with which the bird repeats the performance of holding the head in the direction of the key increases, and the chain of responses has become one response longer. Turning toward the key is followed by the magazine light which is in turn the occasion upon which the remainder of the chain may be emitted and reinforced. The magazine light may then be used to approximate the pecking behavior by differential reinforcement.

When the bird faces the key, his head nods slightly in the direction of the key, and the appearance of the light now occurs only on the occasion of a nod. The result of this change in contingency is an increased frequency of nodding, and the chain of response now consists of a nod in the direction of the key, followed by the magazine light, etc. The occurrence of the magazine light is then progressively made contingent upon larger displacements of the head until, finally, the bird is striking the key. The chain, or sequence of responses may be extended again in an identical manner by now reinforcing pecking at the key only when the light behind the key is green, and allowing pecks at the key to go unreinforced when the light behind the key is red. As with approaching the food magazine, the frequency of pecking at the red key soon declines to near zero (extinction), while the bird continues to peck at the green key. As with the magazine light, we can now reinforce a new response by turning the color of the key to green contingent upon something else which the bird does. For example, every time the bird steps on the treadle on the floor of the cage, the color of the key changes from red to green. In the presence of the green color, the bird pecks at the key producing the magazine light, which is the occasion upon which approaching the food magazine is followed by the sight of food, etc. This chain may be extended indefinitely by establishing explicit stimuli, such as the color of the key or the magazine light. While the development of these performances in the chain of responses depends ultimately upon the receipt of food, the actual stimuli which are manipulated and which, in fact, control the bird's behavior, are the changes in illumination. The same process may be illustrated by a child standing at the door screaming because this behavior leads some personnel on the ward to open the door and take the child out to dinner. The origins of the chain of responses involved may be more complex than with the pigeon because of the long history involved, but the general dynamics of the behavior is completely parallel. Screaming at the door is followed by the appearance of an attendant opening the door, which is the occasion upon which the child may walk through the door and, with the attendant, go into the dining room. Going through the door to the dining room is the occasion upon which the child sits down at the table, which is the occasion upon which delivery of food makes eating possible. Here, as with the pigeon, while the actual receipt of food may ultimately determine the strength of the whole chain of performances, the critical conditioned reinforcers in the chain are in fact the events which determine many crucial aspects of the form of the behavior. Nor is it necessary to assume that ingesting food is the sole consequence maintaining the chain. The actual final reinforcer maintaining most of the behavior may, in fact, be a complex of consequences, including social ones in the dining room. It is not necessary, however, to analyze the total consequence of entering the dining room in order to study the effect of manipulating the prior parts of the chain. The reinforcing effect of a given complex of conditions in the dining room may be measured by the reinforcing properties of going through the door. If we can assume, for purposes of analysis, a constant set of consequences for the child entering the dining room, the form of the behavior of the child at the door leading from the ward is determined by the specific consequences applied to the child's behavior by the attendant. For example, the child at the door may go unnoticed when he stands quietly, and the attendant may notice the child only when it screams. As a result, initial response in the chain begins to take a new form, screaming, because of the differential reinforcement. More and more intense screaming may be reinforced when the attendant is occupied with other matters, and only appears when the intensity of the screams increases to the point where their aversiveness makes the attendant's appearance at the door prepotent over whatever he is doing. Or, conversely, it would be possible to change the form of the child's behavior at the door by withholding the appearance of the attendant when the child is quiet. By arranging the appearance of the attendant analogous to a gradual program of *approximation* or differential reinforcement, it should be possible to produce very different forms of behavior, depending upon what contingencies are arranged. These performances are relatively independent of the consequences in the dining room which are ultimately maintaining the entire chain. Sometimes the form of behavior occurring at the door may be determined completely accidentally as, for example, when the door is opened, regardless of what the child is doing but because of a special history, the child happens to be crying. The appearance of the attendant opening the door when the child is crying will maintain the behavior and increase the frequency of the likelihood that the child will be crying again the next day. This performance may be maintained indefinitely, even though spuriously. The fact that the opening of the door has no planned relation to the child's behavior does not alter the reinforcing effect of opening the door on whatever the child happens to be doing. Such accidental reinforcement occurs very widely in the emerging repertoire of the child. For example, once the infant's crying is reinforced by food brought by the parent, the infant cries as the feeding time approaches (because of past reinforcement and/or the direct effects of food deprivation), the placing of the bottle in the infant's mouth follows a vocalization with a high probability, and the subsequent increased frequency of crying may be maintained spuriously. It does not matter that the parent did not intend crying to be reinforced by (followed by) feeding. This accidental or *spurious* reinforcement illustrates a major aspect of reinforcement: that it is essentially a temporal phenomenon. What behavior we *intend* to develop is less relevant than what behavior is followed by a change in the child's environment which makes possible the reinforcement of a response further along toward some important consequence.

The above example shows that the analysis of the behavior and the ability to control and change it becomes more powerful when we recognize that the child's behavior consists of a sequence of performances, each maintained by specific stimuli. To actually manipulate and control the child's behavior, the important events which need to be altered are the instant and immediate consequences of the behavior. The emphasis on the immediate effects of the child's behavior on the environment, particularly as these effects are occasions for further behaviors in a long sequence of behaviors, does not minimize the importance of the ultimate consequences of these performance sequences in maintaining the performance. These ultimate consequences are in fact crucial, but for purposes of analysis, the actual terms which are manipulated and studied in the analysis of behavior are the immediate consequences.

SOCIAL BEHAVIOR AND CONDITIONED REINFORCEMENT

Many chains of responses in the child's repertoire are possible only by the mediation of another adult. This characteristic is a very basic defining characteristic of social behavior: that the reinforcements ultimately maintaining the behavior of one individual occur as a result of the mediation of another. The mediation of a second organism necessarily implies a chain of responses. Most of the performances in human repertoires consist of verbal and vocal behaviors which, in themselves, have little effect upon the physical environment, except insofar as they are stimuli which are the occasions upon which another individual may make possible some further effect upon the environment. The relevant reinforcing stimuli which need to be analyzed and controlled are the reactions of a second individual, whose behavior is the immediate and specific consequence maintaining the behavior of the first.

In his work on verbal behavior, Skinner (1957) analyzes a simple verbal sequence between a child and an adult in terms of the conditioned reinforcers maintaining both the behavior of the speaker and the listener. Consider the behavior of the child first, as it is diagrammed in the top line of the diagram.

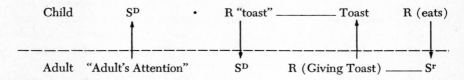

In the presence of an adult, the child says, "Toast, please." This response is followed by receiving toast from the parent which is the occasion upon which the child eats the toast. The delivery of toast reinforces the verbal request, or "mand," as Skinner defines this type of verbal response. For the adult, the sequence begins with the stimulus from the child's verbal response, "Toast, please," the occasion upon which the behavior of giving toast is reinforced by seeing the child eat the toast or, perhaps, because in the past the child has screamed aversively when toast was not forthcoming, and the adult gives toast in order to avoid the aversiveness of the possible tantrum. That this is social behavior may be seen by the interaction (represented by the arrows crossing the dotted line) between the two chains of responses occurring in the adult and the child. The behavior of asking for toast is under the control of the presence of the adult, since the behavior of speaking goes unreinforced in the adult's absence. "Toast, please" is a response emitted by the child, but for the adult it is a stimulus in whose presence the behavior of *giving toast* will be reinforced by seeing the child eat it. The child eating the toast maintains both chains of responses because for the adult seeing the child eat is a positive reinforcement because of a complex of reasons which need not be analyzed for the present purpose; and (2) the delivery of toast reinforced the verbal mand, "Toast, please."

This elaborate analysis of such a small verbal episode is neither trivial nor theoretical because all of the stimuli and responses which are designated refer to actual identifiable events either as responses of the child or the parent's repertoire or specific and observable consequences of these responses. The form and specific features of this simple social interaction could be altered almost arbitrarily by manipulating the specific consequences of any response in the sequence of performances. *Asking for toast* could be weakened simply by the failure of the adult to respond on this occasion. The behavior of the adult in giving toast could be weakened (1) by a failure of the child to eat the toast, or (2) by a change in the relationship between the parent and child no longer making the child's *eating toast* reinforcing to the parent. The stage-by-stage analysis of these two chains and their interactions also makes it possible to understand and control more subtle features of the separate performances of the adult and the child. The intensity and form of the verbal response, "Toast," on the part of the child may be shaped and altered by virtue of a differential response of the parent, as was the case of the child standing outside the door in the example given above. The probability of the adult actually supplying toast depends upon many details of the adult's repertoire as, for example, the other behaviors in which the adult is engaged. The probability of the response, "Toast," being reinforced varies widely with the state of the adult from time to time, as for example, if the adult were under emotional duress. The characteristics differentiating one adult from another (whether the adult is father, mother, or stranger) alter the probability of "Toast" being emitted because of their differential practices. If the parent withholds toast until the child emits strong forms of the response, as for example, shouting and whining, the form of the behavior gradually shifts in that direction. Or, if the consequence of giving toast leads to the child smearing food over himself and the furniture, the child eating the toast may be aversive instead of positively reinforcing, particularly if the adult is a compulsive housekeeper. In all of these cases, it is crucial to identify the instant and immediate consequences of each of the performances involved in the chain and to analyze the subsequent consequence of each stimulus from which its control is derived. Simply identifying food as the reinforcement, as asking for toast, is not a sufficiently detailed analysis to account for the manner in which the specific forms of behavior arise and the manners in which the chains may become distorted or weakened.

Social Chains and Generalized Reinforcers

That the verbal response of the child may go unreinforced on many occasions has broad implications for the role of the adult in maintaining the child's behavior. Because so much of the child's behavior depends upon the mediation of an adult, and because the probability of the child's behavior being reinforced depends crucially on the specific aspects of the adult's bearing, the response of an adult to the child comes to have special significance as a generalized reinforcer. The special reinforcing properties of a generalized reinforcer beyond those present in a simple chain of responses occur because a wide variety of behaviors all maintained by very important consequences to the child become possible only in the presence of the adult, and more specifically, on occasions when the adult has specific characteristics, as, for example, is attending, praising, smiling, not angry or frowning, not preoccupied, etc. For the young child up to the age of two to three years old, the parent (particularly the mother) mediates nearly every important environmental consequence maintaining the child's performance. This occurs largely as a result of the general immaturity of the human infant in comparison with other species. For the first 9 to 15 months of life, the parent is the sole agency upon which the events responsible for the very maintenance of the child's life depends. Even later, when the child acquires more direct control over his environment (technically, acquires performances maintained by the direct effects on the environment, mediated by a variety of individuals, or unmediated by any organism), very substantial portions of its repertoire still continue to be maintained by parental reinforcement. Only in the presence of the parent is the response, "May I have a cookie?" reinforced by the parent saying, "Yes" which, in turn, is reinforcing because this is the occasion upon which the parent hands the child the cookie. Similarly, "May I play with the Tinkertoys?"

Because these characteristics of the adult influence the child in respect to such a wide range of reinforcers and behaviors, they may affect the child without regard to any specific level of deprivation. The praise or attention of the parent is important for the child, even when he is not hungry, because there is likely to be some other behavior in strength whose reinforcement will depend upon the parents' mediation. In other words, consequences in the parental repertoires, such as attention, praise, smiling, etc., continue to be powerful reinforcing stimuli because they are a common element in many chains of responses leading to almost every important consequence maintaining the various elements in the child's repertoire. Such generalized reinforcing stimuli are crucial in the development of much of the social and, particularly, verbal behavior of the child, and are the main means by which the adult exerts educational influences on the child in establishing new repertoires which do not have immediate practical importance for the child. The main reinforcer in teaching a child to comment on his own behavior is a generalized reinforcer involving parental attention, praise, good humor, etc., all of which are related in the child's past history to high probabilities of reinforcement of many important repertoires. Behavior such as "I am playing with blocks" in response to "What are you doing?" must be maintained by some form of generalized reinforcement. In contrast are performances like "Drink of water, please!" which are maintained directly by a reinforcer immediately relevant to a current level of deprivation. Of equal importance in the reinforcing effect of the generalized reinforcer is the nonreinforcement of significant elements of the child's repertoire when the parent is inattentive, frowning, angry, or preoccupied.

It may be seen, therefore, that the development of the generalized reinforcer is a complex behavioral phenomenon which depends upon the existence of many chains of behavior involving many different kinds of performances reinforced by many different kinds of consequences in the environment. As these various chains of responses are variously reinforced or unreinforced, or perhaps occur with different probabilities of reinforcement, depending upon the particular state of the adult who mediates the reinforcers, these particular aspects of the adult come to have the special significance for the child's repertoire as implied by the term *generalized reinforcer*.

Conditioned Reinforcement and Chains of Responses in the Autistic Repertoire

One of the most apparent characteristics of the repertoire of the autistic child is the general lack of long chains of behavior which is typically encountered in the normal child. Most of the autistic child's performances occur in behavioral sequences which are relatively brief and which terminate in a simple consequence. Even performances as simple as moving a chair across the room to look out a window are relatively infrequent. The autistic child, in general, does not look for a toy or go to the shelf to take a box in which blocks are contained, even if the child's repertoire contains some behavior of playing with the blocks or looking out of the window. The same deficiencies are noted in the child's social behavior. That autistic children do not *relate to people* may be very closely tied to the lack of simpler chains of responses, and probably refers to the absence of chains of responses in which other people are the occasions upon which the child may emit some behavior which produces some reinforcer. Most of the chains of responses involving adults are usually of a very simple sort, for example, a child screaming at the door or tugging on an adult's sleeve in the direction of a door when the adult has opened the door for the child in the past. Predominantly, the kinds of chains which may be observed involve little more than a few of the established routines of the ward. This lack of a wide range of performances, chained through the mediation of an adult to environmental consequences important for maintaining the child's repertoire, makes it doubtful that any stimuli may support the autistic child's behavior via the behavioral control of a generalized reinforcer. Since the generalized reinforcer is critical for the development of most complex verbal and social behavior, its absence is perhaps one of the most salient facts characterizing the autistic repertoire.

A commonly cited characteristic of the autistic child's "not looking at an adult" or "indifference to adults" is undoubtedly another manifestation of the lack of chains of responses in these children in which the adult is a link (Kanner, 1943). It is probable that most autistic children do not avoid looking at adults as much as they are simply indifferent to them. A history of aversive control could lead to avoidance of the adult face, but the effectiveness of this kind of control is probably unlikely with large performance deficits. Performances maintained through the mediation of adults involve only very limited portions of the autistic child's repertoire relative to the normal child. It is not at all surprising that the child shows no evidence of "relating to the adult," when one considers the general poverty of the behavioral repertoire. In the normal child, what is described as the child's *relationship to the adult* comes about from a very large repertoire of chains of behaviors in which the adult plays a crucial role involving a wide range of forms of responses and a wide range of environmental consequences. In the autistic child, where the child's repertoire is narrow and limited, much new behavior involving many different behavioral chains would need to be established before the child would come under adult control sufficiently to have a *relationship*.

The development of effective chains of responses requires an initial repertoire with performances capable of exerting more significant changes in the environment than the simple direct reinforcers produced by most of the autistic child's behavior. The existing repertoire and the reinforcers maintaining it have very minimum effects on the environment which are likely to be relevant to any important consequences, either for the individual himself or other children or adults in the environment. The only exception in this regard are temper tantrums. Most of the extensions of the autistic child's repertoire which could potentially occur involve emitting behavior which could alter both the physical and social environment significantly. Building a chain of responses also depends upon some behavior which is strong enough to maintain the chain. The question at issue is "Would the child who sits all day flipping a cup, get a chair and carry it across the room to climb up to a cupboard, in order to get a cup to flip?" In all probability, in spite of the high frequency of the behavior, it is not a strong enough reinforcer to maintain a chain of this sort. An effective sequence of behaviors might be a *child dressing himself* because it makes possible going out to school or to play. Such behavior could not develop if, in fact, there were no disposition to play outside.

The lack of chains of responses in the autistic repertoire is also related to the minimum verbal behavior of the autistic child. Most chains of responses in the normal child involve mediation of another child or adult through speaking to them or attending to their speech.

Chains not Involving Social Reinforcers

Not all chains, however, necessarily involve the mediation of another organism, and many such chains exist in the normal child's repertoire. Consider, for example, a chain of responses involving the behavior of a child moving a chair across the room and using it to climb to a table top to reach the key which, in turn, opens the cupboard containing candy. This complicated sequence of behavior is linked together by critical stimuli which have the dual function of sustaining the behavior they follow (conditioned reinforcement) and setting the occasion for the subsequent response. The chair in the above example is an occasion upon which climbing onto it will bring the child into a position where reaching for food on the table top will be reinforced by obtaining food. Once this behavior is established, the chair in position in front of the table may now be a reinforcer, and any of the child's behavior which results in moving the chair into position will be reinforced because of the subsequent role of the chair in the later chain of behaviors. Even in this type of behavioral chain, generalized reinforcers may occur in the sense that moving a chair produces a state of affairs which is common to the completion of many different sequences of behavior reinforced by a variety of consequences as, for example, opening a lock to go through a door, producing a toy, attracting someone's attention, raising oneself to the level of the window, so that one can see outside, etc. The kind of performances involved in this kind of chain have the common effect of broad changes in the physical world. As a child acquires more and more performances reinforced by a variety of direct effects both on social and non-social environments, conditions emerge which establish simply *changing the environment* as a generalized reinforcer. This occurs because almost all of the reinforcements supporting the child's behavior include direct effects on the social or non-social environment. Merely affecting the environment then, is correlated with many different reinforcers under the control of many different kinds of deprivation. These contingencies establish *control of behavior* as a generalized reinforcer, and are hence capable of affecting the behavior of the individual very broadly. Simply controlling the physical world comes to be an important behavioral consequence which may, in fact, account for much of the "play" behavior of children.

SUMMARY

The analysis of the child's behavior by the basic processes by which behavior is strengthened and weakened in its repertoire provides a framework for characterizing the repertoires of both the normal and autistic

child. Once we have identified the functional relation between the child's
behavior and its environment (including the behavioral processing involving aversive control) we can specify many ways in which its relation to its
environment may be interfered with in such a way as to weaken its behavior. Many divergent processes may contribute to an identical state of
affairs; hence, it is necessary in every case to relate the performance of the
child with its controlling relation in the environment. Such a functional
analysis of the behavior of the autistic child permits a description in which
all of the factors are manipulable events in the environment accessible to
either measurement or control.

REFERENCES

FERSTER, C. B. Positive reinforcement and behavior deficits of autistic children.
   Child developm., **32**: 437-450, 1961.
FERSTER, C. B., and DEMYER, M. K. The development of performances in au-
   tistic children in an automatically-controlled environment. *J. of chron. Dis.*,
   13 (4): 312-345, 1961.
FERSTER, C. B., and SKINNER, B. F. *Schedules of reinforcement*, New York:
   Appleton-Century-Crofts, 1957.
KANNER, L. Autistic disturbances of affective contact. *Nerv. Child*, **2**: 217-250,
   1943.
SKINNER, B. F. *Science and human behavior.* New York: Macmillan, 1953.
SKINNER, B. F. *Verbal behavior.* New York: Appleton-Century-Crofts, 1957.

3. THE PSYCHOANALYTIC MODEL

George Pollock, leader of the Workshop on Scientific Methodology of
Psychoanalysis, at the Institute for Psychoanalysis, Chicago, Illinois, was
invited to have the Workshop formulate and discuss for this volume the
contributions of psychoanalysis to research in psychotherapy. Out of the
Workshop, a group of co-authors produced an up-to-date treatise which
definitively and authoritatively deals with this complex topic.

The authors approached their task by first describing the classical psychoanalytic model and enumerating its research potentials and research
limitations. They highlight the special characteristics and training that
psychoanalytic therapy requires of its practitioners, which has as one of its
principal goals the minimizing of unconscious *blind spots* in the perceptual and integrative functions of the therapist's interaction with his patient.
The psychoanalytic position here is that adverse *counter-transference*
phenomena of the therapist must be eliminated by a personal psychoanalysis in order to avoid disruption of both the therapeutic and research potentials of psychoanalysis. The authors also discuss at this point the reservations that psychoanalysts have about introducing recording equipment

into the psychoanalytic situation to study the analytic process, for fear of disrupting the patient-analyst relationship. (See the chapters by Bergman and by Knapp, *et al.*, which have pertinent comments and somewhat different views on this issue.)

In the oft discussed issue of the difference between psychoanalysis and other psychotherapies, the authors propose that instead of sharp distinctions, it is helpful to consider the various possible processes of psychotherapy on a continuum. Psychoanalysis strives for maximum insight but includes an admixture of education; supportive psychotherapy—at the other end of the continuum—is essentially in the service of the *defensive process* and holds insight at a minimum or manipulates it.

The authors describe and illustrate how the psychoanalytic model has made unique contributions to psychotherapy research. They systematically cover these contributions as they relate to patient variables, such as diagnosis and the assessment of change; therapist variables; and methodological matters, such as data analysis, reduction and classification, and the formulation and testing of hypotheses.

As with other general theoretical chapters in this book, an attempt to summarize more fully the rich contents of this chapter would only provide an inadequate representation. Careful reading of the chapters in this se˘· tion will give the reader a thorough background of the different theoretical positions of the major perspectives in psychotherapy and psychotherapy research.

The chapter by Hans Strupp and his co-authors, Chassan and Ewing, presents first a lucid orientation to one of the central problems of psychotherapy research: the accurate description of the process of psychotherapy with satisfactory consensus among observers. The authors next review a 1956 study by Bellak and Smith which was important because it was the first published attempt of a group of psychoanalysts to describe systematically the events of recorded analytic sessions, and to predict future events. The importance of such a study would seem to be overwhelmingly obvious. The authors point out that it has not been repeated by others. (See, however, Seitz; Knapp, *et al.*; Auld and Dollard; Gottschalk, *et al.*; and Isaacs and Haggard in this volume.)

Using the Bellak and Smith study as a starting point, the authors describe their attempts to develop a rating instrument which can encompass the complexities of the therapeutic hour. Their work constitutes a kind of object-lesson in this type of psychotherapy research, that is, the type which consists of observation of the naturally occurring process, with the observer making judgements on variables in the patient, in the therapist, and in the climate of the relationship. Those who are planning such research will want to study the authors' discussion of (1) the level of inference required in rating the different variables, and the relationship between level of inference and inter-rater agreement; (2) why the overall inter-rater reliability is not higher, and the measures that are needed to improve it; and (3) the results when the rating instrument is applied to ongoing psychotherapy.

These results are in the form of correlations among the variables that were rated. The authors discuss those relationships which were found to be significant. In some cases the results are not at all surprising, for instance, a positive correlation between the patients' hostility and their resistance in therapy. But more interesting relationships are also revealed: for example, a correlation between the patients' insight and their Oedipal strivings; and the general similarity between insight and working through. Findings such as these raise some tantalizing questions about the anatomy of clinicians' judgments, as well as how patients work in therapy. Why should patients develop insight at the same time that they are displaying Oedipal strivings? Or is there some common element in the patients' behavior which makes the therapist perceive both insight development and Oedipal strivings? The authors also find evidence of a relationship between patients' activity and therapists' techniques: those times when the patients were doing well in treatment, the therapists tended to be more "giving," as indicated by deeper and more frequent interpretations.

For a clear and concise statement of where Strupp and his associates feel they stand in present day psychotherapy research, the sections "Recommendations" and "Concluding Comments" at the end of their chapter should be read, along with the "Prospectus" on page 367.

Knapp, Mushatt, and Nemetz cover a large range of issues and problems in research in psychotherapy and psychoanalysis. They report their attitudes about these matters and describe their methods of dealing with them. One of the major topics these authors apply themselves to is the special problems arising in psychotherapy research when psychosomatic and psychoendocrine relationships are also being examined. Reminiscent of the conclusion drawn by Bergman elsewhere in this volume (but in some contrast to Schlessinger, *et al.*), these authors state that the definite clarification, at the onset of the therapy, of the research aspects and conditions of the psychotherapy soon become acceptable constants of the patient-therapist contract for the patient. With these constants as part of regularly anticipated contexts of the psychotherapy, even a task of the patient collecting his urine for 24-hour specimens becomes meaningfully incorporated by the patient into the psychotherapeutic situation. Like Bergman, Knapp and his co-authors find that the psychotherapeutic team member who has the greater difficulty by the introduction into the therapy of research paraphenalia or procedures is the *therapist*.

The authors discuss, with an experienced and knowledgeable eye, a number of other key problems in psychotherapy research including obtaining satisfactory inter-judge reliability in the assessment of complex psychodynamic constellations, a rationale for using sound-recorded instead of sound-film-recorded interviews, and an illustration of the use of a therapist's rough notes as a source of data for certain types of research problems. The latter consideration points up the fact that data pertaining to only part of the interview process (e.g., recording of only the voices) or even sketchy summaries of hourly sessions can be sufficient to answer a large number of research questions.

23. Psychoanalytic contributions to psychotherapy research

Nathan Schlessinger, George H. Pollock, Melvin Sabshin, Leo Sadow, and John E. Gedo

Psychoanalysis presents us with a theory of the mind and its functioning, a theory of personality development, a method of getting primary clinical data, and a therapeutic technique that is employed in the treatment of various disorders. These can serve as baselines for psychotherapy research studies.

The knowledge psychoanalysis has gathered in theory and technique has been utilized in a wide range of non-analytic therapies. Just as psychoanalysis has thus fed the wellsprings of therapy, it has served as a creative force in the evolution of research in therapy. This is of course in keeping with the essence of the development of psychoanalysis itself, for analysts have from the beginning been interested in understanding their patients, themselves, and the complex interactions of the therapeutic process as therapy and research.

The early history of psychoanalysis, recorded in Freud's published cases (1893-1918), reveals vividly the empirical nature of the development of analytic technique in the interest of understanding the riddle of neurotic symptomatology. Throughout its subsequent history, there has been a reciprocal evolution of advances in the theory and technique of psychoanalysis. After the exciting initial discoveries of unconscious processes and their dynamic influence in symptom formation, continuing observations modified psychoanalytic theory which, in turn, modified clinical practice. The structural division of the mental apparatus into ego, superego, and id ultimately facilitated a broadening of the area of analytic exploration to include the ego's defensive operations and the matrix of character structure. In recent years the elaboration of psychoanalytic ego psychology has continued as clinical explorations have extended available knowledge and problems of adaptation to the environment have come under psychoanalytic scrutiny. These developments have had profound implications for all forms of psychotherapy.

In this paper we shall attempt to elucidate the impact of this steadily

From the Workshop on Scientific Methodology of Psychoanalysis of the Institute for Psychoanalysis, Chicago, Illinois.

evolving psychoanalytic theoretical and clinical approach upon research in psychotherapy. No attempt will be made to document or even summarize the full extent of all the contributions; rather, our purpose is to highlight a few major and prototypic trends. The psychoanalytic process itself will first be discussed as a model of a psychotherapy with regard to its research potentials and problems. This will be followed by an effort to describe the contributions of analysis to research in the essential variables of any psychotherapy: the patient, process, and change and outcome variables. The closing section will describe the analytic contribution to an assessment of the therapist and researcher variables in psychotherapy research.

PSYCHOANALYSIS AS A MODEL THERAPEUTIC PROCESS

A brief description of the analytic process will exemplify an entire process of psychotherapy. This model will illustrate research issues at various stages of process. Such an approach recommends itself as useful in the examination of any psychotherapy. It will demonstrate as well that psychoanalysis as a treatment method created a situation for the study of the individual which maximizes research possibilities.

In the practice of psychoanalysis, conditions are arranged that provide for frequent, regular interviews in the same setting, at the same frequency, and reducing external interference to a minimum. Two major factors are taken into account in the rationale of the method: (1) the existence of unconscious mental processes that have to be elucidated in order to understand symptoms, and (2) the fact that the analyst and the patient influence each other in the course of the effort to understand. The patient lies on a couch to facilitate a relaxed state and reduce the possibility of direct influence on the material communicated as a consequence of observing the analyst's movements and facial expressions. Thus, attention is focused on the analysand's internal mental processes. The procedure of free association was the major tool developed to insure that communications reflect the mental content unfolding in the patient. The effort of the patient to set aside all of his objections to the flow of thought, feeling, sensations, imagery, and dreams taps realms of mental functioning otherwise unavailable for examination.

The analyst's task consists in the facilitation of such a free flow of material with interpretive comments which clarify resistances that develop in the patient toward reporting freely what occurs to him. This is differentiated from such techniques as suggestion and reassurance; the analyst listens with "evenly hovering attention" (Freud) to the communications of the patient. His talents of empathy and introspection must, of course, be sharpened by prior training and his personal analysis (Kohut, 1959). He remains as much as possible a person unknown to the patient, about whom the latter is free to fantasy and conjecture as his inner needs dictate. The essential contribution of the analyst is interpretation, a succinct statement pointing out the components and origins of the patient's conflicts and their hidden connections, clarifying patterns of response, and identifying the derivatives of unconscious fantasies and wishes as they enter consciousness transferred to current bits of reality, including the analyst's comments and behavior.

The function of this interaction is to produce insight, i.e., to make conscious with affect the dynamic conflicts between various structures of the mind, between the ego and the superego and the ego and unconscious strivings, and to deepen the understanding of the genetic roots of these conflicts, tracing them to their origins from evidence collected as infantile amnesia is gradually overcome in the analysis. Energy bound up in the defensive process which maintained repression is freed and feelings that were repressed seek conscious expression as the adult ego struggles to make them acceptable and useful.

The natural course of an analysis has been divided into three phases. The opening phase involves the establishment of a therapeutic alliance in which the patient learns to ally the healthy part of his ego with the analyst for the purpose of observing and understanding what happens within him. The necessary trust and confidence develop as resistances are encountered and interpreted and the patient becomes educated in what analysis is. Regularity of visits and the individual attention and implicit support of the analyst who remains objective, non-judgmental, and understanding are crucial as an appropriate emotional environment; and the pressure of suffering and desire for help that brings the patient to analysis moves the patient to reveal intimate, intensely affective, and personal information of a kind rarely brought under examination. The process of free association provides access, then, to material not usually available even to the patient no matter how much the patient trusts another person; namely, to derivatives of unconscious activity revealed in memories, imagery, fantasies, dreams, and transference reactions. The material which the patient brings to analysis bears the stamp of an implicit organization, repeating certain characteristic patterns that have been laid down in the course of the patient's development. The repetition of these patterns in the analysis permits a gradual accumulation of data about their genesis.

In the second phase of analysis, a *transference neurosis* becomes evident in which the analyst becomes the focus of a re-enactment of the patient's patterns of interaction with significant figures from the past. Through repeated confrontation with distortions in the patient's view of the analyst, as well as the recognition and the remembering of repressed material, the patient develops insight and the possibility of a new solution for his conflicts. It is only through repeated, lengthy, and detailed observations which this process provides that reliable data are obtained for accurate genetic reconstructions and proper assessment of psychic structure and the economics of psychic energies.

The third, or termination phase, involves a resolution of the transference in which the patient attempts to overcome the bonds of repetitive behavior dictated by early experiences. Such efforts are, of course, present earlier in the analysis as well; but when the greater part of the work is done, in favorable outcomes, these efforts become concentrated as the patient invests his interest and energy in the satisfactions available in reality. This process of resolution of the transference is a very complex one and it extends beyond the formal termination of the analysis.

In the initial phase of analysis, symptoms may decrease simply because of supportive factors in the analytic relationship; in the middle phase there is a fluctuation of symptom compromises depending on the specific effects of analytic work on the factors involved. In the final phase, as noted by Buxbaum (1950) and Payne (1950), there is commonly a recurrence of symptoms as the neurotic elements are intensified at the threat of separation introduced by thoughts of terminating the analytic experience. The transference functions of the analyst are more sharply focused and interpreted, providing for a resolution of the transference. In the final phase of analysis, childhood experiences are recalled with vividness in reminiscence, and a clarity about the factors entering into the neurosis becomes evident to the analyst and the analysand. The modifications that have occurred in the structures of the mind as a consequence of accumulated insights and the analytic relationship make the symptom compromises unnecessary. The postanalytic course may involve fluctuations in behavior with the degree of utilization of analytic insights as new adaptive patterns are solidified.

RESEARCH POTENTIALS AND PROBLEMS OF PSYCHOANALYSIS

A variety of research issues regarding the psychoanalytic method and process will now be considered, including the function of the analyst, the collection of primary data, the nature of interpretation, the question of prediction, the assessment of change, the evaluation of outcome, and the problem of follow-up studies. Since the function of the analyst is to be a participant observer throughout the analysis, his objectivity and self-awareness are essential. Fleming (1961) has described the special characteristics that analytic work requires of its practitioners. Methodologically, the prerequisite of a training analysis for the analyst is an effort to calibrate the instrument of the analyst's psychic apparatus to reduce distortion to whatever minimum is humanly possible. The analytic tool, interpretation, is based on a complex functioning of this instrument at both unconscious and pre-conscious levels through empathic understanding, connections with available memories and knowledge, and a final filtering through organized conscious thought. The actual interpretive comment to the patient is made according to the analyst's clinical judgment of the meaning of the patient's communication and the level at which it will be meaningful to the patient. It is apparent that the problem of distortion in the analyst's view of the patient is an important one, and it has received much attention, with efforts to become aware of such a mishap through telltale clinical signs and to correct them by self-analysis, re-analysis, or consultation with a colleague.

In fact, considerable literature describing and studying countertransference phenomena in the analyst (Orr, 1954) documents the significance attached to this problem, which may disrupt both the therapeutic and the research potential of analysis. The analyst's objectivity, however, is enhanced by an acute awareness of countertransference as a clinical pitfall. The recognition of unconscious attitudes, reactions, or bias toward a patient is further facilitated by the fact that self-observation and self-interpretation are commonly utilized by the analyst in his understanding of the impact and the nature of the patient's communications.

Efforts at careful research design to study the analytic process pose a number of major methodological problems. Some investigators have made use of tapes or movies to collect comprehensive and objective data. For some purposes this may be useful, but the recording of an analysis may also prove to be an intrusion and a disrupting influence on the patient-analyst relationship, since they are both influenced. It is an effort at precision; however, at best it records only the expressed end product of the analyst's thought processes. Arguments questioning the basic accuracy and meaningfulness of the data gathered by the analyst will hardly be stilled by a tape recording. Such arguments often indicate an underlying skepticism about a necessary part of the instrument of research, namely, the analyst's subjective mental processes. These processes have been described with verisimilitude and imaginativeness in a little-known paper by Erik Erikson (1958).

Another means employed to handle the problem of objective data is supervision in which a consultant receives an account of the analysis from the analyst and can maintain an objective attitude toward the patient-analyst interaction. Further complexities are introduced in this manner, too, of course, but the total advantage appears to outweigh the possible distortion of the analytic process. In the absence of such an external check on the data, questions about distortion may be resolved by a sufficiently large number of cases analyzed by many analysts.

An example of this occurs at the Hampstead Clinic where a number of analysts have combined their efforts in understanding particular types of cases (A. Freud, 1958). This approach permits the accumulation of data about a number of analyses, the cancellation of personal distorting influences in interpretation, and the testing of hypotheses. At the Chicago

Institute, the study of adult patients who lost a parent in childhood (Fleming and Altschul, 1963), and the study of patients with particular types of psychosomatic disorders (Alexander, French, and Pollock, in preparation) employ a group approach to research.

The simultaneous analyses of parents and children, the growing literature on the analyses of marital couples, and the simultaneous analyses of siblings and twin studies, as well as the analysis of young adults who had previously had analysis as children, provide data for investigation and validation of concepts about the therapeutic process.

The nature of interpretation as an essential element in the analytic process has been the object of considerable interest recently. In answer to philosophers who have criticized analysis, interpretation has been defined more precisely by Waelder as an attempt to fill in lacunae in the chain of conscious experiences, undo distortions, and point out connections based on the data of observation provided by the patient in his behavior, memories, dreams, and free associations (1962). He described the hierarchy of conceptualization from data of observation through clinical interpretation, clinical generalization, theory, metapsychology, and philosophy. This schema has been used by us as a promising means of re-examining the origin of analytic concepts for their basis in observed data (Gedo, Sabshin, Sadow, and Schlessinger, 1964).

Freud (1937), in an early methodological comment on technique, made it clear that the interpretation is confirmed or refuted by the productions, behavior, and contributions of the patient rather than by any simple yes or no. The observing ego of the patient is a collaborator in the process of evaluating the correctness of an interpretation. Repetitions of the patterned activity of the patient in the analysis permit utilizing the patient as his own control in a more rigorous manner than has been widely recognized.

The question of prediction has recently been examined with some experimental efforts to test the analyst's ability in this area (Knapp, 1963). There are many kinds of predictions. Some are part and parcel of the analytic process itself. At the beginning, the diagnostic assessment permits a prediction about analyzability and provides evidence for predictions about genetic factors, the nature of the transference neurosis, and the kinds of special problems that may be encountered in analysis. Subsequently, the analyst's effort, although concentrated on the task of understanding past and present as conveyed by the patient's communications, involves a continuing use of limited predictions. These influence the timing and content of the actual interpretations and are checked within the analysis by the patient's response. The shifting compromises which serve the patient's adaptations are not as susceptible to precise prediction in view of the complex and numerous variables that determine behavior. Such variables as are present in external reality or in the unknown content under investigation may produce surprises. However, as the analysis proceeds, the analyst becomes aware of a broad and deep range of motivations, defenses, and patterned responses and observes the changes they undergo. This information does permit prediction. The degree to which such prediction can be successful is open to further study. It may prove a useful method in sharpening quantitative determinants.

The assessment of change in the therapeutic process is of fundamental research importance in the course of an analysis. The factors entering into change are under microscopic scrutiny. The nature of change itself is susceptible to study when a problem comes into focus in analysis and is worked through with a resultant accretion in mental structure. The process permits first an identification of the problem, then an ever-deepening understanding of the contributing factors involved in the development and maintenance of the problem. As the patient overcomes resistances to an awareness of these factors, he is simultaneously modifying attitudes, feelings, and memories in such a way as to promote the possibility of adaptational changes. Examples of such a process will be described below.

It is apparent that the assessment of change goes on continually in the analytic process. However, a more macroscopic view of the nature of change becomes particularly significant in the terminating phase of the analysis. Here the results of the analytic effort are scrutinized as they relate to the analytic ideal and to the general adaptation of the patient. The assessment of change rests most appropriately on a definition of the goal of analysis. The essential goal is to regain for the ego mastery over (or at least awareness of) that which was repressed so that new solutions may be attempted that are closer to reality. In this context, the indicators for change at the end of the analysis are observations bearing on whether this job has been done; whether the patterns and origins of the patient's problems have been brought into clear relief, elaborated, worked through and understood in the transference neurosis, making symptom compromises unnecessary.

An additional factor that enters into the decision about termination is an evaluation of outcome. The sum of the analyst's professional and personal experiences is pressed into service in such an evaluation, since it involves a prediction about the interaction between the changes observed in the patient and the post-analytic environment (Gitelson, 1960). The nature of adaptation itself has become a new focus of analytic interest not yet sufficiently studied.

Freud noted that the end result of a successful analysis is the establishment of a capacity for self-analysis (1937). In this way, problems encountered or focused by environmental or internal pressures are capable of resolution. More recently such a process has been described and explained as based on the acquisition of a new ego function that operates unconsciously (Kramer, 1959). In this contribution Maria Kramer describes her observation of the analysis of a conflict that proceeded unconsciously within her after her conscious efforts at analysis had been to no avail. She ascribes this experience to the acquisition of a new integrative capacity by the analyzed ego, using energies that have been liberated from defensive functions. The full applicability of insights discovered during analysis may await a particular set of post-analytic circumstances.

The evaluation of outcome involves judgments in the measuring of change. The criteria for these judgments about psychic functioning are largely contained in the theoretical framework of analysis. Obviously a scale of movement toward maturity is contained in the descriptions and conceptions about the development of libido, aggression, and object relations and the functions of the ego and superego. In this regard Anna Freud (1963) has recently described a series of "lines of development" providing a very useful research baseline for measuring change. The ego's reality function, object relations, libidinal organization, control, and expression of affect and impulses, etc. can be evaluated and compared with the situation at the start of therapy. Aspects of superego function, particularly archaic elements involved in symptom formation, are elucidated and the growth toward rational judgment can be estimated.

To make careful studies possible, varieties of criteria, confusion of language, and diagnostic differences are barriers that must be overcome. The defect heretofore has been not in a lack of raw data, but in developing an adequate system of data analysis. The work of the group at Hampstead in cataloguing analytic material and clarifying concepts may well provide an appropriate basis for future studies.

Recent efforts at follow-up studies have begun to shed light on the outcome of the analytic process (Pfeffer, 1963). The long-term results of analytic efforts had been studied only in cases of reanalysis. One recent effort employed several follow-up associative interviews by an analyst not known to the former patient. The new relationship acutely recapitulated the previous transference neurosis with a subsequent rapid resolution. Replication studies are indicated to check on the validity of these findings.

Analytic literature does contain, of course, some descriptions of follow-up studies, notably Muriel Gardiner's follow-up of one of Freud's early cases, the "Wolfman," and a 30-year follow-up on two patients by Helene Deutsch. However, analysts have been reluctant, heretofore, to initiate contacts with their former patients after completion of the formal analysis. The Menninger research now in process is studying this area (Wallerstein, 1961) and Pfeffer did investigate it earlier (Pfeffer, 1963). Similarly, discussions about the patient with people who know him intimately are avoided during the analysis as a contaminant of the analytic process and have not been utilized as a source of data post-analytically. Data derived from sequential follow-up studies for some years after analysis combined with data provided by other reporters in the patient's milieu would constitute a fund of information of inestimable value in elucidating the outcome problem in psychoanalysis.

PSYCHOANALYTIC CONTRIBUTIONS TO PSYCHOTHERAPY RESEARCH

The comprehensive scope of its developing theory of human behavior and mental functioning constitutes the most important contribution of psychoanalysis to research in psychotherapy. This comprehensiveness permits the simultaneous assessment of the patient's psychopathology, of the therapeutic technique and resultant transactions, of the characteristics of the therapist, and of the outcome of treatment within a consistent framework.

Psychotherapists may obviously operate quite effectively on the basis of intuition or some implicit structure in their technique without any knowledge of analytic theory. However, an investigation of a variety of methods of treatment to develop an explicit theoretical framework may be useful in providing a broader and deeper understanding of the nature of psychotherapy, with benefits accruing to the teaching and practice of psychotherapy. While the whole field of psychotherapy may be approached from vantage points other than psychoanalysis, recent publications in the study of psychotherapy indicate the exciting prospect that the varieties of techniques practiced may now be fruitfully organized with the conceptual tools provided by psychoanalysis.

Historically the nature of psychotherapy was approached by analysts in attempts to distinguish carefully between other psychotherapies and psychoanalysis. Such a focus does illuminate particularly models of psychotherapy that act to modify or reinforce the defensive organization of the personality with a minimum of insight. Tarachow (1962) has summarized the operations of psychotherapy as supplying the infantile object desired by the patient by entering into a real relationship beyond the limits of the therapeutic alliance described in analysis; supplying stability to the existing personality organization through ego and superego support (educative measures, commands, prohibitions, and expressions of morals and moral values); and supplying displacements through inexact interpretations that accentuate the positive and make life more tolerable. In such supportive therapies, the transference is used for beneficial influence and not interpreted. The model of analysis may be clearly contrasted as striving for a maximum of insight in every aspect of conflict in which the structuralization of personality has been involved. Such a contrast is useful conceptually but perhaps it creates only an illusion of understanding if one considers the various possible processes of psychotherapy as a continuum.

On the one hand, there are therapies which are essentially in the service of the defensive process and in which insight is held at a minimum or manipulated by the therapist; on the other hand, there is psychoanalysis striving for maximum insight. However, in analysis there is an admixture of education, in supportive therapy there is an admixture of insight, and in between there is a territory which requires careful attention.

To some extent there have been elements of theoretical structure erected in this area. Analytic theory has been occupied in defining parameters in practice to permit the utilization of an analytic approach with patients who are not classically neurotic. The essential criteria for analyzability stem from the nature of the process. A patient must have the capacity to engage in a transference neurosis (reliving and remembering the conflicts of the past within the analytic situation) and the ego strength to observe his experiences, understand them, and integrate them. The concept of a parameter has been defined in psychoanalysis as a modification of technique to permit the analytic process to unfold, emphasizing that the treatment can be regarded as the standard model of an analysis only if that modification is later analyzed as to its function and meaning for the patient (Eissler, 1953). An increasing number of character problems and "borderline" personalities have been successfully analyzed. However, the use of specific parameters, even when agreed upon by analysts, only enlarges the area occupied by analysis proper.

New concepts have been suggested to illuminate the area between analysis and supportive therapy (Gedo, 1964). The need to define patient, therapist, process, and outcome variables is an important consideration that has been given insufficient attention. In the area of patient assessment the former descriptive categories may be replaced with constellations based on the metapsychological points of view (which will be described shortly below) and on the advances in analytic ego psychology. Specific patient categories can be defined, based on maturational levels; for example, patients with age-appropriate developmental problems, such as ego identity in the adolescent, constitute a group whose therapy occupies a clear and special area and for whom specific treatment techniques have been discussed (Lorand and Schneer, 1961). Such a category emphasizes a developmental growth factor which is important clinically as well as theoretically since specific supportive measures help the patient progress to the next maturational stage.

In the same context arrests and distortions of ego development may be more carefully defined so that the supportive measures employed may be consciously chosen rather than left to the intuitive response of a skilled therapist. Advances in ego psychology such as contributions on the genesis of the ego and the stages in its organization will reveal specific kinds of ego pathology (Spitz, 1959). This should permit a meaningful diagnosis and a delineation of specific therapeutic tasks.

Psychotherapeutic plans may be directed toward the maintenance of an existing adaptation or toward the preparation of a patient for an analytic

Methods of Research in Psychotherapy

experience. Such preparation has become a common form of treatment but the measures employed and the nature of the process and its subsequent effect as a parameter should be carefully investigated. In an analogous fashion, patients may by virtue of psychotherapy be enabled to master ego developmental tasks left behind in a pathological growth process. The limits and nature of such therapies have yet to be described.

New conceptual tools for studying and defining the nature of the therapeutic process may be provided by current efforts to relate learning theory and analysis in a psychoanalytic theory of learning. One such effort (Piers, G. and Piers, M. W., 1964) describes three types of learning: by conditioning, by identification, and by insight, and discusses the complex interweaving of all three in the analytic process. This provides new perspectives from which to view any therapeutic interaction in order to make more explicit the precise nature of the therapeutic process.

CONTRIBUTIONS TO INITIAL DIAGNOSIS AND THE ASSESSMENT OF CHANGE AND OUTCOME IN THERAPY

Patient assessment is fundamental in psychotherapy research since any measure of change and outcome must utilize an initial baseline. Therefore, we shall first discuss the contributions of psychoanalysis to initial diagnosis and then examine its impact upon studies of change and outcome in therapy.

Most research reports confine themselves to the single case study or attempt only the crudest differentiations, such as *schizophrenia* or *manic-depressive psychosis* or even more general categories (e.g., *neurosis* or *character disorder*). The traditional psychiatric nosology is an almost purely descriptive one. As such, it has some usefulness for naming a patient's gross clinical state at a given point in time (*acute schizophrenic reaction, catatonic type* or *conversion reaction in a chronic neurotic personality pattern disturbance, hysterical type*), but it is ill-suited to the task of estimating manifold reversible dynamic changes as they emerge in the course of psychotherapy. The task of patient assessment does not stop with comparisons of clinical state before and after treatment; because of the frequency of relapses as well as of spontaneous remissions or realignments of the symptoms, ongoing reassessments during treatment as well as systematic follow-up studies after termination are essential.

The initial evaluation of a patient and the definition of that group of patients for whom psychoanalysis is useful have been described by Glover (1949). He emphasizes the need to employ the principles gathered in psychoanalytic investigations in such an assessment, and this is no less true for research in any psychotherapeutic venture. Essentially what is involved is the evaluation of a patient in depth with regard to the nature of the conflict, the early historical determinants of the presenting problems, the structure of the mental apparatus, the quality and nature of impulses and feelings, and the kind of adaptation to the environment. These factors have been formally described in analytic metapsychology as the dynamic, genetic, structural, economic, and adaptive points of view. They will now be discussed briefly and illustrated with clinical vignettes.

The cornerstone of a sound diagnosis is the assessment of the conscious and unconscious conflicts operating in each individual patient, in the integration of instinctual drives, prohibitions and ideals, and external reality. Psychoanalysis has been unique, even among the dynamic psychologies, in its emphasis on Sigmund Freud's greatest discovery, that of the impetus of unconscious forces. The symptoms and characterological difficulties of our patients remained incomprehensible as long as the realm of dynamically active psychic forces not available to their conscious awareness was also ignored by their physicians. The following brief clinical example illustrates how the dynamic framework is utilized in clinical practice:

A 24-year-old medical student sought consultation for depression and anxiety that was seriously disrupting his ability to pursue his studies. The anamnesis revealed that he had for some weeks been involved in an effort to make a decision about marriage to a girl of a religious faith other than his own. On the one hand he was very much in love with the girl; on the other, he did not want to disappoint his parents who reminded him of his obligations to them. His fear of displeasing them and his anger at them, accompanied by guilt, produced a state of anxiety and depression which were the manifestations of his conflict. From the past history, it became clear that the patient had had an intense relationship all his life with an overprotective and seductive mother, which he had attempted to handle as best he could. In part, his involvement with a girl of a group different from his family's related to his need to solve the unconscious conflict with his mother by avoidance, i.e., by choosing a girl as much unlike his mother as possible.

The example cited illustrates the fact that there are levels of conflict ranging from superficial, conscious elements to deeper, unconscious issues which may or may not become evident in the initial evaluation. Of course, the same superficial conflict may exist in patients whose deeper conflicts are quite dissimilar, a point of significance in studying therapeutic outcome in groups of patients. Often intensive work with patients is required to establish the hierarchy of conscious and unconscious conflicts, suggesting the limitations of data gathered from a single interview or a questionnaire for this purpose.

The decisive significance of childhood endowment and experience in personality development, both healthy and pathological, is another of the basic contributions of Sigmund Freud. This has so thoroughly passed into the public domain of the behavioral sciences that its specific origin in psychoanalysis tends to be overlooked; but its actual use in patient assessment is surprisingly underemphasized in much psychotherapy research. It comprises clarification of the precipitating events which produced the latest decompensation as well as of the developmental vicissitudes which led to this specific vulnerability. Studies of *anniversary reactions* are an excellent illustration of the interaction of past and present in producing psychological difficulty as illustrated in the following vignette:

A housewife in her late 30s came for help to disentangle herself from a homosexual affair. Although she had had a few transient extramarital adventures previously, her marriage had remained stable. She continued to love her husband, and she managed to give of herself sufficiently to keep both her husband and her lover satisfied with partial gratification. She could not understand her own unwillingness to relinquish the triangle. Her motivation remained obscure until the emergence of the fact that her father had died at age 45, while she was still a child, leaving her alone with a childlike mother and a schizophrenic sister. Her need for two love objects had arisen when her husband was 45, i.e., when the anniversary of her father's death was imminent in her own marriage.

These anniversary reactions have been studied by Hilgard (1953). The difficulties experienced by the child in meeting adaptive tasks after the death of a member of the family and their exacerbations in adulthood illustrate the genetic point of view. Fleming and her colleagues (Fleming and Altschul, 1963) have conducted research on the consequences of losing a parent during childhood, emphasizing a developmental arrest in the ego. Pollock (1962) reviewed his experiences with adult patients who lost parents or siblings early in life and commented on the comparative significance of such losses in men and women at different age periods.

We attempt to learn of the past in order to be able to appreciate its effect on the here and now. Current behavior and pathology can be viewed as the result of particular external antecedent events and their intrapsychic elaborations occurring at critical points of psychological development. As noted earlier, the psychoanalytic theory of development of personality provides guidelines for the assessment of levels of maturity.

The history of the structural point of view may be briefly sketched for the sake of clarity. Freud's earlier view of the mental apparatus was that it was divided into the conscious and the unconscious. This *topographic* approach was subsequently modified in 1923 in *The Ego and the Id,* when Freud conceptualized the apparatus as consisting of three clusters of enduring personality functions: the instinctual drives as *id*; the internalized ideals and prohibitions as the *superego;* and the perceptual, coordinating, and executive functions grouped in the *ego.* This model has permitted more finite classification of mental functioning and a clearer means of classifying personality disorders. For example, some patients may have hypertrophied superegos as in the obsessive or guilt-laden characters, whereas psychopaths demonstrate a distortion of superego.

Patients with gross deficiencies and distortions of the ego or with variations of drive endowments and expressions present symptoms which can be understood only by reference to the tripartite model of structure. For research purposes, such a categorization has been useful in projects studying change and outcome. The following vignette is an example of the assessment of structure in a patient:

A 33-year-old female psychologist sought psychiatric help, complaining of a profound sense of helplessness, indecisiveness, and depression. She had been unable to fulfill the early promise in her work, becoming increasingly inhibited and self-depreciating. Her problems in this area were particularly acute at the onset of analysis because she had fallen in love with a colleague but found herself blocked in expressing her feelings. Unaccountably, she became involved in meaningless quarrels with him. She was tempted to withdraw entirely from the relationship, had difficulty in identifying her feelings, and began to experience stomach upsets such as she had had as a child. It seemed as though every effort at solution only added to the trouble.

This patient had been raised in a strict, extremely religious household. Her parents had inculcated a rigid and punitive moral code. Sex was a forbidden and mysterious matter and pleasure was suspect. An emphasis on intellectual and scientific pursuits took precedence over pleasurable fantasy in any form.

Structurally, the patient presented a harsh and rigid superego in her self-depreciation, self-criticism, and inability to sustain a pleasurable relationship with a man. Her sexual drives, while normal and strong, were ruthlessly suppressed by her hypertrophied superego. Under the stress of strong sexual temptation in her relationship with her colleague, her ego appeared comparatively helpless and sought solutions in withdrawal, isolation, intellectualization, inhibition, and somatization.

The adaptive viewpoint focuses on the patient's pattern for fitting into his environment through ego functions free from conflict as well as characteristic defenses. The level of adaptation may vary with time and internal and external circumstances. Superficial appearances may be quite deceptive. A knowledge of the patient's past history as it relates to his accommodation of and by the external world, including the nature of his current intimate relationships gives an indication of previous capacity for adjustment which may not be readily evident from the presenting symptomatology and behavior. The assessment of adaptive capacity and type of adaption may be vital for decisions about treatment goals and methods as well as prognosis.

For example, the differentiation of a case of neurotic inhibition with phobic mechanisms of avoidance from one of psychotic isolation may well rest on a history of prior adaptation elicited in an initial evaluation. A past history of a capacity for socialization and significant object relations would point to a neurotic problem; on the other hand, a history of early withdrawn behavior with extremely limited social contacts would indicate a psychotic process.

The following case focuses on a problem in adaptation.

A 48-year-old nurse was employed as a supervisor on a particular closed unit in a psychiatric hospital for several years. She had established a good working relationship with the psychiatrists and staff personnel on the unit. Her role and functions were well defined. Suddenly, because of an administrative reorganization, she was assigned to an open unit that provided quite a different milieu and required many changes in technique and behavior. Her patterns of adjustment and equilibrium were disrupted and the situation precipitated a serious anxiety reaction that prompted her to seek help.

It should be noted that adaptational criteria are in the widest use for patient assessment, often to the exclusion of other metapsychological viewpoints. In the example just cited there were, of course, certain conditions intrapsychically that were very important in a full understanding of the clinical problem. Viewed in isolation, adaptive changes are questionable indicators of the need for or effects of therapeutic intervention, but taken in conjunction with other perspectives, they have value in clinical and research predictions.

In contrast to the common use and abuse of the adaptive point of view, the economic or energetic viewpoint is less frequently utilized for the microscopic assessment of patients because of the difficulty in obtaining reliable data on the nature and quantities of the psychological energies operating within a patient. Gross evaluations, more frequently employed, may be illustrated by contrasting the unchecked bursts of action and expression in an impulse ridden character with the behavior of an inhibited character. However, the subtle elements involved in quantification are seldom available without the intensive study of mental processes afforded by psychoanalysis. Clinical examples cited below to illustrate the analyst's criteria for and indications of change provide some clarification of this issue, emphasizing particularly the use of sequential dreams as a useful source of information.

Having discussed the initial assessment of the patient, we will now consider therapeutic change, outcome, and follow-up studies. As noted in the first section of this paper, analysts are occupied with microscopic views of change in each analytic hour and often with a macroscopic evaluation of the phases of analysis. The complexity of the issues involved is therefore most clear to the analytic researcher. Analysts are accustomed to the problems of an abundance of material in individual cases resulting from frequent contact over a period of years. Questions of data recording, data condensation, data retrieval, and data abstraction are serious problems before evaluation can begin. Analytic experience, however, emphasizes the pitfalls of a ready reliance on superficial data without sufficient regard for the deeper unconscious currents in mental life, the multiple determinants of any human behavior, and the subtleties in interaction between therapist and patient.

The description of change includes a number of factors: the amount of change, the direction of change, the rate of change, the sequence of change, and the duration of change. The measurement of change differs, of course, from the interpretation of its meaning. Whether one considers the measurement or evaluation of change, however, the use of the metapsychological principles as conceptual tools aids in the meaningful ordering and recording of data. Combined with the use of the lines of development as a standard, these concepts then permit a more orderly evaluation of changes.

The data collected in psychotherapy sessions consist of specific content such as the patient's reports of behavior, memories, dreams, fantasies, feelings, affects evident in the process of communication, behavior in the therapeutic hour, posture and psychomotor activity, reactions to the therapist, interventions of the therapist, and responses to these interventions. Outside data bearing on change are available to some extent in evaluations by others, as in job or school reports discussed by the patient. Data from other members of the family may be gathered, for example, from the simultaneous treatment of a sibling, parent, or spouse.

Specific interpretations and generalizations from the data of observation may be organized according to metapsychological principles with the resulting construction of a record of change. Changes occur in symptoms, in memory and recall, in reality testing, in perception, in self-observation and ability to communicate, in freedom from conflict, sexual adjustment, setting of goals and the modes of their attainment, object relations and standards of conduct, to cite a sample list. A specific research design focuses on a particular area, for example, changes in the function of the ego in the handling of conflict. In such a project the available material is then exhaustively studied to delineate precise characteristic modes of ego activity such as introspection or externalization, repression and denial, or defenses based on partial recognition of conflictual elements. The course of action and reaction in conflicts can be studied throughout the therapeutic process. Elements that enter into change can be identified and compared with the original patterns.

In follow-up research designed to establish the outcome of a therapeutic process as in the examination of change, the need for an awareness of the complexity of factors involved is to be stressed. The means of study will be related to what one studies, for example, investigations of post-therapeutic adaptations must recognize the unique features of the method of

treatment employed. However, other tests of consequence using different frames of reference could also be utilized.

Heretofore, most post-therapeutic follow-ups have been conducted by
proponents of the particular technique or theoretical system underlying
the treatment employed. Careful studies stringently assessing recognized
variables have been few. Investigations gathering primary data which
can be subsequently scrutinized in order to identify variables heretofore
undetected, but which may be very important, have been rare. Recognizing the complex problems of data acquisition, data analysis, and data
abstraction, we feel that such researches nontheless are indicated.

Follow-up studies must have fairly clear criteria involving change. As
mentioned above, the quantification of change though exceedingly important cannot be easily determined as there are no absolute units of
change. The direction and sequence of change as it is reflected in the
external environment can more easily be assessed. The permanency and
rate of change require periodic evaluations. Change in the course of
treatment and in the post-therapeutic period requires microscopic evaluation not easily obtained using conventional follow-up techniques. For example, structural and economic alterations may not be evident from a
single interview without the use of extensive inference.

Clinical examples may be useful in clarifying the analyst's criteria for
and indications of change. Obviously such examples must be restricted to
gross phenomena in view of the limits of space. Three examples will be
cited.

Since an important function of any psychotherapeutic effort is the en-
largement of ego capacities and strengthening of ego functions in areas
of conflict, the assessment of change in this regard is of great significance.
The following example describes such a process of assessment.

A writer was neurotically blocked in efforts at productive work because
of conflicts centering on the twin fears of injuring colleagues through his
success and harsh treatment from his critics. Analysis revealed that these
conflicts had their genesis in the jealous rage, fears of retribution, and
wish for love which he had experienced as a child with his father, at the
height of the Oedipal period. The analytic work consisted of a clarification of the origin of the conflict through its enactment and recognition in
the transference with the analyst. The patient's exaggerated fears of his
rage were reduced as some of the magical over-evaluation of the danger
of his childhood feelings became clear. The fears of bitter criticism were
recognized as fears of retribution. The change in circumstances and ego
resources that had intervened in the years since the onset of the conflict
became clearly evident as a factor reducing the old bitterness. Defenses
of inhibition and an accompanying array of compensatory gratifications
were increasingly challenged as the patient turned to efforts at a more
realistic solution of his conflicts. The dream which punctuated the begin-

ning resolution of his conflicts and coincided with an actual remission of symptoms involved the passage of boats on a canal with old and new channels. Since the boats persisted in using the old channel, the patient began to board it up, making it more and more difficult to use. The boats would then become accustomed to using the new route.

In summary form, this example describes changes in dynamics as unconscious conflict is raised to consciousness, in awareness of genetic factors as the specific determinants of the conflict are recognized, in economics as the affect and impulses become manageable, in structure as is symbolized in the dream, and in adaptation as evidenced by the loss of symptoms and the development of a new productivity. The specific changes in structure accompanying such a process are evident in ego defenses, ego ideal, self-image, relations to objects, identifications, the expression and control of affects and impulses, the capacity for integration and synthesis, and the function of the superego, and can be deduced from the data gathered in the therapeutic process (French and Shapiro, 1949).

It is noteworthy that dreams serve a very useful function in indicating and predicting change. This is particularly evident in sequential dreams. A typical series of dreams may depict first a devastated area, go on to various old or dilapidated structures, to laying the foundation of a street and concrete buildings, erecting the steel girders, and finally completing the structure. Such material runs concomitantly with the elucidation and working through of conflicts and serves as a dramatic indicator of the state of the personality. In the area of affects, their neutralization, and control, sequential dreams may typically symbolize angry feelings by the violence and destructiveness of an atomic explosion, gradually diminishing in intensity to the manageable proportions of a firecracker. Or, in another instance, the same affect may be expressed first in fantasies of atomic explosions with very deadly radiation, then concerns about protection from radiation in shelters, and finally in a problem about dirt seeping in through the windows.

The following example illustrates structural changes in the superego of a patient, pointing in an extremely condensed fashion to the kind of data employed by the analyst in assessing change.

The patient was a severely inhibited obsessional bachelor, the younger son of a fundamentalist minister and his fanatically devout wife. He had been ordained in his father's church but sought analysis because he was paralyzed both professionally and in his social life. The major conflicts were clearly expressed in the initial dream he reported, consisting of two parts:

(1) He and his brother find a snake's egg which the latter cracks open. A full-grown poisonous snake emerges; he awakens with panic.

(2) He is in bed with a (non-existent) sister. His mother enters; he awakens with panic.

The sexual and aggressive themes gradually unfolded in the analysis with slow working through, manifested in a series of atomic explosion dreams, among other data. With the resolution of the Oedipal conflicts, the focus of the analytic material moved onto the themes of autonomy and the attainment of independent ideals. These were asserted in the treatment setting by an increasing ability to reach his own conclusions about the analytic data: his dreams and fantasies now dealt with fighting to the bitter end to maintain his own beliefs. He was able to make an appropriate marriage at this time, a particularly striking change in view of the fact that his sexual morality had been such as to make dating impossible. His theology evolved into a liberal one, very different from that of his parents. These evidences of change in his mental functions, especially of relaxation of irrational superego prohibitions and laying down of more independent and rational structure, were confirmed in the dreams he reported in the terminal hour of his treatment which repeated the initial dream pair in a new form:

(1) A helicopter lands near him. He senses danger but when soldiers disembark they turn out to be friendly.

(2) He is in bed with his wife. His mother enters; she goes over to a windowbox to water the flowers and then she tiptoes out.

The patient's associations demonstrated his awareness that the danger he had feared in dreams of hostile soldiers in the past was really based on a fear of his own hostility, most recently mobilized in the task of termination. In the course of the analysis, his projective defense had been identified and worked through in transference reactions, repetitive war dreams, and descriptions of behavior with resultant modifications in intrapsychic structure.

A final illustrative example of the assessment of change will be offered, focusing on the adaptive significance of a defense as traced through the analytic process.

A woman in her 40s routinely made defensive use of a very vivid fantasy life utilizing many unusual animal forms whenever she expressed any feelings in her treatment. Analysis revealed that the images were of particular importance in providing a large measure of control over an unusually powerful sexual drive. The fantasies had begun during her first five to six years when she slept in a crib in the parental bedroom. Recovered memories were consistent in pointing to the frequent witnessing of a variety of sexual practices. Tremendous excitement accompanied the emergence of the memories in the analysis, excitement which was itself a memory, in action, of her response to witnessing parental intercourse. The fantasies clearly were an attempt by the child to deal with affects and tensions for which there was no adequate physiological release. Even crying and thumb sucking had been forbidden by the father. As she grew, there were accretions to the menagerie of images, but the fantasies were invariably brought into play whenever the sexual drive was aroused; for example, when she was attracted to the minister of her church during adolescence, she saw limbless, spirit-like figures playing games among the trees.

Thus, the mechanism which had arisen in response to a physiological need to deal with otherwise overwhelming tensions later became a defense against experiencing sexual impulses during adolescence and, in analysis, served as a resistance against the recognition of similar impulses toward the therapist.

An example of how this mechanism operated can be seen in an hour toward the end of the analysis. Some evidence that the patient was aware that she was ready to complete her analysis had been reported and discussed. The patient's immediate response was that somebody had let her animals loose behind her back and they were "playing around." The prospect of termination of the analysis had just been seen by the patient as a sexual threat, having the meaning of her becoming a woman in relation to the analyst. With simply a reminder of how the fantasied images had been used, the patient promptly recognized the significance of her response and was able to talk about her thoughts and feelings with the analyst directly.

As the patient's fear of expressing her sexual feelings in the transference diminished, the need for the fantasies as a defense against sexuality outside the analysis and as a resistance in the analysis also were reduced. As might be expected, she became more comfortable with her sexual feelings. But simultaneously, she experienced so significant an increase in creative imagination in her work that she was able to conceptualize, organize, and administer a new program of considerable utility. Thus the capacity to create fantasies re-emerged finally as a highly organized adaptive quality.

One must distinguish indicators of change, the meaning of these change indicators, and the actual changes themselves. These can be considered from the intra-analytic framework and the extra-analytic world. Thus, intra-analytic indicators of change include, for example, dreams, transference reactions, self-analytic ability. Extra-analytic indicators include, for example, object relationships, sexual and work activities, behavior. The first group of indicators relate to the internal changes in ego functions and psychic structure; in contrast, thus, we see externally the clear and final disappearance of initial symptoms, the recovery of repressed memories, the great increase in self-observation, self-interpretation, and the realistic and consistent self-image. Structurally ego adaptations cost less in terms of energy; and greater stability, flexibility, and reality oriented superego operations can be noted. These are noted in intra- and extra-analytic situations.

These changes signify new levels of equilibrium in the systemic, intra-personal, and inter-personal spheres.

CONTRIBUTIONS TO THERAPIST ASSESSMENT

In evaluating the contribution of psychoanalysis to the therapist variable, we begin by recalling the crucial significance of the personality of the therapist, for the outcome of psychotherapy emphasized by Freud in the 1890's. Subsequent findings revealed the therapeutic import of the therapist's feelings.

The more familiar aspects of this are the obstacles to therapy caused by the therapist's inability to grasp certain issues in the treatment because of unconscious conflicts of his own. Such failures to understand the patient are referred to as *blind spots*. Their presence precludes the conscious awareness of what was involved in the therapeutic process and may be a serious interference with the significant successful therapeutic change involving those particular conflicts. Excessive therapeutic ambitiousness or unconscious identification with the patient may also interfere with therapy because such attitudes are often experienced by patients as efforts to exploit them. The therapist may utilize the treatment to attempt, usually unconsciously, to gratify or defend against various infantile aggressive or sexual impulses of his own, for example: competitive, voyeuristic, sadistic, exhibitionistic, masochistic, or excessive *altruistic*, giving impulses.

Through insistence on a preparatory personal analysis as part of its training program, the formalized psychoanalytic curriculum has offered an approach to the alleviation of these difficulties and has produced a body of psychotherapists alerted to their own countertransference (i.e., to their own unconscious contribution to any treatment process), and capable of self-analytic activity. This assists in understanding the obstacles created by the therapist's personality problems and the effects produced by whatever the therapist does in the course of treatment as it is reflected in the patient's transference; (i.e., his unconscious tendency to re-experience with the therapist his childhood emotional relationships, whether real or fantasied, with various significant persons). The personal analysis of the therapist maximizes his objective empathic capacity and minimizes his non-rational subjectivity.

One consequence of this is the therapist's greater capacity to facilitate the development of a therapeutic alliance. The therapist can foster such an alliance (or interfere with its flowering) not so much through the particular actions, technical maneuvers, or overt behaviors he performs, but mainly by way of his emotional position, conscious and unconscious, vis-à-vis his patient. Consequently, the elimination of as many as possible of the therapist's unconscious conflicts and of his characterological handicaps to the appropriate attitude of professional helpfulness is one of the prime objectives of a personal analysis as part of the preparation of a psychotherapist. A knowledge of the therapist's countertransference as it influences the therapeutic process must be considered in the design of psychotherapy research. Such countertransference reactions may seriously interfere with an evolving therapy, particularly if unrecognized, lending confusion to the collected data. However, the identification and understanding of such reactions may be of great value in a successful pursuit of therapeutic aims. Estimates of the therapist's significance in the therapy can be assessed via concurrent collaborative or supervisory consultations, and in some instances with data available from the therapist's analytic experience.

CONTRIBUTIONS TO ASSESSMENT OF THE RESEARCHER AND THE RESEARCH SETTING

As psychoanalysis has developed, gradual shifts have occurred in the research methodology utilized. Although the 1932-1933 *Review of the Chicago Institute for Psychoanalysis* already describes the team approach to psychoanalytic research and its early applications to psychosomatic studies of patients in psychoanalysis, the characteristic role of the psychoanalytic researcher has been that of the combined therapist, data recorder, and investigator. We are now more sophisticated in our methodology, extending the tradition of Freud who, acutely sensitive to such issues, repeatedly and extensively discussed research method in various of his works. The same self-searching attitudes required of the psychoanalyst in his therapeutic work are needed by the researcher in his role of scientific investigator.

Data for the systematic study of the different variables involved in the therapeutic process may range from collected observations to controlled experiments. The problem of controls in gathering such data has been extensively discussed in a report by the Group for the Advancement of Psychiatry (1959). A control is broadly defined as any operation designed to test or limit the various sources of error and distortion in knowledge. Variations of controls have been elaborated above in some detail in assessing the variables of psychotherapy, although other aspects of the control problem are still open issues requiring further study. Anna Freud (1958) discussed the issue of planned research in analysis. She pointed out that when psychoanalysis was mainly a matter of private practice, "hedged in by the difficulties and restrictions imposed by the circumstances of the latter," there could be no planned selection of cases, no undistorted publication of material, and follow-up studies depended upon the good will of former patients. Findings relevant to the psychotherapeutic action of psychoanalysis still were possible under the somewhat restricted conditions noted above since "in psychoanalysis the method of therapy is identical with the method of inquiry." Every patient treated

with psychoanalysis for therapeutic purposes could potentially be a research case adding to our knowledge of development, mental functioning, psychopathology, or therapeutic technique. As psychoanalytic clinics
and research centers came into being, planned investigative studies became more possible. At the Hampstead Child-Therapy Clinic, various
research projects have been employed. They use the pooling of clinical
material among a group of analytic workers, planned selection of cases,
simultaneous analysis (by different analysts) of child and parent, second
analyses for comparison with earlier data obtained in the first analysis.
In addition, the study of individuals suffering particular traumas as a
result of fate permits the investigation of situations approximating that
of the experiment. Thus, A. Freud mentions the congenitally blind project
as an example of the latter category. The analytic situation precludes the
setting up of experiments. The repetition compulsion and the transference
neurosis allow for the unfolding of neurotic processes in the analysis itself, thus allowing for observation and testing of prior predictions. Data
obtained from selected analytic patients having particular disturbances
can be pooled and in this way studied for comparability and differences.

More recently, Lustman has addressed himself to "Some Issues In Contemporary Research." He discusses the growth of psychoanalytic research,
various psychoanalytic research methods, as well as questions relating
to the recording of the empirical data coming from psychoanalytic treatments (1963).

In this essay we have attempted to discuss the unique contributions
psychoanalysis makes to psychotherapeutic research. In considering the
patient variables, psychoanalytically-oriented diagnosis and assessment
of the patient, initially as well as throughout the therapeutic process and
in the post termination follow-up study, allows for comparison between
various patients having, for example, similar symptoms, diagnoses, and
psychological configurations, and also permits vertical comparisons of
the same patient with himself at different times during and after the
therapeutic engagement.

The following methodological questions require careful consideration:
data recording and notation; data analysis, reduction and classification;
and data retrieval as it relates to the framing and testing of hypotheses.
Each of these methodological issues can be investigated more fully than
has been the situation to the present time. Primary data consist mainly of
specific contents. One must understand these contents as they relate to
the therapeutic process in toto. The analytic process, on the other hand,
is detected through the careful study of data in depth and over time. Thus
the levels of data analysis to be employed also must be decided upon if
there is to be uniformity and comparability. The question of what are
primary data is not simple to answer. Psychoanalytic or psychotherapeutic
data are not just the verbal productions of the patient. What is not said,

what is felt, what non-verbal happenings occur may be of great significance in the understanding of a "bit of psychotherapy."

Psychoanalysis, as a result of its training requirement of a personal analysis, attempts to increase the objectivity of the therapist during the treatment. Thus, the therapist is an observer as well as a direct participant of the therapeutic process. His own conceptual, emotional, behavioral, and verbal activity provides data that can be studied in a fashion similar to those of the patient. As with the patient, however, all that goes on within the therapist may not be available for later investigation regardless of the elaborateness of the data-recording procedures. The therapist's self-observations obtained through introspection and empathy, as well as his observations of the patient in the ahistorical setting of the therapeutic situation, are examples of these "silent" data that may be crucial to understanding the therapeutic process.

Through its consideration of transference recapitulation, the repetition compulsion, the unconscious, as well as the use of dreams, slips, free association, and the like, psychoanalysis has contributed to understanding certain aspects of the psychotherapeutic situation. This situation, the source of primary data, can be understood separately as part of a process, as well as from the perspective of the ongoing relationship in the continuing therapeutic dyad of patient and therapist. Therapeutic process variables can be studied once primary data are available.

In the harvesting of primary data the therapist is inevitably a researcher in assessing what he will record and how he will record it. Furthermore, it is clear that there are subliminal perceptions which may escape the conscious awareness of the observer but influence the evaluation of observed facts. The critical examination of recorded observations by the therapist may bring to consciousness such preconscious factors. In fact, by virtue of the passage of time and accumulation of information and experience, a review of material that had been puzzling or obscure may stand out very clearly in retrospect. Such experiences of retrospective confidence must be regarded with skepticism, but if carefully examined they may be valuable for research purposes. The very assumption of the role of researcher may be conducive to the development of skills in observation and conceptualization consistent with the research goal. Perhaps it is significant to note that what is observed is influenced by research motivation but this is not necessarily in the direction of unwarranted bias or distortion of the therapeutic process.

If the therapist's prime motivation is that of securing research data to test a particular hypothesis, the therapeutic process itself may become a biased situation. In some instances, simultaneous systematic research occurring during the therapeutic period may interfere with the therapeutic process itself. This problem may be circumvented by either studying the data after the therapy has been completed, or by having the data studied by a researcher unconnected with the therapy. In this instance the therapist serves as primary data gatherer and recorder. The research investigator studies the data from the investigative point of view. As mentioned above, the ever increasing use of pooled clinical data collected by different therapists and studied by a third person or by a team of investigators increases the amount of primary clinical data that can be used to test hypotheses. This method also may reduce the interference and biasing factors in the data collection as well as in the data assessment for any research on therapeutic process.

The problem of data reduction is another area for further study. In order for such second order data to be meaningful, their essence must be retained. This involves questions of criteria used for such condensing and abstracting operations. Data classification and indexing along particular lines bring the primary and secondary data into direct contact with established theoretical frameworks. How shall primary data be used for a problem under current study, yet still be available for investigations in the future that may need information unavailable in the abstracted second order data? These methodological questions require answers as yet not fully agreed upon. Issues of data retrieval also require our attention. Recent developments in mechanical devices may be of assistance in this problem.

Throughout investigations of psychotherapy, however, one must be aware of the need for a sensitive balance between the clinical goals and the research aims. The essence of research is to find new truths which allow prediction and control. The investigator must be aware of the limitations of his studies as well as of the positives he may find. Science is probabilistic. Newer facts that are valid and reliable can overthrow all theoretical formulations. Theories must fit facts; facts may or may not fit theories.

REFERENCES

ALEXANDER, F., FRENCH, T. M., and POLLOCK, G. H. Psychophysiological correlations, Vol. I. (In preparation).

BUXBAUM, E. Technique of terminating analysis. *Int. J. Psa.*, **31**: 184-190, 1950.

DEUTSCH, H. Psychoanalytic therapy in the light of follow-up. *J. Amer. Psa. Ass.*, 445-458, 1959.

EISSLER, K. R. The effect of the structure of the ego on psychoanalytic technique. *J. Amer. Psa. Ass.*, **1**: 104-143, 1953.

ERIKSON, E. The nature of clue and evidence. *Daedalus, J. Amer. Acad. Arts and Sciences*, **87**: 65-87, 1958.

FLEMING, J. What analytic work requires of an analyst: A job analysis. *J. Amer. Psa. Ass.*, **9**: 719-729, 1961.

FLEMING, J., and ALTSCHUL, S. Activation of mourning and growth by psychoanalysis. *Int. J. Psa.*, **44**: 419-431, 1963.

FRENCH, T. M., and SHAPIRO, L. B. The use of dream analysis in psychosomatic research. *Psychosom. Med.*, 11: 110-112, 1949.

FREUD, A. Clinical studies in psychoanalysis (Research Project of The Hampstead Child-Therapy Clinic). *Proc. Royal Soc. Med.*, 51: 938-942, 1958.

FREUD, A. The concept of developmental lines. *The Psa. Stud. of the child,* 18: 245-265, 1963.

FREUD, S. Analysis terminable and interminable. In J. Strachey (Ed.), *The standard edition of the complete psychological works of Sigmund Freud.* Vol. 23. London: Hogarth, 1964. Pp. 209-253. (Original publication, 1937).

FREUD, S. Case histories. In J. Strachey (Ed.), *The standard edition of the complete psychological works of Sigmund Freud.* Vols. 2, 7, 10, 17. London: Hogarth, 1964. (Original publication, 1893-1918).

FREUD, S. Constructions in analysis. In J. Strachey (Ed.), *The standard edition of the complete psychological works of Sigmund Freud.* Vol. 23. London: Hogarth, 1964. Pp. 257-269. (Original publication, 1937).

GARDINER, M. Meeting with the wolfman. *Bull. of the Phila. Ass. of Psa.*, 2: 36-44, 1952.

GEDO, J. E. Concepts for a classification of the psychotherapies. *Int. J. Psa.* 45: 530-539, 1964.

GEDO, J. E., SABSHIN, M., SADOW, L., and SCHLESSINGER, N. Studies in hysteria— A methodological evaluation. *J. Amer. Psa. Ass.*, 12: 734-751, 1964.

GITELSON, M. Seminar on Termination, 1960. Chicago Institute for Psychoanalysis.

GLOVER, E. *Psychoanalysis: A handbook for medical practitioners and students of comparative psychology.* New York: Staples Press, 1949.

Group for the Advancement of Psychiatry. Some observations on controls in psychiatric Research. Report No. 42, 1959.

HILGARD, J. R. Anniversary reactions in parents precipitated by children. *Psychiat.*, 16: 73-80, 1953.

KNAPP, P. H. Short term Psychoanalytic and Psychosomatic Predictions. *J. Amer. Psa. Ass.*, 11: 245-280, 1963.

KOHUT, H. Introspection, empathy, and psychoanalysis; An examination of the relationship between mode of observation and theory. *J. Amer. Psa. Ass.*, 7: 459-483, 1959.

KRAMER, M. K. On the continuation of the analytic process after psychoanalysis. *Int. J. Psa.*, 40: 17-25, 1959.

LORAND, S., and SCHNEER, I. *Adolescents: Psychoanalytic approach to problems and therapy by 19 contributors.* (Foreword by D. Engelhardt.) New York: Hoeber-Harper, 1961.

LUSTMAN, S. L. Some issues in contemporary psychoanalytic research. *The Psa. Stud. of the Child,* 18: 51-74, 1963.

ORR, D. W. Transference and countertransference: A historical survey. *J. Amer. Psa. Ass.*, 2: 621-670, 1954.

PAYNE, S. Short communication on criteria for terminating analysis. *Int. J. Psa.*, 31: 205, 1950.

PIERS, G., and PIERS, M. W. Modes of learning and the analytic process. (Read at Sixth International Congress of Psychotherapy, London, 1964.)

PFEFFER, A. Z. The meaning of the analyst after analysis: A contribution to the theory of therapeutic results. *J. Amer. Psa. Ass.*, 11: 229-244, 1963.

POLLOCK, G. H. Childhood, parent, and sibling loss in adult patients. *Arch. gen. Psychol.*, 7: 295-305, 1962.

SPITZ, R. A. *A genetic field theory of ego formation; Its implication for pathology.* New York: International Universities, 1959.

TARACHOW, S. Interpretation and reality in psychotherapy. *Int. J. Psa.*, 43: 377-387, 1962.

WAELDER, R. Psychoanalysis, scientific method, and philosophy. *J. Amer. Psa. Ass.*, 10: 617-637, 1962.

WALLERSTEIN, R. S. Report of the psychotherapy research project of the Menninger Foundation. *Int. ment. hlth. res. newsltr.*, 3: 12-15, 1961.

24. Toward the longitudinal study of the psychotherapeutic process

Hans H. Strupp, J. B. Chassan, and John A. Ewing

I. PROBLEMS OF METHODOLOGY AND QUANTIFICATION

Accurate description is the first requirement in any science: without it, measurement and prediction are an impossibility. One of the often-repeated criticisms of psychoanalysis and psychotherapy has been aimed at this alleged deficiency, and, one must admit, with considerable justification. Aside from quantitative measurement and prediction which may be viewed as later and more refined developments, it should be possible, minimally, to agree on observable phenomena in the psychotherapeutic situation. Yet, when serious attempts have been made to study this problem, the results have usually been disappointing. The extent of this disillusionment is difficult to gauge because many efforts in this direction which were considered abortive by the investigators have never been published. In the absence of such reports it is difficult to assess whether the difficulties are indeed insuperable. However, if the direction of developments in psychotherapy is toward greater precision, and if psychotherapy aspires to the status of a science, the difficulties must be faced and resolved. The failures which have been experienced are perhaps largely due to faulty methodologies rather than to an inherent impossibility of describing adequately the phenomena of psychotherapy.

The requirement for a consensus among observers is elementary and needs little further elaboration. If Therapist A asserts that Event X is happening at a particular time, but an independent observer, B, describes the occurrence as Event Y, and independent observer, C, describes the occurrence as Event Z, the trustworthiness (reliability) of their observations is seriously in question.

The principal sources of their disagreement appear to be the following: (1) Observers are poorly *calibrated;* that is, they may have different theoretical preconceptions (*orientations*), their level of expertness in observing therapeutic phenomena may differ, etc. (2) The phenomena under observation themselves may be so unclear, fluid, and hazy that observer agreement is in principle impossible and that the observations are little more than the *projections* or fantasies of the observers (this is the usual criticism of the opponents of psychotherapy). (3) The methods by which observations are recorded are faulty, so that it is difficult or impossible to ascertain whether observers in fact agree or disagree.

For the moment we shall disregard sources of disagreement (1) and (2). It will be assumed that observers are equally well trained and that they have a relatively uniform approach to their observations, although it is conceded that unreliability will be introduced in this way. We reject the notion that the phenomena of psychotherapy are *intrinsically* unreliable, and, in contrast, accept as a working assumption that the difficulties lie primarily in the methods used for describing and recording the data.

When one takes a closer look at these difficulties, he finds that they are twofold: (1) the problem of demarcating meaningful units of observation, and (2) the technical problem of specifying dimensions or categories. Solution of these problems is absolutely essential and prerequisite to significant research advances in this area. If one could achieve a level of agreement (reliability) of say, 80 to 85 percent, one would have built a foundation from which a variety of research operations, such as comparisons between the techniques of different therapists and patients' intrapsychic reactions and responses to particular kinds of therapists' communications could be fruitfully undertaken.

With regard to problem (1) the investigator has available essentially two approaches: (a) he can decide on arbitrary units, such as time units, sentences, paragraphs, etc., which are easy to demarcate but which often lack psychological significance; or (b) he can select psychological units, such as *themes,* which emerge in a single hour or over a course of hours (Cohen and Cohen, 1961). These are maximally meaningful but almost impossible to demarcate. In most research studies undertaken so far, course (a) has usually been chosen.

Problem (2) is by far the more difficult one, although since about 1940 many attempts have been made to devise conceptual schemes as well as categories, dimensions, and rating devices to capture "relevant" aspects of the content of psychotherapy. Such schemes are typically attempts at content-analysis, but they vary greatly in their focus, level of abstraction, and the content they include as well as exclude. The review of pertinent content-analysis systems is beyond the scope of this paper; several summaries of the literature have previously been published (Auld and Murray, 1955; Dittes, 1959; Strupp, 1962; Marsden, 1965). A number of schemes described in these sources have been reported as possessing adequate reliability; however, it is noteworthy that no single system has received sustained interest from many investigators other than the originator; instead, investigators have typically preferred to develop systems of their own. It is noteworthy that most systems thus far reported in the literature have been anchored to a particular theory of psychotherapy (the client-centered viewpoint is perhaps best represented), thus effectively precluding comparisons between therapeutic interviews of therapists subscribing to different theoretical orientations. Some systems (like the Bales system of interaction process analysis, Bales, 1950) which are not subject to this stricture, have been considered too general to be of incisive value for research in psychotherapy.

An important advantage of the psychoanalytic situation is that it is unique as a method of observation. This had been stressed by a number of authors including Janis (1958) and Greenacre (1954). If the value of psychoanalysis as a method of observation is granted, a significant question arises: why has it been so sorely neglected by researchers in the area of psychotherapy as well as by personality psychologists in general? The answer may be found in the sharp (and often unjustified) criticisms which have been made against the data generated in this way. Among these, the following may be discerned:

1. In order to make the kinds of observations which analysts claim to be regular, repeatable, and recurrent, one must be indoctrinated in the theory of psychoanalysis. Persons not so indoctrinated do not make the same observations.

2. The data generated in the psychoanalytic situation are purely artifactual, that is, they are a function of the frustrations imposed upon the patient. Consequently they have relatively little bearing upon the patient's attitudes and performance in extra-analytic situations.

3. Whenever one attempts to test the reliability of one analyst's observations (through the use of external observers), the agreement tends to be so low and the contradictions in the inferences drawn from the observations so pervasive that serious doubt must be entertained about the utility of such data.

Criticisms (1) and (3) are related, as we shall presently try to elucidate. Criticism (2) touches upon the question of therapeutic effectiveness and the relevance of studying interpersonal and intrapsychic data in the transference situation for the purpose of effecting changes in the patient's *adjustment*. While this criticism can potentially be refuted by empirical data (although this remains a task for the future), we shall not concern ourselves with it at this time as it lies outside the scope of the present discussion.

Insofar as criticism (1) advocates the abandonment of the psychoanalytic theoretical framework in favor of a completely atheoretical scheme, it can be safely rejected. As Tolman (1953) has shown, the fact that an observer who is trained to make observations along particular lines which another observer not possessing such training would fail to make does not per se disqualify the former as long as the observations are not *automatically* determined by the theoretical frame of reference.

If it were true that inter-rater agreement is of a very low order, the argument against the utility of the psychoanalytic situation as a method of observation (not necessarily as a treatment technique) would indeed be a formidable one. Here we return to our previous contention that the techniques which have thus far been employed for establishing rater consensus have been inadequate or faulty, and that improvement in the techniques would markedly raise the consensus. A distinction must be made here again between the data of observation and the metapsychological (or theoretical) implications. A theory as such cannot be validated by observational means; however, it must be conceded that in the domain of observations with which the psychoanalytic observer deals, almost any observation implies an inference. It is necessary, therefore, to keep the level of inference sufficiently low, but not so low as to become meaningless. For example, observers might agree very well that on a particular day the patient is wearing a green tie (a very low inference but presumably not a very relevant observation); however, they might agree far less on whether the patient is anxious (a relatively high-order inference, but presumably a highly relevant judgment).

One attempt to devise a system for quantifying the therapist's communications was made by one of the authors (Strupp, 1957a). It consisted of three dimensions (depth-directedness, initiative, warmth-coldness) and two sets of categories (type of communication and dynamic focus) which served to quantify each communication by the therapist. In several studies (Strupp, 1957b, 1957c, 1958) it was shown that (1) the system possesses adequate reliability, (2) it discriminates the therapist's activity within single hours and over a series of hours with reasonable sensitivity, and (3) it permits meaningful comparisons between the communications of therapists subscribing to different theoretical orientations, differing in terms of experience and similar variables.

Despite this demonstrated utility, we have come to feel that the system has some significant deficiencies. The main one is that it overemphasizes the structural aspects of the therapist's communication and it is insufficiently sensitive to the attitudinal-emotional facets of his communications. While the system does a reasonably adequate job in specifying whether a communication by the therapist is a question, an interpretation, and the like, and while similarly it assesses reasonably well the degree of initiative, the depth of inference, and the dynamic focus of a communication, it performs poorly in the attitudinal-emotional area.

From the standpoint of the investigator, techniques are needed to assess both (1) the quality of the emotional relationship including subjective, experiential factors in therapist and patient, and (2) the technical operations of the therapist (technique). In addition, of course, there must be developed parallel techniques for quantifying the patient's *state* at a given time, as it is subjectively experienced by the patient as well as it is evaluated by external observers.

The requirements for quantitative assessments are similar whether one is dealing with the communications of the therapist or the patient. It may be stated categorically that existing techniques for measuring essential aspects of the therapeutic encounter are exceedingly primitive and inadequate. New approaches are needed; of this we are convinced, even though we are not prepared to offer radical solutions. The latter seem to lie far in the future. At this time we should like to pursue somewhat further the problem of the deficiency of existing measures.

Bellak and Smith's Contribution

Bellak and Smith (1956) published a paper which represented an original approach to the problems to which the present paper addresses itself.[1] It is regrettable that their study has never been replicated, nor has anyone, to our knowledge, pursued their lead.

In brief, they recorded psychoanalytic sessions and asked two psychoanalysts to make certain ratings of the events in these sessions. Two other analysts were asked to predict, independently, the nature of subsequent analytical sessions, using the same rating instrument. According to Bellak and Smith:

The kind of study we have undertaken forces the participants to attempt to describe more accurately what they see, to agree on definitions of phenomena, and to make more explicit the hypotheses under which they operate. The participants were surprised to find that an implicit prediction was part of their every interpretive statement. (p. 386)

The variables selected by these investigators included transference (positive, negative), acting out, insight, working through, resistance, anxiety, aggression (extra- and intra-), passivity, guilt, depression, elation, oral strivings, anal strivings, phallic strivings, oedipal strivings, genital strivings, homosexuality, scoptophilia. In addition, their list included the following defenses: projection, rationalization, isolation, denial, intellectualization, displacement, reaction formation, regression, reversal, identification with aggressor. The process ratings and predictions were made on an all-or-none basis, and raters were asked to distinguish between *conscious* and *unconscious* phenomena. In addition, there were some features in this investigation which need not concern us in the present context. Without reporting the results in detail, it may be stated that Bellak and Smith found relatively good rater agreement, correlation coefficients ranging from .11 to .78, for variables on which both raters made a rating in a given week. They state:

If ratings had been required on all variables, lower figures would have resulted, (but) such required ratings would be logically and clinically entirely meaningless (since) any scientist addresses himself to a limited area of function-

[1] One of the authors (JBC) has independently pursued research designed to develop adequate systems for quantifying clinical process data. (Chassan, 1962)

ing; to variables which, at the moment, seem important to him. The statistical picture would be rather more distorted than truthful if he were forced to rate variables he considered irrelevant at the time. (p. 406)

They concluded that analysts were able, quantitatively, to agree on the *structure* of the case; that is, they agreed generally on the variables each member of a pair rated relatively high or relatively low. However, they were unsuccessful in predicting the variables in which positive or negative change would occur over a (relatively short) period of time. We agree with the authors' conclusion that despite their failure to demonstrate accuracy of prediction "the results of the study show a gratifying measure of agreement in the description by four or five analysts in psychoanalytic language of the psychodynamics of a patient. This alone is more than has ever been established experimentally and statistically before." (p. 411).

Basing their judgment on the results of their investigation, Bellak and Smith believe that psychoanalytic concepts are poorly defined, and that analysts proceed therapeutically in idiosyncratic ways in accordance with their own personality characteristics, although their subjective preferences may eventually be corrected to produce considerable agreement in the long run. They suggest that a team of psychoanalysts and social scientists be formed to attempt better definitions of the basic vocabulary. In addition, they feel that longer training of participants in the rating procedure as well as better acquaintance with the problems of quantitative rating on the part of the participants would be helpful.

The foregoing recommendations are certainly desirable; however, it may be questioned whether in and of themselves they would produce marked increments in rater agreement. The major obstacle, as we see it, is that even with better definitions of the variables, one still does not know the meaning of a particular rating. Is it an average based upon the fluctuations of a given variable during the hour? Does it represent a single observation at a given point in time during the hour? If so, at what time? It appears that the ratings used by Bellak and Smith are ratings based upon global impressions averaged by the observer for a given hour. On the basis of their findings one does not know the weighting procedures these observers have used and the manner in which they arrived at their ratings.

We disagree with Bellak and Smith in their emphasis upon *predictive* ratings. The task they imposed upon their predictors appears difficult and essentially unrealistic. First, there is the general problem of clinical predictions, which has been well described by Holt (1958). In essence, he argues that often the clinician is asked to generate information in the absence of empirically established relationships between the predictor variables and a given criterion. Bellak and Smith's criterion is so inadequately defined (it is merely a time interval) that the cards are stacked against the clinicians making predictions. If one considers the multitude of intervening events that may influence a patient's feeling state it becomes apparent that his status at an unspecified future date is virtually impossible to predict. The raters were asked to make predictions about impulses and defenses, which by their very nature are unstable. The problem is compounded by the impossibility of controlling the patient's life situation. Obviously, the patient is always in interaction with a complex environment, which somehow must be taken into account in predictive judgments. In the circumstances, the reported failure to demonstrate stable relationships is hardly surprising.

Prospectus

Despite these strictures Bellak and Smith's effort provides an excellent starting point for a system by means of which observations can be made systematically and which yields quantifications of significant aspects of the therapeutic process. Before it can reach maximum usefulness, however, a number of problems will have to be resolved.

1. As Bellak and Smith recognized, it will be necessary to develop better operational definitions of the variables to be rated. The observer-rater must be given specific and unambiguous criteria concerning the observational referents of, say, an anal impulse. The danger is that theoretical preconceptions may automatically determine such ratings. For instance, a patient displaying anger, hostility, and spite may be rated as exhibiting *anal trends* because the theory presupposes a relationship between anality and hostility. Ratings should largely be based on *observable* behavior, without reference to inferred unconscious processes. Ratings also should make minimal theoretical assumptions. These requirements, while difficult to meet, are not impossible.

2. Appropriate units of observation have to be defined. There are indications that smaller units can be more reliably rated than larger units. Because a variable is likely to fluctuate markedly during a therapeutic session, the hour unit is probably much too large. Smaller time units (five minutes, or even less), may prove to be much more satisfactory. (See Section II.)

3. The reliability of ratings will have to be studied extensively, particularly the problem of inter-rater agreement. How well do raters agree on an observation? Are there differences between highly experienced therapists as raters and inexperienced judges? How much training is necessary to achieve a satisfactory level of agreement? What kinds of training are designed to achieve this objective? These are some of the questions to be answered.

4. Variables should be selected in such a way that for the particular unit to be rated a reasonably complete picture of the patient-therapist interaction results. Thus, in addition to ratings aimed at a description of the patient state, there should be parallel ratings of the nature of the therapist's

interventions (technique), his attitudes toward the patient, and the prevailing attitudinal climate of the relationship.

5. Given a rating instrument meeting the above criteria, systematic assessments can be made. It must be decided whether ratings are to be made by the therapist, the patient, independent observers, or in some combination. Once such assessments are made for a number of patient-therapist pairs over an extended period of time, such questions as the following may be approached: (A) What kinds of variables remain relatively stable over time, and which ones change? How does stability or change relate to progress or lack of progress in therapy, as assessed by the more commonly used process notes or clinical observations? (B) How do changes in one clinical variable relate to changes in other variables? What are the relationships to technique, therapist's attitudes, and the emotional climate of the relationship?

It should be noted that the preceding questions may be answered by relying on the empirical data, obviating predictions such as were used by Bellak and Smith.

6. The exploration of these problems requires the solution of a number of statistical issues relative to time-series and the independence of repeated measurements.

The foregoing listing encompasses a program of research in which only the barest beginnings have been made. Obviously, it will not solve *all* the problems with which research in psychotherapy and psychoanalysis is beset. But it could provide an important starting point for more adequate descriptions of the therapeutic process, which at the present stage of development of this amorphous field would indeed constitute a tangible advance.

II. PILOT EXPERIMENTS

In the following pages we shall present the results of some preliminary attempts to develop an instrument which might meet the criteria that have been outlined and to begin experimentation along the lines indicated. The study by Bellak and Smith has been reported in some detail because in important respects the following experiments represent a continuation of their effort. However, on the basis of our results and experience gained in conducting these experiments, we have come to the conclusion that significant modifications of their system are indicated. The nature of the proposed modifications which should be undertaken prior to further experimentation on a larger scale will be made explicit.

A Modification of Bellak and Smith's Instrument

It was our objective to carry further Bellak and Smith's attempt to provide adequate descriptions of the dynamic process of psychotherapy by requiring the therapist to make systematic ratings of the interaction, such ratings to be made following each therapeutic hour. Following these workers, we proposed to use the single hour as a convenient unit of observation, although it now appears that this unit is too large and too global.

For the reasons previously stated, the idea of obtaining predictions from the therapist (or from independent judges) was abandoned. Instead, ratings were to be based on the events transpiring during the hour to be rated. The extent to which such ratings might be predictive of subsequent events in therapy would thus become an empirical question which might be answered by studying changes in the ratings over time.

Second, it was considered inadvisable to require raters to make evaluations of *unconscious* processes, for the reason that such ratings require a very high level of inference. They would be more highly dependent upon the theoretical predilections of the raters than more directly observable events; consequently, it seemed unlikely that a satisfactory level of agreement could be obtained. (Experiment 3 confirmed this assumption.) It was clear that even ratings of so-called observable events required varying degrees of inference which, we anticipated, would dilute rater agreement (as it evidently had in Bellak and Smith's study).

Third, we attempted to distinguish several degrees of intensity (or relative frequency), a possibility which has been considered by Bellak and Smith, but which they abandoned in favor of all-or-none ratings. In order to retain simplicity of the rating process, we devised a uniform five-point scale which therapists were asked to use in rating each variable (see Figure 1).

Finally, several variables from Bellak and Smith's list were eliminated[2] and several new ones added.[3] In addition, we attempted to obtain ratings in two areas not included in the original list. These were: (1) therapeutic technique (seven variables) and (2) the therapist's feelings toward the patient and about the therapeutic process (seven items). The rationale for including these variables derived from previous research in this area in which the potential influence of the therapist's attitudes toward the patient with respect to technique and clinical evaluations had been demonstrated (Strupp, 1958; Strupp and Williams, 1960; Wallach and Strupp, 1960).

[2] Omitted were: Acting out, Aggression (Extra- Intra-), Passivity, Guilt, Homosexuality, Scoptophilia, as well as the 11 "classic" defenses. These variables seemed on an a priori basis too difficult to rate because of their being too general, not sufficiently process-oriented, too inferential, and the like. Bellak and Smith gave no rationale for their list except that the variables had been "agreed upon." Our own list, too, was intuitively derived. It is clear that in subsequent work greater attention must be given to the selection of variables to be rated. The number of empirically distinguishable dimensions is probably limited, and factor analytic techniques might prove useful in isolating such underlying dimensions.

[3] Added were: Dominance, Dependence, Affect, Sadism, Masochism, Hostility (anger), Defensiveness, Competitiveness (rivalry). This left 13 variables common to the two lists.

PSYCHOTHERAPY RESEARCH PROJECT
UNIVERSITY OF NORTH CAROLINA
THERAPIST'S RATING SHEET

Patient Code: _____   Therapist: _____   Therapy Hour No: _____   Date: _____ 196 _

Please rate *all* items using the following code:

0	No evidence, absent	None	Absent, very seldom	Absent
1	Slight evidence	Slight	Occasional	Mild
2	Fairly strong evidence	Moderate	Fairly frequent	Moderate
3	Strong evidence	Great	Frequent	Intense
4	Extremely strong evidence	Extremely great	Extremely frequent	Extremely intense

Note: As far as possible, make ratings on the basis of behavior observed or evidence
obtained during the hour rather than on the basis of inferences or theoretical constructs.

Patient							Therapist					
No.	Variable	0	1	2	3	4	No.	Variable	0	1	2	3	4
1	Dominance						22	Interventions					
2	Dependence						23	Interpretations					
3	Resistance						24	Depth of interpretation					
4	Anxiety						25	Initiative					
5	Affect						26	Warmth					
6	Sadism						27	Coldness					
7	Masochism						28	Support					
8	Hostility, anger												
9	Defensiveness						29	Motivation, dedication, "investment"					
10	Transference-positive						30	Positive attitudes					
11	Transference-negative						31	Negative attitudes					
12	Competitiveness, rivalry						32	Countertransference problems					
13	Depression						33	Empathy					
14	Elation						34	Productivity of hour					
15	Insight						35	Satisfaction with progress					
16	Working through							Comments:					
17	Oral strivings												
18	Anal strivings												
19	Phallic strivings												
20	Oedipal strivings												
21	Genital strivings												

Figure 1

Thus, the modified instrument was designed to provide information in each of the following areas: (1) the patient's feelings, attitudes, emotional reactions in the transference situation; (2) the frequency and kind of interventions by the therapist (technique); and (3) the therapist's feelings and attitudes toward the patient, about himself, and about the therapeutic process.

Experiment 1
Degree of Inference

In this experiment we set ourselves the task of determining empirically the degree of inference entering the rating process. In studying the variables included in the rating instrument it becomes apparent that some are much closer to observable events than others. For example, when the patient expresses hostility (anger) toward the therapist, there are presumably much more direct and specific behavioral manifestations than when he evinces phallic strivings. The latter must be inferred from trends in the patient's free associations and the total context of impulse and defense constellations. Thus, in order to make a rating of the intensity of such a variable, the therapist (or independent observer) must go through a highly complex process of clinical inference, invoke his clinical experience and theoretical knowledge, finally arriving at a quantitative rating which represents a rather high-order abstraction. The farther a variable is removed from directly observable events, the higher is the degree of inference required. Furthermore, it may be hypothesized (and this hypothesis will be tested in Experiment 2) that the greater the degree of clinical inference required in making a rating the lower will be the level of agreement among independent observers (including the therapist). Conversely, observers may be expected to agree best on variables which refer to directly observable events.

This problem of inference has been one of the great stumbling blocks in describing the events in psychoanalysis and psychotherapy. Because many events with which the psychotherapist deals are highly complex and far from being directly observable, and because a high level of clinical inference is often required in describing the nature of the events, it is likely that an independent observer will not traverse the same road of clinical inference traveled by the therapist. The result is that their respective descriptions may fail to agree, or, because the two observers may focus on different levels of abstractions or different facets of the matrix of events, it is difficult to determine from their respective descriptions whether they agree or disagree, or to assess the extent of their agreement.

Another way of stating the problem is to say that, in psychoanalytic terms, there is no one-to-one relationship between behavioral indicators and their psychological antecedents. Long ago Freud differentiated between different viewpoints (such as the dynamic, structural, economic, genetic, and the like). Furthermore, he recognized that any psychic event is complexly determined (*overdetermined*). Accordingly, it is possible (and often highly useful) to give different descriptions of a single event. These descriptions may be given from different *viewpoints* which, however, are (from the observer's position) very difficult to keep apart. Typically, a description of an event in psychotherapy or psychoanalysis represents a mixture, which further complicates the problem of achieving a consensus among independent observers.

For example, a patient at a given point in therapy may become silent. This is a behavioral indicator on which observers presumably can agree with a high degree of precision. The length of the silence can be measured objectively, but not so the determinants. It is readily apparent that a large number of *explanations* can be given of this occurrence. He may be showing resistance to an interpretation given by the therapist earlier, he may be struggling against the expression of erotically tinged feelings toward the therapist, he may mourn a childhood object, he may try to defeat the therapist, there may be a struggle between superego and id resulting in an impasse, and so on. It may be seen that a host of possible formulations may be advanced (many of them considerably more complex than the brief examples given). How is one to decide whether they are in agreement or in disagreement? Which one describes what is *really* going on?

From these considerations it becomes apparent that ideally one should construct rating scales which take account of the multi-dimensionality of events. Such scales should specify not only the particular *viewpoint* one wishes the rater to adopt, but they should be capable of mirroring the total constellation of vectors. It seems unlikely that such scales can be constructed at the present state of knowledge. It must also be recognized that the scales which were posited by Bellak and Smith, as well as our proposed modification, represents a mixture of levels of abstraction and *viewpoints*.

There are essentially two approaches to developing and refining such scales, recognizing that even with highly refined scales accurate measurement of the complex events in psychotherapy may only be approximated. The first approach, followed by Bellak and Smith, is to draw on theoretical and clinical knowledge and to define variables corresponding to what one considers to be important (relevant) concepts. The second is to proceed empirically by selecting variables which stay close to observables, make a minimum of theoretical assumptions, and avoid inference as far as possible. Variables like anger, friendliness, sadness, etc. might exemplify this approach. The possibility exists (and it has much to commend it) to combine the two approaches. Thus, one might posit a number of variables suggested on the basis of theoretical and clinical observations, determine how reliably they can be rated (rater agreement), and study their relative statistical independence. It may turn out, for instance, that hostility and anger are largely synonymous, in which case it would not be necessary to obtain ratings on each as a separate variable. The desideratum would be to develop scales of variables which are highly relevant clinically and theoretically (for purposes of describing ongoing events and making predictions), and highly independent of each other. The latter consideration is dictated by a desire for research economy, since for practical purposes the demands one can make on therapists (or raters) are necessarily limited. Besides, any rating scheme in order to be useful must provide for reduction of the phenomenal complexity and must abstract from the latter a small number of dimensions which are maximally heuristic.

In the present experiment, proceeding from the variables which had already been included in the rating instrument, we addressed ourselves to the problem of assessing empirically the degree of inference required in arriving at a given rating. Our objective was to arrive at a rank ordering of the variables in terms of the degree of inference required for judging each. We did not attempt to treat the three components of the rating instrument (clinical variables, technique variables, and attitudes) as separate entities but proposed to include all variables in the final rank ordering.

Procedure

Eleven judges (trained clinical psychologists having the Ph.D. degree) were given the following instructions:

As part of an ongoing investigation, we should like to request your cooperation in rating the *degree of inference required* in assessing each of the variables listed below. Using the following scale, please indicate alongside each variable how much inference would be required in rating it:

1. virtually no inference required; almost directly observable
2. slight
3. some
4. a fair amount of inference required; a fairly typical clinical judgment
5. moderately high
6. high
7. extremely high degree of inference required; almost impossible to observe directly

The framework for making the above evaluations is the *typical* neurotic patient and the *typical* therapy hour. In other words, we are asking you to put yourself in the position of the therapist (or a direct observer of the therapeutic interaction) and to rate the degree of inference that would be required in making an evaluation of each variable. The unit of observation is the therapeutic hour.

(There followed a list of the 35 variables included in the rating instrument.)

RESULTS

The ratings obtained from the 11 judges were averaged (arithmetic mean) and for each variable a standard deviation was computed. The resulting rank ordering in terms of mean values is presented in Table 1. The results are almost self-explanatory. As might be expected, the more theoretically *neutral* variables grouped themselves at the lower end of the continuum, whereas those referring to impulses and concepts deeply anchored in psychoanalytic theory tended to be given higher (more inference required) ratings. Variables higher on the scale, too, tended to have greater dispersions; however, it is noteworthy that a variable like frequency of therapist's interpretations, which ranked low in terms of inference, had a rather marked standard deviation.

Table 1
Degree of Inference Entering into Ratings by External Observers
N = 11 Judges

Rank	Var. No.	Variable	Mean°	S. D.
1	22	Frequency of therapist's interventions	1.364	.674
2	23	Frequency of therapist's interpretations	1.818	1.789
3	14	Elation	2.182	.874
4	8	Hostility, anger	2.273	.786
5	5	Affect	2.363	1.026
6	13	Depression	2.545	.820
7	4	Anxiety	2.727	1.191
8	25	Therapist's initiative	2.818	1.251
9	1	Dominance	2.909	1.221
10	28	Therapist's support	3.091	1.514
12	2	Dependence	3.182	1.789
12	9	Defensiveness	3.182	1.168
12	27	Therapist's coldness	3.182	1.251
14.5	12	Competitiveness, rivalry	3.273	1.618
14.5	26	Therapist's warmth	3.273	1.272
16	30	Therapist's positive attitudes	3.545	1.440
17.5	31	Therapist's negative attitudes	3.636	1.501
17.5	3	Resistance	3.636	1.120
19	10	Transference—positive	4.000	1.612
20.5	15	Insight	4.182	1.662
20.5	35	Therapist's satisfaction with progress	4.182	1.601
22	11	Transference—negative	4.364	1.501
23	34	Therapist's estimate of productivity of hour	4.545	1.635
25	24	Depth of interpretations	4.636	1.361
25	29	Therapist's motivation	4.636	1.963
25	33	Therapist's empathy	4.636	1.026
27	7	Masochism	4.727	1.555
28	6	Sadism	4.818	1.538
29	16	Working through	4.909	1.700
30	21	Genital strivings	5.000	1.949
31	20	Oedipal strivings	5.182	1.662
32	32	Countertransference problems	5.273	1.555
33.5	17	Oral strivings	5.545	1.573
33.5	18	Anal strivings	5.545	1.635
35	19	Phallic strivings	6.000	1.549

° Based on ratings on a 7-point scale where
1 = virtually no inference required
7 = extremely high degree of inference required (see text).

Experiment 2
A Study of Rater Agreement

This study is an attempt to provide preliminary information on the extent to which independent observers agree when judging the therapeutic interaction by means of the modified rating instrument. To achieve a high level of consensus among independent observers has repeatedly been mentioned as one of the fundamental objectives of research in this area. Unless therapist and independent observers agree in judging the phenomena occurring during the therapeutic hour, little reliance can be placed on results which take such ratings as their point of departure.

Bellak and Smith obtained "considerable agreement" among their judges. As has already been mentioned, their tetrachoric coefficients of correlation ranged from .11 to .78. These results represented the degree of agreement in judgment in those instances in which both raters felt that a judgment was possible. If one of the raters did not rate a given variable, that variable presumably was omitted. Contrary to the results to be presented in this study, their coefficients were based on agreements for *all* variables rated (rather than on *single* variables), called by them the "dynamic structure of the case." There were other important differences in their procedure, which make it difficult to assess the comparability of our results with theirs. The chief difference perhaps is that in the present study the *over-all* agreement among judges and therapist was assessed (rather than among pairs), which represents a more stringent criterion.

Procedure

Four advanced graduate students in clinical psychology (interns) observed therapeutic interviews through a one-way screen and listened to the verbal interchange between patient and therapist by means of a microphone-loud-speaker setup. The patient, a 21-year-old college student, was seen in psycho-analytically-oriented psychotherapy by an experienced clinical psychologist. Interviews were conducted on a twice-a-week basis, although only one interview per week was observed by the raters. The patient's difficulties were essentially characterological and related to a conflict between extreme passivity and rebelliousness toward his father. Observations were made during the first few months of treatment. Following each therapy interview, the therapist met with the student group and discussed problems of psychodynamics and technique. He also informed the group (although not systematically) about events that had transpired during unobserved interviews that had been held in the interim. Ratings were made typically before the discussions, but in some instances contamination may have taken place. If so, this should have led to an artificial inflation of the inter-rater agreement.

The raters had relatively little training and experience in psychotherapy, although they were familiar to some extent with most of the pertinent concepts. No systematic training in applying the rating instrument was given.

Ratings were obtained for 11 therapy hours spaced over a period of three to four months.

RESULTS

Since we were interested in studying the degree of agreement for each variable included in the rating instrument (rather than the overall agreement on all variables during a given hour), we proceeded to analyze each variable separately. The intraclass coefficient of correlation, R, as described by Haggard (1958), was used to determine the amount of agreement among therapist and judges. This measure, a variant of the analysis of variance technique, is a rather rigorous index of the amount of correlation between the ratings of all judges. For example, the R for Variable 1 (Dominance) indicates the degree of agreement among the judges (therapist and raters) on this variable for the 11 hours of therapy under consideration. Table 2 presents the R's for all variables included in the modified rating instrument.

Inspection of this table indicates that the agreement among the judges tended to be rather low: the highest agreement was obtained for Affect (.648), Dependence (.583), and Depression (.504), with most values being considerably lower. In 11 instances the obtained R was a negative value, which for practical purposes signifies no agreement among the raters. There was no evidence that the judges agreed better among themselves than they did with the therapist, which might have been expected on the basis that they represented a more homogeneous (if relatively untrained) group and occupied a similar vantage point as far as their observations and ratings were concerned.

On the basis of these findings, which are considered highly tentative, the reliability of the rating instrument appears deficient. Possible reasons for the lack of reliability are:

1. The variables and scale points were not sufficiently well defined. Bellak and Smith had earlier stressed the importance of arriving at better definitions of the variables to be rated, which, if accomplished, might result in higher rater agreement. Furthermore, providing anchoring definitions for each scale point might give the judges a more uniform frame of reference for making ratings.

2. The judges were inexperienced therapists who undoubtedly had widely different conceptions of the variables they were asked to assess. Greater training and experience in psychotherapy as well as in applying the rating instrument might appreciably augment the rater agreement.

3. The time unit in which observations were made was too large (a full therapeutic hour). The large time unit is considered a major source of unreliability, since under the conditions of this experiment it was not clarified whether a rating was to represent an average rating for the total

Table 2
Intraclass Coefficients of Correlation (R)
Based on Observations during 11 Therapy Hours by 5 Raters

Variable	R
1. Dominance	.345
2. Dependence	.583
3. Resistance	.099
4. Anxiety	.380
5. Affect	.648
6. Sadism	.014
7. Masochism	.138
8. Hostility, anger	.358
9. Defensiveness	.085
10. Transference, positive	*
11. Transference, negative	.178
12. Competitiveness, rivalry	.216
13. Depression	.504
14. Elation	*
15. Insight	.369
16. Working through	.291
17. Oral strivings	.034
18. Anal strivings	*
19. Phallic strivings	*
20. Oedipal strivings	*
21. Genital strivings	.083
22. Interventions	*
23. Interpretations	.046
24. Depth of interpretation	*
25. Initiative	.053
26. Warmth	.204
27. Coldness	.031
28. Support	.060
29. Motivation, dedication, "investment"	*
30. Positive attitudes	.081
31. Negative attitudes	*
32. Countertransference problems	*
33. Empathy	.322
34. Productivity of the hour	.245
35. Satisfaction with progress	*

* negative value (see text)

hour, a measure of the maximum intensity reached during the hour, or whatever. It is considered essential to use much smaller units of observation (perhaps five minutes or even shorter) in future experimentation. (Dr. Henry L. Lennard, in personal communication, has made similar observations.)[4]

Experiment 3
Relationship between Degree of Inference and Rater Agreement

By means of further statistical analysis of the data obtained in Experiments 1 and 2 we tested the hypothesis that an important determinant of rater agreement is the degree of inference required in making a clinical judgment. In other words, the higher the degree of inference entering into a clinical judgment, the lower will be the agreement among independent judges; and, conversely, the closer to observable events the clinical judgment, the higher will be the rater agreement.

Procedure

For purposes of this analysis we rank ordered the first 21 variables in the modified rating instrument (omitting technique and attitudinal variables) in terms of the degree of inference obtained in Experiment 1. We then proceeded to obtain a rank order coefficient of correlation (rho) between these rankings and ranks assigned to the coefficients (R) obtained in Experiment 2, representing the level of agreement among independent judges. The pertinent data are presented in Table 3.

The resulting rho was .712, which is significant beyond the .01 level (one-tailed test), thus strongly supporting the hypothesis. It is concluded that ratings of clinical variables calling for a high degree of inference give rise to deficient rater consensus (at least in the absence of extensive training of judges in observing psychotherapeutic phenomena and/or in the use of the rating instrument). The result also underscores the need for better definitions of the clinical variables to be rated, particularly in the sense of clarifying the behavioral indicators of variables calling for a high degree of inference.

Experiment 4
Three Preliminary Applications of the Modified Rating Instrument

This pilot study is an attempt to apply the modified rating instrument in long-term psychotherapy. The data were provided by two therapists: JAE, an experienced psychiatrist whose psychoanalytic training was nearing formal completion, rated two of his analytic patients (T and R) and

---

[4] In a more recent pilot experiment, each of three experienced psychiatrists conducted 20 psychoanalytic interviews with three college students who had been selected for their "normality" on the basis of psychological tests. The conditions and procedures were highly similar to the ones described in the foregoing experiment, except that the two observers in each instance were more highly experienced. The level of rater agreement did not appear to be superior to that reported here.

HHS, a clinical psychologist, rated one patient (WA). This patient was seen in psychoanalytically oriented psychotherapy.

Table 3
Relationship between Degree of Inference and Rater Agreement

Variable	Degree of Inference		Rater Agreement	
	Mean	Rank	R	Rank
14. Elation	2.182	1	neg.	18.5
8. Hostility, anger	2.273	2	.358	6
5. Affect	2.363	3	.648	1
13. Depression	2.545	4	.504	3
4. Anxiety	2.727	5	.380	4
1. Dominance	2.909	6	.345	7
2. Dependence	3.182	7.5	.583	2
9. Defensiveness	3.182	7.5	.085	13
12. Competitiveness	3.273	9	.216	9
3. Resistance	3.636	10	.099	12
10. Transference—positive	4.000	11	neg.	18.5
15. Insight	4.182	12	.369	5
11. Transference—negative	4.364	13	.178	10
7. Masochism	4.727	14	.138	11
6. Sadism	4.818	15	.014	16
16. Working through	4.909	16	.291	8
21. Genital strivings	5.000	17	.083	14
20. Oedipal strivings	5.182	18	neg.	18.5
17. Oral strivings	5.545	19.5	.034	15
18. Anal strivings	5.545	19.5	neg.	18.5
19. Phallic strivings	6.000	21	neg.	18.5

Patient T, a married woman, was rated for 327 hours. She suffered from a serious character disorder with much impulsive behavior, periodic episodes of overwhelming anxiety, and at times a clinical picture of a borderline psychotic state. Her therapy was characterized by marked fluctuations of mood and a major degree of conscious uncooperativeness for over a year. The gradual elucidation of negative transference led to some marked improvements in the treatment relationship. Following this, it became possible to work on various complex aspects of her development and her current life situation. The latter remained very bad and resulted in her receiving much psychic trauma. Although she grew more able to tolerate many of these blows, they did present a major "outside" interference which led to considerable fluctuation in the psychoanalytic situation. Eventually she decided that such difficulties were ones that she did not have to accept and she took some realistic steps to deal with this toward the end of this period of therapy. Therapist JAE was well aware of the tenuous nature of the therapeutic relationship for most of the first year. This, and the patient's "borderline" state, led to a very special type of handling which JAE believes is reflected in the ratings.

Patient R, a young professional man, was rated for 157 hours. His problem was that of a moderate obsessive-compulsive character neurosis with some recent anxiety attacks connected with increasing awareness of aggressive impulses. Treatment of this case involved dealing with a fairly rapidly developing transference neurosis. There were major defenses against awareness of affects, using typical isolation mechanisms. Considerable satisfactory progress was made during the hours rated, so that throughout this time there was gradual increasing therapeutic interaction. After the period which was rated, the analysis was continued to termination with relief of symptoms and much improvement in interpersonal relations.

Patient WA, a 20-year old girl, in therapy for about three years, was seen typically on a twice-a-week basis. Ratings were made for 173 hours.

She was the daughter of a professional man who was unusually active and devoted to his work although he was advanced in years and on the verge of retirement. The mother was a rather overprotective authoritarian woman. There were two younger sisters.

The patient was originally referred because of difficulties in her schoolwork, both academic and interpersonal. Following verbal disagreements with schoolmates and teachers, she was asked to withdraw from college. She returned home, where she regressed to a passive, helpless state. Her parents alternatively tended to encourage and to condemn her regressive behavior.

Clinically, Miss WA was an extremely dependent and immature young woman. Her passive-aggressiveness was pervasive. She had a severe character problem, complicated by a very impoverished ego development. Her primary defense was to dominate people through her dependency and demandingness.

Therapy was aimed at fostering insight into her unconscious mechanism to maintain the status quo of dependency, and at providing, through the therapeutic relationship, a more suitable reality model than she had experienced in the past. This proved to be an exceedingly difficult task, and progress was slow and halting. Nevertheless, the patient eventually gained enough ego strength to resume her academic work and to become somewhat more outgoing and self-reliant.

All ratings were made for *consecutive* hours. Therapist JAE's patients were rated from the beginning of therapy, but Patient R's therapy continued beyond the 157 hours included here. Patient WA had been in therapy for about two years at the time the ratings were initiated. Her therapy (and that of Patient T) were rated to termination. In other words, Patient T's therapy was rated in its entirety; Patient R was rated from the beginning but continued beyond the cut-off point; and Patient WA was rated from the middle period to termination.

It is apparent that these rating data lack comparability. Not only are there marked differences in type of patient, form of therapy, and background training of the two therapists, but there was also relatively little congruency in terms of the period of therapy being rated. The assumption here is that any course of psychoanalysis or psychotherapy has a relatively regular pattern—a somewhat distinct introductory period, a long middle period (characterized by "working through"), and a termination period.

Eventually, of course, one would hope to obtain ratings covering the complete therapy of different patients who might be matched on a variety of characteristics. In the same manner one might match therapists, different forms of therapy, and other variables. Once such controls are imposed, one would be able to provide empirical answers to the question of whether there is a "typical" course of therapy under specified conditions. One would also be able to investigate deviations from such a typical course once it was established.

This objective far exceeds that of the present pilot study. Our limited goal was to apply the modified rating instrument in a few cases, to study the resulting distributions of ratings, to explore the statistical interrelationships among the variables being rated, and to gather some preliminary data on the rating characteristics of two therapists working with different patients. Whatever tentative comparisons we might make between therapists and between patients must be considered highly speculative. A final objective of this pilot work was to investigate statistical problems relating to repeated ratings of the same patient on identical variables over an extended period of time. The problem of the reliability of ratings, which has previously been discussed, is ignored here, simply because it was not possible to gather pertinent data in the privacy of individual therapy. The findings which have already been presented strongly suggest, however, that this problem must be dealt with systematically before ratings of this kind are collected in the future.

Results

Statistical treatment. The statistical analysis of the data of this study falls under the heading of *time-series analysis*. Tests of statistical significance applied to time-series data, particularly tests for a true or significant correlation between two series, must take into account the extent of redundancy introduced by a succession of observations on the same subject as measured by sets of appropriately defined autocorrelations. The papers by Bartlett (1935, 1946) contain theoretical discussions, and Quenouille (1952) provides a non-mathematical discussion of the methodology.

All ratings were punched on IBM Cards, and distributions for all variables were prepared. We then intercorrelated the ratings for each patient-therapist pair. This procedure resulted in three tables of intercorrelation in which N represents the number of therapy hours rated by each therapist.

In addition, statistical analyses were performed to explore the extent to which a rating on a given variable made during one hour was correlated with comparable ratings in preceding hours.

Distribution of Ratings

Table 4 shows the distributions of each therapist's ratings in percentages. Examination discloses marked divergences in these distributions which appear to be attributable primarily to the following sources: (1) differences between the patients who were being seen in therapy resulting in differences in the clinical phenomena that emerged over the course of treatment; (2) differences in the form of therapy conducted by Therapist HHS and Therapist JAE, as these therapists saw it; (3) differences

Table 4
Distributions of Therapists' Ratings for Three Patients (in percents)

Variable	Patient	None Absent 0	Slight Mild 1	Fairly Strong Moderate 2	Great Frequent 3	Extremely Great or Frequent 4
1. Dominance	WA	49.7	7.5	28.3	12.1	2.3
	T	21.4	19.0	53.2	6.4	
	R	10.8	5.7	70.7	12.7	
2. Dependence	WA	23.7	2.9	26.0	28.9	18.5
	T	46.5	35.5	17.7	.3	
	R	48.4	31.8	19.1	.6	
3. Resistance	WA	2.3	5.2	27.7	42.8	22.0
	T	31.2	22.3	32.1	12.8	1.5
	R	11.5	22.3	54.1	12.1	
4. Anxiety	WA	10.4	20.2	52.0	16.8	.6
	T	43.7	27.8	22.6	5.5	.3
	R	34.4	42.7	18.5	4.5	
5. Affect	WA	16.8	32.9	30.1	14.4	5.8
	T	10.7	26.0	47.7	13.8	1.8
	R	12.1	46.5	35.0	6.4	
6. Sadism	WA	16.2	9.2	29.5	23.7	21.4
	T	99.4	.3	.3		
	R	99.4	.6			
7. Masochism	WA	38.7	11.6	22.5	22.0	5.2
	T	90.2	5.8	3.4	.6	
	R	98.7	1.3			

Table 4 (Continued)

Variable	Patient	None Absent 0	Slight Mild 1	Fairly Strong Moderate 2	Great Frequent 3	Extremely Great or Frequent 4
8. Hostility, anger	WA	8.1	19.1	35.8	16.8	20.2
	T	59.3	19.0	14.4	6.4	.9
	R	61.1	21.0	14.6	2.5	.6
9. Defensiveness	WA	4.0	9.2	28.3	31.8	26.6
	T	41.0	16.2	32.4	10.1	.3
	R	25.5	17.2	48.4	8.3	.6
10. Transference-positive	WA	7.5	6.9	35.8	47.4	2.3
	T	37.0	31.8	26.9	4.3	
	R	51.0	35.0	14.0		
11. Transference-negative	WA	7.5	26.6	31.8	20.2	13.9
	T	71.9	14.4	11.9	1.8	
	R	61.1	28.7	10.2		
12. Competitiveness	WA	72.2	6.4	13.3	6.9	1.2
	T	93.6	3.4	2.4	.3	.3
	R	49.0	23.6	18.5	8.3	.6
13. Depression	WA	43.4	45.1	9.2	1.2	1.2
	T	61.8	21.4	11.6	4.0	1.2
	R	96.2	3.2	.6		
14. Elation	WA	93.1	5.2	1.7		
	T	93.9	3.7	1.8	.6	
	R	99.4	.6			
15. Insight	WA	11.0	35.8	45.1	8.1	
	T	59.3	18.3	19.0	2.8	.6
	R	65.0	19.7	14.6		.6
16. Working through	WA	4.0	20.8	47.4	27.2	.6
	T	29.7	24.5	39.8	5.5	.6
	R	43.3	20.4	34.4	1.9	
17. Oral strivings	WA	86.7	1.7	3.5	4.6	3.5
	T	57.8	19.6	18.3	4.0	.3
	R	46.5	24.8	21.7	7.0	
18. Anal strivings	WA	45.1	1.7	13.3	20.8	19.1
	T	92.4	5.8	1.2	.3	.3
	R	86.0	7.6	5.1	1.3	
19. Phallic strivings	WA	95.4	.6	1.7	2.3	
	T	92.7	2.4	4.0	.9	
	R	79.6	9.6	10.2	.6	
20. Oedipal strivings	WA	65.9	2.3	9.8	18.5	3.5
	T	72.8	15.6	9.2	2.1	.3
	R	78.3	9.6	9.6	1.9	.6
21. Genital strivings	WA	100.0				
	T	95.1	2.1	1.8	.6	.3
	R	98.8	.6	.6		

Table 4 (Continued)

Variable	Patient	None Absent 0	Slight Mild 1	Fairly Strong Moderate 2	Great Frequent 3	Extremely Great or Frequent 4
22. Interventions	WA	1.7	9.8	57.2	30.1	1.2
	T	13.1	43.7	40.1	3.1	
	R	9.6	38.2	52.2		
23. Interpretations	WA	.6	8.1	52.0	38.7	.6
	T	49.5	34.2	15.9	.3	
	R	26.1	56.0	17.2	.6	
24. Depth of inter- pretations	WA		9.2	27.7	47.4	15.6
	T	50.5	8.9	27.5	11.0	2.1
	R	26.7	15.9	31.2	24.2	1.9
25. Initiative	WA	1.2	11.6	38.1	45.1	4.0
	T	88.1	8.6	2.4	.6	.3
	R	91.7	7.6	.6		
26. Warmth	WA	1.2	15.6	52.6	30.1	.6
	T	70.6	24.8	4.6		
	R	90.4	9.6			
27. Coldness	WA	87.3	10.4	2.3		
	T	99.1	.9			
	R	98.1	1.9			
28. Support	WA	2.9	12.7	45.1	38.1	1.2
	T	38.5	46.8	14.4	.3	
	R	71.3	28.0	.6		
29. Motivation	WA	1.2	11.0	40.5	43.9	3.5
	T	76.8	11.3	11.9		
	R	75.8	15.3	8.9		
30. Positive Attitudes	WA	.6	11.0	43.9	42.2	2.3
	T	38.2	38.2	22.9	.6	
	R	35.7	40.1	24.2		
31. Negative Attitudes	WA	75.7	18.5	4.0	1.7	
	T	85.3	9.2	4.0	1.5	
	R	96.8	2.5	.6		
32. Countertransference problems	WA	79.8	17.3	2.3	.6	
	T	72.5	16.8	10.1	.6	
	R	84.1	12.7	3.2		
33. Empathy	WA	1.2	11.0	46.2	38.7	2.9
	T	83.8	7.6	8.6		
	R	71.3	14.6	13.4	.6	
34. Productivity of hour	WA	1.7	15.0	39.3	39.3	4.6
	T	22.6	31.2	36.4	9.5	.3
	R	8.9	30.6	48.4	11.5	.6
35. Satisfaction with progress	WA	.6	16.8	48.6	31.2	2.9
	T	26.0	27.2	37.0	9.2	.6
	R	14.0	26.7	48.4	10.2	.6

in the way the two therapists understood the rating scales and the manner in which they used them; (4) combinations of the foregoing. While the respective influences cannot be isolated apart, there are indications that the two distributions for Therapist JAE are more alike than either is to the ratings of Therapist HHS. Furthermore it will be seen that Therapist JAE sees his therapeutic operations differently from Therapist HHS. We thus infer very tentatively that the observed differences may reflect more strongly different uses of the scales by the two therapists as well as differences in therapeutic technique rather than true patient differences. (Therapist JAE conducted a form of therapy which followed more closely the "classic" psychoanalytic model, whereas Therapist HHS employed a modified form of psychoanalytically-oriented psychotherapy.) These divergencies seem to overshadow true differences between the three patients.

To document these inferences we shall comment upon the empirical findings in somewhat greater detail.

Therapist HHS saw Patient WA as exceedingly passive (showing an absence of *dominance*) which apparently was not true for Patients R and T; similarly, Patient WA was rated high on *dependence* much more frequently than either of the other patients. Passivity and dependence were indeed outstanding features of this patient's psychopathology. Her *resistance*, too, was rated as extremely great. Patient R emerges as more dominant than Patient T, but the degree of their dependence appears about equal, and the distribution of their ratings on resistance do not appear to vary markedly. Anxiety ratings seem to follow a similar pattern.

With respect to ratings of *affect*, Patient T receives the preponderance of high ratings; however, in this instance, all three dyads are reasonably comparable and well distributed over the range of the scale.

Therapist JAE gives virtually nothing but zero ratings on *sadism*, whereas Therapist HHS's ratings are distributed over the entire range. In the case of *masochism*, a very similar situation obtains. It is difficult to believe that one patient was so completely different in these respects and it seems very probably that the two therapists had markedly divergent definitions of these variables and made their ratings in very different ways.

There is little question but that Therapist HHS tended to give more extreme ratings on *hostility* than his colleague, whose two patients appeared very similar in this respect. The same is largely true for ratings on *defensiveness, positive transference,* and *negative transference.* In each instance, Therapist JAE gives sizeable proportions of zero ratings whereas these are very small for Therapist HHS.

Patient T shows very little *competitiveness*, as reflected by the ratings, whereas the remaining two patients, for once, appear more similar.

Patient R emerges as the least *depressed* one of the three; again Therapist HHS tends to give more non-zero ratings.

Elation is one of the few clinical variables which shows very similar distributions for the three dyads, but a very large percentage of all ratings are still zero. Still, non-zero ratings, where they occur, may be important.

Therapist HHS's patient is credited more frequently with achieving *insight* than Therapist JAE's patients. The evidence suggests that we are dealing with a definitional problem rather than a clinical one. *Working through* discloses a similar situation.

The pattern of ratings for the two patients treated by Therapist JAE on *oral strivings* are highly similar; in this instance, Therapist HHS gives a preponderance of zero ratings.

The ratings of *oral, anal, phallic, oedipal,* and *genital* strivings must be suspected of extreme unreliability. (See Experiments 1, 2, and 3.) This is suggested not only by divergent use of the scales by the two therapists, the results of the preceding experiments, but also by comments from various clinicians (including the two therapists) expressing considerable uncertainty about the empirical referents.

The distributions of ratings dealing with aspects of therapeutic technique disclose marked inter-therapist differences. Therapist HHS intervenes and interprets much more frequently (as he sees it), and he regards his interpretations as markedly "deeper" than does Therapist JAE. Therapist JAE seems reasonably consistent with himself, except that he made "deep" interpretations much more frequently with Patient R than with Patient T. Therapist HHS obviously is pursuing a much more active technique, as evidenced by his ratings on *initiative*.

Extremely large differences between the two therapists are disclosed when their self-ratings of attitudes and motivations are examined. For the most part, these discrepancies seem to reflect true differences in the two therapists' approach to psychotherapy, but it is also apparent that their understanding of the various scales must have differed very considerably. For example, in three out of four sessions Therapist JAE rated his motivation as "absent." This simply cannot be true if the ratings are interpreted literally. The rating sheet listed this item as "motivation, dedication, 'investment'," and in fact Therapist JAE scored this as present only when it clearly exceeded the "baseline" motivation which initiated his acceptance of the patients in the first place. At the risk of repetitiveness, let it be said again that the calibration of raters must be achieved through advance training.

It is noteworthy that, making allowance for patient fluctuations, Therapist JAE was reasonably consistent with himself. Therapist HHS, perhaps because he was the originator of the scales and, as a psychologist, more aware of the necessity to achieve "good" distributions, may have attempted to make greater use of the entire range of the scales and, where possible, avoided zero ratings.

The two therapists observed countertransference reactions in 16 to 20 percent of their interviews; here, too, we find reasonable agreement between the two therapists as far as their respective distributions is concerned. Therapist JAE seemed to have the most intense and/or frequent reactions to Patient T. Ratings on negative attitudes showed similar agreement and in general parallel the distributions on countertransference.

Patterns of Intercorrelations

In the following we shall discuss similarities and differences in the correlational patterns obtained for the three patient-therapist pairs. Since one of the two therapists (JAE) contributed two sets of ratings, it will be possible to learn something about his mode of interaction as well as his rating tendencies with *two* patients.

As already indicated, we cannot be sure whether a given finding is idiosyncratic with respect to the therapist, the patient, and their mode of interaction, or whether it represents an invariant relationship which would obtain were we to study *any* therapist-patient pair. Between these two extremes of complete idiosyncrasy and a high generalizability there may be intermediate positions. For instance, a statistical relationship may apply to therapy with a hysterical patient, but not to others; it may apply to a therapist following a particular theoretical orientation (in this case the psychoanalytic), but not to therapists following different persuasions; it may apply to therapists of a given level of experience, but not to others, etc. In brief, the generalizability of any finding here reported is open to question; however, considerable clarification can be obtained empirically simply by studying additional patient-therapist pairs. Therefore, the problem is not insoluble in principle.

Some measure of generalizability is possible by virtue of our having collected data on three patient-therapist dyads. It is for this reason that we shall examine in some detail the patterns of relationships among the variables for each dyad. Where similar patterns of relationships obtain in the three patient-therapist pairs, we may consider ourselves on safer ground than in instances where a relationship is found only for one dyad. However, in any event, the number of dyads is too small for trustworthy conclusions. We shall only discuss those relationships which were stable across the three dyads. For purposes of exposition, we shall subdivide our discussion between clinical, technique, and attitudinal variables (of the therapist).

A. Interrelationships Among Clinical Variables

1. Patient States. Since we are dealing with three different patients who were being seen in psychotherapy for very different clinical problems, a high degree of non-overlap is to be expected. In fact, this is what we found. The relationships, even where they reached statistical signifi-

cance for the three dyads, were for the most part low, and in a number of instances the patterns for the three patients were highly idiosyncratic.[5] Table 5 summarizes the relationships pertaining to patient states.

Table 5
Statistically Significant Coefficients of Correlation (product-moment r's)
Consistent for Three Therapeutic Dyads
A. Clinical Variables: 1. Patient States

Variable	Correlate	Pt. WA N=173	Pt. R N=157	Pt. T N=327
1. Dominance	5. Affect	19*	28	20
	8. Hostility	31	16	14
2. Dependence	7. Masochism	51	18	15
	17. Oral strivings	16	40	26
4. Anxiety	5. Affect	19	32	36
5. Affect	1. Dominance	19	28	20
	4. Anxiety	19	32	36
	8. Hostility	36	24	33
	12. Competitiveness			
7. Masochism	2. Dependence	51	18	15
8. Hostility, anger	1. Dominance	31	16	14
	5. Affect	36	24	33
	18. Anal strivings	50	18	16
12. Competitiveness, rivalry	5. Affect	27	16	16
	20. Oedipal strivings	22	32	23
17. Oral strivings	2. Dependence	16	40	26
18. Anal strivings	8. Hostility	50	18	16
20. Oedipal strivings	12. Competitiveness	22	32	23

* Decimal points omitted

It is somewhat surprising that therapists' ratings of the degree of *anxiety* experienced by the patient were not related systematically to other variables for the three dyads. In fact, only *affect* tends to be systematically related to anxiety for all three patient-therapist pairs. As will be seen in the following, similar observations hold true for a number of clinical variables.

[5] While it would be tempting to discuss "unique" patterns of interrelationships for a particular dyad, this procedure seemed too speculative, for the reasons already indicated.

Oral strivings, as might be expected, show systematic relationships to ratings of *dependence,* which in turn is related to *masochism.*

All three patients, when seen to exhibit *oedipal strivings* are also rated as being *competitive,* which in turn is associated with ratings of *affect.*

Patients are considered to show signs of *affect* when they are *dominant, anxious, hostile,* and *competitive.* It is noteworthy that a number of other variables which are usually considered to have an affective component (e.g., depression, elation, etc.) fail to follow this pattern.

Hostility and *anger* show systematic relationships to *dominance* and *affect,* and, not unexpectedly, they vary concomitantly with ratings of *anal strivings.*

2. Transference. The foregoing variables are of course a function of the transference relationship, but for purposes of exposition we have segregated them from variables which are more specifically and explicitly related to transference phenomena in a technical sense. (See Table 6.)

Resistance and *defensiveness* were found to be appreciably correlated, at least in two of the three dyads. Similarly, there is a fair amount of overlap between ratings of *resistance* and *negative transference.* Patients, too, are rated as *resisting* when they exhibit *hostility* and *anal strivings.* Significant statistical relationships between *resistance* and *affect* were demonstrated, but in one case the relationship was a negative one. A patient who is *defensive* also tended to be seen as *anxious,* but like many of the relationships we have commented upon, this one was at a rather low level.

Positive transference, according to the therapists' ratings, is characterized by *dominance, affect, oedipal strivings,* and the emergence of *insight.*

Negative transference, on the other hand, is accompanied by *hostility,* and, as has already been pointed out, by *resistance.*

The achievement of *insight* and the process of *working through* appear to be markedly similar, at least in terms of the ratings under discussion, and they show highly comparable statistical relationships to other variables such as: *dominance, affect, positive transference,* and *oedipal strivings.* It may deserve comment that in each instance *insight* discloses the higher relationships; possibly this means that ratings on this variable are statistically more reliable.

B. Statistical Relationships Involving Technique Variables (Table 7)

There was some evidence that *frequency of interventions* tended to be correlated with *depth of interpretation* but not with *frequency of interpretation* (only in two instances). On the other hand, *frequency of interpretation,* within the limits of the present study, must be considered virtually synonymous with *depth of interpretation.*

It is difficult to say whether *support* should be considered a technique variable per se, but irrespective of this issue *frequent interventions* tended

Table 6
Statistically Significant Coefficients of Correlation (product-moment r's)
Consistent for Three Therapeutic Dyads
A. Clinical Variables: 2. Transference

Variable	Correlate	Pt. WA N=173	Pt. R N=157	Pt. T N=327
3. Resistance	5. Affect	-18*	21	18
	8. Hostility	35	21	32
	9. Defensiveness	68	17	47
	11. Negative transference	59	19	30
	18. Anal strivings	33	18	20
9. Defensiveness	3. Resistance	68	17	47
	4. Anxiety	19	18	26
10. Positive transference	1. Dominance	29	28	26
	5. Affect	33	33	25
	15. Insight	48	27	35
	20. Oedipal strivings	38	24	42
11. Negative transference	3. Resistance	59	19	30
	8. Hostility	53	30	56
15. Insight	1. Dominance	26	24	38
	5. Affect	17	30	38
	10. Positive transference	48	27	35
	16. Working through	69	43	64
	20. Oedipal strivings	43	28	32
16. Working through	1. Dominance	35	36	43
	5. Affect	33	31	38
	10. Positive transference	61	47	32
	15. Insight	69	43	64
	20. Oedipal strivings	39	17	28

* Decimal points omitted

to be seen as supportive, which was not consistently true for interpretations.

Turning to the relationships between technique and clinical variables, we found the following associations:

Therapists tended to *intervene frequently* when the patient was *dominant,* evincing *positive transference,* achieving *insight,* and *working through.* They tended to *interpret frequently* and *deeply* under similar conditions. In addition, *deep interpretations* were made in the context of *affect, masochistic strivings,* and *oedipal strivings.*

Table 7
Statistically Significant Coefficients of Correlation (product-moment r's)
Consistent for Three Therapeutic Dyads
B. Technique Variables

Variable	Correlate*	Pt. WA N=173	Pt. R N=157	Pt. T N=327
22. Frequency of interventions	24. Depth of interpretations	41**	19	18
	28. Support	55	19	25
	1. Dominance	24	47	32
	10. Positive transference	31	32	18
	15. Insight	37	29	28
	16. Working through	36	43	31
23. Frequency of interpretations	24. Depth of interpretations	61	65	78
	10. Positive transference	43	19	15
	15. Insight	43	24	22
	16. Working through	47	26	17
24. Depth of interpretations	5. Affect	23	32	33
	7. Masochism	22	18	25
	10. Positive transference	48	29	23
	15. Insight	58	24	23
	16. Working through	62	21	16
	20. Oedipal strivings	33	28	35
25. Initiative	26. Warmth	60	40	23
	29. Motivation	59	27	18
28. Support	15. Insight	52	18	18

* In each instance, the correlations between one technique variable and other technique variables are presented first. These entries are followed by the correlations between technique and clinical variables.
** Decimal points omitted

Therapists tended to be more *supportive* when the patient was achieving *insight*.

C. Statistical Relationships Involving Attitudinal Variables (Table 8)

Parallel to the preceding section, let us first examine statistical relationships among attitudinal variables. Here the most pronounced associations were found, suggesting a high degree of overlap among these variables.

In each instance, the therapists felt they were experiencing *positive attitudes* when they had a high degree of *motivation and investment* in the patient, when their *empathy* was high, when the *hour* was *productive*, and when they were *satisfied with the progress*. Under these conditions they also felt they were being *supportive*.

The converse was true for only two variables. Therapists experienced *negative attitudes* when they were *dissatisfied with the progress* and when they considered the *hour unproductive*.

Warmth was appreciably correlated with the therapists' feelings of *motivation, dedication, and investment*, but to no other attitudinal variables. *Coldness* disclosed highly inconsistent relationships, as was true for *countertransference problems*. The latter, in particular, one would expect to be highly idiosyncratic and situationally determined, hence hardly replicable across dyads.

Empathy, productivity of the hour, and *satisfaction with progress* seemed to tap highly similar attitudes, as shown by their high interrelationships, and they appeared to be a function of *positive attitudes*.

How do therapists react attitudinally to different kinds of clinical constellations? If, as we have done throughout this section, we restrict ourselves to statistically significant relationships which were replicated across the three patient-therapist pairs, the following regularities emerged:

Table 8
Statistically Significant Coefficients of Correlation (product-moment r's)
Consistent for Three Therapeutic Dyads
C. Attitudinal Variables

Variable	*Correlate**	*Pt. WA* N=173	*Pt. R* N=157	*Pt. T* N=327
26. Warmth	29. Motivation	69**	27	53
	10. Positive transference	56	29	19
	15. Insight	59	31	20
	16. Working through	59	25	13
	25. Initiative	60	40	23
	28. Support	77	17	31
29. Motivation, dedication "investment"	26. Warmth	69	28	53
	30. Positive attitudes	84	26	49
	10. Positive transference	49	23	26
	15. Insight	54	26	33
	16. Working through	58	28	31
	23. Frequency of interpretations	54	39	18
	25. Initiative	59	27	18
30. Positive attitudes	29. Motivation	84	26	49

Table 8 (Continued)

Variable	Correlate*	Pt. WA N=173	Pt. R N=157	Pt. T N=327
30. Positive attitudes (continued)	33. Empathy	86	39	39
	34. Productivity of hour	77	58	57
	35. Satisfaction with progress	77	54	65
	1. Dominance	16	25	41
	5. Affect	18	39	32
	10. Positive transference	51	47	46
	15. Insight	56	30	54
	16. Working through	57	49	54
	22. Frequency of interventions	48	37	31
	23. Frequency of interpretations	53	32	21
	24. Depth of interpretations	54	44	21
	28. Support	74	27	12
31. Negative attitudes	34. Productivity of hour	-44	-21	-16
	35. Satisfaction with progress	-46	-25	-27
33. Empathy	30. Positive attitudes	86	39	39
	34. Productivity of hour	74	44	42
	35. Satisfaction with progress	76	46	43
	1. Dominance	21	17	21
	5. Affect	19	35	25
	10. Positive transference	54	24	13
	16. Working through	53	18	32
	20. Oedipal strivings	40	27	20
	22. Frequency of interventions	45	25	24
	24. Depth of interpretations	51	29	21
34. Productivity of hour	30. Positive attitudes	77	58	57
	31. Negative attitudes	-44	-21	-16
	33. Empathy	74	44	42
	35. Satisfaction with progress	84	84	79
	1. Dominance	18	41	45
	5. Affect	27	47	39

Table 8 *(Continued)*

		Pt. WA N=173	Pt. R N=157	Pt. T N=327
34. Productivity of hour *(continued)*	10. Positive transference	56	45	44
	15. Insight	59	22	54
	16. Working through	59	36	55
	20. Oedipal strivings	42	31	40
	22. Frequency of in- terventions	43	37	40
	23. Frequency of in- terpretations	47	30	28
	24. Depth of inter- pretations	62	60	44
35. Satisfaction with progress	30. Positive attitudes	77	54	65
	31. Negative attitudes	-46	-25	-27
	33. Empathy	76	46	43
	34. Productivity of hour	84	84	79
	5. Affect	24	48	35
	10. Positive transference	50	41	45
	15. Insight	59	28	53
	16. Working through	59	39	58
	17. Oral strivings	-17	47	32
	20. Oedipal strivings	42	33	36
	22. Frequency of in- terventions	42	47	37
	23. Frequency of in- terpretations	47	30	23
	24. Depth of inter- pretations	52	58	34

* In each instance, the correlations between one attitudinal variable and other attitudinal variables are presented first. These entries are followed, in turn, by the correlations between attitudinal variables and clinical variables and between attitudinal variables and technique variables.
** Decimal points omitted

It seems to make little difference which attitudinal variable is selected for discussion because almost identical patterns of relationships can be demonstrated between them and certain clinical variables. *Warmth, motivation (dedication, "investment"), positive attitudes, empathy, productivity of the hour,* and *satisfaction with progress* each show marked associations with: *positive transference, insight,* and *working through. Dominance* and *affect* seem to follow this pattern, but there are some exceptions, and the coefficients appear to be somewhat lower. Finally, *oedipal strivings* are consistently correlated with *empathy, productivity of the hour,* and *satisfaction with progress.*

It is quite apparent that therapists value manifestations in which the patient is moving in the direction of greater maturity, in which he shows a cooperative attitude with the therapist, in which he seems to be working on his problem, and achieving insight. The emergence of affect and the absence of submissiveness belong to this pattern. Oedipal strivings, at least in part, may be viewed as strivings toward greater maturity. Conspicuous by their absence are comparable negative relationships, such as might exist between resistance and negative attitudes in the therapist. One among many possibilities is that therapists may be more reluctant to acknowledge negative attitudes when they experience them.

Finally, we shall comment upon consistent relationships between attitudinal variables in the therapist and therapeutic technique variables.

Therapist *warmth* was found to be appreciably associated with *initiative* and *support*. Warmth, however, followed a somewhat unique pattern which was not replicated for the remaining attitudinal variables, which in their patterns of correlation appeared to "hang together." With minor exceptions, *motivation* (dedication, "investment"), *positive attitudes, empathy, productivity of the hour,* and *satisfaction with progress* each were markedly correlated with *frequency of interventions, frequency of interpretations,* and *depth of interpretations.* In addition, *positive attitudes* correlated with *support*.

The direction of causation is of course indeterminate, but in general—and this appears to be the most conservative interpretation of the relationships—we may say that therapists feel positively toward a patient when the latter is cooperative, working through, non-defensive, and showing signs of "maturity." At such times, too, they are more likely to be "giving," as evidenced by more frequent and deeper interpretations. It is also this constellation which engenders in them feelings of warmth and empathy, satisfaction with the hour, and progress in general.

This may mean no more than that therapists evince typically "human" reactions: they feel pleased when the work is progressing and they feel frustrated when (presumably for unconscious reasons) the patient is thwarting their efforts. On the other hand, we may have here another demonstration of previously established relationships between therapists' clinical judgments, communications, and attitudes. These relationships were found in an experimental situation in which therapists responded as vicarious interviewers to a patient portrayed in a sound film, as well as in initial diagnostic interviews (Strupp, 1958, 1965; Strupp and Williams, 1960). In the present study we now have evidence that these relationships obtain equally in long-term, intensive psychotherapy. In our earlier publications we called attention to the possibility of a self-fulfilling prophecy which through conscious and unconscious attitudes may influence the therapist's clinical judgments, prognostications, as well as the nature of his interventions. Such attitudinal reactions in the therapist, if communicated to the patient, may reinforce the patient's initial negative attitudes and ultimately result in an impasse.

For example, the patient may be in a state of negative transference and he may be highly resistive during a particular hour. What our findings suggest is that the therapist reacts negatively (rejectingly?) to such maneuvers; he may become silent, withdrawn, etc. in turn and decide to "wait it out." We also glean from our results that under these conditions he becomes dissatisfied with the progress, tends to feel unempathic, and shows less warmth. We are not arguing that under conditions of intense resistance the best clinical and therapeutic procedure may not be for the therapist to remain benevolent, neutral, silent, non-interpretive, etc. It is quite likely, however, on the basis of the present results, that the therapists' maneuvers because of their underlying attitudinal component may reinforce the patient's resistance rather than diminish it. The phenomenon of counter-resistance in the therapist has long been recognized as a countertransference problem. We do not wish to suggest that the therapist invariably falls victim to it; however, the strong likelihood of a relatively frequent occurrence of this phenomenon must be entertained.

In part, therapy consists in *rewarding,* hence reinforcing, those attitudes, moves, feelings, etc. in the patient which are in the direction of what the therapist conceives to be mental health (in terms of our findings, this includes positive transference, dominance, affect, oedipal strivings, and the achievement of emotional insight), and *punishing* (i.e., disregarding, neglecting, treating with silence) those moves which maintain the patient's defensive structure. As far as the evidence from the present investigation can be trusted, it is clear that therapists become *active* (i.e., interpretive) when they see the patient as collaborating, and they tend to become *passive* (at least in terms of frequency of verbal communications) when the patient is "opposing" them. The foregoing has long been known. What this investigation has contributed is certain evidence that both sets of operations by the therapist are not carried out in an attitudinal climate of detachment and neutrality, but rather that the therapist responds rather strongly on an emotional level. It is likely that he may be able to react therapeutically irrespective of these attitudes; the findings do not instruct us about the extent to which he is successful in this endeavor. Ideally, his therapeutic interventions should be largely immune from his personal feelings. We doubt that this is always, or even very often, the case, and suggest that irrespective of the therapist's professional training (including his personal analysis), his therapeutic operations are a function of his emotional and attitudinal response to the patient to a larger extent than is acknowledged by psychoanalytic theory (and most other therapeutic theories extant).

Recommendations

The preliminary nature of the foregoing experiment obviously precludes any conclusions. However, there are a number of lessons to be learned from our experience, and it is in the spirit of facilitating future work that the following recommendations are set forth (see also the section entitled "Prospectus"):

1. The greatest need appears to be for better definitions of the variables to be rated. Factor analysis or similar techniques might be used to isolate major dimensions which might have heuristic value.

2. The number of variables employed in this experiment is too large. Items which are too inferential, too difficult to define, too difficult to rate for other reasons, which are overlapping to an appreciable extent with items that are less beset with the foregoing shortcomings, and items which are judged inadequate on other grounds need to be eliminated or redefined. Contrariwise, a number of items which have shown promise should receive increasing focus.

3. Therapists or other judges using the instrument must be given careful training in its application, and a clear-cut consensus must be reached among judges before further experimentation is undertaken.

4. The units of observation must be clearly demarcated, although it may prove difficult to break the therapeutic hour down into small yet *meaningful* units. Arbitrary time periods do not seem to be the answer to this problem.

5. Once the necessary spadework has been completed, there is need to repeat similar longitudinal observations with the same therapist, but also with similar types of patients and different therapists. When the technical prerequisites have been met, a higher degree of comparability of patient-therapist pairs may be anticipated.

6. Related to the preceding point, there is need to compare different parts of the same therapeutic experience, for example, before and after significant personality modification is believed to have occurred.

7. In all comparative studies (such as might be undertaken under Points 5 and 6) it will prove useful to discuss the quantitative findings in relation to the clinical phenomena as they are observed by the therapist during each hour. The value of such comparisons has been shown by Strupp (1957b) and Auerbach (1963).

8. Despite the inadequacy of the pilot experiments reported in these pages, it seems highly justified to persist in efforts to improve the agreement among judges or between the therapist and a panel of observers. The achievement of a solid consensus among observers of the psychotherapeutic process concerning the phenomena under scrutiny is obviously a task of the highest priority, upon whose satisfactory solution the com-

parative study of psychotherapeutic interviews—whether we are dealing with individual hours or an entire course of therapy—ultimately depends.

Concluding Comments

The reader who has patiently followed the tortuous exposition of the difficulties surrounding the quantification of process phenomena in psychotherapy and the preliminary experiments we have carried out may well wonder concerning the substantive yield of these labors. It is amply apparent that the work here presented allows no definitive conclusions. What we intended to convey in this presention, which may be likened to a visit of the researcher's laboratory, was a close-up of the tremendous obstacles which face the researcher in this area. Our efforts as yet are halting, our methodology is imperfect, and we are not even certain that the direction we have taken will turn out to be promising in the long run. Indeed, there are indications that other "mining techniques" may be more fruitful.

Essentially, there are two courses of action open to the researcher in this area: (1) He can attempt to study the naturally occurring phenomena in psychotherapy and devise ways and means of quantifying them; to do so, he must conceptualize dimensions or categories which, according to his lights, promise the greatest returns. (This course has been followed in the present investigation.) Or, (2) he can turn to experimental approaches, in the course of which he studies part-processes in the laboratory or in quasi-therapeutic situations. This course implies a recognition that the naturally occurring events are intrinsically too complex and not amenable to experimental control or manipulation, at least with our current research technique. (This approach has been followed in other investigations performed by our group, to which reference has been made in this chapter.)

Each of these approaches has its advantages and its shortcomings. Our efforts along both of these dimensions bespeak our uncertainty and our doubts as to which is most deserving of future effort. Perhaps this question cannot be answered at the current state of our knowledge, and considerable work must be undertaken in both of these areas before more definitive answers can be forthcoming. We have made a number of suggestions along the way concerning possible improvements of the methodology we have employed here. We hope they will stimulate others to carry forward the work which is needed.

We have no illusions about the foreseeable future. We do not believe that "break-throughs" are in the offing, although new techniques and advances in seemingly unrelated areas may bring unexpected progress. The field is very young, and research in it is exceedingly difficult. Patience and persistence are perhaps the qualities which are most sorely needed at this stage. We should be wary of gimmicks and easy solutions which promise great returns for small investments of time and energy. On the

other hand, there is no reason to believe that efforts to study the phenomena of psychotherapy by the tools of science are foredoomed to failure. The gold (or, as Freud foresaw, the amalgam) is there: the techniques for assaying it are as yet woefully inadequate. Some may feel that
they are not worth developing; others (among whem we should like to be
counted) remain convinced of the lasting value of the "substance." In the
final analysis, it is a question of values—whether a given researcher considers a particular goal worthy of pursuit.

REFERENCES

AUERBACH, A. H. An application of Strupp's method of content analysis to psy-
chotherapy. *Psychiat.*, **26**: 137, 1963.
AULD, JR., F., and MURRAY, E. J. Content-analysis studies of psychotherapy.
Psychol. Bull., **52**: 377, 1955.
BALES, R. F. *Interaction process analysis.* Reading: Addison-Wesley, 1950.
BARTLETT, M. S. Some aspects of the time-correlation problem in regard to tests
of significance. *J. Royal Statist. Soc.*, **98**: 536, 1935.
BARTLETT, M. S. On the theoretical specification of sampling properties of auto-
correlated time series. *Suppl. J. Royal Statist. Soc.*, **8**: 27, 1946.
BELLAK, L., and SMITH, M. B. An experimental exploration of the psycho-
analytic process. *Psychoanal. Quart.*, **25**: 385, 1956.
CHASSAN, J. B. Probability processes in psychoanalytic psychiatry. In J. Scher
(Ed.), *Theories of the Mind.* New York: Free Press, 1962. Pp. 598-618.
COHEN, R. A., and COHEN, M. B. Research in psychotherapy: a preliminary
report. *Psychiat.*, **24**: 46, 1961.
DITTES, J. E. Previous studies bearing on content analysis of psychotherapy. In
J. Dollard and F. Auld, Jr., *Scoring human motives.* New Haven: Yale
University Press, 1959. Pp. 325-351.
GREENACRE, P. The role of transference: practical considerations in relation to
psychoanalytic therapy. *J. Amer. Psychoanal. Ass.* **2**: 671, 1954.
HAGGARD, E. A. *Intraclass correlation and the analysis of variance.* New York:
Holt, Rinehart and Winston, 1958.
HOLT, R. R. Clinical and Statistical prediction: a reformulation and some new
data. *J. abnorm. soc. Psychol.*, **56**: 1, 1958.
JANIS, I. L. The psychoanalytic interview as an observational method. In G.
Lindzey (Ed.), *Assessment of human motives.* New York: Holt, Rinehart
and Winston, 1958. Pp. 149-182.
MARSDEN, G. Content-analysis studies of therapeutic interviews: 1954 to 1964.
Psychol. Bull., **62**: 298, 1965.
QUENOUILLE, M. H. *Associated measurements.* London: Butterworth Scientific
Publications, 1952, Chap. 11.
STRUPP, H. H. A multidimensional system for analyzing psychotherapeutic
techniques. *Psychiat.*, **20**: 293, 1957. (a)
STRUPP, H. H. A multidimensional analysis of technique in brief psychotherapy.
Psychiat., **20**: 387, 1957. (b)

STRUPP, H. H. A multidimensional comparison of therapist activity in analytic and client-centered therapy. *J. consult. Psychol.*, **21**: 301, 1957. (c)

STRUPP, H. H. The psychotherapist's contribution to the treatment process. *Behav. Sci.*, **3**: 34, 1958.

STRUPP, H. H. Patient-doctor relationships: Psychotherapist in the therapeutic process. In A. J. Bachrach (Ed.), *Experimental foundations of clinical psychology.* New York: Basic Books, 1962. Pp. 576-615.

STRUPP, H. H. A further study of psychiatrists' responses in quasi-therapy situations. *Behav. Sci.*, **10**: 113, 1965.

STRUPP, H. H., and WILLIAMS, J. V. Some determinants of clinical evaluations of different psychiatrists. *A.M.A. Arch. gen. Psychiat.*, **2**: 434, 1960.

TOLMAN, R. S. Virtue rewarded and vice punished. *Amer. Psychologist*, **8**: 721, 1953.

WALLACH, M. S., and STRUPP, H. H. Psychotherapists' clinical judgments and attitudes towards patients. *J. consult. Psychol.*, **24**: 316, 1960.

25. Collection and utilization of data in a psychoanalytic psychosomatic study

Peter H. Knapp, Cecil Mushatt, and S. Joseph Nemetz

The naturalistic approach is important in any branch of science where we are ignorant of the crucial variables or where we lack ways to test their relationships experimentally. Such is the situation in much of current psychiatry and psychosomatic medicine. Here the clinical longitudinal study, usually of a small number of cases, provides information obtainable in no other way (Knapp, 1962). However, on the current scene, such intensive studies have been supplanted to a great extent by the effort to experiment, sometimes prematurely, with groups of subjects or by controlled manipulation of various factors. We suggest that in part this tendency has resulted not just from the wish for experimental accuracy but from discouragement over the problems connected with gathering and utilizing data from the clinical therapeutic situation. This is particularly true of psychoanalytic data, which are in some ways the richest, but also the most complex. We have encountered many of these problems in an interdisciplinary study of bronchial asthma.

Our study investigates the broad hypothesis, stated more fully elsewhere, (Knapp, 1963) that asthma in the adult results from a number of necessary conditions which must be met sequentially: these are an allergic predisposition; some type of reinforcement by the environment, resulting in a long term vulnerability or a "sensitized pathway"; some type of short term vulnerability, resulting in heightened sensitivity, which in combination with biological or psychological precipitants results in primitive impulses to take something into the body and powerful physiologic urges toward riddance.

Our behavioral observations have come from both psychoanalytic and psychotherapeutic interviews. We will emphasize the former, although most of what we shall say applies to both. This presentation will discuss some problems concerned with data collection, although our experience in this regard does not differ radically from that of others (Cf. Fox, 1958; Margolin, 1951, and previous authors in this volume). The particular impact of research upon psychoanalysis is the subject of a separate study we

This work was supported by grants from the National Institute of Mental Health (M-7375-5), the Supreme Council of Scottish Rite, and the Boston Psychoanalytic Society.

are conducting. In the present communication our focus will be on the challenging question: how can psychodynamic material be utilized in combination with more quantifiable biologic data?

1. COLLECTION OF DATA

Our study aims to correlate data gathered simultaneously at different levels, the biochemical, the physiologic, and the behavioral.

Biochemical Data

The biochemical variables have been urinary: adrenal steroids and catecholamines, supplemented by some hematologic ones, plasma steroids, and circulating eosinophiles. The chief difficulties in patient cooperation, as can be surmised, have been those connected with urine—missed urinary collections or incomplete ones (as judged by creatinine determinations). Often there have been obvious motives behind these failures, resistance which is usually intimately interwoven with that to the therapist, probably at times influenced by subtly communicated attitudes of investigators, pressing too hard, or not hard enough for the meticulous effort required of the patient. Whatever its precise meaning, we can say that urine collection has great significance for every subject. When one looks at psychoanalytic material after starting it, one cannot but be impressed by the fantasies of exhibitionism, erotic preoccupation with urinary function, concerns over bodily control, and demands of authority in relationship to bodily function. Yet these childhood residuals become assimilated into adult behavior. We are also impressed by the extent to which most subjects succeed in performing this task, with all of its deeper meaning.

Physiologic Observations and Medical Management

Each patient is in the hands of one internist or allergist, who is the person making the actual requests for research cooperation from the subject. Opportunities for misunderstanding and neurotic behavior on the part of the patient are numerous, calling for careful communication between members of the research team. It is generally impossible to keep the patient from being aware of this communication. In fantasy, at least, he usually feels that he is complying with research demands from the therapist. His transference relationship is often split between various members of the team, or complicated in other ways, which must be understood and dealt with if both therapy and research are to proceed.

Psychologic Observations

We have found it desirable to supplement psychiatric interviews by psychologic testing. If standardized, repeatable, and brief, this permits systematic inquiry about quantitative variables, thereby freeing the clinical situation of the need for such inquiry, and repairing gaps which inevitably occur in the interview data. We have chiefly used a manifest affect scale, an adaptation of the adjective checklist technique, assessing six manifest affect dimensions. In addition we have used other instruments, chiefly human and animal drawings, in an effort to get the same type of regular information about more inferential variables which we assess from interview material (Knapp and Bahnson, 1963).

Therapeutic Interviews

Psychoanalytic and psychotherapeutic interviews are our most important source of behavioral data for assessment of the emotional processes which we postulate to be vital to our understanding of asthma and its disturbed physiology. The data is necessarily uneven. We can testify to the fallacy of the all-knowing interviewer. His information, although enormously valuable, is inevitably selective and limited because of therapeutic needs. On the other hand, the very ebb and flow of material reveals an enormous amount about interpersonal fantasy structure, and thus provides important evidence of underlying dynamic patterns. In addition the interview gives feedback about the meaning of all investigative procedures to the patient.

Obviously the patient's extensive involvement in research has profound significance. Our formal compact is that he receives total medical care and "pays" in the form of cooperation as a research subject. It would be naive to let matters rest there and ignore the conflicts between research and therapeutic aims. These exist at all levels in all participants. The patient experiences a special compound of gratification and frustration, with associated guilt. The internist has frequent confusion between his roles of scientist and healer, which he often adopts in alternation, sometimes to the detriment of both. Nor is the experienced psychotherapist immune to similar conflict. He has narcissistic, exhibitionist, and other concerns. We believe that no one procedure per se creates insoluble problems. Not only can patients collect urine but they can tolerate a vast range of procedures if their motivation is sound. Rather it is conflict in the motivational sphere itself, leading to subtle, pervasive, powerful ramifications in transference and countertransference, which can be damaging both to research and to therapy.

Our manifest guiding principle has been that therapeutic considerations have priority. We believe that this attitude gets communicated to the patient and that the inevitable obstacles which occur in management can be worked out, provided that the therapist understands and takes countermeasures in the conduct of both treatment and research. In general, these remedies center around clear separation of therapeutic and investigative processes. An obvious step is to fill the roles of psychotherapist and psychiatric research worker by two different individuals. This has been our strategy in the longitudinal study of a pair of identical twins, discordant for bronchial asthma. Two therapists, not connected with our formal research, have taken the patients into psychoanalytic treatment on a research basis. Even though both therapists are experienced analysts we have provided each of them with supervision, believing that it is not possible to eliminate irrational reactions to the research. When not part of the immediate investigative group, the therapist may feel excluded from it, or regard the research as an interference or threat.

The alternative possibility should also be mentioned. The dedicated investigator may be able to split roles within himself, so that he can, in fact, be therapist and at a later date examine his own work with relative detachment, the position advocated by Freud (1912). A true scientific curiosity, if free of conflict, may be experienced as helpful by the patient; and certainly it may lead to a richer understanding of his material.

A last measure, helping to prevent therapeutic disruptions, is varying the schedule of data gathering. We have been interested in the formation yielded by periods of one or two weeks of intensive study along with daily urine collection. We have also felt it important to have periods of "psychotherapy as usual," free from added research burdens. Thus we try to elicit the patient's maximum cooperation at certain times and to give him at other times a chance to work out the meaning of the research.

Tape recording of interviews illustrates these issues. With some exceptions we now record all interviews continuously, stating in advance to both patient and therapist that a vast majority of the recording will have to be discarded. Carried out in this way from the start of therapy, tape recording becomes the "normal" atmosphere of the sessions. Thus reactions are lessened in both participants. Our impression is that of the two the therapist is more chronically disturbed by the procedure. Unlike the patient he does not think of the situation as one in which exposure of himself is an intrinsic and necessary evil. As a further note, in our particular scheme of data collection, we have found it vital that the therapist should not depend upon the memory of the tape recorder but should keep his own notes. Tape recording adds many dimensions which lend themselves to use in supervision and teaching as well as in research; but it is hard to grasp the broad sweep of a case over weeks from the voluminous verbatim record.

We have not worked with film and only minimally with direct visual observation. This in spite of the fact that the processes we are studying have to do with emotion. Obviously we lose information, but it is important to remember the kind of question we are trying to answer. As in many studies our problem is not the paucity of information but its superabundance. If one works with more detailed media, one rapidly reaches limits of ground that can be covered. As we will show later, one can obtain extraordinarily useful information and valuable intercorrelations, working from detailed analytic notes. Actually there seems to be a continuum, proceeding from direct audio-visual observations, to utilization of sound recorded tape itself, to working with typescript, to therapist's notes, or even to the report of his contacts with a supervisor. One proceeds from less to more distortion, in terms of what actually took place. As regards impingement on the psychoanalytic situation itself, the spectrum of distortion is in the reverse direction.

If one works with less than verbatim material, the most significant omission is clear and consecutive information as to what the therapist did. When this is required, one needs, at the least, a verbatim typescript.

Two further problems of collection concern timing. In our psychophysiologic and psychoendocrine investigation, detailed observations, which can necessarily be only samples of the extensive course of events, must converge on the same time segment. Our unit has been the 24 hours during which a patient collects urine. Medical assessment covers that span, using a systematic questionnaire about symptoms and medication (Knapp and Nemetz, 1957). Psychotherapeutic data is in ways more difficult, although, as we have stated, it is supplemented by systematic psychological assessment. We attempt to reconstruct the 24-hour period from information provided in the interview. In addition we can examine the course of acute emotional fluctuations and symptomatic flare-ups of asthma, occurring not in hours but in minutes, on an ad hoc clinical basis.

Naturally samples must throw light on the phenomena under scrutiny; here these are the vicissitudes of asthma. Our plan has been to study three conditions: remission, established asthma, and the onset of acute exacerbations. The last is the most elusive. A predetermined schedule may or may not coincide with crises in the disease. We have had to modify data collection according to individual patterns. In this regard pragmatic use of prediction to anticipate times of flux has proved a useful tool.

For example, a 22-year-old student suffered from chronic asthma, which had markedly intensified around the time of his marriage in the spring prior to his starting in our project. When he did start, his wife had just become pregnant. We predicted that as delivery approached he would have a marked exacerbation of his illness. The prediction was frighteningly confirmed. In the eighth month of her pregnancy, he had a fulminating attack of asthma, complicated by infection, which nearly cost him his life.

Predictions of similar stresses, such as separations and other naturally occurring events, have in a similar way modified collection, and served as guidelines for intensive study of segments of our total material.

2. UTILIZATION OF DATA

The selection of particular behavioral variables for study poses separate problems. Recognizing the hazards of pseudo-quantification and fragmentation of a complex field, we nevertheless believe in the feasibility and value of applying quantitative scales to clearly defined dimensions. We began this task by studying a limited number of manifest emotions. Even here we meet problems in deciding, from the wide variety of cues each subject furnishes, which of his emotional responses are actually *manifest*. Our crude clinical criterion has been: would the patient answer "yes," if he were stopped at a given moment and asked whether this or that bit of material indicates this or that predefined feeling? Using seven-point scales of intensity we obtained acceptable reliability in assessing a number of emotions and even some agreement with the patient's own self-rating test results. We realize that the value of such emotional variables is limited. It is often not emotion which the patient is able to report but storms below the surface which are crucial.

In an attempt to define still further what is "below the surface" we encounter semantic issues connected with the term *unconscious emotions* (Knapp, 1958; Knapp and Bahnson, 1963). Pragmatically we mean powerful motivational constellations which when fully expressed would result in strong felt emotion. The problem is to spell out such elements in operational terms. In the sense that factors remain unconscious because they somehow threaten the adaptive balance of the organism, a vast array of unconscious processes must be thought of as "emotional." Yet they are not all equally active at any given immediate moment. Varieties and levels must be distinguished. Some processes are inferred because of their very absence, or because of the existence of countermeasures; others are expressed with varying degrees of completeness, either symbolically disguised or displaced from the primary object arousing them.

We have arbitrarily limited ourselves to certain unconscious aspects. We further have tried to individualize these for each patient. The most important of these we have called "Constellations of Self-Other Fantasy." These are inner guiding fantasies which can be distinguished repetitively in patients. They are the type of mental phenomena referred to as self-images and introjects, or more recently by Jacobson (1964) as the "Self and Object World." They are, of course, a composite of identifications and relationships to others; they have both instinctual and ego components. We find that they vary strikingly in our subjects, though what we postulate about them is undoubtedly valid for a much wider population.

Our choice, then, has been not to attempt quantification of the deepest inferred fantasy level. This can be called the level of *hidden motivational* processes. They themselves remain defended against, inaccessible, and tend to be constant from day to day. Yet they continuously stimulate other more clearly discernible emotional reactions, which often fluctuate strikingly. It is these latter which we have chosen to assess, in our *self-other* fantasies. We have called them *emergent expressive* constellations. These are fantasies having unconscious elements, but also a variety of preconscious and even conscious derivatives. In the next section we shall illustrate our concept of these and our results from assessing them repetitively.

In addition to manifest emotions and latent fantasies, we have felt it important to study factors having to do with general control. After working with a number of concepts, we have settled on a variable called *ego-regulation*. This we conceptualize as representing the activity of a mature part of the personality; it tends to damp down the effects of pathologic thought, action, or emotion. As this control is impaired, these effects increase, although the direction and quality of the pathologic trend varies. Therapeutic *splitting* or *alliance* can be seen as special instances of this variable. Impairment of it is similar to what Menzer-Benaron and her group have called ego-disruption (Menzer-Benaron, 1964).

Our general approach has been to try to establish relationships between behavioral and biologic findings. We have used three specific techniques: precise correlation on the basis of independent ratings, prediction on the basis of more global judgment, and clinical configurational analysis.

A wide variety of correlational techniques are available to compare sets of data, varying in their quantitative precision. Insofar as one can demonstrate mathematical relationships between them the sureness of one's understanding is advanced. In the case material to follow we shall illustrate this approach. The problem it poses is still that of incomplete knowledge. We do not know how deeply our behavioral categories penetrate the complexity of human behavior. More subtle yet important relationships, which evade our crude quantitative net, no doubt exist. Clinical judgment must still supplement attempts at measurement.

Yet what clinician, given a set of findings, cannot discover an explanation for them, after the fact? It is difficult to sort out the role played by bias. One form of control is to use prediction. Besides being put to pragmatic use in guiding the design of data collection, prediction is a way to test the power of judgments which are based on a combination of factors or patterns which are difficult to measure. A desirable feature of the predictive approach in this type of psychosomatic study is that we have a clear, measurable, outcome variable. Feedback of information can be rapid and precise and can lead to progressive refinement of hypothesis. Further discussion of the predictive tool can be found elsewhere (Knapp, 1962). It has pitfalls of its own. The success or failure of a given set of predictions may be hard to interpret; but at least it is free of *post hoc* bias.

Correlation and prediction, no matter how successful, do not exhaust the study of this type of detailed material. Our approach is still naturalistic. This means painstaking search and re-search for new understanding, manifested as new configurations. For example, phases of behavior may stand out, even though their total significance is not clear, and may serve as a basis for looking at a clustering of other variables (the technique used by Sachar *et al.*, 1964, in their study of acute schizophrenia). Hypotheses derived from such configurational analyses lend themselves for subsequent testing.

Case Example: Two Periods of Intensive Study of a Severe Asthmatic

Detailed observations from one psychoanalytic patient will illustrate our approach.

The patient was a male in his early 30's undergoing prolonged psychoanalysis for severe bronchial asthma, associated with a severe personality disorder marked by transvestitism. Elsewhere (Knapp, 1960; Knapp and Bahnson, 1963), we have given some details of his life. He was the oldest of a large family, raised by a mother who was alternately indulgent and harsh, and who quarrelled with an irresponsible father. The patient suffered from long-standing disease, rheumatic fever at the age of six, followed by progressively more severe asthma, which subsided briefly during a period of military service, only to recur with extended violence after his marriage.

In another publication (Knapp, Carr, Nemetz, and Mushatt, 1964) we will more fully describe some of the psychobiologic correlations from these experiments. Here we wish to emphasize our methods of psychologic study and the gain derived from careful behavioral observations alone.

We will present data from two periods of intensive study, an earlier period of approximately three weeks one winter and a later period of approximately one month the following summer. During both periods the patient was collecting urine continuously. During the second period his analytic hours were tape recorded and he was taking a daily manifest affect self-rating scale. All of these procedures were familiar to him from earlier periods of analysis.

Variables and Methods

From interview material three judges assessed independently a group of manifest emotions, chief of which were anxiety, anger, sadness, and erotic feeling, each along a seven-point scale of intensity.

With regard to less conscious processes, the patient appeared to be dominated by extremely primitive wishes and impulses. These were relatively enduring, yet also deeply protected and inaccessible. He was dependent, overwhelmed with terror, rage, and despair when faced with separation. In many ways he was poorly differentiated from the object of his dependence, originally his mother. Thus, his ego structure was also immature and his capacity for insight limited. His primitive fantasies, *oral* in the developmental sense, represented what we called a *hidden motivational* constellation.

Despite these persistent primitive features his day-to-day behavior showed sweeping fluctuations. In these we could distinguish four patterns of identification and other-person fantasy, having unconscious elements, but containing also preconscious and even some conscious components. These we refer to as *emergent-expressive* constellations. Each of the four patterns appeared to represent some attempt at solution of his deeper conflicts. We defined them for this individual as follows:

1. *"Progressive" constellation.* This expressed the fantasy "good boy," obeying and pleasing his parents, particularly the strict, religious mother, hence suppressing his instinctual manifestations, trying to master infantile feelings and impulses, renouncing concrete cravings (though still expecting a reward, as though from a good parent). This constellation represented the highest developmental level this patient attained, though one in which he was still not completely differentiated. It provided the basis for the highest degree of therapeutic alliance he was able to attain. Although freer of anxiety and guilt than the other constellations mentioned below, this "progressive" position meant for him the *loss of pleasure* and of satisfaction.

2. *"Perverse-Pseudogratified" constellation.* This second constellation expressed the illusion that his concrete cravings were being gratified either directly or by substitutive sexual activity. The chief form of this was wearing female clothes, clearly linked associatively to apparel of his mother's. Of this he said "it's like crawling right up inside her." His transvestitism was often accompanied by sexual activity with his wife, or by masturbation. Frequently these practices were aided by ingestion of alcohol and other drugs. Anal and phallic impulses were often intermixed with predominantly oral ones. In his fantasies about self and other person he was largely fused with and incorporating his mother—thus denying her loss, and turning erotically to a masculine object, ultimately the father. These urges, reactivated in the transference, were frightening and remained unclear to him.

3. *"Somatized" constellation.* A third constellation was defined in which he appeared to express through his body and then illness the fantasy of gaining love and nurturance. Thus he attempted to solve his depressive dilemma in a different way. His urges to take in were *oral,* destructive, and often accompanied, too, by primitive notions of impregnation. They led to fearful guilty eliminative urges. In this stage the other person was the nurturing mother; he was the sick child, who by suffering secured love but then paid the price for it. He was also fused to the maternal image. He not only extorted care from the environment but regulated the flow of supplies himself, playing both mother and child.

4. Finally we defined a *"Depleted" constellation.* This expressed the fantasy of himself as a small infant, whose great and very concrete needs were being frustrated, leading to rage and longing, and a mute appeal for love through these affects alone. The other person was fantasied as the all-important mother upon whom he was profoundly dependent (or at times as the "mothering father," with whom he sought to replace her). He felt undifferentiated and helpless, suffering from oscillations of overt rage and sadness. Mixed with his helplessness was guilt over the destructiveness of his impulses. Insofar as this regressive constellation gained strength, it came closer than the others to expressing overtly his deep, hidden fantasies.

These constellations differed in their degree of developmental maturity, the *Progressive* being relatively more mature, the others relatively more immature. In addition the *Depleted* predisposed toward painful affect; the others included varying types of satisfaction. The constellations were not conceived as mutually exclusive. One usually tended to serve as a defense against the others, although rarely was the defense total. More often competition was raging between more than one. Thus we made ratings on all four simultaneously. Seven-point scales were constructed for each, based on the degree to which the constellation was sustained, how completely mobilized it was, and to what extent a major part of current behavior was organized around it.

In the second period of intensive study the constellation *Depleted* was not used but instead a closely related one was employed called *Loss of Defensive Control over Primitive Oral Conflict.*[1] This approached the *ego regulation* variable (mentioned above) with which we are now working.

During the two periods of study these manifest emotions and fantasy constellations were rated independently by three judges, one of whom was the treating analyst. The analyst had had some opportunity to become aware of the biologic findings of the first period. The other two judges were kept in strict ignorance of these. Indeed, they rated a more extended period in which the exact interval of experimental observations was concealed from them by use of edited notes. For the second experimental period all three judges were completely "blind" as to biologic findings. In studying the second period they worked from tape recordings of analytic sessions as well as from analytic notes.

Similarities and differences between the two types of material appear in the following samples. These are: (1) the transcription of the analyst's notes taken during one hour in the second experiment, and (2) a transcription of the first 10 minutes of the taped interview for the same day.

In both samples the analyst's interventions are capitalized. *Italics* indicate material underlined by the analyst while taking notes. ". . ." indicate analyst's original notation of continued conversation not completely covered in notes. S stands for sigh.

A. Analyst's Notes: July 25, Wednesday, Mr. B.

1. *First ten minutes* (Notes)
(Doctor 12 minutes late.) (Long pause) Where to, Doc? When do you leave? CLARIFY REALITIES. *PRESSED FOR ASSOCIATIONS.* "*10 days of asthma, 15 days without . . . a cycle every month.*" KEEP GOING. That's what's happening now. Once a month. Shit. (pause) *PRESSED FOR ASSOCIATIONS.* Not too happy about way things going—battling asthma, and drugs. Free for weeks, then fighting all over again. . . Takes

---

[1] Actually our detailed ratings of this second period took place prior to that of the earlier one. The *Loss of Defensive Control* was a more discriminating variable but this fact only emerged later after statistical analysis of the ratings of both periods.

about a week to stop taking drugs—then he's back sick again. . . . No fucking good. (pause) "As the moon turns. . . ." Gets so after a while so doesn't give a shit about anything. . . . Hard to get back to work. . . . Off the kymograph. MEANWHILE HE AS PERSON LOST. . . AS I SAID—Angry. He is working hard here; but discouraged—here—and at work. Not needed at home or at work. . . . Starts out here with tear in his eye. Yesterday just no ambition for everything. Everything was "neuter." He was "just a stick." . . . Not happy at all.

2. Remainder of Hour (Notes)

Has to keep going. *Against drinking with Gallagher.* Or yesterday *versus Demerol.* . . . What kind of deal is that—to fight against those feelings. . . . Wish for easy way out. Rotten thing. He's standing still. No enthusiasm. Gets nothing from here. Only a chance to open his eyes—doesn't like it. That's why didn't feel like coming—or talking yesterday. . . . And if feels a certain way, he can *influence reality by his will.* Legitimate reasons come up.

Completely free of asthma until right now. Now wheezes coming up. That's why doesn't like to look at self. Makes him sad. Feels like asshole; weekend rough, as it was . . . he was nervous, all shook up. . . . Maybe he should be in-patient, let someone else take over when severe asthma. With Wally this A.M. who suggested he go to Texas. That might be the answer. . . . Get away from what life here. ME? No that—reason against going. Not having me or Carr to talk to . . . (Pause) Demerol. (Pause) Me or Gallagher. Wants to get away. Not have to worry . . . but fears getting dependent on me or Gallagher. . . . Spit out pill when Ma told him to take it. Doesn't like to look at self. . . . His mood. . . .

Kids at grandparents today. Sad. . . . Feels good that David saved a life swimming—but chokes up with sadness. . . . Kids getting older. Bothered. Wants people to rely on him. Bothered by not being needed when gets back to work after illness. . . . Almost stopped off with Gallagher at bar. . . . Shit. . . . When sick it's a "lost weekend." He vegetates. Lives on nourishment that comes out of tubes. LOSES ALL AMBITION. Agrees. He becomes a "nothing." . . . Should come here when has ambition. Doesn't mind struggling when feels is getting somewhere. . . . Whole picture looks good. . . . Not today. . . . Not asthma. Few whiffs on atomizer. . . . Just lethargy. . . . Always that way with illness. . . . Suddenly after a while he rounds corner, then gets started. Hasn't happened yet. . . . Then will get going and what happens. Pow: hit in kisser with breathing trouble . . . not happy picture. That's why doesn't come. . . .

Not really having trouble, yet is sighing and it's similar to way he struggles to get something out with asthma. (Experiments with breathing.) Likes to get stuff out. ALMOST AS IF PARTLY WANTS TO HAVE SOMETHING INSIDE TO GET OUT. Denies—then confirms. It would be excuse for letting go. . . . It's just as bad as drinking but doesn't start voluntarily. If it comes in "back" that's another thing. If Dr. L. gives him injection, then gets asthma, that's her fault. Curses her as fucking Irish Catholic bitch. . . . Though Grandma Munroe was beautiful—never angry at her. Was at Ma. FOCUS ON THAT:

GETS MAD AT ME AND DR. L. HARD TO CAPTURE FEELINGS TO-WARD MA—Blasts Dr. L. more. Did get mad at Ma when wouldn't let him do what he wanted. And at Pa . . . and at Ma when she beat him. REMEM-BER? Equivocates. . . . Pause. Shit. Will go home and vegetate . . . will go back to work. (Pause) So what do I want from him. WHAT DOES HE WANT FROM ME? Good question. Mulls over his sadness. "BASIC DEPRESSION." What do I mean? THAT UNDERNEATH HE'S FULL OF LONGING. PART OF HIM WANTS TO BE SICK. . . . Insists he doesn't feel any of that. CLARIFY: UNCONSCIOUS PROBLEM—Wants drink . . . but can't see it as such. . . Can't see ties or connections. . . . Tries not to get mad when I say part of him wants to get sick. . . . *PART OF HIM GETS ANGRY?* Yes.

B. Typescript, Mr. B. July 25* First 10 Minutes

(Sighs—pause—sighs—yawns) Where to, Doc? You're going when? When are you leaving? 10TH OF SEPTEMBER. 10th of September. ROUGHLY. EITHER THE 10TH OR THE 11TH. That's right after Labor Day anyway. WHAT DID YOU MEAN WHEN YOU SAID WHERE TO? I don't know. Where to from here? (Yawns) WHAT COMES TO YOUR MIND? Ten days of asthma, 15 days without, or something like that. It's a cycle every month. YES, KEEP GOING. SEE WHAT ELSE COMES TO MIND. A CYCLE EVERY MONTH. That's what's happening right now. Once a month. (yawns) Shit. WHAT ELSE DOES IT BRING TO YOUR MIND? I don't know. Not too much of anything, I guess. I'm not too happy about the way things are going. I find myself battling asthma periodically, battling—battling against drugs for a period, then I'm free from asthma for about a week, and then fighting asthma for another week, and then starting the same goddam thing all over again. That's the way it seems. It takes about a week to stop taking drugs or for the effects of them to get over, and then usually from it it seems no more than 12 or 15 days I'm without heavy medication. I live for two fucking weeks every month or whatever it amounts to. This is no good. As the moon turns. It gets so after a while that I really don't give a shit about nothing. (yawns) It's a hard job to get back to work, do this trip. It progresses until I hit the bottom of the paper with the kymograph and then it starts back the other way. (yawns) MEANWHILE, AS I SAY, WE LOSE TRACK OF YOU. As a person? AS A PERSON AND AS A PERSON WITH PROBLEMS. IT ALL GETS HID BE-HIND THE ASTHMA. WHEN YOU'RE SICK YOU DON'T WANT TO TALK ABOUT ANYTHING BECAUSE YOU FEEL SICK. WHEN YOU'RE WELL YOU DON'T WANT TO TALK ABOUT IT BECAUSE YOU'VE JUST BEEN SICK. I don't know. I talk about it during periods that I'm fairly well. If anything, I've been coming more steady during this last stretch than I have any fucking time during the time I've been having asthma, Doc. I don't know what the hell I've gotten out of it. Do you? I get discouraged sometimes and I think I'm hitting a period of discouragement right now. It not only has to do with the way things are going, but like I say it's the withdrawal from medication, it's the other things that happen, it's the events that happen at home and at work.

I see myself at work now as somebody that's really not needed. This is the

* Analyst's remarks are capitalized, as previously.

way it affects me. This goes on, this repeats itself. It isn't something that changes. I'll get back to work after being out and I don't see things as a person that I'm needed at work—somebody that's really needed at home or something— just a fucking drag, and that's the way I feel right now. The whole fucking thing's a drag. I don't even think it outside. It pops out here. I don't know how it pops out. It starts out the other day with a tear in my eye. Yesterday it was nothing. I didn't do anything when I got home. I didn't feel like it. Watch television, I had supper—no feelings to speak of at all. I couldn't put any of the card sort items in the right hand column or in the far right or in the first two rows. They just don't work that way. Everything is neuter. I feel, you know, as a stick or something stuck in place with other things going on. I have no ambition. (sighs) The things go. That's how I feel right now. I don't feel happy.

In comparing these parallel samples, it is obvious that much of the detailed flavor of the transaction eludes the notes. Yet they compress an enormous amount. Looking at the ten minutes covered by both we can see that much which appears to be essential was preserved: the immediate presentation of a transference issue which the analyst did not pursue in the detail it demanded, the fantasy of a cyclic lunar disturbance, the effort of the analyst to get behind the symptom to the emotional problem, the prevailing underlying mood of depression. One can even discern in the notes a precise pattern of associations, twice repeated; there is sequential reference to: asthma → magical cyclic disturbance → feces → a state of generalized dissatisfaction. (One might speculate that asthma leads to fantasies of incorporation, which in turn lead to fantasies of elimination, and finally a sense of emptiness.)

We should also recognize that some notation by the analyst is necessary in order to catch the significant fact that he was 12 minutes late for this session. In spite of all they necessarily omit, such notes, which can be more thorough in the analytic situation than in most, give valuable information about on-going day-to-day process.

They leave particular gaps. In our experience at times of rapid or intense interchange the analyst must, if he is not to be rigid and ineffective, minimize his function of note taking and participate actively. Furthermore, he is almost inevitably bound to be a poor observer about himself. This point is dramatically illustrated by the sample presented here. The typescript reveals that the patient asked "When are you leaving" (for vacation) and the analyst, in a speech slip replied with the date on which he was *returning*. Neither participant remarked upon this slip. In fact, the analyst's notation, about his response in this interchange, was the phrase: *"Clarify Realities."* The issue of separation was a charged one, which had been taken up repeatedly, but not at this moment. Actually the slip proved to be tragically prophetic, because on approximately the day in question the patient left the analyst permanently, as we describe elsewhere (Knapp, Mushatt, and Nemetz, 1964).

This bit of detail illustrates our earlier comment that where such data about the therapist's activity is necessary, one must respect the inevitable limitations placed upon him as observer and find other sources of information.

Results

In both the winter and summer periods reported here reliable agreement between judges was obtained, except for the variable "Depleted." (This may be accounted for by the fact that "Depletion" ran so consistently through the material that it was hard to assess its fluctuations.) Table 1 gives the statistical measure of correlation between three judges. Unless stated otherwise subsequent figures will refer to the judges' averaged ratings.

Table 1
Agreement: 3 Judges Rating Interview Variables

	Experimental Period			
Fantasy	No. 1 (Winter) 17 days		No. 2 (Summer) 20 days	
"Constellations"	w	p	w	p
"Progressive"	.622	$<.02$	.684	$<.01$
"Perverse Pseudo-Gratified"	.830	$<.001$	.620	$<.02$
"Somatized"	.638	$<.02$	.861	$<.001$
"Depleted"	.428	$>.10$		
Loss of Defensive Control over oral conflict			.661	$<.01$
Manifest Emotions				
Erotic feelings	.699	$<.01$	.613	$<.02$
Anxiety	.627	$<.02$	.679	$<.01$
Anger	.587	$<.05$	.840	$<.001$
Sadness	.689	$<.01$	.644	$<.01$

w-Kendall's Coefficient of Concordance

Substantively, these were two periods of dramatic, and in some ways, contrasting interest. Both represented periods which had followed exacerbations of asthma that were severe enough to require treatment with ACTH. This had been an intermittent form of therapy for this patient. The question of whether or not his asthma could be controlled without it had become a central issue for him. He had shown a characteristic tendency to relapse symptomatically usually 10 days to three weeks after a course of steroid therapy. Relapse, in turn, was generally ushered in by an intense period of emotional turmoil.

During the first of these experimental periods rebellious behavior had been an additional issue. The patient had been confronted with this forcefully; he had at first reacted with anger and depression. Then had come four highly unusual days, marked by intense, sexually-colored transference emotion. He had been obsessed by positive feelings about the analyst, associated with great anxiety, having elements of both hypomanic excitement and homosexual panic. These positive feelings appeared to be an attempted solution of his intolerable rage and fear of separation.

Figure 1 shows graphically the last two weeks of this period. It plots a quantitative daily estimate of the severity of the asthmatic process. Below that it shows the level of daily urinary 17-hydroxycorticosteroid (17-OHCS) excretion. At the bottom it plots the ratings of *"Depleted"* constellation, and *Erotic* emotion.

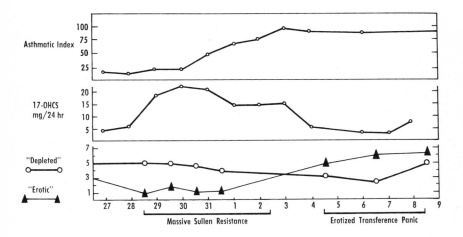

Figure 1
Asthma, Steroids, and Behavior—"B," Winter, 2 Weeks

As we discuss more fully elsewhere (Knapp, Carr, Nemetz and Mushatt, 1964) there was concomitant rise in corticosteroid excretion preceding the asthmatic relapse during this period accompanied by specific emotional tension. The time course of this is shown in Figure 1, not in the two dimensions charted there but in the *massive sullen resistance* characterizing this period: he was surly, covertly rebellious, and disgruntled. Then there was a dramatic swing of his feelings from hostility to intense erotic anxiety. Contrary to our preliminary expectations, the curve of corticosteroid excretion showed a pronounced dip during this interval (cf. Figure 1). During the whole experimental period there were significant negative correlations between 17-OHCS levels in urine and erotic emotion ($r_s = -0.66$ p $< .025$) and anxious emotion ($r_s = -0.70$ p $< .025$).

Figures 2 and 3 and Table 2 give a more detailed view of the psychological variables during this period. They are based on judges' ratings of 17 consecutive interviews. As indicated earlier, these included the period of experimental urine collection, although two of the judges remained in ignorance of exactly when this period occurred. Figure 2 shows the summed ratings of the underlying "constellations." Figure 3 shows the four manifest emotions, *Erotic feelings, Anxiety, Anger,* and *Sadness.*

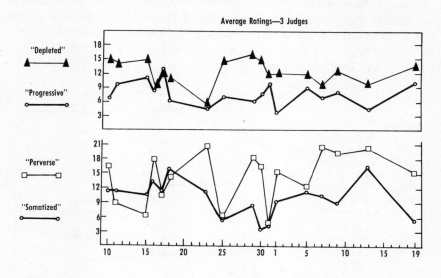

Figure 2

Varying Latent "Constellations"—"B," Winter, 17 Days

Table 2 shows a matrix of correlations obtained by the Spearman Rank Ordering technique (Rho). It illustrates the additional information obtained by such treatment of the data. A variety of patterns, difficult to discern with certainty by eye alone, reveal themselves in the mathematical relationships. Of 28 correlations, 10 are significant at better than the .05 level of confidence. (r_s + or −0.49) and two more are of borderline significance (r_s −0.35 and −0.46).

Looking at Table 2 in conjunction with Figures 2 and 3 the data to some extent confirm logical clinical expectations, to some extent suggest idiosyncratic features in this patient at this time. Among the "constellations," "Progressive" and "Depleted" show a weak positive correlation. So do "Somatized" and "Perverse-Pseudogratified." Figure 3 reveals that at times the members of each of these pairs vary together strikingly, at other times less so. Basically the "Somatized" and "Perverse-Pseudogratified" constellations appear to be in the service of defense against the patient's prevailing depression. This postulation is further supported by the striking

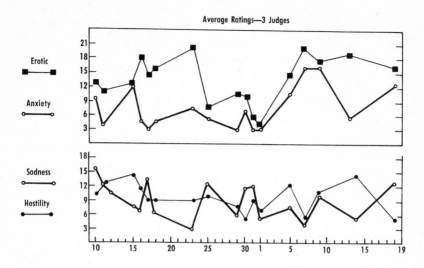

Figure 3

Varying Manifest Emotions—"B," Winter, 17 Days

inverse relationship between "Progressive" and "Perverse-Pseudogratified" ($r_s = -0.57$) and between "Depleted" and "Somatized" ($r_s = -0.51$).

These patterns do not show simple co-variance but instead reveal a complex interplay. The positive correlation between a "Progressive" stance and "Depleted" elements, we suspect, represents an ability to express attitudes connected with loss when the therapeutic alliance was strong; but at the same time adoption of a mature role implied for this man a sense of losing everything. As that would mount, "Progressive" elements would

Table 2

Correlation (Rho) Matrix of Psychological Variables (Patient B—Winter Experiment)

	"Progressive"	"Depleted"	"Perverse"	"Somatized"	Erotic	Anxious	Hostile
"Depleted"	+.23						
"Perverse"	−.57**	−.32					
"Somatized"	−.28	−.51*	+.28				
Erotic	+.14	−.65**	+.71**	+.64**			
Anxious	−.03	−.01	−.06	+.03	+.49*		
Hostile	+.14	+.11	+.19	+.56**	−.11	+.24	
Sad	+.67**	+.50*	−.61**	−.35	−.46	−.03	−.01

* p < .05
** p < .01

start to recede. Similarly "Perverse-Pseudogratified" and "Somatized" constellations appear to represent alternative defensive postures. Their weak positive correlation shows that they emerge with some degree of overlap; the incompleteness of the correlation is consistent with belief that, during this period, one was invoked when the other failed and vice versa.

Among the manifest emotions there is a negative correlation as might be expected, between *Sadness* and *Erotic* feeling. More idiosyncratic is the striking positive correlation obtained between *Erotic* and *Anxiety* ($r_s = +0.49$). This underlines the pervasive nature of anxiety-tinged erotic feeling during this particular period, highlighted clinically as several days of near homosexual panic.

The interrelationships between the latent fantasy "constellations" and the manifest emotions also confirm clinical expectation. This may partially reflect a redundancy in our efforts to formulate unconscious elements. For example, *Sadness* correlates negatively with "Perverse-Pseudogratified" and positively with the "Depleted" constellation, which tells us little new. Of more interest is the striking positive correlation between *Sadness* and "Progressive" constellation. The more "grown-up" this patient became the greater was his mood of nostalgia and sense of losing something. *Erotic* feeling tended to follow a reverse pattern: it correlated positively with "Perverse-Pseudogratified" and negatively with "Depleted."

In this psychosomatic study the "Somatized" variable was of the greatest interest to us. First we should mention that it correlated significantly with independent measurement of his asthmatic manifestations by our internists ($r_s = +0.65$ p $< .05$). For the winter period "Somatized" correlated strongly with *Erotic* feelings, negatively with "Depleted," and negatively with *Sadness*, thus supporting our view that "Somatization" was used as a further defense, when his "Perverse-Pseudogratified" behavior failed to ward off painful feelings.

"Somatized" also showed a strong positive correlation with *Hostile* emotion, the significance of which was more obscure. We can only interpret it clinically. This man seldom experienced directly his deepest and most destructive impulses. These emerged in disguised form, we suspect, in his very symptoms. However, when he was asthmatic, he felt a sort of legitimate "righteous indignation," leading to profuse cursing, swearing, and marked irritability at those around him. The judges' ratings appeared to reflect this *layer* of hostile emotion.

These patterns reveal in this primitive man the picture of two primitive systems in interaction: a dysphoric one, characterized by massive interrelated depressive feelings and fantasies; and a euphoric one, characterized by perverse erotic attempts to ward off pain. "Somatization" appeared at this point to be a supplementary type of defense against dysphoria, tending partially to coincide in time with his perverse defensive trends, and also accompanied by a limited expression of hostile feeling. Anxiety at this juncture was specifically associated with erotic feelings, especially in the transference situation.

The second experiment will be discussed only briefly here. It is treated more extensively in another communication (Knapp, Carr, et al., 1964). In this the judges worked from tapes and typescripts as well as from the analyst's notes. As can be seen from Table 1, their agreement was not significantly changed. Their understanding was perhaps deeper, particularly of the activities of the analyst, though also of the fine detail of the patient's communications.

It was also possible during this period to compare the patient's self-ratings with those of the judges on certain dimensions. What emerged was a similar pattern, although not overall statistically significant agreement. Aberrant days, on which the subject rated himself very low or very high in intensity, generally seemed responsible for the discrepancies. By the usual measures of agreement only the affect of *Sadness*, as rated by judges and by the subject, showed a statistically significant correlation ($r_s = +0.646$ $p < .025$). Figure 4 shows ratings of the judges and self-ratings of the patient on this affect over a 30-day period. Along with it are shown the patient's Asthmatic Index, scored independently by the internist, and his 17-OHCS excretion. It can be seen that despite the configurational agreement there is still a striking quantitative difference in intensity between the clinical ratings and the patient's self-ratings of sadness; the latter are low at the start and rise abruptly at the end of this experiment. This in-

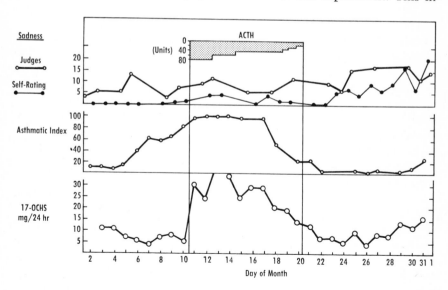

Figure 4

Sadness, Asthma, and Steroid Excretion—"B," Summer, 30 Days

creasing, overt sadness, paralleled by other ratings reflecting depressive emotion, is marked in the last days of this period of study. At the same time there is minimal increase in asthma. This patient was almost at his best physiologically during this phase. As described elsewhere (Knapp, Carr, *et al.*, 1964), this intensity of affect, with minimal expression in the sphere of physiologic symptoms, coincided with a striking increase in another variable, entitled "Loss of Control Over Primitive Oral Conflicts," and at the end, with a brief period of marked fluctuation in 17-OHCS excretion.

This second experiment occurred some time after a major effort on the part of the patient to give up his "Perverse-Pseudogratified" transvestite behavior. Partly as a consequence of this there was, during this period, only minimal evidence of this type of fantasy constellation or of associated manifest erotic affect. On a basis of experience with the winter period, judges, while still blind to biochemical findings for the summer, predicted that if this material did appear it would be accompanied by decrease in his hydroxycorticosteroid excretion. On only one day did he show the faintly hypomanic, highly sexualized material which had been prominent in the earlier period. The specific "blind" prediction was made that this day would reveal a dip in his curve of corticoid excretion. In another communication (Knapp, Carr, Mushatt and Nemetz, 1964) we present the evidence confirming this prediction.

CONCLUDING REMARKS

Elsewhere (Knapp, Carr, Mushatt and Nemetz, 1964) we discuss the extent to which it is possible to generalize findings such as these from one case. We indicate the need for verification by repetition of observations, both in the single individual and in comparable subjects. Here we stress our approach, a flexible, partly individualized study, working toward repeated, quantitative behavioral ratings which can be compared with biologic data.

The approach raises a number of problems. To what extent are judgments really independent, and to what extent influenced by subtle communication between judges, or by shared bias? Ideally, it can be argued, one would strive for a system of rating objective enough to be carried out by a clerk or some other theoretically neutral person. Such systems have been developed by Gottschalk (1963) and other authors mentioned in this volume. We have chosen the alternative strategy of using the "human observer as measuring instrument" (Heyns and Lippitt, 1954), relying on his trained sensibilities to judge complex variables, and exerting our efforts to control the independence of his judgments. It is not always possible to be certain how successful such efforts were. For some purposes absolute success may not be essential. If judgments are truly "blind" with respect to an external criterion of validation, like a biologic finding, and if the predictive power of those judgments can be gauged accurately, they are valuable.

Much thus depends on the external criterion. When one attempts to use this method without such a clear criterion the picture is more complicated. In attempting intercorrelations between psychologic variables we were plagued by the possibility that we were not rating truly distinct categories. For that reason it did not seem worthwhile to attempt more sophisticated study of this data, as might be possible, for example, by multiple regression techniques or by factor analysis.

Obviously, quantification is not a necessary virtue in itself. We would stress again the importance of examining material globally, clinically, naturalistically, and the continued search for naturally occurring units and patterns. However, psychoanalysis and clinical psychiatry have been doing that alone for some time. If scientific advance is to take place, some of the abundant hypotheses which have been derived from purely clinical study must be subjected to more detailed examination. We are impressed by the need for rigorous definition of clearly separate aspects of behavior. When these have been identified they can be scrutinized in various ways to test the durability of apparent regularities and to discover others that are not readily apparent. We regard our efforts to rate a number of manifest affects and certain related less conscious constellations as a preliminary step toward getting the tools which are essential for genuine advance in psychoanalytic knowledge.

Another question relates to distance from the actual interview transaction. We have mentioned a continuum of distortion that takes place as one relies upon an increasingly abridged record. Our data does not contain the wealth of information one finds in a sound film. However, fascinating as such detail is, it may be equally valuable to find ways for dealing with the regularities of broad, underlying fantasy. These are the bedrock of dynamic psychiatry. They are not directly accessible by any technique. In our type of day-to-day and week-to-week study, condensed material has proved to be a highly effective way to get at them.

Our experience actually suggests that all types of material, verbatim recordings, analyst's notes, and also the introspections of the analyst, contain valuable information. Depending upon the questions being asked, they may all be important in a flexible research approach.

In *summary*, our methods in a clinical, longitudinal, psychosomatic study consist of: (1) data collection at various levels, in a psychoanalytically informed setting, which attempts constantly to minimize mutual interference between therapeutic and research aims; (2) selection for study of certain meaningful, quantitatively scaled psychodynamic variables; (3) independent ratings of these by clinician judges; (4) correlation of ratings with biologic data by a variety of techniques; (5) continued search for relationships by use of global predictions; and (6) continued configurational analysis from a clinical, naturalistic viewpoint.

REFERENCES

Fox, H. Effect of psychophysiologic research on the transference. *J. Amer. Psychoanal. Ass.*, **6**: 413, 1958.

FREUD, S. 1912. Recommendations for physicians on the psychoanalytic method of treatment. *Collected Papers*, Vol. II, p. 327. London: Routledge, 1958.

GOTTSCHALK, L. A., GLESER, G. C., and SPRINGER, K. J. Three hostility scales applicable to verbal samples. *Arch. of gen. Psychiat.*, **9**: 254-279, 1963.

HEYNS, R. W., and LIPPITT. R. Selected quantitative techniques. In G. Lindzey (Ed.), Handbook of social psychology. Cambridge, Mass.: Addison-Wesley, 1954.

JACOBSON, E. The self and object world. New York: International Universities, 1964.

KNAPP, P. H. Conscious and unconscious affects: A preliminary approach to concepts and methods of study. *Psychiatric Research Reports No. 8*, 1958.

KNAPP, P. H. Acute bronchial asthma No. 2. Psychoanalytic observations on fantasy. emotional, arousal, and partial discharge. *Psychosom. Med.*, **22**: 88, 1960.

KNAPP, P. H. Models and methods: A psychodynamic predictive approach to bronchial asthma. *J. nerv. ment. Dis.*, **135**: 5, 1962.

KNAPP, P. H. The asthmatic child and the psychosomatic problem of asthma. In H. I. Schneer, M.D. (Ed.), *The asthmatic child*. New York: Harper & Row, 1963.

KNAPP, P. H., and BAHNSON, C. B. The emotional field—A sequential study of mood and fantasy in two asthmatic subjects. *Psychosom. Med.*, **25**: 5, 1963.

KNAPP, P. H., CARR, H. E., MUSHATT, C., and NEMETZ, S. J. Steroid excretion, emotion, and asthmatic crises. (Delivered at Meeting of American Psychosomatic Soc., San Francisco, Calif., Apr., 1964). *Psychosom. Med.* (In press).

KNAPP, P. H., MUSHATT, C., and NEMETZ, S. J. Asthma, melancholia, and death. I. Psychoanalytic Considerations. *Psychosom. Med.* (In press).

KNAPP, P. H., and NEMETZ, S. J. Personality variations in bronchial asthma: A study of 40 patients. *Psychosom. Med.*, **19**: 443, 1957.

MARGOLIN, S. The behavior of the stomach during psychoanalysis. *Psychoanal. Quart.*, **20**: 349, 1951.

MENZER-BENARON, D. Personal communication, 1964.

SACHAR, E. J., MASON, J. W., KOLMER, H. J., and ARTISS, K. L. Psychoendocrine aspects of acute schizophrenic reactions. *Psychosom. Med.*, **25**: 510, 1963.

4. THE CLIENT-CENTERED MODEL

Shlien and Zimring offer a fascinating review of the theoretical evolution through which so-called Rogerian or client-centered psychotherapy has undergone. The authors demonstrate, with a rich documentation of bibliographical references associated with each stage of theoretical development, the prolific output of naturalistic and experimental research studies carried out by students trained in this psychotherapeutic orientation. The reader will note how Rogers' theoretical model for the psychotherapeutic situation began, during Stage I (1940) of his formulations, with a "theory of therapy restricted almost entirely to operations and consequences in the client," and the name for the therapy (*non-directive*) emphasized the relative inactivity of the therapist. The theoretical formulations passed through Stage II (1947-1951), which provided a theory of personality, a theory of self and of change, and an evalution of outcome. Then the theory progressed through Stage III (1955) and Stage IV (1957) which focused on the setting up of a process whereby the patient acquires self-knowledge and the therapist aims to achieve an optimal attitude toward the patient to effect favorably the psychotherapeutic process and the self-understanding. Some readers may notice how client-centered psychotherapy and theory, with the passage of time, has become more complicated and rather similar in some emphases to psychoanalytic therapy. Client-centered therapy has, for instance, steadily moved toward the consideration of goals (self-knowledge) and parameters (the therapist's attitude toward the patient) which have long been a preoccupying interest of psychoanalysis, although other aspects of the theoretical framework of these types of psychotherapies differ markedly. This similarity of some of the clinical aspects of these two schools of psychotherapy should be recognized when a comparison is made of the results of client-centered and psychoanalytic therapy. (See, for example, Cartwright's chapter in this book.)

26. Research directives and methods in client-centered therapy

John M. Shlien and Fred M. Zimring

INTRODUCTION

Methodology

As a method of research in psychotherapy, we take a school of thought as a subject, examining four stages of development to point out the way in which changing theory leads to particular foci and emphases of investigation. It is our general purpose to present and illustrate a functional-historical outline in research methodology. This consists of the *interplay* of (1) developing stages of theory, (2) empirical lines of investigation stemming from and feeding into theory, (3) instruments and sources of data. This chapter is essentially a study of methodology rather than of methods alone. We believe that only the combination of theory and method as it comes out of a program of thought qualifies as research. A technique is not a method, and a method is not by itself a research. Thinking is research. The rest is isolated fact-finding and dilettantism. It is this program of thought, the life-style of a direction of search and a system of research which we have in mind, not as dry bones of methodology but as living interests of people. The portrayal requires a slice of actual history in which we have a unique opportunity to observe a 25-year period covering the life span to date of one school of therapy. We mean to demonstrate the main line of descent and variation in one program of thought and the interadaptation of associated specimen researches.

Intending to throw only main elements into relief, and within the limits of a single chapter, we cannot present all theories conceived throughout this span. The reader can turn to Standal (1954) and Gendlin (1962) for their extensions. We cannot report more than a fraction of the findings, but many of these are available in the notable landmark in outcome studies, *Psychotherapy and Personality Change* (1954). Nor can we catalogue the scores of research efforts but this has been admirably done by Cartwright in his "Annotated Bibliography" (1957). We will not try to characterize the whole effort by presenting only the most sophisticated and complex products; a book such as Butler-Rice-Wagstaff, *Quantitative Naturalistic Observation* (1963) is a methodological study in itself which does not bear reduction to a resumé. Seeman and Raskin (1953) provide excellent coverage of the first dozen years of development. It is beyond our scope to cover, much less do justice to, many researchers who have made weighty contributions to this school. We are working from a narrow perspective which does not admit the whole field of influence but only deals with a *functional microcosm*—a group working so closely in time and space as to be immediately influenced by the shift in theory, or immediately influencing it. These will be primary groups, of which Carl Rogers is an influential and influenced member, working in the Universities of Ohio State, Chicago, and Wisconsin. Because of the immediate functional effect, we will use a dating system which corresponds to the actual schedule of circulation and effect, not publication dates. What we call the "1940 theory" both took effect and was published in 1940, but what we call the "1955 theory" was not published until 1959, with private circulation in the years between. The "1947-51 theory" drew heavily upon the work of Raimy, circa 1943, but was not published until 1948, and upon ideas in Snygg and Combs which were not published until 1949.

Substance

It is then our main intent to present the *natural history* of a set of ideas and methods. First, a digression to relate some actual history and to place this school of thought. Few approaches have such an intense research orientation, or such extensive research production covering so wide a range of methods, as this one. The reasons are worth noting. Client-centered therapy has had an exceptional growth rate, and has grown almost entirely within an academic setting. Most therapies have developed outside universities, and influenced research indirectly and later. Rogers too spent a period of intensive clinical practice during which his views evolved (from an essentially diagnostic base), but when he took his first academic post, he brought with him the new directions of his therapy in a systematic statement already cast in terms which made it a ready research vehicle. When this coincided with the experimental necessities of scholarly careers, many climbed aboard to set off a tradition of hypothesis-and-test which linked research to the therapy from its inception.

Although the new therapy was under pressure to prove itself, both as an upstart going against the main stream and to fit the laboratory atmosphere of American psychology, research was not simply response to the environment. It was rather a consonant expression of one basic thrust of this school of thought: toward a more literal, non-esoteric, fact-based understanding of behavior. Rogers (1960) commented on this in his 1960 review, saying:

There has always been a strong push on the part of those associated with the client-centered orientation to "take a look" at the raw data of psychotherapy. They have not been content with high-flying abstractions, nor descriptions of therapy remote from the actual personal interaction.

The value he places on this thrust is evident as he continues,

It seems probably that whatever memories of different schools of psychotherapy remain 50 years from now, client-centered therapy will at least be remembered for its willingness to take a square look at the facts, at the actual ways in which therapy is conducted, and the operational differences which divide therapists.

Also worth mentioning is the shift from *non-directive* to *client-centered.* This is not incidental revision of nomenclature. It signifies the clarification of a perspective. The reader will see that the therapy and research has always been client-centered. In the second decade of development, it became increasingly clear that *non-directive* is a negative term, a protest contra to *directive,* and misleading in that it suggests merely the absence of direction. Worse, it was not to the main point of the operating theory, which was to stay within the client's complex, shifting, and internal frame of reference. Be, thus, client-centered. In this shift the image of the therapist changes from that of the mirror-like, passively non-influencing listener[1] to that of the sensitive, actively understanding human respondent. What is relevant to research is the way in which this shift in terminology is related to changing assumptions about the therapist's *activity,* with corresponding changes in research interests. When the therapist was viewed as essentially neutral, passive, self-effacing, all therapists would be assumed to be equal, i.e., homogeneous by virtue of their inactivity. When the therapist image changes, the research and theory tend to focus somewhat upon him, though still largely on the client.

Four Stages: The Line of Theoretical Development
Taken as Research Directives

Throughout, the focus of theory is upon *operations* rather than *personality.* This style makes the research orientation. The focus is not upon the static categorical state—an individual's obsessional characteristics, narcissism, introversion, submissiveness, or personality type. Focus is upon the behavioral change, and usually on an *if-then* basis. Given certain conditions (if the therapist, then the client—; or if the client inside therapy, then he will outside—; or if an individual shifts perception, then his behavior, etc.) predictable consequences will follow. The processes are generally examined within the client, often inside therapy itself, but sometimes in the outside world, then called *global.*

---

[1] The apparent passivity and homogeneity seemed entirely characteristic to outsiders. Hoch, in an amusing review of *Psychotherapy and Personality Change* spoke of a "type of treatment that consists of saying nothing to a patient, or at most repeating what he says, acting warmly the while." Of the reported changes, he says "Doubtless many will take heart at such results. They will feel that if such homeopathic psychiatry has measurable effects, other stronger, 'deeper' methods will have correspondingly larger effects." (1954)

Relative Emphasis of Themes and Contexts

Figure 1 is designed to show the relative emphasis of three elements during four periods of time. The elements (therapy, phenomenology, and process theory) interact throughout; but some are more prominent at one time or another. The times, here called *stages* (on the left vertical), are

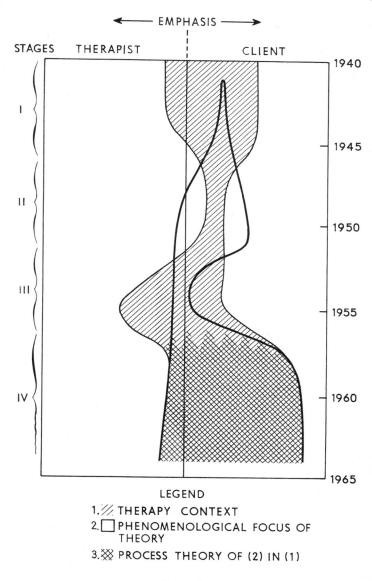

Figure 1

periods in which one or another element takes precedence and directs new phases of research effort. Whether the focus is primarily on one element or another, the emphasis may turn in the direction of therapist or client, as indicated by the center vertical line of the figure. In Stage I, the context is therapy, with emphasis on the client. This is the beginning, in 1940. A thin thread of the phenomenological line begins as an expression of the assumption that there are forces in the client which the therapist needs only to release. In Stage II the line of phenomenology expands to cover developments in the theory of perception and personality which become broader than the shrinking context of therapy. This emphasis changes from one element to another but remains in the client's field. In Stage III, the emphasis shifts for the first time to the therapist, temporarily, while *conditions of therapy* are specified. At this point, the therapist continues to act as a releaser, but his activities expand, while in the client, perception of the therapist's intent is required. In Stage IV, the emphasis returns to the client. Phenomenology again expands, this time in relation to an explanation of experiential processes *within* the client, *in* therapy. Thus all three elements merge. This figure is an approximate visual statement of time spans and the contained research and theoretical emphasis, to help outline what the following text will cover.

It should be understood that currents of influence run back and forth between stages. Researchers may reach back in time for prior directives, and leading theoretical statements were often stimulated by research previously completed. Further, the interaction between stages is additive; not I, II, III, IV, but I, I-II, I-II-III, etc. This is nicely illustrated by the titles of the papers as the stages gather momentum. I was called "The Process of Therapy;" II, "A Theory of Personality and Behavior;" III, "Therapy, Personality, and Interpersonal Relationships."

Characteristics of Stage I (circa 1940)[2]

This (Rogers, 1940) is a theory of therapy restricted almost entirely to operations and consequences *in the client*. It states, as we segment it, that:

If the *client*	and if the *therapist*	and if *both*	then the *client* will
1. feels need of help,	1. operates so as to release rather than intervene,	1. establish rapport,	4. own his expressions,
2. has at least minimal intelligence,			5. recognize and accept his spontaneous self,
3. is not faced by overwhelming environment,			6. make responsible choice,
			7. gain insight,
			8. grow toward independence.

[2] For an easier grasp of the history, each stage is characterized in the same outline of terms: A. Conditions; B. Consequences; C. Focus; and D. Emphasis.

A. The *conditions* reside mainly in the client. This is the beginning of *trust in the organism*, and the source of the phenomenological bent which carries through all the stages.

B. *Consequences* are discrete, non-ordered.

C. *Focus* is the context of therapy.

D. *Emphasis* is on client behavior. The only activity of the therapist, aside from his contribution to rapport, is to release the assumed potential of the client, and to avoid intervention.

Associated Research. This stage led to what has been called *molecular* research. Though relatively little was specified as to the therapist's behavior in Stage I, the therapy was called *non-directive*. This alone introduced a distinction to be studied, and much of the early research attended the questions: What does the therapist actually do? Can non-directive behavior be distinguished from other? The source of the data was verbatim, transcribed interviews, an important innovation in itself. The first study was by Porter (1943). He set up a classification of verbal behavior on a directive-non-directive continuum. Judges found it possible to reliably differentiate between counselors on this continuum, and also to measure the consistency of individual counselor's behavior. The same method was applied a year later by Gump (1944) to Rogerian and psychoanalytic recordings, with the distinctions showing in the predicted directions.

Snyder studied both client and therapist, again using content analysis. He found non-directive therapists to be consistently so (which seemed to end the matter and to leave the therapist as an "assumed" quantity for some time to come). He developed categories for judged analysis of client behavior which showed movement from early to late interviews in emergence of insight, increased planning activity, positive feelings following negative expressions—all fitting the postulated consequences of Stage I theory. In a replication of Snyder's study, Seeman used the same categories and found that non-directive behavior had increased to 85 percent in the later counselors as compared with 63 percent for those in Snyder's cases.

Curran (1945) charted the course of single interviews, carefully inventorying the problems and solutions of the client. He found that problems reduced in number, fell into relationship, and were eventually related to causes. He was dealing with the learning process, and his method of intensive individual study somewhat presaged the later Q-technique.

Bergman (1950) studied the interaction of client and counselor responses. This differs from the earlier studies in that it does not simply tabulate proportions of types of client or counselor behavior in earlier and later phases of therapy, but relates the two as cause and effect. Using category systems similar to those of early studies, it was found that directive (structuring or interpreting) counselor statements were followed by abandonment of self-exploration while counselor's responses classified as non-directive (reflection of feeling) were followed by continued self-exploration or insight. It is interesting to see this later research, carried out in 1950, reaching back to Stage I but executing a more complex study.

The nature of Stage I research contributions may be summarized (except for Raimy's conceptualizing of self-theory) by Raskin's (1952) five steps:

1. The *electrical* recording of cases.
2. The definition of *concepts* which provides an understanding of these cases.
3. The development of objective *measures* of these concepts.
4. The *application* of these measures to the same or similar case material.
5. The interrelating of the results of this application in order to (a) establish the relationships existing between the concepts, and (b) obtain a well-rounded picture of individual cases.

Before moving into the next stage, we note that Stage I, conditions 2 and 3, regarding the client, fade from view. They were not productive of research and did not appear in later theory. Only condition I for the client remains, his *felt need*, a phenomenal quality which will reappear. The condition for the therapist is a somewhat negative statement; it implies much of what is to come in later theory, but for the moment simply says that the therapist will be warm, supportive, but essentially "stay out of the way." He is not powerful, assertive, but *releasing*, so he may be assumed to be an unvarying element. No research is likely to find him a fascinating subject. The vectors of attraction would turn in other directions. But there is the implication of a powerful, highly charged force in the *other* person, the client. This leads to the next stage.

Characteristics of Stage II (circa 1947-51)

This is a phenomenological *theory of personality*, a theory of self and of change. The first statement in 1947 was "Some Observations on the Organization of Personality" (1950). A complete statement is given in the 1951 edition of Roger's book, *Client-centered Therapy*, as the last chapter, "A Theory of Personality and Behavior." It is headed "Implications for Psychological Theory" and, although in a book about therapy, could stand apart from the context. The concepts of personality have little to do with genesis of personality, or personality types. There is only a clear-cut general theory of mechanisms of *how* personality changes, and a theory of adjustment on a continuum of congruence between self and experience. Nothing is stated as to the operations of the therapist. He is assumed, and his conditions are still general prescriptions of non-intervention (though in the book itself, the therapist is beginning to show emotional overtones, and there is emphasis on attitudes vs. technique, which emerges fully in

Stage III). Stage II is the "bulge" of the phenomenological thread running through all stages. A special era of research follows from it. Part A concerns *if-then* changes, Part B concerns general outcomes.

The theory of personality and behavior makes certain assumptions prior to its conditions. These concern the uniqueness of phenomenal reality; the growth motive of the organism; the nature of the self as construct made up of perceptions and experiences. From the 1951 statement of nineteen propositions, we extract the following representative conditions, the first of which is the main basis of this section, and the others of which are derivative:

If	*Then*
1. there is perceptual organization	behavioral change
2. need	the organism will seek satisfaction
3. threatened	perceptions & behavior will be rigid
°4. not threatened	open to experience
5. perceptions are consistent with self-concept	will be accurate, accepted, incorporated
6. perceptions are not consistent with self-concept	will be denied, distorted, or ignored
7. perceptions are congruent with experience	psychological adjustment
8. perceptions are not congruent with experience	psychological maladjustment
9. adjustment	more accepting of others

° It is suggested in the accompanying text that the function of the therapist is to remove threat by his acceptant behavior, but we repeat therapy is *not* the focus of this theory.

A. *Conditions*	are	perceptual change
B. *Consequences*	are	behavioral change
C. *Focus*	is	largely outside of and separate from therapy
D. *Emphasis*	is	the individual person, may be client

Associated Research. One series of coordinated researches (Raskin, 1949) applied several methods and questions to ten recorded complete cases. Some have a particular bearing on Stage II theory. Sheerer (1949) devised categories to measure acceptance of self and of others. Judges reliably rated clients' statements on a 5-point scale, and tested for an increase over therapy of acceptance of self, and subsequent acceptance of others. Stock (1949) analyzed these cases by denoting each client statement in terms of its referent and its affect, and found a correlation between the way a person feels about himself and feels about others. Haigh, using the same ten recorded cases, studied the first and second half of therapy and judged the amount of defensiveness reported by the client, and exhibited by the client. Decreasing reported defensiveness correlated with improvement according to other process measures. Most of these researches, as well as those in Stage I, used raw uncoded units of verbatim interviews, ordered by time in therapy, measured by ratings on category systems applied by judges with sufficiently established reliability. In the ten-case coordinated study, these were supplemented by counselor ratings and by Rorschach evaluation. The latter, in a study by Carr (1949), showed no consistent or reliable changes.

Cartwright (1954) looked for evidence relating to the proposition that experiences not consistent with the self would be repressed or less assimilated. A group of subjects were exposed to a set of items and objects with which they differentially identified. In a later test of memory, he found that stimuli which are consistent with self-structure are better recalled.

The other phase of Stage II produced more research than any other period, with one main topic: *outcomes*. It was timely, almost necessary to prove that therapy, the subject of so much internal investigation, had demonstrable effects. The previously final *then* terms (the client will express himself more openly, etc.) become intermediate *if* terms (and then as a result of more open expression, he will). Since the phenomenological theory of Stage II did not predict consequences for a client inside therapy (as in Stage I) so much as for a person in general, and since there were as yet only general assumptions about the operations of the therapist, the study of outside *global* changes was in order.

Psychotherapy and Personality Change (Rogers and Dymond, 1954) is the basic book reporting this period. In it, a fairly large number of clients and controls (roughly 25 of each) were tested with several measures at various points pre-, post-, and follow-up, with complete recording and transcription of all cases (a very large and expensive procedure). Many variables were examined, the instruments including self-reports, counselor ratings, projective tests (scored "blind" by a diagnostician), judgments of outside individuals, and the problem of experimental controls was attacked. The overall design of this pioneer effort will be depicted in our section on the Q-sort.

A second major outcome study, known as the *change project*, was conducted and is being reported by Cartwright, Fiske, and Kirtner (1963). In the analysis of the first large outcome study, it was observed that there was a low, sometimes negative correlation between observers using the same instrument, or between different instruments. For example, two TAT diagnosticians from differing orientations disagreed on blind interpretations of the same client's stories (Rogers and Dymond 1954), and there was a low correlation between the perception of client, diagnostician, and client's friend, though all exhibit a fairly high degree of self-consistency. This raises the problem of *perceptual vantage points,* a problem to be expected in criterion research. To attack this problem, these researchers chose the tools of factor analysis. They reasoned that the criteria and vantage points could not be so fragmented as to be entirely independent, and sought the factor or factors representing change. They asked, do all criteria change together, and if not, in what relation to one another?

To begin with, this was not solely a study of client-centered outcomes, but a study of change factors for therapy in general. It commenced with a review of the literature for psychotherapy at large (Cartwright, *et al.*, 1963) and fourteen conceptions of possible change were extracted to cover as completely as feasible the range of previous research variables, ratings, test scores, clinical judgments, self-reports. To carry out this study required a large sample (the N was 100) of clients to which all fourteen conceptions of change were applied, at pre-, post-therapy and follow-up through the use of a ten-point evaluative rating scale for each concept. The concepts were represented by such instruments as MMPI, TAT, sentence completion test, self-sort, counselor rating, and diagnostician's evaluation. These and all scales such as *adequacy of contentedness of relationships with others, energy deployment over courses of action,* were intercorrelated. It was found that no single factor or global scale would adequately represent the outcome of therapy, but that factors depended upon instrument-observer combinations. This is surely one of the largest, most energetic and complex studies in the field, and it warns the future researcher that "measures of therapeutic change are highly specific to the observer's role and to the instrument he uses." In a subsidiary research, Kirtner and Cartwright (1962) found that classification of the client's behavior in the first two interviews made differential prognosis possible. Prediction of length of therapy and of success or failure were achieved by observing the manner of experiencing and relating to his problems during this early therapy period. This is an important advance, and could enable future researchers to control outcome studies with much more assurance, since they can relate the power of the treatment effects to the ease with which those effects might be obtained from the particular client involved.

The overall result of the outcome studies points up the very complicated problems of research in psychotherapy.

Characteristics of Stage III (circa 1955)

A second version of a theory of therapy, this one is surrounded by a larger body of theory which subsumes all previous ones. The main new element is the statement of conditions, "The Necessary and Sufficient Conditions of Therapy." (1957) Here the emphasis is much upon the therapist (whereas it was upon the client in 1940). The role of the therapist was limited, in Stage I, to that of non-intervening releaser. Now the therapist is given main responsibility for the "If" conditions. The theory requires that:

1. Two persons are in contact.
2. The client is vulnerable or anxious.
3. The therapist is congruent.
4. The therapist is experiencing positive regard.
5. The therapist is experiencing empathic understanding.
6. The client perceives (4) and (5).

Conditions 1 and 2 restate the 1947 requirements of *rapport*, and *felt need*. Conditions, 3, 4, and 5 are all *positive* specifications of therapist operations. Whereas before he was adjured not to intervene in order to release, he might now intervene, if necessary, in order to be congruent in order to release. If he continues to fulfill conditions 4 and 5, he has made his contribution to the activity of therapy and the process to follow. The larger body of theory in this stage has not stimulated research in inter-personal relationship, for instance, but drew upon previous research for footing. The theory of therapy did have an impact on further research.

A. *Conditions: if* the six stated necessary and sufficient conditions
B. *Consequences: then* a process is set up in the client
C. *Focus:* on the therapist in therapy
D. *Emphasis:* on the therapist's attitude

Associated Research. Halkides (1958) studied the relationship of condi-tions 3, 4, and 5 to success in therapy. When she had judges blindly rate the degree of these conditions in the recordings of interviews of ten cases found to be successful on multiple criteria, and ten unsuccessful cases, she found that all three of these conditions were significantly associated with the more successful cases.

Barrett-Lennard (1959) investigated the effect of the client's experience of these three conditions by having the clients themselves (not judges) complete a Relationship Inventory incorporating statements representing these conditions after their fifth interview, and after the completion of therapy. He found that clients improve in their adjustment according to the extent they perceive their therapist (after five interviews) as under-standing, congruent, positive, and unconditional in his regard for them.

Goodman (1962) investigated the congruence of inner feelings and outer expression of both client and therapist. Each used a (same) variant of the Semantic Differential after every third interview until the twenty-first. On separate sheets of an adjective list, the client scaled the inner feelings he experienced and his outer expression of them. The therapist followed the same procedure for himself. Difference scores showed the distance between each one's self-perceived feelings and expression, thus his *self-disclosure*. For the therapist, this score measured condition 3, his congruence. Each person then predicted the other's self-description. To the extent that the therapist's prediction agrees with the client's self-description, the therapist shows understanding, a fulfillment of condition 5 (understanding). To the extent that the client's prediction agrees with the therapist's self-description, he fulfills half the condition 6, by perceiving condition 5. Goodman found that the match between the two parties increased as therapy progressed. This is a keen example of research following theory.

Stage IV
A Process Conception of Psychotherapy
(1957 to present)

Interest in a particular sort of process is the fourth major theme, from which Rogers' paper (1958) emerged. The word *process* has been so much used as to become somewhat confusing. There have been at least three different methodological aspects. We will try to specify our use of the terms.

The first is the *sequential* or *series* meaning. In this use process refers to a variable examined in segmented sequences over time. For example, one might measure statements of successful clients in terms of self-reference, find an increase from first to last interviews, and discuss the "process of increasing self-reference."

A second aspect is the *cause and effect relationship*, or *interaction*. A study investigating the connections between behaviors of therapist and client might refer to this as the process of therapy.

The third and present meaning of process has reference to the *type of variable involved*. If one examines the position of a physical object at one moment, then at a second moment, and again at a third, the variable *position at a given time* is not of the same nature as a variable such as *motion*. Variables having to do with *movement* or *flow* of the client are now referred to as process variables and should, we think, have a special claim on the term. Rogers is concerned with process in this third meaning.

There has been continuing interest in some type of *process* starting with Snyder's 1943 study and continuing with Porter, Seeman, *et al.* These Stage I studies investigated process in the sequential sense, measuring the change in behavior over therapy.

A substantial methodological advance in the study of sequence was made with Butler's qualitative factor analysis for use in naturalistic observation. The method may be described as a variant of factor analysis in which the basic data are the behaviors of client and therapist rather than scores. This provides a statistical technique for describing sequences of observable events (1962).

There has been little investigation of process in the interaction sense. Comparison of client-therapist behaviors when done in the same study was carried out in either summary fashion, by relating the therapist scores for the first third of therapy to the client's scores in that segment of therapy, or else by comparing a single client response to a single therapist response. Rogers' concern was not with process in the interactive sense. In Stage IV, he assumes that the therapist's conditions are met, and is interested in the change in the *client*.

Gendlin and Zimring (1955) and Gendlin (1962) defined and focused upon a variable which referred to the underlying substrata in the individual as central core in process of change. This variable, called *experiencing*, referred to the ongoing flow of events in the individual. Rogers (1959) used this and a few of the discrete variables investigated in earlier studies as some aspects of what he saw to be the underlying continuum: fixity to changingness, from rigid structure to flow, from static to process. This underlying continuum was conceptualized in terms of seven strands of flow: (1) relationship to feeling and personal meaning, (2) manner of experience, (3) degree of incongruence, (4) communication of self, (5) manner in which experience is constructed, (6) relationship to problems, and (7) manner of relating. The strands are predicted to co-vary within the client. That is, a client judged as being near the fixity end of one strand was likely to be near the fixity end of whatever other strands he exhibited. It should be emphasized that each strand was a particular manifestation of a single underlying continuum of change.

This continuum is divided into seven stages. To illustrate the content of these stages we list the characteristics of the first and seventh stages.

First Stage	*Seventh Stage*
Personal constructs are extremely rigid.	Personal constructs are tentatively reformulated, to be validated against further experience, but even then, to be held loosely.
There is much blockage of internal communication.	Internal communication is clear, with feelings and symbols well matched, and fresh terms for new feelings.
	New feelings are experienced with immediacy and richness of detail, both in the therapeutic relationship and outside.
Feelings and personal meanings are neither recognized nor owned.	The experiencing of such feelings is used as a clear referent.
There is an unwillingness to communicate self. Communication is only about externals.	There is a growing and continuing sense of acceptant ownership of these changing feelings, a basic trust in his own process.
No problems are recognized or perceived.	Experiencing has lost almost completely its structure-bound aspects and becomes
There is no desire to change.	process experiencing—that is, the situa-

Ex. "I think I'm practically healthy."

Close and communicative relationships are dangerous.

tion is experienced and interpreted in this moment, not as in the past.

The self becomes increasingly simply the subjective and reflexive awareness of experiencing. The self is much less frequently a perceived object, and much more frequently something confidently felt in process.

It is of more than passing interest to note that Rogers arrived at the conception of an underlying continuum by listening, with as little bias as possible, to many therapy recordings. The power of this system of naturalistic observation is little recognized by the average researcher, yet it is the basic method of scientists who make history.

A. *Conditions: if* the client perceives himself as fully received
B. *Consequences: then* he will change as described by a continuum from fixity to fluidity
C. *Focus:* movement *in therapy*
D. *Emphasis:* client

Associated Research. Tomlinson and Hart (1962) started with a recording of an early and a late interview from each of ten cases chosen as representative of Counseling Center clients. Nine two-minute segments were chosen from each of these 20 tapes and these 180 segments were then coded and randomized. Two raters with previous experience of the scale then individually decided in what scale portion each of these segments belonged. For this purpose they used typescripts and tape recordings. Since five of these ten clients were successful clients and five unsuccessful, this design enabled them to compare the stages of process of early interview to late as well as success to failure.

Research here returns to old types of operations, i.e., categories of behavior, rated by judges using interview material. There is nothing new in that, except for some advance in showing that scales involving subtle conceptions can be reliably applied to complex interview material. But the real contribution, since the system of analysis is old, lies in the invention of new theory. From this, it seems that if new theory leads to new research with old techniques, theory constitutes a method in itself.

"Q-SORT"—THE CASE HISTORY OF A METHOD AND ITS MODIFICATION

The history of psychology has been said to rest upon available instrumentation. In the *practice* of psychotherapy, where the instruments are people, this is certainly true. In clinical *research,* theory has wandered like an apparition looking for tools with which to make itself visible. Often something is lost in the process. Rich and complicated experience, when phrased in researchable terms, is reduced to the limitations of instruments. The self-concept is somewhat ephemeral, for all its commonness in our language and its brilliant history in social-psychological theory. It was pre-eminent in Stage II of Rogerian theory. But how is one to get at it most directly? The most empathic judges, watching through screens and reading dials connected to all known physiological measures are still once removed from the inner experience of the client's *phenomenal* self. And how is one to quantify the client's own report?

The answer seemed to come from the work of W. Stephenson (1953), fortunately at the University of Chicago when self-theory was burgeoning. His Q-technique offered an idiosyncratic quantitative method in which an individual is applied to a set of statements over time; the correlation between the person arrays is then subjected to factor analysis. Intra-individual rather than inter-individual differences are the issue. This makes it most appealing to the clinical researcher. The technique was applied to single cases in early studies by Hartley (1951) and Nunnally (1955). They had clients describe themselves in terms of a Q-sort at various points over therapy. The result showed details of the movement through therapy in terms of changing factor loadings in the descriptive statements. Exposition of the case in quantitative, hypothesis-testing terms was clearly achieved, but the results, though objective, were still somewhat unwieldy, as in any single case analysis. This first application was genuinely Q-technique.

The next study was a milestone which will be used to represent the major outcome studies mentioned in Stage II and reported in full in *Psychotherapy and Personality Change*. From Q-technique, it took only the Q-sort, aimed at the instrumentation of the self-concept but also adjusted to inter-individual differences. To help the reader visualize the procedure, we shall describe it in some detail. The Q-sort can be considered as essentially an inventory, consisting of a number (usually between 50 and 150) of descriptive statements. This is called the *Q-sort,* and the person describing himself is said to be *sorting.* Typically, the procedure begins with devising or selection of *trait universe.* In this case, the Butler-Haigh study (1954), 100 statements were taken from recordings of clients in different stages of therapy. The items may be phrased positively ("People always like me"), or negatively ("I'm no damned good to anyone"); they may consist of long sentences or single adjectives such as "cheerful." The subject is asked to distribute these items on a continuum of "like me" to "not like me." Instructions under which he sorts vary widely, according to the researcher's interests. One may describe himself in the present, the past, the future, as he wishes he were, as his friends see him, as he sees himself in relation to them, or he may describe others with the same items in equally varying ways.

The technology of Q-sorting is quite advanced. Each item is printed on a card, the cards are placed on a Q-board which holds them up for view so that the sorter can change their placement at will (on a paired comparison basis). The desired distribution is outlined on the board, usually of a forced-normal approximation, so that the number of cards in each pile on the continuum is controlled and thus weighted. Any two distributions may be correlated by recording the differences in placement of each card, squaring and summing the differences, and reading an extrapolation table from which the sum gives an .r, a procedure which takes about two minutes. For non-symmetrical distributions, Cartwright (1956a) devised a rapid computational procedure.

In this illustrative study, the researchers used two instructions: "Sort these cards to describe yourself as you are," and then, "now sort these cards to describe the ideal, the person you want to be." The result provided the widely quoted *self-ideal correlation*, which these authors call a measure of self-esteem. The person who has a large discrepancy between self and ideal is not likely to be acceptant of himself, and probably experiences tension. This is all based on the concept of the phenomenal self, and relates to Stage II, yet it should be noted that congruence of self and *ideal* does not represent the *Congruence* between Self-Structure and *Experience* which Rogers in Stage II postulates as the basis of adjustment. This is an example of the instrumental limitation (*experience* is not as easily encompassed as *ideal*) and also of the way in which individual researchers veer off in their own directions (though Butler and Haigh see the self and ideal coming closer together "on the basis of a broader awareness of experience").

Results demonstrated outcome effects which appear to be desirable, stable, and to have occurred as a consequence of therapy rather than mere passage of time. This is depicted on the chart (Figure 2) which shows mean S-I correlations at pre-, post-, and follow-up points. (These data are essentially the material from the Butler-Haigh study.)

Two *experimental* or *treated* groups are shown. One is the total research population, which moves from a zero-order correlation to a significant .34 at post therapy, and shows no significant change in follow-up. On the assumption that more improved clients should show greater increase in this measure, a subpopulation was selected as improved on the combined basis of two other measures, TAT diagnostic rating and counselor judgments. The "improved" population does indeed show less self-ideal discrepancy, and also shows stability in follow-up. All figures are *averages*, for the groups.

How can this be attributed to therapy? The complicated problem of controls was attacked in two ways. First (line *X*) there is the conventional *matched normal*, equivalent on the basis of age, sex, and socioeconomic status (gross variables which have little meaning, as it turns out) to the

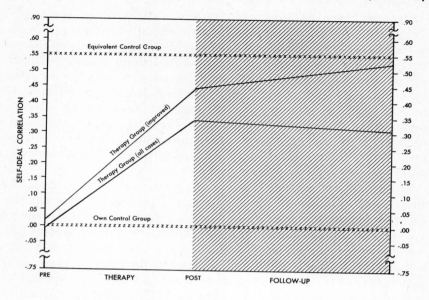

Figure 2
Mean Correlation Chart

matching individuals in the therapy group. As each client is tested, so is his matched control person. Those controls are "normal" in the sense that they volunteered to participate in research for payment, and had not requested therapy. Their status on the measure is significantly higher than other groups at pre-therapy, and does not change, on the average, over time without therapy. However, the matching is incomplete, does not cover the relevant psychological variables, and leaves much to be desired. How does one match for these relevant variables (when not even sure what they are)? Make each person his *own* control. Then he is perfectly matched for himself. This was done by asking half of those who applied for therapy to take the tests, waiting for 60 days, and then beginning therapy (line Z). This group, self-declared as in need of therapy, shows zero-order S-I correlation at time of application for therapy and no change over time until the pre-therapy point. (The *own control* line should actually be outside the chart and to the left, since its position on the follow-up axis really represents the pre-therapy test point and its position at pre-therapy really represents "pre-wait.") These two control groups help to prove the efficacy of treatment vs. no treatment, but they are open to criticism. When people are told that their therapy has yet to begin, there is the complication of possible suggestion (a negative *placebo* effect) in the evidence of no change during the wait period. There is also the need to control for individual growth potential in relation to initial status. That is, study of diet K for children requires not only initial height and weight, but some estimate of likely adult height, such as mean of parents' size, before matching is valid. Differential prognosis is required, and this is a problem only now being attacked in designs. Beside the development of adequate controls, another method with convincing power is that of replication, a method all too rare in clinical research. Shlien (1960) repeated the S-I outcome study with two other groups in a time-limited therapy study and found very similar results.

In a further study of this population, Dymond further separated the Q-sort from Q-technique. Using only the *self-sort* she asked clinicians to divide the items into those describing good and poor adjustment. From this, she was able to make an *adjustment score* of the Q-sort self-description which was framed in terms of the values of outside observers, though the data still came from the self-report. (1954b) At about this time Butler's (1956) factor analysis of the ideal sort showed a single factor which accounted for the variance. This finding restored some of the phenomenological tone to the *adjustment score,* since it proved that clients' ideal sorts were essentially all the same and that they shared a common cultural ideal with the clinicians and the counselors. A later study (unpublished) by Shlien and Jenney confirmed this: on a balanced 80-item Q-sort, the item array of the single ideal factor, when split in the middle coincided *exactly* with the *adjustment-maladjustment* items as judged by clinicians.

In a further modification of the original technique, Shlien removed the self-ideal ratio from any explicit content whatever. No Q-deck was used. Only an apparatus constructed of two moveable semi-transparent spheres, one representing self, the other ideal, was presented. The amount to which the client separated or overlapped these spheres composed a self-ideal correlation (read as the cosine of the formed angle) which correlated highly with the conventional Q-sort-derived self-ideal. This measure, though completely phenomenological (Figure 3) was totally abstracted from its original methodological moorings in Q-technique.

Meanwhile, Butler's work (1960) moved the Q-data toward some of its original purposes. He applied factor analysis to the whole client population (i.e., to matrices of inter-correlations of clients at one time rather than one client at different times) at pre-, post-, and follow-up points, in an *R*- rather than Q-technique. By this means, he found factors representing different types of in-therapy behavior and outcome, and the factor arrays gave, through each client's factor estimation, a description of the clients with high loadings on those factors. These clients were differentiated in terms of self-concept, described in terms of Q-items, and related as types to other outcome measures such as TAT change, ratings by

What ever happened to the Q-sort?

Figure 3

Abstract Apparatus, Rear View

friends of the client, and ratings by the therapist. This method does not follow the single case, but follows and describes groups of cases which cluster as factorial types.

Our effort here has been to illustrate a common event in research activity, and in so doing, to detail some of the design of a research and the viscissitudes of an instrument. All approaches search for methods compatible with their theories, and it so happens that compatible techniques give more favorable results. (When one study found that S-I correlations showed positive results while the TAT showed negative results on the same population, Henry, a leading TAT analyst and theoretician, considered the possibility that "the TAT is unfriendly to client-centered therapy.") Stage II theory seized upon Q-technique, used it in classical form, then converted it to meet contemporary research needs, somewhat departing from the original technique and original clinical theory, as so often happens because usable instruments do not directly express or lend themselves to exact representations of the theory. The modifications moved to a point of complete abstraction from the original technique, then finally back to a more workable reconciliation of method adapted to the actual research situation.

SUMMARY

In this chapter, we have tried to display cross sections of the architecture in a school of therapy built of research-shaped bricks. One can hardly think of research methods that have not been used here. There are actuarial studies, intensive clinical studies, counselor rating scales, hypothesis dictated studies and hypothesis-generating studies, physiological measures, projective techniques, semantic differentials and Q-sorts, prognosis and diagnosis, self-reports and judges' evalutions, uses of diaries, films, sound recordings, longer therapy, shorter therapy, and published research on all of them. Yet it is not these methods which give a research program its character and force. Methods do not tell one what to do with them. Theory does. We have tried to throw into relief four stages of development with associated researches, each stage leading in some line to those behind and ahead. The basic necessities of a foundation have been achieved in the way of theories of therapy and personality. A point of maturity has been reached such that main theoretical directives for research may now come from persons other than Rogers. In any event, we venture to predict the next stage, not from advance information but because our reading of history points that way. The next theory will be a theory of knowledge. And what will that have to do with research? Absolutely everything.

REFERENCES

AIDMAN, T. Changes in self-perception as related to changes in perception of one's environment. *Amer. Psychologist,* **3**: 286, 1948.

ANDERSON, R. P. An investigation of the relationship between physiological and verbal behavior during client-centered psychotherapy. Unpub. Ph.D. thesis, Univ. of Chicago, 1955. (Also *J. counsel. Psychol.,* **3**: 174-184, 1956.)

ASSUM, A. L., and LEVY, S. J. Analysis of a non-directive case with follow-up interview. *J. abnorm. soc. Psychol.,* **43**: 78-89, 1948.

BARRETT-LENNARD, G. T. Dimensions of the client's experience of his therapist associated with personality change. Unpub. Ph.D. thesis, Univ. of Chicago, 1959.

BERGER, E. M. Relationships among acceptance of self, acceptance of others, and MMPI scores. *J. counsel. Psychol.*, 2: 279-284, 1955.

BERGMAN, D. V. The relationship between counseling method and client self-exploration. Unpub. M. A. thesis, Univ. of Chicago, 1950.

BUTLER, J. M. Factorial studies of client-centered psychotherapy. *Counseling center discussion papers*, Chicago, II, 9, 1956.

BUTLER, J. M. Self-concept change in psychotherapy. *Counseling center discussion papers*, Chicago, VI, 13, 1960.

BUTLER, J. M., and HAIGH, G. V. Changes in the relation between self-concepts and ideal concepts consequent upon client-centered counseling. In C. R. Rogers and R. F. Dymond (Eds.), *Psychotherapy and personality change*. Chicago: Univ. of Chicago Press, 1954, Pp. 55-75.

BUTLER, J. M., RICE, L. N., and WAGSTAFF, A. K. *Quantitative naturalistic research*, Englewood Cliffs, N. J.: Prentice-Hall, 1963.

CARR, A. C. An evaluation of nine non-directive psychotherapy cases, by means of the Rorschach. *J. consult. Psychol.*, 13: 196-205, 1949.

CARTWRIGHT, D. S. A study of imbalance in immediate memory. Unpub. Ph.D. thesis, Univ. of Chicago, 1954.

CARTWRIGHT, D. S. A computational procedure for tau correlations. *Psychometrika*, 22: 1956. (a)

CARTWRIGHT, D. S. A rapid non-parametric estimate of multijudge reliability. *Psychometrika*, 21: 17-29, 1956. (b)

CARTWRIGHT, D. S. Self-consistency as a factor affecting immediate recall. *J. abnorm. soc. Psychol*, 52: 212-218, 1956. (c)

CARTWRIGHT, D. S. Annotated bibliography of research and theory construction in client-centered therapy. *J. counsel. Psychol.*, 4: 82-100, 1957.

CARTWRIGHT, D. S., KIRTNER, W. L., and FISKE, D. W. Method factors in changes associated with psychotherapy. *J. abnor. soc. Psychol.*, 66: 164-175, 1963.

CARTWRIGHT, D. S., ROBERTSON, R. J., FISKE, D. W., and KIRTNER, W. L. Length of therapy in relation to outcome and change in personal integration. *J. consult. Psychol.*, 25: 84-88, 1961.

CARTWRIGHT, D. S., and ROTH, I. Success and satisfaction in psychotherapy. *J. clin. Psychol.*, 13: 20-26, 1957.

CHODORKOFF, B. Adjustment and the discrepancy between perceived and ideal self. *J. clin. Psychol.*, 10: 266-268, 1954. (a)

CHORDORKOFF, B. Self-perception, perceptual defense, and adjustment. *J. abnorm. soc. Psychol.*, 49: 508-512, 1954. (b)

CURRAN, C. A. *Personality factors in counseling*. New York: Grune & Stratton, 1945.

DYMOND, R. F. Adjustment changes over therapy from self-sorts, in C. R. Rogers and R. F. Dymond (Eds.), *Psychotherapy and personality change*. Chicago: Univ. of Chicago Press, 1954 (a). Pp. 76-84.

DYMOND, R. F. Adjustment changes over therapy from Thematic Apperception

Test ratings, In C. R. Rogers and R. F. Dymond (Eds.), *Psychotherapy and personality change*. Chicago: Univ. of Chicago Press, 1954 (b). Pp. 109-120.

DYMOND, R. F. (Cartwright), Effects of psychotherapy on self-consistency. *J. counsel. Psychol.*, 4: 1, 1957.

FISKE, D. W., CARTWRIGHT, D. S., and KIRTNER, W. L. Are psychotherapeutic changes predictable. *Counseling center discussion papers*, Chicago, VIII, 4, 1962.

GENDLIN, E. T. *Experiencing and the creation of meaning*. New York: Free Press, 1962.

GENDLIN, E. T., and ZIMRING, F. The qualities or dimensions of experiencing and their change. *Counseling center discussion papers*, Chicago, I, 3, 1955.

GOODMAN, G. Emotional disclosure of therapists and clients over the course of psychotherapy. Unpub. Ph.D. thesis, Univ. of Chicago, 1962.

GORDON, T. and CARTWRIGHT, D. S. The effect of psychotherapy upon certain attitudes toward others. In C. R. Rogers and R. F. Dymond (Eds.), *Psychotherapy and personality change*. Chicago: Univ. of Chicago Press, 1954. Pp. 167-195.

GRUMMON, D. L. An investigation into the use of grammatical and psychogrammatical categories of language for the study of personality and psychotherapy. Unpub. Ph.D. thesis, Univ. of Chicago, 1950.

GRUMMON, D. L. Personality changes as a function of time in persons motivated for therapy. In C. R. Rogers and R. F. Dymond (Eds.), *Psychotherapy and personality change*. Chicago: Univ. of Chicago Press, 1954. Pp. 238-255.

GRUMMON, D. L. and JOHN, E. S. Changes over client-centered therapy evaluated on psychoanalytically based thematic apperception test scales. In C. R. Rogers and R. F. Dymond (Eds.), *Psychotherapy and personality change*. Chicago: Univ. of Chicago Press, 1954. Pp. 121-144.

GUMP, P. V. A statistical investigation of one psychoanalytic approach and a comparison of it with nondirective therapy. Unpub. M.A. thesis, Ohio State University, 1944.

HAIGH, G. Defensive behavior in client-centered therapy. *J. consult. Psychol.*, 13: 181-189, 1949.

HALKIDES, G. An experimental study of four conditions necessary for therapeutic change. Unpub. Ph.D. thesis, Univ. of Chicago, 1958.

HARTLEY, M. W. Q-technique: its methodology and application. Unpub. manuscript, Counseling Center, Univ. of Chicago, 1950.

HARTLEY, M. W. A Q-technique study of changes in the self-concepts during psychotherapy. Unpub. Ph.D. thesis, Univ. of Chicago, 1951.

HENRY, W. E., and SHLIEN, J. M. Affective complexity and psychotherapy; Some comparisons of time-limited and unlimited treatment. *J. proj. Tech.*, 22: 153-162, 1958.

HOCH, P. Book review of *Psychotherapy and personality change*, C. R. Rogers and R. F. Dymond (Eds.). *J.A.M.A.*, 157: 690, 1955.

HOGAN, R. A. A theory of threat and defense. *J. consult. Psychol.*, 16: 417-425, 1952.

JAMES, W. *Principles of psychology.* New York: Dover, 1950.

KIRTNER, W. L. and CARTWRIGHT, D. S. Success and failure in client-centered therapy as a function of client personality variables. *J. consult. Psychol.,* 22: 259-264, 1958.

LECKY, P. *Self-consistency: A theory of personality.* New York: Island Press, 1945.

MOWRER, O. H. "Q Technique"—Description, history and critique. In O. H. Mowrer (Ed.), *Psychotherapy: theory and research.* New York: Ronald, 1953. Pp. 316-375.

MEUNCH, G. A. An evaluation of non-directive psychotherapy by means of the Rorschach and other tests. *Appl. Psychol. Monogr.,* No. 13, Stanford, Calif.: Stanford Univ. Press, 1947.

NUNNALLY, J. C. An investigation of some propositions of self-conception: the case of Miss Sun. *J. abnorm. soc. Psychol.,* 50: 87-92, 1955. (a)

NUNNALLY, J. C. A systematic approach to the construction of hypotheses about the process of psychotherapy. *J. consult. Psychol.,* 19: 17-20, 1955. (b)

PORTER, E. H. The development and evaluation of a measure of counseling interview procedures. *Educ. psychol. Measmt.,* 3: 105-126, 215-238, 1943.

RAIMY, V. C. Self-reference in counseling interviews. *J. consult. Psychol.,* 12: 153-163, 1948.

RASKIN, N. J. An analysis of six parallel studies of the therapeutic process. *J. consult. Psychol.,* 13: 206-220, 1949.

RASKIN, N. J. An objective study of the locus-of-evaluation factor in psychotherapy. In W. Wolff and J. A. Precker (Eds.), *Success in Psychotherapy.* New York: Grune & Stratton. 1952. Chap. 6.

ROGERS, C. R. The processes of therapy. *J. consult. Psychol.,* 4: 161-164, 1940.

ROGERS, C. R. *Client-centered therapy: Its current practice, implications, and theory.* Boston: Houghton Mifflin, 1951.

ROGERS, C. R. Changes in the maturity of behavior as related to therapy. In C. R. Rogers and R. F. Dymond (Eds.), *Psychotherapy and personality change.* Chicago: Univ. of Chicago Press, 1954. Pp. 215-237.

ROGERS, C. R. A theory of therapy, personality, and interpersonal relationships. *Counseling center discussion papers,* I, 5, 1955. (Also in, S. Koch (Ed.), *Psychology: A study of a science.* III, 1961.)

ROGERS, C. R. The necessary and sufficient conditions of therapeutic personality change. *J. consult. Psychol.,* 21: 95-103, 1957.

ROGERS, C. R. A process conception of psychotherapy. *Amer. Psychologist,* 13: 142-149, 1958.

ROGERS, C. R. A tentative scale for the measurement of progress in psychotherapy. In E. A. Rubinstein and M. B. Parloff (Eds.), *Research in psychotherapy.* Washington, D. C.: American Psychological Association, 1959. Pp. 96-107.

ROGERS, C. R. Significant trends in the client-centered orientation. *Progr. clin. Psychol.,* 4: 85-99, 1960.

ROGERS, C. R., and DYMOND, R. F. *Psychotherapy and personality change: Coordinated studies in the client-centered approach.* Chicago: Univ. of Chicago Press, 1954.

SEEMAN, J. A study of the process of non-directive therapy. *J. consult. Psychol.*, 13: 157-168, 1949.

SEEMAN, J. Counselor judgments of therapeutic process and outcome. In C. R. Rogers and R. F. Dymond (Eds.), *Psychotherapy and personality change.* Chicago: Univ. of Chicago Press, 1954. Pp. 99-108.

SEEMAN, J., and RASKIN, N. J. Research perspectives in client-centered therapy. In O. H. Mowrer (Ed). *Psychotherapy: theory and research.* New York: Ronald, 1953. Pp. 205-234.

SHEERER, E. Analysis of the relationship between acceptance of and respect for self and acceptance of and respect for others. *J. consult. Psychol.*, 13: 169-175, 1949.

SHLIEN, J. M. Toward what level of abstraction in criteria? In H. H. Strupp and L. Luborsky (Eds.), *Second research conference in psychotherapy.* Washington, D.C.: American Psychological Association, 1961.

SHLIEN, J. M., MOSAK, H. H., and DREIKURS, R. Effect of time limits: A comparison of client-centered and Adlerian psychotherapy. *Counseling center discussion papers,* VI, 8, 1960.

SNYDER, W. U. An investigation of the nature of non-directive psychotherapy. *J. gen. Psychol.*, 33: 193-223, 1945.

SNYGG, D., and COMBS, A. W. *Individual behavior.* New York: Harper & Row, 1949.

STANDAL, S. W. The need for positive regard: A contribution to client-centered theory. Unpub. Ph.D. thesis, Univ. of Chicago, 1954.

STEPHENSON, W. *The study of behavior.* Chicago: Univ. of Chicago Press, 1953.

STOCK, D. An investigation into the interrelationships between the self-concept and feelings directed toward other persons and groups. *J. consult. Psychol.*, 13: 176-180, 1949.

THETFORD, W. N. The measurement of physiological responses to frustration before and after non-directive psychotherapy. Unpub. Ph.D. thesis, Univ. of Chicago, 1949.

TOMLINSON, T. M., and HART JR., J. T. A validation study of the Process Scale. *J. consult. Psychol.*, 26: 74-78, 1962.

WALKER, A. M., RABLEN, R. S., and ROGERS, C. R. Development of a scale to measure process changes in psychotherapy. *J. clin. Psychol.*, 16: 79-85, 1960.

IV

Evaluation of the Effects or Outcome of Psychotherapy

A prominent psychologist has asserted provocatively that doing process research in psychotherapy is a way to dodge facing the problems of doing outcome research. This assertion disregards the fact-finding function of process research at the various levels illustrated in earlier chapters and the basic contributions such research is making to personality theory and to outcome research. But the statement does, indeed, emphasize the knowledgeable respect and awe that many social scientists have for the formidable problems of outcome research in psychotherapy. The difficult challenge provided by evaluative research in psychotherapy is perhaps well exemplified by the questions raised by Eysenck (1952, 1965) as to whether anyone has demonstrated that psychotherapy does any better than no such therapy or the mere passage of time. Specifically, he asserted that the figures "fail to support the hypothesis that psychotherapy facilitates recovery from neurotic disorder." Scholarly and erudite rebuttals in the literature to Eysenck's arguments by Luborsky (1954), Rosenzweig (1954), and 14 other prominent scholars (See Eysenck, 1965) have somehow not entirely reassured the scientific community that psychotherapy is a definite causal agent in effecting amelioration of personality and behavior disorders. The reader is advised to familiarize himself, if he is not already so, with these papers to acquire a background of knowledge of some of the statistical, methodological, and conceptual issues that have bred and fed this now famous controversy pertaining to evaluative research in psychotherapy. The reader is also referred to two publications of the Group for Advancement of Psychiatry (GAP) which have definite relevance to the problem of measurement of outcome in psychotherapy; these are the GAP publications on controls in psychiatric research and the one on the measurement of change in psychiatric research.

The papers chosen for this part of the book can be classified into two general types: (1) those dealing primarily with outcome research as it relates to general problems of research design, method, and personality theory; and (2) those dealing primarily with tests and measurement instruments.

REFERENCES

EYSENCK, H. J. The effects of psychotherapy: An evaluation. *J. consult. Psychol.*, 16: 319-324, 1952.

EYSENCK, H. J. The effects of psychotherapy (with discussions by 14 prominent psychotherapists). *Int. J. Psychiat.*, 1: 97-178, 1965.

Group for Advancement of Psychiatry. *Some observations on controls in psychiatric research,* Report No. 42. New York: Committee on Research, Group for Advancement of Psychiatry, 1959.

Group for Advancement of Psychiatry. *The Measurement of Change in Psychiatric Research.* New York: Committee on Research, Group for Advancement of Psychiatry. (In preparation)

LUBORSKY, L. B. A note on Eysenck's article: The effects of psychotherapy: An evaluation. *Brit. J. Psychol.*, 45: 129-131, 1954.

ROSENZWEIG, S. A transvaluation of psychotherapy. A reply to Hans Eysenck. *J. abnorm. soc. Psychol.*, 49: 298-304, 1954.

A.

Problems Regarding the Determination of the Pertinent Changes and How to Assess Them

Breedlove and Krause present the problems encountered when one attempts to evaluate the different outcomes occurring with two different casework procedures carried out by independent teams of social workers within the same Family Service Agency. The authors use this actual, ongoing experimental study to point out the major areas requiring attention in the formulation of a satisfactory research design for such an evaluative investigation. Of particular value to the student is the thoroughness with which each problem ensuing in such a comparison is lucidly described. Pertinent references to key articles in the literature are cited. The authors are well aware that in their contribution they have put more of their emphasis on research design in the assessment of pertinent changes than on the evaluative instruments used to measure change. Possible shortcomings or other problems in the use of evaluative procedures are not the aim of this chapter; it is expected that such a topic will be discussed in future publications by these authors.

Chassan and Bellak emphasize the advantages of the so-called intensive or longitudinal design in evaluative research. In the conventional approach to the design of evaluative research the *extensive* design or model is quite often utilized; in this design observations are made and hypotheses are tested on a group of individual patients. On a random basis one group or set of patients is selected for procedure or treatment A and the other group for procedure or treatment B. Relatively few observations are made on each patient along the time axis, and often only end-point observations are carried out. The various hypotheses which can be tested in such a research design are limited to tests between groups of patients. When statistical evaluation is employed of differences in degrees of improvement or change, these mathematical assessments are performed in terms of averaging across the corresponding patient-groups. Hence, the label *cross-sectional* design.

451

The *intensive* or *longitudinal* model of clinical research design, on the other hand, focuses upon the analysis of variation in response within the individual patient in relation to the same or different procedures or treatments. In the intensive design, a given patient is observed at relatively frequent intervals over say, weeks, months, or years. Chassan and Bellak illustrate that it is now possible, if one so desires, to apply sophisticated statistical analysis of the data within each individual patient, because of advances in the applications of mathematical theory.

A particularly important aspect of the intensive model is that in the process of increasing the number of patients studied intensively over time for such obvious purposes as theory seeking, validation of hypotheses, modification or extension of previous findings, the investigator can systematically select and study patients in relationship to various specific patient parameters. The continuing selection of patients for intensive design in practice and theory can in a meaningful way be related to previous results and to specific questions raised by an earlier set of results.

In any intensive study involving people, there are many relevant characteristics which may be at present unknowable, as well as those which can be known, and these are implicitly held constant in the testing of hypotheses within an individual. The patient serves as his own control, and this includes the complete history of all of his anatomy and physiology, his sexuality, intelligence, his possible relevant interpersonal experiences. Obviously, nowhere near this degree of control can ever be achieved in the extensive model.

Wallerstein's chapter is an interim report on the long-term Menninger Foundation Psychotherapy Project, a most impressive program. Its distinguishing feature is the researchers' refusal to compromise with the complexity of the phenomena under study. Faced with all the intricacies of human personality and its changes in psychotherapy, they do not try to reduce this complexity to a few easily managed variables. Instead, they attempt to encompass all pertinent variables in a network of clinical judgments. Their assumption is that such judgments are the most valuable tool presently available for personality description. Since this project represents the most thorough-going application of this instrument (clinical judgment) to psychotherapy research, the project becomes in one sense a test of the value of this methodological approach.

At the same time, the researchers are aware that the instrument itself is in need of much study, and they undertake this. The vehicle for carrying out this study is the set of predictions made by the clinician-researchers before treatment begins. Predictions in psychiatry are, of course, a refreshing change from explanation after the fact, at which clinicians are so adept. The predictions are based upon observed patient characteristics and theoretical hypotheses, the theory in this case being psychoanalytic.

Wallerstein points out that these hypotheses, taken together, comprise the psychoanalytic theory of therapy as understood and applied by the present workers. The subsequent confirmation or refutation of the predictions will inevitably illuminate the nature of the theoretical assumptions, which is a gain of first order. Thus, this project studies clinical judgment and the theory of therapy as well as the actual treatment of 42 patients.

The Menninger Study has other strong points. One is that the assessment of variables is multi-angled: for example, the patient descriptions derive from the reports of different observers including the patient himself, his relatives, the therapist, therapy supervisor, and researchers. The *truth* is bound to lie somewhere near the intersection of the various lines of vision. Another important feature of this study is the quantification of clinical judgement through the method of paired comparisons and by the use of the Health-Sickness Rating Scale. This project can also claim that it does not interfere with the treatment, since there is no direct observation of it.

Certain limitations go hand in hand with these advantages. In the absence of direct observation of therapy, information on it must be gleaned mostly from retrospective reports by patient, therapist, and supervisor. Nowadays, retrospective reports on therapy by the interested parties are somewhat suspect. But this issue has not been explored enough to allow judgment on the validity of the procedure in any particular case. It is quite possible that this type of inquiry provided the Menninger researchers with the data they needed.

The reliance upon clinical judgment naturally raises some questions. When ratings are required on such intervening variables as *ego strength*, one wonders about reliability. Luborsky (1962) states that agreement was high between the two judges who rated the patients' variables before treatment began. The judges discussed the cases before making their independent ratings. Another issue is the reliability between the initial judges and the team that did the termination ratings. And still another is the possible operation of the halo effect in making clinical judgments.

In a lesser project the questions we have raised might be damaging; but in a study with as wide a scope as this one, the most significant thing is not that questions can be raised, but that it has continued to exist and even flourish. Wallerstein names some of the problems involved in the sociology of research. Fortunately, the problems were met. Some results have already appeared, and are mentioned by Wallerstein. Others will be awaited with particular interest because this project, with its thorough and systematic description of patient, treatment, and situation, and with its intelligent awareness of all the problems involved, exemplifies the clinical method at its best.

The existence of different schools of psychotherapy is potentially very valuable heuristically. If there is some fundamental *essence* of psychotherapy, the best way to define it would be to study its expression in the work of the various schools. The treatment of matched patients by different techniques based upon different theoretical principles could go far toward dissecting some aspects of the nature of the psychotherapy process and delineating factors in the process, non-specific with respect to any one personality theory, which lead to change with psychotherapy. Unfortunately, very little of this kind of research has been done, for reasons which probably lie primarily outside the realm of psychotherapy research.

The value of this kind of comparative research is illustrated by Cartwright's chapter. The problem which she set herself is: considering psychoanalytically-oriented and client-centered therapies, what are the effects upon patients of the different therapeutic techniques? To answer this question required control of all variables other than therapeutic technique: the patients were chosen to be as alike as possible, and the therapists were also chosen to be similar, aside from their adherence to client-centered or psychoanalytic principles.

This research required criteria of patient response to treatment. Cartwright found these criteria within the therapeutic hours themselves: the content and style of patient verbalizations. Both psychoanalytic and client-centered theory are explicit about the goals at which they aim. The patient's words can indicate the extent of his progression toward these goals. Client-centered theory has paid particular attention to the changes in the client's psychological functioning within the therapy hours as he improves. (See the critical examinations of the evaluation of client-centered theory in the chapter by Shlien and Zimring in this volume.) Rogers and Rablen developed a Process Scale to rate the patient's verbalizations. These ratings indicate where the patient is on a continuum ranging from a rigid, impersonal type of psychological functioning to a fluid, richly experiencing type.

With regard to progress from the psychoanalytic viewpoint, Cartwright reasoned that this is indicated by improved self-observation, and she devised a scale to measure this. Each of the patient's verbalizations was rated according to its quality and adequacy as a piece of self-observation, ranging from those verbalizations which did not observe the self at all to those which did so in a high level, integrative way. She also scored the patient's and therapist's verbalizations by the Bales Interaction Process system which is theoretically neutral.

One of her findings from this experiment was that there is a discernible difference in the techniques of the psychoanalytic and client-centered therapists. The therapists do not use exclusively the techniques of their theoretical orientation, but they do so enough to be differentiated. As for patient response, the matched patients achieved about the same level of self-observation, regardless of the techniques to which they were exposed. Similarly, the degree of affect expressed appeared to depend more on the patient's personality than on the therapist's technique. Furthermore, the patient influenced the kinds of techniques which the therapist employed: obsessive patients required and elicited more activity from both the psychoanalytic and client-centered therapists than did the hysterics.

These results seem to emphasize the importance, with respect to outcome, of patient-personality over therapist-technique. But Cartwright points out a number of qualifications. One is that all the therapists involved were experienced. She concludes that, given a certain level of skill and experience in the therapist, what happens in treatment depends largely on what the patient brings to it. The author points out that the results may also be taken to indicate that the techniques of client-centered and analytic therapy are after all not that different. She further speculates that one purpose of the rules of therapeutic technique is to organize a beginning therapist's reactions until they become well established in his response hierarchy.

For the purposes of her study, Cartwright lumps together the case treated by psychoanalysis and the one treated by psychoanalytically-oriented once-a-week therapy. Techniques, goals, and theoretical bases differ for classical psychoanalysis and psychoanalytically-oriented psychotherapy and some of these differences, though on a quantitative continuum (e.g., the goal of more insight versus less insight), eventuate in qualitative distinctions between the goals of these therapies. Furthermore, some investigators would argue that it is inappropriate and incorrect to compare results obtained from an incomplete psychoanalysis with a completed course of client-centered psychotherapy. The chapter by Schlessinger et al., in this volume, describes in detail the contrasting technical, clinical, and theoretical differences between psychoanalysis and many other types of psychotherapies. This chapter and the one by Shlien and Zimring should be read in conjunction with the chapter by Cartwright for a thorough appreciation of the theoretical and practical issues involved in Cartwright's study.

REFERENCES

LUBORSKY, L. The patient's personality and psychotherapeutic change. In H. H. Strupp and L. Luborsky (Eds.), *Research in psychotherapy,* Vol. II. Washington, D.C.: American Psychological Association, 1962.

27. Evaluative research design: a social casework illustration

James L. Breedlove and Merton S. Krause

INTRODUCTION

Clinicians within the professions of psychology, social work, and psychiatry increasingly have demonstrated interest in the findings of research studies to supplement their clinical knowledge. The clinician's interest in organized research studies stems primarily from the recognition that demonstrable advances in therapeutic efficacy are dependent upon attaining greater precision in estimating the effects of treatment. Although the observations of the clinician from his practice may provide the bases for hypotheses, his day-to-day practice does not provide the necessary controls for testing the limits of such hypotheses (GAP Report No. 42, 1959; Rychlak, 1959). In most instances, only the organized study which introduces systematic controls on observations of clinical phenomena can demonstrate the utility of the clinician's hypotheses. This is true, of course, in areas other than psychotherapy, casework, and counseling (e.g., see Modell, 1963).

The value of an experimental program to develop knowledge for the clinician lies in the clarity which can be obtained through specifying the limiting conditions that pertain to our knowledge of any observed relationship, for instance the relationship between a treatment method and a particular patient or client outcome. There are at least two major kinds of conditions which limit generalizations about observed relationships. The first of these is the limitation on defining what is observed. For instance, the generalizability of findings from outcome studies depends on their replicability and thus upon the clarity with which both outcome and treatment variables are defined. The second is the limitation on demonstrating cause and effect relationships. Cause and effect relationships can be inferred most unequivocally when the therapeutic variables under study are under experimental control and other variables which may influence treatment outcome can be controlled, at least statistically. This paper is a discussion of some of the problems encountered in defining and estimating these limitations for an evaluative study of social casework. It is unlikely

The study reported here is supported by National Institute of Mental Health grant MH 00764.

at our present stage of knowledge that any practically-oriented research study will contain provisions for defining observations of behavior and establishing the essential nature of their relationships which will be satisfactory in all respects. However, actual experience in coping with these issues within the same study is one way in which progress can be made (Sargent, 1961).

Our intent in this paper is to discuss research principles which apply in the investigations of any therapeutic procedure, somatic therapies, psychotherapy, counseling, or casework. Although we shall speak of *casework, caseworker,* and *clients,* one might as easily substitute the words *psychotherapy, psychotherapist,* and *patients.* Our illustrative study, the design of which is reported here, originated with some Family Service caseworkers' impression that casework efforts have been relatively unsuccessful in bringing about improvements in the functioning or circumstances of families of alcoholics. It was believed, however, that better results could be obtained if caseworkers were to become more knowledgeable and skilled in assisting these families to manage the unique difficulties confronting them. Accordingly, a group of caseworkers at Family Service of the Cincinnati Area developed a modified form of casework practice to deal with these families. Our research objective in this study is the determination of the relative effectiveness of this special casework approach for helping the family in which the husband is an alcoholic. We refer to this study hereafter as the *P.C.F.A.,* or *Preventive Casework with the Families of Alcoholics* study.

THE EVALUATIVE STUDY AS A FIELD EXPERIMENT

The evaluative study, like any other systematic research, is designed to provide a factual answer to a question. The present study has been designed to determine how much more effective an *experimental* casework approach is than the *usual* casework approach with families of alcoholics. The *field experiment* offers a useful approach to evaluating such treatment methods (Thomas, 1960). The determination of the relative effectiveness of two or more casework procedures requires a comparison of the results achieved by each. The objective comparison of the results of two treatments requires that each treatment be given to one of two groups of subjects, each having substantially equivalent potential responsiveness to the treatment variables under study. It also means that a recognizable *a priori* difference must be established between the two treatments if the results are to be replicable.

In this study, however, we are also interested in determining how effective *any* casework approach is with families of alcoholics. To answer this question, a third group of clients receiving minimal treatment will be contrasted with the two groups receiving casework treatment. For practical reasons, such as the increased probability of losing clients, as well as for ethical reasons, it is usually not feasible to refuse to treat clients for research purposes (Imber, *et al.*, 1957). To overcome the practical problem of maintaining contact with clients, the *minimal treatment* group may be accepted for a limited treatment contact, not to exceed two or three interviews, and placed on a waiting list. Since it is expected during the latter half of the study that (due to our public relations efforts) the number of applicants will exceed the caseworkers' ability to accept new cases, there will be some justification for creating a *waiting period* for applicants.

Hereafter, the group of clients receiving the specially developed casework approach will be referred to as the *experimental* or *E* group, the group receiving the usual casework treatment will be referred to as the *control* or *C* group, and the third group receiving minimal treatment will be referred to as the *minimal treatment* or *M* control group. Finally, another control group ought to be included in the study to be treated by caseworkers who would not be aware that their work was being studied. The rationale for such a control group (referred to here as the *second control* or C_2) will be discussed below.

To reduce ambiguity in the comparison of treatments, the basic requirements for an evaluative study design are the same as those necessary in a controlled experiment. In addition to adequate specification of the treatments employed, which will be discussed first below, an adequate experiment requires: (1) elimination of systematic error; (2) reduction of random error in treatment outcome differences, both of which are discussed later in detail; (3) provisions in the experimental conditions for a sufficient range of valid generalization of the findings, referred to below under the subtitle *number of clients;* and (4) arrangements for the statistical calculation of uncertainty, which will be referred to later but not discussed in detail (Cox, 1958, pp. 5-12).

Experimental Control of Treatment Procedures

Establishing Treatment Differences

Although the purpose of an evaluative study is the assessment of the relative efficacy of treatment methods, little attention has been given in evaluative studies to the problems of defining the treatment variables under study (Blenkner, 1962). The Psychotherapy Research Project of The Menninger Foundation is an outstanding example of a current attempt to define treatment variables (Luborsky, *et al.*, 1958). Evaluative studies have made use of distinctions between treatments on qualitative characteristics, e.g., ward milieu therapy, psychotherapy, and group therapy (Fairweather, *et al.*, 1960) and of quantitative characteristics such as number of psychotherapy interviews held (Imber, *et al.*, 1957). Neither of these approaches satisfactorily specifies the substance or content of treatment being studied. Unless manipulable treatment *variables* are clearly defined, the clinical interpretation of the results of the evaluative study will be equivocal. This should not be taken to mean that treatment must be defined in every respect before an evaluative study can be undertaken, but only that two treatments being compared should be different in some manipulable respect which is presumed to have an important bearing on treatment outcome (and otherwise are approximately equivalent and replicable). Choosing such a difference between treatments for an evaluative study requires two prior decisions. First, a decision involving professional values must be made concerning the desirability of specific *outcomes*. Second, a decision involving the logic of treatment practice must be made regarding which *treatment procedures* will be most efficacious in bringing about the desired effects.

Some problems of specifying therapeutic variables in an evaluative study can be demonstrated by the P.C.F.A. Project. Identification of treatment variables for this study began with a practice problem. The agency wanted to improve casework practice to keep the wife of the alcoholic in treatment and to help her cope more effectively with the consequences for the family of her husband's drinking. In addition, it was hoped that better procedures for direct treatment of the alcoholic himself could be found. A period of time was set aside prior to the beginning of the research for the caseworkers assigned to the experimental unit to study these problems, define treatment objectives and methods of practice, and gain experience in using these methods. This trial period provided the opportunity for the caseworkers who were to use the experimental treatment method to specify a treatment approach which presumably would be more effective than that currently used in the field, and to define this approach in sufficient detail that it could be replicated by other caseworkers. Details of the experimental casework procedures will be reported in a later publication; for the purposes of this discussion, we only wish to point out that a considerable amount of effort was put into defining differences between the experimental treatment and the usual treatment on the basis of intensive clinical study.

Maintaining Treatment Differences

It is necessary in any experiment to take precautions to avoid *contamination* of the experimental and control treatment procedures. The caseworkers in the control group, using *ordinary* casework methods about which they are relatively uncertain, might tend to adopt the experimental casework method if they were to learn about it. Thus, no information about the experimental treatment method is to be given to any of the other agency staff and considerable precautions are being taken to minimize "leaks."

A final practical problem in establishing treatment differences is that of determining whether defined treatment differences can be identified and maintained in actual practice. Various means of estimating actual treatment differences between the experimental and control groups can be used. Caseworkers and their supervisors might be asked to complete questionnaires designed to elicit data about casework goals and procedures for each case. In addition, tape recordings of some pre-selected client interviews might be made to provide additional clues about actual differences in treatments.

The remainder of this discussion is concerned with the adequacy of the evaluative research design, that is, with the necessary provisions for reducing uncertainty and ambiguity in comparing treatment results and with estimating the practical significance of the findings. The significance of the results depends on (1) establishing that the effects are due to the treatment rather than to other factors (eliminating systematic error); and (2) determining the conditions under which differences in treatment effects are produced (increasing the precision in the comparison of differences in treatment outcomes by reducing the effects of random error).

Elimination of Systematic Error

One difficulty which typically arises in any experiment is the existence of a number of variables, other than the treatment variables under study, which can or do affect the outcome measures. If such extraneous variables are not known to affect treatment groups equally, it is not possible to attribute a difference in outcome to differences between the treatments. Variables which may affect treatment outcome other than those differentiating the treatment procedures can arise in the *client* and his situation or in the *treatment situation*. Thus, for various reasons, some clients may tend to have more favorable *prognoses* under a broad range of treatment methods. An impartial comparison of the outcome of two treatments can be made only when the treatments are conducted with client groups having, on the average, equivalent potential prognoses. Also, any number of conditions in the treatment situation, such as the caseworker's attitudes toward the client, caseworker morale, and the like, may affect treatment outcome. In order to make an adequate comparison of two treatment methods, some way must be found to insure the equivalence of these variables which are extraneous to the specific treatment methods to be compared. An alternative approach would be to define the experimental treatment in such a way that these *extraneous* variables (such as means of selecting caseworkers and manner of working together), become an intrinsic part of the treatment method itself.

Variables having an effect on the treatment outcome may, for our purposes, be classified according to the way in which they (presumably) operate to affect treatment outcome. For convenience we shall refer to client *motivating* and *facilitating* variables. A discussion of motivating variables as a part of the *placebo effect* may be found in Goldstein (1962, pp. 97-110). The concept of the placebo effect in psychotherapy studies, however, seems less useful to us than the concepts of motivating and facilitating variables (Cartwright, 1956).

By motivating variables, we mean those aspects of the client or his situation which predispose him to make some use of treatment. Such variables as the desire to be helped, the belief that the caseworker can be helpful, and the like, we refer to as motivating the client's *acceptance of treatment.* On the other hand, we refer to variables which contribute to the client's *ability to make changes* in himself or in his environment as facilitating variables. For instance, facilitating variables might indicate the capacity to change one's own attitudes (e.g., *psychological mindedness*) or the ability and freedom to change one's situation (e.g., education), and so on. Our knowledge of extraneous variables which tend to affect the treatment outcome is incomplete and tentative. Nevertheless, in an evaluative study careful consideration of such potentially important extraneous determinants of treatment outcome is essential (Frank, 1959). This point is discussed in greater detail immediately below as well as in a later section of this paper, "Increasing Precision in Treatment Comparisons."

Eliminating Systematic Error in Client Assignment

In general, two ways exist for reducing the systematic effect of such uncontrolled client variables on treatment comparisons.

The first method, factorial design, consists essentially of grouping clients into sets in such a way that all clients in a set are as similar as possible. These sets should differ on one or more interesting or important client variables. Each distinguishable treatment is assigned to the same number of clients in each set. Although such an application of the factorial experimental design has advantages for refined hypothesis testing, data analysis, etc., it is not usually feasible in casework research for two reasons: (1) there is insufficient established knowledge at present about variables which affect treatment outcome, and (2) data for classifying clients are typically lacking or unattainable prior to the assignment of clients for treatment. The second method chosen for this study is the fully randomized assignment of appropriate clients to different treatments. This method is more readily applicable in the social agency field.

Clients will be randomly assigned to one of three treatment groups: experimental, control, or minimal treatment control. That is, each new applicant, when accepted for the study, will be assigned a number selected from a table of random digits. Each applicant will then be assigned to one of the three groups according to this number. The use of a table of random digits assures that (1) each of the three groups receives approximately the same number of applicants since each digit occurs with equal frequency in the whole series, and (2) the assignment of any one applicant would have no relation to the assignment of any other applicant, since the numerical values of adjacent digits are independent of each other. The effectiveness of random assignment is dependent, however, on the cooperativeness of clients in participating in the research procedures (Stephan and McCarthy, 1963, pp. 235-272).

Eliminating Systematic Error in Research Administration

Next, let us consider the systematic error introduced in an evaluative study by (1) the research procedures used directly with clients, and (2) differences in the treatment situations induced by the administration of the research design. That is, differences may arise between the conditions under which the two treatments are carried out which will interfere with the equivalence of the treatment groups in such a way that the treatment effects will be biased (e.g., see Orne, 1962). Even though the variables which are expected to produce specific effects on the clients are in fact different for the experimental and control groups, another set of factors inherent in the way the study is administered may tend to produce systematic differences in the treatment outcomes between the experimental and control groups.

The potential systematic error which may be introduced by conducting research interviews, giving tests, etc., prior to or following therapy, is the most amenable to control, since the administration of these procedures is the direct responsibility of the researcher. Two types of error may be traced to measures used in the evaluative study: (1) the type of outcome data collected directly from the client may provide an opportunity for the expression of bias; and (2) data collection procedures used directly with the client prior to treatment may increase the probability of bias in outcome measures taken after treatment. We will consider each of these sources of error separately.

Systematic Error in Outcome Measures

Measurements of treatment outcome may reflect the conditions of the research design, rather than the results of different treatments. The possibility that the type of procedure used for data collection may itself produce biased treatment results occurs when the conditions of testing have an appreciable but unrecognized effect on the outcome measures (Fiske and Butler, 1963). For instance, the *hello-goodbye* effect has been recognized as one type of distortion (Hathaway, 1948). This refers to the tendency of persons seeking help to overestimate their difficulties early in treatment (to justify their need for help) and to underestimate them at the end of treatment (to justify or indicate gratitude for the therapist's efforts.) Thus, the *improvement* reported by persons receiving prolonged treatment may be artificially greater than for persons receiving short term treatment or those receiving less treatment, e.g., a *minimal treatment* control group. A similar biasing effect may occur in therapists' ratings of improvement of clients. This source of error is most likely to be present when (1) outcome measures between the "no treatment" and the "treatment" groups are compared, and when (2) the subjective impressions of therapists and clients are used. The possibility of this effect can be minimized by using outcome measures which are not dependent on the inferences of subjects (whether caseworkers or clients), whose perceptions may tend to be distorted. To minimize this source of error in the present study, outcome measurements which do not require the subjects to make inferences about "improvement" will be taken in addition to those which require such inference. Another way of handling this problem would be through the data analysis. Outcome measurements could be analyzed separately for clients who received prolonged treatment.

Other sources of systematic error which can be attributed directly to the measurement operations are: (1) interaction effects of pre-treatment measurement procedures with treatment on outcome measurements when two or more treatments are compared; and (2) main or interaction effects of pre-treatment measurement procedures on outcome measurements when a treatment and a no-treatment control group are compared (Campbell, 1957). By *main effects,* we mean the direct and independent effects a variable (e.g., pre-testing) has on measurements of treatment outcome. By *interaction effects,* we mean the indirect and interdependent effects a variable such as pre-testing has on measurements of treatment outcome, when it occurs in the presence of another condition such as a particular treatment method.

If clients have been subjected to testing prior to treatment, the testing itself may influence their response to the treatment. If the changes in response to treatment, due to the testing, were uniform across the two treatment groups (e.g., a main effect), pre-testing would not introduce a systematic error. However, as Campbell (1957) shows, a main effect produced by such pre-testing tends to decrease the overall generalizability or representativeness of the findings. When the treatments compared are quite different, we might expect an *interaction effect,* that is, that the effect of pre-testing, by creating a particular response set in clients, has a greater or different effect on outcome for one of the treatments being compared than for the other. Pre-treatment measures, for instance, may tend to *supplement* one treatment in such a way that it becomes equivalent to the second treatment with which it is being compared. In this case, the first but not the second treatment is affected by the pre-treatment testing. For example, let us assume that the objective of one treatment method (but not of a second) is to sensitize the client to the importance of learning specific attitudes. Tests given prior to treatment, if they tend to increase the client's readiness to learn, such attitudes would have more impact on the results of the second treatment by preparing the client in a

manner similar to that of the first treatment. Thus, the two treatment outcomes would tend to be equalized. The possibility of such an equalizing
affect has been noted in investigations of attitude change, and is a possible
source of bias in evaluative studies (Lana, 1959).

The design for the present study includes the following method for estimating the effect of pre-testing subjects. Only some of the clients assigned
to the three treatment groups requiring pre-testing will actually be pre-
tested. After subjects are randomly assigned to one of the treatment groups
(E, M, or C), they will be randomly assigned within each of these groups
to one of two conditions: (1) pre-treatment testing, or (2) no pre-treatment testing. This design, an adaptation of the "Solomon Four Group Design" (Campbell, 1957), effectively allows us to estimate and avoid the
main and interaction effects of pre-testing. It is schematically represented
below (wherein O refers to observations or measurements, either before or
after treatment). It should be noted that this pre-testing refers to ancillary
measurements only and not a *before* measurement of outcome (change
scores are not used in this study).

P.C.F.A. Research Design
(adapted from "Solomon Four Group Design")

Pre-Treatment Ancillary Measures	Treatment Group	Post-Treatment Outcome Measures
O_1	E	O_2
O_3	C	O_4
O_5	M	O_6
	E	O_7
	C	O_8
	M	O_9
	C_2*	O_{10}*

* If it were possible, it would be desirable to extend the study design to include a control group
of caseworkers who are not aware of their participation in the Project (C_2) and measure the results
of their work (O_{10}).

Caseworker Participation in Research

A contribution to systematic error may result indirectly from the caseworkers' attitudes toward their participation in the research. It has, for instance, been demonstrated that therapists' beliefs in the efficacy of their
methods are transmitted to their patients with corresponding effects on the
patients' attitudes toward treatment (Wolf, 1950). Systematic differences
between experimental and control caseworkers' attitudes toward the treatment procedures thus can bias the comparison of treatment results.

If a large number of caseworkers from different agencies were assigned
at random to the experimental and the control treatment groups, and their
indoctrination were similar with regard to level of aspiration (among

other things), it would be possible to assume that systematic error introduced by the personal and attitudinal characteristics of caseworkers had been minimized or even eliminated. Because relatively little is known about extraneous caseworker variables which may effect treatment outcome (Strupp, 1962), such a procedure would be ideally suited for our design. Unfortunately, in the P.C.F.A. study, it was not possible for the agency administrators to assign caseworkers to the treatment groups in this way. Neither was it possible, because of the limited number of caseworkers participating in the Project, to arrange a factorial experimental design with regard to caseworker attributes.

Caseworkers were selected by the agency administrators to participate in the experimental group on the basis of their interest in devoting full time to the Project. Two of these workers were selected from the agency staff, and two were recruited from other agencies. With one exception, these workers agreed to remain with the Project until its termination, i.e., for three years. Many staff caseworkers decided not to participate because they would have to remain with the Project throughout its duration, as well as carry a caseload consisting exclusively of families of alcoholics.

Other caseworkers were selected for the control group on the basis of their having skill and experience similar to that of the experimental group caseworkers, and also on the basis of their acquiescence in participating on a *part-time* basis in the project. Because of the non-random assignment of caseworkers to the treatment groups, some of whatever differences in treatment outcomes we find may be attributable to systematic differences in the caseworkers assigned to the two groups, e.g., personal differences which led the experimental caseworkers to volunteer for the Project, and those which initially led the control caseworkers not to volunteer. In general, this difference could be interpreted as the degree to which the caseworker is interested in the problem of alcoholism and willing to commit himself to the intensive study and treatment of these families.

We do expect to obtain some measures of both the experimental and control caseworker's attitudes toward alcoholism and study their correlations with outcome measures. This should give us some indication of how much systematic error may stem from this one variable.

The work conditions of the experimental and control group caseworkers provide a second source of potential systematic error. In the experimental group, caseworkers are physically separated from the rest of the agency, have a close "in-group" feeling, and considerable salient experience, skill, and confidence in working with the families of alcoholics. Prior to the beginning of the evaluation phase of the Project, three of the four had worked together intensively for 14 months, developing their knowledge and skill specifically for this work. During this period they devoted their full time and effort to their work, achieving a sense of dedication to the Project and apparently high morale.

On the other hand, the control caseworkers have had no additional opportunity to learn about alcoholism, nor to develop any special confidence in their ability to treat these families. Also, of the control caseworkers' total caseloads, only a small proportion will consist of Project cases. This means that, unlike the *experimental* workers, their efforts will not be devoted exclusively to trying to understand and treat any unique problems which may be presented by these families. This factor alone might contribute significantly to the systematic error, since it may be expected that a caseworker will spend more time and effort on those cases he considers most promising or likely to benefit from casework.

Unfortunately, the inherent differences in the conditions of work for the experimental and control caseworkers will not permit us to conclude on the basis of this experiment alone that any differences found in treatment outcome between the experimental and control groups are due exclusively or even primarily to the experimental treatment method. In order to be able to state with confidence that any treatment differences found are due to the treatment methods, another study in which the other treatment conditions are kept constant will be necessary. This further research objective would be carried out by randomly assigning workers in other agencies to the experimental and control groups. The only difference between the two groups would then be the additional training and skill of the experimental caseworkers in the new methods. As it stands, the present study has a built-in possibility of systematic error, deriving from the probable differences in both the characteristics of the workers and their treatment situations. These differences, discussed above, probably would tend to increase the confidence and effort expended by the experimental caseworkers.

It may, of course, be argued that the caseworker's confidence in his ability to help is an integral part of his casework, and should *not* be considered an extraneous variable as we have done here. However, whether or not the caseworker's belief in the efficacy of his treatment is inseparable from his actual work with the client is not at issue here. We are only noting the possible effects arising from the systematic differences in confidence in the treatment of alcoholics and their families which the experimental and control caseworkers are likely to have when they are pre-selected on a volunteer basis for assignment to a study and prepared differently for it.

Some attempt will be made to minimize this bias by (1) encouraging and supporting the control group workers' confidence in their casework ability with families of alcoholics, (2) arranging for their participation in the data collection procedures to be as active as that of the caseworkers in the experimental group. Thus, both experimental and first control group caseworkers will be constantly aware that they are being studied. Other research studies have indicated that the fact of being studied influences the participants to alter their *usual* behavior, e.g., to increase their productivity or effectiveness (Campbell, 1957). To study and to provide the data for statistical control of this tendency, a third control group ought to be included in the design (in addition to the regular *control* and *minimal treatment control* groups). This additional control group would consist of four caseworkers who would be assigned cases from the Project in the usual way from the agency's Intake Supervisor. Precautions should be taken to keep these four caseworkers from becoming aware that their work is under study. Neither they nor their clients would, therefore, participate in providing research data at the beginning of the study. After these cases were closed, outcome measurements would be taken. Contrasting the results of this second control treatment group (C_2) with those of the experimental (E) and regular control (C) groups, would then provide information relevant to the effect on the caseworkers of knowing they were being studied.

Increasing Precision in Treatment Comparisons

The preceding section has indicated how certain systematic errors may be avoided by random assignment of clients. Although (as we have shown) the treatment methods being compared are confounded with caseworker characteristics and treatment conditions, because of the random assignment of clients, differences between groups of clients in each treatment condition can be considered to be negligible.[1] We can now turn our attention to the next requirement to ensure the adequacy of an evaluative design: *precision* in estimating differences between treatment outcomes. The estimate of such a treatment difference, when systematic error has been eliminated by proper randomization, differs from its true value only by random error, the average size of which is estimated by a conventional statistic, the standard error (see, e.g., Goulden, 1952, p. 20). The magnitude of the standard error, and thus the degree of imprecision in estimating differences between treatment outcomes, depends on: (1) the reliability of the *measuring instruments*, (2) the intrinsic *variability of clients*, (3) the *number of clients* included in the study, and (4) the *research design*. We will discuss each of these factors in turn as they can be employed for increasing the precision of the estimate of treatment comparisons by reducing the latter's standard errors.

---

[1] For many clinicians the possibility that random distribution of subjects between an experimental and a control group will result in equivalent groups seems doubtful. Partly this difficulty in comprehending the efficacy of random assignment may occur if it is thought that the equivalence which is sought refers to persons rather than groups of persons. In addition, however, the effectiveness of random assignment for assuring the equivalence between groups of persons has been questioned because of the vast inherent differences which exist between persons. In general, the greater the variation between subjects, the more subjects will need to be included in order to achieve equivalence between experimental groups. The reader should refer to other sources for a fuller understanding of random assignment: a good introductory discussion of randomization may be found in Cox (1958), pp. 70-90.

Measuring Instruments

The utility of the results of an evaluative study is limited by the kind of reliability of the outcome measures used. This study is problem-centered (Maslow, 1946): outcome measures have been selected or adapted to be directly relevant to the clinical problem under study (i.e., casework treatment of alcoholism and its effects on the family). Our present stage of development in measuring aspects of human behavior does not permit a high degree of accuracy in a study such as this. For example, a growing literature is available on the relative unreliability of clinical diagnosis (Kreitman, 1961). Actually, two kinds of measures of casework results were selected since it seemed desirable to assess as many different aspects of treatment results as possible. The measures selected for use in this study fall into two classifications: (1) primary, or evaluative measures, and (2) secondary, or exploratory outcome measures. They could not be selected on the basis of any empirical evidence for their relative reliability.

Primary Measures of Treatment Results

The primary measures of the results of treatment are those which will be used to determine the effectiveness of treatments for producing desirable results. One major consideration has gone into the selection of measures to evaluate treatment effectiveness. That is, only those measures which seemed to indicate a successful or favorable treatment outcome were selected. Although it is recognized that any search for an *ultimate* success criterion is illusory at present (Jahoda, 1958), the evaluative measures were selected to provide practical clinical indices of treatment success. (See Parloff *et al.*, 1954, for a similarly pragmatic approach to outcome measures.)

The evaluative measures are: (1) continuance in treatment, i.e., the number of treatment interviews kept; (2) the drinking pattern of the husband, i.e., the amount and frequency of drinking, and the existence of associated social problems; and (3) the wife's comfort with her situation. The use of continuance in treatment as an outcome measure not only has practical importance for the clinician but is one way of dealing with the problem of attrition in outcome studies (Lasky, 1962). Each of these variables will be assessed by various methods of data collection, i.e., from caseworker, wife, and (where possible) husband ratings. The use of several sources of data to measure the same variable provides an opportunity to study the observation of many investigators that outcome data collected by the same method on different variables are positively correlated, and data on the same variable assessed by different methods tend to be less correlated (Cartwright, *et al.*, 1963). Reliability can be increased by averaging the several measurements of the same variable where this seems justifiable.

Data will be collected either directly from the caseworkers by means of various questionnaire items, or from clients by research interviewers using a combination of structured interviews and questionnaires immediately upon termination or six months later. We expect to control interviewer bias partially by keeping the research interviewers ignorant of the research design (Rosenthal *et al.*, 1963). Research interviewers will not be made aware that the outcome of casework is being evaluated, or that two case-work methods are being compared. In order to neutralize to some extent the possible biasing effect of interviewers (Hyman, *et al.*, 1954, pp. 83-137), they will be randomly assigned an equal number of respondents from each treatment and control group.

Secondary Measures of Treatment Results

We believe the ultimate purpose of psychological treatment intervention, including casework, is to change behavior through changing attitudes. An evaluative study can contribute to an understanding of the nature of these changes and of how they came about. The primary criteria (discussed above) represent three different facets of casework "success." The most compelling of the three sets of success criteria is the husband's behavioral patterns associated with alcoholism. In addition to such measures which most clearly indicate a favorable outcome, other possibly more sensitive measures of results are needed to indicate limited or partial success. When the problem being studied is one in which treatment successes have been rare, e.g., alcoholism, the need for assessing intermediate degrees of improvement is particularly important. Since we have incomplete knowledge about how the alcoholic's or his wife's attitudes are related to drinking behavior, the investigation of attitudinal outcomes is necessarily tentative. Several direct (verbal) and indirect (behavior) outcome measures of attitudes toward alcoholism and its treatment are included in this study. The manner in which these attitudes are associated with changed criterion behavior can be ascertained in the data analysis.

Administering Outcome Measures

As we noted earlier the design of this study does not rely on *change scores* to determine the effects of treatment. The decision to use only measurements taken after the end of treatment was made upon considering its advantages and disadvantages. One possible disadvantage of the use of *after* scores is a reduction in precision. Greater precision in comparing treatment effects by the use of change scores may be gained, but only if the correlation between the *before* and *after* scores is sufficiently high (Hovland, 1949, P. 323). Despite the possible gain in precision afforded by change scores, at least two possible disadvantages (other than the additional financial expense of taking measurements prior to the beginning of treatment) may be noted. The first of these is the possibility of introducing a systematic error into the study through interaction effects of pre-treatment measurements with the treatments. The second is the possibility of limiting the population to which the findings may be generalized. Both of these possible sources of error are discussed above in the section dealing with systematic error. The decision to use *after* scores rather than *change* scores was made on balance; we recognized that possible gains in avoiding one source of systematic error and maintaining the representativeness of findings might be at the expense of some loss in precision.

Another administrative aspect of outcome measures which may affect both precision and systematic error is the time lapse between termination of treatment and the time scheduled for measuring outcome. A number of factors may affect the time when outcome measurements should be taken. Since we are interested in estimating the ultimate effects of treatments it seemed to us that the factor deserving the most consideration is the possible difference between the *delayed* and the *immediate* effects of treatment. It is possible that the relationship between delayed and immediate treatment effects varies for different treatments. That is, for a given treatment, the immediate effects may gradually *decay* over time. A different type of treatment may show continued improvement over time or *growth*. To provide a basis for the study of such treatment effect curves, a decision was made to measure treatment outcome at two different intervals: (1) immediately following treatment, and (2) six months after treatment. Each client will be interviewed for outcome measurement at both of these time intervals. Three measurements would provide a basis for extrapolating the treatment effect curves as a means of estimating the ultimate effect of treatment.

Client Variability

For various reasons, no attempts are being made to increase precision by reducing the variability of clients, other than limiting the study to families in which the husband is alcoholic. For the purposes of this study, a working definition of alcoholism adapted from Jellinek (1960) has been developed for selecting families from among agency applicants to be included in the study. Applicants are screened by specially trained caseworkers when they initiate contact with the agency by telephone. If the applicant indicates that the male head of the household has a drinking problem, the telephone intake caseworker determines if there are evidences of alcohol *addiction* or alcoholism, e.g., progressively increasing use of alcohol or apparent inability to control alcoholic intake. If evidence of alcoholism is uncovered in the telephone application, the case is referred to the Research Department for random assignment to one of the treatment groups (E or C). It is believed that by including as large a variety of client types as possible, the possibility of gaining further insights into the problem under study is increased, and the basis for generalizing from our results is broadened. Furthermore, not enough is known about the relevant variables of this client population which could be used to increase precision by stratified sampling. (A recent example of an attempt to discriminate client types may be found in Butler, *et al.*, 1962).

When the data are collected, we will be able to describe the sample of clients included in the study and so further delimit the population to which results can be generalized. Two types of descriptive data will be available at that time. The sample will be described first by demographic data including social class position, religion, race, age, etc. Also, the sample will be described according to data which have particular relevance for clinicians and agency administrators, including nature and degree of alcoholism (Jellinek, 1960), extent of family disorganization (Jackson, 1956), referral source, etc.

Number of Clients

Precision in the treatment comparisons can be increased by including a sufficient number of clients to reduce the magnitude of the error in the estimated outcome differences. The probable magnitude of error in estimating the treatment difference can be measured statistically by the standard error.[2]

After the outcomes of several cases have been determined, we can estimate the total number of cases necessary to include in the study to establish a significant treatment effect (Cox, 1958, pp. 182-185). A conventional standard for determining the number of cases needed is the number required for establishing a statistically significant treatment effect. That is, within the time limitation of the study (two years), the number of cases should be increased to the point that the size of the standard error of the differences between the means of the criterion measures is no greater than half the size of those differences themselves. This would yield about a 5 percent level of statistical significance. If the number of cases cannot be increased sufficiently to reach a 5 percent significance level within the two-year period, the study should be extended, if feasible. Of course, differences in outcome measures between the treatment groups may be slight or non-existent; that is, there may be insufficient evidence that one treatment method is any more effective than another (Cox, 1958, p. 160). If this should be the case, we would conclude that if any real difference exists, it

[2] The standard error (*se*) of the difference between the mean outcomes of two treatments is inversely proportional to the square root of the number of clients in that treatment group, i.e.,

$$se = (s) \sqrt{\frac{2}{n}}$$

Here *s* is the standard deviation of an outcome measure. The standard error of the difference of two means therefore can be reduced by increasing the number of clients given those two treatments (Cox, 1958, pp. 154-190).

must be very small or obscured by contrary systematic error (discussed above).

Research Design

In this study (as in most experiments in which subjects have been randomly assigned to treatments), the research design itself is a most useful device to increase the precision of the treatment comparisons (Edwards and Cronbach, 1952). As noted above, we concluded that it was not feasible to use a device such as a factorial or randomized block design (Cox, 1958, pp. 91-153) to reduce uncontrolled (random) variation. However, if the range of clients' potential responsiveness to casework is large, which appears likely, then it will be useful to have supplementary or *diagnostic* information available to help explain this variability. Our alternative choice in design, then, is to reduce this uncontrolled variation by statistical procedures. Other studies (Edwards and Cronbach, 1952; Hovland, *et al.*, 1949) have demonstrated that such supplementary data about client attributes or situations can be useful also for avoiding ambiguous or even erroneous conclusions when outcome data alone are used. (See Klerman, 1963, for a discussion of the problem of ancillary data in pharmacological studies.) In this study we refer to these supplementary data as concomitant measurements of ancillary variables. These variables are discussed below. Only those concomitant measures which (1) are unaffected by the assignment of clients to the treatments, and (2) can be expected to have an effect independent of the treatments on the outcome measures are appropriate for use in reducing the uncontrolled variation by statistical means (Cox, 1958, pp. 48-69). We will take measures of variables which, on the basis of previous empirical findings or on theoretical grounds, are expected to effect treatment outcome.[3]

The kind of analysis of the effect of ancillary variables on treatment outcomes which is appropriate will vary with the scaling properties of the ancillary data. Equal-interval scaled ancillary data may be used to adjust outcome variances (and means) for each of the treatments. The increase in precision resulting from this adjustment varies directly with the correlation between ancillary and outcome measurements. We may, for instance, analyze continuance in each of the various treatments (E and C) in connection with the ancillary variables which are expected to influence continuance in treatment (that is, the motivating variables, e.g., client expectation of benefit, client definition of difficulty, etc.) by the statistical technique of analysis of covariance (Goulden, 1952). This technique arithmetically adjusts the outcome measurements to partition-out the possible influence of the concomitant variables. In the case of qualitative ancillary

---

[3] As discussed earlier, only part of the total sample included in the E and C groups will be pre-tested. Thus, concomitant measurements will be taken on only three-quarters of the clients in the sample.

data, separate analyses may be made for sub-groups of clients (Hovland, 1949, pp. 308-328; for an alternative approach see Finney, 1960, pp. 178-181).

Motivating Variables

We previously referred to client motivating variables, i.e., those characteristics of the client which predispose him to *use* treatment. Earlier empirical findings provide some evidence that the client's attitudes toward his problem or toward treatment tend to be predictive of his use of treatment, i.e., remaining in treatment (Levinger, 1960). Essentially, the major client variables found to be associated with continuance in treatment are (1) degree of discomfort, e.g., anxiety; (2) conception of the problem in psychological or interpersonal terms (Blenkner, 1954); (3) acceptance of responsibility (Rubenstein and Lorr, 1956; Shyne, 1957); and (4) desire to be helped. This study incorporates measures of these variables taken prior to treatment which may be used to adjust the continuance data in each of the treatment groups (E and C). The difference between these adjusted means for continuance data may be taken as the estimate of the effect of the experimental treatment method.

Facilitating Variables

A second type of ancillary data (*facilitating variables*) may be useful to increase precision in the analysis of treatment outcome data. By facilitating client variables, we refer to those aspects of the client which enable him to *benefit* from treatment. Previous findings have indicated several client variables which would appear to predict the clients' *ability to benefit* from treatment: the capacity to conceptualize affective states, e.g., capacity to experience signal anxiety (Siegal and Rosen, 1962) and verbal accessibility (Weber, 1963). Individuals who have achieved a higher level of psychological development, as indicated by less psychopathology (Hunt, *et al.*, 1959) or by greater adequacy in the performance of social roles (Zigler and Phillips, 1961), tend to have more successful treatment outcomes. Still other studies have emphasized the influence of stress and the availability of resources in a person's *environmental situation* on treatment outcome (Voth, *et al.*, 1962; Miles, *et al.*, 1951). Of particular relevance for the present study, alcoholics' attainment of sobriety has been found to be associated with higher economic status, economic adequacy, intelligence, and less pathological behavior (Bailey, *et al.*, 1962; Glatt, 1961). The present study includes several measures of ancillary variables relevant to: (1) *ego strength*, (2) capacity to conceptualize affective states, (3) verbal accessibility, and (4) degree of environmental stress.

CONCLUSIONS

We have described the design of a field experiment to convey the principal ideas of experimental design applicable in evaluative studies of counseling, casework, and psychotherapy. These include the definition of treatments, the selection (sampling) of clients and therapists, the arrangement of control groups, precautions against the possible biasing effects in data collection procedures, and the assessment of promising variables which are not readily controlled. The major purpose of the experiment is to demonstrate the effects of the treatment under study.

As long as an experimenter's knowledge or control of relevant variables is incomplete, his experiments cannot be expected to be conclusive. Under such circumstances findings are contingent on other things being equal. We experiment even though these "other things" are not necessarily equal for treatment and control groups. We experiment because even inconclusive work *can* be cumulative. The cumulative quality of empirical studies may be recognized in two ways: (1) by contributions to planning further scientific work on the same topic, and (2) by the adequacy of description for replicating the study. (Statistically significant findings about a study's hypotheses are neither necessary nor sufficient evidence of its more important quality of cumulativeness; they are only *prima facie* evidence that the results emerge distinctly from their background of sampling error.)

Field experiments, which evaluative studies must be, *can* be as cumulative as laboratory experiments, but only by greater effort. More detailed description of field conditions is necessary to allow replication, since they are not as standard as laboratory conditions on traditional topics. More comprehensive use of population descriptions and (random) sampling plans are necessary for variables which cannot be brought under control. Thus, no doubt contrary to many persons' expectations, proportionally more work should go into the design and preparation of a scientific field experiment than into an analogous laboratory experiment of equal size.

REFERENCES

BAILEY, M. B., HABERMAN, P., and ALKSNE, H. Outcome of alcoholic marriages: endurance, termination, or recovery. *Quart. J. Stud. Alcohol.*, **23**: 610-623, 1962.

BLENKNER, MARGARET. Predictive factors in the initial interview in family casework. *Soc. Serv. Rev.*, **28**: 65-73, 1954.

BLENKNER, MARGARET. Control groups and the placebo effect. *Social Work*, **7**: 52-58, 1962.

BUTLER, J. M., RICE, L. N., and WAGSTAFF, A. K. On the naturalistic definition of variables: An analogue of clinical analysis. In H. H. Strupp and L.

Luborsky (Eds.), *Research in Psychotherapy.* Washington, D.C.: American Psychological Association, 1962.

CAMPBELL, D. Factors relevant to the validity of experiments in social settings. *Psychol. Bull.,* **54**: 297-312, 1957.

CARTWRIGHT, D. S. Psychotherapy: not the placebo effect. Univ. of Chicago Counseling Center Discussion Papers. **2** (Whole No. 29), 1956.

CARTWRIGHT, D. S., KIRTNER, W. L., and FISKE, D. W. Method factors in changes associated with psychotherapy. *J. abnorm. soc. Psychol.,* **66**: 164-175, 1963.

COX, D. R. *Planning of experiments.* New York: Wiley, 1958.

EDWARDS, A. L., and CRONBACH, L. J. Experimental design for research in psychotherapy. *J. clin. Psychol.,* **8**: 51-59, 1952.

FAIRWEATHER, G. W., SIMON, R. GEBHARD, M. E., WEINGARTEN, E., HOLLAND, J. L., SANDERS, R., STONE, G. B., and REAHL, J. E. Relative effectiveness of psychotherapeutic programs: a multicriteria comparison of four programs for three different patient groups. *Psychol. Monogr.,* **74**: (Whole No. 492), 1960.

FINNEY, D. J. *An introduction to the theory of experimental design.* Chicago: Univ. of Chicago Press, 1960.

FISKE, D. W., and BUTLER, J. M. The experimental conditions for measuring individual differences. *Educ. psychol. Measmt.,* **23**: 249-266, 1963.

FRANK, J. D. Problems of controls in psychotherapy as exemplified by the psychotherapy research project of the Phipps Psychiatric Clinic. In E. H. Rubinstein and M. B. Parloff (Eds.), *Research in psychotherapy.* Washington, D. C.: American Psychological Association, 1959.

GLATT, M. M. Treatment results in an English mental hospital alcoholic unit. *Acta Psychiat. Scand.,* **37**: 143-168, 1961.

GOLDSTEIN, A. *Therapist-patient expectancies in psychotherapy.* New York: Macmillan, 1962.

GOULDEN, C. *Methods of Statistical Analysis.* New York: Wiley, 1952.

HATHAWAY, S. R. Some considerations relative to nondirective psychotherapy as counseling. *J. clin. Psychol.,* **4**: 226-231, 1948.

HOVLAND, C. I., LUMSDAINE, A. A., and SHEFFIELD, F. D. *Experiments on mass communication.* Princeton, N.J.: Princeton University Press, 1949.

HUNT, J. McV., EWING, T. N., LaFORGE, R., and GILBERT, W. M. An integrated approach to research on therapeutic counseling with samples of results. *J. counsel. Psychol.,* **6**: 46-54, 1959.

HYMAN, H. H., COBB, W. J., FELDMAN, J. J., HART, C. W., and STEMBER, C. H. *Interviewing in social research.* Chicago: Univ. of Chicago Press, 1954.

IMBER, S. D., FRANK, J. D., NASH, E. H., STONE, A. R., and GLIEDMAN, L. H. Improvement and amount of therapeutic contact: an alternative to the use of no-treatment controls in psychotherapy. *J. consult. Psychol.,* **21**: 309-315, 1957.

JACKSON, JOAN. The adjustment of the family to alcoholism. *Marriage and family living,* **18**: 361-369, 1956.

JAHODA, MARIE. *Current concepts of positive mental health.* New York: Basic Books, 1958.

JELLINEK, E. M. *The disease concept of alcoholism.* New Haven, Conn.: Hillhouse Press, 1960.

KLERMAN, G. Assessing the influence of the hospital milieu upon the effectiveness of psychiatric drug therapy: problems of conceptualization and research methodology. *J. nerv. ment. Dis.,* **137**: 143-154, 1963.

KREITMAN, N. The reliability of psychiatric diagnosis. *J. ment. Sci.,* **107**: 876-886, 1961.

LANA, R. E. Pretest-treatment interaction effects in attitudinal studies. *Psychol. Bull.,* **56**: 293-300, 1959.

LASKY, J. The problem of sample attrition in controlled treatment trials. *J. nerv. ment. Dis.,* **135**: 332-337, 1962.

LEVINGER, G. Continuance in casework and other helping relationships: a review of current research. *Social Work,* **5**: 40-51, 1960.

LUBORSKY, L., FABIAN, MICHALINA, HALL, B. H., TICHO, E., and TICHO, GERTRUDE R. Treatment variables. *Bull. Menninger Clin.,* **22**: 126-147, 1958.

MASLOW, A. H. Problem-centering vs. means-centering in science. *Phil. of Sci.,* **13**: 326-331, 1946.

MILES, H. H., BARRABEE, E. L., and FINESINGER, J. E. Evaluation of psychotherapy: with a follow-up study of 62 cases of anxiety neurosis. *Psychosom. Med.,* **13**: 83-105, 1951.

MODELL, W. Hazards of new drugs. *Sci.,* **139**: 1180-1185, 1963.

ORNE, M. T. On the social psychology of the psychological experiment: with particular reference to demand characteristics and their implications. *Amer. Psychologist,* **17**: 776-783, 1962.

PARLOFF, M. B., KELMAN, H. C., and FRANK, J. D. Comfort, effectiveness, and self-awareness as criteria of improvement in psychotherapy. *Amer. J. Psychiat.,* **3**: 343-351, 1954.

ROSENTHAL, R., PERSINGER, G. W., VIKAN-KLINE, LINDA L., and MABRAY, R. C. The role of the research assistant in the mediation of experimenter bias. *J. Pers.,* **31**: 313-335, 1963.

RUBINSTEIN, E. A., and LORR, M. A comparison of terminators and remainers in out-patient psychotherapy. *J. clin. Psychol.,* **12**: 345-349, 1956.

RYCHLAK, J. F. Clinical psychology and the nature of evidence. *Amer. Psychologist,* **14**: 642-648, 1959.

SARGENT, HELEN. Intrapsychic change: methodological problems in psychotherapy research. *Psychiat.,* **24**: 93-108, 1961.

SHYNE, ANN. What research tells us about short-term cases in family agencies. *Soc. Casewk.,* **38**: 223-231, 1957.

SIEGAL, R., and ROSEN, I. Character style and anxiety tolerance: a study in intrapsychic change. In H. H. Strupp and L. Luborsky (Eds.), *Research in Psychotherapy,* Vol. II. Washington, D.C.: American Psychological Association, 1962. Pp. 206-217.

Some observations on controls in psychiatric research, Report No. 42. New York: Group for the Advancement of Psychiatry, 1959.

STEPHAN, F. F., and McCARTHY, P. J. *Sampling opinions.* New York: Wiley, 1963.

STRUPP, H. H. Patient-doctor relationships: The psychotherapist in the therapeutic process. In A. J. Bachrach (Ed.) *Experimental Foundations of clinical psychology.* New York: Basic Books, 1962.

THOMAS, E. J. Field experiments and demonstrations. In Norman Polansky (Ed.), *Social work research.* Chicago: Univ. of Chicago Press, 1960. Pp. 273-297.

VOTH, H. M., MODLIN, H. C., and ORTH, H. H. Situational variables in the assessment of psychotherapeutic results. *Bull. Menninger Clin.,* **25**: 75-81, 1962.

WEBER, RUTH. Children's verbal accessibility as a predictor of treatment outcome. Unpublished doctoral dissertation, Western Reserve University, 1963.

WOLF, S. Effects of suggestion and conditioning on the action of chemical agents in human subjects. *J. Clin. Invest.,* **29**: 100-109, 1950.

ZIGLER, E., and PHILLIPS, L. Social competence and outcome in psychiatric disorder. *J. abnorm. soc. Psychol.,* **63**: 264-271, 1961.

28. An introduction to intensive design in the evaluation of drug efficacy during psychotherapy

J. B. Chassan and Leopold Bellak

INTRODUCTION

The evaluation of psychotropic drugs shares a good many problems with the evaluation of psychotherapy: the problem of valid and reliable judgments, the effect of time, and the problem of understanding and demonstrating the process of the therapeutic effect, rather than a mere evaluation of the result (Bellak, 1961). Not the least among these difficulties derives from the procedure of testing various hypotheses between groups of patients concerning the relative efficacy of two or more medications. The inability to specify particular patient parameters in relation to the statistical results of such studies, the vagueness of the population of patients from which the study patients are presumably considered as a random sample, and the consequent poverty of operational implications of the results of such studies, are among the many difficulties one encounters in what has been called the extensive model of clinical research design.

From another point of view the use of the extensive model has the effect of exaggerating some of the differences in orientation between clinical research and clinical practice with a consequent feeling of alienation from research on the part of many clinicians who might otherwise be strongly motivated toward it. Research in which statistical comparisons are limited to tests between groups of patients ignore what is happening to the individual patient, to the ebb and flow of his symptoms, to their interpretation within a dynamic framework so important to an understanding of individual psychopathology, and to a more definitive understanding of differential drug effects. There has long been aloft in the land of clinical research the notion that comparisons between groups of patients is the *sine qua non* of statistically valid scientific clinical research, and that the study of the individual case must be relegated at best to a status of intuition and the clinical hunch, not capable of statistical testing and validation. For reasons given in some detail by Chassan (1960, 1961), this view is seen to lack validity in its own right. It has unfortunately tended to perpetuate a basically superficial methodology as a unique prototype for science in clinical research with mental patients.

478

It is noted that what we are stating here is not that the extensive model itself is necessarily unscientific nor that when properly and appropriately performed it cannot be viewed as a statistically valid approach to clinical investigation, but rather that it is quite limiting, and that the clinical-statistical study of the individual case (i.e., the intensive design) is, at the very least, a much needed complementary approach. One of us has made a previous attempt to bridge the difficulties between the clinical and the experimental statistically useful approach by the method of repeated short-range predictions and judgments by independent observers after interaction in psychoanalytic interviews (Bellak, 1956). This study involved not only one psychoanalyst as a clinician but three psychoanalysts working as predictors and judges in a complex experimental setting. The controlled sequence of multidimensional observations was thus made in the framework of testing various hypotheses relevant to the population implicitly defined by the parameters of the single case under study.

The purpose of the present report is to demonstrate a method involving intensive design for the evaluation of drug efficacy within the context of the single case, particularly within the framework of the process and practice of psychotherapy by one therapist. A recognition of the possible advantages of the use of drugs as an adjunct to analytically-oriented psychotherapy antedates the present age of ataraxics (Bellak, 1949), although very little, if any, formal research using the double-blind technique seems to have been done in this area.

INTENSIVE AND EXTENSIVE DESIGN

It may be of some value within the context of this presentation to review some relevant statistical definitions, concepts, and arguments before discussing and developing the clinical data of this study. First, one may begin with the observation that the motivation for the application of statistics to the interpretation of clinical data lies in the existence of what appears to be more than a negligible variation in response to a given treatment of one sort or another despite apparently strong similarities of the conditions under which the treatment is administered. Thus, patient A with syndrome S is treated with medication M and improves markedly, while patient B with the same syndrome is treated with the same medication and shows no improvement at all; or patient C on certain occasions appears to respond most favorably to a particular medication while on other apparently similar occasions shows no response whatever.

An essential purpose of the application of statistics to the design of clinical research, then, is that of attempting to interpret variation in response to treatment in a manner which will provide valid comparisons between two or more treatments. Every statistical test of such a comparison involves in one form or another a comparison of improvement percentages or averages and a determination, e.g., as to whether a difference between an average on medication A is larger than a corresponding average on B by an amount greater than one would expect on the basis of chance alone.

We can interpret "chance alone" in this context somewhat as follows:

1. We are comparing the average of a set of scores on A with a corresponding average of a set of scores on B.

2. In general there will be some difference between these averages. (Let us say the average on A is greater than the average on B.)

3. The difference between these averages may be regarded as consisting of two possible components. First, suppose for the moment that the two sets of data and corresponding average scores, instead of being obtained from observations on two distinct medications, were actually derived from two sets of observations on the same medication. Knowing that there is a certain variation in responses between individuals on the same medication, one should also expect some variation between averages of two sets of data when both sets are derived from the same medication. This can then be viewed as providing the variation between averages due to chance alone. If now we again consider the two averages as derived from two distinct medications, A and B, and if A is to be considered as really better than B, we should like to obtain a difference in average scores between A and B which is significantly larger than is likely to occur by chance alone.

Procedures for applying one or another statistical test for a true difference in effect (i.e., one which is not based on chance alone) between the average obtained from the set of observations on A and that on B involves the concept of a statistical distribution, or hypothetically infinite population. The actual set of observations on medication A is then regarded as equivalent to a sample, randomly selected, from a hypothetical, infinitely large set of results on medication A, in correspondence with the mathematical concept of a *fundamental probability set;* and similarly, for the observations on B. The problem in statistical inference, then, is that of determining, on a probability basis, whether the difference between averages obtained from the samples on A and B, respectively, is sufficiently large, in view of the amount of variation within each sample, to justify the conclusion that the difference would hold up in the long run; i.e., that there is a difference in the corresponding hypothetically infinite population averages.

We have thus far in our discussion referred to the difference between averages based on two sets of observations, one set obtained on medication A, the other on B, without having yet indicated the nature of the sets in relation to their constituent individual observations.

In the conventional approach to the design of clinical research, i.e., in the *extensive model,* the fundamental probability set refers to a hypothetical population of individual patients. On a random basis one group or set of patients is selected for treatment A, the other for treatment B. Relatively few observations along the time axis are generally taken with respect to each patient. Often only end-point observations are employed. The main point in relation to statistical inference about the extensive model is that the various hypotheses which can be tested in the design are limited to tests between groups of patients. Comparisons of degree of improvement between one medication and another, or between a presumably active medication and a placebo are thus performed in terms of averaging across the corresponding patient-groups.

The *intensive model* of clinical research design, on the other hand, focuses upon the analysis of variation of response *within* the individual patient in relation to the comparison of treatments. In intensive design a given patient is observed at relatively frequent intervals over, say, a number of months. During this period the protocol calls for several alternations of treatment between medications A and B. A statistical analysis is then made *within* the data of the individual patient. The observations thus made on a single patient may be regarded as corresponding to a (random) time-sample drawn from corresponding hypothetically infinite subsequences of observations from the same (or a theoretically identical) patient. Results such as a significant difference obtained within the individual patient may then be regarded as specific to that patient with all of his possibly relevant characteristics.

LIMITATIONS OF THE EXTENSIVE MODEL

One of the greatest difficulties in applying the extensive model to the data of clinical psychiatry is found in the rather small number of relatively homogeneous patients in a mental hospital or in a given out-patient setting which can be included in a particular research investigation. Even in hospitals with large patient populations the selection of patients for the investigation of a new treatment for a given symptom, syndrome, and/or diagnostic category almost inevitably will include a considerable variability in many of the following kinds of background variables: age, length of hospitalization, marital status, sex, educational level, various physiological characteristics, etc. In the face of such variability the investigator may have two choices in the direction of the design of a piece of clinical research for testing the efficacy of a new treatment. One approach is to limit the number of patients in a study to as homogeneous a group as can be selected. The other is to include all patients whose symptoms or diagnosis satisfy the purpose of the study without any serious concern about the variability of background characteristics in the sample thus selected. (An even more difficult situation frequently occurs when there may, in addition, be considerable differences between patients selected for a study *in various aspects of the illness or symptoms treated in the study*.)

When the number of patients in a study is limited because of the satisfaction of stringent requirements for a specified degree of homogeneity, the probability of detecting a true difference in efficacy between two treatments within the extensive model will often be quite small because of the generally low statistical power accompanying small samples. On the other hand, increasing the sample size at the expense of the homogeneity of the patient sample will also tend to result in a test of low statistical power because of the increased variability of response. In summary, the extensive model will often fail to detect true effects either because of the inadequacy of the sample size, or because of a lack of homogeneity (including the quality and intensity of symptoms) between patients in a study, or both.

Next, consider the situation in which a statistically significant difference *has* been obtained in the extensive model, reflecting a true difference in effect between treatments A and B. A reasonable question to ask at this point is, how far can one then go with the information contained in such a result insofar as the selection of patients for actual treatment by the medication demonstrated as superior is concerned.

To answer this question let us refer back to the statistical model of the extensive design, or more specifically, to the definition of the elements of the corresponding statistical distribution and then to the logical-statistical conclusions or operational implications which are relevant to a statistically significant result obtained within its framework.

First, to apply the results of a statistically significant effect, one must relate results from the sample (i.e., from the actual clinical investigation) to the hypothetically infinite population, or statistical distribution from which the sample was randomly (or randomly-in-effect) drawn. Thus, if medication A is demonstrated in the study as superior to B, then the expectation is that in the long run, or on an average, a larger percentage of patients drawn from the same (or an identical) population as the study sample may be considered to have been drawn from, will improve on A than on B. An essential difficulty here is that of defining with any reasonable degree of specificity the population from which the clinical sample may be regarded as having been randomly selected. The broad spectrum of patient characteristics which is usually found in such clinical samples results conceptually in a correspondingly vague, and *ad hoc* definition of the population (*ad hoc* because in practice one often selects patients on the basis of pragmatic considerations, rather than as a sample from some clearly defined parent population, so that the only reasonable description or definition of the theoretical or hypothetically infinite population is in terms of an extension of the actual sample).

The *ad hoc* quality of the population to which inferences from the sample apply would in itself not be particularly serious, were it not for wide variation in patient characteristics which, as was noted above, such a sample generally includes. *In practice, it is this variation which makes it difficult, and in most studies impossible, to relate particular patient character-*

istics to the result of treatment. This limitation of the extensive design may be made somewhat clearer if one attempts to relate improvement noted for a given patient in an extensive design to that patient's characteristics. For this purpose let us consider a study in which a significantly greater percentage of patients improved on medication A than among those who had been randomly selected for placebo. Along with our assumption that a significantly greater percentage of improvement occurred on medication A, we also make the realistic assumption that there was some improvement among the group of patients on placebo. Now on the basis of the statistical results obtained in this hypothetical study there is no way of distinguishing between the patients on A who improved because they were on A, and those on A who improved by the same or similar mechanisms as those who improved on placebo. Therefore, the characteristics of a given patient who "improved on A" may have very little to do with patient characteristics relevant to the probability of successful treatment under A in relation to its pharmacological properties.[1]

Just as the extensive model for research design generally does not provide, as a product of the research, possible indications for treatment in relation to specific patient characteristics, extensive design is not likely to provide an organized program of research with respect to a given treatment or set of treatments in which the results of one or more pieces of clinical research logically lead to well-directed possible subsequent ones in an overall integrated approach to a thorough investigation of competing treatments, their indications, and their counter-indications. For, if after a study involving, say, fifty patients based on the extensive model, all one can say is that there is or there is not a statistically significant effect without giving specific clues concerning patient parameters which are associated with such an effect or its lack, not only has the study yielded comparatively little of specific value, but a subsequent one also based on the extensive model will generally have little more to contribute even with the information gained from the earlier one.

ADVANTAGES AND LIMITATIONS OF THE INTENSIVE MODEL

The motivation for the development of the intensive model for the design of clinical research in psychiatry is based upon the awareness of a general underlying variability within the patient, or subject, with respect to his day-to-day or week-to-week affective, psychopathological, or interpersonal states. Such fluctuations form the basis of defining the patient-

[1] While the use of background variables as co-variates in the application of analysis of co-variance and multiple regression techniques to the extensive model may at first glance appear to offer some approach to identifying patient characteristics relevant to successful treatment, the large number of such possible characteristics together with the relatively small number of patients in almost any given clinical investigation would appear to limit the usefulness of such techniques to that end.

state itself in terms of statistical distributions or probabilities estimated from sequences of observations of the individual patient, thereby providing the framework for the application of statistical inference and experimental design to the data of the individual patient.

When a statistically significant effect is obtained within the single-case, the particular patient characteristics and background variables in whose presence the significant result has taken place can be specified. This includes, for example, the patient's age, diagnosis, specific symptoms, and physiological characteristics, as well as many of his possibly relevant early-life and recent experiences.

A particularly important aspect of the intensive model in the design of clinical research is that in the process of increasing the number of patients studied intensively over time for such obvious purposes as validation, modification, and extension of his results, the clinical investigator has, in the intensive model, an instrument for the systematic selection and study of patients in relation to various, specific patient parameters. The continuing selection of patients for intensive design in practice and in theory can in a meaningful way be related to previous results, and to specific questions raised by an earlier set of results. It is in this way that intensive studies can provide the basis for a more integrated approach to research in clinical psychiatry than is at all possible from the use of conventional extensive models.

In discussing these broader aspects of the implications of the use of intensive design it should not be overlooked that many patient-characteristics which are at present unknowable (as well as those which can be known) are implicitly held constant in the testing of hypotheses within the individual. The patient serves as his own control, not merely in the superficial "before-and-after" sense of the evaluations of the extensive design, but in the actual testing of hypotheses on data for which *all possible patient characteristics up until the start of the single-case study are held constant.* This includes the complete history of all of a patient's physiology, his sexuality, intelligence (however one may wish to define it), his possibly relevant interpersonal experiences, neural pathways and mechanisms, etc. Obviously, nowhere near this degree of control can ever be achieved in the extensive model.

One sometimes hears the following argument against statistical inferences drawn from a single-case (intensive) design: "Inferences from a statistically significant result obtained in a single case can apply only to that case. Regardless of whatever disadvantages may accompany the use of the extensive model, a statistically significant result from such a design pertains to a whole population of cases. It therefore is more subject to generalization and is consequently more useful than a result based on a significant finding within the single case."

This type of argument for the extensive model can hardly be maintained once careful thought has been given to the discussion which has thus far been presented. The fallacy of the argument just given within the quotation marks is related to the notion that if a significant effect has been demonstrated by means of an extensive design, the effect necessarily exists for most, or even an appreciable proportion of individuals, in the clinical sample, and hence for the corresponding population. Our earlier discussion has demonstrated clearly that not only is such a conclusion generally quite false, but that from the results of an extensive design one cannot even identify with any reasonable degree of specificity the characteristics of patients in whom the actual pharmacological treatment was effective. We have also noted the way in which this difficulty is related to the vagueness of the population to which inferences are presumably drawn from a clinical sample when the latter must of necessity be heterogeneous with regard to many possibly relevant patient parameters. It has also been noted how this vagueness of the population of reference and its corresponding heterogeneous clinical sample present a serious difficulty in both the selection of patients for treatment as well as for establishing a direction of research effort based on the results of the extensive model. Thus arguments favoring the extensive over the intensive design simply on the basis of the larger number of cases, which can be handled within a given set of resources in the framework of the extensive design, is rather weak, at best, and at worst, can be seriously misleading.

The opposite argument against the apparent overspecification of the population of the intensive single-case design is technically correct to the extent that statistical inferences are strictly valid only when applied to the single case itself. If in the framework of intensive design, one regards the data from the individual patient as a function of all of his relevant characteristics, then the statistical distribution, or population, of a single case can in theory be specified in terms of these characteristics. To the degree that no two patients can possibly have the exact same set of characteristics and life experiences which may be considered *a priori* as related to the particular difficulties which brought them to treatment, no two such corresponding single-case populations can be regarded as identical. However, when a clinician decides upon a course of treatment for a given patient, based on experiences gained through the treatment of other patients, he does not expect or demand that his given patient's relevant, or possibly relevant, parameters and background characteristics all be identical to those of the earlier patients' data which he may be using as precedent. Such decisions are based on similarities rather than upon complete identities. Thus, with respect to the single-case populations, the application of the results of sampling such a population to other single-case populations are performed in terms of similarities of relevant characteristics. From the point of view of purposeful and directed clinical research design, the systematic application of the intensive model to increasing numbers of patients, as representative of single-case populations, carefully selected (rather than *randomly* in this context) for similarities and dissimilarities in particular patient parameters then forms the basis for the identification of factors most relevant to the success of a given treatment.

The purpose of the foregoing discussion was essentially that of acquainting the reader with the approach to clinical research through the use of the intensive model and its advantages. Before going on to the example in double-blind drug evaluation, which forms the illustrative material of this paper, it may be of some value to discuss some of the limitations of the intensive model.

First, it is clear that one needs an appropriate setting for the application of intensive design. A kind of setting, for example, which would rule out the possibility of applying the intensive model would be the admission service of a screening facility where the goal might be that of successfully treating and discharging a patient within two weeks of admission, or, otherwise, transferring the patient to a state hospital. Another, more specific situation, in which intensive design would be out of the question, would be in the investigation of a new agent for the treatment of acute alcoholic psychosis. The inapplicability of the intensive model to such treatment settings obviously lies in the brevity of the total period during which any single patient would be under observation. (These examples are in contrast to the setting of psychoanalytic or psychoanalytically-oriented treatment, in which the patient is seen regularly over a relatively long period and which would therefore be ideal for the application of intensive design.)

A second possible limitation of intensive design is that it can only be applied with difficulty in studies involving shifts back and forth from placebo to active medication when the latter may have a particularly long period of carry-over effect, as for example, is sometimes thought to be the case in the use of monoaminoxidase inhibitors for the treatment of depression. (Here, however, one may possibly think in terms of applying intensive design for the purpose of investigating length of carry-over.)

The longer period of study of the individual patient which is required for the application of intensive design is occasionally viewed with concern, if not alarm, by clinical investigators who may be eager to make important contributions but who also balk at the thought of research commitments which would carry them beyond the briefest possible calendar time per patient. It may be worth remembering that the really significant contributions in both the physical and biological sciences have generally entailed many sequences of careful painstaking observations rather than short-term commitments.

AN ILLUSTRATIVE STUDY USING AN INTENSIVE DESIGN

This investigation was set up mainly as a short, preliminary study to determine whether some of the procedures (as those described below) necessary to establish a tight double-blind study for the evaluation of the efficacy of a drug such as chlordiazepoxide (Librium[2]) by the use of an intensive design, and during a segment of psychotherapy, are feasible. Since this was the primary goal rather than that of testing hypotheses concerning the efficacy of the medication by this method at this time, no attempt was made to provide an adequate time-span for the patient under study to provide a reasonable probability of obtaining statistically significant effects. For the purpose of determining feasibility it was thus estimated that a sequence of ten weekly interviews would be adequate. Contrary to expectations, we did obtain at least borderline significance favoring the active medication over the proverbial identical-appearing placebo in a number of the eight variables which were observed at each interview, and in each of the remaining variables the averages on chlordiazepoxide showed less psychopathology than the corresponding averages on placebo.

However, despite these particular results, the short time span and, concomitantly, the small number of observations made in this study would, in general, have to be regarded as a serious limitation on the chance of securing sufficient data to obtain statistically significant differences toward the detection of true effects. This is, of course, a widely recognized limitation of a very small sample, whether the sample size is based on the number of patients in an extensive design, or on the number of observations along the time axis of the individual case in the intensive design.

There is also a second danger, usually not explicitly stated and perhaps not generally recognized, but nevertheless implicit in the use of very small samples. This second difficulty arises from the influence that just one or two extremely biased observations can have on a total, or on an average, based on a very small number of observations. This kind of bias can occur even when an apparently statistically significant result *does* occur, in both the intensive design when too small a time-sample of the single-case is taken and in the extensive design when too few patients are used. The use of the term, *biased observations,* in this context would apply as well to instances of cases that really do not belong in a study, or to the effect of extremely atypical events (as can be the case in a single-case study based on a small time sample) as well as to isolated instances of observer bias in both types of designs. In larger samples the influence of the singular atypical observation will obviously be less important.

[2] The chlordiazepoxide used in this study was supplied by Dr. L. R. Hines of Hoffmann-LaRoche, Inc.

ASPECTS OF THE DESIGN

1. The Selection of Patient Variables and a Description of the Patient

One of the advantages of intensive design is that, in focusing on the individual case, it encourages the use of items for rating and evaluating psychopathology which, at least in the view of the clinician who is treating and observing the patient, are specific *to* the patient. This is in contrast to the approach which is so often used in the extensive design when patients with diverse symptoms and dynamic patterns are thrust, as it were, onto a single hyperdimensionalized rating sheet and in which statistical analyses take no account of highly relevant individual differences in the interpretability of the direction of a patient's movement along one or another particular scale item, or dimension.

The patient selected for this study was known to the medical author on the basis of a previous course of treatment. The patient suffered from acute anxiety, feeling of depersonalization, and marked dissociation. From this previous contact, together with observations made during an interview with her a week before the beginning of the study proper, he constructed a set of eight variables as follows:

1. Evidence of Primary Process (thought disorder)
2. Anxiety
3. Confusion
4. Depression
5. Hostility
6. "Sexual Flooding"
7. Depersonalization
8. Ability to Communicate Usefully

Each of these items were rated by the medical author at the end of each session of psychotherapy on a 6-point scale. For each of the first seven items a zero rating indicated a complete absence of pathology for an item while a rating of 5 represented its corresponding severest level of pathology. For item (8), a zero represented the most pathological state, and a 5, the most favorable.

2. Medication Treatment Schedule and Administration

At the end of the initial interview, just prior to the beginning of the study proper, the patient was given a bottle of capsules, instructed to take three capsules per day, and to return the bottle at the subsequent interview. At the end of the latter she was given a second bottle of identically-appearing capsules by the therapist with the same instructions. This procedure was repeated until a total of ten bottles were thus received and returned by the patient. Each capsule in a given bottle contained either chlordiazepoxide (10 mg. per capsule) or all capsules in a given bottle were placebos, identical in appearance to those of the chlordiazepoxide. At the end of the study, the set of ratings pertaining to a given interview was then related to the medication the patient was on during the week's period immediately preceding the interview, providing a basis for the comparison between effects on chlordiazepoxide and those on placebo. The actual sequence of medication thus corresponding to each psychotherapy session was as indicated on Table 1.

It is noted that the therapist not only had no information concerning which medication the patient was on during a given week, but also had no way of knowing the points at which a change in medication had been scheduled.

3. Distinguishing Between the Possible Effects of Psychotherapy and Differences in Effect Between Medications

The purpose of the methodology described in this paper is the evaluation of the comparative efficacy of two medications based on observations made during the course of psychotherapy, *and not that of evaluating the effect of the psychotherapy itself*. Nevertheless, in the analysis of the data one must take into consideration the possible effect of psychotherapy (confounded with the effect of time) as a factor in influencing levels of psychopathology as distinct from the influence of differential drug effects. For this reason one cannot, for instance, simply divide the time-span into consecutive halves, with one medication scheduled for the entire first half, and the other for the second. Such a procedure would then obviously confound differential drug effects with those of psychotherapy and of time. In using the intensive design for the evaluation of differential effect between two medications, one must, therefore, utilize a design which allows for a number of alternations back and forth between the medications throughout the course of the study. An elementary statistical approach to the analysis of data thus obtained is suggested in the presentation of Figure 1. Here, as an example, the sequence of *evidence of primary process* ratings is plotted along the time axis (connecting consecutive points, and identifying each plotted point according to whether the observation to which it corresponds was made following a week of placebo or after a week on chlordiazepoxide). A next step is to fit a trend line to the data. Finally, we study and analyze the configuration of plotted points and their identifying medication in relation to their position with respect to the fitted trend line.

A Statistical Description of the Primary Process Series

It may be of some interest to view the data plotted in Figure 1 from a descriptive point of view before presenting the results of any formal statistical analysis. First, it is noted that over the ten weeks of the com-

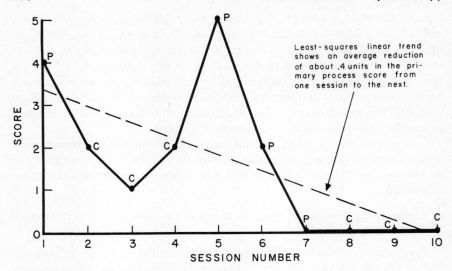

Figure 1
Evidence of Primary Process
(Thought Disorder)

bined administration of psychotherapy and medication (the latter in accordance with the schedule given in Table 1) the fitted trend line describes an *average* decline in the primary process pathology score, of about .4 units per week (i.e., from one session's rating to the next). We note further, that three of the four observations which follow a week of placebo definitely lie above the trend line indicating a worse than average score, while apparently five of the six points relating to the use of chlordiazepoxide are below the trend indicating a better than average score.[3]

Table 2 presents a tabular analysis of the primary process ratings, comparing averages on chlordiazepoxide with those on placebo. These comparisons are made using both the trend-adjusted scores and the raw scores. Averages over the entire run are compared between active medication and placebo, as well as averages based on sub-sequences of observations on the same medication. It is seen that the difference in the average scores favor the active medication over the placebo, and that in this particular set of data the use of the trend-adjusted score reduces the differ-

[3] It should be noted that the singular observation on chlordiazepoxide which lies above the trend line is the last in the series, and it has an actual primary process pathology score of zero (which was also true of the last four observations). Thus its representation as worse-than-average, or rather worse-than-trend, is in this case the result of having selected a straight line trend for reasons of simplicity of exposition. A somewhat more complex trend fitted to the data could have eliminated this feature, perhaps adding slightly to the favorable comparison between active medication and placebo.

Table 1

Session No.	Medication
0*	None
1	Placebo
2	Chlordiazepoxide
3	Chlordiazepoxide
4	Chlordiazepoxide
5	Placebo
6	Placebo
7	Placebo
8	Chlordiazepoxide
9	Chlordiazepoxide
10	Chlordiazepoxide

* Session 0 represents the initial interview.

Table 2
Evidence of Primary Process

Session Number	Medication	Raw Scores		Trend-Adjusted Scores*	
		Session Score	Sequence Average	Session Score	Sequence Average
0	None	5	5.0		
1	Placebo	4	4.0	2.2	2.2
2	Chlordiazepoxide	2		0.6	
3	Chlordiazepoxide	1	1.7	0.0	0.7
4	Chlordiazepoxide	2		1.4	
5	Placebo	5		4.8	
6	Placebo	2	2.3	2.2	2.5
7	Placebo	0		0.6	
8	Chlordiazepoxide	0		0.9	
9	Chlordiazepoxide	0	0.0	1.3	1.3
10	Chlordiazepoxide	0		1.7	
	Placebo mean	2.75		2.45	
	Chlordiazepoxide mean	0.83		0.98	

* Note: The trend-adjusted score was obtained by adding, for the sake of convenience, a constant value large enough to obtain positive trend-adjusted scores, to the difference between the raw score and the score obtained from the fitted trend.

ence from that obtained by the corresponding raw score averages by a small fraction. We also note that in going from one sub-sequence to the next, on the two occasions when the alternation went from placebo to chlordiazepoxide, the average primary process score dropped while the cases in which the direction was from chlordiazepoxide to placebo the average increased. Further, primary process averages for each of the two sub-sequences on chlordiazepoxide are distinctly below each average on placebo in both the raw and the trend-adjusted sequences.

In considering the data plotted in Figure 1, one notes a zero score on placebo at the seventh week followed by three consecutive weeks of zeros on chlordiazepoxide. One might raise the question as to whether the patient had not improved to the point of being free of the symptom by the end of the seventh week, thus invalidating for purposes of comparison the subsequent three zeros on the active medication. A counterargument might then be in the form of an assertion that while the patient first finally achieved a zero score on placebo, it is not unlikely that three consecutive weeks on chlordiazepoxide helped keep her there. Reference to Table 2 shows that taking trend into account has the effect of adjusting the last few scores upward in the manner of a compromise. With regard to the dynamics of the particular case, insofar as an element of clinical judgment may be related to the stability of so rapid a leveling in the rating independently of the medication, it would appear to be unavoidable in such an instance. A longer sequence of observations which would have included a few more alternations between the active and inert medications might have obviated the need for heavy reliance on such a judgment. This is, of course, related to the point made earlier in this paper concerning the shortcomings inherent in small samples, whether dealing with a small time-sample of the individual case in the intensive design, or with small numbers of patients in testing between groups in the more conventional extensive design.

A Summary of Results on the Other Items

As was the case in the ratings on *evidence of primary process*, the weekly observations on each of the other variables namely, *anxiety, confusion, hostility, "sexual flooding," depersonalization, and ability to communicate,* showed more favorable averages on chlordiazepoxide than on a placebo. Table 3 shows a comparison between effects, both within the raw scores and the trend-adjusted scores on each of the observed outcome variables.

In discussing the *evidence of primary process* ratings given in Table 2, it was noted that with respect to both the raw and the trend-adjusted scores, alternations from a sub-sequence of observations on placebo to a sub-sequence on chlordiazepoxide corresponded to an improvement in the average rating for a sub-sequence, while an alternation in the opposite direction (i.e., from chlordiazepoxide to placebo) resulted in a worsening i.e., in an increase in corresponding average primary process pathology. Among the seven other observed items of psychopathology similar fluctuations in sub-sequence-averages occurred in *anxiety, confusion, depersonalization, and ability to communicate.* This did not hold for the trend-adjusted scores in "*sexual flooding*" nor for the raw scores in *hostility*. While this type of alternation in sequence averages also appeared in the raw scores on *depression*, very little significance can be attached to this because of the relatively small difference between placebo and chlordiazepoxide in the overall average rating for *depression* (as can be seen in referring to Table 3).

Table 3

	Average Raw Scores Chlordiaz-epoxide	Placebo	Average Trend Adjusted Scores Chlordiaz-epoxide	Placebo
Primary Process	0.83	2.75	0.98	2.45
Anxiety	0.75	1.75	1.40	2.15
Confusion	0.67	2.00	1.37	2.40
Hostility	0.83	1.50	1.63	2.05
"Sexual Flooding"	0.83	1.75	0.98	1.45
Depersonalization	0.67	2.75	1.45	3.32
Ability to Communicate	0.50*	1.75*	0.35*	1.37*
Depression	1.00	1.25	**	**

* The lower numerical score, the better the ability to communicate.
** Depression is the only item for which a decreasing trend was not at all evident from the data.

Statistical Analysis and Questions of Statistical Significance

Given a set of results showing a preference of one medication over another it is no longer merely the avant-garde who have learned to ask the question: "Are the results statistically significant?" or "What is the level of significance in the difference between drug effects?" Anyone who has had the least exposure to clinical research is aware of the operation of the laws of chance, and of the problem of differentiating between true effects and chance effects. However, what is not always clearly understood is that there is no absolute or unambiguous answer to a question concerning an exact level of significance *without reference to some mathematical statistical model*, which for purposes of statistical inference must be assumed to be correct if probability statements such as those concerning levels of significance are to remain credible. The normal distribution, and the mathematically related Student-t and the chi-square distributions, for example, are mathematical models whose absolute truth in relation to a set of data can never be demonstrated. They can only be assumed to be reasonable models of the reality (sometimes also assumed) to which they are applied. This is, of course, not intended in any way as an argument against the use of the normal and related distributions. There is certainly much empirical evidence to support its use in many diverse areas, and the central limit theorem of statistics,[4] better known to statisticians than to clinicians, adds a theoretical argument in favor of its use. Nevertheless it is by no means always clear whether a given set of data ought to be analyzed by the use of tests based on an underlying assumption of normality or whether a nonparametric approach should be used. The investigator who applies both types of tests to the same set of data will in general obtain two distinct levels of significance. Fortunately, in a great many cases, one such level serves as a fairly good approximation of the other. But when one test yields a level of .04 and the other a level .07, an obsession about reaching *the* .05 level can provide an unfortunate and objectively unnecessary degree of discomfort. The point may be a bit belabored here, but it is made to emphasize that there is generally speaking no single, simple, precise, and unambiguous answer to the question of statistical significance which can be taken as absolute. Judgment, statistical as well as clinical, often has to be invoked with an awareness of one's possible biases.

Another type of problem which relates to the question of how well a statistical model fits the reality of a given clinical design, and one which is often more difficult to handle than the question of parametric versus nonparametric approaches, is that of statistical independence. The question of choosing between a parametric and a nonparametric test is of relatively little consequence if in both cases statistical independence is assumed and the reality of the clinical setting is such that such an assumption may not be tenable. It was suggested by Chassan (1960, 1961) that the assumption of statistical independence in the observation of individual patients on the same ward, as is generally implicit in statistical tests applied to groups of patients, was open to serious question and could consequently result in gross errors in statistical inference. An essential reason for questioning the validity of assumption of statistical independence in such a context lies in the possibility of the communication of mood, affect, or symptoms between patients who may be in close proximity. Consider, for example, a ward in which a presumably active drug is being tested against a placebo in a double-blind study in which the patients have been randomly divided into two treatment groups. Let us now assume that the presumably active drug is indeed active, and that patient X who is rated as improved did in fact improve because he was on the active medication. Next, let us suppose that patient Y who is in the placebo-treated group also improves. The question then arises: was this a

[4] The central limit theorem states that the distribution of an *average* from almost any kind of statistical distribution (e.g., skewed, leptokurtic, platykurtic, bimodal, rectangular, triangular, J-shaped, U-shaped, or whatever), provided that the distribution has a finite variance, approaches the normal distribution, getting closer and closer to it as the sample size upon which the average is based increases.

placebo effect or a random event, or was Y's improvement the result of his proximity to X? To the extent that the last of these explanations may be correct, one is faced with the existence of correlated observations. If such correlations were all positive, this would result in what may be considered as a methodological bias against the probability of detecting true drug effects. Data presented by Kellam and Chassan (1962) provide strong statistical evidence for the existence of both positive and negative correlations between particular respective pairs of patients on the ward. The data from that study were obtained by correlating, for all patient-pairs in the ward, a patient's sequence of daily ratings with that of each other patient's corresponding sequence in turn, over a period which averaged about six months. Thus the coefficient of correlation was obtained for a given patient-pair which reflected the association between the daily clinical state of one patient from the pair as it fluctuated over a six-month period with the corresponding fluctuation in the other. A significant positive correlation between a patient-pair implied that as one tended toward a favorable clinical state, so did the other. A significant negative correlation, on the other hand, indicated that in the patient-pair in which this occurred, the movement toward health and illness was in opposition.

A statistical analysis of the data gathered in this study falls into the area of statistics known as time-series analysis. The question of statistical independence is a matter of concern in the analysis of data from a time-series to the extent that a particular observation may be statistically dependent on the previous observation or on a sequence of immediately preceding observations. Thus, the level of a patient's pathological reactions during an observation period may be statistically dependent on his level during the previous period *in a given setting or context of observation.*[5] The greater the statistical dependence on previous states the less is there an immediate justification for, say, a standard application of the t-test to determine significant differences between time-series segments. However, unlike the situation in extensive designs in which tests between groups of patients are only performed at a single point in time, or even when an initial point is used as a covariate for adjusting end-point observations, the data from the time-series itself provides information concerning the degree of dependence in the series. If this turns out to be quite small, then standard tests, such

[5] The extent of statistical dependence of a given series within a parametric framework of statistical analysis can be estimated by computing a sequence of autocorrelation coefficients from the series. In the data of this study all first-order autocorrelation coefficients (after removal of trend) were uniformly low, seven out of eight being positive. All second- and third-order coefficients were negative. The low positive first-order correlations are first, indicative of near statistical independence, and when considered along with the negative second- and third-order coefficients are consistent with an assumed cyclic fluctuation generated by the alternation between the active medication and placebo in accordance with the (double-blind) schedule followed in the design of the study.

as the t-test, may be expected to provide reasonably valid significance levels.[6]

Applying a t-test to residuals from trend for each of the eight items, the largest t-value, 3.12, was obtained for *depersonalization* which is significant at the .01 level. A t-value of 1.89 was obtained from the *evidence of primary process* residuals which is significant at the .05 level in the single-tailed test. The corresponding t-values of each of the other six items were all smaller, therefore not reaching generally accepted levels of significance. The one closest to significance among these was *ability to communicate*, with a single-tailed level of .09. The least significant difference as noted above was that obtained for *depression*.

Applying a t-test to the *raw scores* on the items which were found to be significant on the trend-adjusted scores still showed acceptable levels of significance in both of these items. The t-value for *evidence of primary process* remained practically unchanged (increasing slightly to 1.90) at the .05 level, while that for *depersonalization* declined from 3.12 to 2.15. The latter value, however, is still significant at a (one-tailed) level of about .035. A third and final test for drug effect applied to the *primary process* and *depersonalization* ratings involved a covariance analysis in which time (i.e., research hour number) was taken as the covariate as a means of adjusting for trend. In this test, the significance level for both variables dropped somewhat, falling between .05 and .06.

The question as to which of the three procedures (we have used in testing for true drug effect) is the most valid can only be answered theoretically in terms of which of the corresponding statistical models is the most valid. This is not always a facile decision, particularly in the case of so small a series of observations. One might ask whether adjustment for trend is valid for this set of data as the trend line itself was not particularly marked in relation to the variation of the data about the trend line. On the basis of so small a set of observations, this may still be a matter of judgment.

In the analysis of covariance as it has been applied here the assumption was implicit that two parallel linear trends exist, namely one corresponding to the placebo and the other to chlordiazepoxide. The analysis of covariance then tested the null hypothesis that the lines are identical.

Analyzing the residuals from the single trend line (corresponding to Figure 1) as was first done does not necessarily test directly or make any direct assumption about two separate trends, but rather tests for a significant difference in departures from a common trend.

---

[6] On the basis of some preliminary theoretical statistical analysis it appears that with even relatively high autocorrelation coefficients (for a fixed treatment) the standard t-test can still be used with a reasonable validity. Much technical statistical research remains to be done in this area, but this does not contraindicate the use of the standard t-test as a reasonably accurate tool.

INTENSIVE DESIGN IN RELATION TO PLACEBO REACTION, FOLLOW-UP, AND SUBSEQUENT TREATMENT OF THE INDIVIDUAL CASE

A particularly valuable property of designs in which one tests *primarily* for significant effects within the individual patient rather than between patients is the specificity of the results (in terms of significance or non-significance) in relation to the patient himself. The procedure not only provides valid data for evaluating whether a treatment is effective, but incorporates the feature of identifying particular patient characteristics which may be relevant to the effect of the treatment in accordance with the results provided by the series of data from each patient in such a study. The comparatively large number of hypotheses which one can thus test by applying an intensive design in a relatively few well-selected (not necessarily randomly selected) patients with some variation in their characteristics makes it possible to develop an organized program of clinical research, with more clearly specified objectives, than can possibly be achieved in a sequence of extensive designs in which hypotheses can only be tested for groups of patients taken as a whole. This can be achieved as has already been stated by a systematic selection of patients, chosen for similarities and dissimilarities in particular patient characteristics and in relation to ongoing results provided by sets of intensive studies.

Apart from the rather broad implications for clinical research methodology as such, the use of the intensive design has, as a corollary, a particular use in the subsequent treatment of the individual study-patient himself.

First, consider such questions as, "Is patient A a placebo reactor?" or "Did A actually benefit from the active medication?" Questions such as these cannot be answered as a consequence of patient A's participation in a clinical research project in which hypotheses are tested between groups of patients. For example, in a study in which one group of patients is on an active medication, and the other on placebo and if A belongs to the group selected for treatment on the active medication, and if, further, A should show an improved score, there would be no way of determining from the data of the study whether A improved because he was on an active medication or whether he merely reacted as he might have to a placebo. If A had instead been selected for treatment with placebo then (1) a failure to improve would give no information concerning how effective treatment with the active medication would have been for him, or (2) if he showed improvement on placebo one still could not state whether improvement might not have been even greater on the active medication. Neither, incidentally, can one state definitively that the reaction would necessarily have been a true placebo effect. Such an effect (i.e., improvement without active medication) can logically result from a complex of circumstances which happened to coincide with the administration of the placebo or with the point in time at which the placebo observation was made and the effect may have been entirely unrelated to it.[7]

Thus, with respect to the continuing treatment of the individual patient participating in the extensive model, the results of a particular study which may show a statistically significant greater improvement on active medication than on placebo, will not, in general, with any degree of confidence provide specific information as to whether a *particular* patient benefited on the active medication and therefore might be benefited by its continued use beyond the study. In a very loose way (because of the wide range of various relevant characteristics of patients) all it does is to indicate that the active medication is a better bet than the placebo. If the study involved one active drug against another (instead of against a placebo) even so gross an assessment would be difficult or perhaps more dangerously misleading, for presumably some of the patients who apparently improved on the drug which came out worse in the comparison might not have been helped by the "better" drug.

Although the use of a simple crossover within the framework of the extensive model may be a little more informative about the individual case, it would still not be anywhere near adequate from the point of view of statistical significance *within* the individual case. Several crossovers back and forth for each patient would, of course, provide data for intensive model analysis.

In an intensive design, irrespective of its broader implications for research, a statistically significant finding is significant, in particular, for a specific patient, and therefore may well indicate the course of further treatment for that patient. The small number of cases that one requires for an application of the intensive model, the minimum number actually being a single case (as in the present study), thus not only allows the practicing psychotherapist to engage in meaningful research to satisfy some of his own interests without requiring elaborate and/or institutional settings, but also represents a use of research methodology in actual treatment and for the maximum benefit of the patient under treatment.

Clinically, the patient under observation in this study did well. Some months after termination of this series of therapeutic interviews, she had some recurrence of anxiety in response to reality difficulties at which time a prescription for a short period of medication with chlordiazepoxide seemed efficacious. An encounter with the patient close to a year after the treatment period indicated that she had been getting along and feeling reasonably well.

[7] It is, at least apparently, this random aspect of psychopathology levels within the individual patient along the time scale that has led to the development of the intensive model (Chassan, 1957, 1959).

REFERENCES

BELLAK, L. The use of oral barbiturates in psychotherapy. *Amer. J. of Psychiat.*, **105**: 849-850, 1949.

BELLAK, L. Research in psychoanalysis. *Psa. quart.*, **30**: 519-548, 1961.

BELLAK, L., and SMITH, M. B. An experimental exploration of the psychoanalytic process. *Psa. quart.*, **25**: 385-414, 1956.

CHASSAN, J. On the unreliability of reliability and some other consequences of the assumption of probabilistic patient-states. *Psychiat.*, **20**: 163-171, 1957.

CHASSAN, J. On the development of clinical statistical systems for psychiatry. *Biometrics*, **15**: 396-404, 1959.

CHASSAN, J. Statistical inference and the single case in clinical design. *Psychiat.*, **23**:173-184, 1960.

CHASSAN, J. Stochastic models of the single case as the basis of clinical research design. *Behav. Sci.*, **6**: 42-50, 1961.

KELLAM, S., and CHASSAN, J. Social context and symptom fluctuation. *Psychiat.*, **25**: 370-381, 1962.

29. The psychotherapy research project of the Menninger Foundation: an overview at the midway point

Robert S. Wallerstein

The Psychotherapy Research Project of The Menninger Foundation has been in operation according to its present design since January 1954. For several years prior to that, the original founding group of clinicians had talked over plans and goals and had evolved some specific instruments (for example, a Health-Sickness Rating Scale) for studying psychotherapeutic processes and outcomes. In 1954 came the rapid expansion of time allocations, of financial support, and of participating personnel, and the concomitant development of the present comprehensive project design. The number of active research participants grew to between 15 and 20; individual time allocations ranged from six hours weekly to full time; the budget (and the grant support) grew to the very substantial levels necessary to maintain such an enterprise.

This overview of the total effort to date stands squarely at the midway point. It was not planned that way. Actually we started with two seemingly simple-minded questions directed at the clinical operation, psychotherapy, whicl. is our central professional activity. We stated our interest in learning more, from an intensive study of representative cases treated in psychotherapy, about (1) What changes have taken place in the patient, along what dimensions? and (2) How have those changes come about or been brought about? That is, from the start, we took it as our goal (in retrospect we appreciate much more fully just how ambitious an undertaking this was) to encompass within one study both the *outcome* question (What has changed?) and the *process* question (How did the change come about?), as both of these are conceptualized within the framework of psychoanalytic theory as it guides our daily clinical work.

We believed, in fact, that in an exploratory, hypothesis-finding study, such as the state of knowledge in this field required, equal attention would

This paper, presented to the Section on Psychotherapy at the Annual Meeting of the American Psychiatric Association, May 9, 1962, Toronto, Canada, is from the work of the Psychotherapy Research Project of The Menninger Foundation. This project is currently supported by the National Institute of Mental Health (MH-08308) and was previously supported by the Ford Foundation and the Foundations' Fund for Research in Psychiatry. Their generous assistance is gratefully acknowledged.

have to be paid to both the process and the outcome components of psychotherapy, since necessarily these are interlocked phenomena. We stated this conviction in an early publication as follows: "Any study of outcome, even if it only counts a percentage of cases 'improved' must establish some criteria for 'improvement' and these in turn derive from some conceptualization of the nature of the course of illness and the process of change, whether or not this is explicitly formulated. Similarly any study of process, in delineating patterns of change among variables, makes at varying points in time cross-sectional assessments which, if compared with one another, provide measures of treatment outcome" (Wallerstein and Robbins, 1958).

Our further original intent was that our research be a naturalistic study of clinical operations. By this we meant that it was to be a study of what happens during and because of therapy as it occurs naturally in our clinical setting, and that therefore the research design would be built in such a way as to neither alter nor impinge upon ongoing therapeutic practice. For instance, neither the patients selected for study nor their therapists (nor the supervisors of the therapy) are made aware that theirs is a research case until the natural termination of the treatment. In such a study in which the research must thus accommodate itself (silently) to the clinical operation (never the other way around) direct access to treatment data becomes sharply limited. Within this stricture on data access created by our commitment to naturalness (as we interpret it), we have designed instruments to collect data at those three major points in time which represent avenues remaining open to us.

First, the *Initial Study* is completed before the patient is in treatment; that is, at the time of the original clinical examination when the materials of the regular diagnostic case study (the psychiatric interviews, the psychological test battery, and the social history obtained from the responsible relative) are all available and all drawn upon for research assessment of the patient and his environment, and for research prognostication about the anticipated course and outcome of the recommended therapy. Second, the *Termination Study* is executed when the patient is no longer in treatment; that is, upon termination of the therapy when the events and outcomes of the treatment are studied by retrospective review of the clinical records that were regularly kept in the case, and by cross-sectional assessment at termination based upon interviews with the patient, the therapist, the therapy supervisor, and significant others in the life of the patient, as well as upon repetition of the original psychological test battery. Third is the *Follow-up Study*, set at only two to two and a half years after treatment termination in order to keep the entire time span of the study within reasonable compass. For this follow-up the ex-patient is invited back to Topeka, together with the spouse or other responsible relative, for a clinical reassessment which includes psychiatric interviewing, repeat clinical psychological testing, again with the identical battery, and social work contact with the significant relative, all as exactly comparable to the initial evaluation undertaken prior to entrance into psychotherapy as the altered circumstances and motivations permit.

The change that is thus assessed in psychotherapy is the resultant of the interactions among three coordinate sets of variables: those in the patient, in his character organization, and in the nature of his illness (called *patient variables*); those in the treatment, in its formal and in its content characteristics, and in the therapist, his attributes and his skills, as well as the climate of the therapist-patient interaction (called, all together, *treatment variables*); and those in the altering life-situation that interact with the changing aspects of the patient and the treatment (called *situational variables*). All these together co-determine the changes that take place. At each of our three vantage points in time (that is, *initial, termination,* and *follow-up*) separate research groups make assessments of current status and of changed status on each of the separately listed variables in each of the three coordinate sets of variables (28 major patient variables, 30 major treatment variables, and 7 major situational variables, a total of 65 variables), in accord with definitions of these variables which represent a consensus of Menninger Foundation clinical usage developed within psychoanalytic theory (Wallerstein and Robbins, 1956; Luborsky, Fabian, Hall, Ticho, and Ticho, 1958; Sargent, Modlin, Faris, and Voth, 1958). Since separately oriented and separately working research groups concern themselves with the assessment of each category of variables, and since assessments at the termination and follow-up points check on predictions made at the initial point and thus must be done independently and by different observers, the need for a multiplicity of working sub-groups and for a large number of investigators in order to properly implement our research design becomes clear.

To this point I have throughout used the phrase *assessment of change* to denote empirical questions that are quite apart from the value judgments that can subsequently be made as to whether particular constellations of changes do or do not add up to overall improvement in terms of any agreed upon consensus about positive mental health and mature functioning. Alongside our 65 separate judgments of variables at each point in time, the patient is also evaluated on another dimension, the Health-Sickness Rating Scale[1] (Luborsky, 1962), which is an effort to study a (value influenced) global judgment of improvement as in itself part of the variable system.

This scale was constructed to represent an overall judgment, in keeping

---

[1] An account of the problems encountered in the development of this scale, as well as reports of the pilot trials and initial reliability studies, is separately published by one of our group elsewhere (Luborsky, 1962).

with a global conception of the concept of health. It is, however, a composite, arrived at by consensus of ratings along seven sub-scales which together embody those value judgments that underlie our agreed-upon thinking about the criteria for mental health. These seven (each of which can be rated on a 100-point scale) are:

1. The patient's need to be protected and/or supported by the therapist or hospital vs. the ability to function autonomously.
2. The seriousness of the symptoms (e.g., the degree to which they reflect personality disorganization).
3. The degree of the patient's subjective discomfort and distress.
4. The patient's effect on his environment: danger, discomfort, etc.
5. The degree to which he can utilize his abilities, especially in work.
6. The quality of his interpersonal relationships (warmth, intimacy, genuineness, closeness, distortion of perception of relationship, impulse control in relationships).
7. The breadth and depth of his interests.

Ultimately we can thus hope to be in a better position to assess our mental health value judgments comparatively and realistically in the same way as each other aspect of psychologic functioning under scrutiny (Wallerstein, 1963).

Thus, our project is centrally concerned with the interaction over time of three major sets of relevant factors (our patient variables, treatment variables, and life-situational variables) that determine through their complex interplay the course and outcome of psychotherapy. The assessments of these variables, and thus the essential data of the project, are the clinical judgments of trained clinician observers. The fuller exposition of our position, this anchoring of our entire research enterprise in clinical judgments as our essential data, and its implications for the methodological issues of psychological science have been fully given by one of our group (Helen Sargent) elsewhere (Sargent, 1961).

Our research instruments have been devised to tap these clinical judgments with the highest level of thoroughness, reproducibility, and explication that we can obtain, and to translate them into empirically testable propositions. These instruments start from the essential clinical data obtained at each of the three points in time in the manner already indicated, transform these into the judgments about the current status and changed status in regard to each of the individual variables in our three coordinate sets of variables, and from the initial configurations of the assessments of these variables generate individual clinical predictions about the anticipated course and outcome of the recommended therapy for that patient, along a variety of postulated relevant dimensions, together with the supporting reasons in observation and/or in theory for each prediction.

Our data as recorded in these various instruments on each of the patients under study, though voluminous, are nonetheless selected data obtained by a variety of approaches applied at only three key vantage points. In making our assessments we, thus, necessarily rely more on criteria of salience, of perspective, of pervasiveness, and of pivotalness of observed phenomena as we have defined these elsewhere (Luborsky, Fabian, Hall, Ticho, and Ticho, 1958) than on the frequency estimation methods more commonly employed by other research groups in this field.

The major interest of our study is in ascertaining change that derives from the interactions within each case and across cases among the three sets of variables. Three major paths of data analysis are outlined. The first is the clinical case study of each case in the total sample, condensed and abstracted from the detailed assessments of the three interacting sets of variables, patient, treatment, and situational, at the three vantage points in time. In each case this is a *clinical* study of the major dimensions of change: what has changed; the outcome question; and how it is conceptualized that those changes have come about, the process question.

The second kind of data analysis is the intraindividual prediction study (Sargent, Horwitz, Wallerstein, and Appelbaum, submitted for publication) in which each individual prediction (these average about 50 per case) is studied in terms of whether its necessary conditions have been upheld, whether the prediction itself was verified or refuted by a subsequent event or judgment, and most important whether the assumptions in observation and/or in theory on which it was based are strengthened by the correctness of the predictive chain or found deficient through its incorrectness. Our manual for this *Prediction Study* encompasses the system for the transformation of the clinical judgments of the prediction study into testable hypotheses in accord with an if-because-then (that is, conditions-assumptions-prediction proper) formal model; and for an evidence form which states, in advance, the predetermined evidence that will have to be found subsequently at the termination and follow-up points to uphold or refute the individual predictions made at the initial point, thus avoiding the pitfalls of *post hoc* reasoning according to which almost any outcome can be plausibly rationalized in terms of retrospectively evident factors.

The third direction of data analysis is that of the quantitative interindividual study of comparative change across the whole sample of patients (Sargent, Coyne, Wallerstein, and Holtzman, submitted for publication). This is based on a modification of the Fechnerian method of Paired Comparisons in which on each variable that lends itself to extrapolation along a more-or-less quantitative dimension, the clinician judge is called upon to judge which of each possible pairing within suitably sized batches is greater than the other, say in the patient variable of level of anxiety, or the treatment variable of extent to which interpretation was a basic treatment technique, or the situational variable of the degree of environmental stress. These paired comparisons are then used to derive ordinal rankings of the patients along each of these relevant variables, and the ordinal rankings, in turn, are converted into individual patient profiles on each set of variables at each point in time. It is these profiles that make possible the selection of groups of patients similar in certain crucial respects but differing in others relevant to particular hypotheses under scrutiny; that is, that permit cross-patient comparisons of factors relevant to specified kinds and directions of change. By this point, techniques have been worked out for merging the ordinal rankings of patients that derive from the paired comparisons within each batch of 12 patients into master ordinal lists, for handling these overall ordinal rankings statistically via intercorrelations and factor analyses, and for assessing the changes in configurations of the three sets of variables at the three points in time, discerned in the changing profiles.

Although our naturalistic design precludes experimental manipulation or the use of formal control groups, since it is based on the study of treatment as it takes place naturally in our clinical setting, principles of control are introduced into this study in four ways (Robbins and Wallerstein, 1959). One is *intra*patient control in the individual prediction study by setting down *in advance* the specific predictions, the assumptions on which they are based, the contingencies (or conditions) to which they relate, and the evidence that will be necessary to confirm or refute them. Thus, observation is controlled and *post hoc* reconstruction and rationalization avoided. The second method is *inter*patient control using the profiles that derive from the paired comparisons study. These profiles facilitate interpatient comparison and contrast, and permit the selection of patients who are alike in respect to certain of our variables, while dissimilar in respect to others, thus controlling some variables while the variability of others is investigated. The third control method is the parallel and independent assessment of variables and the making of predictions by a separate psychological testing team on the basis of the psychological test data alone. Because of time limitations, this has been done in only a portion of the cases. Finally the fourth control method is one that we call that of *inadvertent control*. This occurs where for reasons of finance or geography a treatment plan other than that of choice must be worked out with the patient, or where the clinical staff which recommends and carries out the treatment plan differs in judgment from the treatment recommendations formulated by the research group.

So much for the major elements of the design, the methods, the concepts, and the instruments that have been evolved in our endeavor to seek ways of satisfactorily answering the two seemingly simple-minded questions that, as I began by indicating, set our point of departure. This first major phase of our work, that of the development of the method and design, is now well behind us, and with two significant exceptions, has been already fully presented before a number of professional audiences and in various publications.

In regard to the second major phase, that of data gathering in accord with this design, we stand squarely in mid-stream. As I said at the outset, although it was not planned that way, one of our chief accruals of knowledge in regard to the sociology of research is that every step along the way takes tremendously more in time and energy than even the most cautious of us had anticipated. I hardly think that this is a unique discovery with our group.

Our total sample is only (I use the word advisedly) 42 patients. Our comprehensive *initial studies,* including in each case the evaluation of all the available clinical material, the cross-sectional research assessment of the relevant patient variables, and the relevant situational variables; the clinical prediction study and the translation of these predictions, embedded in clinical context and qualifications, into empirically testable propositions with the predetermined evidence necessary for their confirmation or refutation all set down in advance; and the global clinical judgment about the present and the predicted health-sickness rating—all this on each of the 42 cases at the initial point took four years, from the summer of 1954 to June 1958, to complete.

These 42 cases being studied in the project include 21 in psychoanalysis and 21 in other psychoanalytically-based psychotherapies. Twenty-one are male and 21 are female. All were supposed to be adults between the ages of 20 and 45; actually, there is a youngster of 17 and a lady of 50 among them. All have been in treatment with therapists at least three to five years beyond their residency training, most of them psychoanalysts; and all the patients are individuals for whom psychotherapy was the primary treatment modality, though approximately half have also been hospitalized for some time during their treatment course.

To this point, 32 of the 42 patients have terminated and come to *termination study,* including two who had left Topeka and continued psychoanalysis elsewhere. Of the 32, 29 (including the two who terminated elsewhere) agreed to participate in the *termination study,* which includes interviews and psychological testing of the terminated patient, interviews with the therapist, the therapy supervisor, significant relatives, the hospital doctor, the employer on occasion, etc., as well as review of all available clinical records. In the three instances where the patient refused to participate, termination studies have nonetheless been done on the truncated material available—the clinical records and interviews with all the professional personnel involved with the patient.

Of these 32 cases, the *termination study* built on the evaluation of all this obtained material includes the cross-sectional reassessment of the patient variables and the situational variables at this new point in time, and the assessment based on retrospective study of the treatment (and therapist) variables, as well as clinical judgments concerning the outcomes of each of the individual predictions made about the anticipated course and outcome of that therapy, and concerning the position reached on the health-sickness rating scale. In addition, a new series of individual predictions are made by the research group to anticipated judgments and events over the post-treatment period, to be confirmed according to our same methods, at the follow-up point.

Of the 10 patients still in treatment, three are now with therapists in other cities and seven are still in treatment at The Menninger Foundation. Four of these 10 entered psychotherapy in 1954. We of course should have known that it is not only research but treatment as well that takes longer than one ever estimates. Certainly, within the next year or so we expect to take stock of those still unterminated and decide upon a cut-off point for research reassessment on those few who at that time appear likely to go on in treatment indefinitely.

To date, 22 out of the 32 terminated have arrived at the follow-up point two to two and one-half years after termination, and been invited back (at our expense) for our final research assessment in Topeka. Of the 22, 20 agreed to participate in these *follow-up studies,* all but one being willing to return to Topeka (most often accompanied by the spouse), for several days for this purpose. One patient claimed to be unable to leave his employment in a large metropolitan area, but was willing to be interviewed and tested over a week-end in his own city, which was done by three members of the research group who went there for that purpose. The 20 who have cooperated in the *follow-up studies* include two of the three who, for various reasons, had been unwilling to be seen at the time of termination. The two who did not agree to participate include: first, an individual who had not been willing to be seen at the time of termination either and who ignored our follow-up inquiries as well, but about whom we nonetheless obtained enough information in the process of tracking down his whereabouts, partly from an interview with the family physician currently treating him and partly from telephone conversations with various others involved in his life during the interval after treatment, as to be able to complete a fairly adequate *follow-up study;* and second, an individual whom we *had* seen for *termination study* but who had further decompensated in the interim in a paranoid and malignantly hypochondriacal direction and whom we felt it clinically contraindicated to urge to return to Topeka. In this instance also, a *follow-up study* could be completed with the information obtained by telephone from the ex-patient and from others involved in her life.

On all these 22 cases the research groups have filled out forms involving reassessments of the relevant variables in all the categories and involving confirmation and refutation of individual predictions, just as at the termination point. In addition to all the data gathering detailed to this point, a special psychological testing group has been carrying out the termination and follow-up psychological retest studies, including both the regular clinical test battery and a special battery devised to highlight aspects of the ego identity and of the transference predispositions. Incidentally, one patient of all those seen for *termination study*, while willing to have clinical interviews where she felt she could control the quality and extent of her communications, refused the retesting where she would have felt no such security. However, she subsequently permitted retesting as well as the interviewing at the time of *follow-up study*.

In addition to preparing clinical test reports for integration with the other clinical data in the termination and follow-up assessment of each research patient, the testing group (when the additional time has been available) has carried out independent, parallel assessments of patient variables and made change predictions from the test data alone (as already mentioned under the statement of control methods). Of particular interest to the psychological testing group has been the study of clinical inference and making explicit the inferential process by which raw test data are translated into assessments of patient variables, which in turn generate predictions about the anticipated psychotherapeutic course and outcome.

As can readily be seen, the major preoccupation of most of the project members through these middle years of the project's life has necessarily been keeping abreast of the flow of *termination* and *follow-up studies*. Today, with 32 of the 42 terminations and 22 of the 42 follow-ups behind us, the end of this phase of the work is at last closer than its beginning. Where does that put us in relation to the third major phase, that of data analysis and results? Or stated differently, what, beyond enhanced methodological sophistication—heightened knowledge of how to go about it, and of what we would do the same or much differently if we had it to do over again—what have we learned by now in some substantive sense in relation to our initial key questions: What changes in psychotherapy, and how do we understand that those changes have come about?

You will not be surprised that at this point results in this substantive sense are meagre compared to the elaborate complexity of the design created to search for them. Without denigrating the possible importance of what we do hope to be able to report in the future about results in this usual sense, and I hope without appearing defensive about the relative lack of these to date, I do want to first stress that we have all along regarded as a first kind of *result* of our endeavor the creation of a design, the devising of methods, that would suitably subject the complex data of clinical processes to systematic empirical inquiry without doing violence to their clinical richness and subtlety.

A major, and we believe, a prerequisite first result in the field of psychotherapy research is the demonstration that it *is* possible to evolve a research design that is simultaneously loyal both to the complexity and the nuances of clinical data and also to the search for empirically-based and logically sustained new knowledge in science. It is fashionable to point out when doing psychotherapy research, as we specifically do for our own project, that the state of the field is such that on the *substantive* level one properly aspires to accomplish an explicitly exploratory hypothesis-finding task. Definitive hypothesis testing of more precisely delineated hypotheses is set as a goal for future research endeavor. The counterpart of this research posture on the *methodological* level is the demonstration that ways can be devised to link clinical work to research inquiry in a manner that safeguards the essential canons of each. Toward the successful achievement of this first kind of result, the whole first stage of our project endeavors, that of the creation of the research design, has been devoted.

A second kind of *result*, also prior to the substantive rewards of the results-proper phase, stems from the operations of the second stage of our project, that of data gathering. The difficulties of this level are those of the sociology of research, an area that is only occasionally discussed in the public literature of research, as by Redlich and Brody (Redlich and Brody, 1955) or by Robert and Mabel Cohen (Cohen and Cohen, 1961), but is the *constant* preoccupation of the private discussions among researchers. These are the large issues of maintaining a more or less cohesive and harmonious working together of research colleagues of varying degrees of clinical and research motivation, sophistication, and determination, working with a population of research subjects who are at the same time clinical patients subject to the vicissitudes of varying experiences in both their treatments and their lives that may or may not allow them to remain amenable and accessible to the research requirements over the projected life span of the research design. Add that by its nature research into the process and outcome of psychotherapy is long term, that the subjects have a life span equal to that of the researchers, and that the researchers vary over the course of time in their research commitments and their personal commitments, and the difficulties of the tasks that beset the workers in this field become obvious.

These difficulties of conducting a research study into the nature of the mechanisms of change in psychotherapy are the greater in a dedicated clinical center such as ours with its clinical service ideology and its strongly positive convictions about the high value, the seriousness, and the effectiveness of the psychotherapeutic work which is its central activity. By and large clinicians believe strongly in the great usefulness of their practical clinical endeavors, and of their theoretical guiding principles. Research that explores as open questions the nature of psychotherapeutic change and the effectiveness of psychotherapists as the instruments of that change thus readily evokes anxieties and resistances in such a clinical community. This is the more so, since our research data—the clinical *judg-*

ments about therapeutic changes and outcomes, and about the therapeutic processes by which these changes have come about—can only with difficulty be separated from the *judge* who makes them despite the utmost honesty in the striving for such objectivity. And just as the judge is always part of the judgment, so, to the therapist whose work is being studied must the assessment of the therapy always involve an assessment of the therapist. Indeed an assessment of the therapist, with its inevitably heavy weighting of the unconscious predispositions and biases, the countertransference elements, is specifically built into our research design as part of the system of treatment and therapist variables.

Such factors obviously give rise to interpersonal tensions that beset and often seriously threaten research into the basic operations of a clinical community. That most research is free of such complications has to do with the fact that most research is about phenomena that are not the object of such fierce subjective convictions. It is the difference between doing research on the things that really count as against the things that are emotionally neutral or irrelevant. Thus far we have over a decade of experience in maintaining our complex research group intact in its essential functions, while inevitably losing and gaining individual members along the way. At the same time we have been successful in maintaining a working relationship with the body of treating clinicians despite the kinds of problems discussed here, and maintaining, as well, contact with a population of patient subjects with almost insignificant loss despite the passage of time and the alterations of psychic status. Obviously this can only be accomplished in a clinical institution that is at once large enough, tolerant enough, and convinced enough of the importance of the research enterprise.

Enough has been said to indicate that these operational problems that relate to the ecology of research are at least as difficult of solution as the methodological problems of creating an appropriate design, though as already indicated, they are much more rarely elevated to the forum of public discussion. That they can be coped with to the degree that we feel we have to this point is the second major kind of *result* that we wish to report and to document from our work.

White (White, 1961), in a detailed and sympathetic review of the published work from our project in his survey of "Recent Developments in Psychoanalytic Research," takes this same position about the values of our findings to date and about the nature of results. He states: "Although the final results and conclusions of the study will not be available for several years, here are some of the *notable preliminary findings*." He then lists eight, six of them being results that are clearly methodological and operational, rather than substantive. *His* listing of these six may be condensed as follows:

1. Experienced clinicians can make meaningful predictions about psychotherapy from clinical data.
2. Clinical data can be organized so that quantitative as well as qualitative analyses of them are possible.
3. Patients are surprisingly willing to participate in intensive research interviews despite the anxiety caused by such interviews.
4. If performed tactfully by skilled clinicians, these intensive research interviews are not harmful to patients.
5. Both the patient and the therapist are more willing to discuss the treatment freely with the research team if they feel that it was successful.
6. Such a research study is threatening to the therapist who treats the patient. He almost always feels that his professional ability and his personal worth are being made vulnerable to criticism by the researchers.

Let us turn now to the third or substantive level of results proper in the usual sense. I have stated earlier the three major avenues of data analysis that we have outlined. These are first, the clinical case studies, the integrative clinical judgments about what has changed and how those changes have come about in each case of our total sample of 42; second, the intraindividual prediction study, involving the formal, logical analysis of the conditions, assumptions, and outcomes of each of the 50 or so individualized predictions made about the anticipated course and outcome of the recommended psychotherapy in each case; and third, the interindividual, quantitative study of comparative change across the whole sample of patients using the ordinal rankings and the profiles that derive from the adaptation of the method of paired comparisons to our clinical use.

At this point, we can report beginning substantive results and something of the directions of future results from each of these three major avenues of data analysis. A first effort along the line of clinical study was reported by Siegal and Rosen at the Second Conference on Psychotherapy Research at Chapel Hill one year ago. (Siegal and Rosen, 1962) This paper was a study of the relationship of changes in one aspect of character style, that of how alloplastically vs. how autoplastically one is oriented, to changes in anxiety tolerance consequent upon psychotherapy. The working data of this study were the pre- and post-psychotherapy psychological test reports. Using the 18 patients whose termination studies had been completed at the time of preparation of that paper, Siegal and Rosen found representatives of *each* of *four* possible distinguishable patterns of change; that is, that there were individuals who upon termination of psychotherapy gave clear test evidence of *increased* anxiety tolerance and a somewhat smaller number who gave equally clear test evidence of *decreased* anxiety tolerance. Within *each* of these two subgroups, there was a further subdivision into those in which the change in anxiety tolerance was accompanied by an increased prominence of *autoplastic* behavior modes and discharge patterns and those in whom the same change in anxiety tolerance was accompanied by an increased prominence of *alloplastic* behavior modes and discharge patterns.

Since only psychological test reports from the initial and termination points in time were used in this particular study, no effort could be made at that time to relate the patterns of change in these particular patient variables to any aspect of the concomitant operation of the treatment and therapist variables or the life-situational variables. Rather, in studying the patterns of change in themselves and in particular in studying what we meant by talking, for instance, of increased anxiety tolerance in the presence of increased alloplasticity, or of decreased anxiety tolerance in the presence of increased autoplasticity, we were led to a significant clarification of one of our concepts, and a redefinition of our patient variable, anxiety tolerance. We redefined it in such a way that it became more equally applicable to patients at both ends of the spectrum in their defensive modes, those who bind anxiety autoplastically, as well as those who dispel it or avoid it alloplastically. Prior to this particular study we had unwittingly been using the concept of anxiety tolerance as one particularly relevant to patients at the alloplastic end of the spectrum who must discharge any accretions of anxiety in immediate impulsive actions, that is, who don't tolerate it in its signal function. We had not to that point seen it as equally applicable to patients at the autoplastic end of the spectrum who at the extreme of psychotic or near psychotic disorganization are flooded with traumatic anxiety mounting to panic that is obviously just as poorly tolerated in its signal function. The details of this report of results are available in the proceedings of the conference. The point here is the report of a substantive result at the level of conceptual clarification.

Similarly and more briefly, another result based on the clinical case study method was reported by Voth, Modlin, and Orth at the American Orthopsychiatric Association meeting in New York a year ago. (Voth, Modlin, and Orth, 1962) The pre- and post-treatment assessments of the patient variables and the life-situational variables provided the background for evaluating the process and the outcome of the psychotherapy in two cases. These cases were chosen because they illustrated widely contrasting outcomes in two instances, neither of which indicated significant resolution of core conflict or shift of basic impulse-defense configurations. The outstandingly successful result in the one case could be explained however in terms of the support gained in the psychotherapy to effect a change from a highly conflict-triggering and need-incongruent life situation to one that resonated much more favorably both with the patient's adaptive and neurotic needs. In the other case—the failure—no such environmental shift was effected; in fact the patient had immediately plunged back into the same (for him) neurotogenic environment on the assumption that basic resolution had been achieved of his core neurotic conflicts. Within the follow-up period, the improvement seemingly effected during the treatment was totally undone. In this sample study, it was clear how therapeutic outcomes can be more clearly understood when analyzed within the context of three interacting sets of variables— including the life-situational.

Along the second major avenue of data analysis, that of the intraindividual prediction study, Horwitz and Appelbaum are currently engaged in the classification and the hierarchical organization of the statements that make up the assumptions clause in the 2,000 or so individual predictions (42 cases, about 50 per case) in the *initial studies*. Since many of the assumptions are held in common across a variety of predictions, within a case and across cases, the total list in fact comprises only some 200 distinguishable assumptions statements. These are of course hierarchically interrelated and are of varying degrees of generality and specificity. Together they are the propositions within psychoanalytic theory on the basis of which we predict changes in the patient and happenings in the treatment, and they therefore represent as comprehensive a statement as we can make today about the governing propositions that comprise our body of knowledge of the psychoanalytic theory of *therapy*.

Translated into research terms, these same propositions become the hypotheses formulated and elaborated and refined within the research— in fact, precisely a specific aspect of the *results* explicitly sought for in an avowedly exploratory, hypothesis-finding study. Since the whole network of predictions made in our project rests on these theoretical assumptions within psychoanalytic theory, as predictions are confirmed or refuted, it is these assumptions on which the predictions are based that are strengthened or found wanting. In other words, there are aspects of hypothesis testing as well. In this way the individual prediction study serves both hypothesis-finding, and partially, hypothesis-testing goals as well in the service of elaborating a more precisely defined and more logically articulated psychoanalytic theory of therapy. In contrast to the comprehensive psychoanalytic theory of personality, the theory of therapy is as yet much more fragmentary and tentative, in a state described by Rapaport as consisting essentially of "rules of thumb." (Rapaport, 1960) The kind of classification, hierarchical organization, and partial testing of these theoretical propositions or hypotheses in which we are engaged is thus a major approach to one of the fundamental goals of the project—theory building in the direction of helping to make the theory of therapy comparable in its logical ordering and articulation to the theory of personality.

An effort along the third major avenue of data analysis, that of the quantitative study of comparative change across the whole sample of patients, was reported by Luborsky at the same Second Conference on Psychotherapy Research at Chapel Hill already mentioned. (Luborsky, 1962) Luborsky's paper was a semiquantitative study based on the paired comparisons data of the first 24 patients to come to *termination study,* in which the ordinal rankings of these patients on the patient variables at the initial point in time were correlated with one measure of overall change in psychotherapy, the amount of change in the position of the patient on the health-sickness rating scale as determined on *termination study.* Although it was found that the initial levels of the patient variables in general did not correlate highly with this measure of change, the health-sickness rating, there was one clear exception. The variable, level of anxiety, did correlate significantly with the change measure; that is, the higher the initial anxiety level (the more anxious the patient initially), the greater the amount of change during the ensuing psychotherapy. This correlation was even higher for the half of the patients who began with a moderately high capacity for autonomous functioning as measured by their initial health-sickness ratings. This refinement (independently arrived at) agrees with the formulation from the paper by Siegal and Rosen that the significance of anxiety varies in different patients depending on the differing character configurations, that is, depending on the differing configurations of the other relevant variables. Certainly we know clinically that there are probably as many patients who would be healthier if they were more anxious or could at least allow themselves to become more anxious, as there are those in whom a diminution in anxiety would be looked upon as a favorable sign.

Obviously this *result* is a limited one; we never expected that much of significance to the question of change in psychotherapy could be predicted from the initial level of the patient variables in isolation, let alone from one of them. It is crucial to our thinking that the *patterning* of the patient variables in interaction with the patterning of the treatment and life-situational variables would be required for the elucidation of this problem of change. All of this reported today is rather a beginning in the handling of our data to yield assessments of change that will later come more fully and in a configurational manner from the three paths already charted, the clinical comparisons of the patients at the three points in time, the confirmation or refutation of the predictions of change, and the comparisons of changes in the profiles that derive from the paired comparisons scores at the three points.

I think that by this point you can share with me fully the magnitude of the task our group undertook in creating a psychotherapy research project designed to deal meaningfully and as much as possible, simultaneously, with the two so-called simple questions within which this presentation was set: What changes take place in psychotherapy, and how have those changes come about? In approaching this goal, our set has been explicitly exploratory, hypothesis-finding, and hypothesis-refining. In this presentation today I have discussed three kinds of preliminary results toward the achievement of this goal, results on the methodological level, results on the operational level, and results on the substantive level.

REFERENCES

COHEN, R. T., and COHEN, MABEL B. Research in psychotherapy: A preliminary report. Psychiat., Supplement to No. 2, **24**: 46-61, 1961.

LUBORSKY, L. Clinicians' judgments of mental health. *Arch. gen. Psychiat.*, **7**: 407-417, 1962.

LUBORSKY, L. The patient's personality and psychotherapeutic change. In H. H. Strupp and L. Luborsky (Eds.), *Research in psychotherapy*, Vol. II. Washington, D.C.: American Psychological Association, 1962. Pp. 115-133.

LUBORSKY, L. FABIAN, MICHALINA, HALL, B. H., TICHO, E., and TICHO, GERTRUDE R. The psychotherapy research project of The Menninger Foundation, Second report. II. Treatment variables. *Bull. Menninger Clin.*, **22**: 126-147, 1958.

RAPAPORT, D. The structure of psychoanalytic theory: A systematizing attempt. *Psychological Issues*, **2**: 7-158, 1960.

REDLICH, F. C., and BRODY, E. B. Emotional problems of interdisciplinary research in psychiatry. *Psychiat.*, **18**: 233-239, 1955.

ROBBINS, L. L., and WALLERSTEIN, R. S. The research strategy and tactics of the Psychotherapy Research Project of The Menninger Foundation and the problems of controls. In Eli A. Rubinstein and Morris B. Parloff (Eds.), *Research in psychotherapy*. Washington, D.C.: American Psychological Association, 1959. Pp. 27-43.

SARGENT, HELEN D. Intraphyschic change: Methodological problems in psychotherapy research. *Psychiat.*, **24**: 93-108, 1961.

SARGENT, HELEN D., COYNE, LOLAFAYE, WALLERSTEIN, R. S., and HOLTZMAN, W. H. An approach to the quantitative problems of psychoanalytic research. (Submitted for publication)

SARGENT, HELEN D., HORWITZ, L., WALLERSTEIN, R. S., and APPELBAUM, ANN. Prediction in psychotherapy research: A method for the transformation of clinical judgments into testable hypotheses. (Submitted for publication)

SARGENT, HELEN D., MODLIN, H. C., FARIS, MILDRED T., and VOTH, H. M. The psychotherapy research project of The Menninger Foundation, Second report. III. Situational variables. *Bull. Menninger Clin.*, **22**: 148-166, 1958.

SIEGEL, R. S., and ROSEN, I. C. Character style and anxiety tolerance, a study in intrapsychic change. In H. H. Strupp and L. Luborsky (Eds.), *Research in psychotherapy*, Vol. II. Washington, D.C.: American Psychological Association, 1962. Pp. 206-217.

VOTH, H. M., MODLIN, H. C., and ORTH, MARJORIE H. Situational variables in the assessment of psychotherapeutic results. *Bull. Menninger Clin.*, **26**: 73-81, 1962.

WALLERSTEIN, R. S. The problem of the assessment of change in psychotherapy. *Int. J. Psychoanal.*, **44**: 31-41, 1963.

WALLERSTEIN, R. S., and ROBBINS, L. L. The psychotherapy research project of The Menninger Foundation. IV. Concepts. *Bull. Menninger Clin.*, **20**: 239-262, 1956.

WALLERSTEIN, R. S., and ROBBINS, L. L. The psychotherapy research project of The Menninger Foundation, Second report. I. Further notes on design and concepts. *Bull. Menninger Clin.*, **22**: 117-125, 1958.

WHITE, R. B. Recent developments in psychoanalytic research. *Dis. nerv. System*, **22**: 609-616, 671-679, 1961.

30. A comparison of the response to psychoanalytic and client-centered psychotherapy

Rosalind Dymond Cartwright

The psychotherapy game can be thought of as a team sport involving two players, one a professional, the other an amateur. The aim of the game is to resolve the problems of the amateur according to the rules of the professional, rules which the amateur must learn as the game progresses. Research in this field has concentrated largely on attempts to discover the influence of each of these elements, both singly and in their interactions, on the success of the game, or the resolution of the problems.

In the last few years a number of studies have been reported which show that the major portion of the variance associated with the outcome of psychotherapy can be accounted for by initial patient variables. How successfully the patient can play, that is, use the opportunity of psychotherapy for making positive personality changes, seems to be largely predetermined by the kind of structure he brings to the encounter. A few of these patient variables which have been found to be predictive of response to therapy are the extent of the patient's motivation to change (Cartwright and Lerner, 1963), his ego strength (Barron, 1956; Cartwright, 1958), problem-solving style (Kirtner and Cartwright, 1958), and social class (Hollingshead and Redlich, 1958). While initial patient variables have been found to account for most, they do not account for all of the variance; the therapist, too, contributes to the outcome. Studies have shown that the expertness of the professional (Cartwright and Lerner, 1963), his personal interests and values (Betz and Whitehorn, 1956; McNair, Callahan, and Lorr, 1962), and degree of empathic understanding are all predictive of psychotherapy success.

This state of our knowledge is, however, a very uncomfortable one for most therapists to accept. Does it not make a difference what rules are followed once the patient sits or lies down to begin? Surely a person who is a predicted failure in one type of treatment might have a better pros-

This investigation was supported in part by Public Health Service Research Grant MH 00637 from the National Institute of Mental Health.

The author wishes to acknowledge with gratitude the help of Miss Edith Levitov, Research Assistant, both in refining the instruments used in this study and in applying them to two of the cases.

pect if he were in another. Since most of the studies relating initial status to outcome have not had type of therapy as a variable, the question of the contribution of technique to the resulting therapy process when other important variables are held constant remains an open one. Would patients matched on relevant initial variables, in treatment with matched therapists who differ in theoretical orientation and who employ different techniques, nonetheless respond similarly to treatment, or would patients treated with one technique have a more similar response than those treated by another?

In all studies of this kind the question of the criterion looms large. Perhaps a patient could be deemed to be moving in a positive direction when judged by psychoanalytic standards but might be retrogressing from a client-centered point of view. In whose terms, then, are we to assess the response for the matched cases? In recognition of this problem, the study to be reported made use of three different conceptual schemes: one derived from client-centered theory, one from psychoanalytic theory, and one derived from Bales Interaction Process analysis (Bales, 1950) which is free of direct ties to any therapeutic theory. In this way matched patients in different styles of treatment can be compared on each scheme independently. Having two theory-based scales and a control scale makes it possible to ask a further question: Do patients in one treatment show changes predicted from that theory but not changes expected from another theory? Or is there enough of a general factor involved in therapeutic change so that it will be reflected on all three analysis schemes—despite their differences in conceptual language?

SAMPLE

With these questions in mind, four patients were selected for this study: two female patients in treatment with two male therapists, both of whom had extensive experience, one as a psychoanalyst, the other a client-centered therapist; and two male patients in treatment with two male therapists of moderate experience, one an analyst and another who was client-centered in orientation. The ability to answer the question of the comparability of the process of psychotherapy across different technique models rests very heavily on there being careful matching so that the style of the transactions will stand out as the major differentiating variable. Truly good matches are extremely difficult to make, particularly when there is the requirement that there be fully transcribed protocols of all interviews available for analysis. The four patients chosen were very good matches indeed in terms of age, sex, presenting picture, and total number of interviews although not in total amount of time in treatment. It was a matter of judgment that the number of therapeutic contacts was the more important variable to control here, although this means case

Number 3, on a five-times-weekly basis, was seen for only an eight-week period, and was being compared to case number 4, seen twice a week over a 20-week period. The therapists for these cases were also well matched in terms of their sex, experience level, and reputation for expertness in the technique they practice.

The basic weakness of the design is that the analytic cases are much too short to be good examples of typical analytic therapy. One of these cases was terminated by the patient with the therapist feeling more might be accomplished later but not at this point. The other patient actually continued in treatment but the additional hours were not transcribed and so were not available for analysis at the time of this study.

Table 1
Matching Data for Four Patients

Case No.	Type of Therapy	Therapist Experience	Sex	Patient Age	Sex	No. of Interviews	Presenting Picture
1	1 x week face to face psychoanalytically oriented (PA)	Moderate	M	22	M	33	Both over intellectualizing students with compulsive defenses
2	1 x week face to face client-centered (CC)	Moderate	M	23	M	30	
3	5 x week lying down analysis (PA)	Highly	M	40	F	40	Both housewives with high manifest anxiety and hysteroid defenses
4	2 x week face to face client-centered (CC)	Highly	M	40	F	40	

THE INSTRUMENTS

To scale the patients' productions according to client-centered theory, Rogers' and Rablen's Process Scale (Rogers and Rablen, 1958; Walker, Rablen, and Rogers, 1960) was used. In the language of the authors, it "commences at one end with a rigid, static, undifferentiated, and impersonal type of psychological functioning and evolves through seven distinctive stages to a level of functioning characterized by changingness, fluidity, and rich immediate experiencing of personal feelings which are felt as deeply owned and accepted." This, then, is very largely an *Experiencing* scale although there are actually seven variables involved in the rating of each stage. The seven are: personal meanings (referring to the emotionally tinged experiences and their significance to the individual), manner of experiencing, degree of incongruence between experience and the subject's representation of that experience, communication of self, manner in which experience is construed (rigidly to more loosely held), relationship to problems (from external to existential), and finally, manner of relating to therapist and others. In assigning the patient a place on this scale the rater makes a global judgment on each successive three-minute sample of the patient's verbal behavior throughout the hour. Good reliability has been obtained in a number of studies (Tomlinson and Hart, 1962).

The client-centered therapist plays the game with the assumption that if he does not direct, probe, or interpret for the patient, but stays within the patient's own internal frame of reference, catching the edge of underlying feeling in the communication, and reflects and clarifies this, the patient will become increasingly free in expressing his feelings. Furthermore, feelings that he expresses will have progressively more and more reference to self-experiences which have been previously denied or distorted. The effect of having these denied and distorted experiences understood and accepted by the therapist is that the anxiety associated with them is reduced and, as a result, so is the need to defend against them. They, therefore, can come fully into awareness. It is this movement that the Rogers and Rablen Process Scale is designed to capture.

The scale designed to tap one important aspect of patient change which psychoanalytic therapy attempts to produce is called a *Self-Observation Scale*. In contrast to the Rogers and Rablen Scale, which categorizes only the patients' behavior, this scale has two parts, one for the therapists' statements, the other for the patients' responses. The thinking behind this scale can be traced to Anna Freud (1946) who pointed out that the ego has a self-observing function, and to Sterba (1934) who stated that in the course of psychoanalytic treatment the ego splits into an experiencing ego and an observing ego. It is observing that leads to the understanding of the meaning of what is being experienced. In a recent paper, Miller, Isaacs, and Haggard (1965) suggest that this thinking makes self-observation a prerequisite for insight. From this vantage point, a major part of the psychoanalytic therapist's strategy can be conceptualized as discovering the barriers to the patient's self-observing capacity and applying techniques to free or enhance this capacity. Self-observation, then, is a process which should show movement over a period of therapy of this type.

Since no instrument existed for scaling this process, one was devised for this study and will be given here in some detail since it is not available elsewhere. All the therapist's statements were classified into one of eight categories according to their relation to the patient's job of observing himself:

1. *Non-observational statements.* Remarks or questions by the therapist having no reference to the patient's observing and no interpretative significance.
2. *Instructions.* The therapist attempts to initiate observing directly. The focus is on technique. "This is what I want you to do." "Look within." "Tell me how you see yourself." "What else comes to mind?" etc.
3. *Stimulation or encouragement of all or some part of the patient's observing which is already under way.* "Go on. Tell me more" or "Um hum," if in response to an observing statement.
4. *Redirection.* The therapist switches the focus of the patient by a question or statement in an attempt to elicit something from him which is not yet in the patient's frame of reference.
5. *Identification.* The therapist serves as role model with his own observing attitude. "I wonder about these things." "This is what we have to find out."
6. *Clarification of observation.* The therapist clarifies expressed observations but stays within patient's frame of reference.
7. *Clarification plus additional element contributed by the therapist.* The therapist goes beyond reflection to infer from theory or logic. "You say you are angry and usually when we are angry we are also afraid of something."
8. *Interpretation.* Therapist ties two things together which have been presented separately by the patient. Statements which link or explain observations. "This is what you are doing . . ."

For the patient's responses six categories were used:

1. *Non-self.* The observation is directed to things external to self.
2. *Focusing.* The patient attempts to clarify what it is to be observed. Muses, questions, etc., directed at discovering what therapist is driving at.
3. *Self as object.* Observes or asks about self as fixed and without affect. "I am a dull sort of person."
4. *Self as presently experiencing and not fixed, with appropriate affect.* Cognitive working over of percept in the present. "I think I am a passive guy," where patient is open to the possibility of discovery. Unsynthesized experiences may be expressed but are not often recognized.
5. *Observing of immediate experience.* Contradictions between two inconsistent experiences may be directly felt and dealt with.
6. *Integration of self-observation.* Resolution of conflicted cognitions and affects reached. Two or more threads tied together.

For the analysis in terms of the Bales Scheme, the modification of this system by Noble, Ohlsen, and Proff (1961) was used. This is a 12-category scheme for both patient and therapist, with three categories in each of four general areas: Accepting, Giving, Asking, and Rejecting.

For the patient the Acceptance area has three categories:

1. *Accepting self.* Patient takes positive attitude to himself and his accomplishments. Also classed here are all verbal expressions of happiness and well-being.
2. *Accepting others.* Positive attitudes expressed to or about others, identifica-

tion statements and interest in others, including therapist. Response may be as minimal as "uh huh," "I see," "go on."
3. *Agreement with others.* "Yes, that's as I understand it."

The categories for Giving are:

4. *Giving information.* More objective than category 5.
5. *Giving opinions involving inference or interpretation about his own behavior or evaluation and opinions about the behavior of others or issues in general.*
6. *Giving action-oriented suggestions about problems.*

The Asking area has these categories:

7. *Asking for information.*
8. *Asking for opinions and interpretations.*
9. *Asking for action-oriented suggestions.*

The Rejecting group are:

10. *Disagreeing with others.* Opinions, information, or suggestions.
11. *Rejection of others.* Hostility or hypercriticism toward others, situations, institutions.
12. *Rejection of self.* Anxiety or negative attitudes expressed toward self and his accomplishments. Asks for reassurance and for others to take responsibility for him. Unhappy, discontented, tense, and anxious expressions classified here.

The therapist categories are parallel to these. Under Acceptance the three categories are:

1. *Simple acceptance.* Positive attitude to patient, encouraging communication.
2. *Agrees with, reassures.*
3. *Reflection and clarification of feeling.*

Under Giving:

4. *Giving information.*
5. *Giving his opinions and interpretations.*
6. *Giving suggested plans.*

Under Asking:

7. *Asking for information about patient or others.*
8. *Asking for patients' opinion or interpretation.*
9. *Asking for discussion of plans.*

Finally, under Rejecting:

10. *Taking responsibility for the patient.*
11. *Disagreeing with patient's opinions, information, suggestions.* Discourages communication by patient by interrupting, etc.
12. *Rejecting patient.* Shows negative attitude toward him, ignores him, issues commands.

METHOD

All of the first interview, and of every fifth interview subsequent to it, plus the last interview made up the data sample for the study. Each interchange between therapist and patient was scored according to the Self-Observation and the Bales schemes. For the Rogers scale the typescripts were divided into units, each three pages in length. All the ratings were done on the pair of matched cases at one time. Each interview was coded and all names and dates removed and the order of the interviews from both cases randomized together.[1]

RESULTS

Movement on the Rogers and Rablen Process Scale seems to show that it reflects a process peculiar to the client-centered technique. If the change in the patients' mean experiencing score is taken from beginning of therapy to the highest point reached, then the two analytic cases moved much less during the same number of interviews than the two in client-centered treatment. The three completed cases, Numbers 1, 2, and 4, all show some movement toward this more open and aware type of experiencing and then some closing down following that point, so that the last interview is not at their highest point on this scale. The unfinished case, Number 3, whose highest point is on the last scored interview, may well still be moving.

Table 2
Mean Experiencing Scores on Process Scale

Case No.	Interview Number										Change to highest level
	1	6	11	16	21	26	31	36	40	Mean	
1	3.2	3.1	3.1	3.4	3.4*	3.2	2.7	3.2		3.2	+ .2
2	2.7	3.1	3.6	3.7	3.7	4.2*	3.7			3.5	+1.5
3	3.0	3.0	3.2	3.3	3.4	3.1	3.5	3.3	3.8*	3.3	+ .8
4	4.0	4.8	4.0	3.6	4.5	4.0	5.0	5.5*	4.6	4.4	+1.5

* The highest point reached.

Before turning to the patients' movement on their Self-Observation Scale, let us look at the differences in style of dealing with the patient's job of self-observation adopted by these four therapists. The therapists' observing scale includes technique categories representative of those expected from both client-centered and psychoanalytic therapists. How

[1] All ratings on two of the cases were done by the author, on the other two by Miss Levitov. The raters first established their interjudge reliability on protocols from other cases on all scales to an average 88 percent agreement.

often these are actually used by these therapists tells us something of the purity of the treatment style. Category 3, Stimulation and Encouragement, and category 6, Clarification and Reflection, are the two types of response which the orthodox client-centered therapist has at his disposal for increasing his patient's observing level. The orthodox analyst, on the other hand, is said to make more use of category 4, Redirection; category 7, Clarification plus an addition from the therapist; and category 8, Interpretation. Table 3 shows that the response styles of therapists within the same orientation are in fact more similar than those of therapists of matched cases. Numbers 1 and 3, the two analysts, are like each other and different from therapists 2 and 4, the two client-centered therapists who are very similar. Even though members of each school use the techniques of the other to some extent, it is clear that therapists of different theoretic orientations behave differently even when dealing with very similar patients.

Table 3
Percent Use of Observing Responses by Therapists

Case No.	% CC Technique (Encouragement + Reflection)	% PA Technique (Redirect. + Clarif. Plus + Interp.)
1 PA	48.6	25.8
2 CC	76.8	4.6
3 PA	25.5	37.7
4 CC	75.0	5.1

Table 4 shows equally clearly that although the therapists of the matched patients behaved quite differently, the patients responded to the different techniques quite similarly (patients 1 and 2 are alike and patients 3 and 4 are alike). These data would seem to show that matched patients can work at about the same level of self-observation regardless of the technique employed to help them develop it.

Table 4
Percent Use of Patient Self Observation Categories over Total Sample of Interviews

Case No.	1 Non-Observation	2 Focusing	3 Self as Object	4 Observ. with Present Affect	5 + Observ. of Immediate Feelings	6 Integrative Observ.
1 PA	44	6	31	17		2.0
2 CC	32	.2	34	28		5.8
3 PA	29	.8	20	36		14.2
4 CC	27	4.8	20	36		12.2

The treatment for matched patients 1 and 2 was actually more similar than that of patients 3 and 4 in that they were both being seen in once a week, face-to-face psychotherapy, although one was psychoanalytically-oriented and the other client-centered (see Table 1). Furthermore, from Table 3 it is also apparent that Therapist 1, although an analyst by training, was actually using a high proportion of "client-centered" responses with this patient. This makes patients 3 and 4 the only ones who, though similar, were exposed to sharply contrasting techniques. Table 5 tabulates the style of the therapists' statement which immediately precedes the patients' high level self-observation responses. Looking particularly at patients Numbers 3 and 4, each responded more often with high level observation following a response in the technique style with which their own therapists were most closely identified; the client-centered patient responded to Encouragement and Reflection, and the analytic patient to Redirection and Interpretation. In terms of self-observation, then, it seems that matched patients can reach high levels in response to either technique, although client-centered theory does not specifically deal with observation as a variable necessary to the change process.

Table 5
Style of Therapists' Technique Immediately Preceding Patients' Production of High Level Self-Observation Responses: Immediate Feeling (5) and Integrative Observation (6) Responses

Case No.	Sum of All High Level Observ. Responses: Immediate Feelings (5) + Integrative Observ. (6)	Style of Therapist Preceding Statement: CC Encouragement 3 or Clarification 6		Style of Therapist Preceding Statement: PA Redirection 4 Clarification + 7 or Interpretation 8	
		N	%	N	%
1 PA	14	10	71	4	29
2 CC	25	22	88	3	12
3 PA	34	⎰10	26	24	74⎱
4 CC	50	⎱48	96	2	4⎰

Moving now to the results using the modified Bales System, Table 6 shows that when the therapist's response is classified according to technique style using these categories, much the same pattern emerges as with the Observing categories. Again we see that therapists identified with each school actually play according to the rules of both although they follow their own with greater frequency. Therapist 1 is something of an exception and seems to occupy a kind of mid-position between a client-centered and an analytic treatment style. Table 6 also shows that the type of patient contributes heavily to the amount of responsiveness of the therapist. Both

Therapists 1 and 2 were much more active with their male obsessive patients whom they had to push and prod a good deal than were Therapists 3 and 4 treating the female hysterics.

Table 6

Mean No. of Therapist Responses Per Interview and Percent Use of
Client-Centered and Psychoanalytic Styles in Bales Category Terms

Case No.	Mean Therapist Responses Per Int.	CC Technique: Bales Accepting Categories 1 + 2 + 3	PA Technique: Bales Giving and Asking Categories 4 + 5 + 7 + 8	Others
1 PA	93	49	36	15
2 CC	71	73	14	13
3 PA	34	27	50	23
4 CC	40	77	11	12

In Table 7 the mean patient and therapist use of the category groups is compared. Here the similarity of therapists within schools and the difference between schools in their use of two of the Bales group (Giving and Asking) is clearly demonstrated. It is also clear from this table that the response of the patients is not always reciprocal to their therapists. In fact, the patients' use of Accepting and Rejecting, the two affect categories, seems quite independent of their therapists' use of these responses. The last column of this table in which the affective responses are summed shows that the matched patients resemble each other in the total number of their responses which involve expressivity of their affects. But it is the two client-centered therapists who use these affect categories heavily. In Bales terminology these therapists are more engaged in social-emotional exchanges and the psychoanalytic therapists are more task oriented in their communications. The matched patients, however, are also similar in terms of the way their affective responses are proportionately distributed: case Numbers 1 and 2 express about 80 percent Acceptance of self and others to 20 percent Rejection, while Numbers 3 and 4 divide their responses between Acceptance and Rejection about 50-50.

The patients' use of the Giving categories is *inversely* related to their therapists' use of these responses. The client-centered therapists *Give* very little to their patients in the way of Information (category 4) and of their own Opinions and Interpretations (category 5), yet their patients use these Giving categories most frequently. The proportion of patient and therapist *Asking*, on the other hand, seems to be *directly* related. The psychoanalytic therapists who make more use of asking as a technique seem to free their patients to use it somewhat, too. Client-centered therapists avoid questioning as a technique which seems to constrain this activity on the part of their patients. Perhaps, though, the more general statement that can be made from the data is that patients ask only half as many questions as their therapists.

Table 7
Percent Use of Bales Category Groups by Patient and Therapist:
Accepting, Giving, Asking, Rejecting

Case No.	Categories 1, 2, 3: Accepting		Categories 4, 5, 6: Giving		Categories 7, 8, 9: Asking		Categories 10, 11, 12: Rejecting		Σ Affect Categories Accepting + Rejecting	
	P	T	P	T	P	T	P	T	P	T
1 PA	34.0	53.0	48.9	26.3	11.5	20.4	5.6	.3	39.6	53.3
2 CC	26.8	77.6	60.1	14.8	3.0	6.8	10.1	.8	36.9	78.4
3 PA	14.8	28.4	56.0	34.3	15.1	36.2	14.1	1.2	28.9	29.6
4 CC	13.5	78.5	71.1	10.6	3.9	8.2	11.5	0.0	25.0	78.5

SUMMARY AND DISCUSSION

In summary, then, this study shows that while some specific therapeutic techniques do seem to have an influence in shaping the verbal behavior of patients, there is much more that is similar in the response of matched patients to different treatments than is often credited. A good player can play the game under either set of rules. Actually, the range of verbal behaviors open to psychoanalytic and client-centered therapists is not so very different given the goals they are pursuing; and since the goals for both types of treatment have a good deal in common, the results of this study should not be surprising. Although the two schools of thought differ in their explanation of how and why personality distortions develop, they agree that the aim of treatment is to free patients from inefficient defensive operations by reducing the need for them. Client-centered theory stresses the expression of affect as a necessary condition in the service of this goal, and psychoanalytic theory, while also emphasizing the importance of affective experiencing, uniquely makes observation of the re-experienced material necessary to the working-through process. The study reported here, limited as it is to a small sample of short cases, will need replication. Nonetheless, these data appear to show that both degree of expression of affect and level of self-observation reached by matched patients during their period of treatment are independent of professed style being practiced. In all likelihood, the level reached by the patient depends more on what he brings to treatment than on the rules of the game being followed by the therapist. This statement assumes, of course, that he is in the hands of a well-experienced professional.

What, then, is the function of having different sets of rules and of the care with which we learn and teach them? One answer to this question may well be that they serve as guides to young therapists while they are becoming professionals which keeps the interaction of the game focused on its purpose. In this way the novice is less likely to find himself trying to play several different games at the same time. In other words, the major function of technique models may well be to keep the therapist's behavior with patients role-appropriate until it becomes sufficiently well integrated into his response system so that other competing roles he might play with this patient are not activated.

Of course, this is not all that is involved in being a professional and not sufficient explanation to account for the relationship which has been found repeatedly between the degree of expertness of the therapist and the success of the treatment. To get some real understanding of the variables associated with expertness, which contribute to the finding that patients respond similarly despite technique differences, subtler measures are needed. It is only possible at this time to speculate that the expert probably works more efficiently than the novice in his selection of when to respond and to what material; that is, in the precise location of the crucial data and in his sense of timing of his interventions. In the exercising of these skills, the influence of differences in the formal language properties of the responses could well be minimal.

REFERENCES

Bales, R. F. *Interaction process analysis: A method for the study of small groups.* Reading, Mass.: Addison-Wesley, 1950.

Barron, F. An ego-strength scale which predicts response to psychotherapy. In G. S. Welsh and W. F. Dahlstrom (Eds.), *Basic readings on the MMPI in psychology and medicine.* Minneapolis: Univ. of Minnesota Press, 1956.

Betz, Barbara J., and Whitehorn, J. C. The relationship of the therapist to the outcome of therapy in schizophrenia. *APA psychiatric research reports,* 5, 1956.

Cartwright, Rosalind D. Predicting response to client-centered therapy with the Rorschach PR scale. *J. counsel. Psychol.,* 5, 1958.

Cartwright, Rosalind D., and Lerner, Barbara. Empathy, need to change, and improvement with psychotherapy. *J. consult. Psychol.,* 27, 1963.

Freud, Anna. *The ego and the mechanisms of defense.* New York: International Universities, 1946.

Hollingshead, A., and Redlich, F. C. *Social class and mental illness,* New York: Wiley, 1958.

Kirtner, W. L., and Cartwright, D. S. Success and failure in client-centered therapy as a function of initial in-therapy behavior. *J. consult. Psychol.,* 22, 1958.

McNair, D. M., Callahan, D. M., and Lorr, M. Therapist "type" and patient response to psychotherapy. *J. consult. Psychol.,* 26, 1962.

MILLER, A., ISAACS, K., and HAGGARD, E. On the nature of the observing function of the ego. *Brit. J. med. Psychol.* In press.

NOBLE, N., OHLSEN, M., and PROFF, F. A method for the quantification of psychotherapeutic interaction in counseling groups. *J. counsel. Psychol.*, 8, 1961.

ROGERS, C., and RABLEN, R. A scale of process in psychotherapy. Mimeographed Manual, Univ. of Wisconsin, 1958.

STERBA, R. The fate of the ego in analytic therapy. *Int. J. Psychoanal.*, 15, 1934.

TOMLINSON, T. M., and HART, J. T. JR. A validation of the process scale. *J. consult. Psychol.*, 26, 1962.

WALKER, A., RABLEN, R., and ROGERS, C. R. Development of a scale to measure process change in psychotherapy. *J. clin. Psychol.*, 1, 1960.

B.
Measurement Tools to Assess Change with Psychotherapy

In this section dealing with test and measurement tools in outcome research, we have provided chapters illustrating three major types of psychological test instruments: the self-report test, the projective test, and the behavioral rating scale. These different types of tests each have their specific advantages and disadvantages. A general appraisal of evaluative measures has been given elsewhere by Cronbach (1960) and Anastasi (1963).

The self-report form, e.g., symptom checklists or mood scales, have the advantage of ease of administration and do not require trained test examiners. Some tests of this type are interpreted literally, that is, the items checked or the statements made by the subjects are taken to signify how the person is actually feeling or what his attitude is. Validity studies have not routinely been carried out to test such an assumption. With some self-report types of tests, the subjects' responses are not necessarily believed to indicate literally what his attitudes, interests, or emotions really are. Rather, these are determined on a probabilistic basis by giving the test to groups of individuals with known traits, attitudes, vocational interests, and so forth and then clustering those responses which distinguish one known group from another. Validity criteria of this kind rest on an actuarial basis and in many instances the types of responses made by a subject do not appear to be semantically or logically related to the assessment made. Some examples of such tests are the Minnesota Multiphasic Personality Inventory (MMPI) and the Strong Vocational Interest Blank. All self-report measures have the disadvantage that the subject may aim to present a distorted picture of himself, usually one he considers socially acceptable or desirable, or the subject may simply "fake" his responses to conform to what he sees as the purpose of the test. Methods have been developed to detect such test behavior, for example, the MMPI lie scale and K scale.

Projective tests have the advantage that the subject cannot guess what personality traits are being assessed and hence deliberate distortion of responses cannot readily be carried out. Usually projective tests aim to supply information about a broad range of personality features, including psychodynamic relationships and unconscious psychological drives and conflicts. The precision with which each of these complex constructs can be assessed is probably poor but the test makes up in breadth what it lacks in precision.

Behavioral rating scales, while capable at best of satisfactory inter-rater reliability, indicate what the individual is doing; but if one begins with behavioral ratings one must make inferences if he desires to know the individual's psychological experience. Furthermore, it is obvious that a subject who is not moving or speaking can be having intense and complicated psychological experiences and that the presence of these may be missed by a behavioral rating scale. On the other hand, the observation of overt behavior in the form of patterns and sequences of behavior may, in some instances, leave little doubt about what a person is experiencing and how a person may be likely to behave and feel on similar occasions in the near future. One problem presented by behavioral ratings is whether the ratings validly represent the typical behavior of the individual regardless of the setting or whether such ratings indicate behavior likely to recur in a specific setting. Another problem with such ratings is the difficulty in comparing or equating ratings made by different investigators at different research centers.

Some of the preceding chapters have already described, in one way or another, the basic models or theories, the shortcomings, advantages, or some other features of various evaluative tools of usefulness in psychotherapy research. (See, for example, chapters by Auld and Dollard, Gottschalk, *et al.*, Chance, Haggard and Isaacs, Seitz, Strupp, *et al.*, Chassan and Bellak, Wallerstein, Shlien and Zimring, and Cartwright.) The three chapters following, however, will deal with research that focuses especially on the development of measurement tools to assess personality and personality change.

Schofield describes the use of a standard diagnostic instrument in the assessment of outcome; the instrument is the Minnesota Multiphasic Personality Index, which can be administered both before therapy and at any desired time thereafter. The advantages of the MMPI are its objectivity, relative ease of administration, and the fact that it provides a comprehensive self-description—what Schofield refers to as the "I am" system. The instrument specifies the pre-treatment state of the patient, at least as he sees himself. Before and after comparisons are possible on particular scales of the MMPI profile. Thus, with a depressed patient, one would naturally be most concerned with changes in scores on the depression scale after therapy. But also of interest would be changes in the scores on hypochondriacal trends, psychasthenia, and probably others.

The MMPI has its limitations, too. As we have mentioned, any self-descriptive rating or inventory presents opportunities for distortion by the patient. Such distortion can be detected, Schofield states, by those scales which are built into the instrument to measure test-taking attitudes. However, the detection of distorting factors is not synonomous with their correction.

Another problem of the MMPI is that on repetition of the test there is a tendency toward normalization of the scores. The author accounts for this by the random operation of the error factor in scores. The significance is that the instrument may show "improvement" which is really a function of taking the test again. Schofield explores this issue of comparing pre- and post-therapy profiles. On the one hand, this comparison can be made by clinicians experienced with the MMPI, the experts making their judgments as to degree of improvement. This procedure has the same limitations as any other clinical judgment. More desirable, Schofield says, is a completely statistical handling of the scale scores, but this would require a satisfactory mathematical index of profile similarities. The coding of MMPI profiles is described as an approach intermediate to the former two.

In this connection, Marks and Seeman (1963) have reported elsewhere an investigation which the readers will find to be an interesting methodological contribution in the use of the MMPI. These authors attempted a configural analysis of MMPI scores and explored the statistical relationship of such configurations to various clinical psychiatric and psychological parameters. Their interpretations of MMPI data, a procedure which has been labelled the "cookbook method," can give insightful and accurate psychometric assessments and predictions with respect to change with treatment.

Rightly or wrongly, the MMPI has not won wide acceptance as a criterion measure. The ego strength scale derived from it by Barron (1953) has apparently been more successful. Schofield describes how this scale was developed empirically from MMPI items to predict improvement in psychotherapy, and how a number of studies have borne out its accuracy in this regard.

Schofield emphasizes that the MMPI deals only with the "I am" system; and that the minimum requirements for outcome assessment include delineation of the patient from other vantage points.

The chapter by Samuel Beck is included as a paradigm of projective tests. Other types of projective tests used in evaluative research include the Thematic Apperception Test, The House-Tree-Person Test, the Sentence Completion Test, the Blacky Test, the Szondi Test. These tests provide an impressionistic assessment of personality. Most projective tests are poorly adapted for quantitative measurement, although scores can be derived from them. No test provides an assessment of the personality in isolation; the test is always a sample of social interaction with a specific other person in a specific situation. Hence, it is important in using such tests for evaluative purposes to consider the error variance attributable to the examiner and the context in which the evaluative device is administered. This, of course, applies not only to projective but non-projective personality tests. Finally, the validity studies of projective tests have not tended to be very satisfactory, especially for the prediction of overt behavior. Global impressionistic evaluations from projective tests, when combined with psychometric test data and a clinical history, appear to be more valid. (See, for example, Harrower, 1960.) Also, projective tests often yield valuable hypotheses, in a clinical setting, as to specific conflicts and defenses which can be further explored. Furthermore, some work has been done in relating certain patterns of projective responses to specific clinical groupings to provide actuarial prediction (Piotrowski, 1960, 1961). Appraisals of projective techniques as evaluative measures are given elsewhere by Holt and Luborsky (1958), MacFarlane and Tuddenham (1951), and Gleser (1963).

Maurice Lorr has earned for himself the reputation of a rigorous and resourceful investigator in the development of useful and predictive measuring instruments for the evaluation of the effects of various therapies, including the psychotherapies (1962) used in the Veterans Administration facilities. In a review chapter, written with Douglas McNair, he provides a detailed outline of his working methods and gives descriptions of measurement tools he has developed.

One of the strengths of Lorr and McNair's work is the large number of therapists and patients they have studied. The extensive data they collect receive careful statistical handling. Furthermore, the authors are on sure ground all the way because they stay close to the facts of experience. The data with which they deal are patients' self-reports and those therapist judgments which are no deeper than first-level inferences. Their approach could be characterized as going one step beyond the anecdotal method of clinical description; but this is a very important step indeed. Prior to the objective study of psychotherapy, all information about the process was communicated by way of the anecdote. The basic form, in the profound paper as well as the trivial one, was: "I had a patient who. . . .", followed by a description of whatever happened to impress the therapist. Lorr and McNair have in effect approved such clinical descriptions but have provided for their systematization. Thus, they have developed a rating form on which the psychiatrist records pertinent clinical findings after an interview with a patient (Lorr, et al., 1962). This particular form is not their concern in the present chapter.

The studies which are here reported, however, are based on the same principle, the systematization of the clinician's judgments and the patient's self-reports, so that these can be handled statistically. In this method, factor analysis is an important tool. The issues to which they direct their attention are: patients' mood changes during psychotherapy;

patients' perceptions of therapists' behavior in therapy; therapists' judgments of patients' interpersonal behavior; those therapeutic techniques which therapists endorse, as determined by questionnaire; and therapists' goals in treatment.

The authors conclude their chapter with a study which extends Betz and Whitehorn's well-known work (1956) on Type A and Type B therapists. (In the Betz and Whitehorn study these therapists were differentiated on the basis of their success in psychotherapy with schizophrenic patients, the type A therapists obtaining high success and Type B therapists low success. The two groups could be distinguished on the Strong Vocational Interest Blank: generally speaking, the B therapists were interested in mechanical and technical skills and activities.) In studying a new sample of 40 outpatients, Lorr and McNair found that Type B therapists (as defined by the Strong items) had greater success. In considering why their results are opposite to those of Betz and Whitehorn, the authors find that the major cause for the discrepancy is probably the sex differences between the samples. The Betz-Whitehorn sample included women patients; the Lorr-McNair sample consisted only of men. Since Type B therapists tend to have more masculine interests, they were probably more compatible with the male patients of the second study. Type A therapists are probably more compatible with women patients.

Lorr and McNair's discussion of this and other factors is thorough and closely reasoned, and in fact throws further light on the original Betz and Whitehorn study. All too often, contradictory results in different studies cannot be satisfactorily explained; the achievement of the present authors is therefore notable.

REFERENCES

ANASTASI, ANNE. *Psychological testing.* New York: Macmillan, 1963.

BARRON, F. An ego-strength scale which predicts response to psychotherapy. *J. consult. Psychol.,* **17**: 327-333, 1953.

BETZ, B. J., and WHITEHORN, J. C. The relationship of the therapist to the outcome of therapy in schizophrenia. In N. S. Kline (Ed.), *Psychiatric research reports,* Vol. 5. Washington, D.C.: American Psychiatric Association, 1956. Pp. 89-105.

CRONBACH, L. J. *Essentials of psychological testing.* New York: Harper & Row, 1960.

GLESER, G. C. Projective methodologies. *Ann. Rev. Psychol.,* **14**: 391-422, 1963.

HARROWER, M. *Changes and development.* New York: Grune & Stratton, 1958.

HOLT, R. P., and LUBORSKY, L. *Personality patterns of psychiatrists.* New York: Basic Books, 1958.

LORR, M., KLETT, C. J., McNAIR, D. M., and LASKY, J. J. *The inpatient multi-*

dimensional psychiatric scale manual. Washington, D.C.: Veterans Administration, 1962.

MACFARLANE, J. W., and TUDDENHAM, R. D. Problems in the validation of projective techniques. In H. H. Anderson and G. L. Anderson (Eds.), *An introduction to projective techniques.* Englewood Cliffs, N.J.: Prentice-Hall, 1951.

MARKS, P. A., and SEEMAN, W. *The actuarial description of abnormal personality.* Baltimore: Williams & Wilkins, 1963.

PIOTROWSKI, Z. A. The Rorschach Test. In *The prediction of overt behavior through the use of projective techniques.* Springfield, Ill.: Charles C Thomas, 1960. Chap. 5.

PIOTROWSKI, Z. A., and BRICKLIN, B. A second validation of a long-term Rorschach prognostic index for schizophrenic patients. *J. consult. Psychol.,* **25**: 123-128, 1961.

31. The structured personality inventory in measurement of effects of psychotherapy

William Schofield

I. INTRODUCTION

For reasons that are not obvious, psychiatrists and psychologists were slow to recognize the appropriateness of repeating a diagnostic test in order to get a measure of change that might be related to intervening therapeutic efforts. For a long time, psychiatric diagnostic tests were reserved to the point of diagnosis, and were repeated chiefly in the circumstance of a re-admission to clinic or hospital, again for purely diagnostic purposes. The restriction of diagnostic devices to diagnostic purposes held equally for so-called projective and so-called structured devices.

It is apparent that a valid instrument for diagnosis of psychiatric disorder must be able to measure the extent and nature of symptomatology, or tap the nature of underlying character structure, or both. Since the pathology of mental illness is expressed in behaviors, verbal and nonverbal, a valid diagnostic test must capture the strength and nature of tendencies (response strengths) toward such behaviors. If therapy is successful in any degree in altering these behavioral tendencies, this alternation should be reflected in *changes* in the pattern of response to the diagnostic test. It is obvious that a *valid* diagnostic test should have *potential*, when repeated, as a measure of change, i.e., of response to therapy. It does not follow necessarily that a valid diagnostic test will be equally valid as a measure of therapeutic response, nor that all of the observed changes in test response can be attributed to therapy. Finally, it does not follow that a test of limited but established diagnostic validity may not be of greater validity in the measurement of change.

In the following review of the applications and potential of a particular diagnostic test (the Minnesota Multiphasic Personality Inventory [MMPI]), this writer holds to the following principles:

1. There is *no single* test, observation, rating procedure, behavior sample, or other criterion that is sufficient to stand alone as a determiner of the level of mental health (or illness) of an individual, or of the amount of significant change which has occurred over time. (Meehl, 1955)

2. The best measures of therapeutic effect must entail the application of the same, *standard* methods of observation at not less than two points of time, pre- and post-therapy. The effectiveness of therapy cannot be reasonably inferred from a patient's score on a rating scale (e.g., of ego-strength) which is applied only at the termination of therapy.

3. For perfectly obvious reasons, the evaluations of the patient's clinical status (even pre-treatment, and most certainly post-treatment) must not be exclusively or even primarily provided by the person responsible for the treatment.

4. The patient's evaluation of the effects of treatment and the amount of change, whether given directly and casually or collected indirectly and "objectively," cannot be assumed to be completely free of the contaminating effects of his motives to appear better than he may in fact be and to please the therapist. These are well spelled out in the treatment of the "hello-goodbye" effect. (Hathaway, 1948)

5. The patient's self-concept as revealed in the matrix of statements to which he subscribes as descriptive of his thoughts, feelings, and attitudes (the "I am" system) is equally important at both the diagnostic and post-treatment points of evaluation as is the parallel public concept of the patient's overt behavior (the "He is" system). No adequate study of the patient, no attempt to measure his response to therapy can ignore either of these systems.

II. NATURE OF THE MMPI

The Minnesota Multiphasic Personality Inventory (MMPI) was designed by its authors, a psychiatrist and a psychologist, as a self-administering and objectively scored diagnostic *interview* to be used in screening (especially of general medical patients) for the presence of clinically significant kinds and amounts of psychiatric disturbance, i.e., deviations of thought, affect, or behavior (Hathaway and McKinley, 1940). The subject is required only to give a "True" or "False" response to each of 550 items; these are generally simple declarative statements in the first person singular. The items cover a range of material, including attitudes toward self and others, mental and physical "symptoms," habits, preferences, and some 20 other categories of subject matter. Subjects make their responses either by an actual True-False sorting of item-cards (the individual form) or by recording their responses on a separate answer sheet accompanying a booklet of the statements (the group form).

The test can rarely be completed validly in less than 45 minutes and a cooperative subject with at least a sixth-grade education and normal reading ability will rarely require more than 90 minutes to complete the test. Completely accurate scoring (within the limits of simple clerical error) can readily be learned by the average office worker. A variety of forms are available that permit machine scoring, and even profiling of scores (Glueck, 1963). For research studies, it is strongly recommended that machine-scored forms of the test be utilized.

In constructing the MMPI, its authors instituted a number of features designed to correct for the weakness and criticisms of previous personality inventories. They extended the range of content, adapted the language to the level of the general population, developed specific keys to check on the "honesty" of the responses, and, most important, developed the scoring keys for each of the clinical scales by strictly empirical procedures. The first publication on the MMPI appeared in 1940. By 1960, the bibliography on this instrument was well over 1,000 items (Dahlstrom and Welsh, 1960).

The most commonly reported results from an MMPI-testing are in the form of a profile of standard scores (with a mean of 50 and a standard deviation of 10, for general population norms) on three *validity* indicators and nine clinical scales. As a result of special research investigations, over 200 additional *experimental* scales have been extracted (Dahlstrom and Welsh, 1960).

Figure 1 is an example of a profile obtained from a psychiatric patient. For purposes of a crude "reading" (definitely not the approach to profile analysis used by sophisticated clinicians), the following overly simplified descriptions of each scale will provide some guidance.

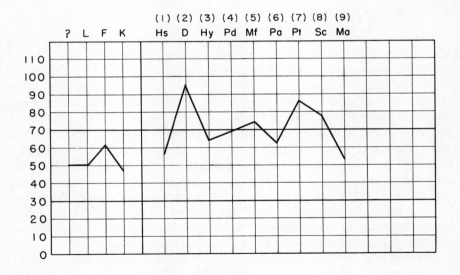

Figure 1
MMPI Profile of 29-Year-Old Male with Diagnosis of
Depressive Reaction

Scale

L—a measure of the extent to which the subject was motivated to a relatively crude attempt to put himself in a good light, to avoid admission of even the mildest of personal defects or conflicts.

F—a measure of the degree to which the test has been invalidated by carelessness in scoring, by carelessness on the part of the subject, by insufficient reading ability on part of the subject, or by tendencies on his part to exaggerate his complaints and to give an unduly "bad" picture of himself.

K—a more sensitive, subtle measure than L or F of "test-taking" attitudes; the higher the K-score, the more "defensive" the subject.

1,Hs—a measure of hypochondriacal trends; all the major organ systems and physical complaint areas are sampled by the items scored on this scale.

2,D—a measure of symptomatic depression.

3,Hy—a measure of hysteroid trends; denial of conflicts, claims of superior personal adjustment, and presence of certain somatic complaints.

4,Pd—a complex scale tapping a mixture of rebellious, resentful attitudes toward authorities, lack of positive emotional experiences, asocial trends, and interpersonal conflicts.

5,Mf—a measure of psychological masculinity-femininity as revealed by interests and preferences.

6,Pa—a measure of trends toward ideas of reference and influence, both subtle and more obvious paranoid mentation.

7,Pt—a measure of the presence of obsessive-compulsive trends, worries, phobias, and extreme anxiety symptoms.

8,Sc—a measure of schizoid mentation and affect, including delusional trends.

9,Ma—a measure of self-confidence, morale, and manic trends.

The patient whose profile is shown in Figure 1 was a 29-year-old male with a diagnosis of depressive reaction. While a picture of the patient's symptomatic status can be derived by examining the size of score on a scale-by-scale basis, the overall diagnostic picture can be best appreciated by appraisal of the configuration of the scores as a *profile*, and this is the manner in which the MMPI is approached by experts. Certain profile types (which are designated by code numbers that reflect the relative deviation, in order of magnitude, of the clinical scales) are of high frequency in psychiatric samples and a sizeable amount of actuarially based diagnostic, prognostic, and general psychopathological information has been accumulated concerning the persons who generate these typical codes (Hathaway and Meehl, 1951; Marks and Seeman, 1963).

The structured nature of the MMPI and its relatively simple format considerably belie its complexity and subtlety as a diagnostic instrument (Meehl, 1945; Seeman, 1952). A superficial knowledge of its construction and of the deviation of the individual scales could suffice for gross errors in clinical use, errors both of over-and under-interpretation. Workers who wish to use the MMPI, either clinically or in research, should be thoroughly familiar with the basic literature on this test. Fortunately, the most critical information has been compiled in a few volumes (Hathaway and Meehl, 1951; Welsh and Dahlstrom, 1956; Dahlstrom and Welsh, 1960).

While the validity of the MMPI as a diagnostic device would not either directly limit nor express its validity as a measure of changes attributed to therapy, a brief word is in order concerning its utility. As a structured inventory designed to afford screening diagnoses of psychiatric symptomatology, it is without question the best instrument of its kind. While it is by no means completely free of the criticisms that have been made of its forerunners, its authors have been notably successful in overcoming most of the weaknesses of the older neurotic inventories. (For reviews of its validity see Calvin and McConnell, 1953; Buros, 1959.)

III. EVALUATION OF PRE- AND POST-THERAPY PROFILES

A. The Reliability of Scores

A psychometric score on any measure of a personality variable or psychiatric dimension always involves two components: the subject's *true* score and an error component. The error factor at any one testing may serve either to cause a false inflation or a false suppression of the subject's obtained score as a reflection of his true status on the measured variable. On the assumption that error factors operate randomly, it is unlikely that they will lend themselves uniformly to an elevating or to a depressing effect on scores when the subject is retested. The error factor is probably most readily perceived in the instance of extreme scores (either very high or very low). When the individual with such scores is retested (over too brief an interval to permit the operation of any variables that would validly change his *true* score) his retest score will generally be less extreme than his original scores. This phenomenon is acknowledged in the statistical notion of *regression toward the mean*.

The regression phenomena is a particular concern in clinical work since the patient typically presents his pathology in the form of elevated scores, statistically deviant scores (i.e., of a magnitude having infrequent occurrence in the normal population), and it is not easy to know how much of the elevation is a function of an error increment to the true score. Upon retesting, the statistically probable reduced score may be primarily a function of a change in the *error* variable. Thus, in examining pre- and post-therapy scores, the clinician or researcher must ask how much of the observed change in scores is to be accounted for by chance, that is, by the random fluctuation associated with the error variance in the measurement.

The same question may be put differently. How stable are the scores in question with repeated testing when the subject has *not* been exposed to any procedures or experiences, such as psychotherapy, that are likely to influence the measured variable? The stability over time of personality test scores is usually expressed as test-retest reliability coefficients; these represent a statistical estimate of the correlation between the paired scores of individuals when tested on two different occasions, usually with a short time intervening. The higher the coefficient the greater the stability of the measure and the smaller the error factor.

In estimating the reliability of personality test scores as measures of the response to psychotherapy, it is most appropriate to obtain coefficients on samples of psychiatric patients; these are the persons with whom psychotherapy is used. Furthermore, it is the nature of some psychiatric variables (such as mood) to be variable over time. It is important to know the amount of fluctuation in these generally less stable variables so that shifts in scores on appropriate measures will not be erroneously assigned to the effects of treatment. (This same fact, i.e., that it is the nature of certain personality dimensions to fluctuate over brief time intervals, also serves as a reservation against the usual interpretation of test-retest reliabilities as a measure of accuracy of measurement. Thus, a low reliability coefficient for a measure of a presumably stable, structured element of character is undesirable. But, a high coefficient obtained for a measure of a presumably variable component, such as hysteroid symptomatology, would suggest an undesirably insensitive measure.)

The ideal data for appraising the stability of MMPI scores (freedom from error) as a base for evaluating the significance of score changes presumably associated with intervening psychotherapy would be provided by test-retest scores over an interval of not more than a few days (preferably not more than one week) in out-patient neurotics who were candidates for psychotherapy. Such ideal data have not been reported, but an approximation is afforded in data obtained from a sample of 40 patients who were tested with the MMPI after an average of three days following hospital admission and retested after an average interval of four days before any formal treatment was started. (Rosen, 1953) The test-retest reliability coefficients from this study are reported in Table 1. For com-

Table 1
MMPI Test-retest Coefficients for Normals, Control Patients, and Treated Patients

Study	Sample	N	Test-retest	Hs (1)	D (2)	Hy (3)	Pd (4)	Mf (5)	Pa (6)	Pt (7)	Sc (8)	Ma (9)
Rosen (1953)	VA Hospital	40	2-7 days	.85	.80	.88	.88	.64	.75	.80	.83	.56
Cottle (1950)	College students	100	1 week	.81	.66	.72	.80	.83/.79*	.56	.90	.86	.76
Schofield (1950)	Outpatient	25	5-330 days	.66	.42	.66	.57	.83	.37	.71	.80	.75

* Male/Females

parative purposes, similar data is reported for a sample of 100 college "normals" who were tested and retested after an interval of one week. (Cottle, 1950) (For a comprehensive review of MMPI reliability data see Dahlstrom and Welsh, 1960)

The data of Table 1 are illustrative of other comparable data that support several generalizations:

1. As a group measure of major psychiatric dimensions, the MMPI scales reveal generally satisfactory levels of reliability.

2. There is variation among the scales in the relative stability of the measures they yield. In general, the more *characterological* scales (right-hand side of the profile, scales 7 and 8 in particular) yield more stable measures than the more *symptomatic* scales (left side of the profile, scales 1, 2, and 3).

3. Other things being equal, marked reductions in scores on the more stable measures are more likely to reflect clinically significant and therapy-related changes in a patient's status than are comparable fluctuations in measures which are inherently variable, such as depression. Thus, estimations of the standard error of measurement of each scale would support confidence in the *clinical significance* (as against random error variation) of T-score changes in either direction of the following size, Scales: 2, D—14 points; 6, Pa—12 points; 3, Hy; 4, Pd; and 9, Ma—10 points; 1, Hs; 5, Mf; 7, Pt; and 8, Sc—8 points (Cottle, 1950).

B. Profile Analysis

The correlation of pre- and post-therapy scores, when compared with the stability of scores obtained over a brief interval from untreated control subjects, yields one kind of evidence as to whether therapy has been influential and in what particular ways. Table 1 reports such coefficients for a small sample of psychiatric patients who received out-patient psychotherapy (Schofield, 1950). It may be seen that the treated patients showed considerably more fluctuation in the measures of mood (Scale 2), of somatic symptomatology (Scales 1 and 3), and of paranoid sensitivity (Scale 6) than was found in the non-treated samples. It would be appropriate to infer from such evidence of score fluctuation that a significant clinical process had intervened between the two testings. Such correlational analysis, however, is insufficient to reveal the amounts of change or whether the shifts in score tended to be in one direction, either on particular scales or on the profile as a whole. For such appraisal, it is desirable to compare directly the mean profiles obtained before and after therapy.

Figure 2 shows the mean profiles obtained before and after psychotherapy by a sample largely of neurotic patients who were seen in an outpatient clinic where they received weekly interviews; from two to

18 therapy sessions occurred between the two testings (Schofield, 1950). Comparison of these mean profiles with the test-retest correlations reported for the same patients in Table 1 is instructive. The correlational data suggest that at least some of the patients were affected by their clinic experience in ways that resulted in changes in their MMPI response patterns, and it suggests that at least some of the patients may have changed sizeably. By contrast, the mean profiles suggest that the particular treatment of this sample was ineffective. Statistical tests of the reliability of the changes in the pre- and post-therapy mean scores revealed that none of them exceeded chance fluctuation. It would be inferred from the mean profiles that, *as a group,* the patients were not significantly helped by the therapy they received. The changes suggested by the correlational data appear either to be unsystematic or otherwise hidden by the mean profiles.

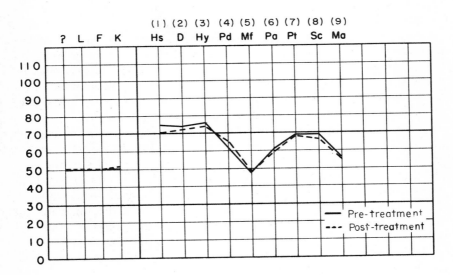

Figure 2

Mean Pre- and Post- Therapy MMPI Profiles for 25 Outpatients Who Received Weekly Psychotherapy

Source: William Schofield. Changes in responses to the Minnesota Multiphasic Inventory following certain therapies. In H. S. Conrad (Ed.), Psychol. Monogra., *64*, No. 5, 1950. Reproduced with permission of The American Psychological Association, Washington, D. C.

It might be noted that with a single exception (Scale 4-Pd), all of the mean post-therapy clinical scores of Figure 1 are lower than the pre-therapy scores. It would be tempting to infer from the general trend toward lowered pre-treatment scores that the mean profiles reveal the operation of a general albeit weak effect of therapy in the direction of slightly improved clinical status. Such an inference is unjustified in light of the finding in several studies (Darley, 1938; Kaufmann, 1950; Schofield, 1950) of a generalized tendency for retest mean scores of control groups to shift downward. It has been demonstrated that patients who are required (by clinical circumstance or by experimental design) to endure a waiting period before the beginning of therapy will show shifts in symptomatic scores which are very similar both in direction and size to those found in matched patients who received therapy (Barron and Leary, 1955). It is a general finding that psychotherapy, especially in its earlier stages, may be accompanied by an increase in the 4, Pd-score, while other scores show diminution. The elevation of this scale appears to reflect the opportunity (and encouragement) that therapy affords the patient to become aware of and to ventilate his interpersonal conflicts and hostilities. Perhaps this is an instance in which an increase rather than decrease of score is to be looked upon as evidence that an active process is under way.

At this point, no satisfactory conclusion can be made as to whether the psychotherapy of these patients was effective. Examination of the pre- and post-treatment profiles of individual patients presents more direct evidence. In such examination, significance of score changes must be evaluated with respect to the range of likely random fluctuation as reported above. It is a matter of clinical judgment whether the paired profiles of a patient reveal significant improvement. In such analysis, depending upon the particular goals of therapy (or research), attention may be given primarily to particular scales or to the profile in its entirety. For example, if patients have been grouped for homogeneity of somatic complaint, attention might be directed primarily to the changes in scores on the *neurotic triad* (1-Hs, 2-D, 3-Hy). When the general health or pathology of the patient's self-concept, attitudes toward others, and mental and emotional life are the criteria, the MMPI profiles should be examined for overall change. It is to be emphasized again that this data from the "I am" system constitutes only one of multiple criteria that should be examined in appraising the efficacy of therapy.

Because of the complexity as a clinical task of the reading of a single profile of scores, let alone the comparison of two profiles, judge error should be compensated by use of multiple readers who are requested to sort the pre- and post-therapy profiles of a sample of patients into groups showing one or more degrees of "improvement." The proportion of a treated sample with profiles judged so as to reflect improvement provides a more direct measure of therapeutic response than is afforded by any group statistics. Figure 3 shows the profiles of one patient drawn from the sample reported in Table 1 and Figure 2. In general, the kind of improvement in clinical status suggested in the two profiles of Figure 3 has been found to correlate well with other independent clinical ratings of the patient's behavioral response to a treatment regime. (Pacella, Piotrowski, and Lewis, 1947; Hales and Simon, 1948; Carp, 1950; Feldman, 1951, 1952; Simon and Gilberstadt, 1954) Clinicians experienced with the MMPI demonstrate a high degree of agreement in classifying retest profiles as "improved" or "unimproved" (Briggs and Schofield, 1958).

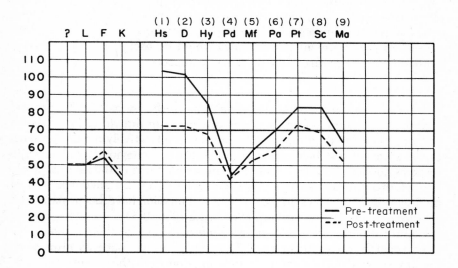

Figure 3

Pre- and Post-Treatment MMPI Profiles of a 25-Year-Old Psychoneurotic Who Received Outpatient Psychotherapy

The clinical reading of profiles, both because of the time required and the fallibility of the clinician as an analyzer and integrater of complex data, is less desirable than an actuarial approach that entails strictly clerical or computer production of numerical indices (Meehl, 1959). As yet, there is no large agreement as to what constitutes the best index of profile similarity, but a variety of such indices have been explored in various researches (Dahlstrom and Welsh, 1960). Obviously, indices of profile similarity, when applied to pre- and post-therapy profiles of individuals, can yield an index of dissimilarity, or of amount of change, presumably due in part to the effects of treatment. Such indices when distributed for a research sample, and a cutting-score selected, permit objective specification of groups of *changed* and *unchanged* patients. Of course, profile inspection would be necessary to distinguish between therapeutic and deleterious changes.

A procedure that is intermediate to that of clinical reading of profiles and score-by-score arithmetic analyses of profiles is afforded by a system of coding the MMPI profiles (Hathaway, 1947; Welsh, 1948). The elevation and conformation of the separate clinical scale scores are by this method reduced to a single numerical index. These indices (or codes) may then be directly compared. In research on psychotherapy, it would be meaningful to ascertain the relative frequency of various code-types among pre-therapy profiles and post-therapy profiles for the same patients, as an indication of the effects of therapy in shifting profile types. Study of post-therapy codes found in patients who are homogeneous with respect to pre-treatment profile codes would be useful in generating hypotheses as to the nature of the therapeutic impact.

C. Internal Analyses

The examination of the MMPI profiles produced by patients before and after psychotherapy, either in terms of change in individual scale scores or by reference to profiles, may be considered a relatively molar approach to the study of test behavior and of associated behavioral tendencies in response to therapy. It is pertinent to know something of the internal workings of the instrument at a more molecular level. Detailed analyses of therapy-related changes in item-response behavior have been made and lead to some interesting findings (Schofield, 1950, 1953).

Control groups retested over brief intervals change their responses to approximately one-sixth of the 550 items. Neurotic patients after some therapy show a shift in approximately one-fourth of their item responses. The relationship between the number of item responses altered and the amount of related change in scale scores is positive but not very high. This is in part a function of the fact that only 307 of the 550 items are scored on any of the nine standard clinical scales; it is in part a function of the fact that some of the scored items appear on more than a single scale. Thus, it is possible (and in fact happens) that certain patients will show marked shifts in their profile of scale scores as a result of changing their responses to relatively few items; by contrast, other patients may change their responses to many items but produce relatively little change in their profiles.

In general, it is found that the response changes of neurotic patients after *brief* psychotherapy are concentrated on those items with content pertaining to somatic complaints, sexual attitudes, and general morale. By contrast, such patients show relatively infrequent change in responses to items in the area of depressive affect, family and marital relations, and cognitive distortion. The item changes appear to be consistent with what would be expected as responses to brief, relatively supportive therapy in an outpatient clinic.

D. Special Scales and Scores

It was noted previously that a large number of special scales have been evolved out of MMPI research on special patient groups or directed to particular psychiatric problems. Among these are to be found some with particular revelance to research on psychotherapy.

A scale to measure ego strength (Es) was developed empirically by identifying initial item responses that distinguished patients who showed improvement after six months of outpatient psychotherapy from a comparable group of patients who failed to respond in the same setting (Barron, 1953). A variety of validational studies have revealed this scale to have considerable accuracy in predicting response to psychotherapy; the higher the pre-treatment Es score the greater the likelihood that the patient will benefit from therapy. It has been demonstrated that the Es score provides a better prediction of therapeutic response than do judgments of the MMPI profile by clinicians (Wirt, 1956). Apart from its predictive use, it has been generally found that the Es score tends to rise with therapy and may afford an additional index of therapeutic response.

The Ev scale (evaluation of improvement) was constructed by identification of those items showing a pre- to post-treatment *response change* in improved patients that was not found in unimproved patients (Feldman, 1958). The research patients involved received electroconvulsive therapy, but the resulting scale appears to be a measure of *severity of illness* and, hence, should have general applicability as a summative statement of pre- and post-treatment status for any patient or treatment.

Somewhat related to the Ev scale, as a general measure of pathology, is the general maladjustment (Gm) scale (Welsh, 1952). This is composed of the 34 items which are scored on three or more of the basic clinical scales. Score on these items affords a general measure of the degree of pathology and can be used as one index (in terms of pre- to post-treatment change) of therapeutic impact.

The Pc scale (prediction of change) was isolated by identifying those items revealing the greatest frequency of response change in patients undergoing various forms of therapy (Schofield, 1950). The higher the score on this scale the greater the amount of clinical scale scores to be attributed to items having a likelihood of change under treatment; by inference, high Pc scores are predictive of changed MMPI profiles, with such change of a nature found associated with psychiatric treatment.

Of these special scales for predicting response to therapy (and hence, also, for evaluating degree of change in those personality functions most related to psychotherapeutic effort, viz. Introduction), the Ego-strength scale has the most extensive research literature and appears most promising.

In addition to these specially constructed *scales* which are relevant to predictions and evaluations of psychotherapy response (and to measure of the particular sectors of personality affected by therapy), several special *scores* have been proposed as providing useful summations or integrations of the more complex data of the clinical profile. Most notable among these are the Anxiety Index (AI) and the Internalization Ratio (IR) (Welsh, 1952). The Anxiety Index was derived from theoretical, empirical, and clinical considerations and is a weighted summation of scores and differences between scores on the neurotic triad and scale 7, Pt. The Internalization Ratio is the ratio of the three complaint and mood scales (1, Hs; 2, D; 7, Pt) to the three *character* scales (3, Hy; 4, Pd; and 9, Ma). As the names imply, AI reflects the degree of overt, external somatic expression of anxiety, while IR reflects the extent of pathology of a more *behavioral* nature. Various studies have revealed sizeable *construct validation* (Cronbach and Meehl) for each of these complex scores. In particular, it has been noted that improved patients, in contrast to unimproved patients, show post-treatment reductions in each of these indices. In general, psychotherapy appears to be more effective with patients having higher scores on each of these indices, although therapy appears to have more impact on the disturbances reflected in AI than in those measured by IR.

IV. SUMMARY

The MMPI is an instrument with multiple potentials for contribution to research in psychotherapy. As a diagnostic test, it provides an objective, quantified summary of the "I am" system that permits (especially with reference to the profile coding operation) a specification of the homogeneity of research samples that considerably exceeds what is available by reference to clinical diagnosis. In addition, by use of various summative scores (e.g., A.I. Ev. Es.) it permits concrete specification of the level of pre-treatment pathology and of the likelihood of positive response to psychotherapy; these are objective indices against which post-treatment status may be directly compared. The generation of research findings that can be meaningfully appraised and, most important, replicated, demands precise description not only of the extent and nature of the psychotherapy entailed but also objective specification of the nature of the patients and especially of their pre-treatment status.

A very significant aspect of the pre-treatment status of candidates for psychotherapy is to be found in their attitudes, values, self-concepts, and complaints, and in the *empirically* established behavior correlates of their behavioral reports. The MMPI is an instrument which by format, ease of administration, objectivity of scoring, and richness of research literature is ideally suited to provide a standardized expression of this "I am" system, one with sufficient complexity and subtlety to provide a description of the pre-treatment status of the patient that is relevant to the goals of therapy. Furthermore, both in its basic profile and in the special scales and scores that have been derived, it provides standard measures, the repetition of which during psychotherapy or at the close of therapy can afford one kind of objective evidence of the impact of treatment.

It cannot be too strongly emphasized that the MMPI taps in one fashion a certain set of variables which are of criterion quality for research on psychotherapy. Ideally, this test or other comparable structured inventories should be used in combination with observational schedules and other measures designed to tap the "He is" system of the personality. For this purpose, because of certain features of format, a psychiatric rating procedure such as that of Wittenborn (1950) provides an excellent complement to the MMPI.

It is particularly desirable in research on psychiatric treatment to begin with standard, objective descriptions in as comprehensive form as possible of the pre-treatment status of the patient, especially because matching of this status for large numbers of patients is essential in order to determine the effect of a particular program of therapy. In this regard, it is particularly desirable to have a precise picture of congruities or incongruities of the patient's "I am" and "He is" system at the start of treatment. The degree to which the patient moves toward a fuller compatibility in these two systems of his personality may well constitute the primary measure of the success of treatment.

REFERENCES

BARRON, F. An ego-strength scale which predicts response to psychotherapy. *J. consult. Psychol.*, **17**: 327-333, 1953.

BARRON, F., and LEARY, T. F. Changes in psychoneurotic patients with and without psychotherapy. *J. consult. Psychol.*, **19**: 239-245, 1955.

BUROS, O. K. (Ed.) *The fifth mental measurements yearbook.* Highland Park, N.J.: Gryphon Press, 1959. Pp. 158-169.

CALVIN, A., and McCONNELL, J. Ellis on personality inventories. *J. consult. Psychol.*, **17**: 462-464, 1953.

CARP, A. MMPI performance and insulin shock therapy. *J. abnorm. soc. Psychol.*, **45**: 721-726, 1950.

COTTLE, W. C. Card versus booklet forms of the MMPI. *J. appl. Psychol.*, **34**: 255-259, 1950.

CRONBACH, L. J., and MEEHL, P. E. Construct validity in psychological tests. *Psychol. Bull.*, **52**: 281-302, 1955.

DAHLSTROM, W. G., and WELSH, G. S. *An MMPI handbook. A guide to use in clinical practice and research.* Minneapolis: Univ. of Minnesota Press, 1960.

DARLEY, J. G. Changes in measured attitudes and adjustments. *J. soc. Psychol.*, **9**: 189-199, 1938.

FELDMAN, M. J. A prognosis scale for shock therapy. *Psychol. Monogr.*, **65**: No. 10 (Whole No. 327), 1951.

FELDMAN, M. J. The use of the MMPI profile for prognosis and evaluation of shock therapy. *J. consult. Psychol.*, **16**: 376-382, 1952.

FELDMAN, M. J. An evaluation scale for shock therapy. *J. clin. Psychol.*, **14**: 41-45, 1958.

GLUECK, B. C. (Institute of Living, Hartford, Connecticut). Personal communications.

HALES, W. M., and SIMON, W. MMPI patterns before and after insulin shock therapy. *Amer. J. Psychiat.*, 105: 254-258, 1948.

HATHAWAY, S. R. A coding system for MMPI profiles. *J. consult. Psychol.*, 11: 334-337, 1947.

HATHAWAY, S. R. Some considerations relative to nondirective counseling as therapy. *J. clin. Psychol.*, 4: 226-231, 1948.

HATHAWAY, S. R., and McKINLEY, J. C. A multiphasic personality schedule (Minnesota): I. Construction of the schedule. *J. Psychol.*, 10: 249-254, 1940.

HATHAWAY, S. R., and MEEHL, P. E. *An atlas for the clinical use of the MMPI.* Minneapolis: Univ. of Minnesota Press, 1951.

KAUFMANN, P. Changes in the MMPI as a function of psychiatric therapy. *J. consult. Psychol.*, 14: 458-464, 1950.

MARKS, P. A., and SEEMAN, W. *The actuarial description of personality. An atlas for use with the MMPI.* Baltimore: Williams & Wilkins, 1963.

MEEHL, P. E. The dynamics of "structured" personality tests. *J. clin. Psychol.*, 1: 296-303, 1945.

MEEHL, P. E. Psychotherapy. *Ann. Rev. Psychol.*, 6: 357-378, 1955.

MEEHL, P. E. A comparison of clinicians with five statistical methods of identifying psychotic MMPI profiles. *J. counsel. Psychol.*, 6: 102-109, 1959.

PACELLA, B. L., PIOTROWSKI, W., and LEWIS, N. D. C. The effects of electroconvulsive therapy on certain personality traits in psychiatric patients. *Amer. J. Psychiat.*, 104: 81-91, 1947.

ROSEN, A. Test-retest stability of MMPI scales for a psychiatric population. *J. consult. Psychol.*, 17: 217-221, 1953.

SCHOFIELD, W. Changes in responses to the MMPI following certain therapies. *Psychol. Monogr.*, 64: No. 5 (Whole No. 311), 1950.

SCHOFIELD, W. A further study of the effects of therapies on MMPI responses. *J. abnorm. soc. Psychol.*, 48: 67-77, 1953.

SCHOFIELD, W., and BRIGGS, P. F. Criteria of therapeutic response in hospitalized psychiatric patients. *J. clin. Psychol.*, 14: 227-232, 1958.

SEEMAN, W. "Subtlety" in structured personality tests. *J. consult. Psychol.*, 16: 278-283, 1952.

SIMON, W., and GILBERSTADT, H. MMPI patterns before and after carbon dioxide inhalation therapy. *J. nerv. ment. Dis.*, 119: 523-529, 1954.

WELSH, G. S. An extension of Hathaway's MMPI profile coding system. *J. consult. Psychol.*, 12: 343-344, 1948.

WELSH, G. S. An anxiety index and internalization ratio for the MMPI. *J. consult. Psychol.*, 16: 65-72, 1952.

WELSH, G. S., and DAHLSTROM, W. G. (Eds.) *Basic readings on the MMPI in psychology and medicine.* Minneapolis: Univ. of Minnesota Press, 1956.

WIRT, R. D. Actuarial prediction. *J. consult. Psychol.*, 20: 123-124, 1956.

WITTENBORN, J. R. Symptom patterns in a group of mental hospital patients. *J. consult. Psychol.*, 15: 290-302, 1950.

32. The Rorschach test, communication, and psychotherapy

Samuel J. Beck

I. THERAPY IS COMMUNICATION

Every psychotherapist can lament over the frustration that he has suffered from the patient who defeats himself and his doctor because he does not communicate meaningfully. My contribution to the central interest in this volume, psychotherapy, is on the Rorschach test as an instrument of communication. Psychotherapy always is an undertaking in communication. This proposition would by now appear to have the force of the axiomatic. Yet a large amount of literature today in the field of psychopathology devotes itself to linguistic and other expressive behavior that forms the discourse between a patient and his therapist. It has long been known that the idiom of the mentally ill is frequently not the same as that of his society. Sometimes it is a different language. This observation is "as old as organized psychiatry," Birdwhistell notes (1959). He comments, "The sheer fact that successful therapy has something to do with communication, however, provides us with a basic line from which to operate." A moment later he emphasizes the need for becoming ever "more explicit" about the "communication system."

But what constitutes this system? Which is to say who communicates with whom? The most obvious fact is that the patient talks to his therapist and the therapist to the patient. Together they are one system, a transactional unit. The functioning of this system constitutes the therapy and it operates toward the person's healing.

What is less obvious, because it is unseen, is that another dialogue has been going on. This has consisted of the messages within the patient himself. The therapist, to be sure, has been the instrument for initiating and sending these messages. They have had meaning because as they pass back and forth the patient changes. The treatment interactions have opened up channels hitherto obstructed between his higher mental processes and the affective states in his personality. Connections are being established between the upper layers of his brain and the lower ones (Jackson); between ego-functions and id forces (Freud). The successful therapy "throws light" on the person's conflictual and destructive processes. Light is understanding and the essence of healing.

The Greeks' penetration to internal stress as breeding insight is superbly stated in one of the Aeschylean tragedies. Its central character, Orestes, suffers the anguish that derives from the moral code under which he lives. It orders a son to avenge the murder of a parent by killing the murderer. According to another rule in the code, any slayer of a parent was handed over for punishment to the Furies. Orestes' father, Agamemnon, has been murdered by his mother, Clytemnestra. This was the impasse into which the Greek mind, brooding over the human condition, has deposited Orestes. He kills Clytemnestra and his agony takes on its logical course. He is possessed of the Furies, embodiment of madness. But as the Aeschylean trilogy progresses we have a glimpse of Apollo making contact with the tragic hero. Apollo is light. He is atonement and purification. The psychosis has been to Orestes an ordeal through which he has been groping his way to light. It is the patient's understanding of himself.

However, one does not attain this goal unaided. He does so while transacting within the system consisting of himself and his therapist. But the patient and his therapist are obstructed by that major barrier, the language of the mentally ill. The patient's words taken separately are recognizable, but the syntax and grammar are alien and even idiosyncratic. Also the interactions include many messages in media other than words; gestures, body poses, art productions. There are the mute withdrawals, with violent outbursts. In Birdwhistell's exposition, the patient "may move or make noises, he may emit odors, he may emit certain chemicals, he may resist pressure, he may see, he may hear, smell, taste, or feel. . . ." (Ibid.) Birdwhistell at the same time accents the interaction function of communication: "an individual does not communicate; he engages in or becomes part of communication." Again, "as a system it (communication) is to be comprehended on a transactional level." (Ibid.)

The language disorders, in schizophrenia particularly, have by now held the interest of many investigators. These always include Freud (1938) and Bleuler (1924). Among the others are Cameron (1945), Sullivan (1953), and Ruesch (1957), who have centered an especially high focus on this behavior area. In a volume intended for the layman, and entitled *The Power of Words,* another writer, Chase (1953), lays open the many meanings and implications to which words are subjected in our social communication. He lists a variety of reasons for communication failures, ranging from simpler confusions, through some persistent logical errors, to "gobbledy-gook."

The system, patient-therapist, suffers then from a fatal internal defect. Its members talk in different dialects. Hermann Rorschach (1884-1921) was as sensitive as any psychiatrist to these barriers in his field. He devised an instrument that cut through the obscuring fog between the patient and the therapist. In experimenting with ink blots Rorschach had tried several hundred. Eventually one set of ten elicited responses which his alert and trained brain recognized as the messages which his patients' minds were transmitting. Associations out of the preconscious and unconscious, emotion-weighted ideas, they both concealed the patient's thinking from, and exposed it to, Rorschach. With his test (1942) he had assembled a new system, one in which the transactions were among three participants: the patient, the ten ink blot stimuli, and himself. He followed up his surmises with the essential scientific steps of (1) statistical ordering of his observations; and (2) studying the regularities he observed against clinical data as his frame of reference. So (3) he deduced his hypotheses empirically concerning the psychological meanings of the behaviors by the patients as they reacted to his ink blots. His test was a tool that reached into the depth layers of his patients' personalities, and as in an archaeological research it dug out ideas long buried. His technical problem was that of deciphering the meanings in the visual perceptions which his patients reported. Eventually his test became a *lingua franca*, one open to any investigator who knows its syntax and grammar.

II. PRINCIPLES OF THERAPY AND RORSCHACH VARIABLES

Since the present volume is one about therapy, and my chapter is an exposition of the Rorschach test as promoting therapy, my points of departure in this exposition will be the psychological principles of clinical interest upon which the therapist concentrates. In connection with these I describe the relevant test variables and theory.

The ego's functioning and its stamina will therefore be the first topic. Next in order, equal in importance, are the emotions in their several dimensions. Those operations which the ego interposes against the emotions, the defenses, are a third major factor which the therapist needs to evaluate. Does the patient engage in a fantasy activity as one of his defense tactics, converting the fantasy, however, into a sublimative achievement? The resultant of these trait forces (ego, emotions, defenses, fantasying) is the person's total adaptive pattern. This pattern sets the direction for the diagnostic thinking. Implicit in this is the therapeutic thinking. Plans begin to form then concerning the goals of the treatment and the level at which to make the effort. Personality dynamics for which, additionally, the therapist is continually on the alert include the super-ego forces in the patient, the repressive needs, and his self-percept.

The ego is a first topic of interest. Activities for identifying this major force and for which the Rorschach test has its own language are: knowing reality as most people see it; the synthesizing, meaningfully, of the objects perceived; control over the emotions; the setting up of goals and maintaining a direction looking toward attaining them.

Regarding his contact with reality, the patient communicates in the test by way of his perception of forms (Rorschach's F+). His accuracy in knowing the objects and events of his world and his wish to adhere to values that are those of his society enter into the information implicit in this (F+) variable. Another aspect of this ability is his recognition of his society's proprieties, even if surface values, its conventions (the *P* responses). In the content of his associations he discloses the extent to which his mental processes may be bound to the simplest and easiest aspects of what he sees (the percent of animal forms). Is his thought content stereotyped? Commonplace? Or can his ideas be original? Diversified? Do they go to the extreme of being unique? The patient is at the same time telling about the spread of his interests: How distributed are they between human beings and the inanimate? What specific fields of effort attract him: The world of nature? Art? Science? Some profession? Or some other vocation? He reveals something about the orderliness and smoothness with which he carries on these intellectual activities (indicated in the test in the sequence which he follows in attending to the large and minute configurations of the blots). His ability to shift his attention with the shift of stimuli in his perceptual field is another important test datum (Rorschach's *mode of approach*). We determine from this whether or not the patient can adjust to the conditions of his situations as these vary. This test variable is therefore valuable also as index of the patient's ability to change, even if only superficially, at the intellectual level. Since treatment is change, this datum is that much communication in the test language of the person's treatability.

The empiric facts are that the patients who are clinically refractory to treatment are found with invariant modes of approach in the test. They portray in this a rigid style of life and the treatment goals in them can only be of limited scope. The range of findings for the above test variables has been statistically established in normals and in the major mental disorders (Beck, 1954). It is now possible to evaluate a patient's functioning for each psychological activity indicated in those variables, to measure it within by the frames of reference known for normals and the several clinical groups.

III. ONE GIRL'S INTELLECTUAL FUNCTIONING

Let us now illustrate the working of these principles.

In a girl of 11 years the F+ percent turns out to be 70. This is within neurotic ranges in children and in adults.[1] It shows her controlling her perception adequately toward carrying on her affairs at expectancy for a neurotic child. But she is also inaccurate from time to time (F— percentage of 30). Inaccurate perceptions by anyone may be due to his sheer inability to recognize the object and point thus to mental deficiency or to

---

[1] For the statistics, the means, and the measures of distribution used as frames of reference in evaluating the findings for this girl see Beck (1954) and Thetford, Molish, and Beck (1951).

brain impairment. Or they may result from emotional pressures in a person who is ordinarily capable of seeing his world correctly. It is the latter that are the cause of this girl's deviations as we know from another test finding (lambda index[2] at 1.30, which is below, but not seriously, the normal range). This tells us that she is more than normally responsive to her emotions: affective forces can be too strong to be controlled by the intellect. Another test variable shows her acquaintance with conventions to be quite at expectancy (P score of 5): she has enough ego to want to know and to respect propriety. As regards the content of her thoughts: she follows the well-worn paths at just about the mean for children (animal percent of 43). But she also diverges from these paths as she associates around some original topic: nature scenes, a household theme, clothing, a "T-shirt." In moments she even enriches one of her very common forms, as when she identifies a "dog" seen by most persons as a "French poodle." Her interests can spread out to objects beyond the stereotyped. More important for therapeutic purposes, this interest embraces other persons: her six whole human percepts are more than twice the number of those typically seen by our normal children. Her thinking has then a large amount of room for other persons. She is capable of interpersonal relations. An inference that follows regarding her ego's growth is that she can bend her efforts toward a socially appropriate goal. Another Rorschach sign is evidence that she has the ability to integrate her ideas and her other psychological assets so as to direct them toward her goals. This we can know from her ability to grasp the meaningful relationships between her percepts (Z score of 45.5). She actually rates above the mean of the average adults and approaches that of the very superior. This high score derives in part from her nine responses to the blots as wholes. She perceives holistically in larger quantity than is to be expected for her years. And in this she manifests too much drive. It is more than she can successfully cope with, as we can know from her total association productivity of 30

---

[2] The *lambda index* technically is the numerical ratio between the responses determined only by form and those in which one of the emotional variables contributed. The Rorschach test assumption is that form (F) responses refer to a person's perception of external reality. Responses determined in any degree by color (C), shading (Y,V,T), or the movement (M) variables are to that degree a result of emotional reactions. Psychologically, then, the lambda index tells of the relative extent to which the person attends to environmental data and to those in which an inner, emotional experience participates. As an example of how the lambda index is obtained, suppose the patient's response total to the test is 32. Out of these responses 16 are scored $F+$ and 4 are scored $F-$; and the others are distributed M-2; C-1; CF-2; FC-3; FY-3; and VF-1. The lambda index is a ratio of *all* F, over all in which any non-F is scored. In the example it is $20/12 = 1.67$. The range in normal groups is 1.60 to 2.75. When a person's lambda is noticeably below this range he is excessively responsive to his own emotions, whether there are excitements that are externalized (C); anxious, painful mood tones (Y); or internalized (M). The excessively high lambda index I have found in feeble-minded, some organics, some schizophrenics, depressives; that is, in patients with too little emotional flexibility, rigid persons.

which is slightly below the mean for the average adult. In the discrepancies between these two variables, between high synthesizing ability and modest actual achievement, the test reports that in her present personality state the girl is in some imbalance. At the same time, in the uneven orderliness of her procedures (sequence) she discloses some, but at no time serious, irregularity. She was judged as essentially at normal in this respect and provided evidence in this of adequate ego development for her to be habitually methodical.

The foregoing Rorschach test findings are all part of the formal quantitative summary for this child's response record. They are all in the intellectual sphere. But the test reports much about a person that can never enter into the quantitative, formal structure. Some of her misperceptions are noticeably far from the usual departures and so disclose that her judgments can sometimes be seriously erratic. At times they are so because of the girl's personal involvement in the theme. She has strong emotional need to see what she sees. At times she is uncritical because she is too excited. In either event the ego is vulnerable to emotional forces. It can weaken enough to tolerate some pathology. Such for example was her "seal with a snail on it . . . the snail climbed on to rest," as she interpreted two details, one of which is superimposed on the other. This is an example of accidental thinking.

Her Rorschach symptoms of this kind were few, however, and remained within neurotic limits. She established the neurotic pattern in some shock phenomena. The evidence for this was as follows: She was more inaccurate at two of the color cards of the test (Figures 8 and 10). She blocked at another color card (Figure 9). These are stimuli in the test that stir up urges either to pleasure or to impulsive acting out. Two test cards that carry prominent genital configurations, the one feminine (Figure 2), the other masculine (Figure 6) also disturbed her. Even more revealing of anxiety on this topic, she both blocked and was disturbed at the most characteristically feminine figure of the test (Figure 7), one that vividly arouses female genital imagery. Shock data in any language are information about interactions within the patient between his intellectual and his emotional forces.

In the Rorschach test the shocks make themselves known through some kinds of intellectual breakdown. The ego's forces are in disorder; yet the shocks are paradoxical evidence of strength in the ego. They point to awareness of social values in the patient and his compulsion to observe them. They are signs of clinical anxiety and the ego's warning to the individual that he is thinking or tempted to an act of which he does not approve. "I am shocked at the idea," our 11-year-old girl is essentially saying, as unconscious reaction in the test's color shocks and shading shocks. But equally important to the fact of her disturbances were the signs in our girl that she has mastered her anxiety. The Rorschach technique for identifying this self-mastery belongs under the topic of the defenses (see, p. 564). The relevant point here is that the test showed her strong enough to regain her poise after having been dislodged from her controls.

On the question of ego strength the indications in the test were for a favorable therapeutic outlook. The girl has learned to know reality adequately and appropriately; she can grasp the larger meanings of her percepts and can purposefully direct them toward a goal; and in this goal her object relations and her values can be such as to draw social approval.

The treatment implications for this girl as stated in the report of findings for her concluded with the statements:

The child should be salvaged; she may have a superior mind and imagination. She presents a real challenge to a preventive therapeutic program.

IV. ABOUT EMOTIONAL STATES

For the full considerations on which this favorable recommendation was made we must necessarily scrutinize the child's emotional traits. How did they contribute to her maladjustive total condition? What resources in them can she utilize in attaining a healthier mental state?

Among the attributes of the emotions of high clinical interest for which the test has indications are: affective quality (Is it pleasurable or painful?); intensity (Of what degree?); level of maturity (What are the relative influences of ego and id forces on each other, and therefore on the net emotional reaction?).

The several technical problems in recognizing these influences have been dealt with by Rorschach and in the several texts and numerous other literature since his time.[3] The techniques can only be mentioned here: the patient's relative weighting of color or form in determining his associations; the number of responses with which he associates in the all-color figures (8, 9, 10) as compared with response total in the other seven; the absolute number of his associations determined in whole or in part by color; the content in his color-determined associations; and other unique themes in the three all-color test figures.

The content is the lead to how socially appropriate or self-serving are the ideas that excite the patient's pleasurable trends: have they socially useful potential or do they only stem from the patient's narcissistic urges? The test stirs up latent wishes that were not apparent clinically. A nonmeasurable trait of importance, one that is usually obvious in the patient's tone and language is a state of elation, or some nuance of it. We have seen that the three color figures played their roles in identifying a neurotic

[3] Aside from Rorschach's monograph (1942), the important tools are those by Schafer (1954), Rabin and Haworth (1960), Klopfer and colleagues (1956), Bohm (1958), Piotrowski (1957), Loosli-Usteri (1961), Beck (1960).

anxiety disturbance. So also do the two test figures in which bright red details sharply break into the overall black (Figures 2 and 3, although the latter less frequently has a shock effect). Regarding the importance of the color associations in indicating the patient's net inner emotional state (Rorschach's Experience Balance) and in his total emotional potential (my Experience Actual), I comment below.

It is the person's assets in the form of the lively feeling reactions, his acting out trends, to which the test penetrates by means of its color stimuli. Can the person release his feelings at all? And how spontaneously does he do so? How appropriately? Is his mood usually a pleasant one? Does he have a broad range of emotional interests? And, something especially critical for treatment purposes, can he reach to others emotionally? Can he have sympathetic understanding of the other?

How surcharged with emotion the patient is always becomes a question of high priority to the therapist especially at the start of the treatment. This high charge can be either in the pleasurable or painful feeling modality. It may be the over-reaction of the hysteric; the ebullience of the manic; the inappropriate excitement of the schizophrenic. Or it may be somewhere on the anxious and depressive dimension of the feelings, ranging in severity to the disabling obsessional states or depressions.

A person's painful affects are drawn out of him in the Rorschach test by his sensitivity to the darks and greys of the ink-blot figures. Again, three broad modalities have been identified in the tests and I can only mention them here. They are the vague greys, e.g., "a fog," product of a diffuse anxiety. Second is the vista association, a three-dimensional percept, i.e. "a rugged mountain," "trees in the distance." These are product of the discomfort that goes with feelings of inferiority. Both of these response categories were known to Rorschach (1942), although he had not yet developed their full significance (but see Oberholzer, 1944). The most thorough exposition of the shading associations is one published by Binder (1932). Oberholzer demonstrated their application in patients with brain pathology (1931). In collaborating with the anthropologist DuBois (1944) he did this also in a subliterate population. The third is the texture response, first described by Klopfer (1956); e.g., "a kitten's soft fur"; "silk, it's so smooth." Klopfer sees it as a generic index to "sensuality or a general desire for contact.") While the contact need is the core of the texture determined association I have been able to relate it more specifically to the affect hunger described by Levy (1937). It is the unhappy feeling that goes with sensed erotic deprivation, a feeling with its roots in infancy and persisting in some neurotics into adult life.

Nuances of painful affect are thus depicted by the test in the shading variables. In these, too, the relative weights of the shading and the form elements need to be known. As with the color-determined associations this offers information about whether the emotion or the intellect is dominating. Does the person master his painful reaction? Does it master him? Which core of his personality rules, affect or ego? Oberholzer uses the technique of weighting the form and the shading similarly to Rorschach's rule for the color associations (1944).

The emotional experience which the color and the grey-black cards activate is a critical factor in the shock reactions which they set off. While shock is always work of anxiety, that which develops in the grey-black test figures differs dynamically from the kind stirred up by the color stimuli. At the latter it is the impulse toward some relationship with an object outside the individual that initiates the anxiety. At the grey-black figures it is a state of mind long resident within. Both are warnings to the individual that his thinking is a source of danger to him. In the one instance, i.e., at the color stimuli, it is a present temptation. In the other, at the somber-toned cards, it is a guilt attitude which rests in some event long past. The test in its grey-black figures opens up a line of communications to the superego; in the color figures, to the id. Since now (a) anxiety is the essence of both, and as such is (b) an ego-defense operation, and hence, (c) the person's reaction to a social value, it follows (d) that both kinds of shock disclose moral sensitivities, and so (e) both are basically activities of the superego.

The specific sources of clinical anxiety about which the dark figures of the Rorschach test are informative are the following; the patient's attitude about a father figure (card 4 of the test); the phallus (Figure 6); the mother (Figure 7). A person's concern over homosexuality may also be stirred up, (more common in Figure 5, but found elsewhere). Bohm (1958) notes a pattern which he relates to anxiety centering around the parent of the same sex as the patient's (shock disturbances in *both* Figures 1 and 4). Certain topics about which humans are sensitive are recalled by some particular details in the several test cards: menstrual blood (Figure 2, lower red); the female genital (Figure 4, upper center folds; and Figure 7, "hinge" detail at bottom); also a maternal figure (in Figure 1, center detail). The anxiety that the female genital can release is the cause of disturbances that the white spaces of the test may trigger, Bohm reports (1958). Orr (1961) and Loosli-Usteri (1961) who also observed these white space shock phenomena in women and girls are reporting them as anxieties stirred up by the fact of femininity more generally. Bohm (1958) also reports a specific *red* shock. He sees it as a symptom of anxiety hysteria or of anxiety neurosis (varying with certain variances in the test pattern). He cites Loosli-Usteri to the effect that the red shock may be indicative of patient inhibiting his aggressive pressures. The lead may be to a deep inhibition and an ambivalent attitude to it, or inhibition with liability for violent discharge (again varying with other test reactions).

The incidence of disturbances and their severity will vary with the age and sex of the patient. Phallic imagery can be very disturbing to adolescent girls and young adult women, married or single, and less frequently so to males. The menstrual blood percept is upsetting to some adult males; rarely to females. But father or mother imagery I have been finding about as frequently distracting and blocking to the growing child, the adolescent boy or girl, and the grown man or woman.

Other categories of content can as a general rule be set down as activating conflict, anxiety, or fear. Among these are themes related to reproduction in nature generally; body organs, and the more so as they relate to vital processes; aggression implements; body injury or distortion; death. The literature reports a diversity of others. In my own observation, any topic can be interpreted specifically only within the context of the person's total adjustment. This caution holds especially with regard to ideas considered to be paranoid or those thought to be of suicidal significance. Any association may vary in symptomatic value with the individual that produces them. Hence, only each individual can clear up the meaning of a symptom or of an association to himself. This may take many sessions of therapeutic groping in the labyrinth which the unconscious is.

Among other leads of dynamic import in the patient are whether or not his percepts in the test are so erratic as to be distortions of reality. One should be especially curious also about deviations that emerge at the shock points. But throughout the protocol, the patient may uncover highly personal needs in any unique themes and in ideas less unique but original. The associations determined by any of the emotional variables as scored in the test's language are always to be scrutinized for dynamic leads. The color, shading, vista, texture, fantasy responses are the test's mirroring of the person's trend to acting out, to diffuse anxiety, inferiority attitudes, erotic hunger; or the wishes and fears implicit in his fantasy activity.

These emotional variables are information about psychological reactions as impersonal processes. Regarding the personal fortunes that move the patient, this information about processes is as neutral as are any cold numerals. For the therapist to help the patient use his emotions with healing results he must know what the personal foci are that stir up those emotions; what thought excites gladness in the patient, and what agitates him; what arouses his fears, his hostilities; and what fond wishes his dreams are fulfilling.

V. FANTASY LIVING: THE EMOTIONS INTERNALIZED

We turn now to the technique so unique to Rorschach's test and which lays the internalized emotions open to view. The *movement* responses are the test's pipeline to the unconscious. They are ideas heavily weighted with feelings, the feelings which the patient's ego has found too uncomfortable to face, and with which he turns inward, living them only in his imagination or in the disguise of the daydream. The repressed ideas, which these fantasy responses are, can be aired painlessly in the innocent play of the Rorschach test. The person is toying with ink blots and the meanings in these responses elude the censoring ego. They thus escape out of the repression. Since they are feelings, *introversive,* to use Rorschach's terminology, the attribute of the emotions described above hold also for the movement responses. They can be painful or pleasurable in affective tone; they can represent a wish (repressed) for acting out or a passive adaptation; they can be intensely experienced or mildly.

Certain attributes are specific for the fantasy activity as delved out by the test. Depending on whether the person sees an integrated form or a distortion, he is verbalizing imagery out of his preconscious or out of his deeper unconscious layers. The exotic condensations of the true dream world can be readily identified in many fantasy productions. The patient is in this way telling his therapist what his ego has most resisted telling. He does it with the innocence and amusement of a child relating his dream at the breakfast table. It can be seen therefore why the movement-determined association was such an important discovery. A brilliant act of the imagination on Rorschach's part when its potential dawned on him, it was a truly creative idea. He converted it into something real, the very real tool that it is for exploring personality.

VI. OUR GIRL'S EMOTIONS

Let us now examine what our 11-year-old girl communicates in the test language about her emotions. She tells us for one thing that her dominant affect and mood are decidedly painful. She discloses something about the nature of her unhappiness in the formal summary: inferiority feelings (vista responses) and a vague, passive-anxious reaction (shading). In both of these the feeling is of secondary importance for its total effect since the form determinant takes precedent over the emotional one. The ego has both of these affects under control. If we relied only on the data in the formal summary, we would not, however, be listening to all that the girl tells us. Her individual associations are rich in information not subject to quantitative notation. Among her first responses, a maternal form (in Figure 1, the large central detail) elicits the expression "sort of mean . . . a dead frog." Belatedly she had seen the humans of Figure 3 as "witches." In the "mother" figure (7) she introduces a sour note in her first association "teen-agers . . . not attractive." She elaborates the same "girls" into something unusual and significant, a separation theme: "good friends . . . saying good-bye . . . both on a long journey in the opposite way." Out of her unconscious she is here communicating both an important need, "good friends," and their loss to each other. She suffers, too, one of her most erratic perception lapses at this figure. In this she is breaking with reality. The emotion stirred up by mother imagery has had that traumatic effect on her. She produced only two responses here. She did not perceive the objects most commonly seen in this test figure, the two maternal profiles. In this way, she shuts the mother out from her vision and does not identify with her.

She associates with the "father" figure (4): "very big and fierce . . . don't all giants . . . look it! . . . chasing Jack." She blocks following this vivid and phobic fantasy, "I can't . . . can't," while turning the card in the effort to see more, i.e., motor symptoms of her tension. Her anxiety has bound her too tightly and she cannot free her mental processes.

It is germane to note here that the child was conceived prior to her parents' marriage although they married prior to her birth. One excerpt from the report of findings in this girl's Rorschach test is:

She fears her father . . . her mother has provided her with no psychologic support . . . and is a loss as identification figure. Hence the child has neither parent to cling to.

Such are the personality deficits which this test protocol opened up to the psychiatrist who referred this child. It told of other signs of tension. It disclosed her too little able to release her feelings (only two color-determined associations). This is a serious lack in so young a child; it speaks of damage to her spontaneity. In such release as she permits herself she is either impulsive without check on herself (pure color) or she is only partially controlled, labile (color having primacy over form). Her perceptions became erratic at these points, i.e., her ego's controls have loosened. She thus betrays a weakened grip over her emotions, evidence that she was suffering anxiety at the opportunity for a pleasurable experience. Her inability to act out satisfactorily is in contrast with her urge to do so. This we know from her responding so freely to the three all-color test figures (affective ratio is 0.57 which is near the upper end of the normal range). "While the potential is there she can not now make use of it," the report states.

Finally the girl engaged in much fantasy activity, well above the expectancy for her age, a total of eight such associations. Through these responses she informs us that she does experience emotions; but she is containing them. Containment, however, is not necessarily adjustment. In a mentally ill person it is likely to be the undischarged affect fermenting as the repressed needs which are pushing for satisfaction. (See in this connection, Grinker, 1961; also Kubie, 1954). The emotions are being pressed back by a defending ego, and the person is pathogenically diverting his resources from objectives that could be healthy to him and constructive in society. The fantasies that this girl released in her first test cards were quite dereistic, a child's dream-world. They had an ominous look and they, too, were thus symptom of her anxiety disengaging her

from her controls. However, "all the producti
healthy in structure and much of it carried the ;
propriate and cheerful wishes," the report contir
therapeutic significance I return below.

VII. THE EXPERIENCE BALANCE AND EXPERIENC

Rorschach's *Erlebnistypus,* or *Experience Bc*
tion. The concept is a unique one in psychol·
Rorschach formulated it very simply. It is the num.....
the total number of fantasy (movement) associations to the weighted sum
of the person's color-determined responses. Is the total of fantasy or of
color high? Low? And what is the balance between them? In the psychological significance of the Experience Balance, Rorschach is opening up a
new vista toward understanding the human personality. He states it as the
person's net emotional state (more extratensive than introversive, or vice
versa). More important, he emphasizes it as an inner experience and as
determining one's style of life. He thus identifies the varieties of Experience Balance in accordance with the Jungian ideas of personality types.
In his careful exposition of the concept he is, however, developing thinking that takes in the emotional life in its breadth and depth, and sounds
it in many of its tonal nuances.

The *Experience Actual* is my extension (Beck, 1960) of the Rorschach
concept. It is constructed directly out of the ingredients of his Experience
Balance. As a technical finding it is again simple: the *sum* of the movement and color scores. Psychologically it is an index to the total emotional
forces that stir the individual. He may introvert and he may externalize
them, pleasurably or painfully. They are his innerly sensed affective experience, that immediacy of emotional life which the phenomenologists
Dilthey and Husserl have made the object of their psychological science.
Rorschach devised an instrument for breaching the gap from phenomenology to a behavioral discipline. This is the essence of the Experience
Actual.

In our child, since the fantasy count was 8 and the color sum was
2, her Experience Actual came to 10. This is a rich enough reservoir of
feelings for one of her age. From her Experience Balance we know that
she characteristically lived her emotional life in her inner world. This is
her style of life. From her unresolved neurotic state we know that she is
not converting her Experience Actual, not utilizing the total emotional
richness which is hers, into something creative. She is not sublimating it.
The child has assets in the emotional spheres, but they are wasting within
unproductively. She has also, as we have seen, assets in the intellectual
sphere. A wide range of thematic content is evidence of potential. Some
of this did have the flavor of symptomatic preoccupation. But some dis-

s able to contemplate broad horizons, sign, that is, of widen-
oundaries.

is wasting these emotional resources, too. The reason for her par-
seeking psychiatric help for her was that she was poor in her schoolwork. But a Stanford-Binet administered on the day of her Rorschach
yielded an Intelligence Quotient of 113. As her mother reported the girl's
behavior in school it was "balk, block, stares out of the window . . . she
seems to be frightened in the area of learning."

Our test findings thus pattern out the genetic reconstruction behind
the child's defeat in learning, important activity which that is in the
present phase of her life. I reasoned in my report that, aware of her having
been conceived prior to her parents' marriage, she sensed herself as a
blemished personality and that this "may well be the dynamic factor,
with both parents probably being resentful and hostile to her. The result
is an inferiority state, already deep in her character." We see that owing
to her unhappy mood state and lack of identification with either parent
she is without drive and ambition, without effort, and quoting from the
test report again, "due to loss of interest, symptomatic of her pathologic
reaction to her painful mood state, her lack of urge for gratification and
for self-esteem. Meanwhile she can compensate by too easy flight into her
fantasy world." The treatment implications reported for the test findings
overall (the Stanford-Binet, a C.A.T., and the Rorschach) follow:

This child critically needs kindness, encouragement and a positive recognition
of herself as a worthwhile person. She has had so little approval yet her response
is so quick and favorable when she senses herself as accepted. The assurance to
her of her fine intelligence could be the start for confidence, and so activate ambition and self-esteem. She further needs identification with a mother she can
love, and a father she can respect and love. Her conception of the parental roles
can highlight one area of the treatment program. The indications are for a supportive, warm, and understanding therapy; the child has ample assets with
which to respond. An understanding teacher could be an additional source of
encouragement and security, and it may be helpful to draw the school into the
treatment program. But most important of all are the parents. A realization by
them of this child's clear potential, and the dangers as well, may help them
set aside their marital difficulties and make it a child-centered home. The child
should be salvaged; she may have a superior mind and imagination. She presents a real challenge for a preventive psychiatric program.

VIII. ABOUT DEFENSES

While words reveal, they as often conceal, the person within. This
peculiarity of language is well known in life generally, is a truism in psychotherapy, and in the Rorschach experience frequently presents us with

enigmas. The central fact is that the patient resists and defeats the very purpose for which he has come. He needs the help pathetically. He fights opening himself up to it desperately. Such are the consequences of that peculiarly human psychologic invention, the defenses. They are adaptive devices, critically essential to humans if we are to get along with one another. But like all other adaptations they have their price. One of these is that the individual fences himself in: the constrictive defenses. In another variety he binds himself tightly to some firmly fixed attitude, as in the days of sailing vessels when mariners lashed themselves to the mast, the last resort in a storm that was about to break up their ship. Some neurotics are always in a storm. Their safety lies in lashing themselves tightly to their pathologically obsessive mechanisms.

In still another expedient the person distorts what he sees. He transforms his data into something more satisfying to him emotionally, more palatable to his ego. The various grades of paranoid misconstructs belong here. Taking one further step along this dimension the patient creates a world altogether out of whole-cloth. These are the escapes into fantasy, a living in a world of dreams.

The Rorschach test has its several techniques for discerning these subterfuges. They have been identified in terms of the test's variables. The clinical varieties of patients who use each kind of defense are understood. We are thus enabled to make judgments concerning the kind of maladjustment with which each kind of Rorschach defense pattern is related. Since the levels of treatability of the several clinical conditions are understood, we can arrive at some conclusions concerning a person's treatability from the defense mechanisms which are built into his test protocol.

How fixed are the defenses? How amenable to change is the patient? We derive this information in the signs of rigidity or fluidity in the intellectual and the emotional spheres. The Rorschach data in which these traits are manifest have been published (Beck, 1960). Condensing here: In his perception does the patient restrict himself to naked accuracy? This assures present safety but it is a rigidity which does not bear up under stress. In their thought content these persons can only recognize what is most trite. The associational productivity in some of these patients is very low; for some it is high, discrepantly so for the quality of their total pattern. The ones show themselves overly cautious; the others defend by being overly inclusive. The more seriously impaired in this respect are limited in their ability to synthesize their percepts into larger meanings: it can be dangerous or painful to know too much. The emotional range of these persons as found in the test is narrow. They neither externalize their feelings nor internalize any as fantasy activity. Impassive and unimaginative they inure themselves against troublesome affective experiences. Their interest spread is a diminished one and niggardly. Interspersed with their test responses are qualitative signs betraying their distrust of their own mental processes and they not unfrequently undo their own thinking.

The uniform psychological meaning that runs through these defenses is that they impoverish the patient intellectually and emotionally. These persons are refractory to change. How deeply indurated any of these defenses are in the patient's character structure can usually be judged from the context of his Rorschach reaction pattern as a whole. These are inferred from the severity of the patient's conflict and stress and the intensity of his need for defenses. The reconstruction of the dynamics of the illness is frequently possible in the test data (as in the child's case above), but not always. Such reconstruction enables a surmise concerning the probable growth phase in which the defenses had set in: infancy, childhood, adolescence. The fixity of the defenses varies inversely with the recency of their inception. The older they are the more difficult, naturally, is the therapist's task.

Special comment is always in order concerning the fantasy activity. In it the patient is engaging in a double role relative to his therapist. He is both resisting and communicating to him. In a pathologic total reaction pattern the fantasy is likely to be a defense operation. It is resistance, however, because in his overt language the patient does not tell what he is wishing or fearing in his unconscious. His fantasy associations are screening this critical information both from himself and from his therapist. Yet these associations are communications because they tell of needs and attitudes which the patient has been unable to ventilate clinically. His ego has compelled him to repress what they mean to himself. So he can live within his inner world impulses which would be very dangerous for him to carry out in the external one. He can also revel in satisfactions which reality denies him. In these ways his fantasy living is a defense.

The therapist's problem with his patient's fantasy is that it is a message which he must still decode. Rorschach's movement response is actually a dream induced through the instrumentality of the test. It can be characterized in the language which Freud uses of the dream:

It is plausible to suppose that the dream censorship, which we regard as being responsible in the first instance for the distortion of the dream thoughts into the manifest dream, is a manifestation of the same mental forces which during the day-time had held back or *repressed* the unconscious wishful impulse (1938).

The Rorschach fantasy is similarly a distortion since it says overtly something other than what it means. The patient's ego is still fighting. But in associating with these fantasies the patient is opening up what can be therapeutically a most effective dialogue between his therapist and himself.

IX. SPECIALIZED CLINICAL FIELDS

By now the test has been extensively applied in all personality pictures, both sexes, adults and children. In the clinical field, experience, as is to be expected, has been most widespread in the neuroses and the schizophrenias, and one can only note the ever-burgeoning literature on the test in these areas. In addition, it has been tried out in more specialized fields. Brief notes on these follow.

In the large areas of organic pathology investigators have addressed themselves (1) to the test's potency for establishing the sheer fact of brain damage; (2) with some investigators boldly specifying the brain area affected; and (3) others correlating test patterns with some of the recognized organic syndromes. Piotrowski's investigations have long led in this field (1957). Baker has definitely described the test findings as index to brain pathology (1956). Molish has surveyed the literature and evaluated the results (1959). My own especial effort in brain-damaged patients has been to inspect for the psychologic factors overlying the deficits resulting from organic impairment, whatever the method by which the organicity has been diagnosed. The psychological questions are: To what degree is the patient's awareness of and reaction to the fact of his impairment a significant element in his total adjustment? Can we reason regarding a neurotic or other maladjustive condition prior to the trauma to the brain? The focus of interest is on the patient's present residual assets. These are what he presents to the therapist as his amenability to therapy within the limits set upon him by his organic pathology.

Among the unfortunates classified as mentally defective, some find the test a great boon. It is their opportunity for displaying themselves mentally in a medium other than one dependent on formal school learning. The Rorschach task preserves them from failures and the attendant further depreciation of a self already depreciated. Many feeble-minded disclose, in their test patterns, resources which have been submerged in the social and psychological investigations. They may manifest, by way of the test, an affective fluidity which is an urge for warm contact. Some of these children uncover a latent interest such that they can be educated vocationally. Now and then one even displays a flash of imagination. To the personnel who have in hand the destiny of these boys and girls, the test thus opens up information of critically important value toward managing them. They can set a course for these children that salvages their assets, and pulls them out of the doldrums of dependency so expensive to their community. A certain proportion of these can be directed into lives in which they care for themselves and enjoy a commensurable esteem.

Adolescents, when the topic is therapy, always command a special consideration. These more-than-children and not-yet-adults poignantly disclose in their test patterns the severity of their tensions. They themselves can detect no resolution of their impasse, pressured as they are by biological urges on one front and by ego ideals on the other. They provide in their test patterns measures of their egos' strength in bearing up under the additional stress which a therapeutic experience generates. (See Ames and others, 1959; Hertz, 1960; Beck, 1960.) Some show that their defenses are barely holding against the batterings from the two fronts and are thus warning the therapist against a treatment under which the personality may disintegrate. Gitelson strongly warns against this hazard in adolescence. As he phrases it, they are in need not of *analysis* but of *synthesis* (1948). Other writers, Balser (1958) and Blos (1962), accent this view, and some especially accent the identification needs of adolescents. A prominent aspect of Rorschach reactions in adolescents, one presenting the hazard of misdiagnosis, is that the pattern sometimes strongly resembles those of schizophrenics. The tensions, released affects, and the related intellectual disturbances can be very acute. Mood and shock phenomena, i.e., signs of ego carrying on the struggle are the signs of counterforces against the disintegrated pressures. The ego is under emotional impact and the person may be in regression. But the evidence can be detected that the regression is temporary. The boy's or girl's stress, as evident in the test, is his or her cry for help and the therapist's opportunity.

Not infrequently a psychiatrist refers both husband and wife in a marriage that is heading for a break-up. Divorce is contemplated; in some instances proceedings have already started. The psychiatrist's question is: Can the marriage be saved? Is it advisable to do so? The help that he looks for in the test is with regard to the mental health or disorder in each partner. What is the degree of the disorder and its variety? The situation is likely to be grave since it usually involves care for children and litigation of the issues. The test's information may be relevant to questions which the court may put to the psychiatrist. In such referrals husband and wife must take the test separately. It is essential to schedule so that they will not be able to talk about the test experience to each other. Administration of the test during the morning and afternoon of the same day usually provides this assurance. Each protocol is evaluated by itself in accordance with the procedures and criteria in any Rorschach test. The next task is to make an appraisal of the marital pair as a unit. The questions are again: What are the signs of integration in each and what is the psychological resource which would enable a homeostasis in the marital unit? Or are husband and wife so differing in basic personality structures, one or the other so impaired psychologically, as to warrant their not living together? How will the mental health of either or both be affected by a separation or by a reconciliation? What will be the effect on the life patterns and mental health of the children?

I have been attempting to answer these questions strictly from Rorschach test data and am still in the exploratory and groping stages. The number of such pairs available to me is small. A topic of first interest to ponder is: what are the chances for emotional harmony between husband and wife? High focus of attention therefore centers on the Experience Balance and the Experience Actual of each. The ego's stamina and reserve in husband and wife will necessarily be studied with equal care. Inherent in these findings are indices regarding the vulnerability of the two persons. When their tests show either of the pair as the more infantile, narcissistic, or with a neurosis of character depth or latent serious disorder, it is of course possible to make recommendations with that much more assurance. In at least one such referral the test results supported the psychiatrist's judgment pointing against a divorce, at least at the time of the Rorschach studies of that marital pair.

X. SUMMARY

Following is a compendium of the psychological lines of force or traits to which the test has access. The results obtained with it are translated into the language of the clinic. Findings in these terms are the essence of diagnostic thinking. Yet a Rorschach test report is clinically more realistic when stated in descriptive language. Diagnostic formulation is less consistent with the test's implications. The usual diagnostic terms cannot, however, be discarded. They are the established means of communication in the science of psychopathology. Nevertheless, a finalistic outlook is too often assumed as the significance of a nosologic classification. Such finalistic indication is not, in my experience, faithful to the portrayal of the open system which, in the great majority of cases, the test develops. A descriptive statement is therefore more accurate. To the sophisticated psychotherapist such description is meaningful regarding the treatment that he can undertake: whether to treat in depth, supportively and directively; to hospitalize; to activate surface insight; to limit the effort to situational rearrangements.

In overview then the test data enable psychological description as follows. The ego's stamina is judged by the patient's intellectual controls along a dimension from the degrees of integration to those of disruption. Manifestation of the latter range into the perceptual and thinking disorders that identify the schizophrenias. The emotions are viewed within frames of reference ranging from uninhibited discharge to anergic states, with the indicators also of controlled release. In the information regarding these two fundamental personality forces the test depicts the individual's ego-affect balance. In the fantasy activity which it liberates, the test discloses a mental process with which some patients accommodate to their intrapsychic imbalances. While using this fantasy the individual may be having recourse to autistic living, to regressions. Or he may utilize it constructively, sublimating it as imaginative talent. Fourth, the test uncovers a number of defensive expedients.

All of these trait findings, together with the thematic content in the associations, create a picture of the patient's adaptive pattern socially. This mirrors his ego as adjustive agent in the management of his affairs. This adjustment is manifest in numerous behavior samples for which the test has equivalent data. For example, Does he reject his environment? Does he construct reality in terms of his own needs? Is he capable of engaging in the usual and appropriate pleasures and enjoyments? Is he content with a social level lower than that for which his abilities give promise? On the other hand, Is he mastering his drives and energies by intellectual control? Can he sympathetically grasp the needs of others and be regardful of them? What about his aspirations and achievements? Does he hold an adequate concept of himself?

As these trait forces are being identified the descriptive diagnostic thinking has been crystallizing and emerging. Within the broad areas of the neuroses the test makes clear-cut distinctions between the hysteric and the obsessive-compulsive groups. It differentiates the psychologic structures which make up the depressed and the manics. In these two latter groups it may analyze the relative roles of reactive and endogenous factors, critical information in planning therapy. Especially rich has been the Rorschach contribution in the schizophrenias. The phenomena which it brings to light include the thinking dysfunctions, perceptual deviations, affective pathology, fantasy regressions, and varieties of overall patterns. I have commented about its usefulness in evaluating assets in the brain damaged and the feeble-minded. In some cases of marital stress, by exploring the personalities of the marital pair the test can appraise the resources in each and arrive at some surmise as to whether the marriage can be saved. It can be decisively helpful to adolescents in penetrating to the relative strengths of ego and affect and in tracing out the uneasy personality equilibria which these young people present. Many in adolescence appear close to a schizophrenic break. It is a temporary regression. Evaluation of ego resources is critically essential.

Such, then, is the information which is available in a Rorschach test protocol. Our 11-year-old girl exemplifies some of its diagnostic principles and the therapeutic implications. As she demonstrates, a major construct in Rorschach's theory is his Experience Balance from which I have derived the Experience Actual. This concept has its roots in phenomenology and existentialist thinking. Rorschach's test when used as an objective instrument is a bridge from a phenomenological to a behavioral method. To the degree of the validity of the psychological significance attributed to the Experience Balance and the Experience Actual, the patient is communicating in these variables the breadth and depth of his emotional life. He thus informs the therapist about the asset which is so important in the treatment process: the mental fluidity which enables one to change, to learn, to adapt, and so to survive psychologically.

Whether the therapist can help the patient to utilize this resource will vary with his own Experience Actual. For, as stated at the beginning of this chapter, a treatment situation is a communication system. The units in a communication system, however, are not only senders of messages; they also receive them. The therapist's Experience Actual is his receiving set. It is the measure of his own breadth and sensitivity. With it he knows his patient emotionally. With it, too, he himself obtains the necessary light regarding his patient's very human condition. As a result, he can guide another man or woman toward opening up the communication between his or her intellect and emotions, thereby generating the light which is the essential antecedent to the treatment.

REFERENCES

AMES, L. B., METRAUX, R. W., and WALKER, R. N. *Adolescent Rorschach responses, developmental trends from ten to sixteen years.* New York: Hoeber-Harper, 1959.

BAKER, G. Diagnosis of organic brain damage in the adult. In B. Klopfer, *et al.* (Eds.), *Developments in the Rorschach technique*, Vol. 2. New York: Harcourt, Brace & World, 1956. Chap. II, pp. 318-375.

BALSER, B. H. Dynamic psychiatry of the adolescent. In J. H. Masserman and J. L. Moreno (Eds.), *Progress in psychotherapy*, Vol. III. New York: Grune & Stratton, 1958. Pp. 166-170.

BECK, S. J. The six schizophrenias. *Res. Monogr.*, No. 6. New York: Amer. Orthopsychiat. Association, 1954.

BECK, S. J. *The Rorschach experiment.* New York: Grune & Stratton, 1960.

BINDER, H. *Die Helldunkeldeutungen im psychodiagnostichen experiment von Rorschach.* Zurich: Fussli, 1932.

BIRDWHISTELL, R. L. Contribution of linguistic-kinesic studies to the understanding of schizophrenia. In Auerbach, A. (Ed.), *Schizophrenia, an integrated approach.* New York: Ronald, 1959. Chap. 5, pp. 99-123.

BLEULER, E. *Textbook of psychiatry.* Trans. by Brill, A. A. New York: Macmillan, 1924.

BLOS, P. Intensive psychotherapy in relation to the various phases of the adolescent period. *Am. J. Orthopsychiat.*, 32: 901-910, 1962.

BOHM, E. *Lehrbuch der Rorschach psychodiagnostik fur psychologen, Arzte und Padgogen.* Huber, Bern, 1951. Trans. by A. G. Beck and S. J. Beck. New York: Grune & Stratton, 1958.

CAMERON, N. Experimental analysis of schizophrenic thinking. In J. S. Kasanin (Ed.), *Language and thought in schizophrenia.* Berkeley, Calif.: Univ. of California Press, 1945.

CHASE, S., with CHASE, M. T. *Power of words.* New York: Harcourt, Brace & World, 1953.

FREUD, S. The interpretation of dreams. Wit and its relation to the unconscious. In *The basic writings of Sigmund Freud*, Modern Library Edition. New York: Random House, 1938.

FREUD, S. Psychoanalysis. In J. Strachey (Ed.), *Collected Papers*. London: Hogarth, 1950. Pp. 107-130.

GITELSON, M. The psychotherapeutic problem of adolescence. *Am. J. Orthopsychiat.*, **18**: 422-431, 1948.

GRINKER, R. R. *Psychosomatic research.* (rev. ed.) New York: Grove, 1961.

HERTZ, M. R. The Rorschach in adolescence. In A. I. Rabin and M. R. Haworth (Eds.), *Projective techniques with children.* New York: Grune & Stratton, 1960. Chap. 3, pp. 29-60.

KLOPFER, B., et al. *Developments in the Rorschach technique.* 2 vols. New York: Harcourt, Brace & World, 1956.

KUBIE, L. S. The fundamental nature of the distinction between normality and neurosis. *Psychoanal. Quart.*, **23**: 167-204, 1954.

LEVY, D. M. Primary affect hunger. *Am. J. Psychiat.*, **94**: 643-652, 1937.

LOOSLI-USTERI, M. *Praktisches Handbuch des Rorschachtests.* Berne: Huber, 1961.

MOLISH, H. Contributions of projective tests to psychological diagnoses in organic brain damage. In S. J. Beck and H. B. Molish (Eds.), *Reflexes to intelligence.* New York: Free Press, 1959. Pp. 190-230.

OBERHOLZER, E. Zur Differentialdiagnose psychischer Folgezustände nach Schädelträumen mittels des Rorschachschen Formdeutversuchs. *Ztschr. f.d. ges. Neurol. u. Psychiat.*, **136**: 596-629, 1931.

OBERHOLZER, E., in DuBois, C. *The people of Alor.* Minneapolis: Univ. of Minnesota Press, 1944. Chap. 22, pp. 588-640.

ORR, M. Unpublished paper cited by Loosli-Usteri, M. in *Praktisches Handbuch des Rorschachtests.* Berne: Huber, 1961.

PIOTROWSKI, Z. A. *Perceptanalysis.* New York: Macmillan, 1957.

RABIN, A. I., and HAWORTH, M. R. (Eds.) *Projective techniques with children.* New York: Grune & Stratton, 1960.

RORSCHACH, H. *Psychodiagnostik: Methodik und Ergebnisse eines wahrnehmungsdiagnostischen Experiments* (2nd ed.), Bern and Berlin: Huber, 1932. Trans. by P. Lemkau and B. Kronenberg. New York: Grune & Stratton, 1942.

RUESCH, J. *Disturbed communication. The clinical assessment of normal and pathological communicative behavior.* New York: Norton, 1957.

SCHAFER, R. *Psychoanalytic interpretation in Rorschach testing.* New York: Grune & Stratton, 1954.

SULLIVAN, H. S. *The interpersonal theory of psychiatry.* New York: Norton, 1953.

THETFORD, W. N., MOLISH, H. B., and BECK, S. J. Developmental aspects of personality structure in normal children. *J. proj. Tech.*, **15**, No. 1, 1951.

33. Methods relating to evaluation of therapeutic outcome

Maurice Lorr and Douglas M. McNair

The purpose of this chapter is to present brief descriptions of the development and application of a set of procedures useful in the evaluation of therapeutic outcome. Initially attention will be focused on patient self-reports. These are designed to measure the patient's moods and attitudes and his perception of his therapist. An instrument to describe characteristic patient interpersonal interactions and relationships is next discussed. Since individual psychotherapy is a dyadic relationship it is necessary to account for the therapist as well as his client. Procedures developed for assessing the therapist's techniques and his goals for the patient are, accordingly, described. Finally, a scale devised to assess therapist attributes that contribute to successful treatment is presented.

The philosophy of the present approach is consistent with that sketched by Parloff, Kelman, and Frank (1954). If psychotherapy and its relative effectiveness are to be appraised certain basic conditions must be satisfied. It must be possible (1) to describe patients objectively in terms relevant for psychotherapy; (2) to measure change in terms permitting comparison of different types of treatment; (3) to describe the therapeutic techniques employed; (4) to describe the personality of the therapist as it relates to his ability to influence different types of patients. It will be seen that the methods and procedures described here touch on every one of the above conditions. They offer at least a beginning to the satisfaction of these needs.

THE MOOD SCALES

Scale Development

The initial form of the Psychiatric Outpatient Mood Scales (*POMS*) was constructed and first applied in connection with a study of the effects of Meprobamate and Chlorpromazine in psychotherapy patients (Lorr, McNair, Weinstein, Michaux, and Raskin, 1961). The customary inventories were bypassed as inappropriate since no time reference is built into such devices. Subjects may interpret questions as referring to events occurring in the past week, the past month, or the past year. Moreover, only two possible responses are ordinarily offered except for an uncertainty

573

category. Since a statement must be checked as true or not true, small changes cannot be reported. There is good reason to believe that these two conditions, ambiguity of time set and coarseness of scale, reduce considerably an instrument's sensitivity to change.

The initial form of POMS included 55 adjectives so selected as to represent the hypothesized moods of anxiety, tension, anger, depression, vigor, and fatigue. To emphasize the current feelings of the patient a one-week time-set was specified. The set was: "How much have you felt the way described during the past week including today?" Each adjective was rated on a 4-point intensity scale extending from "Not at all," "A little," "Quite a bit," to "Extremely." For scoring the intervals were assigned weights of 0, 1, 2, 3. The adjectives were selected from those assembled by Nowlis and Green (1957), Sells, et al. (1956), a dictionary, and a thesaurus. The Thorndike-Lorge word lists (1944) were used to confine the adjectives to those understandable by persons of average intelligence.

The pre-therapy ratings of 200 male outpatients from 23 Veterans Administration clinics were obtained. The product-moment correlations among the scaled adjectives were correlated and factored. Except for Anxiety, which could not be differentiated from Tension, all postulated mood factors were confirmed. To determine whether psychiatric patients could be discriminated from normal persons, a group of 45 normals were also administered POMS twice. Normal subjects scored significantly differently from patients on all mood scales in expected directions. Pre-post therapy evaluations revealed significant reductions in score for the combined treatment groups over an eight-week period, in Tension-Anxiety, Hostility, Depression, and Inertia. Normal subjects, however, did not show change over the same time interval.

A revision of POMS was included as a measure of clinical status in a study of correlates of length of stay (Lorr and McNair, 1964). POMS was administered once to a random sample of 523 males in psychotherapy in 44 clinics. All patients had been in therapy continuously for periods ranging from three months to ten years. The revision included 57 adjectives including a set to define Confusion-Bewilderment. The factor analyses, however, failed to confirm the Confusion cluster but supported the findings of the previous analysis.

The third form of POMS was administered prior to therapy and at weekly intervals in a five-week study of the early effects of a tranquilizer and psychotherapy (Lorr, McNair, and Weinstein, 1963). The subjects were 150 male outpatients newly accepted for psychotherapy at 23 clinics. A modified POMS consisted of 60 adjectives designed to measure Tension, Depression, Anger-Hostility, Fatigue, Vigor, and an expanded group entitled Confusion. When the correlations among pre-therapy ratings were factored, seven mood factors emerged including Confusion and a Friendliness factor.

Description of the Factors

The Tension-Anxiety (T) factor or scale is defined by adjectives descriptive of heightened muscle tension although quasi-psychic elements are presented. The adjectives given below are most consistent in correlating well with T.

tense	restless
nervous	(not) relaxed
on edge	anxious
shaky	uneasy

Factor A, Anger-Hostility, appears to reflect an angry, irritable, belligerent mood with a touch of suspicion. The adjective definers of A are shown below.

angry	annoyed
furious	resentful
ready to fight	spiteful
grouchy	deceived

Factor D, is labeled Depression as it seems to reflect feelings of worthlessness and hopelessness. In analyses of psychotic behaviors a similar factor called Intropunitiveness has been identified (Lorr, McNair, Klett, and Lasky, 1962).

worthless	blue
helpless	lonely
unhappy	gloomy
discouraged	miserable

A Vigor-Activity factor (V) also appears consistently. The mood is one of carefree liveliness as shown below.

lively	active
vigorous	carefree
full of pep	alert

A Fatigue-Inertia factor (F) has been confirmed twice. F is not simply the opposite of V, but represents an independent source of variation.

tired	sluggish
fatigued	weary
worn-out	sleepy

The last two factors to be described, Friendliness and Confusion, are brief and yet to be confirmed. The first is defined by the following: friendly, cooperative, good-natured, understanding, and cheerful. The second factor, Confusion, is marked by forgetfulness, inability to concentrate or to think clearly, inefficiency, and confusion. Further study may clarify whether Confusion is a mood state or simply a report on cognitive inefficiency.

Relation to Prior Studies

How do POMS factors compare to those identified by Nowlis and Green (1957) and Borgatta (1961)? Nowlis and Green found eight mood factors. Of these, Activation-Deactivation is similar to Vigor and Fatigue combined. The difference in findings is most likely a function of the observation period. POMS ratings were based on a one-week period while Nowlis and Green (N-G) ratings were based on mood at the time of self-report. There is fair resemblance between the N-G factors of Aggression, Anxiety, Social Affection, and Depression and POMS Anger, Tension, Friendliness, and Depression. However, the N-G factors are at best sharply defined by two or three adjectives, whereas POMS factors are clear-cut. Borgatta (1961) found six factors in an analysis of 40 adjectives taken from N-G. Borgatta's Loneliness, Defiant, Tired, and Warmhearted resemble POMS Depression, Anger, Fatigue, and Friendliness.

Clyde (1963) has developed the Clyde Mood Scale (CMS) consisting of 48 adjectives. Some of the factors measured by CMS resemble those measured by POMS. However, the number of adjectives clearly identifying each factor are relatively few. The CMS Friendly factor resembles POMS factor of the same name. The Clear-thinking factor appears to be the obverse of POMS Confusion scale. The Sleepy scale corresponds closely to POMS Fatigue-Inertia. The CMS Unhappy scale has some resemblance to the POMS Depression scale. The CMS Aggressive scale seems to have no correlative factor in POMS nor does the Dizzy scale.

Validity of POMS

The POMS mood scales have demonstrated factorial validity and content validity, but what other construct validity evidence is available? All five mood scales detected short-term changes over an eight-week and a four-week period respectively in the first and third studies previously cited. In the third study significant differences between an active drug (chlordiazepoxide) and a placebo were detected by Tension and Vigor after only one week of drug treatment. The control sample of normals of the first study showed no significant changes on the five mood scales after an eight-week interval.

Support for concurrent validity, that is, evidence that similar measures correlate well with the POMS factors, is also available. The data that follows is intended to be illustrative only. The Tension factor correlated .80 with the Taylor Manifest Anxiety scale in the first study, and .24 with the therapist rating of motivation for psychotherapy in the third study. The Anger-Hostility scale correlated .32 with therapist ratings of Hostility and .31 with ratings of Mistrust on the Interpersonal Behavior Inventory (Lorr and McNair, 1963). The Depression scale correlated .21 with Abasiveness and .21 with Passivity, two measures from the Interpersonal Behavior Inventory (Lorr and McNair, 1963).

The POMS thus represents a fairly sensitive measure of transient affective changes for periods up to 12 weeks. Not only drug and placebo effects are reflected but also early effects of psychotherapy, the relief of such complaints as undue tension, fatigue, and irritability.

PATIENT PERCEPTIONS OF THERAPISTS

Theory and Construction

The patient's feelings and attitudes toward the therapist have long been recognized as important features of the therapeutic relationship. This aspect of the relationship has become identified with Freud's term *transference*, although he differentiated between *earned* and *unearned* transference. In defining transference some investigators (Apfelbaum, 1958) emphasize the patients' strongly held expectations regarding their prospective therapists. Others (Snyder, 1961) consider transference as the actual experienced feelings and attitudes toward the therapist.

The view taken here is similar to that expressed by Schutz (1958), although the latter did not express his hypothesis in terms of transference relationships. The basic notion is that when a patient perceives his adult position in an interpersonal situation to be similar to his own childhood relation, the adult behavior evoked will be similar to his childhood behavior toward significant others. For example, a patient may perceive and react to his therapist as though the latter were a rejecting parent, a competitive sibling, or a nurturant mother figure. In brief, knowledge of how a patient *perceives* his therapist at any given stage of therapy is likely to be a good predictor of his way of *relating* to him. It is the neurotic ways of relating to others interpersonally, and the conflicts that ensue, that represent a large share of a patient's problems. The patient's perceptions of his therapist are thus of value in understanding and modifying the former's behavior.

In view of the importance of such perceptions, an inventory was designed to identify the main dimensions of clients' perceptions of their therapists. The eight constructs postulated were in part based on conceptualizations proposed by Fiedler (1950) of what constitutes a good therapeutic relationship and the interpersonal categories developed by Leary and his colleagues (1957). The constructs hypothesized were as follows: Directiveness, Nurturance, Understanding, Acceptance, Equalitarianism, Independence-Encouraging, Critical Detachment, and Hostile Rejection.

An inventory of 65 statements was constructed in which each dimension was defined by four to ten statements to be rated on a scale of frequency of occurrence. The inventory was completed by 523 male patients under individual psychotherapy, in 43 veteran's clinics, as part of a larger study. All patients had been in treatment continuously at least bi-weekly from three months to ten years. Approximately 50 percent of the sample were neurotics, 32 percent were psychotics, and the remainder were classed as personality disorders and psychosomatic cases. The 65 variables were correlated and, following a number of operations described more fully elsewhere (Lorr, 1963), five correlated factors were identified.

The Dimensions of Therapist Behavior

The five isolated dimensions of perceived therapist interpersonal behavior were Understanding, Accepting, Authoritarian, Independence-Encouraging, and Critical-Hostile. The first, Understanding, is defined by statements concerning the therapist's ability to understand what the patient is expressing, feeling, and communicating. Examples are: Seems to know exactly what I mean; Understands me even when I don't express myself well; Realizes and understands how my experiences feel to me. This dimension corresponds closely to Rogers' postulated condition for an adequate therapeutic relationship (1957).

The factor entitled *Accepting* is characterized by therapist interest in, emotional support of, and equalitarian attitude toward the patient. Illustrative statements are as follows: Shows a real interest in me and my problems; Is easy to talk to; Acts as though we were co-workers on a common problem; Makes me feel that he is one person I can really trust. Patient ratings of overall improvement, and therapist ratings of observed improvement and judged patient satisfaction with treatment, were obtained at the same time the patients' perceptions of their therapists were obtained. Factors of Understanding and Accepting correlated .31 and .24 respectively with patient ratings of improvement; correlations with therapist ratings of improvement were .19 and .16. Judged patient satisfaction with therapy correlated .30 and .24 respectively with Understanding and Acceptance. All these correlations are significant at $P < .02$. These findings are, of course, supportive of the suspected role of patients' perceptions of their therapists.

The Authoritarian dimension is characterized by statements that indicate the therapist offers advice, gives directions, offers assistance in reaching decisions, and tends to be controlling in his operations. Examples are the following: Is full of advice about everything I do; Tells me what to do when I have difficult decisions to make; Expects me to accept his ideas and opinions. Correlation of Authoritarian scores with patient ratings of improvement is -.16 and -.19 with judged satisfaction with treatment. The Critical-Hostile category has similar relations to rated improvement. The patient perceives his therapist as critical, cold, and disapproving. Illustrative are the following: Becomes impatient when I make mistakes; Acts smug and superior as though he knew all the answers; Talks down to me as if I were a child.

The last dimension, Independence-Encouraging, is defined by statements such as: Expects an individual to shoulder his own responsibilities; Encourages me to work on my own problems in my own way. The scale, however, is brief and is in need of expansion to increase reliability. In some respects it corresponds to the concept of non-directiveness but emphasis is on the active encouragement of independent patient operations rather than simple permissiveness.

Fiedler (1950) employed three concepts in his study of a good therapeutic relationship. One, the therapist's ability to communicate with and understand the patient, appears to be confirmed in the Understanding factor. The emotional distance which the therapist assumes toward the patient (close versus far), Fiedler's second dimension, appears to be represented both by Critical-Hostile and Accepting. The third Fiedler variable, therapist status in relation to the patient (equal, superior, or subordinate), appears also to be a composite. The attitude of superiority is reflected in the Authoritarian factor. The equalitarian tendencies are absorbed in the Accepting factor. Rausch and Bordin (1957) analyzed the concept of therapist warmth and found it divisible into commitment, understanding, and spontaneity. The first two correspond well with the constructs of Accepting and Understanding measured by the Inventory.

The inventory factors thus correspond well to some of the concepts utilized or formulated by Fiedler, Rausch, and Bordin. There is a question, however, as to the extent to which the perceptions of the patients represent distortions and to what extent they reflect actual therapist behavior. The data available do not permit an unequivocal answer. Additional experiments will be necessary to explore this problem. On the other hand, the inventory does measure a set of perceived interpersonal behaviors associated with response to treatment useful in understanding therapeutic relationships.

AN INTERPERSONAL BEHAVIOR INVENTORY

Background

The Interpersonal Behavior Inventory (IBI) arose out of a need for a sound set of measures of the patient's interpersonal relations. Such a system is needed to predict what will happen in therapy and to measure change during and after treatment. Emphasis is placed on interpersonal relations because neurotic and character disorders are viewed as arising out of maladjusted interpersonal behaviors. Symptoms and complaints also become most meaningful within a social or interpersonal context.

The Interpersonal Check List (ICL) developed by Coffey, Freedman,

Leary, and Ossorio was bypassed for a number of reasons. The authors fail to provide adequate supportive data for the number, nature, independence, or ordering of their interpersonal categories. The adjectives and phrases that comprise their check-list are heavily weighted with or influenced by social desirability. In fact, the social desirability variable is sufficiently prominent to raise the question as to what the ICL is measuring. The adjectives themselves provide a weak base for interpersonal assessment; a behavioral definition is needed. Single adjectives have a wide range of connotations and thus do not mean the same to different raters. They lack the precision needed to describe the variety of behaviors subsumed under an interpersonal category. Thus, while the important conceptual advances provided by the Kaiser Foundation researchers were acknowledged, it was felt that a more objective device was needed.

Development of the IBI

The construction and development of IBI has been carried through three revisions involving data from three independent patient samples and a non-patient sample. In each instance a set of interpersonal interaction categories were postulated, and a set of new or revised behavior statements was assembled. Next the form was completed by therapists on patients undergoing individual psychotherapy.

The hypothesized interpersonal constructs of IBI-1 were formulated on the basis of Murray's (1938) *need definitions,* the Leary *circle variables,* Schutz's *FIRO* (1958), and the Stern (1958) *activities list.* Schutz postulates three basic interpersonal needs as sufficient to account for interpersonal behavior. These are inclusion, control, and affection. Stern's device measures 42 needs proposed by Murray. Only a portion of his assumed needs are interpersonal in nature. The Leary ICL consists of 16 scales defined by adjectives and short phrases.

In the initial experiment (Lorr and McNair, 1963) an inventory of 171 manifest behaviors was used by 163 psychologists and psychiatrists in private and public practice to describe a few of their clients. Factor analysis of the IBI of 446 male and female patients and 80 non-patients revealed nine interpersonal categories which could be arranged into a circular rank order resembling the ICL circle.

In the second experiment 14 interpersonal categories were postulated. A set of new items were constructed and combined with the revision of statements retained from IBI-1 to form IBI-2. The revised form consisting of 144 statements was completed by therapists on 523 veteran patients seen in individual psychotherapy in 39 mental hygiene clinics. A factor analysis confirmed all except one category but only 11 categories fit a circular order.

The third experiment was designed to expand still further the categories of the interpersonal circle and to secure a normative sample of patients in therapy. Sixteen interpersonal interaction categories were postulated. Ten statements descriptive of manifest behaviors were used to define each of the 16 constructs. A nationwide sample of therapists in private and public clinics provided data on 366 patients seen in treatment for at least four months on a once-a-week or more frequency basis.

A factor analysis of the correlations among the 160 variables confirmed all of the 16 categories assumed. However, one construct, Autonomy, failed to fit well into the circular order. The 15 interpersonal categories in circular rank order are as follows:

Dominance	Succorance
Recognition	Abasement
Aggression	Deference
Mistrust	Agreeableness
Detachment	Nurturance
Inhibition	Affection
Submission	Sociability
Exhibition	

Since the sample included only neurotics and character disorders, there is the possibility that non-patient interpersonal behavior categories might be different in composition or in number. For this reason ratings were secured on 290 non-patients from seniors and graduate students in psychology. These raters described persons they knew well for at least one year. Immediate family, spouses, and close friends of the opposite sex were excluded. Separate factor analyses were made on the first 80 and the second 80 variables in IBI-3. Since statements were presented in cyclical order on the form, half of the variables defining each category were present in each set. Again all assumed factors were confirmed. However, Autonomy and Agreeableness were not as well defined as in the patient sample.

The IBI presently consists of 140 statements of manifest interpersonal behaviors that yield 15 category scores. Meaningful profiles may thus be determined for each patient descriptive of a wide range of interpersonal behaviors. Relatively little validity data is yet available. However, judging from the success of the ICL, the IBI should have much promise as a method for predicting therapy behavior, for understanding the patient, and for evaluating changes resulting from treatment. Table 1 presents 3 illustrative statements for each of the 15 categories.

PSYCHOTHERAPIST TECHNIQUES

Another important aspect of the Laboratory's research program has been the development of methods for objectively characterizing psychotherapists and testing their contribution to treatment outcome. While the

Table 1
Abbreviated Descriptions of Several Statements Defining
Each of the IBI Categories

Dominance

Takes charge of things
Bosses his friends
Volunteers advice and information

Succorance

Asks others to look after his interests
Seeks unreciprocable favors
Dumps his problems on others

Recognition

Strives for status symbols
Seizes opportunities to surpass others
Seeks membership in prestige associations

Deference

Takes role of helper to authorities
Obeys zestfully his superior's orders
Readily accepts superior's advice

Aggression

Belittles the successes of others
Ridicules or belittles others
Uses sarcastic humor

Agreeableness

Contributes positively as member of group
Treats people as equals
Gains rapport and liking from others

Mistrust

Mistrusts intentions of others
Is suspicious of people nice to him
Says people criticize him unjustly

Nurturance

Listens sympathetically to people's troubles
Comforts others who are feeling low
Puts aside work to help others

Detachment

Acts impersonal with co-workers
Is emotionally reserved with others
Keeps aloof from his neighbors

Affiliation

Shows a real liking for people
Shows affection to family
Acts personal with people

Inhibition

Shows discomfort when watched
Shows self-consciousness with strangers
Keeps in background at social affairs

Sociability

Invites friends to his home
Encourages informal visits from friends
Visits friends just to socialize

Abasement

Apologizes for not doing a task better
Blames self for interpersonal friction
Accepts blame when things go wrong

Exhibition

Amuses others at parties
Draws group's attention by telling jokes
Makes startling remarks

Submissiveness

Appeases others
Lets others push him around
Gives in rather than fight

therapist is usually recognized as an important factor in the treatment situation, few devices are available for evaluating his influence. The approach has been to identify or hypothesize some of the relevant therapist variables, to develop methods for the quantitative measurement of such variables, and then to ascertain their relationship to patient and outcome variables.

A major therapist influence is commonly considered to reside in his psychotherapeutic techniques. Most schools of psychotherapy have their origins in differences of opinion over what constitute the most effective therapeutic techniques. One major approach to the problem of assessment has been content analysis (Strupp, 1957; Snyder, 1945; Murray, 1956; Dollard and Auld, 1959). After much exploratory but rather fruitless work, this approach was discarded. Typically, each investigator develops his own system for content analysis (if he does not borrow the Bales' [1950] system) which is not highly appropriate for the therapy situation. Typically the new system is applied in a single study or, occasionally, in several studies. Because of their complexity, content analysis studies are rarely based on more than a handful of cases. Thus, results are not cross-validated and their generalizability is severely limited. Even though most investigators publish respectable indices of inter-rater agreement in categorizing the responses, these are open to serious question. Usually the published inter-rater agreement is based on two people who have worked together intimately in the development of a coding system, and who have engaged in much discussion of definitions and disagreements. Inter-rater agreement for a new set of judges given a reasonable but a practical period of training with a system would represent a more realistic index of reliability. Trials with some existing systems for content analysis suggested that reliabilities obtained by a new set of judges, using only the formal coding rules, definitions, and examples, are much lower than is usually reported. Often they do not meet minimum standards for scientific work.

Another approach has been to classify therapists into schools on the basis of global, qualitative criteria and then to relate orientation to outcome by statistical or experimental methods. Sometimes the investigator simply has the therapist state whether he is Freudian, Rogerian, or eclectic. Statistical tests for an association between orientation and outcome then follow. A major problem here is that it is not known to what extent theoretical orientation is reflected in the behavior of therapists toward patients. Another is the gross oversimplification involved in characterizing therapeutic approach by school labels. A more rigorous variation of this approach is to identify and manipulate a set of techniques as an experimental variable. One such method is to train therapists to assume specific roles and then to study the relation of role to outcome. Ashby, Ford, Guerney, and Guerney (1957) have made the most sophisticated application of this method in their comparison of leading and non-leading therapists. Their therapists, however, were inexperienced, and they had some problems adhering to the experimental roles. A preferable procedure would be to select therapists who actually practice different techniques.

A third approach to the study of psychotherapeutic technique is a multi-stage program. It involves an empirical study of the domain of treatment techniques, identification of the major dimensions of that domain, development of quantitative measures of therapist behavior on each major dimension, multi-variate classification of common therapeutic roles, and study of the relation of therapist role to other treatment variables, such as outcome measures.

Fiedler (1950) reported some early work in this area. He assembled a Q-sort deck of descriptions of therapist behaviors. In one study, he asked experienced therapists, inexperienced therapists, and novices to describe with the deck their concept of the ideal therapeutic relationship. He found no differences among the judges in their descriptions. Correlations among raters could be accounted for by assuming only one factor which he called *degree of idealness*. Later, Fiedler (1951) had raters of different schools use the same Q-sort deck to describe actual interviews conducted by ten therapists of different schools and levels of experience. Four factors were required to account for the correlations among the ratings of the ten interviews by each judge. One factor in each judge's ratings clearly separated expert and non-expert therapists, but none separated orientations. The factor separating experts from non-experts was defined by ability to communicate, therapist security, and emotional distance from the patient. Aside from the extremely small samples involved, a major problem in Fiedler's studies is the selection of items for his Q-deck. The sample is extremely limited, covering only characteristics of communication, emotional distance, and status relationships between patient and therapist. Very few describe specific techniques associated with particular schools. Sundland and Barker (1962) later found that the Fiedler type items were non-discriminating among therapists. In the former's sample nearly all therapists agreed in endorsing or rejecting the Fiedler items as characteristic of their behavior and aims. With these limitations, it is hardly surprising that technique factors did not appear in Fiedler's studies.

Sundland and Barker (1962) made the most thorough study of the technique domain as a basis for their sampling and measurement of specific techniques and subsequent identification of the major technique dimensions. They identified 252 points of difference in the literature of the various schools of therapy and constructed a 95-item questionnaire for assessing therapeutic approach. They mailed the questionnaires to a random sample of 400 psychologists who were interested in psychotherapy, and later factored the response correlations of 139 persons who returned the form by a cutoff date. Their analysis revealed three interpretable technique factors which the authors considered to be only variants of a single, general factor. They concluded that therapeutic orientation could be measured on this single bi-polar dimension which they defined as *analytic* vs. *experiential*. This dimension was defined as follows:

. . . the analytic pole stresses conceptualizing, the training of the therapist, unconscious processes, and a restriction of therapist spontaneity. The experiential pole de-emphasizes conceptualizing, stresses the personality of the therapist and unplanned approach to therapy, and accepts spontaneity. (Sundland and Barker, 1962, p. 205).

Development of AID

The work of Sundland and Barker served as a springboard for several attempts at assessing therapist techniques (McNair, and Lorr, 1964).[1] For reasons detailed in the full report three independent factors were postulated. A set of scales (AID) was then constructed to test the hypotheses. The three postulated technique factors were: Psychoanalytically-oriented techniques (*A*), impersonal vs. personal affective approaches to patients (*I*), and directive, active therapeutic interventions (*D*).

The original form of AID consisted of 57 scales. A majority of statements represented modifications of those used by Sundland and Barker, but some were suggested in an earlier article by Fey (1958); the remainder were original. AID included 17 scales to represent psychoanalytic techniques, 21 scales to represent impersonal vs. personal modes of relating to patients, and 19 scales to represent directive techniques and an active therapist role. All AID scales were written as descriptions of how therapists should conduct therapy or behave during interviews. Therapists indicated degree of agreement or disagreement on eight-point scales.

AID was administered to 192 male and 73 female psychotherapists who were actively engaged in the practice of outpatient psychotherapy at 43 VA Mental Hygiene Clinics. There were 67 psychiatrists, 103 clinical psychologists, and 95 social workers in the sample. About 57 percent of the therapists had some personal psychotherapy or analysis. They averaged ten years of experience. While not a representative sample, the principal missing source of variance appeared to be the psychoanalysts.

Details of the factor analysis of the 49 questions included are given elsewhere (McNair, and Lorr, 1964) and will be summarized only. All three of the hypothesized factors were clearly confirmed. Table 2 gives condensed descriptions of the scales defining each factor.

Description of the Factors

The scales defining factor *A* (Analytic) derive from a psychoanalytic heritage, and the continuum appears to represent the extent of use of such

[1] Sundland and Barker generously supplied numerous statistical details concerning their questionnaire. This is gratefully acknowledged.

Table 2
AID Scales Defining Therapist Technique Factors

Factor A: Psychoanalytic Techniques
    Analyzes resistance
    Discusses childhood events
    Uses free association
    Interprets dreams
    Looks for causes of behavior
    Finds concept of unconscious of limited value*
    Interprets mannerisms, slips of tongue
    Emphasizes understanding childhood
    Interprets unconscious motives
    Analyzes transference
    Believes learning causes of behavior is the major result

Factor I: Impersonal vs. Personal Techniques
    Keeps office free of personal photos, mementoes, etc.
    Takes a detached, impersonal approach
    Believes training and technique are most crucial to outcome
    Uses patients' first name*
    Spontaneously expresses feelings*
    Feelings are unchanged if patient is critical or appreciative
    Acts reserved and uninvolved
    Considers spontaneous remarks and reactions unwise
    Believes emotional involvement defeats therapy
    Never shows anger at patient
    Considers walking about therapy room acceptable*
    Acts spontaneously on basis of feelings*
    Sometimes discusses news, movies, sports, etc.*
    Considers therapist personality more important than technique*

Factor D: Directive Techniques
    Sets long-range treatment goals
    Makes overall treatment plan for each case
    Aims at social adjustment of patient
    Considers treatment plan unnecessary*
    Accepts patients' own goals*
    Assumes different roles with different patients
    Considers case history and diagnosis essential to treatment
    Leads the interview into fruitful areas
    Thinks all goal-setting should be left to patient*
    Takes fairly passive, silent role*

* Scoring reversed.

techniques. Factor *I* (Impersonal) represents a continuum of expression vs. control of affect toward patients. Therapists with high scores on the factor endorse an aloof, detached, impersonal approach. Those with low scores appear to act spontaneously and practice a relationship-type therapy. Factor D (Directive) appears to tap the extent to which therapists assume active control of the treatment task. It is defined by techniques for planning therapy, for actively implementing those plans, and for shaping the therapeutic interaction in a therapist-determined direction. Therapists with low scores on Factor D appear to prefer a non-directive approach.

Relations among the first-order factors and among factor scores based on the defining items are low to moderately positive, ranging from .24 to .46. In brief, at least three dimensions are required to adequately characterize a therapist's approach. AID thus provides a feasible, reliable method for quantifying therapeutic technique, and for studying relations between technique and other treatment variables.

After the three technique factors were identified, therapists in the sample were classified into one of eight technique patterns on the basis of whether their factor scores were above or below the median on each factor. The resulting patterns of technique were clearly related to other therapist characteristics. Each professional group exhibited distinct preferences for one or two of the patterns, suggesting a strong relation between therapeutic approach and training of the therapist. Male and female therapists preferred different approaches, with women more often endorsing patterns with high scores on the Impersonal factor. As expected, therapists who had some personal analysis were more likely to endorse the four patterns characterized by high scores on the Analytic factor. Experience of therapists was unrelated to the techniques they endorsed.

THERAPIST GOALS

It is generally accepted that psychotherapy is a multi-purpose, not a single purpose, method of treatment. Most clinicians recognize that specific treatment goals can and must differ, depending on the nature of the patient's problem and diagnosis, the approach of the therapist, the setting in which therapy is undertaken, the time available for treatment, the intellectual and financial resources of the patient, and many other factors. Some therapists deliberately select the aims of treatment. Others claim such choices are the patient's prerogative. Most schools of therapy at least implicitly assume that the aims of treatment influence its course and outcome.

The laboratory's approach to the evaluation of treatment goals and their relation to outcome has been similar to that taken toward therapeutic techniques. Much groundwork necessarily preceded experimental attempts to relate goals and outcome. The initial stages included the identification and quantitative measurement of the major kinds of goals. Its study began as part of research on the effects of interview frequency on psychotherapy outcome (Lorr, McNair, Michaux, and Raskin, 1962). A sample of goals was obtained by asking therapists to provide free response descriptions of their specific goals in treating the 282 cases assigned to the study. Michaux and Lorr (1961) developed and reported a three-category qualitative schema for classifying the goal statements. The three categories were: (1) Reconstructive goals, where the major aims are personality change with insight; (2) Supportive goals, where the aims are stabilizing current adjustment patterns; and (3) Relationship goals, where the aims are to improve the patient's adjustment by fostering his relationship with the therapist.

Subsequently, an attempt was made to quantify the measurement of goals and to determine by factor analysis whether the qualitative categories accurately reflected the principal kinds of goals (McNair and Lorr, in press). A Goal Statement Inventory (GSI) was constructed as a device for assessing the kinds of goals therapists hold for specific patients. The items for the GSI were selected to sample the kinds of goals classified into Michaux and Lorr's three categories. The GSI was then administered to the same group of 259 therapists who participated in the development of AID. Therapists indicated whether each goal on the GSI was or was not one of their specific goals for the next six months in treating 523 outpatients. The GSI was designed to measure three factors corresponding to the three qualitative categories, with each factor defined by the goals selected to represent each category. In the process of factor analyzing the correlations among the goals endorsed, it became apparent that the original categories were unsatisfactory and required considerable revision. The three factors actually defined in the analysis and the goals defining each factor are given in abbreviated form in Table 3. Full statements of the goals are available elsewhere (McNair and Lorr, 1964).

Factor R corresponds closely to Michaux and Lorr's Reconstructive category. The goals in this category are the conventional goals of psychotherapy with neurotics. The goals defining the factor have in common the therapeutic aims of shaping personality change and developing insights. The second factor, St, appears to be a Stabilization factor. The defining goals have in common the aims of maintaining the patient's current adjustment pattern and preventing worsening. Four of the six goals from Michaux and Lorr's supportive category correlate significantly with Factor St. Factors St and R correlated negatively ($-.27$). This suggests that goals of personality change and stabilization tend to be incompatible, as is commonly believed, but that they are not polar opposites. The third factor, Situational Adjustment (Si), is defined by aims which emphasize adjustment to the current life situation. These include attempts to improve job adjustment, social difficulties, and other specific problems. Four of the five goals defining Si were originally classed as supportive goals by Michaux and Lorr. Factors St and Si are moderately correlated (.45), suggesting that the two represent jointly a more general factor. No factor corresponding to a *relationship* category emerged. The goals included to represent this category correlated significantly either with Factor R or St, suggesting that therapists' aims to develop a good therapeutic relationship are subsidiary to broader aims.

Table 3
Goals Defining GSI Factors

Factor R: Reconstructive Goals
  Relate past experiences to present problems
  Awareness of unconscious motives and conflicts
  Relate emotions to life situation
  Work through a pathological pattern
  Reduce defenses
  Improve relations with authority
  Awareness of reactions to significant others
  Release hostility
  Improve motivation for psychotherapy
  Corrective experiences within therapy relationship
  Understand responsibility for problems
  Relate physical symptoms to emotions
  Increase self-esteem
  Improve sexual adjustment
Factor St: Stabilization Goals
  Remain out of NP hospital
  Prevent worsening
  Reassure to alleviate a specific concern
  Accept present limitations
  Strengthen defenses
  Develop reality testing
  Satisfy dependency within therapy
  Help patient accept and trust therapist
Factor Si: Situational Goals
  Improve job adjustment
  Achieve specific reality goal (change residence)
  Develop more control over behavior (reduce acting out)
  Relate to others with less friction
  Handle a current crisis

Results of the work with the GSI indicate that there are at least three distinct kinds of aims in psychotherapy which may be measured objectively. While there well may be still other kinds of aims, the GSI probably samples rather well the more common goals of outpatient psychotherapy. Together GSI and AID help to meet two objectives of psychotherapy research. They provide a means for operationally defining some of the major features of treatment. This means that the treatment employed in a study can be more rigorously described and that results of different studies may be more meaningfully compared. Quantification of some major features of the treatment situation also means that treatment variables may be more precisely related to outcome variables.

THERAPIST PERSONALITY AND OUTCOME

Although a distinction between the therapist's personality and his techniques is probably somewhat artificial, it is convenient both for exposition and for classifying therapist variables in the treatment situation. The therapist's techniques and his personality characteristics are generally considered his two major resources for influencing outcome. Some schools of therapy consider personality more vital to results of treatment, whereas others regard the impact of particular techniques as more crucial. Factor *I*, in the AID scales, appears to assess the extent to which the therapist's personality is emphasized and utilized in treatment, although it does not attempt to measure any specific personality characteristics.

There is little solid research evidence to indicate that the therapist's personality influences the results he obtains. However, the assumption has the status of a clinical truism. The requirement of a personal analysis for the practice of psychoanalysis is based on wide acceptance of the assumption. Cutler (1958) has demonstrated some influences of personality on the therapists' interpretation and evaluation of what transpires during psychotherapeutic interviews. In a series of papers, Betz and Whitehorn (1956) and Whitehorn and Betz (1954, 1960) reported findings on two groups of therapists which they designated as types A and B. They first divided psychiatrists and psychiatric residents at Johns Hopkins Hospital into two groups. One group (Type A) obtained high success rates with schizophrenic patients. The other group (Type B) obtained low improvement rates with schizophrenics. They then searched for personality differences between the two groups of physicians. Most of their impressions were based on clinical notes, observations, and recollections about the members of the groups. However, they presented some statistically supported evidence of differences between the groups on the Strong Vocational Interest Blank (SIB) which they cross-validated on two very small additional samples of therapists. More specifically, they found that 15 A and 11 B therapists gave significantly different responses to 23 SIB items (A-B Scale). Since the SIB includes 400 items, significant differences on about 20 items could be expected by chance. The replication, however, made it difficult to dismiss the finding as simply a chance result.

Accordingly, a study was designed to check the Betz and Whitehorn findings with a sample of non-schizophrenic outpatients. It was also hoped to obtain evidence about which personality characteristics the scale measured. The study is reported in full detail elsewhere (McNair, Callahan, and Lorr, 1962), and will only be summarized here.

A large group of therapists had completed the SIB at the beginning of another study (Lorr *et al.*, 1962). The SIBs were scored on the A-B scale and 40 therapists were selected for the study of therapist *types*. Included were 20 *A* therapists (high scores) and 20 *B* therapists (low scores) selected so that both groups were matched as closely as possible for profession, experience, and rated competence. No women therapists were included because the A-B Scale correlated —.56 with the SIB Masculinity-Femininity (M-F) Scale, and nearly all women therapists were classified as Type *A*.

The patient sample included 40 male patients who were treated in outpatient psychotherapy for at least four months. Each patient was treated by one of the above therapists. The patients treated by the two groups of therapists did not differ significantly in number of psychotherapy sessions during the four-month period. They also did not differ significantly in age, education, or rated severity of their disorders.

Patients were tested prior to treatment, 16 weeks later, and one year after treatment began. Therapists also evaluated the patients at each time period. Results of covariance analyses indicated a consistent pattern of significantly greater improvement by patients of Type *B* therapists. Both therapists and patients agreed in reporting more improvement by Group *B* after four months of therapy. Patients reported significantly greater increases on a measure of Ego Strength and significantly greater reduction of symptoms. Type *B* therapists saw significantly greater reduction in Severity of Illness and significantly more observable changes in their patients. Further, the relatively greater gains by Group *B* were also maintained one year after treatment began.

At this point, it was felt that the A-B Scale had demonstrated its sensitivity. The fact that the results were opposite in direction to Betz and Whitehorn's could easily be due to patient sample differences. However, the scale had a strictly empirical basis—it worked. Why it worked or what it measured were much less clear. Examination of the item content (cf. Betz and Whitehorn, 1960, for a listing of items) appeared to defy interpretation concerning what personality characteristics the scale measured.

One question was whether the A-B Scale measured one or several personality characteristics. Correlations among all 23 items were computed for a group of 99 therapists who completed the scale in a subsequent study. Fifteen of the items formed a very homogeneous cluster, if the scoring of the two items is reversed from the Betz and Whitehorn key. The internal consistency of the 15-item set (Table 4) is .91. They are interpreted as measuring therapist interest in mechanical and technical skills and activities. The remaining eight items in the Betz and Whitehorn key clearly do not belong in the same measure as the 15 items. Correlations between the remaining items are near zero with the 15 in the core group. Also, since no other clusters appear among the eight remaining items, there is no suggestion that these assessed some other therapist characteristic.

Several explanations can be offered for the discrepancy between our results and those of Betz and Whitehorn. The samples differed in at least three important respects. Betz' patients were schizophrenics; the present sample consisted of neurotics and a few personality disorders. About 30 percent of Betz' sample came from lower or lower-middle class backgrounds; about 70 percent of the present sample came from such backgrounds. Although Betz does not indicate a sex breakdown for her sample, it is likely that more than half her patients were women, since more women than men are hospitalized in university psychiatric facilities. Only male patients were included in the sample described here.

Table 4
Abbreviated A-B Scale Items[1]

SIB Item No.	Item
17	Building contractor
19	Carpenter
59	Marine engineer
60	Mechanical engineer
68	Photo engraver
87	Ship officer
94	Toolmaker
121	Manual training
122	Mechanical drawing
151	Drilling in a company
185	Making a radio set
187	Adjusting a carburetor
189	Cabinet making
290	Public addresses about a new machine
368	Mechanical ingenuity

[1] Key: B Therapists profess these interests.

Thus, Types A and B therapists may be differentially effective with different diagnostic groups. Or the A-B Scale may tap a set of interests which B therapists are likely to share with patients from lower socioeconomic groups. Such shared interests may have had generalized effects on factors important to treatment, such as ease of communication. The high correlation between the A-B scale and the SIB masculinity-femininity scale, plus the fact that few women therapists are classified as Type B, strongly suggests that sex differences between the samples may have been the major reason for the discrepant results. Types A and B male therapists may be relatively more compatible with women and men patients respectively. This compatibility may facilitate the development of the therapeutic relationship or it may be translated into more effective therapeutic interventions.

REFERENCES

APFELBAUM, B. *Dimensions of transference in psychotherapy*. Univ. of California Publications in Personality Assessment and Research, No. 2. Berkeley, Calif.: Univ. of California Publications, 1958.

ASHBY, J. D., FORD, D. H., GUERNEY, B. G., and GUERNEY, LOUISE F. Effects on clients of a reflective and a leading type of psychotherapy. *Psychol. Monogr.*, 71, No. 24, 1957.

BALES, R. F. *Interaction process analysis*. Reading, Mass.: Addison-Wesley, 1950.

BETZ, BARBARA J., and WHITEHORN, J. C. The relationship of the therapist to the outcome of therapy in schizophrenia. *Psychiat. res. Rep.*, 5: 89-140, 1956.

BORGATTA, E. F., Mood, personality, and interaction. *J. gen. Psychol.*, 64: 105-137, 1956.

CLYDE, D. J. *Clyde mood scale*. Coral Gables, Fla.: Biometric Laboratory, Univ. of Miami, 1963.

CUTLER, R. L. Countertransference effects in psychotherapy. *J. consult. Psychol.*, 22: 349-356, 1958.

DOLLARD, J., and AULD, F. *Scoring human motives: A manual*. New Haven: Yale University Press, 1959.

FEY, W. F. Doctrine and experience: their influence upon the psychotherapist. *J. consult. Psychol.*, 22: 403-409, 1958.

FIEDLER, F. E. The concept of an ideal therapeutic relationship. *J. consult. Psychol.*, 14: 239-245, 1950.

FIEDLER, F. E. Factor analysis of psychoanalytic, nondirective, and Adlerian therapeutic relationships. *J. consult. Psychol.*, 15: 32-38, 1951.

FIEDLER, F. E. Quantitative studies on the role of therapist feelings towards their patients. In O. H. Mowrer (Ed.), *J. Psychotherapy: theory and research*. New York: Ronald, 1953.

GREEN, R. F., and NOWLIS, V. A factor analytic study of the domain of mood with independent validation of the factors. Technical report No. 4. Research Program on Mood and Attitude Change. Rochester, N.Y.: Univ. of Rochester, 1957.

LEARY, T. *Interpersonal diagnosis of personality*. New York: Ronald, 1957.

LORR, M. Client perceptions of therapists: A study of the therapeutic relationship. *J. consult. Psychol.*, 29: 146-149, 1965.

LORR, M., and MCNAIR, D. M. An interpersonal behavior circle. *J. abnorm. soc. Psychol.*, 67: 68-75, 1963.

LORR, M., MCNAIR, D. M., MICHAUX, W. W., and RASKIN, A. Frequency of treatment and psychotherapy outcome. *J. abnorm. soc. Psychol.*, 64: 281-292, 1962.

MCNAIR, D. M., CALLAHAN, D. M., and LORR, M. Therapist "types" and patient response to psychotherapy. *J. consult. Psychol.*, 26: 425-429, 1962.

McNair, D. M., and Lorr, M. An analysis of mood in neurotics. *J. abnorm. soc. Psychol.*, **69**: 620-627, 1964.

McNair, D. M., and Lorr, M. An analysis of professed psychotherapeutic techniques. *J. clin. Psychol.*, **28**: 265-271, 1964.

McNair, D. M., and Lorr, M. Three kinds of psychotherapy goals. *J. clin. Psychol.*, **20**: 390-393, 1964.

Michaux, W. W., and Lorr, M. Psychotherapists' treatment goals. *J. consult. Psychol.*, 250-254, 1961.

Murray, E. J. A content-analysis method for studying psychotherapy. *Psychol. Monogr.*, **70**, No. 13, 1956.

Murray, H. A. *Explorations in personality.* New York: Oxford, 1938.

Parloff, M. B., Kelman, H. C., and Frank, J. D. Comfort, effectiveness, and self-awareness as criteria of improvement in psychotherapy. *Amer. J. Psychiat.* **111**: 343-351, 1954.

Rausch, H. L., and Bordin, E. S. Warmth in personality development in psychotherapy. *Psychiat.*, **20**: 351-363, 1957.

Rogers, C. R. The necessary and sufficient conditions of therapeutic personality change. *J. consult. Psychol.*, **21**: 95-103, 1957.

Schutz, W. C. *Firo: A three-dimensional theory of interpersonal behavior.* New York: Holt, Rinehart and Winston, 1958.

Sells, S. B., Barry, J. R., Trites, D. K., and Chinn, H. I. A test of the effects of pregnenolone methyl ether on subjective feelings of B-29 crews after a 12-hour mission. *J. appl. Psychol.*, **40**: 353-357, 1956.

Snyder, W. U. An investigation of the nature of nondirective psychotherapy. *J. gen. Psychol.*, **33**: 193-223, 1945.

Snyder, W. U. and Snyder, B. June. *The psychotherapy relationship.* New York: Macmillan, 1961.

Stern, G. G. *Preliminary Manual: Activities index and college characteristics.* Syracuse, N.Y.: Syracuse University Psychol. Res. Center, 1958.

Strupp, H. H. A multidimensional system for analyzing psychotherapeutic techniques. *Psychiat.*, **20**: 293-306, 1957.

Sundland, D. M., and Barker, E. N. The orientations of psychotherapists. *J. consult. Psychol.*, **26**: 201-212, 1962.

Thurstone, L. L. *Multiple factor analysis.* Chicago: Univ. of Chicago Press, 1947.

Whitehorn, J. C., and Betz, Barbara J. A study of psychotherapeutic relationships between physicians and schizophrenic patients. *Amer. J. Psychiat.*, **111**: 321-331, 1954.

Whitehorn, J. C., and Betz, Barbara J. Further studies of the doctor as a crucial variable in the outcome of treatment with schizophrenic patients. *Amer. J. Psychiat.*, **117**: 215-223, 1960.

V

Research in the Teaching of Psychotherapy

Research in the *teaching* of psychotherapy—like research in psychotherapy—can be classified into several types: research in the process of teaching, outcome of teaching, and theory of teaching psychotherapy. Such research is actually a kind of educational research that is in the very early stages of development, for the psychotherapies have only recently evolved as systematic therapeutic procedures and skills with identifiable theoretical structures.

Many books and technical articles have been written, it is true, on "how to do it," that is, how to do psychotherapy, from this theoretical vantage point or that. Some of these are excellent works, quite instructive to the would-be craftsman or the aspiring, and even the experienced, teacher of psychotherapy. Although representative writings of this sort might conceivably be reviewed or listed, such literature has become too voluminous to give it adequate space here.

On the other hand, evaluative research in the teaching of psychotherapy has been meager. Hence, we believe this type of educational research in psychotherapy deserves some serious consideration in this book. We realize that the selection of one group of authors to discuss such a research area might provoke controversy from researchers, teachers, and psychotherapists preferring to follow some rival theoretical frame of reference. But this research area is so sparsely populated insofar as active work is concerned, that to locate a group of co-workers willing to pioneer in writing about such research is a rare find.

We present, therefore, a chapter on the subject by Matarazzo, Wiens, and Saslow. To do justice to the other research workers in this area, they have provided an extensive review of the literature followed by a description of their own experiments in the teaching and learning psychotherapy skills. We trust that their excellent chapter will stimulate other investigators and teachers to report their research in the teaching of psychotherapy.

34. Experimentation in the teaching and learning of psychotherapy skills

Ruth G. Matarazzo, Arthur N. Wiens, and George Saslow

INTRODUCTION

"Considering the fact that one-third of present-day psychologists have a special interest in the field of psychotherapy, we would expect that a great deal of attention might be given to the problem of training individuals to engage in the therapeutic process. . . . For the most part this field is characterized by a rarity of research and a plenitude of platitudes" (Rogers, 1957). While there have been numerous attempts by psychologists, psychiatrists, and psychoanalysts to improve the teaching of psychotherapy, only a handful of these could be called *research* efforts designed to answer the question whether particular student behaviors were altered.

The fact that there is virtually no research in this area is probably attributable to a number of factors. The *experiential* learning, which all psychotherapeutic schools agree is necessary, involves complex behavioral and cognitive changes which are far more difficult to assess than facts learned in a didactic course. The postulated learning, even when teaching innovations have been introduced, appears to have been evaluated only through such indirect and subjective criteria as whether or not the students' patients improve or feel that they have improved; whether the students believe that their skills and attitudes have changed; whether the instructor's subjective opinion is that the students have benefited; and whether the students value the instruction highly.

Unfortunately, students' attitudes, statements, and feelings about what they have learned stand in marked contrast to independent, objective measures of what in fact the learning retention is (McGuire, Hurley, Babbott, and Butterworth, 1963). It has also been shown that when students are asked to write down what they would say in a client-centered interview, their predicted responses fall into categories markedly different in percentage distribution from those in fact observed when their interviews are recorded (Blocksma and Porter, 1947). Hence, it is clear that one

This investigation was supported by research grants MH-01938 and M-158-63 from the National Institute of Mental Health, of the National Institutes of Health, U. S. Public Health Service, and by the Medical Research Foundation of Oregon, Inc.

cannot rely on information other than students' observed behavior in live (actual or simulated) psychotherapeutic situations.

This chapter will be divided into three major sections. The first section summarizes program descriptions, innovations, and conceptual frameworks; the second mentions possible approaches to experimental study; and the third describes examples of research in the field.

I. PROGRAM DESCRIPTIONS

Psychoanalytic School

The psychoanalytic school sees the ideal learning situation as one which facilitates *growth* in the student, freeing him from neurotic blind spots and defenses which otherwise would preclude the possibility of increasing his capacity for creativity. The teaching method is related to the theory of psychoanalysis per se, first with the working through of a personal analysis, and then with the controlled observation of oneself while attempting to analyze a patient. The student's counter-transference to the patient is found again in the student's counter-transference to his supervisor, although the supervisor's counter-transference to the student is not analyzed. The working-through of the student-to-supervisor transference is a long and difficult process, the resolution of which is a prerequisite to the necessary learning of psychotherapy. (Since other schools, such as the Rogerian, pay practically no attention to this aspect of learning we have here an important question about the utility of a particular procedure which needs to be settled by objective inquiry.) Ekstein and Wallerstein's (1958) book describes in a detailed and comprehensive fashion the program at an important psychoanalytic center. Their book presents a viewpoint representative of current literature. The student's *problems in learning* are defined as his defense against learning and are ascribed almost entirely to his neurotic characteristics. In this case an available theory of psychotherapy is thought to provide answers to teaching and learning problems which arise, and the material presented is unsupported by actual research findings.

In addition to personal analysis and several control analyses with continued emphasis upon the student's personality as revealed in his counter-transference problems, psychoanalytic training has also utilized the case conference method. Perhaps because the former are essentially private, two-person interactions, there seems to be no literature describing innovations in such supervisor-student interactions. In regard to the case conference, the major questions seem to revolve about the method of obtaining data regarding the student-patient interaction: whether by verbal summary, recording, live interview with a patient or a role-playing situation. There are no data establishing the superiority of one method above another, although Fleming and Hamburg (1958) present the advantages and disadvantages of a variety of supervisory and instructional methods. However, Covner's (1944) studies of Rogerian counseling interviews indicate that significant omissions and distortions are likely to occur in the student's verbal summary.

The Non-Directive or "Rogerian" School

The Rogerian school was the first to become concerned about the lack of both objective data which record what occurs in psychotherapy and explicit evaluation of training techniques for the would-be psychotherapist. Thus, Rogers' group was the first to make extensive use of electrical recordings and the first to describe specific, brief training programs in psychotherapy. His collaborators, Blocksma and Porter (1947), were also the first to obtain objective evaluation of the results of training. Their experiment will be described in Section 3 of this chapter.

Despite the fact that Rogers is concerned with more explicit training techniques, he is in agreement with the psychoanalytic philosophy of training that clinical experience, the actual *doing* in psychotherapy, is the most important aspect of the training program. "I would like to propose that it is experiential learning and not cognitive learning which is essential in the training of an individual to engage effectively in therapy. When we speak of learning that is experienced we have to realize that this *cannot* be communicated. It can only be facilitated" (Rogers, 1957). Thus the acquisition of facts, theory, or intellectual learning is not seen as providing the kind of knowledge necessary to conduct *good* psychotherapy.

Intellectual training is seen by Rogers as facilitating therapeutic skill only insofar as it matures the individual and gives a broader awareness of some phenomena occurring in psychotherapy. He reviews a series of graded procedures which can facilitate the kind of experiential learning which he deems necessary to learning to become a psychotherapist. While there has been no objective evaluation of the effects of these training techniques, they differ from the techniques used by the psychoanalytic school[1] by virtue of their public observability or reproducibility, and thus are a step further in the direction of scientific analysis. The student-patient behavior which is evaluated does not depend upon the student's subjective report, but rather upon recordings or actual observed interviews.

Length of training is not specified, but it is pointed out that any period of training is helpful and that optimum length depends upon goals and practical considerations; perhaps even five years would not be enough to reach one's peak of therapeutic effectiveness, but this goal and expenditure of time would not be practicable.

Rogers (1957) presents the most explicitly formulated plan for teach-

---

[1] While we are aware that at least some training analysts use recordings, the psychoanalytic literature does not make it appear that this is emphasized as an important mechanism for teaching.

ing psychotherapy. As an *introduction* to therapeutic relationships he suggests listening to recordings of experienced and inexperienced therapists, and students' interviewing of each other. The next stage is that of *obtaining a direct acquaintance* with psychotherapy through observing a series of interviews conducted by the supervisor, participating in group therapy, and undertaking personal individual therapy, if he desires it. Lastly, when he *actually carries on psychotherapy*, himself, the suggested teaching techniques are recording of interviews, multiple therapy, and facilitative, non-directive individual supervision.

While the client-centered group developed within psychology and has involved the teaching of psychotherapy to psychology students, the group has had an impact upon training within the medical profession. Teaching within medical schools, to medical undergraduates and to psychiatric residents, appears to have evolved from both psychoanalytic and Rogerian methods and theory. Because of the necessity, in any medical setting, of attending to the biological dimension of human functioning, the incorporation of psychotherapy instruction into medical education programs has led to an orientation toward the patient which is more comprehensive than that found either in the psychoanalytic institute or in the Rogerian counseling center.

Teaching of Psychotherapy in Medical Schools

Two conference reports have been important in the development of the teaching of psychiatry, psychotherapy, and interviewing skills in medical schools (Group for the Advancement of Psychiatry, 1948; Whitehorn, Jacobsen, Levine, and Lippard, 1952). These reports recommended that medical students obtain training in interviewing skills over the four undergraduate years. The aim of such instruction would be to help students to learn how to obtain all the data needed for an adequate delineation of medical problems and to develop appropriate psychological attitudes toward patients so that the doctor-patient relationship could be utilized constructively in medical study and treatment of the patient.

In 1947, Coleman recommended the early introduction into medical education of training in psychotherapy as a necessary counterweight to the authoritarian, directive attitude commonly fostered in medicine. He suggested such teaching could be done in stages. The student could begin with a non-directive, listening approach, proceed to acceptance of a patient's superficial feelings, then to exploration of deeper conflicts, and finally to acquisition of knowledge of dynamic psychopathology. Aring (1949) discussed the rarity of comprehensive teaching in a medical curriculum despite the recommendations of many committees. He felt the reason for this difficulty was that: "Teachers of medicine in general reflect the lack of instruction in their own occupation; a degree in medicine does not fit one for teaching." Romano (1950) points out that psychiatry is less systematized than other areas of medicine and does not have discrete variables which can be isolated for analysis. The kind of assimilation necessary for learning to do psychotherapy needs to be extended over a long period of time. He is thus in agreement with the GAP report suggesting that psychiatry be taught over the entire four years of medical school. Strauss (1950) described a four-week junior clerkship in psychiatry in which the students observe four consecutive therapy interviews between a staff member and patient, and after each interview participate in a discussion of the psychodynamics and rationale of the therapy. One student takes notes each time, and presents the material during the discussion hour. Sometimes family members are interviewed also, so that the students obtain a more complete picture of the patient's interaction with his immediate social environment.

Guze, Matarazzo, and Saslow (1953) presented a conceptual framework for teaching a procedure of psychotherapy which is congruent with the treatment procedures in medicine. This framework involved the identification of these factors in the individual: the stresses operating (allergens, family conflict, etc.); the state of the individual at the time the stress is operating (genetic background, pattern of adjustive mechanisms, etc.); the physiological changes in response to the stressor (bronchial or colonic hyperfunction, etc.); the associated drive state (anxiety, depression, etc.); and the behavioral responses (repression, avoidance, rationalization, etc.). Identification of these several factors helps the patient to label those environmental cues to which he is sensitive and to which he responds with various physiological dysfunctions. He is helped to learn to manipulate pertinent environmental factors as in any other kind of disease (avoidance or desensitization, altering a family constellation or one's perception of it, etc.), and his new ways of dealing with environmental stress (more appropriate use of direct problem-solving techniques) are given as vitally important a place as in other illnesses.

No systematic data supplemented the personal experiences summarized above. Motivated by dissatisfaction with the existing theory and technique of initial interviewing, Gill, Newman, and Redlich (1954) presented the complete transcripts of three initial interviews, with running commentary on the interviewer's behavior. Some of their specific recommendations are that a therapist "engage in minimal activity; remain flexible in planning the course of the interview; engage largely in classifying the vague thoughts and feelings of which the patient complains; avoid interpretations; refrain from attempting to impress the patient, or in any way attempt to gain personal satisfaction; question the patient's conventional statements to make sure he understands what the patient really means; elucidate the presenting complaint, its significance to the patient, and possible causes." They emphasize that listening to recordings of oneself is a valuable teaching method, improved by listening with another person, who helps one to identify not only the words but emotions and attitudes.

The liaison program between medicine and psychiatry at the University of Rochester takes advantage of the opportunity to teach medicine comprehensively in a medical school program when psychotherapy instruction is added (Engel, Green, Reichsman, Schmale, and Ashenburg, 1957). The instructors in this program were trained first as internists and then received *psychological training*. As part of the *liaison program,* the students take turns interviewing unselected medical patients before their colleagues and two instructors. Emphasis is not on differential diagnosis, but on "psychological and communication aspects of the interview process for both student and patient. . . . The student learns to take an initial history which will include information about the setting of the illness and the identity of the patient, past and current, without the patient's being made to feel that an irrelevant or intrusive inquiry is being made."

Adams (1958) describes a two-month clerkship in comprehensive medicine at Western Reserve University: a major feature is that the student can have continuity of contact with his medical patient and his patient's family, despite the specialization of the modern medical center. A close relationship is maintained between the student and staff consultants, with the psychiatric consultant on call for difficult situations and regularly joining the student for a demonstration interview to pull together the material the student has obtained. Weekly student-staff conferences are the setting for student presentation of a particular case or problem. "The psychiatrist helps teach history-taking, physical examination, and interviewing. Help is offered in medical management and formulation of treatment goals by helping the student attain a more thorough knowledge of his patient's emotional life; the patient's feelings about and concept of his disease, his habitual ways of reacting, his motivation and potentiality are shown to be important in this. This broadening process seems to have been successfully accomplished."

Werkman (1961) has focused on the student's problems in dealing with the *final* interview in which findings are discussed and recommendations made. He noted students' difficulties in organizing the information to be imparted to patients as well as student tendencies to work around difficult problems, give false reassurance, blame the patient, suggest magical solutions (e.g., that the child will outgrow the problem, etc.). To conduct the final interview more effectively he has suggested an outline for the student to follow and he has had students role-play this interview situation with the supervisor taking the role of the parents or child in question. The student's non-specific reassurance and ineptitude is not viewed as a function of neurosis but rather as "a simple lack of knowledge of how to handle specific situations."

Pfouts and Rader (1962) report an experimental program in which all fourth-year medical students serve full-time, five-week clerkships in the Psychiatric Outpatient Clinic in groups of eight. The authors observed all initial interviews and, immediately following each one, discussed with each student his technique and relationship with the patient. Discussion of interview technique involved such things as emotional climate; avoiding biasing the patient's responses; handling resistance; how to recognize and follow up leads; making transitions; ending the interview, etc. They also found that "Almost all the medical students seemed to have difficulty in recognizing and controlling the influence on their interviews of their hostile and disapproving feelings about certain patients. . . ." They found that the students were resistant to observation, experiencing "natural anxiety and reluctance to expose themselves." The students were asked to make unsigned, written evaluations at the end of the service, and 80 percent of them were positive, ranging "from mild acceptance to extreme enthusiasm."

Lester, Gussen, Yamamoto, and West (1962) point out that one of the student's greatest assets in helping the patient is a *positive attitude* toward him. In order to maintain this attitude he must have expert backing to avoid feelings of helplessness, anxiety, and hostility toward patients who may not have an immediate, favorable response to therapy. They call for further study in the development of teaching methods in this area. "Without some systematic attempt to evaluate and revise teaching methods, little progression can be made in our efforts to help future physicians to understand the vicissitudes of the doctor-patient relationship."

Heine, Aldrich, Draper, Meuser, Tippett, and Trosman (1962) have described teaching and evaluating the results of a clerkship in psychotherapy for medical students at the University of Chicago Medical School. Senior students spend 17 weeks in the Psychiatry Outpatient Clinic doing short-term psychotherapy under intensive supervision. The problems of supervision are discussed and verbatim excerpts from supervisory sessions are presented in order to substantiate their observations. They discovered many interesting facts, such as that the students wanted to develop *the appearance* of a skillful interview technique more than basic understanding of psychopathology; that students believed their patients were, to some extent, dissatisfied with the therapy experience.

They attempted to evaluate student learning through the students' self-report on a questionnaire. Between 80 and 90 percent of the students reported gains in insight, confidence "in using their personality as a medium of treatment," and "sensitivity to the feelings and attitudes of patients." In an attempt to estimate the credence such self-reports warrant, the authors examined the relationship between these responses and the students' behavior and attitudes in other contexts. For example, they found that students who rated themselves as having profited most from the program came to regard psychotherapy as more "scientific" than intuitive;

liked their patients; and had patients who were rated as improving the most over the course of therapy.

This is an excellent comprehensive collection of observations and subjective ratings, providing hints for further research. However, it does not contain controlled, objective data and does not attempt to evaluate teaching method.

In another report from the same department (University of Chicago), Aldrich and Bernhardt (1963) describe a new four-year sequence in psychiatry. This included a threefold increase in teaching time, seminar case-study instruction, and longer supervised patient contact. They compared knowledge of psychiatric facts and modification of these students' attitudes with those of students instructed by the traditional program. The latter students had had less overall teaching time and less patient contact. The comparison measure was made on a Problem Cases Test which presented seven vignettes of patients. The student was asked to outline the problems presented in each vignette, to list additional information that would improve his understanding of each problem, and to describe action he would take as the doctor in the case. Instructors also graded the students on their actual performance. There was no significant difference in the test performance of students instructed by the two methods, although instructors' subjective impressions were to the contrary. However, reliability of grades based on these impressions was low. The authors conclude that better measures of student performance (particularly, sensitivity to interpersonal relationships) are necessary. In view of the results of Blocksma and Porter (1947), to be quoted in the next section, it would appear that Aldrich and Bernhardt are justified in their suspicion of the validity of students' written reports about what they would do under given circumstances. Thus, the above study is inconclusive on two counts.

Post-Graduate Programs for the General Physician

A number of articles have described post-graduate programs which attempt to compensate for the lack of psychiatric training in the undergraduate program from which a practicing physician may have come. Such programs do not attempt to make the general physician into a psychiatrist nor do they attempt to teach him to do psychotherapy. Rather, they are based on the assumption that, in order to be a good physician and in order to use his time most effectively, the practitioner must have interviewing skill and must be able to develop a positive, therapeutic relationship. Typically these programs involve group supervision of a kind similar to that of the case conference. The physician may present the case of a baffling patient in his practice.

Whitaker (1949) trained practitioners, through multiple therapy, to promote the "ability to develop a more therapeutic doctor-patient relationship" so that the practitioners might handle mild psychiatric disturbances.

Balint (1954) feels that doctors in practice are "better material for training in psychotherapy than are medical students." He holds case conferences with six to eight physicians in which they discuss their day-to-day work with neurotic patients in their practice. The goal of the course is "to help the doctors to become more sensitive to what is going on, consciously or unconsciously, in the patient's mind when doctor and patient are together."

In training general physicians to deal with "the kinds of patients who might turn up in any physician's office," Enelow, Forde, and Gwartney (1962) conducted case conferences with groups of eight to ten physicians in practice. A psychiatrist interviewed a patient typical of patients seen in general office practice. Following the interview a psychiatrist and internist led a group discussion of interview techniques and observations, and the medical and psychiatric aspects of the illness. In an abstract summarizing an ongoing program, Enelow, Adler, and Manning (1963) describe a special clinic designed to reproduce something of the "actual situation of the family doctor." The physician-student examines and treats his assigned patients comprehensively, for both physical and psychological ailments. In addition, three instructors (internist, psychiatrist, and sociologist) observe the physician-student in a demonstration therapy session each week and participate in a group supervision session with all of the physician-students. In addition, the psychiatrist demonstrates ongoing psychotherapy. Cognitive learning gain is measured by content analysis of responses to open-ended questions presented during a filmed patient interview viewed at the beginning, middle, and at the final session of the course. Proposed criteria of learning gain are enhanced ability for accurate observation of the patient's behavior toward the interviewer and ability to draw meaningful conclusions for diagnosis and management. A questionnaire form completed at the beginning and end of the course is used to measure change in conception of the role of the physician along four dimensions: "(1) use of professional medical skills in the treatment of illness; (2) use of the authority he commands as an expert; (3) behavior expressive of the physician's humanitarian concern for the patient; (4) recognition of his own feelings toward the patient."

Teaching Devices and Specific Innovations

The first use of electrical recordings, two decades ago, was a major breakthrough in the teaching of psychotherapy. A second breakthrough was the one-way screen. Since then, there have been numerous devices which their inventors believe increase the effectiveness of the supervisory process.

The Mechanical Third Ear

Korner and Brown (1952) developed a device which they called *The Mechanical Third Ear* which is a hearing-aid device with an extended cord leading to a microphone in the observation room. The student's supervisor can talk into the microphone and directly transmit suggestions to the student regarding observations to consider, comments he might make, etc. The current version of this approach is reported by Ward (1960, 1962) who describes feeding his comments to the student via a small radio receiver (*electronic preceptoring*). Two patterns of preceptor intervention are reported. (1) Constant Intervention: The teacher attempts to react to nearly every sequence. (2) Nodal Intervention: The teacher reacts only at important junctures. Two types of intervention have been recognized. (1) Dialogue Formulations: The teacher tells the student what to say, how to handle a particular situation. (2) Dynamics Formulations: The teacher points out meanings and relationships and leaves dialogue and action pattern to the student. They report that thus far students prefer nodal intervention and dynamics formulations.

Closed-Circuit Television

The opportunity for a large number of students to hear and observe psychotherapy in progress via closed-circuit television viewing is being utilized in a number of medical centers, including the Universities of Kansas, Mississippi, and Nebraska.

The Content-Free Interview

Thompson and Bradway (1950) emphasized the significance of tone and expressive movements as indicators of emotional interchange in addition to the words the patient might choose. They felt the inexperienced therapist was largely unaware of nonverbal cues and developed a procedure to increase such awareness. Their students (playing therapist and patient roles) were asked to conduct an interview in which they used no words, but counted, or used numbers in any sequence, instead. They note: "It is our feeling that these content-free interviews are valuable teaching devices because they force the "over-ideational pre-Ph.D." (with apologies to Rapaport) to examine the intangibles which are so foreign to his academic experience."

Multiple Therapy

Lott's (1957) survey revealed that numerous training centers, of diverse theoretical persuasions, utilize this method which consists of the supervisor, student-therapist, and patient meeting in joint conference. Another variation has been for the two therapists to play different roles; for example, one taking an authoritarian, directive stance and another a nondirective, supportive role. Lott reports general agreement that multiple therapy is a good teaching method, that most patients are favorably inclined toward it, and improve with it.

Peer Supervision

Brugger, Caesar, Frank, and Marty (1962) have attempted peer supervision, consisting of weekly meetings in which four student-therapists discuss the recorded interviews of each of the four without direct staff supervision. This method of supervision has seemed to facilitate greater spontaneity and aggressiveness, discussion of therapist-patient relationships and reactions to each other, and frank discussion of group processes. Exposure and recognition of shortcomings and felt inadequacies were reported to be less anxiety-provoking than when a supervisor was present. While coverage was perhaps less incisive and comprehensive than would have been possible with individual staff supervision, there was continuity in the group membership and enthusiasm for the "stimulating nature of the group sessions."

Is There a Psychotherapist Personality?

In view of the heavy emphasis upon the interactional, experiential character of training for psychotherapy and the characteristically close supervision of a student-therapist's initial efforts, it is not surprising that considerable thought has been given to what would constitute the necessary or desirable qualifications of a psychotherapist. Schwartz and Abel (1955) describe the psychoanalytic school's earlier "omnipotent reliance upon the sufficiency of the personal analysis to insure the training risk." However, they report that in their own more recent selection efforts they have tried to eliminate individuals who are "too conventional and constricted" and those with severe personality disturbance. "Obviously, too, the wider his experience with people has been, the more secure he is in his own development and his feeling about himself, the better he will be able to enter into the personal relationship with a patient in a helpful and therapeutic way" (Fleming 1953).

In his review of the literature to find the personality characteristics that were felt to be most desirable for the psychotherapist, Krasner (1963) reports that he ran into an "avalanche of adjectives" which varied widely and sometimes were contradictory. Kelly and Goldberg (1959), in their review of psychologist-therapists, found a few variables which discriminated therapists from psychologist administrators and academic psychologists but they suggest as more significant the fact that almost all of the large number of variables considered in their study failed to differentiate therapists at all. They found therapists to be an extremely heterogeneous group. Similarly, Holt and Luborsky (1958) found little differentiation in the personality characteristics of psychiatrists, psychotherapists, and psychoanalysts or, for that matter, from "the kind of man one might hope to encounter in any profession and who might be expected to do well in almost any type of work." Typically desired personality attributes were superior intelligence, capacity for understanding, empathy, flexibility, breadth of interests, respect for the dignity and integrity of the individual, etc.

The necessary conclusion would seem to be that many different kinds of persons are engaged in psychotherapy and that to some extent, perhaps, effective therapeutic work involves the appropriate pairing of therapist-patient interaction characteristics. The relevant characteristics are still largely unspecified and it is necessary for each therapist to discover empirically with what kind of patients or patient-problems he works effectively.

II. POSSIBLE APPROACHES TO EXPERIMENTAL STUDY

From the studies cited, and from our review of the literature, we have concluded that there is essentially no published research regarding the teaching of psychotherapy, the supervisory process, how learning of effective psychotherapy takes place, and how to teach psychotherapy efficiently. Many reports of training programs are available and it is evident that many psychotherapists talk about teaching, but few report systematic innovations, comparison of methods, and/or student skill before and after a course of instruction. Admittedly, the complex behavioral and cognitive changes in *experiential* learning are difficult to define. It is equally or even more difficult to reliably define growth experience, enhanced creativity, therapeutic doctor-patient relationship, and resolution of a counter-transference neurosis.

What seems to be needed is a more precise delineation (including behavioral definition) of at least three important variables (situation, patient, therapist) in the psychotherapy interview. Each of the variables has stimulus value that *evokes* certain interview behaviors from patient and (student) therapist which the student should learn to recognize and with which he must learn to deal.

Situation

First, the context or psychotherapeutic interview situation, itself, contains demands for particular role performance. Jones and Thibaut (1958) suggest that in trying to understand social interaction, knowledge of the roles of the participants conveys much information and ". . . for the most part, we interact with others within fairly well-defined situations, and in terms of rather constraining roles. Our main requirement, therefore, is for information relevant to adequate role performance." The psychotherapy interview situation obviously focuses on *doctor* and *patient* roles, and it is of considerable importance to the student-therapist how he plans to enact this role. One assumption that seems to affect interaction between patient and doctor is the expectation that the patient should do most of the talking in the interview. Thus, one possible research question would concern the amount of talk-time actually utilized in ongoing psychotherapy, as well as the amount of talk-time utilized by individuals (students) assigned alternately to *patient* and *doctor* roles. Saslow, Goodrich, and Stein (1956) have emphasized that the interviewer role is not genetically determined or invariable but is flexible. Furthermore, they demonstrated that the range of behavior available to the therapist in general was much greater than that which he used with his patients. Therefore, the therapist's behavior with his patients would appear specific to that interactional situation, presumably learned, and if learned, teachable.

Patient

A second major variable in psychotherapy interview behavior is the patient, and it is likely that favorable patient factors are an exceedingly important key to a successful psychotherapy relationship. What patient factors should a student-therapist learn to assess, recognize, compensate for, etc.? Such patient variables as social class, verbal facility, and intelligence have been related to the likelihood of receiving psychotherapy in the first place as well as to probable outcome of a series of psychotherapeutic sessions. Strupp (1962) suggests that studies of patient variables point to the probability of successful psychotherapy if the patient and therapist hold mutually congruent expectations of what therapy is to accomplish; if the patient is intelligent, well educated, psychologically minded, able to communicate his feelings; recognizes his problems as psychological and wants psychological help. Heller, Myers, and Kline (1963) enacted specific client roles and demonstrated that interviewers who were faced with dominant versus dependent client behavior responded, in turn, with passive versus hyper-responsible behavior, and when faced with hostile versus friendly client behavior they responded, in turn, with hostile and likeable, agreeable behavior. Thus, specific kinds of interviewee behavior appeared to evoke predictable interviewer behaviors. Such research results suggest that it is possible to conduct experimental studies to determine some of the relevant dimensions of interview behavior.

Another effort to introduce some constancy of stimulus to which student-therapists might react is Dugan's (1963) use of a *coached client*. The *coached client* was described (personal history data) in the same way to all of the students and was given a series of behavior topics to introduce as similarly as possible in the interviews. Inasmuch as the observer knew what topics were to be introduced by the client, it was easy to see when the counselor obstructed the development of the interview; i.e., the client often had a real problem in getting himself and the situation into the interview. This was mainly the result of counselor domination, teaching, and interpreting. Dugan's observations on the students' behavior in these interviews included the following: The counselor was very conscious of himself; he tended to teach; there was a high ratio of student talk (the counselor talked 60 to 65 percent of the time); there was a tendency to use probing and interpretive responses and a general tendency not to listen to the client. The pacing of the interview was too rapid (use of pauses was very limited); there was generally little use of simple acceptance (the counselor's attention was not on the client as much as on himself); psychological test interpretation was too often involved; on request for decision, the counselor usually hastened to reassure the client (little objectivity involved); there was considerable difficulty in termination.

Therapist

A third major variable in the psychotherapy interview is the therapist himself. While it has been recognized that many different personality and behavior patterns may characterize psychotherapists, it would seem important for the student-therapist to become aware of his own stimulus characteristics. There has been increasing recognition that the therapist is actively evoking patient behavior not only with explicit verbal interest and response, but also with a number of non-verbal tactics. Subtle mechanisms for controlling interview behavior include such indications of therapist interest as questioning glances, focus of visual attention, head nodding, saying mm-hmm, and clearing of the throat. The marked interview effect of some of these subtle therapist behaviors has been described by J. D. Matarazzo, Wiens, and Saslow (1965). Furthermore, the therapist who believes he should be active will elicit patient behavior different from that which is elicited by the therapist who thinks he should be more passive and silent; similarly, warm versus cold, or friendly versus distant stances will evoke different interviewee response.

Heller (1963), in collaboration with Myers, has studied the influence of some therapist behaviors. The interviewers were instructed to vary their behavior along the dimensions of activity-passivity and hostility-friendliness. The interviewees were found to prefer friendly interviewers, with active-friendly interviewers best liked and passive-hostile interviewers least liked. The proportion of subject speaking-time was directly influenced by the interviewer; with active interviewers, regardless of affect condition, eliciting a high level of verbal output and silent interviewers eliciting sharply reduced verbal output from the interviewees. The active-hostile condition was not the most inhibiting although in this condition punishing remarks were frequent and openly stated. Lack of communication and lack of orientation cues (in the passive conditions) were more *punishing* and inhibiting to verbal output than openly stated, clearly structured disapproval. Interviewer style, however, did not affect specific content.

Reece and Whitman (1962) have reported, similarly, that experimenter *warmth* increased verbalization but did not change the rate of emission of the reinforced class of behavior (i.e., did not determine what they talked about).

Studies on the effect of some additional therapist characteristics are reported by Parloff (1956, 1961) who notes that the therapist able to establish better social relationships in his non-professional life also established better therapeutic relationships; the therapist who perceived his patient as more like the *ideal patient* created the better therapeutic relationship; and incidence of premature termination was negatively associated with the goodness of the relationship. Whitehorn and Betz (1954) have reported that therapists with certain personality characteristics are likely to be more successful with schizophrenic patients than are other therapists. The therapist's verbal reinforcement behavior is another important area to study (Krasner, 1963). One goal of research on the effect of therapist behavior might well be to enhance awareness of the full range of its potential for influencing others.

In the delineation of these variables (situation, patient, therapist) in psychotherapy interview behavior it has been possible to specify questions regarding the teaching of student-therapists. It would seem that many of the assertions made by teachers of psychotherapy, and quoted in Section I of this chapter, could be treated as hypotheses for further study and then would lend themselves to systematic before-and-after-training studies, comparison of methods, and so forth.

III. RESEARCH STUDIES

In our review of the literature we have found three studies that examine the pre- and the post-instruction behavior of students receiving psychotherapy instruction. All three studies measure the verbal behavior of the student-therapist but in different ways. Analysis of verbal content is not the only way to deal with verbal activity, as will be seen below.

Blocksma and Porter

In 1946, a course for V. A. "Personal Counselors" was planned by the staff of the University of Chicago Counseling Center. The course lasted for six weeks and Blocksma and Porter (1947) measured some differences in counselor interview behavior, before and after instruction. This was the first objective research on attitudes and behaviors of counselors' pre- and post-training. There were approximately 100 counselors who were trained in seven groups, each consisting of from 10 to 25 members. Just as psy-

choanalytic training programs have used some of their own psychotherapeutic methods in producing changed behavior in their students, the client-
centered staff attempted to inculcate the client-centered viewpoint by
implicit demonstration of its principles in a *learner-centered* climate.

The course consisted of: (1) daily lectures, the topics influenced greatly
by the interests of the learners; (2) daily group and sub-group discussions
which were, in part, group therapy; (3) first-hand experience with counseling, and discussion of recorded sessions; (4) analyses of recorded and
transcribed interviews which had been conducted by trained staff members and therapists of differing orientations; (5) opportunity for personal
therapy; and (6) concentrated, intimate, informal association among the
participants. The members were together for a minimum of eight hours
per day, and often continued informal "bull" sessions well into the evening.

Thirty-seven of the counselors were studied in order to measure: "(1)
the extent to which client-centered procedures were learned, and (2) the
extent to which these learnings were related to later success on the job."
The pre- and post-measures consisted of a paper and pencil test (Porter,
1950) and two live interviews in which the same two staff members took
the role of the same, specific patient, playing the role as consistently as
possible with each student. The paper and pencil test required a trainee
to select a response to given client statements. In every case the student
selected from five different response classes assumed to communicate
different intentions of the counselor: moralization or evaluation; diagnosis
or formulation; interpretation or explanation; support or encouragement;
and reflection or understanding.

There was very little relationship between what, on the paper and pencil test, the students *said* they would do and what they *actually* did in the
interview. For example, during the pre-training evaluation they used 89
percent reflection in the written test but only 11 percent reflection in the
interview. However, marked changes took place in the students' interview
behavior over the six weeks of training. In their pre-training interviews,
the students' comments were 84 percent directive and 11 percent non-
directive, whereas in the post-training interview their responses were 30
percent directive and 59 percent nondirective. The authors also found that
in pre-test 60 percent of the responses suggested that the student was
thinking *about* the client and evaluating him, whereas in post-test 61 percent of the responses indicated that the student was thinking *with* the
client and allowing him to evaluate himself.

The paper and pencil test did not predict later job success as a counselor. However, the use of client-centered techniques in the post-training
interviews, and especially the tendency to think *with* rather than *about*
the client, were significantly related to high supervisor ratings at the end
of the counselor's first year of employment. Such a counselor was likely to
hold his counseling cases, rather than having early terminations.

Palmer, Fosmire, Breger, Straughan, and Patterson

The above authors (1963) have described a pilot project in which two training procedures were compared. Their basic assumption was that imitation is a major aspect of the learning process in psychotherapy training. Their exploratory study compared the relative effectiveness of conventional personal supervision with teaching based on therapy tape recordings plus certain supplementary materials. Learning, under both control and experimental conditions, was estimated by comparing each student's pre- and post-training interview behavior with that of his supervisor and noting to what extent he became more like or unlike his supervisor. The training material consisted of tape recordings of four consecutive interviews in which the students' supervisor was conducting psychotherapy. The supervisor wrote a critical commentary on each of his own responses. The tape was spliced so that the student could listen to the patient's comment and then, during the pause that followed, dictate the response he thought he would make as therapist. As the recording continued, he could listen to the therapist's (supervisor's) response, and finally, read the supervisor's discussion of the interaction. Pairs of students, matched for experience, reading, and attitudes in regard to psychotherapy, were assigned to each of four supervisors. One member of the pair received only personal supervision, and the other member received only tape-and-commentary training. All patients were temporarily transferred from the supervisors to the students for a series of four therapy sessions. Both groups of students spent about equal amounts of time in therapy sessions plus personal supervision or study of tape and commentary. They were assessed, before and after the training experience, with ten criterion measures including: ". . . a number of Snyder's coding categories . . . Harway's depth of interpretation scale . . . a questionnaire designed to measure one's theoretical rationale for therapy, a set of 'self' ratings (self as therapist, ideal therapist, and effective therapist), ratings of appropriateness of response, and a number of objective measures of verbal activity." The authors concluded that the experimental students, trained with tape and commentary, changed their responses to be more like their supervisors than did the control students who were given individual supervision. There was noticeable variability among the supervisors as to "their relative effectiveness in training by the two procedures," e.g., one supervisor was equally effective with either method.

R. G. Matarazzo, Phillips, Wiens, and Saslow

R. G. Matarazzo, Phillips, Wiens, and Saslow (1965) reported on the first of three groups of sophomore medical students who had elected to take summer clerkships in psychiatry in 1960, 1961, and 1962. None had had any previous interviewing experience: all had taken a two-term (six-month) psychiatry course which included lectures, discussion of general interviewing principles, and interview demonstrations with written exercises on the students' interview observations. The first aim of the study was to define certain dimensions of the students' initial interviewing behavior before an intensive eight-weeks' experience and instruction in psychotherapy. The second aim was to measure the amount and direction of change, post-instruction.

In 1960 there were six students who were observed while interviewing the same six patients in counterbalanced order. The patients had been treated previously on the inpatient psychiatric service, were now no longer hospitalized, were considered by two staff members unlikely to change during the course of the summer, and had agreed to take part in the study. They were also selected for variation in verbal fluency, sex, and type of emotional problem. The students were not given any prior information about the patients, but received the written instructions: "You are to conduct an interview with the patient, lasting about 35 minutes, in which you should try to get to know the patient and understand his (her) present problem. Do not conduct a systems review or medical questionnaire, but concentrate largely on the patient's emotional or behavioral problems." The post-instruction interviews, after eight weeks of instruction and experience, were conducted in the same manner with the same patients. The students had no contact with these patients other than in the two experimental series of interviews.

Following his first six experimental interviews each student was assigned two new psychiatric inpatients for intensive psychotherapy: he attended group therapy and all of the administrative and therapeutic conferences of the psychiatric ward which is maintained as a "therapeutic community" (Saslow and Matarazzo, J. D., 1962). Two psychiatrists each supervised three students, meeting them two times a week. Each student reported to his supervising psychiatrist on his psychotherapy interviews, and was given suggestions for the tactics and strategy of therapy. Readings in Rogers (1942), Wolberg (1954), and other texts were suggested to the students. The supervisors were requested not to observe student interviews during the course of the summer and were not acquainted with the ratings being made. Neither were the students given any feedback by the research observers (RGM, JSP) who continued to observe their assigned psychotherapy patients twice a week over the course of eight weeks.

"Error" Scale Measurements

A checklist of potential interviewer *errors* (shown in Table 1) was developed and required, first, a rating of the general quality of each therapist statement as "Good," "Fair," or "Poor." If the quality rating was either "Fair" or "Poor," the rater checked as many of the specific errors as were embodied in the statement. The list of thirty potential errors was drawn

Table 1
Check List of Therapist "Error" Behavior

General Quality of Statement (Check one for each therapist verbal unit.)
Good statement or question—no error
Fair statement—comment generally appropriate but partly
   ineffectual, embodying at least one error listed below
Poor statement—comment expected to produce serious
      block to communication or distortion of relationship

(Check as many as are applicable for each therapist verbal unit.)

I. *Errors of Focus*
   Narrow focus or focus on irrelevant material
   Focus on symptoms in non-productive manner
   Neglects to label or explore important content
   Allows sidetrack
   Changes topic abruptly
   Stops exploration
   Inaccurate reflection or question indicating lack of
      understanding of what patient has said
   Fails to structure sufficiently—patient rambles
   Non-contributory statement or question

II. *Faulty Role Definition*—authoritarian or social
   Argues—is authoritarian or dogmatic
   Criticizes, belittles patient—condescending
   Cross-examines patient
   Participates in criticism of another professional person
   Gives information or advice inappropriately
   Makes personal reference or gives opinion inap-
      propriately
   Gives reassurance or agreement where inappropriate
   Flatters patient
   Laughter when inappropriate

III. *Faulty Facilitation of Communication*
   Guesses facts (asking yes or no)
   Asks yes, no, or brief answer question
   Interrupts
   Interrupts silence too soon
   Allows silence too long
   Awkwardness—awkward pause, abrupt, makes long
      speech, structures too much

IV. *Other Errors*
   Irrelevant or unprofessional statement
   Asks patient own interpretation or question to which
      he could not be expected to know the answer

largely from books by Rogers (1942) and Wolberg (1954) with the addition of other errors which had been noted empirically as errors the students committed and for which no prior descriptive term had been found. The errors could be grouped into three broad types: (I) Errors of Focus; (II) Faulty Role Definition—Authoritarian or Social; (III) Faulty Facilitation of Communication. The two residual errors which seemed not to fit exclusively into any of these categories were classified as (IV) Other Errors. Errors of Focus involved unprofitable questions about physical symptoms, grossly inadequate reflections, questions obviously irrelevant in the ongoing context, etc. Faulty Role Definition included, for example, the interviewer's giving the patient direct advice, or telling the patient about himself (the student). Faulty Facilitation of Communication included *yes-no* type questions, interruptions, failure to respond within a reasonable time when a response was clearly indicated, etc. Two observers, who rated errors in these major categories, obtained agreement ranging from 84 to 93 percent.[2] The frequency of individual errors was small so that only the major categories were analyzed for reliability and for measurement of change in student behavior.

Table 2
Mean Number of Errors of Each Student in Interview Series 1 and 2

Student	C	J	P	R	V	Y	M	Sigma
Series 1	56	80	30	52	65	54	56.2	27.9
Series 2	28	36	20	16	35	19	25.6	15.2
						F-test	4.53	
						p	.01	
						r	.54	
						p	.01	

Table 2 shows the total number of errors made by each student in Interview Series 1, before instruction (mean of 56.2 errors) and the marked decrease in Series 2, after instruction (mean of 25.6 errors): this difference is significant at the .01 level of confidence. While the students varied greatly among themselves in their initial skill (sigma of 27.9 errors), they are more homogeneous in their error behavior at the end of the training period (sigma of 15.2 errors). As shown in Table 2, they tended to retain their relative position in regard to total number of errors per student, with an r of .54 for total number of errors made by each student in Series 1 and Series 2. Although the students as a group had altered their error behavior in a direction desired by the instructional staff, individual differences among them persisted.

[2] The authors wish to express appreciation to Dr. F. H. Kanfer for making the reliability ratings on the checklist.

Table 3
Number of Therapist Errors Elicited by Each Patient

	Ba	Hu	Ma	Ro	Sch	F-test	p
			Patients				
Series 1							
Mean	41.2	45.5	85.3	47.5	61.7	4.74	.01
Sigma	26.6	17.8	37.2	18.4	16.1		
Series 2							
Mean	27.7	11.7	31.2	22.8	34.5	2.99	.05
Sigma	13.5	7.5	20.1	15.2	10.5		

Table 3 shows that the student therapists tended to make more errors with certain patients than with others ($F = 4.74$, p of .01 for Series 1; and $F = 2.99$, p of .05 for Series 2). This tendency is consistent with suggestions in the literature that the patient influences therapist behavior (Heller *et al.*, 1963).

The five most common student therapist errors were: interruptions; asking yes-no or brief-answer questions; focusing on material that was irrelevant to the patient's current emotional or behavioral problems; and awkwardness, consisting of long speeches, abruptness, unusually long silences which seemed unrelated to their antecedents or consequents. In Series 1, errors were predominantly in the Facilitation of Communication category, whereas in Series 2 they were mainly Errors of Focus. By Series 2, then, the students had learned a few simple rules about what *not* to do (interrupt, ask yes-no type questions, focus on medical symptoms), but they had substituted *some* other poor behaviors (guessing facts and asking yes-no questions about these), and still did not know what to *do* in responding sensitively to significant cues (ineffective focusing).

Interaction Chronograph Measurements

Other aspects of the students' interview behavior were measured by the Chapple Interaction Chronograph (J. D. Matarazzo, Saslow, and R. G. Matarazzo, 1956). Of the several temporal measures of interviewer-interviewee interaction which can be recorded, those analyzed in this study were the frequency and duration of single units of interviewer and interviewee speech and their silence behavior (latency).

One criterion of good interviewing technique is the facilitation of patient verbalization. Therefore, *good* interviewer statements might be expected to result in longer patient utterances, generally, than those given a lower quality rating. With numerous interviewer *errors* the patient might be expected to have numerous, short, relatively non-self-exploratory statements and to use less of the total interview time. To study the association between interviewer errors and patients' verbal behavior, the ten interviews with the greatest number of interviewer errors were compared with the ten in which number of interviewer errors was smallest. With six student-interviewers and five patient-interviewees there was a total N of 30 interviews for *each* of the two interview series (30 different student-patient pairs).

In Series 1, the mean number of interviewer errors was 87 for the ten interviews in which they were maximal; this contrasted with a mean of 29 errors ($t = 7.25$, p of .001) for the ten interviews in which interviewer errors were minimal. In the ten *maximal error* interviews, the patients spoke with an average speech duration of 24 seconds compared with an average speech duration of 42 seconds ($t = 2.68$, p of .02) when interviewer errors were minimal. In Series 2 (after instruction) the mean number of errors for the ten *maximal error* interviews was 44, and for the ten interviews with the fewest errors the mean was 9 ($t = 10.96$, p of .001). When interviewer errors were maximal the patients spoke with a mean speech duration of 20 seconds and with minimal interviewer errors the associated interviewee mean speech duration was 43 seconds ($t = 2.43$, p of .05). In addition, a correlational analysis of the relationship between the total number of interviewer errors in all interviews and the mean speech duration of the interviewees in all interviews resulted in a product-moment correlation of $-.53$ (p of .01) for Series I, and $-.47$ (p of .01) for Series 2. When the correlational analyses were done separately for each interviewer and his five interviews, the correlation was significant in each instance and was replicated in the second series.

The students were given uniform, written instructions that the interviews should last for 35 minutes. Although the length of all the interviews approximated this (range 24 to 38 minutes), in Series 1 the interviews tended to be shorter when the patient talked a relatively small percent of the time and the student therefore "had to" talk a relatively large percent of the time. Thus, there was a significant positive association ($r = .43$, p of .05) between the length of the interview session and the percentage of time that the patient talked, and a significant negative association ($r = -.43$, p of .05) between the length of the interview and the percentage of student talk-time. This pair of correlations was not replicated in Series 2, and one could speculate that by the second series of interviews the students were sufficiently comfortable during the interviewing either to be more precisely aware of the actual duration of elapsed time or to be able to plan flexibly during the interviews so as to continue them for the prescribed length of time.

In Table 4 it can be seen that the students spoke an average of only 5.8 minutes out of the average total interview length of 31 minutes in Series 1. This was a 19 percent talk-time as opposed to 81 percent talk-time for the patients (not shown in the table). In Series 2 the students obtained an average speaking time of 3.3 minutes, taking up 13 percent of the talk-

Table 4
Mean Values, Correlations and t-ratios of some Interview Variables in 30 Replicated Interviews of Six Interviewers and Five Patients

	Students					
	Series *1*	Series *2*	*r*	*p*	*t*	*p*
Total duration of speech (minutes)	5.8	3.3	.28		6.68	.001
Sigma	1.4	1.5				
Percent talk-time	18.7	13.0	.34	.06	3.77	.001
Sigma	5.2	6.3				
Number of speech units	94.7	50.6	.36	.05	6.23	.001
Sigma	33.8	19.0				
Single speech unit duration (seconds)	4.1	4.3	.38	.05	.33	
Sigma	1.7	2.5				
Single speech latency duration (seconds)	1.4	3.0	.34		5.20	.001
Sigma	.9	1.4				
Number of interruptions	25.2	5.0	.00		8.38	.001
Sigma	11.8	5.5				
Percent of speech units that are interruptions	27.5	9.7	−.28		6.30	.001
Sigma	13.0	8.4				
Total number interviewer errors	56.2	25.6	.54	.01	5.28	.001
Sigma	27.9	15.2				

time, as opposed to the patients' 87 percent (not shown in the table). The decrease in student percentage talk-time was significant, as was the increase in patient percentage talk-time ($t = 3.77$, p of .001). J. D. Matarazzo, Wiens, and Saslow (1965) found an interviewee-interviewer mean single speech duration ratio of roughly 5 or 6 to 1 in a number of studies. In Series 1 the patients' total speech duration was 4.4 times that of the students', and in Series 2 this ratio was 6.9 to 1. Thus, the students approximated this aspect of the experienced interviewer's role on both occasions, although they appeared to be more skillful in facilitating patient talk in Series 2. This would be consistent with the finding of decreased student errors in Series 2, and the previously demonstrated relationship between this and the increased duration of patient utterances. It may be also that the students were less *wasteful* in their speech

in Series 2, and that less surplus rather than more provocative speech
was the case. When one looks at the decrease in the number of speech
units for the students in Series 2 from Series 1 (95 to 51), it might be
suggested that the students have less surplus speech in Series 2. Certainly, the fact that the number of their speech units approximated that
of the patients would suggest a more regular alternation in speech behavior. The mean number of patients' speech units in Series 1 was 58; in
Series 2 it was 58. The students, however, changed a great deal. They
interrupted less, had a more regular alternation, and made fewer irrelevant comments.

The students spoke only about half as much in Series 2 as they had in
Series 1, and did not maintain their rank order within the group (r of .28,
p n.s.). This would not have been predicted, since J. D. Matarazzo,
Saslow, Wiens, Weitman, and Allen (1964) have shown that individuals
do tend to retain their relative status on such interview variables when
in groups that are being subjected to various experimental conditions,
even though the group mean may be considerably changed. Furthermore,
earlier studies have demonstrated that an individual's temporal speech
interaction characteristics are very reliable (Saslow and J. D. Matarazzo,
1959). It appears that, in our present study, the training experiences and
supervision affected the students *differentially* in regard to speech duration *in their role as interviewers*. Indeed, the instructors presumably
hoped that those who spoke a great deal initially might decrease their
activity, and that those who spoke very little might increase their activity
in this role.

While the mean duration of speech units was not changed from
Series 1 to Series 2[3], the latency in student speech was significantly
lengthened. Presumably, after training the student could allow himself a
longer time interval to formulate a response or comment, or to allow the
patient some opportunity to initiate another comment. The latency value
reported here is a combined measure of two types of latency: (1) the
passage of time from the point at which one participant terminates his
speech until the other person begins, i.e., reaction-time latency; and (2)
the type of silence duration that occurs when the second person (often
the interviewer) does not respond following the termination of the first
person's (interviewee's speech), i.e., initiative-time latency between two

[3] In their first and second year courses in psychology and psychiatry at this school
the students are exposed repeatedly to the idea, through research presentation, lecture
material, and interview demonstration, that an interviewer can say a great deal in
about five seconds. This may account for the short mean duration of speech units
with which the students both began and ended the interview training. However, it is
of interest to note that, when we chronographed the interview by the student interviewer from the phonographic recording presented by Gill, Newman, and Redlich
(1954), we discovered that average speech duration of this student was three seconds, not too dissimilar from the mean speech duration of our students.

utterances by the same person. Therapists often may remain silent in order to permit the interviewee to speak again.

Goldman-Eisler (1952) investigated differences among psychiatrist interviewers and demonstrated that each had his own individual inter-action pattern. However, this pattern could be adjusted somewhat to the type of patient (within the limits of each interviewer's own pattern). Thus, different patients could elicit somewhat different patterns of inter-viewer behavior. To what extent would differences in various character-istics of student interviews be determined by the patients and by the student-interviewers? To answer this question we did an analysis of variance on such interview characteristics as total speech duration, per-centage talk-time, number of speech units, mean speech duration, mean speech latency, number of interruptions, percentage of speech units that were interruptions, and total number of interviewer errors.

Table 5
Sources of Variability in Student and Patient Interview Behavior

Patient Interview Behavior

	Series 1				Series 2			
	Patients		Students		Patients		Students	
	F	p	F	p	F	p	F	p
Total speech duration	4.36	.05	4.67	.01	20.48	.001	5.53	.01
Percent talk-time	5.75	.01	2.25		19.90	.001	11.01	.001
Number of speech units	27.47	.001	1.10		18.51	.001	2.61	
Mean speech duration	8.06	.001	1.02		12.53	.001	.84	
Mean speech latency	14.75	.001	.80		241.01	.001	1.16	
Number of interruptions	5.70	.01	1.64		.85		1.35	
Percent of speech units that are interruptions	1.78		3.73	.05	.33		1.19	

Student Interview Behavior

	Series 1				Series 2			
	Patients		Students		Patients		Students	
	F	p	F	p	F	p	F	p
Total speech duration	6.47	.01	2.00		10.47	.001	15.14	.001
Percent talk-time	5.76	.01	2.25		19.90	.001	11.01	.001
Number of speech units	3.16	.05	1.95		3.69	.05	7.31	.001
Mean speech duration	.38		2.62		2.36		12.14	.001
Mean speech latency	2.71		.95		5.81	.01	3.62	.05
Number of interruptions	2.81		1.64		.06		1.47	
Percent of speech units that are interruptions	.59		2.31		.15		.53	
Total interviewing errors	4.74	.01	3.33	.05	2.99	.05	2.20	

It appears (Table 5) that, on most patient variables, the patients be-have "like themselves" regardless of which student is interviewing them. That is, a patient who tends to speak in long utterances, takes up a large proportion of the talk-time, interrupts frequently, and maintains his status relative to the rest of the patients while interacting with each of the student interviewees. The students did, however, have some influence upon the patients' total speech duration and tendency to interrupt. The patients as a group talked more and interrupted more with some interviewers than with others. It appears, then, that the patients presented quite different stimulus values to the interviewers and that patient behavior was affected relatively little by differences among the students.

Looking at the *student* interview behavior in Series 1, the students did not exhibit consistent differences among themselves at all, although the patients apparently elicited different behaviors from them in regard to total speech duration, percentage talk-time and number of speech units (i.e., how often and how long the student spoke and how much of the total interview time he used was determined largely by the patient). Again, one might guess that each student had not yet established his own stable interviewing style, and thus that his individual behavior from interview to interview was as variable as were the behaviors among the students as a group. In Series 2 this is no longer the case, with differences among students being significant at the .001 level in regard to total speech duration, percentage of talk-time, number of speech units, and mean speech duration. The students were also significantly different from one another in their mean speech latency. While the patients contribute significantly to the variance in the students' total speech duration, percentage of talk-time, number of speech units (as they did in Series 1), and mean speech latency in Series 2, it appears that the students have established a more stable, somewhat individual (different from each other) style for themselves as interviewers.

Our analysis of the variance of the temporal factors, as shown in Table 5, thus suggests in general that differences among the *patients* were largely responsible for differences in their interview behaviors with the student interviewers, and that differences in the students' interview behavior imposed minimally on the patients either in Series 1 or Series 2. The patients also contributed significantly to some of the *students'* interview behavior in both Series 1 and 2; however, while in Series 1 student variability was generally random, in the Series 2 interviews the students were more consistent in their behavior and different from each other.

An experienced psychiatrist interviewed the same five patients on two occasions, just prior to the students' Series 1 and 2. This same psychiatrist also interviewed the student therapists prior to Series 1 and subsequent to Series 2. It was possible, then, to compare some interview interaction characteristics of these patients when being interviewed by student-therapists and by an experienced psychiatrist; to compare the interviewer behavior of student-therapists and that of an experienced psychiatrist when interviewing the same patients; and to examine and contrast the interview behavior of the student therapists when serving as interviewers of patients and when serving as interviewees. The psychiatrist followed with both the students and the patients a partially standardized interviewing plan; this procedure has been described by J. D. Matarazzo, Saslow, and R. G. Matarazzo (1956). Some of the data obtained from these comparisons are shown in the tables which follow.

Table 6
Mean Values of some Interview Variables when Six Students* and an Experienced Psychiatrist** are Interviewing Five Patients

| | | | Patient Means | | |
Interviewer	Series	Percent Talk-time	Single Speech Unit Duration (Seconds)	Single Speech Latency Duration (Seconds)	% Speech Units that are Interruptions
Student Y	1	78	24.2	1.7	41
	2	84	35.0	3.6	13
Student P	1	79	36.7	2.8	37
	2	91	28.8	4.0	3
Student R	1	79	26.9	2.7	21
	2	88	20.1	3.8	10
Student C	1	84	37.3	2.7	21
	2	86	28.1	3.4	11
Student V	1	80	36.1	1.9	46
	2	81	30.9	3.9	27
Student J	1	85	35.1	2.0	29
	2	92	33.3	3.3	9
Psychiatrist	1	87	30.1	2.2	26
	2	86	25.2	1.7	25
6 Students	1	81	32.7	2.3	32.5
Total Mean	2	87	29.4	3.7	12.2

° Free-style interviewing
°° Partially standardized interviewing technique

Patients' Behavior when Interviewed by a Psychiatrist

Table 6 presents the mean values of some interview variables for the five patients when interviewed by the psychiatrist just before Series 1; by the six student-therapists before instruction; and again by all of these interviewers after the students had completed their eight weeks of instruction (Series 2). It may be noted that the mean percentage talk-time, speech duration, speech latency, and percentage interruptions for the patients when interviewed by the experienced psychiatrist with a partially standardized procedure are all within the range of their means with the student-therapists in free-style interviews. Further, when the means of the patient variables are averaged for the six students, they approximate closely the mean patient behaviors with the psychiatrist. In their percentage of talk-time and mean speech duration the patients' values are very similar for student and psychiatrist interviewers. Patients' mean speech latency and percentage of interruptions are more difficult to compare inasmuch as the psychiatrist, utilizing the partially standardized interview, had to introduce both latencies and interruptions in a uniform fashion during the course of his interview.[4] A large part of the variance in all of the interviews was contributed by the patients as indicated by the fact that patient behavior is the same whether in a free-style or partially standardized interview.

Table 7

Mean Values of some Interview Variables when Six Students* and an Experienced Psychiatrist** are Interviewing Five Patients

Interviewer Means

Interviewer	Series	Percent Talk-time	Single Speech Unit Duration (Seconds)	Single Speech Latency Duration (Seconds)	% Speech Units that are Interruptions
Student Y	1	22	5.6	1.0	23
	2	16	5.5	3.0	6
Student P	1	21	3.7	1.3	24
	2	9	3.0	4.1	9
Student R	1	19	4.9	2.0	45
	2	12	3.2	3.5	8
Student C	1	16	3.4	1.7	23
	2	14	3.1	1.8	15
Student V	1	20	4.3	1.3	27
	2	19	8.2	2.4	12
Student J	1	15	2.6	1.2	23
	2	8	2.6	3.0	9
Psychiatrist	1	13	4.1	.7	.4
	2	14	4.3	.3	2.4
6 Students	1	18.8	4.1	1.4	27.5
Total Mean	2	13.0	4.3	3.0	9.8

* Free-style interviewing
** Partially standardized interviewing technique

Interviewer Behavior of Students and Psychiatrist

Table 7 indicates that the percentage of talk-time of the student-interviewers and the psychiatrist was grossly similar; and even more so after the students' instruction period when their mean percentage of talk-time was 13 percent as compared with the psychiatrist's 14 percent. The mean duration of speech units was identical for the psychiatrist

[4] Although the psychiatrist used the partially standardized interview technique described in the reference (J. D. Matarazzo, Saslow, and R. G. Matarazzo, 1956), only Periods 1, 3, 5, the relatively free give-and-take periods of the interview, were analyzed for comparison with the students' free-style interview.

and the students, although the former was aiming for standardized speech units of 5 seconds' duration while the students were not constrained in this fashion. The psychiatrist, however, was much more consistent in his speech durations (sigma of .3 and .1 seconds) than the students (sigma 1.7 and 2.5 seconds). Speech latency and interruption behavior cannot be compared since the psychiatrist was supposed to do *no* interrupting and to respond within one second. The students *did* interrupt, even in Series 2, and their responses were not immediate. It is not known whether this would be the interruption and latency behavior of the psychiatrist with these patients were he not using the partially standardized interview. Wiens, Saslow, J. D. Matarazzo, and Allen (1963) report that this psychiatrist, in free-style interviews with his own psychotherapy patients, did interrupt.

Table 8
Mean Values of some Interview Variables when Six Students and Five Patients are Interviewed by an Experienced Psychiatrist**, and Comparison of Students as Interviewers* and Interviewees

Interviewees	Series	Percent Talk-time	Single Speech Unit Duration (Seconds)	Single Speech Latency Duration (Seconds)	% Speech Units that are Interruptions
5 Patients	1	86.6	30.1	2.1	26.4
	2	85.5	35.2	1.7	25.0
6 Students	1	82.4	22.7	1.5	20.7
	2	80.5	21.7	2.6	13.7
Comparison of Students as Interviewers and Interviewees					
6 Students (Interviewers)	1	18.7	4.1	1.4	27.5
	2	13.0	4.3	3.0	9.7
6 Students (Interviewees)	1	82.4	22.7	1.5	20.7
	2	80.5	21.7	2.6	13.7

* Free-style interviewing
** Partially standardized interviewing technique

Students' Behavior as Interviewees

It will be recalled that part of our experiment involved casting our students in the role of interviewees, with the experienced psychiatrist using the procedure of the partially standardized interview. The students were told that this was for the purpose of discussing their expectations of the summer's work with this senior faculty member. Since the patients were also interviewed by the technique of the partially standardized interview by the same psychiatrist, it was possible to compare the interviewee behavior of student and patient. Furthermore, student behavior as interviewee could be compared with student behavior as therapist. Table 8 shows some of these comparison data. In the role of interviewee the students' behavior was very different from their behavior in the role of interviewer. In Series 1, as *interviewers,* the students' mean percentage talk-time was 18.7 percent, their mean speech duration was 4.1 seconds, mean speech latency. 1.4 seconds and percentage of interruptions, 27.5 percent. As *interviewees* the students' mean performance was as follows: 82.4 percent talk-time, 22.7 seconds' duration of utterance, 1.5 seconds' latency, and 20.7 percent interruptions. As interviewees, the students' behavior is grossly similar to that of the patients as interviewees. In comparison with their behavior as interviewers, they took up a much larger percentage of interview time, spoke in considerably longer utterances, had a longer latency, and interrupted less. Thus, role definition was an important determinant of some aspects of their verbal behavior.

Replication of the "Error" Scale Measurements

The study described above was repeated, in part, during the two ensuing summers with the 1961 and 1962 groups of sophomore medical students. No interaction chronograph measures were made, but the students were evaluated on the *error* rating scale pre- and post-instruction (R. G. Matarazzo, 1963).

In June of 1961, the four sophomore medical students interviewed four selected patients, in counterbalanced order, and the procedure was repeated in late August.

Figure 1 shows, for this 1961 group, the percentage of utterances which were rated by the judge-observer as "Good," "Fair," or "Poor" at the beginning of the summer, prior to any experience or instruction, and the percentage so rated after eight weeks of intensive experience and instruction. The arrow in the figure shows the point at which instruction in interviewing began. (The 1960 group was not rated initially on "Good-Fair-Poor" so no comparable prior ratings are available). In 1961 "Good" statements increased by 73 percent (from 30 percent to 50 percent of the total number of utterances); "Fair" statements decreased by 13 percent (from 50 percent to 43 percent); and "Poor" statements decreased by 71 percent (from 21 percent to 6 percent).

Figure 2 presents similar data for the 1962 group of sophomore medical students. There were five students who interviewed the same two patients in mid-May, one month prior to the beginning of instruction; in mid-June, at the start of instruction; in mid-July, after one month of instruction; and in mid-August, after two months of instruction. For each series of interviews the arrow marks the point at which instruction was begun. It can be seen for the 1962 group that, between interview Series 1 and 2, with no intervening interviews or instruction, there was a small

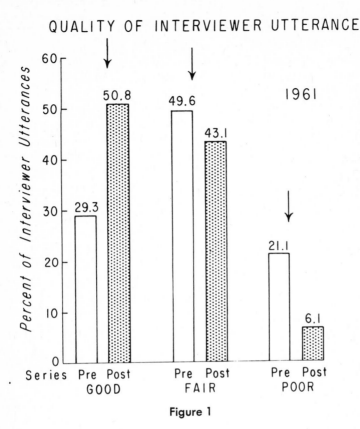

QUALITY OF INTERVIEWER UTTERANCE

1961

Figure 1

rise (from 19 to 24 percent) in "Good" statements; a small decrease in "Fair" statements (64 to 57 percent), but also a small rise (from 16 to 19 percent) in "Poor" statements. However, between interview Series 2 and 3, during which time there was one month of intensive instruction and experience, there was a considerably greater (68 percent) increase in the percentage of statements which were rated "Good" (from 24 to 40 percent), and a sizeable (42 percent) decrease in "Poor" statements (from 19 to 11 percent), as well as a continuation of the decreasing (15 percent) trend for "Fair" statements (from 57 to 49 percent). It appears that following their test interviews during the 1962 experience, the students improved somewhat in their interview behavior with no intervening instruction, perhaps on the basis of lessened anxiety; perhaps on the basis of having "taken stock" of their technique, studied their class notes and general reading with more thought to putting this knowledge to specific use, etc. Their comments late in the summer suggest that at least some of the latter took place. However, the beginning of specific instruction

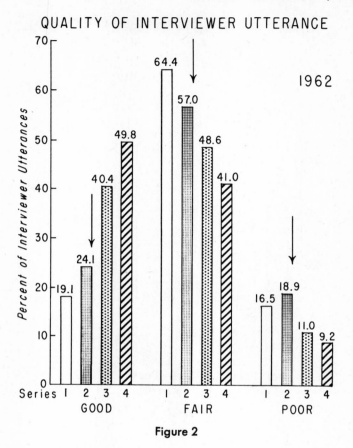

Figure 2

produced a much greater change (between Series 2 and 3); and it would appear that the period of greatest improvement in *interview method* occurred during the first month of instruction. Improvement continued at a somewhat slower rate during the second month due, in part, to the *kind* of scale items used (i.e., there was no attempt to rate the students on more subtle or complex skills such as therapeutic plan or understanding of patient dynamics).

To return again to the 1961 data, Figure 3 shows the changes in specific *types* of errors for the four 1961 students, pre- and post-instruction. The type of error which was most prevalent in the 1960 group of beginning interviewers was *Faulty Facilitation of Communication* (Series 1, 52 percent). In the 1961 group this occurred in 54 percent of the Series 1 utterances (yes-no type questions, awkwardness, abruptness, structuring too much, etc.). Thus the student initially tended to stand in his own way or prevented the patient from telling his story. The greatest amount of

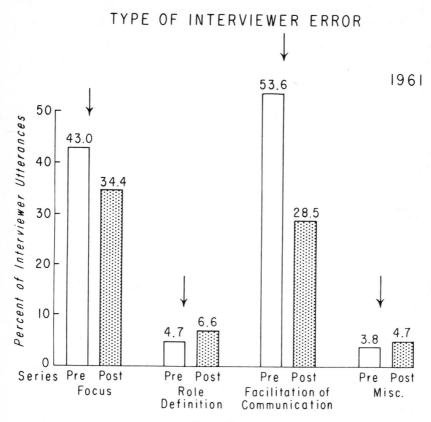

Figure 3

improvement (decrease of 47 percent) also took place in this area, from 54 percent (Series 1) to 28 percent (Series 2) in the 1961 group (and from 52 to 26 percent in the 1960 group). Moderate improvement also took place in the category *Errors of Focus* (or failure to focus on material of probable importance), which showed a 20 percent decrease, from 43 percent to 34 percent. However, errors in the category *Faulty Role Definition,* while small, appeared not to change (i.e., the occasional student who tended to be authoritarian or dogmatic remained so; and the one who made the interview a social rather than professional relationship had similar difficulty in altering his role). The number of *Miscellaneous Errors* did not change either. (Note that the percentages of errors for pre- and post-instruction do not add up to 100 percent because in the pre-instruction series, there was an average of slightly more than one error per utterance, whereas in the post-instruction series, there was less than an average of one error per utterance.)

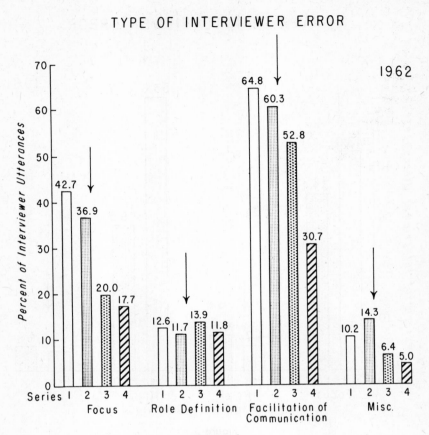

Figure 4

Among the 1962 group of students the same phenomena can be observed. That is, again the greatest source of initial error is in *Faulty Facilitation of Communication,* and it is also the area of greatest improvement. *Errors of Focus* are a smaller source of error (although possibly of equal importance). *Errors of Role Definition,* once present, seemed difficult to alter.

A few words should be said about the nature and intensity of the 1962 instructional experience. The students were given two therapy inpatients each, whom they interviewed for a minimum of two hours weekly. (Each student had many additional experiences such as group therapy, attendance at clinics, taking part in the therapeutic community activities, etc.) The supervisor observed the students through a one-way screen once a week with each therapy patient (who was not included in this research). In turn, each observed other students interviewing their respective therapy patients. Following the supervisor and student observation of two interviews by two different students, there was group discussion of interview technique. For ten weeks, approximately two hours per week were spent in such discussion. The supervisor of interview and therapy skills, however, did not know the nature of the ratings being made by the experimenters, as this supervisor was purposely kept uninformed of the research procedures. Thus, little contamination was possible.

Table 9
Mean Number of Errors Per Utterance

	Interview Series			
	1	2	3	4
1960	—	—	—	.99
1961	1.05	—	—	.74
1962	1.30	1.23	.95	.65

Table 9 (last column) permits some comparison of the three small student groups (1960, 1961, and 1962) with regard to the average number of errors per utterance. There is a trend toward progressive improvement in the number of errors over the three years. The table indicates that this cannot be accounted for by initial mean difference in number of errors. We know that we have been altering our methods of instruction over the years, and hypothesize that this may be responsible for the improvement in student performance.

There have been two major changes in instructional method over the years: (1) In 1960, the supervisor discussed the students' patients with them but was instructed not to observe any interviews. (2) The major change between 1960 and the two succeeding years was the use of supervisor observation of actual interviews. While in 1961 and 1962 the general instructional procedures were essentially the same, in 1962 there was increased use of group discussion, with the students observing and discussing each other's interview technique. This enabled each one to (a) analyze the interview technique of a student at the same experience level, and (b) obtain feedback regarding his own interviews from peers as well as from an instructor.

EPILOGUE

Clearly, research about the learning of psychotherapy is possible. Some of the difficulties in designing and executing investigations on the learning of psychotherapy are evident from the material presented in this chapter. They include the small size of experimental samples; the need for highly trained research clinicians to observe the learners for considerable periods of time; the unavoidable complexity of the independent variable, *instructional procedures;* the difficulty in selection and definition of appropriate variables for evaluation, etc. Nevertheless, current researches, such as those reported at the 1962 and 1963 Annual Conferences on Research in Medical Education of the Association of American Medical Colleges, demonstrate a rapidly increasing awareness of the necessity to increase our effort and sophistication in the design of experiments to assess the effectiveness of a wide variety of instructional procedures involving complex cognitive, affective, attitudinal, and behavioral functions. Presumably this sophistication will extend into the domain of instruction in psyschotherapy.

REFERENCES

ADAMS, W. R. The psychiatrist in an ambulatory clerkship for comprehensive medical care in a new curriculum. *J. Med. Educ.*, 33: 211-220, 1958.

ALDRICH, C. K., and BERNHARDT, H. Evaluation of a change in teaching psychiatry to medical students. *Am. J. Orthopsychiat.*, 33: 105-114, 1963.

ARING, C. D. The medical curriculum and the teaching of psychiatry. *J. Assoc. Am. Med. Coll.*, Sept. 3-8, 1949.

BALINT, M. Method and technique in the teaching of medical psychology. II. Training general practitioners in psychotherapy. *British J. Med. Psychol.*, 27: 37-41, 1954.

BLOCKSMA, D. D., and PORTER, E. H., JR. A short-term training program in client-centered counseling. *J. consult. Psychol.*, 11: 55-60, 1947.

BRUGGER, T., CAESAR, G., FRANK, A., and MARTY, S. Peer supervision as a method of learning psychotherapy. *Comprehensive Psychiat.*, 3: 47-53, 1962.

COLEMAN, J. V. The teaching of basic psychotherapy. *Am. J. Orthopsychiat.*, 17: 622-627, 1947.

COVNER, B. J. Studies in phonographic recordings of verbal material: III. The completeness and accuracy of counseling interview reports. *J. gen. Psychol.*, 30: 181-203, 1944.

COVNER, B. J. Studies in phonographic recordings of verbal material: IV. Written reports of interviews. *J. appl. Psychol.*, 28: 89-98, 1944.

DUGAN, W. E. Coached client: a technique for supervised counseling practicum. Personal communication, 1963.

EKSTEIN, R., and WALLERSTEIN, R. S. *The teaching and learning of psychotherapy.* New York: Basic Books, 1958.

ENELOW, A. J., ADLER, LETA M., and MANNING, P. R. A supervised psychotherapy course for practicing physicians. Paper read at Assn. Am. Med. Coll., Chicago, October, 1963. (Abstract)

ENELOW, A. J., FORDE, D. L., and GWARTNEY, R. H. Psychosomatic medicine: an avenue for the psychiatric education of medical practitioners. *Dis. nerv. System*, 23: 1-3, 1962.

ENGEL, G. L., GREEN, W. L., JR., REICHSMAN, F., SCHMALE, A., and ASHENBURG, N. A graduate and undergraduate teaching program on the psychological aspects of medicine: A report of the liaison program between medicine and psychiatry at the University of Rochester School of Medicine. *J. Med. Educ.*, **32**: 859-871, 1957.

FLEMING, JOAN. The role of supervision in psychiatric training. *Bull. Menninger Clin.*, **17**: 157-169, 1953.

FLEMING, JOAN, and HAMBURG, D. A. An analysis of methods for teaching psychotherapy with description of a new approach. *A. M. A. Arch. Neurol. Psychiat.*, **79**: 179-200, 1958.

GILL, M., NEWMAN, R., and REDLICH, F. C. *The initial interview in psychiatric practice.* New York: International Universities, 1954.

GOLDMAN-EISLER, FRIEDA. A study of individual differences and of interaction in the behavior of some aspects of language in interviews. *J. ment. Sci.* **100**: 177-197, 1952.

Group for the Advancement of Psychiatry: Committee on Medical Education. *Report on medical education.* No. 3, 1948. Pp. 1-12.

GUZE, S. B., MATARAZZO, J. D., and SASLOW, G. A formulation of principles of comprehensive medicine with special reference to learning theory. *J. Clin. Psychol.* **9**: 127-136, 1953.

HEINE, R. W., ALDRICH, C. K., DRAPER, E., MEUSER, MARY, TIPPETT, JEAN, and TROSMAN, H. *The student physician as psychotherapist.* Chicago: Univ. of Chicago Press, 1962.

HELLER, K. Interpersonal style in an interview analogue. Paper read at Am. Psychol. Ass., Philadelphia, August, 1963.

HELLER, K., MYERS, R. A., and KLINE, LINDA V. Interviewer behavior as a function of standardized client roles. *J. consult. Psychol.*, **2**: 117-122, 1963.

HOLT, R. R., and LUBORSKY, L. *Personality patterns of psychiatrists.* New York: Basic Books, 1958.

JONES, E. E., and THIBAUT, J. W. Interaction goals as bases of inference in interpersonal perception. In R. Tagiuri and L. Petrullo (Eds.), *Person perception and interpersonal behavior.* Stanford, Calif.: Stanford University Press, 1958.

KELLY, L., and GOLDBERG, L. R. Correlates of later performance and specialization in psychology. *Psychol. Monogr.*, **73** (Whole No. 482), 1959.

KORNER, I. N., and BROWN, W. H. The mechanical third ear. *J. consult. Psychol.*, **16**: 81-84, 1952.

KRASNER, L. The therapist as a social reinforcer: man or machine. Paper read at Am. Psychol. Ass., Philadelphia, Aug., 1963.

LESTER, B. K., GUSSEN, J., YAMAMOTO, J., and WEST, L. J. Teaching psychotherapy in a longitudinal curriculum. *J. Med. Educ.* **37**: 28-32, 1962.

LOTT, G. M. Multiple psychotherapy. *Psychiat. quart. Supplement, Part 2.* Utica, N.Y.: State Hospitals Press, 1957.

MATARAZZO, J. D., SASLOW, G., and MATARAZZO, RUTH G. The interaction chronograph as an instrument for objective measurement of interaction patterns during interviews. *J. Psychol.* **41**: 347-367, 1956.

MATARAZZO, J. D., SASLOW, G., WIENS, A. N., WEITMAN, M., and ALLEN, BERNADENE V. Interviewer head nodding and interviewee speech durations. *Psychotherapy: theory, research and practice,* **1**: 54-63, 1964.

MATARAZZO, J. D., WIENS, A. N., and SASLOW, G. Studies in Interview Speech Behavior. In L. Krasner and L. P. Ullman (Eds.), *Research in behavior modification: New developments and their clinical implications.* New York: Holt, Rinehart and Winston, 1965.

MATARAZZO, RUTH G. The process of acquiring skill in interviewing. Paper read at Western Psychol. Ass., Santa Monica, Apr., 1963.

MATARAZZO, RUTH G., PHILLIPS, JEANNE S., WIENS, A. N., and SASLOW, G. Learning the art of interviewing: A study of what beginning students do and their pattern of change. In *Psychotherapy: theory, research, and practice.* (In press).

McGUIRE, CHRISTINE, HURLEY, R. E., BABBOTT, D., and BUTTERWORTH, J. S. Auscultatory skill: gain and retention after intensive instruction. Paper read at Ass. Am. Med. Coll., Chicago, Oct., 1963. (Abstract)

PALMER, B., FOSMIRE, F. R., BREGER, L., STRAUGHAN, J. H., and PATTERSON, G. R. Quasi-programmed instruction in psychotherapy. *M H R I Res. Bull. (Ft. Steilacoom, Washington),* 7: 11-14, 1963.

PARLOFF, M. B. Some factors affecting the quality of therapeutic relationships. *J. abnorm. soc. Psychol.,* 52: 5-10, 1956.

PARLOFF, M. B. Therapist-patient relationships and outcome of psychotherapy. *J. consult. Psychol.,* 25: 29-38, 1961.

PFOUTS, JANE H., and RADER, G. E. Instruction in interviewing technique in the medical school curriculum: report of a trial program and some suggestions. *J. Med. Educ.,* 37: 681-686, 1962.

PORTER, E. H., JR. *An introduction to therapeutic counseling.* Boston: Houghton Mifflin, 1950.

REECE, M. M., and WHITMAN, R. N. Expressive movements, warmth, and verbal reinforcement. *J. abnorm. soc. Psychol.,* 64: 234-236, 1962.

ROGERS, C. R. *Counseling and psychotherapy.* Boston: Houghton Mifflin, 1942.

ROGERS, C. R. Training individuals to engage in the therapeutic process. In C. R. Strother (Ed.), *Psychology and mental health.* Washington, D. C.: American Psychological Association, 1957.

ROMANO, J. Basic orientation and education of the medical student. *J. Am. Med. Assoc.* 143: 409-412, 1950.

SASLOW, G., GOODRICH, D. W., and STEIN, M. Study of therapist behavior in diagnostic interviews by means of the interaction chronograph. *J. clin. Psychol.,* 12: 133-139, 1956.

SASLOW, G., and MATARAZZO, J. D. A technique for studying changes in interview behavior. In E. A. Rubinstein and M. B. Parloff (Eds.), *Research in psychotherapy,* Washington, D. C.: American Psychological Association, 1959.

SASLOW, G., and MATARAZZO, J. D. A psychiatric service in a general hospital: a setting for social learning. *Int. J. soc. Psychiat.,* 8: 5-18, 1962.

SCHWARTZ, E. K., and ABEL, THEODORA M. The professional education of the psychoanalytic psychotherapist. *Am. J. Psychother.,* 9: 253-261, 1955.

STRAUSS, B. V. Teaching psychotherapy to medical students. *J. Ass. Am. Med. Coll.,* July, 1950, pp. 1-6.

STRUPP, H. H. Patient-doctor relationships: Psychotherapist in the therapeutic process. In A. J. Bachrach (Ed.), *Experimental foundations of clinical psychology*. New York: Basic Books, 1962.

THOMPSON, CLARE W., and BRADWAY, KATHERINE. The teaching of psychotherapy through content-free interviews. *J. consult. Psychol.*, 14: 321-323, 1950.

WARD, C. H. An electronic aid for teaching interviewing techniques. *Arch. gen. Psychiat.*, 3: 357-358, 1960.

WARD, C. H. Electronic preceptoring in teaching beginning psychotherapy. *J. Med. Educ.*, 37: 1128-1129, 1962.

WERKMAN, S. L. Teaching the interpretive process to medical students. *Am. J. Psychiat.*, 117: 897-902, 1961.

WHITAKER, C. A. Teaching the practicing physician to do psychotherapy. *Southern Med. J.*, 42: 899-903, 1949.

WHITEHORN, J. C., and BETZ, BARBARA J. A study of psychotherapeutic relationships between physicians and schizophrenic patients. *Am. J. Psychiat.*, 111: 321-331, 1954.

WHITEHORN, J. C., JACOBSEN, C., LEVINE, M., and LIPPARD, V. W. (Eds.) *Psychiatry and medical education*. Report of the 1951 Conference on Psychiatric Education, Cornell University. Washington, D. C.: American Psychiatric Association, 1952.

WIENS, A. N., SASLOW, G., MATARAZZO, J. D., and ALLEN, BERNADENE V. Interruption behavior during interviews: a detailed analysis. Paper read at Western Psychol. Assoc., Santa Monica, Apr., 1963.

WOLBERG, L. R. *The technique of psychotherapy*. New York: Grune & Stratton, 1954.

Author Index

Abel, T. M., 607, 634
Abraham, K., 144
Acheson, G. H., 125
Adams, H. E., 299, 307
Adams, W. R., 602, 632
Adler, A., 130, 144
Adler, L. M., 605, 632
Adler, M., 166 n.
Aidman, T., 443
Aldrich, C. K., 603, 604, 632, 633
Alexander, F., 339, 358
Alexander, J. M., 226, 227, 228, 239
Alksne, H., 474
Allen, B. V., 620, 625, 633, 635
Altschul, S., 339, 346, 358
Ames, L. B., 568, 571
Anastasi, A., 530, 534
Anderson, R. P., 443
Apfelbaum, B., 577, 593
Appelbaum, A., 504, 513, 515
Apter, N., 58
Aring, C. D., 600, 632
Arnold, J., 134, 144
Artiss, K. L., 422
Ashby, J. D., 583, 593
Ashby, W. R., 266, 285
Ashenburg, N., 602, 632
Assum, A. L., 443
Auerbach, A., 3, 397, 399
Auld, F., Jr., 83, 85, 89, 92, 96, 124, 187, 210, 225, 362, 399, 583, 593
Ayllon, T., 302, 306, 307

Babbott, D., 597, 634
Bahnson, C. B., 403, 406, 408, 422
Bailey, M. B., 473, 474
Baker, G., 567, 571
Bales, R. F., 132, 144, 363, 399, 518, 521, 523, 526, 528, 583, 593
Balint, M., 605, 632
Balser, B. H., 568, 571
Bandura, A., 293, 307
Bar-Hillel, Y., 288
Barker, E. N., 583, 585, 594
Barker, R. G., 285, 287

Barnett, C. D., 306, 307
Barrabee, E. L., 476
Barrett, B. H., 306, 307
Barrett-Lennard, G. T., 434, 444
Barron, F., 517, 528, 532, 534, 544, 547, 549
Barry, J. R., 594
Bartlett, M. S., 381, 399
Basowitz, H., 126
Bateson, G., 65, 147, 152, 267 n., 282, 283, 285, 287
Bateson, M. C., 288
Bavelas, A., 287
Beck, A. T., 124
Beck, S. J., 532, 551, 554, 563, 565, 568, 572
Beecher, H., 96, 124
Bellak, L., 187, 196, 204, 207, 210, 215 n., 225, 289, 331, 365 ff., 399, 451, 452, 478, 479, 499
Benedict, R., 266, 285
Bently, A. F., 287
Berger, E. M., 444
Bergman, D. V., 429, 444
Bergman, P., xi, 35, 332
Berlo, D. K., 287
Bernard, C., 284, 285, 287
Bernhardt, H., 604, 632
Bernstein, L., 51 n., 161
Bertalanffy, L. V., 272, 285, 286
Betz, B. J., 517, 528, 543, 590, 591, 592, 593, 594, 611, 635
Bierer, J., 58
Bijou, S. W., 306, 307
Binder, H., 558, 571
Birdwhistell, R. L., 60, 74, 82, 263, 264, 267 n., 271 n., 285, 286, 287, 288, 551, 552, 571
Blake, K., 298, 307
Blenkner, M., 458, 473, 474
Bleuler, E., 552, 571
Blocksma, D. D., 597, 599, 604, 611, 632
Bloom, V., 92
Bloomberg, 299
Bloomfield, L., 89, 92, 287
Blos, P., 568, 571

Board, F. A., 126
Bock, P. B., 287
Bohn, E., 557 n., 559, 571
Bond, I. K., 302, 307
Bordin, E. S., 185, 187, 189, 192, 205, 207, 579, 594
Borgatta, E. F., 576, 593
Boronsen, H. W., 287
Boyd, R. W., 289
Bradway, K., 606, 635
Brady, J. V., 126
Breedlove, J. L., 451, 456
Breger, L., 291, 613, 634
Brekstad, A., 14
Bricklin, B., 535
Brierly, M., 239
Briggs, P. F., 545, 550
Brill, A. A., 192, 207
Brody, E. B., 58, 509, 515
Brosin, H., ix, 265, 267, 285
Brown, E. M., 154
Brown, W. H., 606, 633
Brugger, T., 607, 632
Buros, O. K., 540, 549
Butler, J. M., 190, 208, 285, 424, 435, 438, 439, 441, 444, 462, 471, 474, 475
Butler, J. R., 299, 307
Butterworth, J. S., 597, 634
Buxbaum, E., 337, 358

Caesar, G., 607, 632
Cain, A., 197 n.
Callahan, D. M., 517, 528, 590, 593
Calvin, A., 540, 549
Cameron, N., 552, 571
Campbell, D., 463, 464, 466, 475
Cannon, W. B., 95, 124
Carmichael, H. T., 40, 49, 50
Carnap, R., 288
Carp, A., 545, 549
Carr, A. C., 432, 444
Carr, H. E., 408, 420, 422
Cartwright, D. S., 424, 432, 433, 439, 444, 445, 446, 461, 468, 475, 517, 528
Cartwright, R. D., 187, 454, 455, 517
Cattell, R. B., 95, 102, 124
Chance, E., 83, 127, 128, 134, 135, 140 n., 142, 143, 144, 240
Chapman, J., 25, 33, 49, 51 n., 53, 59
Chapple, E. D., 289
Charney, E. J., 288
Chase, M. T., 571
Chase, S., 552, 571
Chassan, J. B., 331, 361, 365 n., 399, 451, 452, 478, 494, 495, 498 n., 499
Cherry, C., 268, 285
Chinn, H. I., 594

Chodorkoff, B., 444
Cleghorn, J. M., 124
Clyde, D. J., 576, 593
Cobb, W. J., 475
Coffery, H. S., 132, 144, 579
Cohen, M. B., 40, 49, 362, 399, 509, 515
Cohen, R. A., 40, 49, 362, 399, 509, 515
Colby, K. M., 194, 206, 207, 269, 285
Coleman, J. V., 600, 632
Collins, B. J., 301, 303, 309, 310
Combs, A. W., 425, 447
Conrad, D., 126
Conrad, H. S., 543 n.
Cottle, W. C., 542, 549
Covner, B. J., 58, 599, 632
Cox, D. R., 458, 467 n., 471, 472, 475
Coyne, L., 504, 515
Cronbach, L. J., 472, 475, 530, 534, 548, 549
Curran, C. A., 429, 444
Cutler, R. L., 590, 593

Dahlstrom, W. G., 538, 540, 542, 545, 549, 550
Danehy, J. J., 80, 82, 146 n., 152, 274, 286, 289
Darley, J. G., 544, 549
Darrow, C. W., 95, 124
Darwin, C. R., 288
Day, J., 147, 152
Delay, J., 124
DeMascio, A., 289
DeMyer, M. K., 302, 307, 316, 330
Deniker, P., 124
Deutsch, F., 153, 166, 167, 169, 170, 288
Deutsch, H., 341, 358
Deutsch, K., 287
Dewey, J., 287
Dibner, A. S., 146, 152
Dignam, P. J., 303, 309
Dinoff, M., 303, 307
Dittes, J. E., 362, 399
Dittmann, A. T., 25, 40, 49, 81, 82, 145, 146
Di Vesta, F. J., 298, 307
Dollard, J., 25 n., 33, 59, 83, 85, 92, 187, 210, 225, 289, 291, 293, 304, 307, 583, 593
Draper, E., 603, 633
Dreikurs, R., 447
DuBois, C., 558, 572
Duckert, A. R., 287
Dugan, W. E., 609, 610, 632
Duheim, P., 14
Dulany, D. E., Jr., 295, 307
Dymond, R. F., 189, 208, 229, 230, 231, 239, 432, 441, 444, 445, 446

D'Zmura, T., 124

Eastman Kodak Co., 24
Edwards, A. L., 472, 475
Eichhorn, M., 170
Eissler, K. R., 343, 358
Ekman, P., 298, 301, 307
Ekstein, R., 598, 632
Eldred, S. H., 289
Ellis, N. R., 306, 307
Enelow, A. J., 605, 632
Engel, G. L., 602, 632
English, O. S., 60
Erbaugh, J., 124
Erikson, E., 338, 358
Erikson, M. H., 61
Evans-Pritchard, E. E., 287
Ewing, J. A., 331, 361
Ewing, T. N., 475
Eysenck, H. J., 293, 302, 303, 307, 449

Fabian, M., 476, 502, 504, 515
Fadiman, C., 149
Fahmy, S. A., 298, 307
Fairweather, G. W., 458, 475
Faris, M. T., 502, 515
Feibleman, J. K., 272, 285
Feldman, J. J., 475
Feldman, M. J., 545, 547, 549
Fenichel, O., 93, 124, 130, 144
Ferster, C. B., 289, 290, 291, 302, 307, 312, 316, 320, 330
Fey, W. F., 585, 593
Fiedler, F. E., 577, 579, 584, 593
Finesinger, J. E., 476
Finney, D. J., 473, 475
Fiske, D. W., 432, 444, 445, 462, 475
Fleischmann, O., 58
Fleming, J., 337, 339, 346, 358, 598, 607, 633
Ford, D. H., 583, 593
Forde, D. L., 605, 632
Forgays, D. G., 298, 308
Fosmire, F. R., 613, 634
Fox, H., 401, 422
Frank, A., 607, 632
Frank, J. D., 293, 308, 461, 475, 476, 574, 594
Frank, L. K., 288
Freedman, M. B., 132, 135, 144, 579
French, T. M., 185, 186, 210, 212, 216, 217, 225, 339, 351, 358, 359
Freud, A., 338, 341, 355, 356, 359, 520, 528
Freud, S., 130, 131, 141, 142, 144, 192,

212 n., 226, 239, 266, 268, 285, 334, 335, 339, 340, 341, 345, 346, 359, 371, 404, 422, 551, 552, 566, 572
Fries, C. C., 89, 92
Frisch, K. Von, 274, 275, 286
Fromm, E., 130, 131, 132, 144
Fromm-Reichmann, F., 267 n.
Funkenstein, D. H., 95, 124

Gajdusek, D. C., 22, 24
Galanter, E., 286
Gardiner, M., 341, 359
Gebhard, M. E., 475
Gedo, J. E., 334, 339, 343, 359
Gelfand, D. M., 301, 310
Gellhorn, E., 95, 124
Gendlin, E. T., 424, 436, 445
Gilberstadt, H., 545, 550
Gilbert, W. M., 475
Gill, M. M., 57, 58, 601, 620 n., 633
Gillespie, J. F., Jr., 196, 208
Gitelson, M., 340, 359, 572
Glatt, M. M., 473, 475
Gleason, H. A., Jr., 73, 82, 266, 271 n., 272, 285
Gleser, G. C., 93, 96, 98, 101, 102, 123, 124, 125, 225, 422, 533, 534
Gliedman, L. H., 475
Glover, E., 344, 359
Glueck, B. C., 538, 550
Goldberg, L. R., 607, 633
Goldenberg, G. M., 89, 90, 92
Goldiamond, I., 302, 308
Goldman-Eisler, F., 621, 633
Goldstein, A., 295, 308, 460, 475
Goodman, G., 434, 435, 445
Goodrich, D. W., 609, 634
Gorton, T., 445
Gottschalk, L. A., 3, 83, 93, 94, 96, 98, 100, 101, 102, 104, 119, 122, 123, 124, 125, 210, 225, 240, 268, 285, 289, 420, 422
Goulden, C., 467, 472, 475
Green, R. F., 574, 576, 593
Green, W. L., Jr., 602, 632
Greenacre, P., 363, 399
Greenblatt, M., 190 n., 208
Greenhill, M. H., 9
Greenson, R. R., 92, 226, 239
Greenspoon, J., 293, 297, 298, 308
Grinker, R. R., 126, 562, 572
Grobstein, C., 286
Group for Advancement of Psychiatry, 355, 359, 450, 456, 476, 600, 601, 633
Grummon, D. L., 190, 208, 445
Guerney, B. G., 583, 593
Guerney, L. F., 583, 593

Gump, P. V., 429, 445
Gussen, J., 603, 633
Guze, S. B., 601, 633
Gwartney, R. H., 605, 632

Haberman, P., 474
Haggard, E. A., 13, 14, 152, 154, 157 n.,
    187, 188, 226, 228, 239, 376, 399, 520,
    529
Haigh, G., 438, 439, 444, 445
Hales, W. M., 545, 550
Haley, J., 147, 152
Halkides, G., 435, 445
Hall, B. H., 476, 502, 504, 515
Hall, E. T., Jr., 75, 82
Hambidge, G., Jr., 119, 124, 125
Hamburg, D. A., 126, 598, 633
Hampton, P., 89, 90, 92
Handler, J. S., 51 n.
Harl, J. M., 124
Harris, Z., 287
Harrower, M., 533, 534
Hart, C. W., 475
Hart, J. T., Jr., 447, 520, 529
Hartley, M. W., 438, 445
Hathaway, S. R., 289, 291, 462, 475, 537,
    539, 540, 545, 550
Haughton, E., 302, 306, 307
Hawkins, D., 286
Haworth, M. R., 557 n., 572
Hayes, A. S., 288
Heath, H. A., 126
Heine, R. W., 603, 633
Heller, K., 609, 610, 633
Henry, W. E., 443, 445
Hertz, M. R., 568, 572
Herz, M., 126
Herzog, E., 9
Hewes, G. W., 288
Heyns, R. W., 420, 422
Hilgard, J. R., 346, 359
Hines, L. R., 487 n.
Hirsch, S. I., 147, 152
Hoch, P., 426 n., 445
Hockett, C. F., 80, 82, 146 n., 152, 266,
    267 n., 271 n., 272, 274, 285, 286, 287,
    289
Hogan, R. A., 445
Holland, J. L., 475
Hollingshead, A., 517, 528
Holt, R., 366, 399, 533, 534, 607, 633
Holtzman, W. H., 504, 515
Horner, R. F., 303, 307, 309
Horney, K., 130, 131, 132, 144
Horowitz, L., 504, 513, 515
Horst, P. A., 208
Hovland, C. I., 469, 472, 473, 475

Hunt, J. McV., 473, 475
Hurley, R. E., 597, 634
Hutchison, H. C., 302, 307
Hyman, H. H., 469, 475

Ikman, P., 310
Imber, S. D., 458, 475
Isaacs, K. S., 187, 188, 226, 227, 228, 239,
    520, 529
Isaacs, W., 302, 308
Iverson, M. A., 299, 308

Jackson, D. D., 64, 147, 152
Jackson, J., 471, 475
Jacobsen, C., 600, 635
Jacobson, E., 93, 125, 406, 422
Jaffe, J., 105, 125, 289
Jahoda, M., 468, 471, 475
James, W., 446
Janis, I. L., 363, 399
Jellinek, E. M., 470, 476
Jenney, 441
John, E. S., 445
Jones, E. E., 608, 633
Joos, M., 73, 82, 288
Jourard, S. M., 308
Jung, C. G., 130, 132, 144

Kahn, J. B., Jr., 125
Kanfer, F. H., 293, 300, 308, 616 n.
Kanner, L., 328, 330
Kaplan, S. M. A., 102, 122, 123, 125
Kapp, F. T., 125
Karas, S. C., 300, 308
Kaufman, P. E., 210, 225
Kaufmann, P., 544, 550
Kavanagh, J., 154
Keet, C. D., 190, 208
Kellam, S., 495, 499
Kelly, G. A., 129, 144
Kelly, L., 607, 633
Kelman, H. C., 476, 574, 594
Kepecs, J. G., 210
Kirtner, W. L., 432, 433, 444, 446, 475,
    517, 528
Klein, L. S., 89, 90, 92
Klerman, G., 472, 476
Klett, C. J., 534
Kline, L. V., 609, 633
Klopfer, B., 557 n., 558, 572
Klopfer, P. H., 281, 286
Knapp, P., 93, 125, 187, 332, 339, 359,
    401, 403, 405, 406, 407, 408, 413, 420,
    422
Koehler, W., 286

Koffka, K., 266, 286
Kogan, L. S., 58
Kohut, H., 212 n., 225, 335, 359
Kolmer, H. J., 422
Korchin, S. J., 126
Korner, I. N., 606, 633
Kramer, E., 145
Kramer, M. K., 340, 359
Krasner, L., 190, 289, 290, 291, 292, 293, 298, 300, 301, 303, 305, 306, 307, 308, 309, 310, 311, 607, 611, 633
Krause, M. S., 451, 456
Kreitman, N., 468, 476
Kubie, L. A., 93, 125
Kubie, L. S., 562, 572
Kurpiewski, B. S., 303, 307

Lacey, J. T., 95, 125
LaForge, R., 475
Lamb, R., 59
Lana, R. E., 464, 476
Lang, P. J., 302, 309
Langer, S. K., 283, 286
Lasky, J., 468, 476, 534
Latil, P. de, 287
Lawson, C. A., 287
Lazarus, A. A., 302, 309
Lazarus, R. S., 293, 310
Lazovik, A. D., 302, 309
Leary, T., 132, 144, 544, 549, 577, 578, 593
Lecky, P., 446
Lennard, H. L., 378
Lerner, B., 517, 528
Lester, B. K., 603, 633
Levin, S. M., 295, 310
Levine, M., 600, 635
Levinger, G., 473, 476
Levitov, E., 517 n., 523 n.
Levy, D. M., 558, 572
Levy, S. J., 443
Lewin, B., 226, 239
Lewin, K., 266, 286
Lewis, N. D. C., 545, 550
Lewis, W. C., 210
Lichtenstein, E., 197 n.
Liddell, H. S., 14
Lindemann, E., 289
Lindsley, O. R., 302, 306, 307, 309
Lippard, V. W., 600, 635
Lippitt, R., 420, 422
Lissitz, R. W., 154
Loofbourrow, G. N., 95, 124
Loosli-Usteri, M., 557 n., 559, 572
Lorand, S., 343, 359
Lorenz, 164, 281, 286, 287
Lorr, M., 473, 476, 517, 528, 533, 534, 573, 574, 576, 577, 578, 580, 585, 587, 588, 590, 591
Lott, G. M., 606, 633
Lowinger, P., 92
Luborsky, L., 9, 190, 208, 449, 450, 453, 455, 458, 476, 533, 534, 607, 633
Lumsdaine, A. A., 475
Lundin, R. W., 293, 309
Lustman, S. L., 356, 359

Maanen, E. F. Van, 125
Mabray, R. C., 476
MacFarlane, J. W., 13, 14, 533, 535
MacIntyre, A. C., 83, 84
MacLean, P. D., 95, 125
MacLeod, J. A., 125
Magliocco, E. B., 124, 125
Mahl, G. F., 25 n., 33, 59, 95, 125, 146, 152
Mandelbaum, D. G., 288
Mangon, G., Jr., 126
Manning, P. R., 605, 632
Margolin, S., 401, 422
Marks, P. A., 532, 535, 539, 550
Marmor, J., 293, 297, 309
Marsden, G., 82, 84, 362, 399
Marty, S., 607, 632
Maruyama, M., 287
Maslow, A. H., 468, 476
Maslow, J. W., 95, 126
Mason, J. W., 422
Masserman, J. H., 95, 126
Matarazzo, J. D., 191, 302, 310, 601, 610, 614, 617, 619, 620, 623, 624 n., 625, 633, 634
Matarazzo, R. G., 596, 597, 613 ff., 633, 634
May, R. R., 293, 309
McCarthy, P. J., 462, 476
McConnell, J., 540, 549
McGaugh, J. L., 291
McGuire, C., 597, 634
McKinley, J. C., 537, 550
McNair, D. M., 517, 528, 533, 534, 573, 574, 577, 580, 585, 587, 588, 590, 593, 594
McQuown, N. A., 146, 150, 152, 267 n., 287, 288
Meehl, P. E., 128, 144, 536, 539, 540, 545, 548, 549, 550
Mees, H., 306, 311
Mendelsohn, R., 197 n.
Mendelson, M., 124
Menninger, K., 269, 286
Menzer-Benaron, D., 407, 422
Merrill, R. M., 190, 208
Metraux, R. W., 571

Meunch, G. A., 446
Meuser, M., 603, 633
Michael, J., 302, 307
Michaelis, A. R., 289
Michaux, W. W., 573, 587, 588, 593, 594
Miles, H. H., 473, 476
Miller, A., 228, 239, 520, 529
Miller, G. A., 286
Miller, N. E., 8, 9, 293, 304, 307
Miller, R. E., 126
Minard, J., 300, 310
Mirsky, I. A., 95, 126
Modell, W., 456, 476
Modlin, H. C., 477, 502, 512, 515
Molish, H., 554, 567, 572
Molitor, H., 298, 308
Mosak, H. H., 447
Mowrer, O. H., 132, 144, 210, 225, 293, 304, 309, 446
Murphy, J. V., 126
Murphy, W. F., 169
Murray, E. J., 96, 124, 362, 399, 580, 583, 594
Murray, J., 293, 303, 304, 306, 309
Mushatt, C., 332, 401, 408, 413, 420, 422
Myers, R. A., 609, 610, 633

Nash, E. H., 475
Nemetz, S. J., 332, 401, 405, 408, 413, 420, 422
Newman, R., 57, 58, 59, 601, 620 n., 633
Noble, N., 521, 529
Noblin, C. D., 299, 307, 309
Novey, S., 226, 239
Novikoff, A. B., 266, 286
Nowlis, H. H., 95, 126
Nowlis, V., 95, 126, 574, 576, 593
Nunnally, J. C., 438, 446

Oberholzer, E., 558, 559, 572
Ohlsen, M., 521, 529
Oken, D., 103, 126
Olim, E. G., 154 n.
Oppenheimer, J. R., 127, 145
Orlando, R., 306, 307
Orne, M. T., 295, 309, 462, 476
Orr, D. W., 338, 359
Orr, M., 559, 572
Orth, M. H., 477, 512, 516
Osgood, C. E., 288
Ossorio, A. G., 132, 144, 580

Pacella, B. L., 544, 550
Palmer, B., 613, 634
Parloff, M. B., 9, 190, 208, 468, 476, 574, 594, 611, 634

Patterson, C. H., 293, 309
Patterson, G. R., 613, 634
Pavlov, I. P., 14
Payne, S., 337, 359
Pennicker, R. E., 289
Percy, W., 269, 286
Persinger, G. W., 476
Persky, H., 95, 126
Pfeffer, A. Z., 341, 360
Pfouts, J. H., 602, 634
Phillips, J. S., 613 ff., 634
Phillips, L., 473, 477
Piers, G., 344, 360
Piers, M. W., 344, 360
Pike, K. L., 288
Piotrowski, W., 544, 550
Piotrowski, Z. A., 533, 535, 557 n., 567, 572
Pisoni, S., 297, 309
Pittenger, R. E., 80, 82, 146 n., 147, 152, 274, 286, 288, 289
Pollock, G., 210, 330, 334, 339, 358, 360
Pool, I., 82, 84
Porter, E. H., 429, 435, 446, 597, 599, 604, 611, 612, 632, 634
Pribram, K. H., 286
Price, D. B., 289
Proff, F., 521, 529
Pryer, M. W., 306, 307

Quenouille, M. H., 381, 399

Rabin, A. I., 557 n., 572
Rablen, R., 447, 454, 519, 520, 523, 529
Rader, G. E., 602, 634
Rafi, A. A., 302, 309
Raimy, V. C., 210, 225, 425, 430, 446
Rangell, L., 226, 239
Rapaport, D., 93, 126, 204, 205, 208, 513, 515
Raskin, A., 573, 588, 593
Raskin, N. J., 424, 430, 431, 446, 447
Rausch, H. L., 579, 594
Reahl, J. E., 475
Redfield, 287
Redlich, F. C., 25 n., 33, 57, 58, 59, 509, 515, 517, 528, 601, 620 n., 633
Reece, M. M., 611, 634
Reich, W., 130, 145
Reichsman, F., 602, 632
Reid, J., 126
Reynard, M. C., 299, 309
Reznikoff, M. A., 9
Rice, L. N., 285, 424, 444, 474
Rickard, H. C., 302, 303, 309
Riesman, D., 130, 145

Rioch, D., 126
Risley, T., 306, 311
Robbins, F. P., 210
Robbins, L. L., 501, 502, 505, 515, 516
Robertson, R. J., 444
Rogers, C. R., 58, 59, 132, 145, 189, 208,
    210, 225, 229, 230, 239, 422, 423, 425,
    427, 430, 432, 435, 436, 437, 439, 446,
    447, 454, 519, 520, 523, 529, 578, 594,
    597, 599, 614, 616, 634
Rohovit, D. D., 125
Romano, J., 600, 634
Rorschach, H., 552, 553, 557 n., 558, 563,
    572
Rosen, A., 541, 550
Rosen, I., 473, 476, 511, 515
Rosenthal, R., 295, 296, 309, 469, 476
Rosenzweig, S., 449, 450
Ross, W. D., 125
Roth, I., 444
Rotter, J. B., 293, 309
Rubinstein, E. A., 9, 190, 208, 473, 476
Ruesch, J., 147, 152, 287, 552, 572
Rychlak, J. F., 456, 476
Ryckoff, I. M., 147, 152
Ryder, R., 197 n.

Sabshin, M., 126, 334, 339, 359
Sachar, E. J., 422
Sadow, L., 334, 339, 359
Salzberg, H. C., 303, 309
Salzinger, K., 293, 297, 309
Sanders, J. L., 475
Sapir, E., 80, 82
Sapolsky, A., 299, 310
Sarason, I. G., 300, 310
Sargent, H., 96, 97, 126, 457, 476, 502,
    503, 504, 515
Saslow, G., 191, 302, 310, 596, 597, 601,
    609, 610, 613 ff., 633, 634
Saussure, R. de, 226, 239
Schaflen, R., 557 n., 572
Scheflen, A. E., 60, 83, 153, 219, 240, 263,
    267, 272, 280, 282, 286, 288
Schlessinger, N., 332, 334, 339, 359, 455
Schmale, A., 602, 632
Schneer, I., 343, 359
Schneider, S. F., 193, 208
Schneirla, T. C., 265, 286
Schofield, W., 531, 532, 536, 542, 543,
    544, 545, 546, 547, 550
Schorer, C., 92
Schutz, W. C., 577, 580, 594
Schwartz, E. K., 607, 634
Sebeok, T. A., 288
Seeman, J., 424, 435, 447
Seeman, W., 532, 535, 539, 550

Segel, R. H., 51 n.
Seitz, P. F. D., 95, 126, 185, 186, 187,
    209, 212 n., 225, 240
Sells, S. B., 594
Shaffer, G. W., 293, 310
Shakow, D., 25, 33, 49, 51 n., 52, 53, 57,
    59, 289
Shannon, C. E., 268, 286
Shanon, J., 125
Shapiro, L. B., 210, 351, 359
Shaw, F. J., 293, 310
Sheerer, E., 447
Sheffield, F. D., 475
Shepard, M., 295, 310
Shlien, J. M., 422, 424, 441, 445, 447,
    454, 455
Shoben, E. J., Jr., 293, 304, 306, 310
Sholiton, L. J., 102, 126
Shyne, A., 473, 476
Siegal, R., 473, 476, 511, 515
Silver, H., 125
Simkins, L., 298, 310
Simon, R., 475
Simon, W., 545, 550
Simpson, G. G., 266, 272, 286
Skard, A. G., 14
Skinner, B. F., 293, 295, 310, 312, 320,
    324, 330
Sklansky, M., 51
Slack, C. W., 302, 310
Smith, H. L., Jr., 73, 82, 147, 152, 288
Smith, M. B., 187, 215, 331, 365 ff., 399,
    499
Snyder, B. J., 577, 594
Snyder, W. U., 89, 90, 92, 190, 208, 435,
    447, 577, 583, 594
Snygg, D., 425, 447
Solomon, H. C., 289
Sorenson, E. R., 22, 24
Speisman, J. C., 196, 208
Spielberger, C. D., 295, 310
Spitz, R., 281, 286, 343, 360
Spottiswoode, R., 289
Springer, K., 93, 102, 124, 125, 225, 422
Standal, S. W., 424, 447
Starkweather, J. A., 151, 152
Stein, M., 609, 634
Stein, S. N., 25
Stekel, W., 297, 310
Stember, C. H., 475
Stephan, F. F., 462, 476
Stephenson, W., 187, 438, 447
Sterba, R., 520, 529
Stern, G. G., 580, 594
Sternberg, R. S., 25, 33, 40, 49, 51 n., 53,
    59
Stock, D., 431, 447
Stone, A. R., 475

Stone, G. B., 475
Straughan, J. H., 613, 634
Strauss, B. V., 601, 634
Strom-Olsen, R., 58
Strupp, H. H., 9, 187, 190, 208, 268, 286,
    289, 331, 361, 362, 364, 395, 397, 399,
    400, 465, 477, 583, 594, 609, 634
Sullivan, H. S., 552, 572
Sundland, D. M., 583, 585, 594
Szasz, T., 305, 310

Taffel, C., 296, 297, 310
Tarachow, S., 342, 360
Taylor, J. A., 95, 126
Temerlin, M. K., 193, 208
Thetford, W. N., 447, 554, 572
Thibaut, J. W., 608, 633
Thomas, E. J., 457, 477
Thomas, J., 302, 308
Thompson, C., 129, 145, 606, 635
Thurstone, L. L., 594
Ticho, E., 476, 502, 504, 515
Ticho, G. R., 476, 502, 504, 515
Timin, M., 197 n.
Timmons, E. O., 299, 303, 307, 309
Tinbergen, N., 287
Tippett, J., 603, 633
Tolman, R. S., 363, 400
Tomlinson, T. M., 437, 447, 520, 529
Toomey, L. A., 9
Tourney, G., 90, 92
Trager, G. L., 69, 70, 73, 75, 76, 77, 82,
    145, 147, 151, 152, 288
Trites, D. K., 594
Trosman, H., 603, 633
Tuddenham, R. D., 533, 535

Ullmann, L. P., 298, 300, 301, 303, 307,
    308, 309, 310, 311

Vikan-Kline, L. L., 476
Vlack, J. Van, 15, 16, 24, 270, 289
Voth, H. M., 473, 477, 502, 512, 515

Waelder, R., 339, 360
Wagstaff, A. K., 285, 424, 444, 474
Walker, A., 447, 519, 529

Walker, R. N., 571
Wallach, M. S., 400
Wallerstein, R. S., 341, 360, 452, 453,
    500, 501, 502, 503, 504, 505, 515, 598,
    632
Ward, C. H., 124, 606, 635
Watson, R. I., 292, 310
Weaver, W., 268, 286
Weber, R., 473, 477
Weekland, J., 147, 152
Weigert, E., 44 n.
Weiner, N., 287
Weingarten, E., 475
Weinstein, 573, 574
Weiss, R. L., 301, 309, 310, 311
Weitman, M., 633
Welsh, G. S., 101, 538, 540, 542, 545,
    546, 548, 549, 550
Wenar, C., 13, 14
Werk, E. E., Jr., 126
Werkman, S. L., 602, 635
West, L. J., 603, 633
Whitaker, C. A., 604, 635
White, A. M., 89, 92
White, R. B., 510, 516
Whitehorn, J. C., 517, 528, 534, 590, 591,
    592, 593, 594, 600, 611, 635
Whitman, R. M., 210
Whitman, R. N., 611, 634
Wiens, A. N., 596, 597, 610, 613 ff., 633,
    634, 635
Williams, J. V., 395, 400
Winget, C. M., 93, 125
Wirt, R. D., 547, 550
Wittenborn, J. R., 126, 549, 550
Wohl, T. H., 126
Wolberg, L. R., 614, 616, 635
Wolf, M., 306, 311
Wolf, S., 464, 477
Wolpe, J., 293, 301, 311
Wright, H. F., 285
Wynne, L. C., 81, 82, 145, 146, 147, 152

Yamamoto, J., 603, 633
Yates, A. J., 302, 311

Zigler, E., 473, 477
Zimring, F. M., 422, 424, 436, 445, 454,
    455
Zuckerman, M., 95, 126

Subject Index

A-B Scale, 590 ff.
Abasement, 285
Abstract ideas, free association and, 200–201, 202
Accent light, 16
Acceptability scale, 132, 143
Acceptance, 521–522, 526, 578, 579
Acoustics, 27–28, 32
ACTH, 414
Acting out, 365, 389 n.
Action-reaction models, 269
Activation-Deactivation factor, 576
Activities list, 580
Adaptation, 347–348
Administration, research, error in, 462
Adolescents, Rorschach and, 567–568
Adrenals, 284, 402
Aeschylus, 552
Affect, 369 n., 374, 376, 377, 379, 382, 385, 388 ff.
  definition of, 96
  meaningfulness of patient statements and, 232 ff.
  quantification of, 93 ff.
  relatability and, 227 ff.
  verbalization, clinical interview and, 231–232
Affiliation, 582
Agamemnon, 552
Aggression, 365, 369 n., 576, 582
Agreeableness, 582
Agreement, interpretational, 213
  See also Consensus
Agreement and difference method, 273
AI, 548
AID, 585
Alcoholic study, 457 ff.
Alloplasticity, 512
Ambiguity, free association and, 192
  meaning of unit and, 283
Ambivalent hostility, 94, 103, 109, 115–116, 121
Anal character, 130
Anal strivings, 365, 374, 377, 379, 382, 386, 388, 389, 390
Analysis phase of filming, 23

Anatomy, 6–7
Ancillary variables, 472–473
Anger, 372, 416
Anger-Hostility factor, 575, 576
Anniversary reactions, 346
Annotation, film, 22
Anthropology, 7, 79–81, 266
Anxiety, 365, 374, 379, 382, 385, 388, 389, 390, 416, 417, 418, 576
  Index, 548
  in intensive design, 488
  reliability of scoring, 100–101
  Rorschach and, 559
  sequential changes in, 117–118
  speech disturbance and, 146
  therapist's, in filmed therapy, 44, 55
  validation studies of, 101–102
  verbalizations of, 94, 99–100, 106, 110–112, 134
Apollo, 552
Asking, 526, 552
Associative anamnesis, 168
Asthma, 401 ff.
Atavism, 319–320
Atmospheres, 301
Attitudes, 130, 374, 377, 382, 386, 391 ff., 464–465
Attractiveness, interpersonal, 299
Audio in filming, 17–19, 25 ff., 31–32
  room construction and, 27–28
Authoritarian factor, 578, 579
Autistic child, 312 ff.
  community and, 318
  conditioned reinforcement and, 320 ff.
  durability of reinforcer and, 316–317
  environment and, physical, 314–315
  indifference to adults of, 328
  intermittent reinforcement and, 318–320
  shaping repertoire of, 315
  social behavior and, 315, 324 ff.
  specifying reinforcer for, 317–318
Autonomic arousal, 102
Autonomy, 581
Autoplasticity, 512
Aversion conditioning, 302

Aversive stimulation, 319
Avoidant response, 86–87
Awareness, conditioning and, 295, 298, 300, 301
Axiomation, 77

B roll, 21
Background, 35 ff.
Bales Interaction Process analysis, 518, 521, 522, 524 ff.
Bee dance, 275
Behavior modification, 292 ff., 313 ff.
Behavioral rating scales, 531
Bias, 134, 296–297, 487
Biotrophic vs. sociotrophic dichotomy, 303
Bisexuality, 76, 77
Blacky Test, 532
Blind spots, 354
Blond women, MME and, 162
Bodily expressions, 166 ff.
    See also Kinesics
Bodily mobilization, 86
Body set, 74
Breaking in with new thought, 146
Brunette women, MME and, 162

Camera operation, 19, 30
Casework, social, 456 ff.
Castrative impulse, 220–221
Catecholamine, 102, 402
Categorization, 362
Catharsis, 226
Cause and effect relationships, 435, 456
Censorship, temporal, 165
Centralist theory, free association and, 192
Centrality in verbal expression, 97
Chain of responses, 320 ff.
Change in therapeutic process, 340, 349 ff., 432, 469, 502, 504–505
    See also Outcomes of therapy
Character, scales, 542, 548
    splitting, 131
    types, 129–130
Childhood development, 345–346
Children, autistic, 312 ff.
    MME and, 162, 164
Chlordiazepoxide study, 487 ff.
Chlorpromazine, 573
Chronology, cultural, 78
Cigarette-lighting as structural unit, 273–274, 276, 281–282
Cinematographer viewpoint of filming, 15 ff.
Circle variables, 580

Clarification of observation, 521, 524, 525
Clause analysis, 105 ff.
Client-centered therapy, 424 ff.
    compared with psychoanalysis, 517 ff.
Clinical study of change, 504
Clinical variables, 387–389
Clytemnestra, 552
Coached client, 609
Code, information storing, 21
Coder-decoder models, 269
Coding, facial expresions, 155–156
    linguistic, 80–81, 87 ff., 134 ff., 147–148
Coldness, 374, 377, 382
Communication, 7, 70–71
    as abstract system, 268–269
    culture as, 75 ff.
    intensive design and, 488, 493, 496
    kinesic, 70, 74, 152 ff., 166 ff.
    motion picture facilities and, 25 ff.
    natural history method and, 263 ff.
    paralanguage, 70
    therapy and, 551–553
    variables in general, 69 ff.
Community reinforcement, 318
Competitiveness, 134, 369 n., 374, 377, 379, 382, 385, 388, 389
Complex processes, 185 ff.
Conditioning, 289–291
    reinforcement, 320 ff.
    verbal operant, 293 ff.
Conditions of therapy, 433–435
Confidentiality of filming, 22
Conflict, interpersonal, 130, 131, 132, 136
    unconscious, 345, 350–351
Confusion factor, 488, 493, 575–576
Congruence, 439
Consensus in interpretation, 185–187, 209 ff., 361 ff.
    meaningfulness and, 232, 233
Contamination of experiment, 459
Content, free association, 199 ff.
Content analysis, 82–83, 362
    in characterization of therapist, 583
    emotional changes in interview and, 93 ff.
    motivational variables in, 85 ff.
    of verbalizations about interpersonal experience, 127 ff.
Content-free interview, 606
Contentedness, 433
Context analysis, 264 ff.
    as abstract system, 268–269
    application to human communication, 267 ff.
    basic assumptions of, 269–270
    communicational frame of reference of, 268

recording and transcribing in, 270–271
setting up experiment in, 284
structural units in, 271 ff.
synthesizing larger picture, 278 ff.
Continuous case, consensus in, 211
Contrasting, 273, 274–275
Controls, 355, 505
Conversion reaction, 91
Correlation of data, 407
Corticosteroid, 415, 420
Countertransference, 13, 142, 330, 338, 355, 374, 377, 382, 387
Critical-Hostile factor, 578, 579
Cross-sectional design, 451
Culture, 71–72, 75 ff.
Cybernetics, 266

Dark and grey sensitivity, 558, 559
Data recording, 13–14
background problem in, 35 ff.
in context analysis, 270
filming, 15 ff., 25 ff., 64–65
observers and, 61–63
reactions of patient and therapist to, 34 ff.
sound film therapist's experience, 50 ff.
subjective reactions to, 60
Data reduction, 358
Death anxiety, 102, 106
Defenses, 342–343
adaptation and, 352–353
multiple, 219
primitive oral conflict and, 410
Rorschach and, 564–566
Defensiveness, 369 n., 374, 377, 379, 382, 385, 389, 390, 432
Deference, 582
Defiant factor, 576
Defining variables, 367, 456
Delineation, 273–274
Demand characteristics, 295–296
Denial, 365
Dependence, 369 n., 374, 376, 377, 379, 382, 385, 388, 389
Depersonalization, 488, 493, 496
Depleted constellation, 409, 410, 414, 415, 416, 417, 418
Depression, 365, 374, 376, 377, 379, 382, 385
hostility and, 103
in intensive design, 488, 493, 496
personality inventory of, 538–539
in POMS, 575, 576
verbalizations and, 134
Desensitization, 302
Detachment, 582
Diagnosis, 231, 344 ff.

Diffuse anxiety, 106
Directive, active intervention, 585, 586
Disease model, 304–305
Displaced concern of therapist, 44–45
Displacement, 365
Dissociation, 131
Disturbing motives, 217, 218, 224
Doctorality, 76
Documentary film, 15, 16 ff.
Dominance, 369 n., 374, 376, 377, 379, 382, 385, 388 ff., 582
Dreams, change during therapy, 351–352
first, consensus and, 211
Drive vs. external stimulation, 204–205
Drug efficacy, intensive design and, 478 ff.
Dubbing, 18
Dymond Scale of Adjustment, 230

Eastern Pennsylvania Psychiatric Institute, 20
Ego, 295, 343, 346, 347
disruption, 407
facial expressions and, 154 ff.
free association and, 191
regulation, 407, 410, 414, 420
Rorschach and, 553, 556
self-observation scale and, 520
strength, 350, 473, 547
Elation, 365, 374, 377, 379, 382, 386
Electronic preceptoring, 606
Emergent expressive constellations, 406–407, 409
Emotional change in interview, 93 ff., 146 ff.
Emotional states, Rorschach and, 557 ff., 561–563
Emotionally toned words, 231
Emotions, unconscious, 406
Empathy, 374, 377, 382, 392, 393, 394, 395
Energy deployment, 433
Entertainment film, 15
Environmental reinforcement, 313–315
Environmental stimuli, free association and, 200, 201
Eosinophiles, 402
Erlebnistypus, 563
Erotic emotion, 415, 416, 417, 418
Errors, interviewer, 91, 614 ff.
scale measurements, 626 ff.
systematic, 461 ff.
Es scale, 547
Evaluations of filmed therapy, 47
Evaluative research design, 456
    See also Outcome of therapy
Evocative situation, 86
Examiner variables, 296–297, 300, 301

Exhibition, 582
Expectancies, patient-therapist, 295, 296
Experiencing, 436, 519–520, 563–564
Experimental film, 15
Exploitative orientation, 130–131, 132
Expression, emergent, 406–407, 409
Extensive design, 451, 479 ff.
    limitations of, 481–483
Extinction by interpretation, 299
Extroversion, 130, 132

Facial expressions, correlates of rapid
        changes in, 159 ff.
    ego mechanisms and, 154 ff.
    methods of measuring, 155–156, 163–
        164
    reliability of measures of, 156–158
    theoretical considerations of, 164–165
    variability of changes in, 159
Facilitating variables, 461, 473
Facilitation, faulty, of communication,
        615, 616, 628, 630
Family service casework, 456 ff.
Fantasy, 220, 406, 414
    Rorschach test and, 560–561
Fatigue, hostility and, 103
Fatigue-Inertia factor, 575, 576
Fatty acid levels, 102
Fear, 94, 117–118
Felt need, 430, 434
Field theory, 266
Filming, 25 ff.
    analysis phase in, 23
    annotation, 22
    audio considerations, 17–19, 27–28, 31–
        32, 51
    camera operation, 19, 30
    cinematographer's viewpoint of, 15 ff.
    in context analysis, 270–271
    facial expressions, micromomentary,
        146 ff.
    identification, 21
    lighting for, 16–17, 29
    observers and, 61–63
    patient's reactions to, 41 ff.
    as personal experience, 64–65
    photographic considerations, 29–31
    playback considerations, 32
    room construction and, 27–29, 51
    scripting, 16
    segment judgment units, 155–156
    teaching, 23
    technical consultants, 26–27
    therapist's reactions to, 44–46, 50 ff.,
        60, 64–65
    transcript of interview, 240 ff.
FIRO, 580

Fixed-ratio schedule of reinforcement, 320
Focal conflict, 185–186, 212, 214–215,
        218, 221–222, 224
Focus, 521, 524, 615, 616, 629, 630
Follow-up, 341, 349–350, 497–498, 501,
        507–508
Free association, 193 ff., 336
    areas needing investigation, 203 ff.
    control and simplification, 189 ff.
    dissection of process, 206
    freedom, 198–199, 203, 204
    interventions, 206–207
    posture and, 168
    ratings of performance, 196 ff.
    task significance, 192
    training and agreement of judges, 202–
        203
Friendliness factor, 575, 576
Function of unit, 284
Functional microcosm, 425
Fundamental probability set, 480

General maladjustment scale, 547
General systems theory, 266
General physician, post-graduate program
        for, 604–605
Generalizability of data, 387
Generalization, 301
Generalized reinforcer, 326–327
Genital strivings, 365, 374, 377, 379, 382,
        386
Gestalt theory, 266
Gestures, 166 ff.
Giving, 522, 526
Global impressionistic evaluations, 533
Global processes, 426
Gm scale, 547
Goal Statement Inventory, 588–590
Goals, research, 5–6
    therapist, 587 ff.
Grey-black sensitivity, 558, 559
Groups, small, theory, 7
GSI, 588–590
Guilt, 106, 365, 369 n.

Habitual reactions, 130
Healer, 304
Health-Sickness Rating Scale, 502
Hello-goodbye effect, 462
Helper, role of, 191–192
Hematologic data, 402
Hidden motivation, 406, 408
Hierarchy of levels, 272
Hoarding, 130
Homosexuality, 365, 369 n.
Hostility, 94, 99–100, 369 n., 371, 372,

374, 377, 379, 382, 385, 388, 389, 390, 417, 418
ambivalent, 94, 103, 109, 115–116, 121
in intensive design, 488, 493
inward, 94, 108–109, 114–115, 121
outward, 94, 107–108, 112–114, 119–121
reliability of scoring, 100-101
rivalry, 220 ff.
validation studies, 102–104
House-Tree-Person Test, 532
Hunch, 216
17-Hydroxycorticosteroids, 102, 415, 420

IBI and ICL, 579–581
Iconic communication, 74–75
Id, 346
Idealness, degree of, 584
Identification, with aggressor, 365
of film, 21
therapist's statements and, 521
Illumination of filming, 16–17, 29
Imitation in learning, 613
Immediate context, 278
Immediate experience observing, 521, 524, 525
Impersonal vs. personal affective approaches, 585, 586
Improvement, 462
See also Outcome of therapy
relatability and, 228 ff.
scale, evalution of, 547
Inadvertent control, 505
Independence-Encouraging factor, 578, 579
Independent assessment, 505, 508
Inference in rating process, 371 ff., 378
Inflection, affect and, 116–117
Information storing code, 21
Inhibition, 582
free association and, 198–199
reciprocal, 302
Initial study, 501, 506
Initiative, 374, 377, 382, 386, 391, 392
Insight, 300, 365, 374, 377, 379, 382, 386, 389 ff.
Instinct, 130
Instructional set, 298
Instructions, 521
Integration of self-observation, 521, 525
Intellectualization, 365
Intelligence quotient, 102
Intensive design, 451–452, 478 ff.
advantages of, 483 ff.
extensive design and, 479–481
illustrative study with, 487

placebo reaction, follow-up and, 497–498
Interaction, chronograph measurements, 617 ff.
effects, 463
models, 269
process analysis, 435, 518, 521, 522, 524 ff.
Intermittent reinforcement, 318–320
Internalization Ratio, 548
Interpatient control, 505
Interpersonal aspect of verbal conditioning, 301
Interpersonal attraction set, 299
Interpersonal behavior inventory, 579–581
Interpersonal experiences, classification of, 132, 133
content analysis and, 127 ff.
free association and, 200, 202
Interpretation, 386, 389, 521, 524, 525
consensus in, 185–187, 209 ff.
as structural unit, 279
by subject, in conditioning, 299–300
by therapist, 336, 338, 339, 374, 377, 382, 391 ff.
Intervention, interviewer, 237–238, 370, 374, 377, 382, 389, 391, 393, 394, 395
Interview, 4–5
affect verbalization and, 231–232
communication aspects of, 81
content-free, 606
emotional changes during, 93 ff., 146 ff.
errors, 614 ff.
observers and, 61–63
verbal conditioning and, 297–298
Intraindividual prediction study, 504
Intrapatient control, 505
Introjection, 143
Introversion, 130, 132, 561
Intuition, 216, 342
Involvement, free association, 198, 203, 204
IR, 548
Isolation, 265, 365

John Scale, 22, 230
Judges, 61–63, 361 ff.
free association, 202–203
meaningfulness and, 232, 233
Judgment units, film, 155–156
Junctures in speech, 148, 150

Kicker light, 16
Kin structure, 78

Kinesics, 70, 74, 152 ff.
    facial expressions and, 154 ff.
    verbal communication correlation with,
        166 ff.

Lambda index, 55 n.
Language, 70 ff., 82 ff., 145
Leader, film, 21
Learning, 7, 292 ff.
    imitation in, 613
    Personal Counselors course, 611–612
    teaching and, 597 ff.
Liaison program, 602
Librium study, 487 ff.
Lighting for filming, 16–17, 29
Lines of development, 341
Linguistic analysis of emotion, 146 ff.
Linguistic coding, 80–81
Linguistics, structural, 266
Loneliness, 576
Loss of defensive control over primitive
    oral conflict, 410, 414, 420

Main effects, 463
Maladjustment, genral, scale, 547
Markers, 282
Marketing character type, 130
Marriage, Rorschach test and, 568
Masochism, 369 n., 374, 377, 379, 382,
    385, 388, 389, 391
Meaning of unit, 282
Meaningfulness of patient statements,
    232 ff.
Measurement, criticism of, 265
    of emotional changes, 93 ff., 146 ff.
    of facial expressions, 155 ff.
    goals of therapist and, 587 ff.
    mood scales, 548, 573 ff.
    of motivational variables, 85 ff.
    interpersonal behavior inventory, 579–
        581
    personality inventory, 536 ff.
    Rorschach test, 551 ff.
    theory, 8
    of therapist, 587 ff.
    tools to assess change, 468–469, 530 ff.
Mechanical Third Ear, 606
Mediate context, 278
Medical schools, teaching in, 600 ff.
Menninger Foundation project, 452, 500 ff.
Mental Health Centers (Chicago), 229
Mentally defective, Rorschach and, 567
Meprobamate, 573
Methodology, 356–357, 361 ff., 509
Microcosm, functional, 425
Microlinguistic techniques, 146 ff.

Micromomentary expressions, 154 ff.
Microphone placement, 31
Mill's canons, 273
Minnesota Multiphasic Personality, Index,
        531–532, 537 ff.
    lie scale, 103
    psychasthenia scores, 101
Mistrust, 582
MME's, 154 ff.
Molar biology, 266
Molecular research, 429
Mood scales, 548, 573 ff.
Motion pictures, See Filming
Motivational variables, 85 ff., 374, 377,
        382, 386, 391 ff., 460, 461, 473
    categories for sentence, 87–89
    evaluation of coding, 91–92
    guidelines for inferring unconscious,
        86–87
    reliability of coding, 89–90
    unitizing task, 89
    validity of coding, 90–91
Motives, disturbing, 217, 218, 224
    free association and, 191
    hidden, 406, 408
    patient vs. volunteer, 195
    reactive, 217, 218
Movement responses, 560
Multiple defenses, 219
Multiple therapy, 606–607
Music, 74
Mutilation anxiety, 102, 106

Naming with denial, 87
Natural history method, 263 ff.
    application to communication, 267 ff.
    evolution of, 264 ff.
    setting up experiment, 284
    sound motion picture recording, 270
    structural units, 271 ff.
    synthesizing larger picture, 278 ff.
    transcribing data from film, 270–271
Need, definitions, 580
    felt, 430, 434
Negative attitudes, 374, 377, 382, 386,
        393, 394
Negative practice, 302
Neurophysiologic bases of affects, 95
Neurosis, basic conflict of, 130, 131, 132
    transference, 336
Neurotic triad, 544
Noise level, 28
Non-affective words, 231
Non-directive therapy, 426, 429
    learning and, 599–600
Non-observational statements, 521, 524
Non-self response, 521

Nonverbal communication, 166 ff.
  See also Kinesics
Number of patients, 471–472, 481–482
Nurturance, 582

Object relations, 227
Observation, psychoanalysis as method of, 363
Observers, consensus, 361 ff.
  interviewing in presence of, 61–63
  See also Judges
Oedipal striving, 221, 223, 350, 352, 365, 374, 377, 379, 382, 386, 388 ff.
Office setting, 36 ff., 55
Oral striving, 130, 365, 374, 377, 379, 382, 386, 388, 389, 410, 414, 420
Orestes, 552
Other concept, 227
Outcome of therapy, 340–341, 349 ff., 449 ff.
  client-centered, 432–433, 517 ff.
  criteria for, 228 ff.
  evaluative research design, 456 ff.
  goals and, 587
  intensive design for, 478 ff.
  interpersonal behavior inventory for, 579–581
  measurement tools for, 468–469, 530 ff.
  Menninger Foundation project, 500 ff.
  mood scales, 548, 573 ff.
  patient perceptions, 577–579
  personality inventory, 536 ff.
  psychoanalyses, 579–581
  Rorschach test, 551 ff.
  systematic error in, 462–464
  therapist's personality and, 590 ff.
Overdetermination, 186, 212, 214–215

Paralanguage, 70, 73–74, 145, 147 ff.
Parallel assessment, 505, 508
Parental role, 162, 326
Passive-aggressive character disorder, 141
Passivity, 365, 369 n., 385
Patients, 370, 502, 609–610
  alliance with, 336, 354
  meaningfulness of statements of, 232 ff.
  number of, 471–472, 481–482
  perceptions of therapists, 577–579
  reactions of, to research setup, 34 ff., 41 ff.
  role of, in disease, 304
  states of, 387–388
  verbalizations of, 87–88, 617 ff.
Pc scale, 547
Peer supervision, 607
Perception of facial expressions, 164

Perceptual vantage points, 433
Persona, 131
Personal Counselors course, 611–612
Personal equation, 13
Personal experience, filming as, 64–65
Personality, 430 ff.
  free association and, 204–206
  interview process as method of affecting, 4–5
  inventory, 531–532, 536 ff.
  research, goal and, 6
  of therapist, 590 ff., 607–608
Perverse-pseudogratified constellation, 409, 414, 416, 417, 418, 420
Petulance, 150
Phallic striving, 220–221, 365, 371, 374, 377, 379, 382, 386
Phonemes, 147, 151
Phonetics, 73
Phonology, 73
Photographic considerations in sound filming, 29–31
Physical appearance, 55
Pigeon reinforcement, 316–317, 321–322
Pitch in speech, 148, 150
Placebo effect, 460, 486, 490, 491, 493, 494–495, 497–498
Plasma steroids, 402
Playback considerations, 32
POMS, 573 ff.
Positive attitudes, 374, 377, 382, 386, 392 ff.
Post-graduate programs, 604–605
Posture behavior, 166 ff., 279, 280
Pragmatics, 76, 77
Precision in treatment comparisons, 467
Preconscious, consensus and, 212, 214–215
Prediction, 339, 504, 547
  consensus in, 214, 266, 267
  as control, 407
Prestige of examiner, 301
Pre-therapy measurement, 230, 463, 542 ff.
Preventive Casework with Families of Alcoholics study, 457 ff.
Primary process, evidence of, 488, 489 ff., 496
Prior interaction, 300
Privacy, invasion of, 53 ff.
Process research, 435–437
  goal of, 5–6
  longitudinal study of, 361 ff.
  personality and, 262 ff.
  scale, 519–520, 523
  selected variables in, 69 ff.
Productivity of therapy, 374, 377, 382, 393, 394, 395

Profile, personality, 536 ff.
Programmed reinforcement, 302
Progress, satisfaction with, 374, 377, 382, 393, 394, 395
Progressive constellation, 409, 410, 414, 416, 417, 418
Projection, 143, 365
Projective tests, 530–531, 532–533
Psychiatric Outpatient Mood Scales, 573 ff
Psychoanalysis, 330 ff., 334 ff., 585, 586
    client-centered therapy compared with, 517 ff.
    diagnosis and outcome of therapy, 344 ff.
    learning and, 598–599
    as model therapeutic process, 335–337
    research contributions of, 342 ff.
    research potentials of, 337 ff.
    researcher assessment, 355 ff.
    therapist assessment, 354–355
Psychopathology theory, 7
Psychosomatic study, 401 ff.
Psychotherapist, techniques for characterizing, 581 ff.
    See also Therapist
Psychotropic drugs, 478 ff.
Punishing in therapy, 396

Quantification, 85, 265, 361 ff.
    See also Measurement
Quantitative interindividual study, 504
Q-sort, 437 ff., 584
Q-technique, 438, 441

Rapport, 434
Rater consensus, 361 ff.
Rating, inference in, 371 ff.
    instrument for psychoanalysis, 368 ff.
    reliability, 367
    See also Judges
Rational ego, 191
Rationalization, 365
Reaction formation, 365
Reactive motive, 217, 218
Real self, 131
Receptive orientation, 130, 132
Recognition, 582
Reconstructive goals, 589
Recording, 338
    in context analysis, 270
    patient and therapist reactions to, 34 ff.
Recruiting studies, 194–195
Redirection, 521, 523, 525
Regression, 196, 365
Regression toward mean, 540

Reinforcement, 292, 293, 312 ff., 396
    chains of response, 327–329
    community, 318
    durability of, 316–317
    generalized, 326–327
    intermittent, 318–320
    physical environment and, 314
    social, 302–303, 315–316, 324 ff.
    specification of, 317–318
    spurious, 323
    verbal conditioning, 293 ff.
Rejecting, 522, 526
Relatability, 227 ff.
Relaxation, 302
Releasers, 281
Reliability of rating, 367
    personality profile, 540–542
Remote context, 278
Repressed affect, 98
Research, criteria, 228 ff., 472–473
    goals and problems in, 3 ff.
    setting, 37–39, 55
Research Document Film (R.D.), 16 ff.
Researcher variable, 355–356
Resistance, 365, 374, 377, 379, 382, 385, 389, 390, 402, 415
Resistant sentence segments, 90
Resolution in filming, 29
Responses, chain of, 320 ff.
    class characteristics of, 301
    reinforcement strength and, 316–317
    verbal conditioning, 297
Reversal, 365
Rivalry, hostile, 220 ff.
Robotism, 306
Roger's and Rablen's Process Scale, 519–520, 523
Rogerian school, 599–600
Role definition, faulty, 615, 616, 629, 630
Room construction, filming and, 27–29, 51
Rorschach test, 551 ff.
    communication and, 551–553
    defenses and, 564–566
    emotional states and, 557 ff.
    fantasy living and, 560–561
    experience balance and experience actual, 563–564
    specialized clinical fields and, 567–569
    therapy principles and, 553–554

Sadism, 369 n., 374, 377, 379, 382
Sadomasochism, 141
Sadness, 416, 417, 418, 419
Schizophrenia, childhood, 312 ff.
    verbalization and, 147, 552

Schedule varying in data collection, 404
Scientific filming, 16
Scoptophilia, 365, 369 n.
Scripting, 16
Selection of variables in intensive design, 488
Self-analysis, 340
Self-concept, 227, 438, 527
Self-criticism, 103–104, 108–109
Self-disclosure, 434
Self-ideal correlation, 439 ff.
Self-images, 131, 406
Self and object world, 406
Self-observation, 520, 521, 524–525
Self-other fantasy, 406
Self-rejection scores, 136 ff.
Self-report tests, 530, 537 ff., 573 ff.
Semology, 73
Sensuality, MME and, 162
Sentence, change, 146
    coding, 87 ff.
    completion task, 297, 532
Separation anxiety, 106
Sequential meaning of process, 435
Setup, research, reactions to, 37 ff., 55
Sexual flooding, 488, 493
Shame anxiety, 102, 106
Shaping of behavior, 292 ff., 313 ff.
Shifting, tactical, 279, 280
Signal, 72, 73
Signal-to-noise ratio, 26
Signs, 72
Silence in therapy, 199, 201, 372
Situational goals, 589
Situational variables, 502, 608–609
Skinnerian conditioning, 293–294, 297, 302, 303, 312, 324
Sociability, 582
Social Affection factor, 576
Social casework, 456 ff.
Social psychology, 292–293
Social reinforcement, 302–303, 315–316, 324 ff.
Socioeconomic background, 139–140
Sociology, 7
Somatized constellation, 409, 414, 416, 417, 418
Sorting, 438
Sound for filming, 17–19, 25 ff., 31–32, 51
    room construction and, 27–28
Sound of voice, affect and, 116–117
Soundproofing, 28
Spatiotemporality, 76, 77
Spearman Rank Ordering, 416
Speech disturbance, 146 ff.
Speech rate, 98, 159 n., 160

Spontaneity, free association and, 199, 203, 204
Spouse, MME and, 162
S-R models, 268–269
Stabilization goals, 589
Statistical analysis, 493 ff.
Steroids, 402
Stimulation by therapist, 521, 524, 525
Stimulus, aversive, 319
    generalized reinforcing, 326
    verbal conditioning, 299
Story-telling task, 297–298, 303
Strategy, 77
Stress in speech, 148, 150
Strong Vocational Interest Blank, 534, 590
Structural units, context analysis, 271 ff.
Structure of case, agreement on, 366
Structuring maneuvers, 280
Students as interviewees, 625–626
Subjects' ego involvement, 295
Subliminal change of facial expression, 164
Submissiveness, 582
Substantive level, 509, 511
Succorance, 582
Superego, 341, 346, 347, 351–352
Superiority, achievement of, 130
Supervision of psychoanalysis, 338
Support, 374, 377, 382, 389, 391, 393, 395
Supportive therapy, 343
Suppressed affect, 98
Symbolism, language, 71, 72, 76, 77
Symptom, operant conditioning and, 304
Symptomatic scales, 542
Synergy, 77
Systematic error, 461 ff.

Tactile-sensory communication, 74
Taffel Sentence Completion Task, 297
Tape recording, 53, 338, 404
Task, free association and, 200, 202
    verbal conditioning, 297–298
Teaching, 595–596
    devices and innovations, 605–607
    experimental study of, 608 ff.
    film, 15, 23
    in medical schools, 600 ff.
    non-directive, 599–600
    post-graduate, 604–605
    psychoanalytic, 598–599
Technical consultants, film, 26–27
Technique variables, 389–391
Technology, cultural, 78
Television, 606

Temple University interview transcript, 240 ff.
Temporal censorship, 165
Tension, verbalizations and, 134
Tension-Anxiety factor, 575, 576
Termination study, 501, 506, 508
Testing in context, 273, 275–277
Texture response, 558
Thematic Apperception Test, 228, 230, 441, 443, 532
Themes, 362
Therapeutic technique, 369, 374
Therapist, activity and passivity, 396
  biases, 296–297
  in client-centered therapy, 433–435
  dimensions of behavior of, 578–579
  errors, 91, 614 ff.
  feelings, 369, 370
  filmed therapy and, 44–46, 50 ff., 56–57, 60, 64–65
  objectivity, 357
  patient attitudes toward, 577–579
  patient reciprocals, 282
  personality of, 607–608
  predictions, 366
  psychoanalysis and, 354–355
  recording procedure and, 34 ff.
  sentences, caegories for, 88–89
  teaching and, 610–611
  Type A and Type B, 534, 590 ff.
Therapy, communication and, 551–553
  multiple, 606–607
  Rorschach and, 553–554
Thought disorder, 488, 489 ff.
Time-series analysis, 381, 495
Timing in psychosomatic study, 405
Tired factor, 576
Trait universe, 438
Tranquilizers, 574
Transcribing data in context analysis, 270–271
Transference, 141–142, 167, 212, 336, 365, 374, 377, 379, 382, 385, 389 ff., 396, 577
Typescript, affect measurement from, 104–105
  verbal behavior analysis from, 96–97

Unconscious, conflicts, 345, 350–351
  consensus and, 214
  emotions, 406
  motivation, 86–87
  ratings and, 365, 369
Understanding, 578
Units, in context analysis, 271 ff.
  of observation, 362, 367
Unreasonableness, 47
Urinary data, 402

Value theory, 7
Variable-ratio schedule of reinforcement, 319
Verbal behavior analysis, 93 ff.
Verbal conditioning, 293 ff., 324–325
  biases and, 296–297
  demand characteristics and, 295–296
  reinforcement, 293–294, 295, 297, 302–303
  response classes, 294–295
Verbal vs. nonverbal communication, 166 ff.
Verbal samples, scoring of, 105 ff.
Verbalization, 617 ff.
  affect, 231–232
  interpersonal experience analysis and, 127 ff.
Vigor-Activity factor, 575, 576
Vista association, 558
Vocalizations, 148, 149
  paralanguage, 73–74
Voice quality, 146, 147, 148, 150
Voice set, 148

Warmhearted factor, 576
Warmth, 374, 377, 382, 391, 392, 394, 395
Work conditions, systematic error and, 465, 466
Working through, 365, 374, 377, 379, 382, 386, 389 ff.

Zondi Test, 532